Families and Work

In the series
Women in the Political Economy,
edited by Ronnie J. Steinberg

FAMILIES AND WORK

Edited by Naomi Gerstel and Harriet Engel Gross

Temple University Press   Philadelphia

Temple University Press, Philadelphia 19122
Copyright © 1987 by Temple University. All rights reserved
Published 1987
Printed in the United States of America

The paper used in this publication meets the minimum
requirements of American National Standard for Information
Sciences—Permanence of Paper for Printed Library Materials,
ANSI Z39.48-1984

Library of Congress Cataloging-in-Publication Data

Families and work.

   (Women in the political economy)
   Includes bibliographies.
   1. Work and family.   I. Gerstel, Naomi.
II. Gross, Harriet.   III. Series.
HD4904.25.F35   1987   306.8'5   86-30151
ISBN 0-87722-467-6 (alk. paper)
ISBN 0-87722-469-2 (pbk. : alk. paper)

Acknowledgments

We wish to acknowledge the help, encouragement, and criticism of a number of colleagues and friends. Robert Zussman read and discussed the Introductions more times than we had any reason to expect. His insights were invaluable. Toby Ditz, Mark Martin, and Sarah Rosenfield listened sympathetically and pushed us to clarify our prose. Joan Smith and Lois Hoffman provided important feedback about the outline and premises of the book. Linda Steiner's intellectual and practical help, as well as good cheer, came at critical moments. Mary Ann Clawson, Fran Deutsch, Barrie Thorne, Eleanor Gorman Miller, and Judith Wittner provided needed encouragement along the way. Ronnie Steinberg wrote extremely incisive and useful commentary on the entire volume. Michael Ames provided both practical assistance and editorial expertise at several points in the process. Jane Barry provided careful and thoughtful copyediting and Jennifer French eased the production process. Howard Gross provided much needed support. We are grateful, too, for the generous cooperation of the University of California Press, the University of Toronto Press, and Sage Publications in the permissions process. Finally, we want to thank the contributing authors for their efforts and patience as well as those authors whose good material we considered but could not ultimately include.

Contents

Introduction and Overview

Lamenting the fate of the family is something of a cottage industry these days. The demographic litany is familiar: decreasing fertility rates and increasing divorce rates parallel the obsolescence of single-earner families. Yet scholars recently have come to recognize that what is changing is not just "the family" but the relationship between families and work. A growing body of research about work and families has moved social scientists, if not the public, beyond what Kanter in the mid-seventies deplored as the "myth of separate worlds"[1] toward an understanding of their "systematic interconnectedness."[2] Much of this new scholarship, unfortunately, is widely scattered and poorly synthesized. This book, through its organization, introductions, and articles, provides a framework for the study of work, families, and their changing relationship.

Four premises inform the book. First, the historical legacy of a spatial and ideological separation of work and families in the nineteenth century both shapes and hides the ongoing relationship between them. Second, the conventional monolithic conceptions of contemporary work and family obscure the existing complexities in each as well as their connections. Third, the characterization of these separate yet dependent spheres legitimates the distinctiveness and inequality of men, women, and children—with important differences by race and class. It did so in the past and it does so today.

Finally, and most generally, understanding and changing work, families, and the economy depends upon analyses that are both macro-sociological and critical. Rather than focusing on the stresses endured by individuals or the coping mechanisms they use to adapt to the effect of daily work roles or family roles, we must recognize the connections between work and families that produce historically specific and socially structured conflict, adaptation, and resistance (at home as in the market). Thus, we see not only conflicts within families but also among different families whose interests vary. Our final premise, then, incorporates the idea that families are themselves agents of change, making choices and struggling against economic constraints instead of reacting passively to them.

Definitions of Family

By the mid-seventies, a cacophony of voices challenged the idea of "The Family"—a monolithic entity consisting of a breadwinning husband, a homemaking wife, and at least one child—as the only legitimate family form. In fact, for at least a decade now such families have been in the minority: today, this family form accounts for only 14 percent of U.S. households. In 1976 diverse groups (including, for example, Parents Without Partners, the Gay Task Force, the National Alliance for Optional Parenthood, and the Family Services Association) successfully pressured President Jimmy Carter to change the name of the promised "Conference on the American Family" to "Conference on Families." To be sure, a politically powerful "New Right" now seeks to restore the hegemony of the heterosexual couple, permanently wed, in which the husband is the breadwinner and household head, the wife a housekeeper and mother, and the children (there are always some) subject to parental control. But their program is little more than reactive; it neither represents the opinions of the majority of the American public nor addresses the predominant structural trends in family life.[3]

Changing empirical and political realities, however, have not been the only bases for challenges to the concept of a monolithic family. Equally important are the scholarly (especially feminist) challenges to the belief that "any specific family arrangement is natural, biological, or functional in a timeless way."[4] Although historians and anthropologists have for some time investigated variation among families, many have nonetheless sought to discover universal characteristics of family life.

In his now-classic analysis of some five hundred societies, Murdock developed a universal definition of the family: "a social group characterized by common residence, economic cooperation, and reproduction. It includes adults of both sexes at least two of whom maintain a socially approved sexual relationship and one or more children, own or adopted, of the sexually cohabiting adults."[5] Though widely cited, Murdock is equally often challenged on each criterion that he advances—for the conflation of household and family (see Hareven [Chapter 2] and Gerstel and Gross [Chapter 21] in this volume), for the assumption of economic cooperation among family members (see Jones [Chapter 3] and Morrissey [Chapter 14] in this volume), for the presumption that only units with two adults of both sexes who have children constitute this universal that is "family."

More important, recent scholarship suggests that the search for a universal hides historical change as it sets in place an ideology of "the family" that obscures the diversity and reality of family experience in any particular time and place. In colonial America family members were defined in terms of productive contribution and household membership. Thus, servants who lived and worked in a household, but were not related by blood, were often viewed and treated as family members by those with whom they shared a home. They provided labor as they were taught productive skills, religious doctrine, and moral values. They were family members because they shared a household and were subject to the authority of its head, not because they were treated with nurturance, affection, or love.[6]

Many scholars argue that the defining characteristics of the "modern American family" (with its roots in the nineteenth century) are altogether different: it is formed on the basis of love and affection;[7] it operates on behalf of the personality to provide psychological security and tension management;[8] and its spouses are companions as its parents (especially mothers) are nurturant and self-sacrificing.[9] Moreover, whereas the colonial family (a "little commonwealth") was all but indistinguishable from the community, scholars suggest that the modern family has become increasingly privatized, quiet, and secluded. Relations within the family become more intimate and valued as relations outside it become more remote, specialized, and tenuous.[10]

Given these new meanings, many now lay claim to the title "family" or promote their own restricted definition. Lesbians and gay men demand that the state and church legitimize their unions. Single parents argue that they and their children are "family" because they are tied together by both blood and emotion. At the same time, as Collier et al. argue, "when anti-feminists attack the Equal Rights Amendment, much of their rhetoric plays on the anticipated loss of the nurturant, intimate bonds we associate with The Family."[11] But all these groups—whether on the left or the right—obscure the actual conditions of modern families. Clarifying these conditions is fundamental to the reconceptualization of work and family.

By understanding the modern family as an emotional unit, we hide the labor that still goes on in families and miss the ways in which economic responsibilities and opportunities bind family members. The childcare and housework provided by women become acts of love because the family is a unit based on love. (See DeVault [Chapter 6] and Cowan [Chapter 7] in this volume.) Men who believe that they need their jobs to support the families they love are castigated for not contributing to the family's emotional life. (See Halle, Zussman, as well as Fowlkes [Chapters 15, 16, 17] in this volume.) So, too, children's labor in the home becomes a means to build character, serving the primary modern familial goal of emotional growth. (See White and Brinkerhoff as well as Greenberger [Chapters 9 and 19] in this volume.)

By understanding the family as privatized, we also apply a distinctly middle-class ideology that hardly characterizes the middle class itself and surely misrepresents the poor. In the late fifties and sixties, a large body of research showed that even the American middle class typically lived in "modified extended families" rather than the "isolated nuclear" ones previously proposed. Americans, by and large, keep in touch with kin, even those who live at some distance from them.[12] Furthermore, the modified extended family's very existence depends on a good deal of work, typically done by women, who provide the care and connections for their kin. [13]

Such research extends our conception of the modern family beyond the conjugal unit. But it still focuses primarily on the middle-class. In contrast, Liebow and Stack both describe how poor blacks turn friends into "fictive kin" because family is supposed to be more reliable than friendship. [14] Friends become kin because they can be counted on to exchange money, goods, and services, not simply love. From her ethnographic research in the Flats, Stack develops a new definition of family:

> Ultimately I defined "family" as the smallest, organized, durable network of kin and non-kin who interact daily, providing domestic needs of children and assuring their survival. The family network is diffused over several kin-based households. . . . An arbitrary imposition of widely accepted definitions of the family, the nuclear family, or the matrifocal family blocks the way to understanding how people in the Flats describe and order the world in which they live. [15]

Indeed, as Rapp has suggested, the debate within the feminist movement about the value and future of the family is based on experiences that vary by class and race. The Third World feminist who defends the family and the middle-class feminist who thinks it ought to be abolished "aren't talking about the same families." [16]

Finally, the ideology of the family not only hides the different experiences within families but shapes them. Seeing the husband as the family's primary breadwinner and head contributes to the subordination of women and children in the labor force. They can be offered low-paying, intermittent jobs, fired in times of labor surplus, and hired in times of labor shortage, because employers believe (or can assert) they work for "pin money" and have a husband/father who makes a "family wage." (See Chapters 1, 4, and 14 in this volume by Smith, May, and Ferree.) And if they should lose that husband or father, their dependence is shifted to the state, whose welfare policies produce a growing feminization of poverty. (See Chapters 5, 14, and 25 in this volume by Boris and Bardaglio, Morrissey, and Folbre.)

Definitions of Work

Humans have always needed to produce their own livelihood and probably have always understood that effort as work. But the definition and evaluation of work—how to distinguish it from other expenditures of human effort and what significance to attach to economically productive activity—has varied historically. Thus, for example, the Greeks regarded such effort as drudgery fit only for slaves; the Old Testament tradition believed it was punishment for original sin; Protestantism elevated work to a religious duty; and Marx argued that humans created themselves and became distinctively human through freely performed labor.[17]

More recently, the U.S. Department of Health, Education and Welfare developed a broad definition of work as "an activity that produces something of value for other people."[18] This recent concern with broadening the definition of work came from two sources: (1) feminists trying to incorporate into the concept of work the efforts that women undertake on behalf of family and household members; and (2) futurists concerned that the changing circumstances of production would mean that work as now constituted—that is, paying jobs—will no longer be available for many who need it. For feminists, the issue has been to make visible the unpaid efforts and activities involved in "house" and/or "domestic" and/or "family" work. For futurists, the issue has been to reconsider distinctions between "leisure" and "work" so that people may be better prepared for the "jobless economies" that they foresee in post-industrial societies.[19] Both have produced a growing understanding that a single, timeless definition of work may be as illusory as were similar definitions of family.

John Robertson, a British futurist, contends that post-industrial societies are in the early stages of a shift from an old work ethic based on employment to a new one based on what he calls "ownwork"—activity which is "purposeful and important and which people organize and control for themselves."[20] In Britain, the rise in self-employment, community businesses, and cooperative commercial enterprises testifies to the growing trend to "ownwork" even within the formal economy.[21] He argues that the traditional equation of economic activity with the operation of the formal economy obfuscates this growing trend. Moreover, like feminists, he criticizes both neoclassical and Marxist theories of value and work for emphasizing the formal economy at the expense of the informal economy. He argues that people are engaged in a considerable amount of significant, though unpaid, economic activity, as when neighbors do repair services for each other and community-based volunteers care for the elderly. Such activities, though a part of the informal economy, are nonetheless important contemporary "ownwork."[22]

Feminists have been equally critical of the equation of "work" and "worth" with the operation of the formal economy. Discussion of these issues (which came to be known as the "domestic labor debate") began when Marxist feminists attempted to elevate women's unpaid work to theoretical parity with waged work. Since then, other feminist scholars have extended the concept of "work" to include a range of women's responsibilities that had previously gone unrecognized—not only as work, but as effort of any sort. Thus, for example, Fishman calls attention to the "interaction work" that women do to sustain communication with their mates.[23] And Weinbaum and Bridges focus on the effort involved in selecting goods and making purchases, or the "consumption work" women do to link their family's needs with products in the market.[24] Hochschild analyzes the management of feelings (characteristically women's responsibility), distinguishing "emotional work" from "emotional labor." The former, she says, is management of feelings in a private context, whereas the latter is done for a wage by an employee.[25] In this volume (Chapter 7), DeVault sees meal planning, preparation, and coordination as part of the work that contributes to and creates family. Much of this effort, she suggests, is invisible not only in the sense that it goes unacknowledged as work but also in the sense that it is literally not seen. Meal preparation, for example, involves mental activities (like thinking about food choices and menus) that go on at the same time as, and fit around, other activities and thus cannot be isolated from them. Such work is recognized only when it is not done—meals are unprepared, clothes are unwashed, beds are not made.

These definitions of work, unlike that proposed by HEW, focus on work as a social activity (instead of simply a physical or mental one) that "not only produces a social product but also constitutes the worker as a particular social being."[26] This includes the unpaid work typically done by women, though sometimes by men and children, both inside the home (e.g., meal preparation or communication work) and outside it (e.g., consumption work and kinkeeping). And it includes the social relations this work creates, not only the role of "house"-wife, but the family itself.

Though these examples illustrate feminists' attempts to broaden the concept of work, the diverse experiences they identify defy easy categorization. One useful attempt to locate a common thread among the activities of women that feminist scrutiny has brought to light is Murgatroyd's concept of "people-producing work." This work, she suggests, involves:

the direct manipulation of people in such a way that they embody more (or a different quality of) energy or productive capacity from that previously embodied. Those who nurture, procreate, feed, educate, give physical care (medical or otherwise) or manipulate others psychologically in such a way as to increase the amount, or ameliorate the quality of human energy and potential labor power embodied by directly manipulating people, are doing people-producing work.[27]

The lasting import of all such attempts to reconceptualize "work" is the visibility they give to efforts that produce "value," even when such efforts are not easily isolated, restricted to job sites, or compensated with wages. Furthermore, the efforts of both feminists and futurists have revealed the ideological underpinnings of previous definitions of work. So, too, they suggest that an invariant definition may not be possible. As Nona Glazer (Chapter 11) contends, work cannot be universally defined; its definition must be economy-specific. For a capitalist economy, she suggests that we define work as "those activities which produce goods and/or provide services and/or provide for the circulation of goods and services which are directly or indirectly for capitalism."

Finally, the concerns feminists and others have raised about the distinction between the "public" and "private" spheres is relevant to the definition of work and family.[28] We have come to acknowledge the distortion in such dichotomies; to see the ideology that, in part, created and ratified the separations these dichotomies appeared to describe. Instead of trying to locate the distinction between work and family, we should be looking for the specific ways in which each set of activities comes to be defined among different social classes and for the actual relationships that constitute "work" and "family" in different historical contexts and circumstances.

Redefining "Family" and "Work": An Agenda

Reconceptualizations of both work and family shaped this volume's origin and development in a number of ways. First, because gender inequality inheres in the social activities of the home and the market (indeed, the stratification of each depends on the stratification of the other), a book about families and work is necessarily about gender relations. More specifically, it is about the inequality that is socially constituted through men's and women's different work and family activities.

Second, narrow conceptions of work have made children's labor invisible. This book brings children back in. It makes visible their labor both at home and in the market, and it highlights the labor that goes into preparing children to be workers.

Third, because contemporary men, women, and children live in and rely on a wide range of family structures, this book necessarily examines the ways in which the shifting economy produces, even demands, diverse family forms—including, for example, female-headed households, extended kinship units, dual-career couples, and lesbian collectives.

Fourth, these broad reconceptualizations force us to realize that neither specific family arrangements nor work and job conditions are timeless and that the relationship between them is dialectical. Transformations in each, whether over centuries or decades, depend on changes in the other. And such changing connections produce a series of contradictions. For example, the nineteenth-century ideology of separate spheres that made women guardians of the home also set the foundation for struggles for equality in the "public domain." Industrial capitalism, and the technology it spawned, produced household devices and services marketed as labor-saving. These very same developments maintained, as they transformed, women's unpaid work. At the same time, families increasingly depended upon two incomes. Yet the reliance on wives' services at home produced husbands who both resisted and encouraged their wives' employment and women who were ambivalent—not simply resentful—about their double burden. The modern "crisis in the family" allowed increasing numbers of women to rely on their own resources at the same time that their limited economic opportunities forced them to find wage-earning husbands or depend on the provisions of the welfare state. Cuts in welfare expenditures, increases in divorce, and a growing gender-stratified service economy produced both increases in women's labor-force participation and the feminization of poverty. So, too, the acceleration of women's employment has brought an increasing depreciation of those who stay at home, which, in turn, creates political divisions among women newly defensive about their varied styles of life. In examining the changing connections between work and families, this book details such contradictory forces and the varied responses to them—within and between families.

These rationales provide a broad agenda for the book. Because of limits of space and available scholarship, however, the collection necessarily omits significant topics. Most important, we focus primarily on the "developed" nations, such as the United States, West Germany, Canada, and England. Although we address the differences that race brings to the linkages of work and family, we have not included as much as we would have liked on black, Hispanic, or other minority-group variation. While we suggest that contemporary developments can be understood only in the context of the past, the historical section addresses principally the nineteenth century. Finally, we were forced by the limits of available research to truncate the stages of both jobs and families, omitting, for example, retirement and the post- (or, more accurately, "late-") parental stage.

Part I elaborates the existence and implications of the temporal, normative, and spatial separation of jobs and family that occurred with the development, in the nineteenth century, of industrial capitalism. It suggests that industrial capitalism not only separated job site and household but produced a new distinctiveness in women's and men's lives. In the nineteenth century this distinctiveness was the basis of their dependence on one another and therefore of the actual—though hidden—connection of worksite and household.

Over the twentieth century, women's labor-force participation rose steadily. Indeed, the last two decades have seen an especially sharp increase in married women's employment. Whether viewed as a "subtle revolution"[29] or the "single most outstanding phenomenon of our century,"[30] women's employment has forced scholars to reconsider the seemingly new relationship of work and family that is now eroding the ideology of separate spheres.

Just as the separation between job site and household in the nineteenth century was the catalyst for the development of an ideology of separate and gendered spheres, so has women's increasing labor-force participation in the twentieth century helped to erode these ideas. When married women went out "to work" only to find that they also came home "to work," some began to realize the inadequacy of the nineteenth-century ideological equation of work with what men do for a wage and related notions about "women's nature" and the home as "women's place." And they came to see how work outside the home was intimately tied, in fact and ideology, to their obligations and experiences inside it. Women's unpaid "family work" provided "a haven in a heartless world" and, in doing so, contributed to the comforts and job security of husbands as it contributed to the profits and stability of the capitalist economy. Moreover, in socializing their children to become the next generation of workers (at home and in the market), women helped reproduce, albeit incompletely, a gender-stratified family and economy. They also discovered that women were doing a good deal of unpaid "family work" outside the home—be it volunteer work that maintains the family's class position as it maintains the stratification system or unpaid service work that links the family to the economy as it maintains both of them. Such work in and for the family makes the family a worksite. And the fact that their family work transcends the boundaries of the home shows that the home is not so distinct from the marketplace.

Part II examines the many faces of family work. It begins with women's unpaid work in families; it moves on to the family work that children do; and finally it considers the types of labor done from, though not in, the home, blurring the boundary between the world of family and the world of the economy and government.

Part III turns to paid labor. It begins with the idea that nineteenth-century conceptions about the home as women's proper place and the market as men's have shaped women's and men's employment in the twentieth century. Breadwinning became (and remains) men's primary family responsibility. Most women still have access only to low-paying, intermittent, low-mobility jobs that often require "emotional labor" or tasks like those they perform in the home; a small number are expected to become superwomen, outperforming their colleagues on the job and at home. Family responsibilities, then, shape not only employment opportunities but also orientations to jobs and the very structure of the labor market itself. In turn, the organization of the twentieth-century economy and the demands of particular jobs held by women and men surely shape families at every point in the life course.[31]

Part III considers these reciprocal effects: the way the economy and jobs shape families and the way families shape occupational experiences. Just as in the nineteenth century men's dominance and women's relegation to domestic life vary by class, such variation remains as important as gender and gencration in the twentieth century. The essays in Part III specify the linkages between work and family among these hierarchically ordered segments of American society. They look at women, men, and children separately, enabling us to locate the experiences of each in a class- and gender-stratified economy and in a variety of family forms.

All too often people attempt to adapt individually to widely shared conflicts between work and family. They blame themselves for those private troubles that are really public problems. As an attempt not to privatize solutions, Part IV addresses the political and economic policies now heralded as strategies to ameliorate these shared conflicts. Although many argue that the United States has no family policy, this volume claims that it does have one, if only by default, that shapes the economy as it shapes the family in a gender-stratified way.

This section divides current social remedies and policy directives into two groups. First, it examines employers' policies which focus (on a largely piecemeal basis) on one source of strain or another—schedule incompatibility, childcare problems, home-centered employment. Next it turns to the policies of the state, especially its welfare programs. The inadequacies of both sets of policies suggest that only a simultaneous revamping of both the economic underpinnings of the privatized family and the familial assumptions on which the labor force is built can address the urgent needs of working families. The essays in this volume represent, we hope, a contribution to this effort.

Notes

1. Rosabeth Moss Kanter, *Work and Family in the United States: A Critical Review and Agenda for Research and Policy* (New York: Russell Sage Foundation, 1977), p. 7.

2. Joan Kelly, "The Doubled Vision of Feminist Theory: A Postscript to the 'Women and Power' Conference," *Feminist Studies* 5, no. 1 (1979): 222.

3. See Naomi Gerstel, "Domestic Life: The New Right and the Family," in B. Haber (ed.), *The Woman's Annual* (New York: G. K. Hall, 1982).

4. Barrie Thorne and Marilyn Yalom (eds.), *Rethinking the Family: Some Feminist Questions* (New York: Longman, 1982), p. 2.

5. George Murdock, *Social Structure* (New York: Macmillan, 1949), p. 1.

6. See Edmund Morgan, *The Puritan Family* (New York: Harper & Row, 1966); Michael Gordon, *The American Family* (New York: Random House, 1978).

7. Carl Degler, *At Odds: Women and the Family in America from the Revolution to the Present* (New York: Oxford University Press, 1980).

8. Talcott Parsons and R. F. Bales, *Family, Socialization and Interaction Process* (New York: Free Press, 1955).

9. Edward Shorter, *The Making of the Modern Family* (New York: Basic Books, 1975).

10. Ibid.; Eli Zaretsky, *Capitalism, the Family, and Personal Life* (New York:

Harper & Row, 1973); Christopher Lasch, *Haven in a Heartless World: The Family Besieged* (New York: Basic Books, 1977); Mary P. Ryan, *The Cradle of the Middle Class: The Family in Oneida County, New York, 1790–1865* (Cambridge: Cambridge University Press, 1981).

11. Jane Collier, Michelle Z. Rosaldo, S. Yanagisako, "Is There a Family? New Anthropological Views," in Thorne and Yalom, *Rethinking the Family*, p. 33.

12. Eugene Litwak, "Extended Kin Relations in an Industrial Democratic Society," in Ethel Shanas and Gordon T. Strieb (eds.), *Social Structure and the Family: Generational Relations* (Englewood Cliffs, N.J.: Prentice-Hall, 1965); Marvin B. Sussman, and Lee Burchinal, "Kin Family Network: Unheralded Structure in Current Conceptualizations of Family Functioning," *Marriage and Family Living* 24 (1962): 231–40.

13. Carol Rosenthal, "Kinkeeping in the Familial Division of Labor," *Journal of Marriage and the Family* 47 (1985): 965–74.

14. Elliot Liebow, *Tally's Corner: A Study of Negro Street Corner Men* (Boston: Little, Brown, 1967); Carol D. Stack, *All Our Kin: Strategies for Survival in a Black Community* (New York: Harper & Row, 1974).

15. Stack, *All Our Kin*, p. 31.

16. Rayna Rapp, "Family and Class in Contemporary America: Notes Toward an Understanding of Ideology," *Science and Society* 42 (1978): 278–300.

17. For a discussion of the history of changing conceptions of work, see Stanley R. Parker, *The Future of Work and Leisure* (New York: Praeger, 1971), chap. 3.

18. Cited in Alice Kessler-Harris, *Women Have Always Worked* (Westbury, N.Y.: Feminist Press, 1981), p. 18.

19. C. Jenkins and B. Sherman, *The Collapse of Work* (London: Eyre Methuen, 1979); C. Jenkins and B. Sherman, *The Leisure Shock* (London: Eyre Metheuen, 1981); C. M. Handy, *Future of Work* (London: Basil Blackwell, 1984), S. S. Parker, *Leisure and Work* (New York: Allen and Unwin, 1983); John Robertson, *Future Work* (New York: Universe Books, 1985).

20. Robertson, *Future Work*, p. x.

21. Ibid., pp. 184–85.

22. As Robertson writes, "the orthodoxy of the industrial age has been that the formal economy is the only real economy and that responsible thought and action on economics and social questions should concentrate only on those activities that have a money tag attached" (ibid., p. 102). See also R. E. Pahl, *Division of Labor* (New York: Basil Blackwell, 1984), for a discussion of the informal economy.

23. Pamela Fishman, "Interaction: The Work That Women Do," *Social Problems* 25 (1978):397–406.

24. Batya Weinbaum and Amy Bridges, "The Other Side of the Paycheck: Monopoly Capital and the Structure of Consumption," in Zillah Eisenstein (ed.), *Capitalist Patriarchy and the Case for Socialist Feminism* (New York: Monthly Review Press, 1979), pp. 190–205.

25. Arlie Hochschild, *The Managed Heart* (Berkeley: University of California Press, 1983).

26. Julie A. Matthaei, *An Economic History of Women in America: Women's Work, the Sexual Division of Labor and the Development of Capitalism* (New York: Schocken Books, 1982), p. 34.

27. Lois Murgatroyd, "Production of People and Domestic Labor," in P. Close and R. Collins, *Family and Economy in Modern Society* (London: Macmillan, 1985), pp. 45–62.

28. See, for example, Eva Garmarnikow, David H. J. Morgan, Jane Purvis, and Daphne Taylorson (eds.), *The Public and the Private* (London: Heinemann, 1983); Close and Collins, *Family and Economy in Modern Society*.

29. Ralph E. Smith (ed.), *The Subtle Revolution: Women at Work* (Washington, D.C.: Urban Institute, 1979).

30. Eli Ginzberg, "Women and Employment," *New York Times*, September 12, 1976.

31. Indeed, a large literature now specifies these effects. But because many of the insights from such research on the effects of employment (largely done before and during the 1970s) are now working assumptions of sociologists, we do not include many examples of it in this volume. The conclusions it yielded, however, are worth summarizing. First, and most important, the employment (or unemployment) of fathers (and increasingly mothers) locates all family members in the class structure. Although individual achievement rather than familial ascription is a fundamental principle of modern life, the contemporary family nonetheless determines the class position of children while they are young and shapes their aspirations and life chances as adults. Second, jobs set the spatial and temporal boundaries of family life, determining where family members live and the quality and quantity of time that they spend together. Third, daily experience on the job shapes the personality of workers, affecting not only their daily moods and interaction but the values they bring home for the socialization of children. Fourth, the power, influence, and control awarded (or denied) by the occupational structure shape expectations for power, influence, and control at home. Men, typically more empowered than women (or children) on the job, gain power at home. For reviews of this literature, see Rosabeth Kanter, *Work and Family;* R. Rapoport and R. Rapoport (eds.), *Working Couples* (New York: Harper & Row, 1978); Karen E. Feinstein (ed.), *Working Women and Families* (Beverly Hills, Calif.: Sage, 1979); Patricia Voydanoff (ed.), *Work and Family* (Palo Alto, Calif.: Mayfield, 1984); Helena Lopata (ed.), *Research in the Interweave of Social Roles: Families and Jobs,* vol. 3 (Greenwood, Conn.: JAI Press, 1983); Joan Aldous (ed.), *Two Paychecks: Life in Dual-Earner Families* (Beverly Hills, Calif.: Sage, 1982).

PART I

Work and Families in Historical Perspective: The Making of Separate Spheres

Introduction

In colonial America economic and family life were merged. Contributing to the family, the majority of husbands, wives, and children lived on family farms or in artisan households and were all co-workers. Though colonial husbands were—in politics, religion, and culture—patriarchs and household heads, the property-owning family (especially in the North) jointly engaged in a common enterprise of subsistence.[1] Despite the division of labor between husbands and wives, this agrarian society was a "family economy" or "family system of production": In turn, "In the sphere of economics, colonial spokesmen defined sex roles that often blurred the distinction between women and men."[2]

In the nineteenth century, job site and household fractured into separate spheres. This split became the basis for a vision of work and family as distinct, not only spatially and temporally, but also normatively. It differentiated social institutions as it became a new basis for the segregation of women and men. Over the course of that century, men—in most social classes—became the family's primary wage-earner. In so doing, they consolidated on new grounds their position as the family's agent outside the home. At the same time, most married women were excluded from the marketplace. Homemaking became their vocation. The relegation of women to a privatized, domestic sphere ensured their economic dependence on husbands. And it ensured that husbands would be dependent on their wives for moral and emotional support, maintenance of their home, and the upbringing of their children.

These are now widely accepted historical facts. Yet over the last thirty years, various schools of thought have assessed these facts quite differently, deriving different causal sequences and different social consequences from them. According to the functional theory popular until the 1960s, modernization (or the combination of industrialization, urbanization, and specialization) established worksites away from households. Because this major shift in economic organization put a premium on the small, mobile family that could move to follow jobs, ties between extended kin attenuated and ties within the nuclear family intensified. Functions previously performed by extended kin were transferred to specialized institutions: schools provided education, welfare institutions provided care for the indigent and elderly, and, most important, production was removed from the home to industry. However, the nuclear family remained an important, specialized institution devoted primarily to childrearing and expressive functions (i.e., those performed "on behalf of the personality").[3]

Functionalists argued that these specialized activities produced a new set of complementary roles for women and men. With this split between worksite and household, between nuclear family and kin, portable wives and mothers *naturally*—not because of historical precedent, but because of biology and early socialization—remained in the small private home. They nurtured their children and managed the tensions husbands brought home from jobs. Because of women's primacy in the home, the husband had to become the primary breadwinner and as such served as the only link between the now-separated occupational and familial systems. The interests of both men and women were met in their newly created roles. The spheres of employment and family, and the roles of husbands and wives, though separated, thus "fit" together in a necessary and easy equilibrium.[4]

Instead of tying the separation of work and family to the amorphous process of industrialization, some Marxists in the 1970s focused on how first industrial and then monopoly capitalism created, fueled, and profited from that separation. In this formulation capitalism destroyed extended kin ties as it curtailed home production.[5] The development of monopoly capitalism set in place a process in which even the relations of nuclear family members were shaped to serve the voracious search for profits of an ever-expanding "universal market."[6] In this formulation, too, the family is derivative: the newly privatized family is shaped to fit the demands of capitalist production. But for Marxists, commodity production not only changes but destroys the family, as the marketplace and state gradually seize all functions previously provided by it. That is, "the family has been slowly coming apart for more than a hundred years."[7]

These Marxists do not explain the sexual division of labor inside and outside the home except insofar as it is rooted in biological and economic imperatives. They explain inequality between husbands and wives as a result of wives' exclusion from, or devaluation in, the market. But they do not explain why it is women, rather than men, who are excluded. Instead, they operate with categories that can be termed "sex-blind."[8]

Detailed historical research has shown both these theoretical formulations to be wrong on a number of counts. It has suggested that the image of the extended household before industrialization as well as the incapacitation of extended ties with the development of industrial capitalism are both misleading. Extended family members did not typically share a household throughout the life course in preindustrial settings.[9] And nineteenth-century relatives were a vital resource for nineteenth-century factory workers. [10]

It remained for feminist scholars to question and unravel the assumptions about the causes and consequences of historical development for women and men. From careful attention to historical detail, feminists recognized that the separation and inequality of women and men was inherited and redefined, but not created, by industrial capitalism. A gender-based division of labor, the degradation of women, and the characterization of the "public" as men's domain and the "private" as women's existed in preindustrial settings. [11] By studying a wide range of economic systems, they uncovered enormous variations in the sexual division of space, labor, and power. This discovery pointed to the social (rather than biological) construction not only of the relationship between families and the economy but of the relationship of gender to both. [12]

To explain inequalities between women and men that could not be explained solely as a result of capitalist relations of production, feminists invoked and developed the concept of "patriarchy." This led to a debate among feminists over the definition and use of the term. For some, "patriarchy" was used broadly to refer to all systems of male domination. For example, Hartmann defined patriarchy as "a set of social relations which has a material base and in which there are hierarchical relations between men, and solidarity among them, which enables them to control women. Patriarchy is thus the system of male oppression of women." [13] But other feminists argued that the term "patriarchy" should be reserved for historically specific situations and that it was confusing to place control over children under the same rubric as control over women. [14] For example, Rubin argued that the specific form of male dominance known as patriarchy is "more properly confined to pastoral nomads and other such groups where one man holds absolute dominance over wives, children, herds and dependents as an aspect of the institution of socially defined fatherhood." [15] In response to these criticisms, a number of feminists have attempted to distinguish among different historical stages of patriarchy. To describe the period in which individual fathers garner economic benefits from and have power over their children as well as their wives, Brown uses the term "private patriarchy," and Boris the term "family patriarchy." These scholars (though they too have differences) typically argue that the power of individual fathers is replaced by the power of men who use the state to establish laws and public policies that help preserve "public" or "state" patriarchy.[16]

Although they realized that male domination over women preceded and shaped capitalism, feminists also understood the need to explain how capitalism both reshaped and used gender inequality. As Jaggar puts it, socialist feminists in particular "claim that a full understanding of the capitalist system requires a recognition of the way in which it is structured by male dominance and, conversely, that a full understanding of contemporary male dominance requires a recognition of the way it is organized by the capitalist division of labor."[17]

At the same time, feminists' discussion of the social construction of gender inequality confirmed the independent and formative influence of ideology on behavior.[18] Through analyzing the prescriptive literature and daily lives of men and women at different historical moments, feminists uncovered transformations in the ideology applied to and used by them. In particular, in looking at the nineteenth century, when women and men moved to inhabit increasingly separate spheres, feminist historians uncovered a "domestic code" or "cult of true womanhood." Here women were conceived of as moral guardians—pious, sexually pure, naturally domestic and nurturant. This guardianship was viewed as necessary to preserve the home as haven and, just as important, to civilize an increasingly competitive world. Men, who were to achieve in the occupational world, were rational, calculating, and unemotional: "Manliness became equated with success in the economic competition; indeed man's position in the household came to be described as bread*winner*."[19] These men needed wives who were emotionally supportive of them and their children and who could competently manage the domestic front.

Some historians have argued that this ideology, and the separation it entailed, gave women a certain power—a "domestic feminism"—in their own realm.[20] But others argue that the ideology that exalted housewives condemned those forced to do wage work.[21] The implementation of this domestic code also offered industry the services of an unpaid labor force at home whose primary tasks were to replenish the work force and stretch the husband's "family wage." Yet it also set the foundation for struggles for equality. As Welter suggested in her discussion of the cult of true womanhood, "The very perfection of True Womanhood carried within itself the seeds of its own destruction. For if woman was so very little less than angels, she should surely take a more active part in running the world."[22]

In the process of refining the idea of separate spheres for women and men, feminists uncovered the changing position of children. Children of the middle class were, like women, excluded from paid employment and viewed as needing their mother's home-based protection in order to maintain their innocence and attain a conscience or sense of *self*-control [23] Indeed, that new innocence and sense of self required that mothers focus all the more on the home. Yet children of the immigrant poor, just like black children, had to labor outside the home to keep their families out of poverty. As Early writes of the children of French-Canadian immigrants in nineteenth-century Massachusetts: "Family survival was—literally—in their hands." [24] And working-class parents—who did not think of childhood as a separate stage of life but rather as a time to learn to shoulder the burdens of labor—struggled with middle-class reformers who believed that the development of children's moral sense depended on their protection within the home. [25]

Finally, by focusing on women feminists uncovered the systematic interconnectedness of employment and family even as industrial capitalism advanced. First, they saw that women's work in the home was essential in shaping men's employment and the family's class position, the development of the economy, and the moral order. Second, they saw that among the poor, immigrants, and blacks, men and women did not inhabit the same separate spheres occupied by the white, the native-born, and the old and new middle class. Despite the spatial, temporal, and normative separation of worksite and household, feminists began to discover that just as the structure and allocation of labor and power within the household depend on the stratification of the economy, the stratification and operation of the economy depend on the contribution of the household.

The essays in this section highlight important aspects of the feminist reinterpretation. In a complex article that repays several readings, Dorothy Smith examines in broad strokes the displacement of an agrarian economy by industrial and corporate capitalism. She speaks not so much to the weakening of the family as to its transformation. Her article specifies the connected economic and familial conditions that constitute the transition from the early stages of agricultural economies to early industrial and then corporate capitalism as well as the development of an ideological and institutional separation of jobs and family. Her analysis affirms the indispensability of simultaneous consideration of gender and class inequality. In the process, she shows how class relations and inequalities are organized and sustained by women's daily domestic activities and how these activities, in turn, are organized through the collaboration of capitalists, professional "experts," unions, and the state. Finally, Smith shows in detail both how family organization in a capitalist system is the basis for women's subordination to men and how women's family work—providing personal services for their employed husbands and cultural background, appearance, and training in conduct for their children—

maintains the capitalist economy. But she also shows how the advance of capitalism simultaneously increases women's dependence on men *and* provides the basis for their independence.

The two articles that follow show the limits of the conception of work and family as distinctive spheres even in the nineteenth century. In her analysis of the French-Canadian working class, Tamara Hareven affirms the ongoing commingling of work and family in the very establishment of industrial production. She reveals the extensive use of kin in industrial recruitment and training as well as the ways in which industrial opportunity maintained kin ties and served household economies. Though her work does not speak to the relative contribution of men and women in maintaining these kin networks, she does show that—at least under conditions of labor surplus—these networks could manipulate the economic system to their own ends. Her work, then, corrects an earlier emphasis on the passivity of the family in the face of forces unleashed by industrial capitalism.

Jacqueline Jones's discussion (Chapter 3) shows how a similar use of conjugal and blood ties helped blacks both adapt to, and rebel against, slavery in the nineteenth century. This article shows how both slaveowners and slaves used and manipulated ideologies of gender to serve their own contradictory purposes. While they upheld the ideology of virtuous and delicate womanhood for women of their own race, owners downplayed gender differences in the work assignments and punishments meted out to slaves, at least insofar as these did not interfere with black women's capacity to bear a future work force. Slaves—men and women—upheld a sexual division of labor in their own quarters in order to resist the masters' opportunistic use of ideology. Finally, freed slaves resisted racism by reestablishing the authority of black men over black women and removing black women from fieldwork to their own homes. From such analyses we see how gender, race, and class inequality sometimes reinforce and sometimes undermine one another.

Jones and Hareven, looking at different social classes and races, affirm the ongoing reciprocity between work and family in industrializing America. But to bear in mind the continuous connection of work and family is not to deny the movement toward institutional separation and gender segregation. Martha May's essay (Chapter 4) offers a detailed documentation of the changing meaning and significance of the family wage, an ideology originating in the nineteenth century whose influence reached into and shaped twentieth-century economic developments and family life. She shows that in the 1830s the ideology served the working-class struggle to obtain a decent standard of living. In the twentieth century, however, it became a means to ensure the Ford Motor Company's control both at home and in the shop. May finds that although the family wage originated in class conflict over workers' livelihood, its objective consequence was female subordination both at home and at the workplace. In the end, working-class men had joined their corporate bosses to make the ideology and practice of the family wage an affirmation of the public roles of men and the private roles of women.

But the affirmation rested on something more. From the nineteenth century to the twentieth, state policy increasingly sustained separate spheres and orchestrated gender relations, with different themes and variations by race and class. In Chapter 5 Eileen Boris and Peter Bardaglio analyze the ways in which the domination over women shifted out of the hands of male heads of households into those of the state, through legislative and judicial as well as executive action. Their discussion shows how state policy reinforced the separate spheres of women and men as it excluded working-class and nonwhite women from the private sphere. Their analysis is useful as well because it brings in children, showing how control over them shifted from fathers to the state. At a moment when their children were no longer economically productive, this change celebrated women as mothers and put new obligations on them. Finally, the authors bring us to a late twentieth-century dilemma: as the state undermined men's authority in the home while rendering women and children more autonomous there, state policy also sustained women's and children's economic dependence or even impoverished them. Boris and Bardaglio remind us that the state's construction of the family and the economy remains an important arena for the struggle of competing interests, among women and between women and men.

Together, these articles analyze the nineteenth-century foundation on which contemporary realities are built. Thus, they set the stage for the following sections in which we consider each of the "separate spheres"—the family and its unpaid work; the market and paid employment—and examine their connections in the twentieth century.

Notes

1. Although it is agreed that the colonial family was a "common enterprise of subsistence," historians still disagree about the extent to which the family produced for exchange in outside markets or produced for their own use and that of neighbors. See Toby Ditz, *Kinship and Property in Early America: Inheritance in Five Connecticut Towns, 1750–1820* (Princeton: Princeton University Press, 1986); Michael Merrill, "Cash Is Good to Eat: Self-Sufficiency and Exchange in the Rural Economy of the U.S.," *Radical Historians' Review* 4, (Winter, 1977):42–66.

2. Mary P. Ryan, *Womanhood in America: From Colonial Times to the Present*, 3d ed. (New York: Franklin Watts, 1983), p. 31. It should be stressed that though sex roles may have blurred in the economic sphere, women's labor nonetheless did not bring them control over economic resources (which still remained with husbands and fathers). As Folbre writes: "In colonial New England, men, women and children may have worked together in the same location, but proximity did not imply equality. The work of women and children may have been quite important, but it did not necessarily

guarantee them any significant power within the family'': Nancy Folbre, ''Patriarchy in Colonial New England,'' *Review of Radical Political Economics* 12, no. 2 (1980):4–13. See also Mary Beth Norton, *Liberty's Daughters: The Revolutionary Experience of American Women, 1750–1800* (Boston: Little, Brown, 1980). For good overviews of work and family in colonial America, see Ryan, *Womanhood in America*, as well as Alice Kessler-Harris, *Out to Work: A History of Wage Earning Women in the United States* (New York: Oxford University Press, 1982), chap. 1; Julie A. Matthaei, *An Economic History of Women in America: Women's Work, the Sexual Division of Labor and the Development of Capitalism* (New York: Schocken Books, 1982), chap. 1 and 2.

3. Talcott Parsons and R. F. Bales, *Family, Socialization and Interaction Process* (Glencoe, Ill.: Free Press, 1955), p. 16.

4. See, for example, Parsons and Bales, *Family, Socialization and Interaction Process;* E. W. Burgess and H. J. Locke, *The Family: From Institution to Companionship,* 2d ed. (New York: American Books, 1955); William Goode, *World Revolution and Family Patterns* (New York: Free Press, 1963).

5. Eli Zaretsky, *Capitalism, the Family and Personal Life* (New York: Harper & Row, 1976).

6. Harry Braverman, *Labor and Monopoly Capital* (New York: Monthly Review Press, 1974).

7. Christopher Lasch, *Haven in a Heartless World: The Family Besieged* (New York: Basic Books, 1977), p. xiv.

8. For good summaries of the ''sex-blind'' character of Marxist analysis, see Heidi Hartmann, ''The Unhappy Marriage of Marxism and Feminism: Towards a More Progressive Union,'' in Sargeant, *Women and Revolution* (Boston, Mass.: South End Press, 1979), pp. 1–41; and Michelle Barrett, *Women's Oppression Today* (London: Verso Editions, 1980).

9. See Peter Laslett and Richard Wall (eds.), *Household and Family in Past Time* (Cambridge: Cambridge University Press, 1972).

10. In addition to Chapter 2 in this volume, see Michael Anderson, *Family Structure in Nineteenth-Century Lancashire* (Cambridge: Cambridge University Press, 1972).

11. As Reiter puts it: ''The radical separation of home and workplace in industrial capitalism transforms and buttresses the distinction between public and private domains that had long had ideological legitimacy''; ''Men and Women in the South of France,'' in R. R. Reiter (ed.), *Toward an Anthropology of Women* (New York: Monthly Review Press, 1975), p. 281. But as Ryan points out, women's association with the ''private'' in preindustrial settings should not be confused with their insulation in the family or even be interpreted as meaning that the family was ''coterminous with some private sphere.'' See Mary P. Ryan, *The Cradle of the Middle Class: The Family in Oneida County, New York, 1790–1865* (New York: Cambridge University Press, 1981), p. 42.

12. For a good review of cross-cultural variation, see Charlotte G. O'Kelly and L. Carney, *Women and Men in Society* (Belmont, Calif.: Wadsworth, 1986).

13. Heidi Hartmann, ''Capitalism, Patriarchy and Job Segregation by Sex,'' *Signs* 1 (1976): 138.

14. See, for example, Barrett, *Women's Oppression Today.*

15. See Gayle Rubin, ''The Traffic in Women,'' in Reiter, *Toward an Anthropology of Women,* p. 168.

16. Carol Brown, "Mothers, Fathers and Children: From Private to Public Patriarchy," in Lydia Sargent (ed.), *Women and Revolution: A Discussion of the Unhappy Marriage of Marxism and Feminism* (Boston: South End Press, 1981); Eileen Boris and Peter Bardaglio, "The Transformation of Patriarchy: The Historic Role of the State," in Irene Diamond (ed.), *Families, Politics, and Public Policy: A Feminist Dialogue on Women and the State* (New York: Longman, 1983). See also Chapters 5 and 25 in this volume. Ferguson distinguishes between "father patriarchy" and "husband patriarchy" as different phases of what others have called "private patriarchy"; see Ann Ferguson, "On Conceiving Motherhood and Sexuality: A Feminist Materialist Approach," in Joyce Trebilcot (ed.), *Mothering: Essays in Feminist Theory* (Totowa, N.J.: Rowman & Allanheld, 1984).

17. Allison Jaggar, *Feminist Politics and Human Nature* (Totowa, N.J.: Rowman and Allanheld, 1983), p. 125.

18. As we use it, "ideology" is not simply the norms and values attached to gender, but, as Dorothy Smith writes, "a procedure for sorting out and arranging conceptually the living actual world of people so that they can be as we know it ideologically. It is a practice which has the effect of making the fundamental features of our society mysterious because it prevents us from recognizing them as problematic." See Dorothy Smith, "Theorizing as Ideology," in R. Turner, *Ethnomethodology* (Baltimore: Penguin Books, 1974), pp. 41–44.

19. From Matthaei, *Economic History of Women*, p. 105.

20. See, for example, Daniel Scott Smith, "Family Limitation, Sexual Control, and Domestic Feminism in Victorian America," *Feminist Studies* 1, nos. 3–4 (1973).40–57.

21. Kessler-Harris, *Out to Work*, p. 53.

22. Barbara Welter, "Cult of True Womanhood: 1820–1860," in Michael Gordon (ed.), *The American Family in Social Historical Perspective* (New York: St. Martin's, 1973), p. 386. See also Nancy F. Cott, *The Bonds of Womanhood: "Women's Sphere" in New England, 1780–1835* (New Haven: Yale University Press, 1977).

23. For an interesting discussion of the creation of conscience in middle-class children of the nineteenth century, see Ryan, *Cradle of the Middle Class*.

24. F. H. Early, "The French-Canadian Economy and the Standard of Living in Lowell, Massachusetts, 1870," in Gordon, *American Family*, p. 491.

25. Christine Stansell, "Women, Children and the Uses of the Street: Class and Gender Conflict in New York City: 1850–1860," *Feminist Studies* 8, no. 2 (1982):309–26.

1

Women's Inequality and the Family

DOROTHY E. SMITH

Although it is a serious oversimplification to treat the family as the sole basis of women's inequality, it is the social organization of women's labor in the home and outside and the relations between the two which *are* women's inequality. It will be argued here that the character of inequality and its history differ in different class settings.

The strategy adopted here is that of a consciously open-ended inquiry into the actual processes which are now and have been at work in our society. Such an inquiry is grounded less in the theoretical and political debate— however important that has been in formulating the central issues addressed—than in the experience from which the theoretical debate arises and which it originally expressed directly. The concept of patriarchy as it has been developed in the women's movement locates and conceptualizes women's direct personal experience of inequality in their personal, and indeed sometimes intimate, relations with men. [1] By contrast, as intellectuals we begin ordinarily *outside* experienced actuality and *within* the discourse— the conversation-in-texts going forward among an intelligentsia. In this inquiry I have sought to return to the actuality in which such experience arises and to explore the larger social and historical process which is the matrix of that experience. Rather than detaching patriarchy as a phenomenon to be examined in relation to capitalism, this inquiry turns, however partially and imperfectly, to that world in which we have needed such terms to speak politically of our experience.

Engels' *The Origin of the Family, Private Property, and the State* suggests the method of analysis which will be used here. [2] This method takes an actual work process and locates it in a determinate social relation. When we do this we can see how the articulation of an individual's work to the social relations

Adapted from Dorothy Smith, "Women's Inequality and the Family," in Allan Moscovitch and Glenn Drover (eds.), *Inequality: Essays on the Political Economy of Social Welfare* (Toronto: University of Toronto Press, 1981). Reprinted by permission of the author and University of Toronto Press. © University of Toronto Press 1981.

of a given mode of production determines how *she* is related and the ways in which she becomes subordinate. There is, on the one hand, a work process, an actual activity, and on the other, social relations (and activities) which articulate and organize that work as part of a division of labor in society.

Engels did not see the division of labor simply as a distribution of work in work roles. Rather, he saw the work process as articulated to social relations, which defined its relation to other processes and hence defined how the doer of that work was related in society. Here we don't draw a boundary between the mode of production and the door of the home. Instead, we see that home and family are integral parts of and moments in a mode of production. Our method of work is one which raises as an empirical question the work which is done and the relations which organize and articulate that work to the social, economic, and political processes beyond and outside the home. Thus, we don't cut across class or other divisions such as rural/urban differences in a society to discover the lineaments of the family and then return to the abstracted family to discover how it "varies" in differing class and historical contexts. We begin with a method which locates the family and women's work in the home and in the actual social relations in which they are embedded. Thus, we shall be trying to understand the inner life and work of the family and the personal relations of power between husband and wife as products of how family relations are organized by and in economic and political relations of capitalism. The relation between internal and external, between the personal dimensions of relations—those relations wherein particular individuals confront, cooperate, and work together as individuals—and those relations which are organized as economic and political ones are all key to women's experience of the personal as political and as a relation of inequality.

Behind the personal relations of women and men in the familial context are economic and political processes which provide the conditions, exigencies, opportunities, powers, and weaknesses of the interactional process. The economic and political processes are there as a continual presence giving shape, limits, and conditions to what goes forward, and—as in every other aspect of a capitalist mode of production—supplying change and necessitating adaptation, rendering the examples of lifetime experience of previous generations irrelevant as models for each succeeding generation. Our strategy seeks for the determination and shaping of the interpersonal forms of domination and oppression of women in the economic and political relations in which the family is imbedded.

In the analysis which follows, class and family—or class and patriarchy— will not be viewed as opposing and incompatible terms placing us in an either/or situation at every point. Rather, our strategy will be one relating the specific form of the family to the class organization of a changing capitalist society. The conception of class we will use is a Marxist one, which identifies classes on the basis of differing relations to the means of production. For instance, the ruling class appropriates and controls the means of production. In turn, it is supported by a class which labors to produce the subsistence of the ruling class as well as its own. In a capitalist society this relation takes the form of the mutual constitution of capital and wage labor. Surplus value is the form in which surplus labor appears and is then appropriated by the ruling class. This dichotomous class structure, however, does not become visible in a simple way for reasons which will be discussed, in part, throughout this paper. We shall see that an analysis of family relations, rather than leading us away from an examination of class, brings them into focus as a feature of an everyday world. By beginning with class as a dynamic relation central to capitalism; by recognizing families as organized by and organizing social relations (among them, class relations); and by avoiding the use of the abstracted concept of the family to make differences between classes unobservable, we can begin to see the social organization of class in a new way. We discover that the forms of family work and living are integral to the active process of constructing and reconstructing class relations, particularly as the ruling class responds to changes in the forms of property relations and in the organization of the capitalist enterprise and capitalist social relations.

It is important to preserve a sense of capitalism as an essentially dynamic process which continually transforms the "ground" on which we stand, so that we are always looking at a continually changing historical process. It is one of the problems of the "head world" strategy that our categories and concepts fix an actuality into seemingly unchanging forms, and then we do our work in trying to find out how to represent society in that way. We must avoid this. We must try to see our society as part of a continually moving "surface" and avoid introducing an artificial fixity into our perceptions. The society as we find it at any one moment is the product of an historical process. It is a process which is not "completed," in that the various "impulses" generated by the *essentially* dynamic process of capitalism do not come to rest in their own completion or in the working-out to the point of equilibrium of systemic interactions. The process of change is itself unceasing, and at any moment we catch only an atemporal slice of a moving process. Hence, to understand the properties, movement, and "structure" of the present, we must be able to separate the strands of development which determine their present character and relations.

Our discussion here of the present bases of women's inequality and its relation to class and family will sketch the differing histories of women and the form of the family in the historical development of classes within capitalism. Behind the course of change and the experience of women in different classes is the same overall historical course which capitalism has taken in North

America. That common course of development has shaped the histories of classes and the widely different experiences of family living for middle-class and working-class women.[3]

The Petit-Bourgeois Family

Our analysis of the forms and bases of inequality among women of different classes follows a historical course, tracing changes in key relations over a period of some two hundred years. For some writers the change in women's status from precapitalist to capitalist forms of the family coincides with the shift of production from the family to the factory. Women's work in the home was no longer part of a productive enterprise; hence, its value as an essential contribution to the productive process declined.[4]

A rather different picture will be presented here. Here we will focus on a process of development in the social relations of capitalism, taking property as that key relation which has organized the relation of the bourgeois and petit-bourgeois family. This is not a fixed relation. Rather, it is a reciprocal process, on the one hand, of changes in the forms of property relations *fundamental* to capitalism, and on the other hand, of processes of advance and elaboration of capitalist social relations and of a deepening penetration by capital of all aspects of society. Capital reorganizes the *forms* of property relations and the specific character of the relation of property-owning "units" to capitalist social relations. At the outset the characteristic form of property holding, the characteristic property basis of capitalist enterprises, is that of the individual—a man—whose civil person subsumes that of his wife, so that in marriage they constitute a single person equatable to him. Over the last hundred years in particular, that form of property basis for the capitalist enterprise has been displaced, though not eliminated, by the corporate form, whereby the unit becomes the corporate entity (of whatever kind) and not the individual. The implications for the family and for women's status in the family are major, for the emergence of the second form of property relation as a predominant form means that capital has been disconnected from its grounding in the bourgeois family. It means that family relations, which were formerly penetrated and organized by this relation to the individualized property form and the individualized organization of the enterprise, are now severed from the direct relation. The family is no longer constitutive of property relations under monopoly capitalism.[5]

Nevertheless, the enterprise identified with an individual owner who participates directly in the labor process has persisted, most notably in agriculture, but also as a generally recurrent form.[6] This is the typically petit-bourgeois type of enterprise. Here, perhaps most distinctly, we can see two aspects of the process described above. On the one hand, forms of property ownership permit the husband to appropriate the wife's labor in the enterprise. On the other hand, the reorganization of the relation of household to enterprise—of women's domestic work and her work directly for her husband's enterprise as being that enterprise—is articulated to changing capitalist social relations, including changing financial institutions and fiscal practices, and, in general, to the increased domination of monopoly capitalist forms and thereby of finance capital.

In the context of this history we can contrast earlier forms, in which the commodity-producing enterprise and the household producing the direct subsistence of both domestic and productive ''workers'' formed complementary sides of a single economic unit, with the more advanced forms of capitalist social relations. Where accounts were kept of this economic unit, domestic and personal expenses were included in the overall accounting for the enterprise.[7]

The reciprocal dependence of household and enterprise is visible in nineteenth-century Canada in more than one form. At least one of the households Katz describes in his study of late nineteenth-century Hamilton suggests just such a relation between household and enterprise:

John Mottashed, a 52-year old Protestant shoemaker, born in Ireland, lived on Hughson Street in a two-storey stone house which he rented from T. Stinson. With him in 1851 lived his 40-year-old second wife Mary Ann; his married, 24-year-old son Jonathan, a miller, and his 20-year-old daughter-in-law, Mary Anne; his other sons, John, twenty-two, George, seventeen, Roger, fourteen, Joseph, six, and Charles, one; his daughters, Mary, twelve, and Anne, eight; and his stepchildren, John Calvert, an 18-year-old shoemaker, and Sarah Calvert, fifteen years old.[8]

This was the household in 1851. It is not clear whether the adult sons were working as shoemakers, but in 1861 the relation of household to enterprise is more clearly established. Mottashed's three older sons have taken up his trade, and his son the miller and his daughter-in-law are no longer part of the household.

For a farm of slightly later period, Nellie McClung's autobiography gives us a picture of this type of organization of household and enterprise:

An Ontario farm, in the early '80's was a busy place, and everyone on our farm moved briskly. My father often said of my mother that she could keep forty people busy. She certainly could think of things for people to do. Maybe that was one reason for my enjoying the farmyard so much. I loved to sit on the top rail of the fence, and luxuriantly do nothing, when I was well out of the range of her vision. Mother herself worked harder than anyone. She was the first up in the morning and the last one to go to bed at night. Our teams were on the land, and the Monday morning washing on the line well ahead of the neighbours'.[9]

It is clear from McClung's account that the woman in charge of the household with this relation to the enterprise has a role going beyond that merely of laboring to produce subsistence. It is an organizational and managerial role. The daily scheduling of work, the mobilizing of available labor resources to get the work done—these were part of the housewife's work role. Characteristically, men produced the means of production and produced for the largely local market while women produced the means of direct subsistence. Dependence upon money was minimal in the farming context. As far as possible, the subsistence of family members, servants, and hired hands employed for harvesting would be produced by the women—wives, daughters, and servants. A substantial farm, such as that described by Nellie McClung, would have employed servants of both sexes. Women in such households established rights in their own products so that when there was a surplus they could market it themselves.

At an earlier time the successful homestead would develop toward the type of household-enterprise organization described by Nellie McClung. At later stages homesteading enters a very different set of economic relations: it constitutes a subsistence economy. The division of labor between husband and wife and children as they become of age to participate produces their own survival. The contribution each makes is indeed essential, and it is hard to see how issues of relative power and status arise in such a context. However that may be, when the homestead develops to the point of producing a marketable surplus and enters economic relations already formed to constitute an economic unit of a determinate type, in which men are the economic agents, the force of these relations becomes apparent. In the midwest this experience was part of the impetus to women's suffrage and to the changes in matrimonial property laws (minimal though they were) which followed on the success of the campaign for suffrage.

There is an experience which is superficially similar to the work organization and division of labor of the Ontario farm described by McClung but very different in its actualities, both as an experience and in its underlying structure. In a Canadian novel based on her own experience as a schoolteacher boarding with a farm family, Martha Ostenso tells a story of tyranny of a farmer over his wife and daughters, and of the special drudgery of his wife's existence.[10]

To understand this radical difference in the internal organization of the farm family we must examine how the later farm family is articulated to the later agricultural economy. The change is a departure from the form in which the production for the subsistence of those laboring on the farm was integral to its economy. In this farm, as we've seen, women played a key role. What has happened in between the childhood scene described by Nellie McClung and that described by Ostenso in her novel are changes in the political economy of Canadian farming. Political and economic policies in Canada during the late nineteenth and early twentieth centuries combined railroad expansion with land settlement through promoting extensive immigration. [11] The later was a political imperative in defense of the threat of incorporation of western Canada into the United States and also served to develop a commodity (wheat) on which the railroad could depend for freight. As a bonus, the railroad created, and to a large extent dominated, a highly speculative real-estate market. The immigrants who built up the wheat economy of the Canadian prairies were, in many instances, financed by mortgages on their land and bank loans for tools, seed, and other necessities for which their crop stood as collateral. They did not begin, as homesteaders characteristically did, by producing their own subsistence and remaining to a large extent outside the market economy.

Ostenso's novel attests to the fact that survival for the immigrant farmer in this squeeze depended on the production of a single cash crop. Everything must be subordinated to that. In this context, then, women's labor is substituted for hired labor both in working the land and in the production of subsistence for the family. Furthermore, her labor is substituted as far as possible for labor in the form of manufactured commodities for which money must be found. Increased inputs of her labor eke out the lack of money at every possible point in the enterprise. Her time and energy, indeed her life, are treated as inexhaustible. She must, in addition, bear children because their labor is also essential. Women were virtually *imported* into Canada at this period to serve these functions.

Further, in this relation she is totally subordinate to her husband. She has no independent economic status or independent source of money. There are no local sources of employment for women. And while such laws as property, debt, and credit endow him with full economic status, they do not do the same for her. He is responsible for the debts on the land; he owns it insofar as he can be said to own it; the monetary income from the crops is his. Her labor contributes to his capacity to act in the economic sphere but does not further her own. These forms of matrimonial property law establish title to land in such a way as to provide for its standing as collateral to loans, or for being mortgaged. They are integral to the constitution of that type of economic organization in which the family functions as a small business in a fully developed capitalist economy. Moreover, the functioning of a highly speculative real-estate market was facilitated by single and unencumbered titles to real property. The patterns of drudgery and tyranny described as the farm woman's experience by Ostenso and others are generated by a political economy of this kind.

The extraction of surplus labour through mortgages and loans to farmers and homesteaders at this period took a distinctive form in relation to this rural petite bourgeoisie. The interest on loans and mortgages concealed, as did the wage, a relation of exploitation in which the farming household produced surplus value for the capitalist. The property form identified the farm with the individual male farmer. His success in accumulating over and above what he had to pay out in interest depended generally upon exploiting the labor of women, both domestically and as supplementary labor on the land. This is the situation Nellie McClung presents to typify the injustices and suffering of farm women:

I remember once attending the funeral of a woman who had been doing the work for a family of six children and three hired men, and she had not even a baby carriage to make her work lighter. When the last baby was three days old, just in threshing time, she died. Suddenly, and without warning, the power went off, and she quit without notice. The bereaved husband was the most astonished man in the world. He had never known Jane to do a thing like that before, and he could not get over it. In threshing time, too![12]

Farm women of that period were vividly conscious of this relation and of the injustice of laws which deprived them of the fruits of their own labor and permitted its appropriation by men as a basis for economic activity. For example, in 1910 a Saskatchewan farmeress (self-styled) stated the issue as follows:

It may not be so in every part of the province, but here it is not the bachelor who is making the most rapid progress, buying land and in every way improving the country, but it is the married men—and why? One wonders if the women have nothing to do with this. Who does the economizing if not the women? And pray tell me what incentive a woman has to work longer hours everyday than her husband, if she is to have no say in the selling or mortgaging of land her hard work has helped to pay for? Is it not the women who deny themselves most when the bills come due? It is not for myself that I so much want our rights as for our unfortunate sisters who, no matter how hard they toil, can never get what they merit. Several women in this neighbourhood have land, and I do not know of one who is not anxious for the dower law and homesteads for women, and most of them for equal suffrage.[13]

In the political economy of prairie development, women at this period were doing much the same kind of work as they did in the farm of the nineteenth century. Yet the social relations organizing their work and their relation to their husbands were very different. Rather than playing a leading managerial role in the household/enterprise as a whole, they became subordinated to a market and financial structure through their husband, who, as property owner, acted as economic agent. The husband extracted surplus labor from his wife, the results of which were allocated through the mortgage and loan system between him and those to whom he paid interest. Writings of this period expressing the perspective of women—whether in novel or journalistic form, such as those of the Saskatchewan farmeress[14] or Nellie McClung[15] or the U.S. writer Mary E. Wilkins Freeman—show an implicit or explicit hostility of women to men and a sharp recognition of women's interests as opposed to those of men. Women sought various means of limiting and controlling how they were exploited. Securing some rights in the property they helped to accumulate was only one way. Suffrage also was a means to this.

There were other ways. One major form was the withdrawal of women's participation in the labor on the farm, which accompanied the increased affluence of farming. A friend in British Columbia described how her mother prevented her from acquiring the manual skills and strength which would make her useful in "his" enterprise and thus make it less likely that she would be called upon to help.[16] Kohl indicates that this may be a more general practice.[17] Property rights constituting the man as economic agent have only very recently begun to be modified. The celebrated Murdoch case drew the attention of rural women to the fact, of which many were unaware, that their labor did not entitle them to a share in the property. Mrs. Murdoch had worked for twenty-five years on her husband's ranch, doing more than the domestic work. A large part of the work of cattle ranching she did herself, since, in addition to what she did when her husband was there, she took over the whole enterprise for the five months of the year he took paid employment. Yet her labor did not, in the view of the courts, entitle her to a share in the property she had helped to create. Even the dissenting opinion of Bora Laskin did not recognize the wife's contribution of labor to the overall enterprise as constituting a claim on the property. He dissented only on the grounds that her contribution had been exceptional. Women's labor as such—as the labor of a wife—had no claim.

Though petit-bourgeois forms of production are no longer the predominant form in Canada, the farm as an economic unit and other independent businesses still organize and incorporate women's labor in much the same way. The husband is constituted as economic agent appropriating his wife's labor as part of the enterprise. He cannot pay her a wage and deduct it from his income tax. A wife working in her husband's business cannot pay into the pension plan and is not insured for injuries on the job.

In the farm setting there is no physical separation of household and enterprise. Women's work in and around the household—both as direct producer of primary resources (gardening, keeping hens, etc.) and in processing and storing farm produce in general—sharply reduces the monetary costs of maintaining the family labor force. Nevertheless, the earlier complementary relation has disappeared, and with it the managerial role played, for example, by Nellie McClung's mother.[18] The organization of the farm as an economic unit is vested in the person of the husband. Wives, according to Carey, are not viewed as part of the enterprise: "Men view women as helpers, and women themselves often underestimate their own indispensable contribution to the farm.''[19] The man as economic agent and property owner articulates the farm as a productive process to the structure of large-scale agribusiness. In this relation, a woman's domestic labor, the economies she can achieve, combined with work on the farm and sometimes part-time employment outside, contribute to the profits of agribusiness. Carey points out that ''agribusiness corporations have indirectly admitted that they cannot pay anyone to work for them as cheaply as a farmer, his wife and children would work for a family farm.''[20] Individual ownership by the man and his legal capacity to appropriate the unpaid labor of his wife enter into very different relations at different points in the development of capitalism. It is in this relation that ''value'' arises, and it is this relation which organizes the internal relations of the family.

The Rise of Monopoly Capital and the Changing Middle-Class Family

The development of the corporate forms of ownership and economic agency increasingly separate the spheres of economic relations and of the family and household unit. The social construction of the individual man as agent or actor arises at the juncture of these two spheres. The forms of property and the social relations of the economy organize domestic labor in relation to the individual man in determinate ways. Under capitalism these relations are in a continual process of change, producing an ever-increasing concentration of capital. Quantitative changes have been accompanied by major modifications in the forms of property ownership, in the organization of the market and of financial and commercial processes, as well as of management and technology. These changes have also radically modified the organization of the middle-class family.

Over a period of time the corporate form becomes the legal constitution for all sizes of business, although for small business it is elective. Organizationally, it completes the separation of family and household from economy—or rather from the economy as differentiated and specialized processes. Economic relations are increasingly differentiated and specialized at national and international levels. Earlier forms of externalized economic relations still depended upon networks of kinsfolk in varying degrees. The middle-class family was a broader conception than the household, representing an organization of common interests vested in more than one privately owned enterprise or professional occupation. The separation of family and business world was blurred. Economic organization was supported and organized by kin and familial relations. The primarily domestic work of women was not isolated from the relational politics of business, quite apart from other ways in which women's skills could be involved in business enterprise. The advancement and security of the family involved the active participation of women in more than one way. Allegiances, decisions about character, the back-door informational processes known as gossip—these were all part of the ordinary world in which business was done and were integral to it. But the corporate form supplants these processes with its own. Those employed must owe allegiance to the organization and not to the family. Specific competencies and qualifications become of greater importance than family ties. Alliances established within the business structures and networks themselves become more central than alliances in the local area or within a kin network. As the economic process is sealed off, women in the household are isolated, and the domestic world becomes truly privatized. The locus of advancement for the individual ceases to be identified with his family connections and with the advancement of the kin constellation. It becomes identified with his individualized relation to the corporate enterprise. It is this which later becomes institutionalized as a career. The domestic labor of the middle-class household is increasingly organized as a personal service to the individual man. Its relation to the business enterprise in which he is an actor arises in how the household work and organization are subordinated to its requirements as they become his.

The relation through which men appropriate women's labor is changed. The relation is no longer part of the organization of the enterprise in relation to the economy, in which women are included. Now an individual man appropriates as his the work done by his wife or other women of his family. The individual man becomes the enterprise so far as the family is concerned. The earliest and most typical form of this is that of the individual professional. It becomes general as the *career,* rather than individual ownership, structures the entry and activity of the individual as economic agent. As the corporate form of organizing agency and ownership become primary, the individual's agency and relation to the means of production are organizationally mediated. The relation of appropriation becomes highly personalized. It becomes a general form characterizing the relations of middle-class women and men in work situations in the home and outside.

This is visible in many forms. It is present, for example, in what we do not know about women in the past. It is present in our ignorance, until recently, of the fact that the public figure of British astronomer William Herschel concealed that of a second astronomer, his sister Caroline, who shared his work, perhaps shared his discoveries, made discoveries of her own, kept house for him, and acted as his secretary.[21] When a group of eminent sociologists wrote accounts of how one of their major pieces of work was done, some described a very substantial contribution by their wives. No one raised questions about the fact that the husband appropriated that work as his and that the wives' work contributed to the advancement of their husbands' careers and reputations and not to their own.[22]

The middle-class relation of appropriation by men of women's work is incorporated into professional, bureaucratic, and managerial organizations. It appears as a differentiation of men's and women's roles, providing for the structuring of a career for the former in positions which are technically specialized and superordinate, and a truncated structure of advancement for the latter in positions which are skilled but ancillary and subordinate to those of men and, of course, lower- paid. Women were and still are secretaries, graduate nurses, dental hygienists, and elementary classroom teachers. Men were and still are managers, doctors, dentists, and principals and vice-principals of elementary schools. Until recently these forms of employment for middle-class women were institutionalized as a transitional status between childhood and marriage. Possible competition and social contradiction between women's occupational status and marriage and subordination to the husband were avoided by terminating employment on marriage or by ensuring that married women did not occupy professional positions of any authority.[23]

In these developments we find the social and material bases of the form of family which we have taken as typical. We only now become aware of it as a distinct, historical, and cultural form in moving away from it. This is the household and family organization which is a distinct economic unit, primarily a "consuming" unit; that is, one in which women's domestic labor producing the subsistence for the individual members depends upon a money income. Household and family are increasingly tied to the individual man's career and less to an interlinking of family relations and enterprises. Household and family are enucleated. The interests of the wife are held to be intimately bound up with her husband's career. In various ways she is expected to support him morally and socially, as well as through the ways in which her domestic labor ensures both his ordinary physical well-being and his proper presentation of self.[*] His career should pay off for her in increments of prestige in the relevant social circles and in home furnishings, a larger home—in general, in the material forms in which his advancement in the organization may be expressed in relations between neighbors, friends, and colleagues. As corporations increase in size and the managerial structure is increasingly objectified, a sharp contradiction arises between individual autonomy and subordination to authority. There is a peculiarly difficult combination of the need to exercise initiative, to give leadership, and to take risks as ingredients of a successful career and the requirements of conformity to organizational exigencies, norms, and criteria of achievement in a hierarchical structure.

*Editors' note: See Fowlkes (Chapter 17) in this volume.

Hence, "tension management" comes to be seen as an important responsibility of middle-class wives.

As the professional, government, and corporate apparatuses become consolidated as a ruling apparatus, forms of action in words and symbols become fully differentiated. Language is constituted as a discrete mode of action. This requires a division of labor which will organize and provide for the necessary material aspects of communication. Processes of action which are merely communicative depend on specific divisions of labor as well as a technology—hence the elaboration of clerical work. But women's domestic labor also comes to be organized specifically to service this conceptually organized world of action. As I have written elsewhere:

It is a condition of man's being able to enter and become absorbed in the conceptual mode that he does not have to focus his activities and interest upon his bodily existence. If he is to participate fully in the abstract mode of action, then he must be liberated also from having to attend to his needs, etc. in the concrete and particular. The organization of work and expectations in managerial and professional circles both constitutes and depends upon the alienation of men from their bodily and local existence. The structure of work and the structure of career take for granted that these matters are provided for in such a way that they will not interfere with his action and participation in that world. Providing for the liberation from the Aristotelian categories [of time and space] of which Blerstedt speaks, is a woman who keeps house for him, bears and cares for his children, washes his clothes, looks after him when he is sick and generally provides for the logistics of his bodily existence.[24]

The home, then, becomes an essential unit in organizing the abstracted modes of ruling in the context—the necessary and ineluctable context—of the local and particular.

These changes introduce a new subordination of the home to the educational system. The technological, accounting, and communicative practices of the emerging ruling apparatus require appropriate skills as a condition of entry and of action in its modes. Language skills—indeed, perhaps just those styles of speech identified originally by Bernstein as an elaborated code[25]—are essential to participation in this form of action and being. The work of mothering in relation to the work of the school becomes an essential mediating process in the production and reproduction of class relations among the bourgeoisie and against the working class.

The educational system and access to the educational system, mediated and controlled by family, home, and, above all, by the work of women as mothers, come to provide the major transgenerational linkage of class. Children are no longer prospective actors in the moving history of family relations entwined with property and economic enterprise. Sons are no longer prospectively those who will carry on family businesses and hence provide for the continuity of capital built in the work of one generation toward the next. Daughters are no longer those who will consolidate alliances or relations linking social, economic, and political relations into a network of kin. The child progressively becomes the object of parental work, particularly the work of mothers, aimed at creating a definite kind of person, with distinct communicative skills in speech and writing and with capacities to take advantage of an educational process through which he or she can become advantaged.

Much of the literature on the relation between family, class, and education fails to recognize that it is the product of the work of women. The school as an organization of work presupposes prior and concomitant work which is done by women in the home. This work is never named as such. It is seen in ways which render the time, skill, and effort involved as invisible. It is translated into love and responsibility or is merely treated mechanically— home as an "influence" on school performance; the family as an "influence" on school achievement; etc. But the relation is not recognized as an actual work process. Here, for example, is a description of a "home" setting which is favorable to the successful child:

David is the son of professional parents who have themselves been educated in a grammar school. They provide him with facilities for doing homework in a separate room and light a fire when necessary. There is therefore little interruption from other members of the family or from television and radio. If he has trouble with his homework he can turn to either his mother or father for help, and many books of reference are available. His cultural background is constantly a help to him at school and in his homework. Mother or father may even inspect his homework regularly or occasionally.[26]

The authors are properly aware of the significance of economic factors in this picture, and it is indeed contrasted with the situation of a working-class boy of similar age and abilities. What is not visible to them, apparently, is the work of mothering, which provides the facilities, inhibits interruption, cleans, lays the fire, feeds, provides an orderly environment—and, indeed, the work involved in providing the "cultural background" which becomes his. In general, middle-class mothers are both expected to and do spend a great deal of time and work on organizing the home to facilitate their children's work in school and in developing their children's skills in the nonspecific ways summed up in "cultural background" or "language abilities." Somehow it is often described as if the language skills of a child are acquired by some kind of osmosis merely from the atmosphere of the home. There is a lack of recognition of the amount of actual work and thought which middle-class women, having time, opportunity, and skills, expend upon their children. Mothers train their children in the responsibilities of schoolwork, in scheduling, in "mood control," and in the organization of physical behavior, adapting them to the classroom. Mothers may correct their children's deficiencies and prevent errors, lapses, and delays from becoming visible at school and, hence, from being consequential in the child's record. This is work. It is an important part of how middle-class women's work in the home serves to organize and sustain the inequalities of class.

The emergence and progressive integration of the new form of ruling apparatus, distinctively a communicative practice, is also an ideologically informed and organized practice. Determinate social organization differentiates and separates the enterprise from particular individuals and particular places. We can find in Weber's analysis of the bureaucratic type of authority the essential prescription for the formation of a managerial or administrative structure serving the objectives of an enterprise quite independent of the objectives of those who "perform" it, make its objectives theirs, and thereby bring it into being. The bases of access to positions in the ruling apparatus change. As these no longer clearly differentiate on sex lines but call for technical knowledge, qualifications, and so forth, the barriers to women's entry are weakened. In response, the barriers are artificially and actively reinforced, and ideological forms aimed specifically at the organization of middle-class women's relation to the ruling apparatus are developed.

The rise of monopoly capitalism, rather than instantly precipitating women into the private sphere, initiates a struggle. On the one hand, the barriers to women's participation are reinforced and reorganized; and on the other, women strive to break through barriers already weakened by the advance of capitalism. This struggle has focused particularly on women's education. The conception of a specialized education for women preparing them for domesticity points to a new need to plan and organize women's relation to the home. It is also provides that the very ideological channels through which women's potential access to a wider arena opens should be those through which they would learn the practice of their confinement. Ideological organization has been central in organizing the role and social relations of middle-class women.

As education became the key link in the access to economic agency, women's access to education had to be regulated. Steps were taken to exclude women from professional, bureaucratic, and political positions as these were found to be vulnerable.[27] Active forms of ideological and state repression responding to incursions by middle-class women were developed. An educational system systematically differentiating boys from girls was put in place. Girls were streamed so that they would be disqualified for the kinds of advanced training giving access to the professions. The hidden curriculum trained them to be open and conforming to the ideological initiatives and technical practices increasingly originating from experts located in academic settings.

Women's postsecondary training, insofar as it is not in subordinate forms of professional training, such as nursing, pharmacy, and teaching, emphasizes arts and social science. The stress of school and postsecondary education is on women's language abilities, on their knowledge of social science, on psychology, on art and literature.[28] Women are prepared for their ancillary clerical roles in management. They are provided with the language skills needed to give the "cultural background" on which their future children's success in school will depend. They are also trained to respond to the work of psychological and sociological experts, to psychiatrists, and to physicians as authorities, and to make practical use of their understanding of the new ideologies produced by such specialists. These ideological skills link the private domestic sphere to the professional, bureaucratic, and managerial controls of the ruling apparatus. The ideological organization coordinated and still coordinates the family and women's roles in relation to the changing and various needs of the ruling apparatus. Education not only ensured that middle-class women would not end with the types of skills which would give them an undeniable claim to entry as active participants to the ruling apparatus, but it also laid down specific ideological controls through which the changing relations of a rapidly shifting capitalist development could be reformulated and reorganized as they were fed through to the family and to women's work in the family. What mothers did in the home affected what children did in school. But what went on in the home was the "wild" factor uncontrolled by the hierarchical structure of the educational process. Ideological organization, originating in a scientific establishment and mediated by the mass media, came to coordinate the private and state sectors of responsibility for children, as indeed it did in other spheres.

These relations among ideological organizations—first, a family form subordinating women in a subcontractual relation[29] to a ruling apparatus of government, management, and professions mediated as personal services to husband and children, and second, an educational system preparing women for these family functions and for the essentially subordinate clerical and professional roles—are the matrix of the experience of patriarchy among middle-class women. The authority of men over women is the authority of a class and expresses class "interests." The inner complicity of women in their own oppression is a feature of class organization. The concept of "patriarchy" explicates as a social relation between women and men the conjunction of institutions locking middle-class women into roles which are ancillary but essential to the ruling apparatus and specifically silencing them by giving them no access to the ideological, professional, and political means in which their experience might be communicated to other women.

The Changing Material Bases of Dependency

Dependence of married women, and particularly women with children, on men and men's salaries or wages is a feature of both middle-class and working-class family relations in contemporary capitalism. This is not simply a matter of a universal family form characteristic of a species rather than a culture or mode of production. Women's dependency must be seen as arising in a definite social form and, as we have suggested, must be organized rather differently in differing class settings and relations. One view identifies the emergence of this type of family organization with the rise of capitalism. As the productive process is increasingly taken over by the industrial organization of production, the family becomes a consuming, rather than a producing, unit, and women's domestic labor ceases to play a socially productive role and becomes instead a personal service to the wage-earner. Her domestic labor reproduces the labor power of the individual worker. Here is Seccombe's account:

With the advent of industrial capitalism, the general labour process was split into two discrete units: a domestic and an industrial unit. The character of the work performed in each was fundamentally different. The domestic unit reproduced labour power for the labour market. The industrial unit produced goods and services for the commodity market. This split in the labour process had produced a split in the labour force roughly along sexual lines: women into the domestic unit, men into industry.[30]

But as we acquire more historical knowledge of women we find that the sharpness of this supposed historical moment becomes blurred. The emergence of the dependent family form is slow and seemingly contingent upon elaborations and developments of the original separation of the domestic economy from the industrial process. As we explore the dynamic process at work we can recognize a contradiction in the rise of capitalism so far as women and their relation to the family are concerned. It seems that the same industrial capitalism leading apparently to a restriction and narrowing of the scope of women's work in the home and to her own and her children's dependence on a man's wage is also a process which potentially advances women's independence by creating conditions under which women can earn enough to support themselves, and perhaps even to support their children. Earlier productive labor was tied to sex differences by varying physical and biological situations and also by the intimate ties of skills, which represented a true specialization of persons from childhood or youth onward. As production is increasingly mediated by machines and increasingly organized as a form of enterprise specifically separated from particular individuals and their local relations, it also becomes increasingly indifferent to social differentiations, such as gender or race.[31] At every new level in the development of productive capacity in capitalism, this contradiction is apparent. Capitalism continually presents the possibility of women's independence and, at the same time, engenders conditions and responses which have constituted a fully dependent form of family unit. The dependence of both middle-class and working-class women on the individual man's salary or wage must be examined in relation to the organization of the labor market and employment possibilities for women outside the home.

Let us look first at one rather straightforward and simple picture of the relation. In the Canadian census data for 1961, the majority of men's average earnings are at the break-even level or better, and only workers in service and recreation, farm workers, and laborers earn less than the basic income for a four-member family. Women's earnings are insufficient to provide for the four-member family in every category of women workers. Indeed, the average earnings for women in most categories fall below the basic, no-frills income needed for a two-member family. Women's average earnings would not, for the most part, support a woman and her child. It is clear then, that as soon as a woman has a child to support, her options are sharply reduced. Quite apart from the lack of adequate childcare and other sources of support, such as school meals, etc., women's earning possibilities incapacitate them from independence. Men can (or could) count on earnings which would provide for both children and a wife. Women cannot count on earnings sufficient for themselves and children.[*]

Over time, working-class and middle-class patterns of family organization have become more alike with respect to the wife's dependence on her husband's wage or salary. But the history of that relation is very different. Among the middle class the earlier civil status of a man simply obliterated his wife's as she was subsumed in the family economic unit identified with him. She had no place in civil society, no capacity for economic action, at least so long as she was married. What she produced and what she earned, if she did earn, were his. Later, her domestic labor becomes subordinated to the enterprise of his career, and employment outside the home is organized to ensure that the jurisdictions of male authority and appropriation of women's labor inside the home and outside it do not interfere with one another. Dependency is part of a perpetuated pattern of excluding women, and married women in particular, from functioning as independent economic agents and making their domestic and other services available to those who do.

The history of the present family form among the working class is very dif-

---

*Editors' note: Although this analysis was based on 1961 Canadian census data, the general points still apply to both the United States and Canada. (See Introductions to Parts III and IV of this volume.)

ferent. It does not begin with women's exclusion from economic activity, and it does not involve the formation of a property-holding unit identified with the man. The legal forms were the same, and these gave men the right to women's earnings, but the actual practice and organization of work relations and economic contributions did not conform to the middle-class pattern. The exclusive dependence of women on men's wages is only gradually established and is differently structured. For working-class women, dependence is directly on the man's wage-earning capacity and role, and the man's status and authority in the family are directly linked to his capacity to earn. Moore and Sawhill summarize the sociological studies on the effects of wives' employment outside the home on marital power relations, drawing attention to the greater effect among working-class women: "A number of studies have found that wives who are employed exercise a greater degree of power in their marriages. Marital power is higher among women employed full-time than those working for pay part-time or not at all, and it is greatest among women with the most prestigious occupations, women who are most committed to their work, and those whose salaries exceed their husbands'. Working women have more say especially in financial decisions. This tendency for employment to enhance women's power is strongest among lower- and working-class couples."[32]

As we learn more of women's history, we find that the emergence of the dependent form of the family among the working class was far from an abrupt and immediate consequence of the rise of industrial capitalism. The subsistence work of women in relation to the household as an economic unit has only gradually been supplanted by the industrial process. And only gradually have women been weaned from contributing to the *means* of household subsistence, as contrasted with labor applied to the direct production of the subsistence of its members. On the one hand, women came into competition with men for jobs in industry; on the other hand, their labor was essential in the house, so that home and family were in competition with industry for women's labor. The dependence of the mother-children unit on the male wage-earner emerges rather slowly. Anderson describes, for early nineteenth-century-Lancashire, a form of family in which all its members, with the exception of the very young and the very old, worked outside the home and pooled their earnings.[33] Scott and Tilly have identified a distinct form of working-class and petit-bourgeois family economy, which they describe as the "family wage economy."[34] It is one in which each member earns and contributes to a common fund out of which the family needs are met. They argue that although a relatively small proportion of married women were employed in industry until relatively late in the nineteenth century, the pattern of women not working outside the home and not contributing actively to the household economy came very late. A wife who did not work and contribute directly to the means of subsistence, and who had to depend upon her husband's wage, was most definitely undesirable. Married women worked outside the home and brought money or goods into the home in all kinds of ways. Many had gardens and produced for their families and could sell the small surplus they might produce. Women were small traders, peddlers, went into domestic service, were laundresses seamstresses, farm laborers, scavengers, as well as industrial workers.[35] Women also did productive work in the home. Manufacturers put work out to women at piece rates. Sometimes manufacturers supplied machines to women working at home. Other paid work done by women at that period included running a boarding house and working in small businesses.[36]

Of course, many women workers were single, but it is also clear that many were married. It is married women who would have been working in the home. Moreover, the very rapid response to the *salles d'asile* (day-care nurseries) established by women's religious orders in the 1850s indicated the extent of the need. The surviving records of two such *salles d'asile* show that many children were from families in which both parents went out to work.[37]

Under the "family wage" economy, children are essential contributors. Children might be employed in factory work, but they had also a wide variety of opportunities for contribution, ranging from the care of younger children while parents were at work, to housekeeping, gardening, many ordinary chores such as fetching water, and, as well, odd jobs when these were available. As attendance at public school came to be enforced, the school came into competition with the needs of the family for children's labor.[38]

With the institutionalization of universal education, children cease or have already ceased to be regular wage-earners contributing to the family wage. They cease progressively to contribute to the everyday work activities of household tasks and childcare. Previously the work of children would have relieved the mother of at least some of her household obligations and made it easier for her to undertake employment outside the home. The withdrawal of child labor from the household, as well as from the labor force, required the presence of mothers in the home. Indeed, the home comes to be organized around the scheduling of school and work so that the mother is tied down to the household in a way which was, in fact, new. Both the husband and children might come home for a midday meal. The school imposed standards of cleanliness, which represented a serious work commitment on the part of women, who had to pump and heat water for washing.[39] In the school context the child appears as the public "product" of a mother's work. Her standards of housekeeping and childcare begin to be subject to the public appraisal of the school system through the appearance and conduct of her child in the school. The working-class home as a work setting began to be organized by a relation to the school, as well as to the place of work. The school itself set standards for women's work and, in various ways, enforced them.

Hence, the family wage economic organization is shifted to the new enucleated family form, in which wife and child make no contribution to the family economy in terms of inputs from outside, and in which both depend upon the man as wage-earner. The wife, in addition, depends upon the husband for the means to reproduce the domestic order, while she is to provide him with personal service in the form of domestic labor in the home, as well as other more immediate personal services. These changes were part of the developments in capitalism and of the institutionalization of responses and adaptations to such developments. The segregated labor force we find today results from these changes. This process is the other face—that which regards the working class—of the same developments in capitalism, earlier described in relation to the bourgeoisie and middle class.

The Subordination of Women in the Working-Class Family

The dynamic process of capital accumulation is also one of an increasingly extensive use of machines, making labor more productive, displacing labor, and making the productive process more generally indifferent to differentials of physical strength. From this process, two consequences flow for working-class women. One is the actual or potential broadening of the range of jobs and industrial settings in which women work. A second is the tendency of capitalism to generate a surplus labor population which cannot be absorbed into developing sectors and hence functions as a reserve army of labor. These factors together create a highly competitive situation, which becomes acute at times of recession.

The traditionally lower wages of disadvantaged groups such as women and blacks give them an advantage in competing for jobs. Through the nineteenth and twentieth centuries, this problem was a recurrent theme in male working class views concerning women in the labor force and in policies of trade and labor unions. The issue of women displacing men in the work force is complemented by a concern for the implications for the family and men's status therein.[40] Conceivably, women might be paid a wage which would effectively compete with the family for women's labor. Conceivably, women might be economically independent of men. Certainly it happened that some women were earning when husbands, brothers, and sons could not.[41] These complementary themes recur again and again in the attack on women workers made by leading sectors of the trade union movement from the early nineteenth century on. Even in the 1960s the American Federation of Labor refused its support to any kind of quota system which might rectify the inequalities experienced by blacks and women. Of the early nineteenth century, Malmgreen writes:

There was a psychological as well as an economic basis for the male workers' uneasiness, for the chance to earn a separate wage outside the home might free wives and daughters to some extent from the control of their husbands and parents. The piteous image of the sunken-cheeked factory slave must be balanced against that of the boisterous and cheeky "fact'ry lass." Lord Ashley, speaking on behalf of the regulation of child and female labour in factories, warned the House of Commons of the "ferocity" of the female operatives, of their adoption of male habits—drinking, smoking, forming clubs, and using "disgusting" language. This, he claimed, was "a perversion of nature," likely to produce "disorder, insubordination, and conflict in families."[42]

The voice here is that of the ruling class, but on this issue the working-class man and the ruling class have often been united. Malmgreen notes that in the early nineteenth century this view appears particularly prevalent among leading artisans in the working-class movements of Britain. It is the interests of a similar type of worker—crafts and trades workers—which were represented in the American Federation of Labor (AFL). The AFL played a leading role in the organization of a sex-stratified (as well as a racially stratified) labor-market as corporate capitalism began its great rise in North America in the late nineteenth and early twentieth centuries.[43] During this period the AFL contributed to the institutionalization of the sexually stratified labor force we find today. Under Samuel Gompers' leadership, the trade union movement in North America became for women a systematic organization of weakness relative to men, and a systematic organization of preferential access to skills and benefits for men. In marked contrast to the class orientation of the Industrial Workers of the World (IWW), there was little interest in unionizing women other than as a means of control.[44] There was a fear that bringing numbers of women into a union would result in "petticoat government."[45] Women's locals were sometimes given only half the voting power of men on the grounds that they could only contribute half the dues.[46]

Struggles to restrict women's participation, and particularly married women's participation, in the labor force went on under various guises.* It does not seem likely, however, that union efforts, even when supported by at least some sections of the women's movement at that period, would have been effective in reconstituting the family in a way that maintained women's dependence on men's wages without the active intervention of the bourgeois state apparatus. The corporatist ideology enunciated by Mackenzie King formulated the principles of, and legitimated, the administrative and regula-

*Editors' note: See May (Chapter 4) in this volume.

tory forms through which trade union organization was articulated to state mechanisms aimed at controlling and deploying the labor force in the service of monopoly capital.[47] In these contexts the implicit alliance between state and trade unions with a common interest—stemming from very different bases—becomes effective in subordinating women to domestic labor and in restricting their participation in the labor force.[48]

The emergence of national and international market and financial organizations; of an organization of productive processes implanted into local areas rather than arising indigenously and conforming to standardized technical plans and standardized machines, tools, and other equipment; and of a universalizing of managerial and technical processes called for a new kind of labor force. Similar exigencies arose also in relation to the military requirements of imperialist expansion and the devastating wars resulting from the conflict of rival empires. This new labor force had to be capable of entering the industrial process anywhere in the society. The need was not only for technically skilled workers, but more generally for a *universalized* labor force, stripped of regional and ethnic cultures, fully literate, English-speaking, familiar with factory discipline and the discipline of the machine, and, in relation to the military enterprise in particular, physically healthy. In the production of this labor force, mothering, as a form of domestic labor, was seen as increasingly important.

In the legislation passed during this period, we can see two aspects of state interest: on the one hand, a concern to restrict the ways in which industry competed with the home for women's labor; on the other hand, an interest in laying the legal and administrative basis for a family form in which the costs of supporting the wife and of providing for children would be borne by the wage of the man.[49] The latter motive has obviously special attractions during periods of economic depression.

From the early twentieth century through to the mid-twenties there are a series of legislative measures directed toward the family and women.[50] These served to reorganize the legal and administrative basis of the family.* Laws which earlier entitled the husband and father to appropriate the earnings of his wife and children disappeared. New legislation was passed requiring men to support their families whether they lived with them or not.[51] Welfare policies were developed incorporating similar principles. These have been built into the welfare practices of today so that, for example, a man sharing the house of a woman welfare recipient may be assumed to be supporting her and her children, hence permitting the suspension of her welfare payments.† Unemployment insurance and pension plans, introduced subsequently, also created an

---

*Editors' note: See Boris and Bardaglio (Chapter 5) in this volume.
†Editors' note: See Folbre (Chapter 25) in this volume.

administrative organization enforcing women's dependence on men in marriage. The seemingly genial and recent legal recognition of the common-law relation is in fact part of the same theme. Futhermore, the state entry into the socialization of children through the public education system provided an important source of control. Streaming patterns to those characterizing the experience of middle-class women prevented working-class women from acquiring the fundamental manual and technical skills on which access to skilled, and even semiskilled, work in industry came increasingly to depend. Thus, a significant part of the increased cost of producing the new kind of labor force, including the costs of women's specialization in domestic labor, would be borne directly by the working man's wage. [52]

It would, however, be a serious mistake to view the interests of the trade unions at the earlier period as representing a simple patriarchal impulse. Subsistence of both men and women and their children depended upon the work of women, in a way which is no longer so. The provision of shelter and heat, the purchase and preparation of food, the making and maintenance of clothing, and the overall management of wages were survival work and survival skills. The physical maintenance of the male breadwinner was essential. When food was short, women and children went without to ensure that the ''master'' got enough, or at least the most of what there was. [53] It must be emphasized that this was an interdependent unit which maximized the survival possibilities of all its members. Black describes the dilemmas arising for women when unemployment or low wages made it impossible to support a wife and family, thereby forcing women to wage labor. She must choose at that time between the care she could give her children by staying home, which meant that they would starve, and the risks of leaving them to go out to work to earn enough for them to eat. [54]

Characteristic of the working-class family, in which the man is the breadwinner and the women and children are dependent, is a marked subordination of women to men. Control over funds is a distinct male prerogative. A husband's resistance to his wife's going out to work goes beyond the practicalities of the family's economic well-being. [55] Working-class women learn a discipline which subordinates their lives to the needs and wishes of men. The man's wage is his; it is not a family wage. Varying customs have developed around the disposal of this. Sometimes there appears to be a survival of the ''family wage'' tradition whereby the wife takes the whole wage and manages its various uses, including a man's pocket money. But it is also open to men not to tell their wives what they earn and to give them housekeeping money or require them to ask for money for each purchase. It is clearly *his* money, and there is an implicit contract between a husband and wife whereby he provides for her and her children on whatever conditions he thinks best, and she provides for him the personal and household services that he demands. The household is organized in relation to his needs and wishes; mealtimes are when he wants his meals; he eats with the children or alone, as he chooses, sex is when he wants it; the children are to be kept quiet when he does not want to hear them. The wife knows at the back of her mind that he could take his wage-earning capacity and make a similar "contract" with another woman. As wages have increased, the breadwinner's spending money has enlarged to include leisure activities which are his, rather than hers—a larger car, a motorcycle, a boat. Even a camper often proves more for him than for her, since for her it is simply a transfer from convenient to less convenient conditions of the same domestic labor she performs at home.

For working-class women this relation has a political dimension. The discipline of acceptance of situations over which they have no control and the discipline of acceptance of the authority of a man, who also has in fact no control over the conditions of his wage-earning capacity, are not compatible with the bold and aggressive styles of political or economic action which are characteristic of working-class organization. Women's sphere of work and responsibility is defined as subordinate and dependent to that in which men act. The children's well-being, the production of the home—these require from women a discipline of self-abnegation and service as exacting sometimes as that of a religious order. Masculinity and male status are, in part, expressed in men's successful separation from, and subordination of, the sphere of women's activity, as well as the visibility of his success in "controlling" his wife (what may go on behind the scenes is another matter).

The fact that the wage relation creates an uncertain title to male status and authority, by virtue of how its conditions are lodged in the market process, makes the visible forms of relations all the more important. Men subordinate themselves in the workplace to the authority of the foreman, supervisor, and managers. A condition of their authority in the home is this daily acceptance of the authority of others. Men assume also the physical risks and hazards of their work. They live with the ways in which capital uses them up physically and discards them mentally and psychologically. They also undertake a lifetime discipline, particularly if they elect to marry and support a wife and children. That responsibility is also a burden, and it can be a trap for working-class men as much as for working-class women. Through that relation a man is locked into his job and into the authority relations it entails. His wife's subordination, her specific personal and visible subservience, her economic dependence, are evidence of his achievement. Her "nagging," her independent initiatives in political or economic contexts, her public challenges to his authority—these announce his failure as a man. In the political context, we find a subculture prohibiting women's participation in political activity other than in strictly ancillary roles essentially within the domestic sphere. Thus, when women organized militant action in support of the men striking in the Flint, Michigan, strike in 1937, they had to go against norms restraining women from overt forms of political action.

Earlier we cited Malmgreen's description of an instance of ruling-class fear of the "ferocity" of female operatives. Lord Ashley clearly identified the subordination of women to men in the home with their political suppression. The ideology of weak and passive women, needing protection and support, and subordinated "naturally" to the authority of men in the home—as it was adopted by working-class men and working-class political and economic organizations—served to secure the political control of one section of the working class by another.[56] The subordination of working-class women to men in the family, which was progressively perfected over the latter half of the nineteenth and the first quarter of the twentieth centuries, was part of the attempt of the ruling class to establish a corporate society subordinating workers through their union organization. The range of organized working-class action was progressively narrowed to economic organization restricted to the workplace. A whole range of concerns and interests arising outside the workplace in relation to health, housing, pollution, and education, remained unexpressed or expressed only indirectly. Inadvertently, working-class men combined to suppress and silence those whose work directly engaged them with such problems. Indirectly, and through the mechanism described above, they came to serve the interests of a ruling class in the political and economic subordination of half the working class.

As we have examined the development of a form of the family in which women depend upon men, and the ideological and political institutions which enforce this dependency, we can begin to see patriarchy (in the sense of men's political and personal domination over women) in relation to class as part of the institutions through which a ruling class maintains its domination. At different stages in the transformation of property relations from the individual to the corporate form, middle-class women have been subordinated to the changing requirements of class organization and of the transgenerational maintenance of class. For working-class women we have seen the emergence of a dependent form of family subordinating women to men, locked in by legal and administrative measures instituted by the state, and a stratified labor market fostered by trade unions, capitalists, and the state. These are the institutional forms which have secured the uses of women's domestic labor in the service of a ruling apparatus, ensuring and organizing the domination of a class over the means of production. They are political institutions in the sense in which the women's movement has come to understand that term, in that they involve the exercise of power as such, whether it is a feature of specialized political institutions, such as political parties, government, and the like, or not.

Throughout the foregoing analysis we have been aware of capitalism as continually generating changes in material conditions, and of these changes as they are fed through to the "surface," necessitating innovations, adaptations, and reorganization. Forms of political and ideological organization which are relatively successful in stabilizing the position of the ruling class at one point may, at the next, confront situations in which they are no longer effective or appropriate. This is surely the situation with respect to women today. The institutions of patriarchy organize and control in a material context that which they can no longer handle effectively. The ground has shifted under our feet.

We have pointed to a major contradiction arising for both middle- class and working-class women as capitalism advances. It is the contradiction between a capital which is becoming essentially indifferent to the sex of those who do its work, and the claims of domestic economy as an essential basis for its property relations and the reproduction of class and the labor force. With the rise of corporate capitalism, the balance begins to shift away from the domestic. In relation to middle-class women, the extension of corporate capitalism, the professions, the governmental process, the elaboration of the ruling apparatus characteristic of contemporary capitalism—these require skills based on education and specialized advanced training which are not differentiated by sex. Women's exclusion becomes, then, a political institution built into the organization of education, into the uses of power characteristic of the self-governing process of professions and professional organizations, and into the conjunction of the interests of a ruling class and its male members. Earlier the contradiction emerged as a latent, and sometimes actual, competition between the domestic and the political economies for women's labor—a competition resolved for some time by restricting women's access to the labor force after marriage and, in general, by a limited range of occupations with an earning capacity below that enabling them to maintain a family unit without a husband. The political aspects of women's subordination are the institutions of patriarchy. But they could not have been effective without a corresponding material base.

Earlier, too, women's domestic labor was essential to subsistence. There were no alternatives. Domestic labor has also been essential to advances in the family standard of living, which would have been originally unobtainable without the interposition of women's work in the home. Women of both the middle and working classes at different income levels could, by their personal skills, hard work, and commitment, take the wage and salary, purchase materials and tools, and combine these with labor and skill—their knowledge of cooking, cleaning, managing, laundering, shopping, etc.—to produce a subsistence level (or better) essential for family health, comfort, and, under minimal income conditions, survival. Over time, the labor women contributed to the domestic production of subsistence was displaced by labor and skill embodied in the product of industry. Progressively, capital has interposed a labor process into the home and has reorganized the work process there.* At some point, what women can contribute in the form of labor no longer balances off in a comparison with what she can earn and hence add to the purchasing power of the family. The wife can no longer reduce costs to the wage-earner by contributing more of her labor to the household process.

The slow but consistent upward creep of the labor-force participation of married women, and, indeed, of women in general, points to the diminishing power of the domestic economy to compete with paid employment for women. The demand for certain types of women's labor increased greatly as corporate capitalism called for clerical, sales, and service workers at low cost, a demand which has more and more been met by women. The "compact" restricting the employment of married women, and hence the direct competition of paid employment with the domestic economy controlled by the husband, has been weakened and is in decline. The assertion of individual authority by a man in restraining his wife from taking on paid employment outside the home is weakened by the disappearance of complementary restrictions in the work setting. With inflation and increasing levels of unemployment, more and more married women enter the labor force. Money earnings are essential to the family, and if the man's wage or salary does not bring in enough, then a woman's responsibilities to her home and family increasingly demand that she seek employment outside the home.

The same developments within capitalism which elaborate the apparatus of ruling are also those which result in the ever-increasing problem of the surplus labor population. Rates of unemployment have been slowly and steadily increasing, but in the current period of economic crisis they have risen sharply. For the first time, the concentration of capital in a machine technology has begun to create a surplus labor population among the middle class. The state, management, and professional organizations respond to these problems by a resort to the measures which worked earlier and, on the part of professions, by the adoption of protectionist strategies reinforcing discriminatory practices against women. The state attempts to reduce unemployment and reduce state responsibility for unemployment by using the well-worn mechanisms for forcing women into dependence upon men through its welfare policies, unemployment insurance practices, the withdrawal of subsidies for childcare, etc. But these measures now function vacuously. The relation of dependency is no longer fully viable. The status quo

*Editors' note: See Cowan and Glazer (Chapters 6 and 11) in this volume.

ante cannot be reinstated. These measures, rather than having practical force in articulation to a material base, merely become the arbitrary exercise of political power.

The earlier political and ideological accommodations, institutionalized in the labor market and the educational system, function so as to depress arbitrarily women's capacity to earn a living, to survive, and to provide for children. Of course, there are segments of both the middle class and the working class where earlier forms are successful because the underlying relations have not disappeared. Contemporary capitalism is a complex form, and the political economy characteristically develops unevenly and via transitions which are often abrupt, as new levels of capitalist organization invade and overlay earlier forms. At the same time, the dislocations and the arbitrary oppression of the patriarchal forms begin to emerge. Among middle-class women and sections of the organized working class, the women's movement advances an ideology and establishes political and economic organizations through which the latent inequities are given objective expression and become the focus of organized action.

In the course of this inquiry, what the women's movement has made visible as patriarchy has been explicated as an integral part of the institutional process by which the capitalist ruling class has maintained its domination over society. It has taken different forms in relation to women in the middle classes and in the working class. The differences in class are real. They are the bases of differing formations of interest among women struggling against inequality, but the enemy is the same.

Notes

Acknowledgments: I am very much indebted to David Smith for criticisms and editorial comments. Thanks also to Vivian Crossman, Beverly Bingham, and Gordon Reichelt, who typed the drafts, pieces of drafts, and final version of the paper.

1. Kate Millett's *Sexual Politics* (New York: Avon, 1970) was a key work in establishing this formulation.

2. Frederick Engels, *Origin of the Family, Private Property, and the State* (Moscow: International Publishing, 1968), p. 73 (emphasis in original).

3. The terminology of class used here is descriptive rather than analytic. The current state of the debate on class and stratification is quite inconclusive and does not yield a decisively satisfactory terminology, let alone a theoretical account. I am currently working on the topic of women and class, and in doing so, I have treated the capitalist elite, the middle classes, and the petite-bourgeoisie as a single class in relation to contemporary forms of property. It is an internally differentiated class articulated to the regional basis of the capitalist economy, actively organized and reorganized as a class by ideological processes, by the organization of networks of personal relations, and by the maintenance of privileged access to state services, including education, governmental regulation, and so forth. Within this class we can

distinguish between a petite bourgeoisie in which the individual owner contributes his/her own labor to the enterprise, a middle bourgeoisie (which I have continued to describe here as the middle class, since this is the customary term and I don't want to introduce new terminologies in this paper), and a great bourgeoisie occupying key positions in the ownership and marketing of capital as a commodity. The working class can also be seen to be stratified, but its overall internal structure as a class is not actively organized by the working class itself but largely as responses and adaptations to conditions and events originating in the economic process. Trade unions do not organize the working class as a whole.

4. See Naomi Griffith, *Penelope's Web* (Toronto, 1976), p. 141; Eli Zaretsky, "Capitalism, the Family and Personal Life," *Socialist Revolution,* nos. 13–14 (1973): 69–125, and 15 (1973): 19–71; and Wally Seccombe, "The Housewife and Her Labours Under Capitalism," *New Left Review* 83 (Jan.–Feb. 1974): 3–24.

5. This development will be examined later in this paper in the section entitled "The Rise of Monopoly Capital and the Changing Middle-Class Family."

6. Seena B. Kohl, *Working Together: Women and Family in Southwestern Saskatchewan* (Toronto, 1976). Kohl also describes a perpetuation of father-son inheritance of the family enterprise among farm families in Saskatchewan. This pattern of inheritance consolidates as capital the accumulated surplus of the previous generation's work.

7. See Alfred D. Chandler, Jr., *The Visible Hand: The Managerial Revolution in American Business* (Cambridge: Harvard University Press, 1977), p. 66; and Leonore Davidoff, "The Rationalization of Housework," in Diana L. Barker and Sheila Allen (eds.), *Dependence and Exploitation in Work and Marriage* (London and New York: Longman, 1976).

8. Michael Katz, *The People of Hamilton, Canada West: Family and Class in a Mid-Nineteenth Century City* (Cambridge: Harvard University Press, 1975).

9. Nellie McClung, *Clearing in the West: My Own Story* (Toronto, 1964), p. 27.

10. Martha Ostenso, *Wild Geese* (Toronto, 1967).

11. V.C. Fowke, *The National Policy and the Wheat Economy* (Toronto, 1973).

12. Nellie McClung, *In Times Like These* (Toronto, 1972), p. 114.

13. Ramsay Cook and Wendy Mitchinson (eds.), *The Proper Sphere: Women's Place in Canadian Society* (Toronto, 1976), p. 111.

14. Ibid., p. 111.

15. McClung, *Clearing in the West,* and *In Times Like These.*

16. Mary E. Wilkins Freeman, *The Revolt of the Mother and Other Stories* (Old Westbury, N.Y.: Feminist Press, 1974). The title story is a moving and humorous drama on this theme.

17. Kohl, *Working Together,* pp. 70–71.

18. McClung, *Clearing in the West,* p. 27.

19. Patricia Carey, "Farm Wives: The Forgotten Women," *Canadian Women Studies 1,* no. 2 (1978): 4–5.

20. Ibid.

21. See H. J. Mozans, *Women in Science* (Cambridge: Harvard University Press, 1974), pp. 182–90.

22. Philip E. Hammond, *Sociologists at Work: Essays on the Craft of Social Research* (New York: Basic Books, 1964).

23. See Kathleen Archibald's account of the establishment of this structure in the federal civil service, in her *Sex and the Public Service: A Report to the Public Service Commission of Canada* (Ottawa, 1973), pp. 14–17.

24. Dorothy E. Smith, "Women's Perspective as a Radical Critique of Sociology," *Sociological Inquiry* 44, no. 4 (1974): 10.

25. Basil Bernstein, *Class, Codes and Control: Theoretical Studies Towards a Sociology of Language* (St. Albans: Methuen, 1973).

26. R. R. Dale and S. Griffith, "The Influence of the Home," in Maurice Craft (ed.), *Family, Class and Education: A Reader* (London: Methuen, 1970), p. 86.

27. See, for example, Mary Roth Walsh, *Doctors Wanted, No Women Need Apply: Sexual Barriers in the Medical Profession, 1835–1975* (New Haven: Yale University Press, 1977), and Albie Sachs and Joan Hoff Wilson, *Sexism and the Law: A Study of Male Beliefs and Judicial Bias in Britain and the United States* (Oxford: Free Press, 1978).

28. See A. Leslie Robb and Byron G. Spencer, "Education, Enrolment and Attainment," in Gail C. A. Cook (ed.), *Opportunity for Choice: A Goal for Women in Canada* (Ottawa and Montreal, 1976), and J. Vickers and J. Adam, *But Can You Type?* (London: Unipub, 1977).

29. Dorothy E. Smith, "Women, the Family and Corporate Capitalism," in Marylee Stephenson (ed.), *Women in Canada* (Toronto, 1973).

30. Seccombe, "The Housewife," p. 6.

31. See Patricia Connelly, *Last Hired, First Fired: Women and the Canadian Work Force* (Toronto, 1978).

32. Kristin A. Moore and Isabel U. Sawhill, "Implications of Women's Employment for Home and Family Life," in Ann H. Stromberg and Shirley Harkess (eds.), *Working Women: Theories and Facts in Perspective* (Palo Alto, Calif.: Mayfield, 1978), p. 206.

33. Michael Anderson, "Family, Household and the Industrial Revolution," in Michael Anderson (ed.), *Sociology of the Family* (Harmondsworth: Penguin, 1971), pp. 78–96.

34. Louise A. Tilly and Joan W. Scott, *Women, Work, and Family* (New York: Holt, Rinehart & Winston, 1978).

35. Ibid., pp. 123–29.

36. Suzanne D. Cross, "The Neglected Majority: The Changing Role of Women in Nineteenth Century Montreal," in S. Trofimenkoff and A. Prentice, *The Neglected Majority: Essays in Canadian Women's History* (Toronto: University of Toronto Press, 1977), p. 73.

37. Ibid., pp. 74–75.

38. See, for example, the records of truant officers excerpted by Alison Prentice in Alison L. Prentice and Susan E. Houston (eds.), *Family, School and Society in Nineteenth Century Canada* (Toronto, 1975).

39. Mrs Pember Reeves, *Round About a Pound a Week* (London, 1913).

40. See, for example, Edward O'Donnell, "Women as Bread Winners: The Error of the Age," in Rosalyn Baxandall, Linda Gordon, and Susan Reverby (eds.), *America's Working Women: A Documentary History—1600 to the Present* (New York: Random House, 1976). R. Geoffroy and P. Sainte-Marie provide a number of instances of such views; see, for example, their *Attitude of Union Workers to Women in Industry*, Studies of the Royal Commission on the Status of Women, no. 9 (Ottawa, 1971), pp. 57, 58, and 101–2; see also Philip S. Foner, *History of the Labor Movement in the United States*, vol. 3: *The Policies and Practices of the American Federation of Labor, 1900–1909* (New York: International Publishing Co., 1964), p. 244.

41. O'Donnell, "Women as Bread Winners," p. 168, writes: "The rapid displacement of men by women in the factory and workshop has to be met sooner or later, and

the question is forcing itself upon the leaders and thinkers among the labour organizations of the land. Is it a pleasing indication of progress to see the father, the brother and the son displaced as the bread winner by the mother, sister, and daughter?''

42. Gail Malmgreen, *Neither Bread Nor Roses: Utopian Feminists and the English Working Class, 1800–1850,* a ''Studies in Labour History'' pamphlet (Brighton, 1978), p. 23.

43. Foner, *Policies and Practices,* pp. 219–55.

44. Joan Sangster, ''The 1907 Bell Telephone Strike: Organizing Women Workers,'' *Labour: Le Travailleur* 3 (1978): 109–30.

45. Ibid., p. 126. Other unions simply refused to admit women or to recognize locals organized by women. See Foner, *Policies and Practices,* pp. 224–25.

46. Sangster, ''Bell Telephone Strike,'' p. 127.

47. See Reginald Whitaker ''The Liberal Corporatist Ideas of Mackenzie King,'' *Labour: Le Travailleur* 2 (1977): 137–69.

48. The state, of course, also represented the specific interests of segments of the capitalist class in the low-cost labor provided by women. For an account of the state process coordinating the various interests and the exclusion of working-class women, see Marie Campbell, ''Early Twentieth Century Trade Unionism and Women in British Columbia: Discovering Oppression,'' forthcoming in *Our Generation.*

49. See National Council of Women in Canada, *Legal Status of Women in Canada* (Ottawa, 1924).

50. Sachs and Wilson, *Sexism and the Law.*

51. National Council of Women, *Legal Status.*

52. Mary Inman, ''In Women's Defense'' (Los Angeles: Committee to Organize the Advancement of Women, 1940), in Gerda Lerner, ed., *The Female Experience: An American Documentary* (Indianapolis: Bobbs, 1977).

53. Richard Hoggart, *The Uses of Literacy* (London: Oxford University Press, 1958).

54. Clementina Black, *Married Women's Work* (London: Merrimack, 1915); for examples, see pp. 91 and 138.

55. Lillian Breslow Rubin, *Worlds of Pain: Life in the Working Class* (New York: Basic Books, 1976), pp. 177–84.

56. Malmgreen, *Neither Bread nor Roses,* p. 35; see also Jill Liddington and Jill Norris, *With One Hand Tied Behind Us: The Rise of the Women's Suffrage Movement* (London: Merrimack, 1978), pp. 216–17.

2

The Dynamics of Kin in an Industrial Community

T A M A R A K. H A R E V E N

Introduction

This essay examines the role of kinship in the process of migration and the
adjustment of immigrant workers to industrial conditions. It focuses on three
interrelated areas of kin activities: first, the recruitment of immigrant workers
to the textile industry through the services of kin—a process which joins migratory origin and destination into one social system; second, the role of kin
within the factory, particularly in hiring, job placement, and the control of
work processes; and third, overlapping both processes, the general function
of kin in critical life situations, most notably during periods of unemployment
and insecurity. These three areas are explored empirically in a case study of
French-Canadian immigrants in an American industrial community, Manchester, New Hampshire, from 1880 to 1930, a period encompassing both the
peak of Manchester's industrial development and its subsequent decline. The
essay interprets these empirical findings in the context of sociological theories
of kinship. In doing so, it points to those areas of research where sociological
theories have influenced historical analyses of kinship; and, conversely, it
suggests the extent to which historical findings can reorient current thinking
about the role of kin and modify historical and sociological generalizations
about family change.

Historians have only recently begun to view the role of kin as an important
aspect of family behavior in the past. The recent literature on the history of
the family has focused primarily on household structure, rather than on the
organization and functions of kin. Historians' concentration on the household
has led to a restricted definition of the functions of "family" to the household, thereby overlooking functions of extended family members who did not

Reprinted from *Turning Points: Historical and Sociological Essays on the Family,* by John
Demos and Sarane Spence Boocock (eds.), *American Journal of Sociology* 84 Supplement, by
permission of The University of Chicago Press. © 1978 by the University of Chicago.

reside with the nuclear family. This concentration of the nuclear family was also partly a result of the recent historical effort to document the persistence of nuclear household structures in Western society over the past three centuries.[1]

This emphasis has reinforced the confusion of *household* with *family* and, except for preindustrial society, has confined most analysis of family structure to the household unit. Historical scholarship has thus contributed inadvertently to the myth of the "isolated nuclear family" in modern urban society, a myth reinforced by sociological theories. The theory of social breakdown pointed to the erosion of primary group relationships under the stress of the urban, industrial system, while its counterpart in modernization theory has emphasized the "fit" between the isolated nuclear family and the modern industrial system (Parsons 1943: 22–23).[2]

Revisionist sociological studies by Litwak, Sussman, and others have documented the pervasiveness of informal kin relationships outside the confines of nuclear households in contemporary American society. Sussman has focused on patterns of mutual assistance to their aging parents from married children, and Litwak, one of the major challengers of the stereotype of the "isolated nuclear family" in modern American society, has viewed extended kin structures as a series of interconnected nuclear families. The focus of most of these studies is limited, however, to the relationships between extended kin members and the nuclear family. Kin interaction with larger social institutions, especially their role as intermediaries between individuals and nuclear families and the industrial system, has received less attention (Sussman 1959; Sussman and Burchinal 1962; Litwak 1960). Nor have changing functions and adaptations of kin been examined historically in relation to the process of industrialization. Smelser's contribution was significant in analyzing the role of the family in the early process of industrialization in England. His documentation of the recruitment of entire families as work units in the early factory system in England has challenged prevailing theories of family breakdown under the impact of industrialization. However, Smelser's claims that the phenomenon was limited to the first phase of the industrial revolution, that by the early 1830s, under the impact of advanced technology, family work had become differentiated, and that the family was dissolved as a work unit in the factory have been challenged recently by Anderson (1972). Anderson's study of family structure and the functions of kin in nineteenth-century Lancashire has documented the survival of vital kin functions among industrial workers in Preston, especially the continuation of family involvement with textile factories in the period 1830–50. Anderson also provides significant documentation for the vital role of kin in the process of migration and in adaptation to industrial conditions. His analysis is limited primarily to kin assistance in crisis situations, rather than to their continuing active role in the workplace. No comparable historical analysis of kinship in industrial communities has been attempted so far for the United States.

The Historical Context: Manchester, N.H.

This study examines the role of kin among French-Canadian immigrant textile workers during the period 1880–1936. French Canadians comprised at least one-third of the labor force in the Amoskeag Manufacturing Company in Manchester, New Hampshire, at the peak of the corporation's industrial development during the first two decades of the twentieth century and during its subsequent decline. The Amoskeag Company provides an important setting for this study because it enables us to document the interaction between the family and industrial work in the context of corporate paternalism at the turn of the century. Manchester, a city of 55,000 inhabitants at the beginning of the twentieth century, was the site of the world's largest textile mill, the Amoskeag Manufacturing Company, which employed an average of 14,000 workers each year [3]

Originally developed by the Amoskeag Company as a planned textile community, Manchester, unlike the sister communities of Lawrence and Lowell on which it was modeled, continued to be dominated by the corporation that originally founded it in the 1830s. Following the example of the textile manufacturing towns on which Manchester was patterned, the Amoskeag Company recruited its early labor force from among rural New Englanders. From the 1850s on, immigrants from England, Scotland, and Ireland began to replace native American workers. In the 1870s, following the textile industry's discovery of French Canadians as a most "industrious" and "docile" labor force, the corporation embarked on the systematic recruitment of laborers from Quebec. By 1900 French Canadians constituted about 40 percent of the labor force in the mill and more than one-third of the city's population. While their migration continued through the first two decades of the twentieth century, the corporation also absorbed small numbers of Germans and Swedes, followed by increasing numbers of Polish and Greek immigrants in the second decade of the twentieth century. [4]

As a planned industrial town, Manchester did not experience the classic problem of social disorganization generally attributed to urban living. The carefully designed and maintained corporation space, encompassing the millyard and housing for a large segment of the work force, enclosed the workers in a total environment. The industrial environment was augmented by cohesive neighborhoods organized along kinship and ethnic lines which, from the late nineteenth century on, developed in a fan shape, radiating east, south, and west of the millyard.

As will be detailed later, the social environment of the city, and particularly the changing history of the Amoskeag Company, significantly affected roles and relationships of kin. The period 1890–1919 represented the peak in the corporation's development as the world's largest textile factory under one roof. With the exception of a temporary slump during the recession of 1907, the Amoskeag Company reached its peak of production in 1911. During World War I the corporation made its largest profits. Following the war, however, a curtailment of production set in, and from that point on the corporation went into a gradual decline resulting from its inability to confront southern competition because of antiquated machinery, inefficiency, and relatively higher wages.

During the pre–World War I period, the Amoskeag Company introduced a series of efficiency measures and launched a new company welfare program which was grafted onto the continuing tradition of nineteenth-century paternalism. Following the war, the corporation was forced to curtail different aspects of production and gradually to taper its labor force. During this period, the workers began to experience an increasing breakdown in job security and a general deterioration in working conditions. The strike of 1922, the first major one in the company's history, lasted for nine months and marked a point of no return in the corporation's history. It virtually paralyzed the city. Following the strike, which failed completely from the perspective of both management and workers, the corporation never recovered full production. The labor force gradually dwindled, and most of the welfare programs were abandoned. Manchester began to experience serious unemployment from about 1926 on, and by 1933 the Amoskeag's labor force was reduced until it reached a mere 400 in 1936, the year of its shutdown (Creamer and Coulter 1939).

The role of kin in relation to the corporation is best understood in the context of industrial paternalism. Initially there was a close fit between corporation policy and the function of kin as intermediaries, paternalism in the factory system closely matching the hierarchical organization of the workers' families. As long as the corporation followed a policy of family employment, the balance between corporation policy and kin-group interest continued. After World War I, when a conflict of interest emerged, the balance was gradually shaken, and workers pitted their own interests against those of the corporation (Hareven 1975: 365–89).

These historical changes in the corporation are particularly significant for our understanding of its interaction with the workers' families. The first half of the period studied here was marked by labor shortages, while the later half was marked by labor surplus and resulting unemployment, and therefore a weakening of the influence of kin on the corporation system. Preceded by a prolonged decade of decline, the sudden shutdown of the mills in 1936, which left two-thirds of the city's working population unemployed, placed a heavy burden on kin. It is possible, therefore, to examine the role of kin in periods of relative stability as well as in times of crisis.[5]

The dynamics of kin, particularly modes of adaptability, emerge more clearly when viewed over time than when examined at one point in time. Within the relatively short time period between 1880 and 1936, successive changes in the functions and effectiveness of kin can be examined in relation to the changing organization of production and labor policies within the corporation. This study utilizes longitudinal data files which have been reconstructed from individual employee files in corporation records and which have been subsequently linked with vital records and insurance records. It is thus possible to reconstruct, to some extent, the life and work histories of a sample of workers employed by the Amoskeag Company between 1910 and 1936. The individual employee files kept by the Amoskeag Company were particularly valuable for this study because they recorded all fluctuations in each worker's career within the mill, including stated reasons for leaving or dismissal. Beyond the reconstruction of individual careers, the project reconstructed family and kinship clusters of individual workers by linking the employee files with the city directory, vital records, and fraternal insurance records. In addition to these quantitative data, the study utilizes corporation records and oral history interviews. While the quantitative analysis provides structural evidence for organization and behavior of kin, the oral history interviews offer insight into the quality of relationships and into their significance to the participants. The empirical analysis reported here—while attempting to weld both types of evidence—actually presents two different levels of historical reality, each derived from a distinct type of data. While these two different types of evidence are mutually reinforcing, they also often reflect divergent experiences. For example, both the quantitative and the qualitative data provide documentation for the effectiveness of kin in initiating workers into the factory system, but only the qualitative data provide insight into the internal conflicts between siblings or between children and parents resulting from the pressures of joint work situations.[6]

The Functions of Kin: Recruitment and Migration

From approximately the beginning of the century through World War I, workers fulfilled the corporation's expectations that they would bring their relatives to the factory, assist in their placement, and socialize them into industrial work. In their interaction with the corporation, kin served as an informal recruitment and hiring agency. As the Amoskeag Company began to recruit French Canadians systematically, management again relied primarily on the workers' efforts to bring their relatives to Manchester and to introduce them to work in their departments. The corporation thus utilized the workers' own informal patterns by encouraging those already living in Manchester to attract their Canadian kin and to provide the necessary support for newly arriving relatives. The corporation could thus restrict its own efforts to organizing transportation and did not need to concern itself with assistance to new workers.[7]

French-Canadian migration to Manchester was part of the general process of recruitment of French Canadians to New England textile towns which had begun shortly after the Civil War. By 1882 there were approximately 9,000 French Canadians in Manchester; according to the 1890 census, they constituted 28 percent of the city's population; and by 1910 they comprised one-third of the labor force in the Amoskeag Company. Informal recruitment through relatives continued throughout the first two decades of the twentieth century. Workers who went to visit Canada on their vacation or to dispose of farmland back in their village encouraged others to migrate and often brought relatives back with them. The Amoskeag Company embarked on a formal recruitment campaign in Quebec, through *Le Canado-Americain,* the newspaper published by the Association Canado-Americaine in Manchester: "More than 15,000 persons work in these mills. . . . It is true that the large company to which they sell their labor treats them as its own children."[8] Kin recruitment and assistance in migration and placement meant, in effect, that the trainloads of workers from Quebec were not crowds of helpless people, moving in a disorganized fashion into completely unknown territory. They had already received some firsthand descriptions of the place to which they were going and most likely had someone awaiting them upon arrival. They also had many relatives who were still left behind in Canada. If things failed in Manchester, there was still a place to which they could return.

Chain migration formed the basic pattern. First came the young, unmarried sons and daughters of working age or young married couples without their children. After they found work and housing, they sent for other relatives. The S. family provides a classic example of chain migration: Eugene S. and his wife first migrated to Lisbon Springs, Maine, in the 1880s and worked in the textile mills there. Their first three children were born in Maine, and the S. family subsequently returned to Canada where the remaining four children were born. After the mother's death, the oldest son migrated to Manchester in 1908 and started working as a weaver; he then brought his father and all his younger brothers. The father entered the same weaving room that the son was working in; subsequently, each child entered the mills upon reaching age fourteen or sixteen.[9]

In families where most of the children had passed school age, first the oldest son went to Manchester, and the other children followed in age sequence. Once they were established, they encouraged their children and other relatives in Quebec to come to work in Manchester. Chain migration also ran through New Hampshire and Maine towns. While the major migration route led from Quebec to Manchester, there was also a good deal of circular and back-and-forth migration. One former worker articulated the migratory character of kin most strikingly and succinctly: "Our family was five minutes in Canada, and five minutes here. . . . One child was born here, one in Canada" (oral interview with Jean Dione).

Chain migration thus joined families in Manchester and Quebec into one social system. Kin assistance continuously flowed back and forth between Manchester and Quebec. Those who went to the United States spearheaded the migration for those left behind and prepared the housing and jobs, while those who remained in Quebec took care of the property and family responsibilities. In order to migrate, individuals needed not only assistance upon arrival but also psychological and economic support to be able to leave. In most cases French-Canadian immigrants to New England industrial towns during the early part of the century did not consider their migration final. It was necessary, therefore, to have the informal approval of relatives, so the migration would not sever family ties, and to assure that the relatives remaining behind would help take care of the property or tend to the farm (often still functioning) while the owners migrated on a provisional basis.

While historians have already recognized the importance of kin in facilitating migration to the new country, they have paid less attention to the role of those relatives remaining behind. In this case, some of those left behind in Canada provided the security of someone to fall back on if the migrating family members failed in Manchester. The prospect of finding assistance, either upon a return to Canada during slack periods in Manchester or upon a return to settle permanently, was an essential aspect of the decision to migrate. Kin as backup were particularly instrumental for the first generation of immigrants, which was normally drawn to Manchester before the establishment of cohesive immigrant neighborhoods. The interaction between kin in Manchester and in Quebec was conditioned on exchanges in a variety of services.[10]

While the young or middle-aged people who were fit to work in the mills constituted the bulk of immigrants to Manchester, older parents, aunts, and uncles remaining in Quebec were cared for by those relatives who had stayed behind. Parents also tended to leave their young children with relatives until they were able to find jobs and housing in Manchester. Some parents did not send for their children until they reached the legal work age, or at least could pass for the legal work age, and then brought them down to start working in the mills. The birth of additional children led some to forget the older children who were left behind. Relatives remaining in Canada also performed important services in case of family breakdown. Young orphans were often sent back from Manchester to Quebec. Parents also sent back their sick children if they felt that the industrial enviroment was the cause of their illness (particularly in cases of eye, skin, or lung disease). Old people in Manchester also depended on their kin in Quebec. After having worked until their later years of life, some returned to their villages of origin to spend their last days with their own relatives and ''to die at home.''[11]

Quebec also served as a refuge for pregnant but unmarried daughters for whom life in Manchester became unbearable because of shame and social pressure. Such women were sent to convents, where they were kept until they bore their children. The unwanted children were given up for adoption or were taken to be raised by relatives, and the mothers either stayed in Canada or returned to work in Manchester.

The backup system provided by kin in Quebec proved particularly valuable during periods of unemployment, during the strike of 1922, and during the shutdown in 1936, when entire families returned to Quebec following the curtailment of production and layoffs. Men who had left small towns of Quebec and Canada to search for quick advancement in industrial Manchester returned shamefaced during the strike of 1922 to seek assistance and employment.

The interaction between immigrants in Manchester and their kin in Quebec contributes to our understanding of the territoriality of kin. Most recent historical studies documenting the survival of kinship ties in the industrial environment have utilized geographic proximity as the chief measure of kin interaction. Bott has provided an important model of urban networks which has been subsequently applied to a variety of neighborhood and community studies in England and in the United States, most notably Peter Young and Michael Willmott's study of East London and Herbert Gans's study of Boston's West End. While the Manchester data offer important examples of the interconnectedness of kin with neighborhood, which is central to Bott's model, they also extend to the examination of kin as mobile units transcending the specific boundaries of one neighborhood community (Bott 1964; Young and Willmott 1957; Gans 1962).

The French-Canadian textile workers of Manchester studied here held many of the characteristics which Bott lists as generally conducive to forming strong kinship networks: geographic proximity, similarity in work (particularly where one local industry dominates the employment market) and in occupational status, similarity in migration patterns, and little opportunity for social mobility. Despite these common characteristics, the French-Canadian workers in Manchester differed considerably from Bott's London East Enders in their geographic mobility. While in Bott's community kinship networks gained their strength from the neighborhood, the Manchester study reveals that geographic mobility and kin dispersion over a wider region can be conducive, in their own way, to strong kinship networks.

In Manchester, as in mid-ninteenth-century Preston and twenticth-century East London, kinship networks were embedded in the industrial town. But the social space of French-Canadian kin extended from Quebec to Manchester and spread over other New England industrial towns. The local networks in Manchester and Quebec were obviously more intensive and provided help locally on a daily basis. Continuing ties with kin between the different communities fulfilled important functions, different in character from those of neighboring kin. Relatives back in Quebec or in Berlin, New Hampshire, Sacco and Brunswick, Maine, or Lowell and Lawrence, Massachusetts, provided some insurance in case of industrial disasters, layoffs, and shutdowns or when personal problems necessitated migration. The networks of relatives, besides serving as important backup systems, also enabled workers to experiment with different employment opportunities, to send their sons to scout out better jobs, or to marry off their daughters.

French-Canadian kinship behavior in Manchester thus demonstrates the importance of intensive networks in both one's immediate neighborhood and one's workplace, as well as the persistence of long-distance kinship ties laced through larger communities. Long-distance kin performed significant functions for migrant populations and were particularly effective for temporary migrants, at least at the initial stages of their migration. Geographic distance did not disrupt basic modes of kin cooperation, but rather revised and diversified priorities and modes of interaction. Under certain conditions, migration strengthened kinship ties and imposed new functions upon them, as changing conditions dictated. Kin affiliations in the new setting not only facilitated migration to and settlement in Manchester but also served as reminders and reinforcers of obligations and ties to premigration communities.

Appalachian mountain migrants to the North in the post–World War II period followed similar patterns. In their study of migration from Appalachia to Ohio, Schwarzweller and his colleagues concluded that "the kinship structure . . . provides a highly persuasive line of communication between kinsfolk in the home and in the urban communities. It channels information about available job opportunities and living standards directly, and therefore, it tends to orient migrants to those areas where kin groups are already established." In this context, their definition of a "migration system" is particularly pertinent to this study: "Two subsystems together form the interactional system in which we wish to consider the adjustment of a given group of migrants, individually and collectively. We have, then, *one migration system* to consider, namely, the Beech Creek–Ohio migration'' (Schwarzweller, Brown, and Mangalam 1971: 94–95).

Hiring, Placement, and Job Control

Kin fulfilled a major role in labor recruitment and in the placement of workers in Manchester. Routine functions in this area started with simple assistance in finding employment for newly arrived immigrants or young relatives coming of age and later developed into the more complex service of specifically placing relatives in preferred jobs and departments. Workers utilized the good offices of their relatives who were already working in the mill and were able to exploit their good relations with the overseers to place their kin, especially the young ones, in rooms where the "bosses" were known to be safe and paternal and where parents did not fear their daughters' exposure to bad habits. As will be detailed later, these informal patterns of placement eventually influenced the composition of workrooms and the work process within them. Workers continued to influence these informal patterns of recruitment, through the overseers, even after the introduction of a formal employment office by the Amoskeag in 1911.

Under the centralized employment system, an overseer still retained the privilege of requesting a specific worker through the employment office. If a worker did not immediately find an appropriate place, relatives were watching, and when an opening appeared in a suitable workroom they arranged for a transfer.[12] The size of the corporation, with its many departments and the existence of several workrooms for each operation, made such transfers possible. The presence of a relative in a desirable workroom facilitated matters, particularly if he or she interceded with the overseer to request a particular worker from the employment office. The clerk who ran the employment office from its establishment in 1911 until 1929 articulated the degree of family control of the employment process. Having been appointed to introduce a centralized and depersonalized hiring system, he proceeded to hire his own relatives, one after another: "First I came, then I brought my father, then my brother and my sister, and then my wife. That's how you do it. Don't misunderstand me. You can't make a job . . . but if there is a job, family comes first."[13] His statement in itself contradicts his *raison d'être*. Overseers supported recruitment through kin because they were thus assured of having a position filled by someone they trusted. They could also rely on workers to teach their jobs to newly arrived relatives and to hold some responsibility for the new workers. As a result of this informal recruitment process, clustering along kinship and ethnic lines in the mill became common practice.

Analysis of the kinship networks of the French-Canadian workers in the different workrooms reveals patterns of kin clustering: out of 717 French-Canadian workers in the original sample of the individual employee file, 75.6 percent had relatives working in the mill at any time, without necessarily overlapping (Table 3-1). These findings are conservative, since the reconstruction of kinship work clusters is limited to those retrieved through the linkage of employee files with vital records and thus does not include all kin working in the mill but only those whom we were able to identify. Even so 75.6 percent of the entire sample of French Canadians had one or more relatives working in the mill.

These figures reveal the tendency of members of the same family to work in the Amoskeag mills. Of 121 clusters for whom kin relationships were established, 20.7 percent included both husband and wife working in the mill, 23.1 percent had couples and their parents working in the mills, and 24.1 percent had extended kin as well as members of the nuclear family working in the mills (Table 3-2).

The most frequent correlation, which involved two members of the same kin group working in the same department, was repeated 93 times and constituted 61.6 percent of all coincidences of kin (Table 3-3). These figures represent kin working in the same department, but not necessarily at the same time. They demonstrate, however, the tendency of members of the same family to hold certain occupations in the same departments. Once a family member was established in a particular department, it was only natural for

---

Table 3-1 Percentage of French-Canadian Workers with Relatives Working in the Mill at Any Time

Relatives Ever in the Mill	% (N = 717)
None	24.4
1	29.9
2	17.5
3	9.9
4	5.9
5	3.5
6	3.1
7	2.1
8	1.8
9 and more	1.9
Mean N relatives ever working in the mill	2.0

Note: I am grateful to Merle Sprinzen for advice in the presentation of these tables.

Table 3-2 Kinship Clusters Working in the Mill

Cluster	N	Adjusted %* (N = 121)
Original informant only	31	25.6
Husband and wife only	25	20.7
Husband and/or wife and their parents	34	28.1
Husband and wife and their children	2	1.6†
Nuclear and other members	29	24.0

*Total number of kinship clusters working in the mill for which exact relationships of all members are known.
†The small percentage of children working with their own parents is a result of the linkage and trace process: since marriage and employment records were used predominantly for the trace, it was impossible to retrieve larger numbers of sons and daughters who were still unmarried, living at home.

other relatives to follow, even if the original family member was not working there anymore.

Even more significant for socialization and mutual assistance was the tendency of relatives to coincide in the mills at the same time. This tendency is evident in Table 3-4. Of 103 instances of overlap of kin, there were 65 instances (63.1 percent) involving two or more members at the *same* time and 21 instances (20.4 percent) involving three members. Of the 105 clusters working in the mill, 59 percent had two or more members working at the same time (Table 3-5). Members of two generations in the same kin group coincided or overlapped frequently; of the kinship clusters with known relationships, 65.7 percent had two generations of the same family work in the mills at the same time (Table 3-6).

The frequency of these overlaps in different workrooms is also significant. Out of 151 instances of departmental overlap, the highest incidence occurred

Table 3-3 Percentage of Times Members of Kinship Clusters Worked in the Same Department at Any Time

Kin in a Department	No. Times This Occurred	% of Times This Occurred (N = 151)
2	93	61.6
3	23	15.2
4	18	11.9
5 or more	17	11.3

Table 3-4   Percentage of Times Members of Kinship Clusters Worked in the Same Department at the Same Time

Kin in a Department	No. Times This Occurred	% of Times This Occurred (N = 103)
2	65	63.1
3	21	20.4
4	7	6.8
5 or more	10	9.7

Table 3-5   Percentage of Relatives Coinciding in Kinship Clusters with Members Working in the Same Department at the Same Time

Members Coinciding	Clusters	% (N = 105)
1	43	41.0
2	31	29.5
3	17	16.2
4	14	12.3

Table 3-6   Generations in Each Cluster Working in the Mill at the Same Time

Generations Working in Mill at Same Time	Clusters	% (N = 105)
None	6	5.7
1	29	27.6
2	69	65.7
3	1	1.0

in the weave room and the spinning room. Thirty-one percent of all overlaps occurred in the weave departments and 34 percent in the spinning departments. This high frequency reflects the character of these two departments: they had the highest concentration of semiskilled workers, were the two most populated departments, and attracted French Canadians in large numbers. These were also the departments to which sons and daughters were typically sent for their apprenticeship. The dress room, the card room, and the spool room also accounted for 7.6, 5.3, and 8.0 percent, respectively, of all instances of overlapping. Kin also overlapped in the boiler room (6.0 percent), in the yard (2.6 percent), and in the bleach room (6 percent). The tendency of relatives to drift to certain workrooms was common to most of the family clusters analyzed.

In assessing the significance of these patterns, it is important to keep in mind that the large number of French Canadians in the mills is in itself merely the natural outcome of the high concentration of French Canadians in the city and the dependence of a major part of the working population on the Amoskeag. The critical fact, though, is that so much clustering occurring in the same workrooms suggests a conscious tendency of kin to work in related occupations and in the same place. There were in fact family-specific workrooms: rooms to which members of the same family tended to return again and again, while members of another family turned to a different workroom.

The advantages of kin clustering for the development of individual careers have not yet been systematically analyzed for this project. All other factors remaining constant, were workers with kin present in the workrooms or with strong kin connections more likely to advance than others? Preliminary findings on this project have begun to suggest that those whose parents or other relatives had developed stable work lives in the mill were more likely to find better jobs, to have more options, and to advance occupationally. Kin were particularly important in the beginning of one's career, when their presence in the same workroom not only might have made the difference between finding or not finding a job but also offered the guidance and support needed on first entry into the factory by their young relatives. The presence of kin helped initiate the new worker into the techniques and social regulations involved in the job. But the development of a successful career in the mill depended on more than the mere presence of kin. It was related to how well connected these kin were, to their reputation, and to their status in the mill.

Given the nature of textile work and the size and structure of the mill, kin assistance cushioned the first encounter of young men and women with their job. Generally, young men and women started their first job at fourteen or sixteen; they were typically brought to the employment office or to a workroom by a relative, at first for temporary work during school vacations and subsequently for full-time employment. They learned their first jobs from their own relatives in a specific workroom; this saved time for the corporation and made special training and apprenticeship programs superfluous. Workers were able to continue their own work while teaching their relatives, at least in the period preceding the piece-rate system. The significance of this practice is clear, especially in the context of what is generally considered an impersonal industrial system, where each worker presumably represents only one link in the production system and where the factory environment is considered alienating and threatening. In reality the workers created their own world within the factory, a world in which kinship ties and family status were used to manipulate the system. Parents, older brothers and sisters, aunts and uncles, and cousins invested in the training of their progeny or young kin because the work was essential to the household economy, because they wanted their relative to succeed in the factory, and because they wanted to transmit their own work ethic to the younger generation and to newly arrived immigrants.

A worker who already had relatives in the mill did not walk into a social vacuum when starting to work. Relatives were present to help, to instruct, to facilitate, and to prod. Beyond the immediate assistance extended by present kin, kinship ties also carried with them a specific frame of reference. Workers entering the factory bore the label of their kin. An individual was identified and often judged by the family to which he or she belonged or by association with other known relatives in a department. Incoming workers partly inherited the status of relatives already present in the mill. A young girl would be labeled immediately as Joe DuBois's daughter or Anna Gagnon's niece. The sins of the fathers were not necessarily being visited upon the sons, but neither was a worker uniformly treated as an independent agent. The reception accorded a worker depended largely on the standing and interpersonal relations of his or her relatives. In this respect, kinship ties bestowed advantages as well as disadvantages.

Some workers preferred, therefore, to enter as free agents rather than to carry the assets or bear the stigma of their kinship ties. Several young men mentioned unwillingness to work with their father as a reason for leaving their jobs. Children or close relatives of overseers preferred not to be in the same workroom as their overseer father in order to allay any suspicion that they were being treated more favorably than the other workers—a suspicion which might provoke a conflict situation or cause them to be discriminated against.[14]

The continuity between family ties and work relationships in the factory was pervasive even though the workplace was separated from the home. In contrast with modern society, where taking a job generally involves an individual's separation from the family of orientation and the assumption of at least a partially independent career, young Amoskeag workers carried their family affiliations into the factory system. Family ties in the workplace, along with continued residence of unmarried daughters and sons at home and their contribution of most of their wages to the family, show how little individual autonomy was actually achieved with the commencement of a first job.

Learning jobs from relatives and carrying out the first few weeks of work under their supervision had the tremendous advantage of obtaining tips on shortcuts and "tricks" along with established work procedures. Particularly important were the nonverbal techniques which workers could transmit to each other, primarily through observation, and which had a personalized style. By imitating such techniques or by adapting them to one's own tempo, it was possible to control the pace of work and even secure some leisure time between rounds. Older relatives in the mill also provided comfort, reassurance, and a sense of belonging. The unspoken but clearly conveyed code of behavior in the workrooms, and the presence of more experienced workers from one's family group, made new workers—particularly young women—less vulnerable to the liabilities in the system. Parents took this into consideration when trying to decide which room to send their children to.

Relatives were also instrumental in making arrangements in work loads or conditions which could not be achieved through regular channels. Marie Landry, for example, wanted to be assigned a set of window looms because she had problems with her eyesight. The "boss" told her that she would have to wait her turn till such a set became available. One day she asked permission to switch with her son, who had window looms, and the next morning the son gave notice. The overseer knew that the timing of the switch was premeditated, but there was little he could do about it.

Relatives present in the same workroom provided some protection from accusations by second hands or from misunderstandings and conflicts, particularly where filing a formal grievance was involved, because they were able to support each other and corroborate each other's statements. Susan Gagne was dismissed by the "boss" because she had missed one day without notifying him that she was sick. When she reported for work the next day the second hand asked her to leave. She was ready to leave when her sister, who spoke English, interceded on her behalf and filed a grievance with the Adjustment Board. Susan was reinstated (Grievance Files, Amoskeag Company 1920, 1922). When workers lost their tempers with one another or with the "bosses," relatives frequently interceded on their behalf to smooth things out, to apologize, or to bring about a compromise. Having the relatives or close friends present was also particularly important where different aspects of the work process were structurally interconnected and where the speed of one worker depended on that of his fellow workers.

Relatives took turns running machinery and taking breaks, and substituted for each other during illness, childbirth, or trips to Canada. They helped their slower kin to complete their piece-work quota, and, most important, out of consideration for each other they rarely exceeded what they had established as the generally accepted limit. This type of family work pattern was particularly important insofar as older workers were concerned. It gave them the opportunity to trade their know-how and skill for assistance from younger relatives in more speedy and taxing jobs. Where a family group was together, as in the case of the Scottish dye-house workers, it was possible for them to keep Old Spence or Old Joe on the job, as long as younger relatives were carrying out the more physically taxing tasks. Old Spence traded skill and know-how for physical assistance (interview with Tom Smith, former overseer of the dye house). Relatives thus provided mutual support in facing supervisors and in handling the work pace. The presence of relatives in the same workroom, especially if they were well respected or in supervisory positions, sheltered workers from being laid off, protected them against fines, and provided support in case of mistreatment by management or conflict with other workers.

Family manipulation of the work process could provide a partial explanation for the absence of unions from the Amoskeag until World War I. As long as the corporation's paternalism was in harmony with the workers' familistic orientation, and as long as the flexibility in the system enabled the workers to exercise controls informally, they showed little enthusiasm for union membership. Perhaps it is no coincidence that the union recruited its first large membership and was in fact successful in calling a strike during a period when family control of the work process was on the decline.

Limitations of Kin Assistance

So far, we have discussed the role of kin as intermediaries in providing important support mechanisms for the workers. In the ensuing pages, we will examine the areas in which kin manipulation of the system and the strong family character of the work process carried built-in weaknesses.

The integration of kin into the work process occasionally posed serious challenges. In a setting where relatives were considered responsible for each other's performance and where new workers were hired on a relative's recommendation, how did one deal with a relative who was incompetent or who abused the system by lack of discipline or violating basic rules of behavior? How far did loyalty to kin go? Workers were not held responsible for the misbehavior of a relative, but if that particular relative was hired on their recommendation, this diminished their chances of having other relatives hired in the future. Another problem was competition with one's own kin. Did one hide the fact of being a better worker? Did one slow down in order to protect a slower relative, or give up one's lunch break to fix the warps for young relatives (as many fathers, mothers, aunts, and uncles actually did), or forfeit a share of the piece rate?

The introduction of piece work and the increase of speed of production imposed additional pressures on relatives. While once they had been willing to teach skills to their younger relatives, they now had to be more jealous of their time. One woman recalled that when she started working as a learner in the spinning room, her sisters warned her specifically not to alert the employment office to their presence in the mill, because they did not want to be saddled with teaching her the job. She started work, therefore, in another room, and only after she had learned how to spin did she ask to be transferred to work with her sisters. A number of grievances reflect the workers' anxiety over being pressured by the boss to teach a skill to other workers without the proper adjustments for loss of piece-rate time. In all the grievances on this issue, management upheld the worker's rights not to be forced to engage in such teaching without being compensated on an hourly rate (Grievance Files, Amoskeag Company, 1919–21).

Under a system where most of the working members of a kin group worked for the same employer, the efficacy of kin depended greatly on the factory system itself. Kin functioned best under the conditions of labor shortage and a more loosely organized hiring system which prevailed prior to World War I. During periods of labor surplus, which became increasingly common after World War I, kinship ties were still extremely useful in finding a job, particularly as daily and nightly lines in the employment office became at once endless and hopeless. At the same time, having an entire family group work in the same place made all members vulnerable to changing economic conditions in the factory. The strike of 1922, the subsequent decline of the mill, and particularly its final shutdown in 1936 revealed the family's liabilities to the insecurities of the industrial system. Even prior to the strike, some of the workers interviewed had tried to prevent such situations by having certain relatives work in shoe factories. This type of foresight was rare, however. [15]

During tense periods, the Amoskeag's workers gradually discovered the built-in liabilities in the dependence of a family group on one employer. It meant that they were unable to assist each other, because they found themselves unemployed at the same time. During the strike and the shutdown, families were unable to share their resources, because, having continuously functioned on a narrow margin of subsistence, they had very few or no resources left to transfer. The strike also pitted relatives against each other. The issue of whether to strike or be a scab divided many families and caused conflicts which took years to overcome, long after the strike. Certain relatives, in fact, have not been on speaking terms since 1922. [16]

As external conditions rendered local kin assistance ineffectual, long-distance kin proved extremely valuable. Workers in Lowell and Lawrence, and in certain cases in Rhode Island, found jobs for unemployed Manchester relatives and shared housing with them while they had to commute. Some families migrated to Lowell and Lawrence, never returning to Manchester or returning only in the early forties, when small individual textile mills opened up in the empty structures of the giant mill complex. Others returned to Canada temporarily and worked in the textile mills in Trois Rivière. For the commuters, the presence of relatives in other New England industrial towns was critical. Women with a mother or an aunt nearby were able to work in those towns during the week while their children were being cared for by relatives.

In many instances husband and wife went to Lawrence and an older female relative kept the children for the entire week. During such periods of failure in the factory system, the effectiveness of kin as migrant agents continued. In this instance, the route of migration was reversed. Earlier, workers brought their kin into the factory in Manchester; now other kin enabled them to find temporary or more permanent work in other towns or to migrate back to Canada. The existence of fluid kinship networks throughout New England ensured that the needs of unemployed workers for temporary jobs and housing would continue to be met. [17]

Instrumentality of Kin

In his study of nineteenth-century Lancashire, Anderson uses exchange theory as an explanation for mutual assistance among kin. Anderson's emphasis on instrumental relationships is particularly relevant for Manchester, New Hampshire. Although the time period is different, Manchester shares several characteristics with Preston. In a low-resource working-class community, consisting of a high proportion of immigrants, kin provided a crucial economic and social resource. The Manchester experience also points to the areas in which economic exchange theory could be revised in relation to a different social and historical setting. The oral history interviews of former workers in Manchester—which, of course, were not available for Preston in 1850—provide vital information on their own perceptions of instrumental relationships (Anderson 1972).

What did instrumental relationships mean in the context of Manchester? Basically, they fell into two categories: short-term routine exchanges in services and assistance in critical life situations, and long-term investments in exchanges along the life course. Short-term assistance involved sharing in housing, food, babysitting, tools, and supplies; assistance during illness or death; short-term loans; and assistance in the construction of a house. In an urban setting, exchanges in skills, goods, and services were routine, rather than being limited strictly to crisis situations. For example, mill workers supplied their relatives with cheap cloth and received farm products in exchange. Plumbers, masons, etc., traded services with each other, and storekeepers exchanged merchandise for medical or legal assistance from relatives.

Long-range investments were more demanding and less certain in their future returns. The classic exchange along the life course is that between parents and children, based on parents' expectations of old-age support in return for their investment in childrearing. The choice of godparents also represented long-term exchanges. In return for the honor of the position, godparents assumed obligations of future assistance to their godchild. Well-to-do relatives were, therefore, preferred as godparents. Under conditions of high migration, exchanges across different stages of the life course also took place between aunts and uncles and their nieces and nephews. The former frequently acted as surrogate parents for their newly arrived young relatives in Manchester (oral history of Anna Champagne and Simone St. Laurent).

Such exchanges were horizontal as well as vertical. Horizontally, aunts and uncles were fulfilling obligations to brothers or sisters by taking care of nieces and nephews; vertically, they were entering into exchange relationships with their nieces and nephews who might assist them later in life. In large families, given the wide age discrepancy between siblings in the same family, exchanges along the life course also took place between older and younger siblings, particularly in one-parent families where an older brother or sister acted as a surrogate parent for the younger siblings. While the benefits in short-term exchanges are more clearly understandable, it would be difficult to conceive of long-range exchanges as resting exclusively on a calculative basis. For example, many men and women sacrificed their opportunity for marriage because of the need to support their parents. Many couples interviewed in Manchester carried on twenty-year-long courtships, and some did not marry until they reached their late thirties or forties, because they had to support their parents while their sisters were getting married. With these economic constraints and insecurities, personal preferences clearly had to give way to collective family strategies. Members of the nuclear family took priority over more distant kin, even if a more distant relative might have been potentially a better contributor to the exchange bargain. The young women who postponed their marriage or never married did so out of a sense of responsibility and affection for their parents or siblings. In particular, those women who acted as surrogate parents did so because preservation of family autonomy was essential for their self-respect and standing in the neighborhood and ethnic community (oral history of Joanna Duchesne).

Self-reliance was one of the most deeply ingrained values, but in this case it meant familial autonomy rather than individualism. When asked where they turned for help in case of need, very few of the interviewees mentioned the church or ethnic mutual aid associations. (The latter provided social activity and fraternal insurance.) For assistance, one turned to the family. Very few workers actually turned to strangers for help. Most of the workers were too proud to accept help from the city welfare office or the union store during the strike. The first large-scale acceptance of public welfare occurred in the 1930s when, after enduring unemployment and the subsequent shutdown of the mills, workers turned to the Federal Emergency Relief Administration and the Works Progress Administration as they opened up in Manchester.

Family considerations, needs, and ties guided or controlled most individual decisions. Migration to Manchester, the finding of jobs and housing, leaving the mill, or returning to Canada were all enmeshed in collective family strategies, rather than individual moves. Families, as seen by participants in this study, might be described as units consisting of multiple interchangeable molecules which could be switched around as the need arose. Each unit could be relied upon and utilized when appropriate. Families followed internal schedules of timing as to when to migrate, whom to leave behind, when to return, when to bring those who were left behind to rejoin the family in Manchester, whom to send to boarding school with the nuns, whom to send back to the farm, whom to encourage to explore working conditions in other New England industrial towns, whom to allow to marry, and whom to pressure to stay home and at what point in time.

Collective family needs were not always congruent with individual preferences. Nor did subordination of individual needs to family decisions take place without conflict. Many of the interviewees who had sacrificed personal preferences for familial needs expressed long-repressed anger and pain during the interview. The family was the matrix within which career as well as economic choices were made. But internal family decisions were closely connected to the changing fortunes and organization of the workplace. Work careers did not spring from individual choices, and work itself was not an isolated undertaking. The family offered its members the main incentives, but it also presented them with the major obstacles. Even the metaphor by which other organizations and aspects of life were perceived and judged was based on the family. Good working relations in the mill were perceived like good family relations: "We were all like a family."[18] It is not surprising, therefore, that many of the workers perceived the shutdown of the mill not only as a personal catastrophe but also as the breakdown of the mill family.

While such historical studies of kinship as Anderson's reveal the strength of kin in providing support during critical life situations, the Manchester study also points to areas of real or potential conflict resulting from the pressures imposed on individuals to subordinate their own needs to family strategies. Anna Champagne, for example, later resented the fact that she had to start working at age fourteen and to postpone her own marriage because she was left as the last child of working age who could support her parents, while her older sisters all decided to get married. Being the youngest child in her case meant having to leave school and to start work earlier and subsequently to continue to support her mother. Her mother made up for this, however: while the other daughters had to assemble their own dowry chests and buy their own wedding gowns, Anna received from her mother a dowry chest with a complete set of household equipment and eventually also the family's sewing machine. Having sacrificed her youth, she felt that she should have at least inherited the parental home. But the older sister who came back into the

picture shortly before her mother's death was the one to receive the home because she cared for the mother in the last years of her life. Having grown up in
a large family and having had firsthand experience of the pressures imposed
by kin, Anna drew the lines with her husband's family immediately after marriage: she refused to pay her mother-in-law's credit charges and made it very
clear to her husband and her mother-in-law that: ''I put my foot down the first
year that I got married and we got along swell. When they used to come and
visit and ask to borrow money, I said: 'Listen, I don't go down to your house
to bother you. I'm happy with my husband and get the hell out. Don't come
here and try and borrow anything from him or from me' '' (interview of Anna
Champagne). Interestingly, despite her resentment of large families and her
own bitterness toward her siblings, it is Anna Champagne who keeps the
most complete family albums and who follows the traditional Quebec custom
of maintaining a family genealogy. Her personal resentment of the intrusions
of kin into her own privacy was divorced from her ideological commitment to
keeping a complete family record for posterity.

Louise Duchesne and her fiancé postponed marriage until their mid-thirties
because he had to support a widowed mother and an old-maid sister. After the
mother finally died, they decided to get married. The old-maid sister went to
live in an apartment, but Louise always instructed her housekeeper ''to give
her a hot meal when she'd come by'' (interview of Louise Duchesne). Laura
DuBois, the youngest of six sisters, all of whom worked in the mills, has become isolated from her sisters ever since they accused her of cashing in their
father's insurance money after his death and of using it for her own needs.
Since she was the last remaining daughter at home, and took care of her father
until his death, she felt that she was entitled to the money. Marie Duvall
resents even now the fact that she was sent to work in the mill at age fourteen,
while her two brothers were sent to the Priests' Seminary. At age sixty, she is
now finally graduating from high school and is expressing this repressed
resentment to her eighty-five-year-old mother and to her brother (interview of
Laura DuBois and Marie Duvall).

Changing Functions of Kin and the Modernization Process

Recent historical evidence has tended to reverse sociological stereotypes of
family breakdown under the impact of migration. There is the danger, however, that an oversimplified revisionism may generate new stereotypes. The
notion of premigration networks transferred *intact* into a new setting
represents one such stereotype. Some out-of-context misunderstandings of
the concept of ''urban villagers'' have led to a filiopietistic interpretation,

which views immigrants in modern American cities as "old-country" peasants. A systematic differentiation among intact transfers, modifications of traditional patterns, and new adaptations will considerably advance our understanding of the role of kin in the process of modernization. The Manchester experience suggests that what has been considered a survival of premodern patterns may actually represent modern responses to new conditions. French-Canadian immigrants initially carried over kinship ties and traditional practices of kin assistance into Manchester. They subsequently adapted their kin organization to the new industrial system developing new modes of interaction and adopting new functions. [19]

Although the basic kinship structures had been imported from rural Quebec, their functions were responsive to the demands of industrial production. Such functions were considerably different from those customarily performed by kin in rural society. They required familiarity with bureaucratic structures and organizations, adherence to modern work schedules, planning in relation to the rhythms of industrial employment, specialization in tasks, and technological skill. The roles assumed by kin in organizing the work process, hiring young relatives, and negotiating the pace of production and the quality of materials all entailed a mastery of advanced, "modern" activities. So did the handling of industrial schedules and piece rates, as well as the understanding of interrelated industrial processes and the relative significance of different factors in turning out high-quality products at a rapid pace. All this required a level of expertise and sophistication that would be expected of overseers and management. The role of kin in all these areas, as well as in handling the Manchester housing market, required an understanding of the complexity and diversity inherent in an urban, industrial system. The use of kinship ties by the workers of Manchester represented, therefore, an important step in the direction of modernization, but it also represented an important carry-over from the past.

Modernization theory has frequently cited individuals' integration with kin as an obstacle to modernization. The Manchester data suggest that, rather than "holding down individuals" and delaying their mobility, kin conveyed individuals and families from preindustrial to industrial settings. Kin also served as agents of adaptation and modernization by providing examples and role models, as well as by offering direct assistance. The historical process was not "either/or." Under the insecurities of the factory system, the selective use of kinship ties was part of survival strategy and, under certain circumstances, was essential for mobility (Moore 1965: 77). [20] The functions of kin varied considerably with the industrial conditions and at different points in the life course. Continuing research on this project will hopefully distill those conditions under which kin served to facilitate matters from those where they added burdens.

The model which has been employed most frequently to explain historical changes in the family is that of differentiation. According to this model, the transfer of functions previously held by the family to other social institutions was generally followed by a weakening in the formal functions of kin. [21] The consummation of this process is the takeover by the welfare state of the reciprocity and mutual assistance functions previously held by kin, particularly child welfare and old-age support. This model considerably oversimplified the process of historical change, particularly insofar as working-class life is concerned. In the United States, the social security system has partly eliminated the elderly's economic dependency on kin for subsistence. Beyond that, however, the welfare system has not replaced most of the other functions of kin discussed above. One particular area in which kin still retain a viable role is in sociability and psychological support. The segregation between age groups and their isolation from each other which has characterized middle-class family life has not yet fully penetrated working-class life. Most of the former workers interviewed in Manchester still interact frequently with their relatives and are dependent upon them not only for sociability but also for various services which are unavailable or considered undesirable if obtained through state or city programs. This is particularly true for the cohort now in its eighties, which survived the shutdown and the Great Depression without turning to city welfare and to relief.

The increase in the value of privacy and individualism, particularly as enshrined in the ideology of the modern nuclear family, has further tended to enforce the stereotype of the structural and functional isolation of the nuclear family in modern society. [22] But a number of sociological studies since the fifties have begun to disprove this isolation and to document the continuing interaction between middle-aged and older parents and their adult children as well as among other relatives (e.g., Litwak 1960). In American society in general, and in the working class in particular, kin has continued to function as an important resource. The nature and uses of kin vary considerably among the different ethnic groups and socioeconomic classes and along different stages of the life course. These variations are subject to continuing and future exploration.

Conclusion

This study obviously represents only the first stage of a more comprehensive analysis of kinship patterns in industrial communities. It still leaves a series of questions for further exploration: How did degrees of intensity in kin interaction correlate with different degrees of affinity? What was the difference, for example, between interaction with kin on the mother's side and kin on the father's side?[23] What were the relative roles of men and women in developing and maintaining kinship networks and in shaping different modes of interaction? To what extent did kinship ties hinder or advance social and occupational mobility outside the mill? The extent to which kin also facilitated the movement of individuals into urban white-collar or mercantile occupations also remains an open question.

Another major area which is still subject to exploration is the relative role of several *overlapping* but not completely identical networks. Most of the individuals studied here were involved in kinship networks, workroom networks, ethnic networks, and neighborhood networks, all of which were enmeshed with each other. Further analysis will have to differentiate, however, among these networks and to identify the functional boundaries and sources of potential conflict between them.

Serious questions must be raised also about the degree of typicality of this study. The textile industry has been particularly alluring to students of the family because of its practice of family employment. This study shares, therefore, the limitations of Smelser's and Anderson's studies, namely, its lack of comparability with other industries involving a role segregation between men and women, such as mining or metal industries. Hopefully future historical research will examine such communities as well.

Despite these limitations, these findings, although incomplete, begin to suggest some direction for a reconsideration of theories of kin and family behavior. First, the Manchester study documents the survival of premigration kinship networks in an urban, industrial setting. Second, and more important, it shows that the function of kin in modern industrial communities represented not merely an archaic carry-over from rural society but rather the development of new responses to needs dictated by modern industrial conditions. Third, this study suggests some direction for a reassessment of the territoriality of kin. The Manchester study offers a dual model of kin organization: one views kinship ties as embedded within the territorial boundaries of the community and is most effective in studying interaction with local institutions; the other views kinship networks strung over several communities. The strength of the former lies in its stability; the latter's utility is drawn from its fluidity and continuous reorganization. Under certain historical or life-course conditions, neighborhood networks are more valuable. Under other conditions, intercommunity kinship networks are more instrumental. Kinship is a process; kinship ties can be latent at one point in time and can be revived at some other point, depending on circumstances. Fourth, the functions of kin can be examined more effectively by looking from the nuclear family outward—not only as it relates to extended kin, but also in its relationship to larger social institutions. The brokerage model of kin interaction examined in this study can be extended from the factory to other bureaucratic institutions.

Finally, this study raises some questions about the relationship between social change and family behavior. Recent scholarship has generally accepted a model of change over time which sees the history of the family as one of retreat from interaction with the community into an isolated nuclear family. The Manchester data point to the value of examining those areas in which the family has taken on new functions in response to the complexity of modern society.

Notes

Acknowledgments: Different aspects of this project were funded by the National Endowment for the Humanities, the Norwin and Elizabeth Bean Foundation, the Merrimack Valley Textile Museum, and the New Hampshire Council of the Humanities. Support of the Ford Foundation is gratefully acknowledged for a faculty research fellowship during the spring semester, 1976, when this essay was written, as is the assistance of the Radcliffe Institute and the Harvard Center for Population Studies, where I was a fellow during the preparation and revision of this essay. I am grateful to the Manchester Historic Association and to the Manuscript Division of the Baker Library, Harvard University, for the use of their materials; to Steve Shedd for computer programming; to Yale Bohn for statistical assistance; and to the research assistants at different stages of this project, especially to Robert and Denise Perreault, Ron Petrin, and Sally Boynton. I am also grateful to Howard Litwak and Blanche Lindow for editorial assistance. Earlier versions of this essay were presented at the Radcliffe Institute, the Shelby Cullom Davis Center, Princeton University, the Harvard Center for Population Studies, the economic history seminar at All Souls College, Oxford, the social history seminar at Warwick University, and the Cambridge Group for the History of Population and Social Structure. This essay has benefited from the comments of David Montgomery, Glen Elder, John Modell, Michael Anderson, Peter Marris, Richard Vann, Randolph Langenbach, and members of the Cambridge Group, especially Peter Laslett and Lawrence Stone. All names of oral history interviewees cited in this text are fictitious, except for Joseph Debski and Thomas Smith.

1. For an overview of the field, see Hareven (1971, 1974), Demos (1970), and Greven (1970). The emphasis on the nuclearity of families over time is most striking in Laslett and Wall (1972) and Sennett (1971).

2. One challenge to this point of view is provided by Goode (1963).

3. See Brown (1915), a company history, and Creamer and Coulter (1939). On classic, planned New England textile towns, see Ware (1942), Armstrong (1968), and Shlakman (1935).

4. These figures were computed from the nationality charts which the Amoskeag Company assembled for each year, from 1911 to 1929, found in the Amoskeag Records, Baker Library, Harvard University, Cambridge, Mass.

5. The United Textile Workers Union made its first inroads into the Amoskeag in 1918 during the World War I boom. A number of grievances heard before the union's grievance committee revolved around the protest of workers who were laid off or not rehired in the order of seniority, and who were replaced by relatives of other workers

or of the overseer (Amoskeag company papers, Labor Records: Adjustment Files, Baker Library, Harvard University).

6. The oral histories in the project consist of 300 two-to-four-hour interviews of all surviving former workers in the Amoskeag Mills who are still living in Manchester and whom we were able to locate and interview. The edited interviews were published in *Amoskeag: An Oral History* (New York: Pantheon, 1980). Oral history has only recently been introduced as a source of historical research. Its validity depends on the methods followed in gathering the interviews. In this instance, individuals were interviewed only after their family and work histories were reconstructed, and narratives were checked carefully against the demographic and employment data. Oral histories were utilized here as evidence of the manner in which historians have traditionally employed other subjective sources, such as diaries or family letters. By comparison to such sources, oral history suffers from being narrated many years after the event and therefore possibly being weakened by faulty memory. On the other hand, it has several advantages over literary documents. First, the interviewee recounts past events with the perspective of hindsight, and second, the interviewer can address questions about the specific topics which are vital to the subject under investigation.

7. No corporation records exist explicitly indicating an official recruitment policy based on kin, but this practice was generally followed until the 1920s, when the agent began to instruct overseers to refrain from hiring members of the same family or same ethnic group in one workroom.

8. *Le Canado-Americain* (November 10, 1913). This newspaper was published in Manchester by the Association Canado-Americaine, a fraternal insurance company founded by Theophile Byron, the French-Canadian overseer in the Amoskeag Company, and the only one for a long time to come. The Amoskeag utilized this paper for advertisement.

9. The history of the Simoneau family has been reconstructed from corporation records, vital records, and oral history interviews.

10. Based on oral history interviews of twenty-five French-Canadian immigrants who reconstructed their migration routes.

11. This recurring pattern has emerged from the oral history interviews. Because of the unavailability of systematic immigration data, the project has not reconstructed immigration routes quantitatively.

12. On the establishment of the employment office of the Amoskeag Company, see "Notices to Superintendents and Overseers," 1910 (Amoskeag Company papers).

13. Interview of a former employment office clerk in the Amoskeag, Joseph Debski.

14. The reluctance to work with fathers, husbands, wives, or siblings was mentioned in five instances of oral interviews

15. The increase in intermittent employment has been documented (see Creamer and Coulter 1939: 271–80).

16. This was a recurring theme in the interviews of twenty workers who had experienced or witnessed the strike.

17. Over the decade 1920–30, Manchester lost 10,580 individuals, or 13.5 percent of the city's population, to out-migration (Creamer and Coulter 1939: 290). Part of this migration was temporary, however. The oral history interviews provide ample evidence for the circular migration which these individuals experienced. What appear, therefore, as final separations were actually only temporary absences.

18. The statement "We were all like a family" was repeated by most former workers interviewed.

19. This study has not yet analyzed comparatively kinship patterns in the Quebec communities of origin. The current discussion relies, therefore, on Horace Miner's analysis of rural kinship in the parish of St. Denis (Miner 1939) and for urban kinship patterns on Philippe Garigue (1956).

20. For a critique of modernization theory in relation to the history of the family, see Hareven (1976).

21. Smelser (1959) is the most detailed explanation of the process of differentiation as it applies to the history of the family. Anderson (1972) uses differentiation theory as an explanation for the transfer of welfare functions from kin to public welfare institutions.

22. On privatism in middle-class family life, see Ariès (1962) and Sennett (1971).

23. See Bott (1964) and Gans (1962). Both document the difference between kin interaction on the wife's and husband's sides, respectively.

References

Anderson, Michael. 1972. *Family Structure in Nineteenth-Century Lancashire*. Cambridge: Cambridge University Press.

Ariès, Philippe. 1962. *Centuries of Childhood*. Trans. R. Baldick. New York: Knopf.

Armstrong, John B. 1968. *Factory Under the Elms: A History of Harrisville, N.H. 1774–1969*. Cambridge: M.I.T. Press.

Bott, Elizabeth. 1964. *Family and Social Network: Roles, Norms, and External Relationships in Ordinary Urban Families*. London: Tavistock.

Brown, Waldo. 1915. *A History of the Amoskeag Company*. Manchester, N.H.: Amoskeag Co.

Cambridge, Mass. Baker Library, Harvard University. Amoskeag Records.

Canado-Americain, Le. November 10, 1913. Manchester, N.H.

Creamer, Daniel, and Charles W. Coulter. 1939. *Labor and the Shutdown of the Amoskeag Textile Mills*. Philadelphia: Works Projects Administration.

Demos, John. 1970. *A Little Commonwealth: Family in Plymouth Colony*. New York: Oxford.

Gans, Herbert. 1962. *The Urban Villagers: Group and Class in the Life of Italian-Americans*. New York: Free Press.

Garigue, Philippe. 1956. "French Canadian Kinship and Urban Life." *American Anthropologist* 58: 1090–101.

Goode, William. 1963. *World Revolution and Family Patterns*. New York: Free Press.

Greven, Philip. 1970. *Four Generations: Population, Land, and Family in Colonial Andover, Massachusetts*. Ithaca, N.Y.: Cornell University Press.

Hareven, Tamara K. 1971. "The History of the Family as an Interdisciplinary Field." *Journal of Interdisciplinary History* 1:399–414.

———. 1974. "The Family as Process: The Historical Study of the Family Cycle." *Journal of Social History* 7: 322–29.

———. 1975. "Family Time and Industrial Time: Family and Work in a Planned Corporation Town, 1900–1924." *Journal of Urban History* 1:365–89.

———. 1976. "Modernization and Family History: Perspectives on Social Change." *Signs* 2: 190–206.

———. 1980. *Amoskeag: An Oral History*. New York: Pantheon.

Laslett, Peter, and Richard Wall (eds.). 1972. *Household and Family in Past Time*. Cambridge: Cambridge University Press.

Litwak, Eugene. 1960. "Geographical Mobility and Extended Family Cohesion." *American Sociological Review* 25: 385–94.

———. 1965. "Extended Kin Relations in an Industrial Society." In Ethel Shanas and Gordon T. Streib (eds.), *Social Structure and the Family: Generational Relations*. Englewood Cliffs, N.J.: Prentice-Hall.

Miner, Horace M. 1939. *St. Denis, French-Canadian Parish*. Chicago: University of Chicago Press.

Moore, Wilbert E. 1965. *Industrialization and Labor: Social Aspects of Economic Development*. Ithaca, N.Y.: Cornell University Press.

Parsons, Talcott. 1943. "The Kinship System of the Contemporary United States." *American Anthropologist* 45: 22–38.

Schwarzweller, Harry K.; James S. Brown; and J. J. Mangalam. 1971. *Mountain Families in Transition: A Case Study of Appalachian Migration*. University Park: Pennsylvania State University Press.

Sennett, Richard. 1971. *Families Against the City: Middle-Class Homes of Industrial Chicago, 1872–1890*. Cambridge: Harvard University Press.

Shlakman, Vera. 1935. *Economic History of a Factory Town: Chicopee, Massachusetts*. New York: Octagon.

Smelser, Neil J. 1959. *Social Change and the Industrial Revolution*. Chicago: University of Chicago Press.

Sussman, Marvin B. 1959. "The Isolated Nuclear Family: Fact or Fiction." *Social Problems* 6: 333–41.

Sussman, Marvin B., and Lee Burchinal. 1962. "Kin Family Network: Unheralded Structure in Current Conceptualizations of Family Functioning." *Marriage and Family Living* 24: 231–40.

Ware, Caroline F. 1942. *The Early New England Cotton Manufacture*. New York: Houghton Mifflin.

Young, Michael D., and Peter Willmott. 1957. *Family and Kinship in East London*. London: Routledge & Kegan Paul.

3

Black Women, Work, and
the Family Under Slavery

JACQUELINE JONES

The burdens shouldered by slave women represented in extreme form the dual nature of all women's labor within a patriarchal, capitalist society: the production of goods and services and the reproduction and care of members of a future work force. The antebellum plantation brought into focus the interaction between notions of women *qua* "equal" workers and women *qua* unequal reproducers; hence a slaveowner just as "naturally" put his bondwomen to work chopping cotton as washing, ironing, or cooking. Furthermore, in seeking to maximize the productivity of his entire labor force while reserving certain domestic tasks for women exclusively, the master demonstrated how patriarchal and capitalist assumptions concerning women's work could reinforce one another. The "peculiar institution" thus involved forms of oppression against women that were unique manifestations of a more universal condition. The following discussion focuses on female slaves in the American rural South between 1830 and 1860—cotton boom years that laid bare the economic and social underpinnings of slavery and indeed all of American society.[1]

Under slavery, blacks' attempts to maintain the integrity of family life amounted to a political act of protest, and herein lies a central irony in the history of slave women. In defiance of their owners' tendencies to ignore gender differences in making work assignments in the fields, the slaves whenever possible adhered to a strict division of labor within their own households and communities. This impulse was exhibited most dramatically in patterns of black family and economic life after emancipation. Consequently, the family, often considered by feminists to be a source (or at least a vehicle) of women's subservience, played a key role in the freed people's struggle to resist racial and gender oppression, for black women's full attention to the duties of moth-

Adapted from " 'My Mother Was Much of a Woman': Black Women, Work, and the Family Under Slavery," *Feminist Studies* 8, no. 2 (Summer 1982): 235–70, by permission of the publisher, Feminist Studies, Inc., c/o Women's Studies Program, University of Maryland, College Park, MD 20742.

84

erhood deprived whites of their power over these women as field laborers and domestic servants.[2]

Interviewed by a Federal Writers Project (FWP) worker in 1937, Hannah Davidson spoke reluctantly of her experiences as a slave in Kentucky: "The things that my sister May and I suffered were so terrible. . . . It is best not to have such things in our memory." During the course of the interview, she stressed that unremitting toil had been the hallmark of her life under bondage. "Work, work, work," she said; it had consumed all her days (from dawn until midnight) and all her years (she was only eight when she began minding her master's children and helping the older women with their spinning). "I been so exhausted working, I was like an inchworm crawling along a roof. I worked till I thought another lick would kill me." On Sundays, "the only time they had to themselves," women washed clothes, and some of the men tended their small tobacco patches. As a child she loved to play in the haystack, but that was possible only on "Sunday evening, after work."[3]

American slavery was an economic and political system by which a group of whites extracted as much labor as possible from blacks through the use or threat of force. A slaveowner thus replaced any traditional division of labor that might have existed among blacks before enslavement with a work structure of his own choosing. All slaves were barred by law from owning property or acquiring literacy skills, and although the system played favorites with a few, black females and males were equal in the sense that neither sex wielded economic power over the other. Hence property relations—"the basic determinant of the sexual division of labor and of the sexual order" within most societies[4]—did not affect male-female interaction among the slaves themselves. To a considerable extent, the types of jobs slaves did, and the amount and regularity of labor they were forced to devote to such jobs, were all dictated by the master.

For these reasons the definition of slave women's work is problematical. If work is any activity that leads either directly or indirectly to the production of marketable goods, then slave women did nothing *but* work.*[5] Even their efforts to care for themselves and their families helped to maintain the owner's work force and to enhance its overall productivity. Tasks performed within the family context—childcare, cooking, and washing clothes, for example—were distinct from labor carried out under the lash in the field or under the mistress's watchful eye in the Big House. Still, these forms of nurture contributed to the health and welfare of the slave population, thereby increasing the actual value of the master's property (that is, slaves as both strong workers and "marketable commodities"). White men warned prospective mothers that they wanted neither "runts" nor girls born on their plantations, and slave

*Editors' Note: See the discussion of definitions of work in the Introduction and Overview.

women understood that their owner's economic self-interest affected even the most intimate family ties. Of the pregnant bondwomen on her husband's expansive Butlers Island (Georgia) rice plantation, Fanny Kemble observed, "they have all of them a most distinct and perfect knowledge of their value to their owners as property," and she recoiled at their obsequious profession, obviously intended to delight her: "Missus, tho' we no able to work, we make little niggers for Massa." One North Carolina slave woman, the mother of fifteen children, used to carry her youngest with her to the field each day, and "when it get hungry she just slip it around in front and feed it and go right on picking or hoeing," symbolizing in one deft motion the equal significance of the productive and reproductive functions to her owner. [6]

It is possible to divide the daily work routine of slave women into three discrete types of activity. These involved the production of goods and services for different groups and individuals, and included women's labor that directly benefited, first, their families, second, other members of the slave community, and third, their owners. Although the master served as the ultimate regulator of all three types of work, he did not subject certain duties related to personal sustenance (that is, those carried out in the slave quarters) to the same scrutiny that characterized fieldwork or domestic service.

The rhythm of the planting-weeding-harvesting cycle shaped the lives of almost all American slaves, 95 percent of whom lived in rural areas. This cycle dictated a common work routine for slaves throughout the South, though the staple crop varied from tobacco in the Upper South to rice on the Georgia and South Carolina Sea Islands, sugar in Louisiana, and the "king" of all agricultural products, cotton, in the broad swath of "Black Belt" that dominated the whole region. Of almost four million slaves, about one-half labored on farms with holdings of twenty slaves or more; one-quarter endured bondage with at least fifty other people on the same plantation. In its most basic form, a life of slavery meant working the soil with other blacks at a pace calculated to reap the largest harvest for a white master. [7]

In his efforts to wrench as much field labor as possible from female slaves without injuring their capacity to bear children, the master made "a noble admission of female equality," observed one abolitionist sympathizer with bitter irony. Slaveholders had little use for sentimental platitudes about the delicacy of the female constitution when it came to grading their "hands" according to physical strength and endurance. Judged on the basis of a standard set by a healthy adult man, most women probably ranked as three-quarter hands; yet there were enough women like Susan Mabry of Virginia, who could pick four or five hundred pounds of cotton a day (150 to 200 pounds was considered respectable for an average worker), to remove from a master's mind all doubts about the ability of a strong, healthy, woman fieldworker. As a result, he conveniently discarded his time-honored Anglo-

Saxon notions about the types of work best suited for women, thereby producing many "dreary scenes" like the one described by northern journalist
Frederick Law Olmsted: during winter preparation of rice fields on a Sea Island plantation, a group of black women, "armed with axes, shovels and
hoes . . . all slopping about in the black, unctuous mire at the bottom of the
ditches." Although pregnant and nursing women suffered from temporary
lapses in productivity, most slaveholders apparently agreed with the (in
Olmsted's words) "well-known, intelligent, and benevolent" Mississippi
planter who declared that "labor is conductive to health; a healthy woman
will rear most children." In essence, the quest for an "efficient" agricultural
work force led slaveowners to downplay gender differences in assigning
adults to field labor. [8]

Together with their fathers, husbands, brothers, and sons, black women
were roused at four A.M. and spent up to fourteen hours a day toiling out of
doors, often under a blazing sun. During the winter they performed a myriad
of tasks necessary on nineteenth-century farms of all kinds: repairing roads,
pitching hay, burning brush, and setting up post and rail fences. Like Sara
Colquitt of Alabama, most adult females "worked in de fields every day from
'fore daylight to almost plumb dark." During the busy harvest season, everyone was forced to labor up to sixteen hours at a time—after sunset by the light
of candles or burning pine knots. Miscellaneous chores occupied women and
men around outbuildings regularly and indoors on rainy days. Slaves of both
sexes watered the horses, fed the chickens, and slopped the hogs. Together
they ginned cotton, ground hominy, shelled corn and peas, and milled flour. [9]

Work assignments for women and men differed according to the size of a
plantation and its degree of specialization. However, because cotton served
as the basis of the southern agricultural system, distinct patterns of female
work usually transcended local and regional differences in labor-force
management. Stated simply, most women spent a good deal of their lives
plowing, hoeing, and picking cotton. In the fields, the notion of a distinctive
"women's work" vanished as slaveholders realized that "women can do
plowing very well and full well with the hoes and equal to men at
picking." [10]

To harness a double team of mules or oxen and steer a heavy wooden plow
was no mean feat for any person, and yet a "substantial minority" of slave
women mastered these rigorous activities. White women and men from the
North and South marveled at the skill and strength of female plow hands.
Emily Burke of eastern Georgia saw women and men "promiscuously run
their ploughs side by side, and day after day . . . and as far as I was able to
learn, the part the women sustained in this masculine employment, was quite
as efficient as that of the more athletic sex." In preparing fields for planting,
and in keeping grass from strangling the crop, women as well as men

blistered their hands with the clumsy hoe characteristic of southern agriculture. "Hammered out of pig iron, broad like a shovel," these "slave-time hoes" withstood most forms of abuse (destruction of farm implements constituted an integral part of resistance to forced labor). Recalled one former slave of the tool that also served as pick, spade, and gravedigger: "Dey make 'em heavy so dey fall hard, but de bigges' trouble was liftin' dem up." Hoeing was backbreaking labor, but the versatility of the tool and its importance to cotton cultivation meant that the majority of female hands used it a good part of the year.[11]

The cotton-picking season usually began in late July or early August and continued without interruption until the end of December. Thus, for up to five months annually, every available man, woman, and child was engaged in a type of work that was strenuous and "tedious from its sameness." Each picker carried a bag fastened by a strap around her neck and deposited the cotton in it as she made her way down the row, at the end of which she emptied the bag's contents into a basket. Picking cotton required endurance and agility as much as physical strength, and women frequently won regional and interfarm competitions conducted during the year. Pregnant and nursing women usually ranked as half-hands and were required to pick an amount less than the "average" 150 or so pounds per day.[12]

Slaveholders often reserved the tasks that demanded sheer muscle power for men exclusively. These included clearing the land of trees, rolling logs, and chopping and hauling wood. However, plantation exigencies sometimes mandated women's labor in this area, too; in general, the smaller the farm, the more arduous and varied was women's fieldwork. Lizzie Atkins, who lived on a twenty-five-acre Texas plantation with only three other slaves, remembered working "until slam dark every day"; she helped to clear land, cut wood, and tend the livestock in addition to her other duties of hoeing corn, spinning thread, sewing clothes, cooking, washing dishes, and grinding corn. One Texas farmer, who had his female slaves haul logs and plow with oxen, even made them wear breeches, thus minimizing outward differences between the sexes. Still, FWP interviews with former slaves indicate that blacks considered certain jobs uncharacteristic of bondwomen. Recalled Louise Terrell of her days on a farm near Jackson, Mississippi: "The women had to split rails all day long, just like the men." Nancy Boudry of Georgia said she used to "split wood jus' like a man." Elderly women reminisced about their mothers and grandmothers with a mixture of pride and wonder. Mary Frances Webb declared of her slave grandmother, "in the winter she sawed and cut cord wood just like a man. She said it didn't hurt her as she was strong as an ox." Janie Scott's description of her mother implied the extent of the older woman's emotional as well as physical strength: she was "strong and could roll and cut logs like a man, and was much of a woman."[13]

Very few women served as skilled artisans or mechanics; on large estates, men invariably filled the positions of carpenter, cooper, wheelwright, tanner, blacksmith, and shoemaker. At first it seems ironic that masters would utilize women fully as field laborers, but reserve most of the skilled occupations that required manual dexterity for men. Here the high cost of specialized and extensive training proved crucial in determining the division of labor; although women were capable of learning these skills, their work lives were frequently interrupted by childbearing and nursing; a female blacksmith might not be able to provide the regular service required on a plantation. Too, masters frequently "hired out" mechanics and artisans to work for other employers during the winter, and women's domestic responsibilities were deemed too important to permit protracted absences from the quarters. However, many young girls learned to spin thread and weave cloth because these tasks could occupy them during confinement.[14]

The drive for cotton profits induced slaveowners to squeeze every bit of strength from black women as a group. According to the estimates of Roger L. Ransom and Richard Sutch, in the 1850s at least 90 percent of all female slaves over sixteen years of age labored more than 261 days per year, eleven to thirteen hours each day. Few overseers or masters had any patience with women whose movements in the field were persistently "clumsy, awkward, gross, [and] elephantine" for whatever reasons—malnutrition, exhaustion, recalcitrance. As Hannah Davidson said: "If you had something to do, you did it or got whipped." The enforced pace of work more nearly resembled that of a factory than a farm; Kemble referred to female field hands as "human hoeing machines." The bitter memories of former slaves merely suggest the extent to which the physical strength of women was exploited. Eliza Scantling of South Carolina, only sixteen years old at the end of the Civil War, plowed with a mule during the coldest months of the year: "Sometimes me hands get so cold I jes' cry." Matilda Perry of Virginia "use to wuk fum sun to sun in dat ole terbaccy field. Wuk till my back felt lak it ready to pop in two."[15]

At times a woman would rebel in a manner commensurate with the work demands imposed upon her. "She'd git stubborn like a mule and quit." Or she took her hoe and knocked the overseer "plum down" and "chopped him right across his head." When masters and drivers "got rough on her, she got rough on them, and ran away in the woods." She cursed the man who insisted he "owned" her so that he beat her "till she fell" and left her broken body to serve as a warning to the others: "Dat's what you git effen you sass me." Indeed, in the severity of punishment meted out to slaves, little distinction was made between the sexes: "Beat women! Why sure he [master] beat women. Beat women jes' lak men." A systematic survey of the FWP slave narrative collection reveals that women were more likely than men to engage in "verbal confrontations and striking the master but not running away," probably because of their family and childcare responsibilities. [16]

Family members who perceived their mothers or sisters as particularly weak and vulnerable in the fields conspired to lessen their work load. Frank Bell and his four brothers, slaves on a Virginia wheat farm, followed his parents down the long rows of grain during the harvest season. "In dat way one could help de other when dey got behind. All of us would pitch in and help Momma who warn't very strong." The overseer discouraged families from working together because he believed "dey ain't gonna work as fast as when dey all mixed up," but the black driver, Bell's uncle, "always looked out for his kinfolk, especially my mother." James Taliaferro told of his father, who counted the corn rows marked out for Aunt Rebecca ("a short-talking woman that ole Marsa didn't like") and told her that her assignment was almost double that given to the other women. Rebecca indignantly confronted the master, who relented by reducing her task, but not before he threatened to sell James's father for his meddling. On another plantation, the hands surreptitiously added handfuls of cotton to the basket of a young woman who "was small and just couldn't get her proper amount." [17]

No slave women exercised authority over slave men as part of their work routine, but it is uncertain whether this practice reflected the sensibilities of the slaveowners or of the slaves themselves. Women were assigned to teach children simple tasks in the house and field and to supervise other women in various facets of household industry. A master might "let [a woman] off fo' de buryings 'cause she know how to manage de other niggahs and keep dem quiet at de funerls," but he would not install her as a driver over people in the field. Many strong-willed women demonstrated that they commanded respect among males as well as females, but more often than not masters perceived this as a negative quality to be suppressed. One Louisiana slaveholder complained bitterly about a particularly "rascally set of old negroes"—"the better you treat them the worst they are." He had no difficulty pinpointing the cause of the trouble, for "Big Lucy, the leader, corrupts every young negro in her power." On other plantations, women were held responsible for instigating all sorts of undesirable behavior among their husbands and brothers and sisters. On Charles Colcock Jones's Georgia plantation, the slave Cash gave up going to prayer meeting and started swearing as soon as he married Phoebe, well known for her truculence. Apparently few masters attempted to coopt high-spirited women by offering them positions of formal power over black men. [18]

In terms of labor-force management, southern slaveowners walked a fine line between making use of the physical strength of women as productive workers and protecting their investment in women as childbearers. These two objectives—one focused on immediate profit returns and the other on long-term economic considerations—at times clashed, because women who spent long hours picking cotton, toiling in the fields with heavy iron hoes, and walking several miles a day sustained damage to their reproductive systems immediately before and after giving birth. For financial reasons, slaveholders might have "regarded pregnancy as almost holy," in the words of one medical historian. But they frequently suspected their bondwomen (like "the most insufferable liar" Nora) of shamming illness—"play[ing] the lady at your expense," as one Virginia planter put it. These fears help to account for the reckless brutality with which owners forced women to work in the fields during and after pregnancy. [19]

Work in the soil thus represented the chief lot of all slaves, female and male. In the Big House, a division of labor based on both gender and age became more apparent, reflecting slaveowners' assumptions about the nature of domestic service. Although women predominated as household workers, few devoted their energies full time to this kind of labor; the size of the plantation determined the degree to which the tasks of cleaning, laundering, caring for the master's children, cooking, and ironing were specialized. According to Eugene Genovese, as few as 5 percent of all antebellum adult slaves served in the elite corps of house servants trained for specific duties. Of course, during the harvest season all slaves, including those in the house, went to the fields to make obeisance to King Cotton. Thus, the lines between domestic service and fieldwork blurred during the day and during the lives of slave women. Many continued to live in the slave quarters, but rose early in the morning to perform various chores for the mistress—"up wid de fust light to draw water and help as a house girl"—before heading for the field. James Claiborne's mother "wuked in de fiel' some, an' aroun' de house sometimes." Young girls tended babies and waited on tables until they were sent outside—"mos' soon's" they could work—and returned to the house years later, too frail to hoe weeds, but still able to cook and sew. The circle of women's domestic work went unbroken from day to day and from generation to generation. [20]

Just as southern white men scorned manual labor as the proper sphere of slaves, so their wives strove (often unsuccessfully) to lead a life of leisure within their own homes. Those duties necessary to maintain the health, comfort, and daily welfare of white slaveholders were considered less women's work than black women's and black children's work. Slave mistresses supervised the whole operation, but the sheer magnitude of labor involved in keeping all slaves and whites fed and clothed (with different standards set according to race, of course) meant that black women had to supply the elbow grease. For most slaves, housework involved hard, steady, often strenuous labor as they juggled the demands made by the mistress and other members of the master's family. Mingo White of Alabama never forgot that his slave mother had shouldered a work load "too heavy for any one person." She served as personal maid to the master's daughter, cooked for all the hands on the plantation, carded cotton, spun a daily quota of thread, wove and dyed cloth. Every Wednesday she carried the white family's laundry three-quarters of a mile to a creek, where she beat each garment with a wooden paddle. Ironing consumed the rest of her day. Like the lowliest field hand, she felt the lash if any tasks went undone.[21]

Although mistresses found that their husbands commandeered most bondwomen for fieldwork during the better part of the day, they discovered in black children an acceptable alternative source of labor. Girls were favored for domestic service, but a child's sex played only a secondary role in determining household assignments. On smaller holdings especially, the demands of housework, like cotton cultivation, admitted of no finely honed division of labor. Indeed, until puberty, girls and boys shared a great deal in terms of dress and work. All children wore a "split-tail shirt," a knee-length smock slit up the sides: "Boys and gals all dress jes' alike. . . . They call it a shirt iffen a boy wear it and call it a dress iffen the gal wear it." At the age of six or so, many received assignments around the barnyard or in the Big House from one or more members of the master's family.

Between the ages of six and twelve, black girls and boys followed the mistress's directions in filling woodboxes with kindling, lighting fires in chilly bedrooms in the morning and evening, making beds, washing and ironing clothes, parching coffee, polishing shoes, and stoking fires while the white family slept at night. They fetched water and milk from the springhouse and meat from the smokehouse. Three times a day they set the table, helped to prepare and serve meals, "minded flies" with peacock feather brushes, passed the salt and pepper on command and washed the dishes. They swept, polished, and dusted, served drinks and fanned overheated visitors. Mistresses entrusted to the care of those who were little more than babies themselves the bathing, diapering, dressing, grooming, and entertaining of white infants. In the barnyard black children gathered eggs, plucked chickens, drove cows to and from the stable and "tended the gaps" (opened and closed gates). (In the fields they acted as human scarecrows, toted water to the hands, and hauled shocks of corn together.) It was no wonder that Mary Ella Grandberry, a slave child grown old, "disremember[ed] ever playin' lack chilluns do today."[22]

In only a few tasks did a sexual division of labor exist among children. Masters always chose boys to accompany them on hunting trips and to serve as their personal valets. Little girls learned how to sew, to milk cows and churn butter, and to attend to the personal needs of their mistresses. As tiny ladies-in-waiting, they did the bidding of fastidious white women and of girls not much older than they. Cicely Cawthon, age six when the Civil War began, called herself the mistress's "little keeper": "I stayed around, and waited on her, handed her water, fanned her, kept the flies off her, pulled up her pillow, and done anything she'd tell me to do.'' Martha Showvely recounted a nightly ritual with her Virginia mistress. After she finished her regular work around the house, the young girl would go to the woman's bedroom, bow to her, wait for acknowledgment, and then scurry around as ordered, lowering the shades, filling the water pitcher, arranging towels on the washstand, or ''anything else'' that struck the woman's fancy.[23]

Sexual exploitation of female servants of all ages (described in graphic detail by Harriet Jacobs in Lydia Maria Child's *Incidents in the Life of a Slave Girl*) predictably antagonized white women. Jealousy over their husbands' real or suspected infidelities resulted in a propensity for spontaneous violence among many. Husbands who flaunted their adventures in the slave quarters increased the chance that their wives would attack a specific woman or her offspring. Sarah Wilson remembered being ''picked on'' by the mistress, who chafed under her husband's taunts; he would say, '' 'Let her alone, she got big, big blood in her,' and then laugh.''[24]

A divorce petition filed with the Virginia legislature in 1848 included a witness's testimony that the master in question one morning told his slave favorite to sit down at the breakfast table ''to which Mrs. N [his wife] objected, saying . . . that she (Mrs. N.) would have her severely punished.'' Her husband replied ''that in that event he would visit her (Mrs. N.) with a like punishment. Mrs. N. then burst into tears and asked if it was not too much for her to stand.'' This husband went to extreme lengths to remind his spouse of slave-mistress Mary Chesnut's observation that ''there is no slave, after all, like a wife.'' In the black woman the mistress saw not only the source of her own degradation, she saw herself—a woman without rights, subject to the impulses of an arrogant husband-master.[25]

To punish black women for minor offenses, mistresses were likely to attack with any weapon available—a fork, butcher knife, knitting needle, pan of boiling water. Some of the most barbaric forms of punishment resulting in the mutilation and permanent scarring of female servants were devised by white mistresses in the heat of passion. As a group they received well-deserved notoriety for the ''veritable terror'' they unleashed upon black women in the Big House.[26]

Interviews with former slaves suggest that the advantages of domestic service (over fieldwork) for women have been exaggerated in accounts written by whites. Carrying wood and water, preparing three full meals a day over a smoky fireplace or pressing damp clothes with a hot iron rivaled cotton picking as back-breaking labor. Always ''on call,'' women servants often had to snatch a bite to eat whenever they could, remain standing in the presence of whites, and sleep on the floor at the foot of their mistress's bed (increasing the chances that they would sooner or later be bribed, seduced, or forced into sex-

ual relations with the master). To peel potatoes with a sharp knife, build a
fire, or carry a heavy load of laundry down a steep flight of stairs required
skills and dexterity not always possessed by little girls and boys, and injuries were common. Chastisement for minor infractions came with swift severity; cooks who burned the bread and children who stole cookies or fell
asleep while singing to the baby suffered every conceivable form of physical abuse, from jabs with pins to beatings that left them disfigured for life.
The master's house offered no shelter from the most brutal manifestations of
slavery.[27]

For any one or all of these reasons, black women might prefer fieldwork to
housework. During his visit to a rice plantation in 1853, Olmsted noted that
hands "accustomed to the comparatively unconstrained life of the negro-
settlement detest the close control and careful movements required of the
house servants." Marriage could be both a means and an incentive to escape a
willful mistress. Jessie Sparrow's mother wed at age thirteen in order "to go
outer de big house. Dat how come she to marry so soon." Claude Wilson recalled many years later that "his mother was very rebellious toward her duties
and constantly harassed the 'Missus' about letting her work in the fields with
her husband until finally she was permitted to make the change from the
house to the fields to be near her man." Other women, denied an alternative,
explored the range of their own emotional resources in attempting to resist
petty tyranny; their "sassiness" rubbed raw the nerves of mistresses already
harried and high-strung. A few servants simply withdrew into a shell of
"melancholy and timidity."[28]

The dual status of a bondwoman—a slave and a female—afforded her master a certain degree of flexibility in formulating her work assignments. When
he needed a field hand, her status as an able-bodied slave took precedence
over gender considerations, and she was forced to toil alongside her menfolk.
At the same time, the master's belief that most forms of domestic service required the attentions of a female reinforced among slave women the traditional role of woman as household worker.

The authority of the master in enforcing a sexual division of labor was absolute, but at times individual women could influence his decisions to some
extent. In certain cases, a woman's preferences for either fieldwork or domestic service worked to her advantage. For example, the rebelliousness of
Claude Wilson's mother prompted her removal from the Big House to the
field, a change she desired. Similarly, masters might promise a woman an opportunity to do a kind of work she preferred as a reward for her cooperation
and diligence. On the other hand, a slave's misbehavior might cause her to
lose a position she had come to value; more than one prized cook or maid was
exiled to the fields for "sassing" the mistress or stealing. A system of rewards and punishments thus depended on the preferences of individual

slaves, and a servant determined to make life miserable for the family in the Big House might get her way in any case. [29]

In the field and Big House, black women worked under the close supervision of whites (the master, overseer, or mistress) at a forced pace. The slaves derived few, if any, tangible benefits from their labor to increase staple-crop profits and to render the white family comfortable (at least in physical terms). However, their efforts to provide for their own health and welfare often took place apart from whites, with a rhythm more in tune with community and family life. For slave women, these responsibilities, although physically arduous, offered a degree of personal fulfillment. As Martha Colquitt remarked of her slave grandmother and mother who stayed up late to knit and sew clothes "for us chillun": "Dey done it 'cause dey wanted to. Dey wuz workin' for deyselves den." Slave women deprived of the ability to cook for their own kinfolk or discipline their own children felt a keen sense of loss; family responsibilities revealed the limited extent to which black women (and men) could control their own lives. Furthermore, a strict sexual division of labor in the quarters openly challenged the master's opportunistic approach to slave women's work. [30]

A number of activities were carried out either communally or centrally for the whole plantation by older women. On smaller farms, for example, a cook and her assistants might prepare one or all of the meals for the other slaves each day except Sunday. Similarly, an elderly woman, with the help of children too young to work in the fields, often was assigned charge of a nursery in the quarters, where mothers left their babies during the day. To keep any number of little ones happy and out of trouble for up to twelve to fourteen hours at a time taxed the patience of the most kindly souls. Slave children grew up with a mixture of affection and fear for the "grandmothers" who had dished out the licks along with the cornbread and clabber. Other grannies usurped the position of the white physician (he rarely appeared in any case); they "brewed medicines for every ailment," gave cloves and whiskey to ease the pain of childbirth, and prescribed potions for the lovesick. Even a child forced to partake of "Stinkin' Jacob tea" or a concoction of "turpentine an' castor oil an' Jerusalem oak" (for worms) would assert years later that "Gran'mammy was a great doctor," surely a testimony to her respected position within the slave community, if not to the delectability of her remedies. [31]

On many plantations, it was the custom to release adult women from field-work early on Saturday so that they could do their week's washing. Whether laundering was done in old wooden tubs, iron pots, or a nearby creek with batten sticks, wooden paddles, or washboards, it was a time-consuming and difficult chore. Yet this ancient form of women's work provided opportunities for socializing "whilst de 'omans leaned over de tubs washin' and a-singin' dem old songs."

Much of the work black women did for the slave community resembled the colonial system of household industry. Well into the nineteenth century throughout the South, slave women continued to spin thread, weave and dye cloth, sew clothes, make soap and candles, prepare and preserve foods, churn butter, and grow food for the family table. Slave women mastered all these tasks with the aid of primitive equipment and skills passed on from grandmothers. Many years later, blacks of both sexes exclaimed over their slave mothers' ability to prepare clothing dye from various combinations of tree bark and leaves, soil and berries; make soap out of ashes and animal skins; and fashion bottle lamps from string and tallow. Because of their lack of time and materials, black women only rarely found in these activities an outlet for creative expression, but they did take pride in their resourcefulness and produced articles of value to the community as a whole. [32]

Black women's work in home textile production illustrates the ironies of community labor under slavery, for the threads of cotton and wool bound them together in both bondage and sisterhood. Masters (or mistresses) imposed rigid spinning and weaving quotas on women who worked in the fields all day. For example, many were forced to spin one "cut" (about three hundred yards) of thread nightly, or four to five cuts during rainy days or in the winter. Women of all ages worked together, and children of both sexes helped to tease and card wool, pick up the loom shuttles, and knit. In the flickering candlelight, the whirr of the spinning wheel and the clackety-clack of the loom played a seductive lullabye, drawing those who were already "mighty tired" away from their assigned tasks. [33]

In the quarters, group work melded into family responsibilities, for the communal spirit was but a manifestation of primary kin relationships. Here it is possible only to outline the social dynamics of the slave household. The significance of the family in relation to the sexual division of labor under slavery cannot be overestimated: out of the mother-father, wife-husband nexus sprang the slaves' beliefs about what women and men should be and do. Ultimately, the practical application of those beliefs (in the words of Genovese) "provided a weapon for joint resistance to dehumanization." [34]

The two-parent, nuclear family was the typical form of slave cohabitation regardless of the location, size, or economy of a plantation; the nature of its ownership; or the age of its slave community. Because of the omnipresent threat of forced separation by sale, gift, or bequest, this family was not "stable." Yet in the absence of such separations, unions between husbands and wives and parents and children often endured for many years. Marital customs, particularly exogamy, and the practice of naming children after the mother's or father's relatives (the most common pattern was to name a boy after a male relative) revealed the strong sense of kinship among slaves. Households tended to be large; Herbert G. Gutman found families with eight living children to be quite common. Out of economic considerations, a master would encourage his work force to reproduce itself, but the slaves welcomed each new birth primarily as "a social and familial fact." A web of human emotions spun by close family ties—affection, dignity, love—brought slaves together in a world apart from whites. [35]

In their own cabins, the blacks maintained a traditional division of labor between the sexes. Like women in almost all cultures, slave women had both a biological and a social "destiny." As part of their childbearing role, they assumed primary responsibility for childcare (when a husband and wife lived on separate plantations, the children remained with their mother and belonged to her master). Women also performed operations related to daily household maintenance—cooking, cleaning, tending fires, sewing and patching clothes. [36]

Fathers shared the obligations of family life with their wives. In denying slaves the right to own property, make a living for themselves, participate in public life, or protect their children, the institution of bondage deprived black men of access to the patriarchy in the larger economic and political sense. But at home women and men worked together to support the father's role as provider and protector. In the evenings and on Sundays, men collected firewood; made shoes; wove baskets, constructed beds, tables, and chairs; and carved butter paddles, ax handles, and animal traps. Other family members appreciated a father's skills; recalled Molly Ammonds, "My pappy make all de furniture dat went in our house an' it were might' good furniture too," and Pauline Johnson echoed, "De furn'chure was ho-mek, but my daddy mek it good an' stout." Husbands provided necessary supplements to the family diet by hunting and trapping quails, possums, turkeys, rabbits, squirrels, and raccoons, and by fishing. They often assumed responsibility for cultivating the tiny household garden plots allotted to families by the master. Some craftsmen, like Bill Austin's father, received goods or small sums of money in return for their work on nearby estates.

These familial duties also applied to men who lived apart from their wives and children even though they were usually allowed to visit only on Saturday night and Sunday. Lucinda Miller's family "never had any sugar, and only got coffee when her father would bring it to her mother" during his visits. The father of Hannah Chapman was sold to a nearby planter when she was very small. Because "he missed us and us longed for him," she said many years later, he tried to visit his family under the cover of darkness whenever possible. She noted, "Us would gather 'round him an' crawl up in his lap, tickled slap to death, but he give us dese pleasures at painful risk." If the master should happen to discover him, "Us could track him de nex' day by de blood stains," she remembered. [37]

Hannah McFarland of South Carolina well remembered the time when the local slave patrol attempted to whip her mother, "but my papa sho' stopped dat," she said proudly. Whether or not he was made to suffer for his courage is unknown; however, the primary literature of slavery is replete with accounts of slave husbands who intervened, at the risk of their own lives, to save wives and children from violence at the hands of white men. More often, however, fathers had to show their compassion in less dramatic (though no less revealing) ways. On a Florida plantation, the Minus children often rose in the morning to find still warm in the fireplace the potatoes "which their father had thoughtfully roasted and which [they] readily consumed." Margrett Nickerson recalled how her father would tenderly bind up the wounds inflicted on her by a maniacal overseer; in later years, her crippled legs preserved the memory of a father's sorrow intermingled with her own suffering.[38]

The more freedom the slaves had in determining their own activities, the more clearly emerged a distinct division of labor between the sexes. During community festivities like log rollings, rail splittings, wood choppings, and corn shuckings, men performed the prescribed labor while women cooked the meals. At times, male participants willingly "worked all night," for, in the words of one former slave, "we had the 'Heavenly Banners' (women and whiskey) by us." A limited amount of primary evidence indicates that men actively scorned women's work, especially cooking, housecleaning, sewing, washing clothes, and intimate forms of childcare (like bathing children and picking lice out of their hair).

The values and customs of the slave community played a predominant role in structuring work patterns among women and men within the quarters in general and the family in particular. Yet slaveholders affected the division of labor in the quarters in several ways; for example, they took women and girls out of the fields early on Saturdays to wash the clothes, and they enforced certain task assignments related to the production of household goods. An understanding of the social significance of the sexual division of labor requires at least brief mention of West African cultural preferences and the ways in which the American system of slavery disrupted or sustained traditional (African) patterns of women's work. Here it is important to keep in mind two points. First, cotton did not emerge as the South's primary staple crop until the late eighteenth century (the first slaves on the North American continent toiled in tobacco, rice, indigo, and corn fields); and, second, regardless of the system of task assignments imposed upon antebellum blacks, the grueling pace of forced labor represented a cruel break from the past for people who had followed age-old customs related to subsistence agriculture.[39]

Though dimmed by time and necessity, the outlines of African work patterns endured among the slaves. As members of traditional agricultural societies, African women played a major role in producing the family's food as well as in providing basic household services. The sexual division of labor was more often determined by a woman's childcare and domestic responsibilities than by any presumed physical weakness. She might engage in heavy, monotonous fieldwork (in some tribes) as long as she could make provisions for nursing her baby; that often meant keeping an infant with her in the field. She cultivated a kitchen garden that yielded a variety of vegetables consumed by the family or sold at market, and she usually milked the cows and churned butter.[40]

West Africans in general brought with them competencies and knowledge that slaveowners readily exploited. Certain tribes were familiar with rice, cotton, and indigo cultivation. Many black women had had experience spinning thread, weaving cloth, and sewing clothes. Moreover, slaves often used techniques and tools handed down from their ancestors—in the method of planting, hoeing, and pounding rice, for example. Whites frequently commented on the ability of slave women to balance heavy and unwieldy loads on their heads, an African trait.[41]

The primary difficulty in generalizing about African women's part in agriculture stems from the fact that members of West African tribes captured for the North American slave trade came from different hoe-culture economies. Within the geographically limited Niger Delta region, for example, women and men of the Ibo tribe worked together in planting, weeding, and harvesting, but female members of another prominent group, the Yoruba, helped only with harvest. In general, throughout most of sub-Saharan Africa (and particularly on the west coast), women had primary responsibility for tilling (though not clearing) the soil and cultivating the crops; perhaps this tradition, combined with work patterns established by white masters in this country, reinforced the blacks' belief that cutting trees and rolling logs were "men's work." In any case it is clear that African women often did fieldwork. But because the sexual division of labor varied according to tribe, it is impossible to state with any precision the effect of the African heritage on the slaves' perceptions of women's agricultural work.[42]

The West African tradition of respect of one's elders found new meaning among American slaves; for most women, old age brought increased influence within the slave community even as their economic value to the master declined. Owners, fearful lest women escape from "earning their salt" once they became too infirm to go to the field, set them to work at other tasks—knitting, cooking, spinning, weaving, dairying, washing, ironing, caring for the children. (Elderly men worked as gardeners, wagoners, carters, and stocktenders.) But the imperatives of the southern economic system sometimes compelled slaveowners to extract from feeble women what field labor they could. In other cases they reduced the material provisions of the elderly—housing and allowances of food and clothing—in proportion to their decreased productivity.[43]

The overwhelming youth of the general slave population between 1830 and 1860 (more than one-half of all slaves were under twenty years of age) meant that most plantations had only a few old persons—the 10 percent over fifty years of age considered elderly. These slaves served as a repository of history and folklore for the others. Harriet Ware, a northern teacher assigned to the South Carolina Sea Islands, reported in 1862, " 'Learning' with these people I find means a knowledge of medicine, and a person is valued accordingly." Many older women practiced "medicine" in the broadest sense in their combined role of midwife, root doctor, healer, and conjurer. They guarded ancient secrets about herbs and other forms of plant life. In their interpretation of dreams and strange occurrences, they brought the real world closer to the supernatural realm and offered spiritual guidance to the ill, the troubled, and the lovelorn.[44]

For slaves in the late antebellum period, these revered (and sometimes feared) women served as a tangible link with the African past. Interviewed by an FWP worker in 1937, a Mississippi-born former slave, James Brittian, recalled his own "grandma Aunt Mary" who had lived for 110 years. A "Molly Gasca [Madagascar?] negro," she was plagued by a jealous mistress because of her striking physical appearance: "Her hair it was fine as silk and hung down below her waist." Ned Chaney's African-born Granny Silla (she was the oldest person anyone knew, he thought) commanded respect among the other slaves by virtue of her advanced age and her remarkable healing powers: "Ever'body set a heap of sto' by her. I reckon, because she done 'cumullated so much knowledge an' because her head were so white." When Granny Silla died, her "little bags" of mysterious substances were buried with her because no one else knew how to use them. Yet Chaney's description of his own mother, a midwife and herb doctor, indicates that she too eventually assumed a position of at least informal authority within the community.[45] In the quiet dignity of their own lives, these grandmothers preserved the past for future generations of Afro-American women.[46]

Within well-defined limits, the slaves created—or preserved—an explicit sexual division of labor based on their own preferences. Wives and husbands and mothers and fathers had reciprocal obligations toward one another. Together they worked to preserve the integrity of the family. Having laid to rest once and for all the myth of the slave matriarchy, some historians suggest that relations between the sexes approximated "a healthy sexual equality."[47] Without private property, slave men lacked the means to achieve economic superiority over their wives, one of the major sources of inequality in the ("free") sexual order. But if female and male slaves shared duties related to household maintenance and community survival, they were nonetheless reduced to a state of powerlessness that rendered virtually meaningless the concept of equality as it applies to marital relations.

Developments during the turbulent postwar years, when the chains of bondage were loosened but not destroyed, made clear the significance of black women's work in supporting the southern staple-crop economy. They also revealed the connection between patterns of women's work and black family life—a connection that had, at least to some degree, remained latent under slavery. Black women did their part in helping to provide for their families after the war. Female household heads had a particularly difficult time, for under the "free labor" system, a mother working alone rarely earned enough to support small children who were themselves too little to make any money. Relatives in a better financial situation often "adopted" these children, or took the whole family under their care.[48]

After the war, black women continued to serve as domestic servants, but large numbers stopped going to the fields altogether, or agreed to work only in harvest time. Indeed, from all over the South came reports that "the negro women are now almost wholly withdrawn from field labor." Ransom and Sutch, in their study of the economic consequences of emancipation, estimate that between one third and one-half of all the women who worked in the fields under slavery provided proportionately less agricultural labor in the 1870s. This decline in overall female productivity was the result of two factors: many wives stayed home, and the ones who did continue to labor in the fields (like black men) put in shorter hours and fewer days each year than they had as slaves. Crop output in many locales dropped accordingly, and white landowners lamented their loss, "for women were as efficient as men in working and picking cotton."[49]

In their speculation about the sources of this "evil of female loaferism," whites offered a number of theories, from the pernicious influence of northern schoolteachers to the inherent laziness of the black race. Actually, black women and men responded to freedom in a manner consistent with preferences that had been thwarted during slavery. Husbands sought to protect their wives from the sexual abuse and physical punishment that continued to prevail under the wage system of agricultural labor. Wives wanted to remain at home with their children, as befitted free and freed women; many continued to contribute to the family welfare by taking in washing or raising chickens.[50]

By 1867 freed people who wanted to assert control over their own productive energies had reached what some historians term a "compromise" with white landowners anxious to duplicate antebellum crop levels. This "compromise" came in the form of the sharecropping system, a family organization of labor that represented both a radical departure from collective or "gang" work characteristic of slavery and a rejection of the wage economy so integral to the (North's) fledgling industrial revolution. Freed families moved out of the old slave quarters into cabins scattered around a white man's plantation; they received "furnishings" (tools and seed) and agreed to pay the landlord a share of the crop—usually one-half of all the cotton they produced—in return for the use of the land and modest dwelling. Under this arrangement, black husbands assumed primary responsibility for crop management, and their wives devoted as much attention as possible to their roles as mothers and homemakers. During the particularly busy planting or harvesting seasons, a woman would join her husband and children at work in the field. In this way she could keep an eye on her offspring and still put to use her considerable strength and skills unmolested by white men.[51]

The Reconstruction South was not the best of all worlds in which to foster a new order between the races—or the sexes. Faced with persistent economic exploitation and political subservience within white-dominated society, black men sought to assert their authority as protectors of their communities and families. Outwardly, they placed a premium on closing ranks at home. This impulse was institutionalized in the freed people's churches ("Wives submit yourselves to your husbands" was the text of more than one postbellum sermon) and political organizations. One searches in vain for evidence of female participants in the many black conventions and meetings during this period, although this was perhaps in part attributable to the fact that women did not have the right to vote. Black women remained militantly outspoken in defense of their families and property rights, but they lacked a formal power base within their own communities. And in an atmosphere fraught with sexual violence, where freedwomen remained at the mercy of white men and where "the mere suggestion" that a black man was attracted to a white woman was "enough to hang him," a black husband's resentment might continue to manifest itself in his relations with those closest to him. A Sea Island slave folktale offered the lesson that "God had nebber made a woman for the head of a man." In the struggle against white racism this often meant that black women were denied the equality with their men to which their labor—not to mention justice—entitled them.[52]

The sexual division of labor under slavery actually assumed two forms—one system of work forced upon slaves by masters who valued women only as work-oxen and brood-sows, and the other initiated by the slaves themselves in the quarters. Only the profit motive accorded a measure of consistency to the slaveholder's decisions concerning female work assignments; he sought to exploit his "hands" efficiently, and either invoked or repudiated traditional notions of women's work to suit his own purposes. In this respect, his decision-making process represented in microcosm the shifting priorities of the larger society, wherein different groups of women were alternately defined primarily as producers or as reproducers according to the fluctuating labor demands of the capitalist economy.[53]

Within their own communities, the slaves attempted to make work choices based on their African heritage as it applied to the American experience. Their well-defined sexual division of labor contrasted with the calculated self-interest of slaveowners. Slave women were allowed to fulfill their duties as wives and mothers only insofar as these responsibilities did not conflict with their masters' demands for field or domestic labor. As sharecroppers, freed people sought to institutionalize their resistance to the whites' conviction that black women should be servants or cotton pickers first, and family members only incidentally. In working together as a unit, black parents and children made an explicit political statement to the effect that their own priorities were inimical to those of white landowners.

To a considerable extent, the freed family's own patriarchal tendencies—fathers took care of "public" negotiations with the white landlord while mothers assumed primary responsibility for childcare—resulted from the black man's desire to protect his household in the midst of a violently racist society. The postbellum black nuclear family never duplicated exactly the functions of the white middle-class model, which (beginning in the late eighteenth century) drew an increasingly rigid distinction between masculine and feminine spheres of activity characteristic of commercial-industrial capitalism. Clearly, the peculiar southern way of life suggests that an analysis of black women's oppression should focus not so much on the family as on the dynamics of racial prejudice. However, black women and men in the long run paid a high price for their allegiance to a patriarchal family structure, and it is important not to romanticize this arrangement as it affected the status and opportunities of women, even within the confines of black community life. Women continued to wield informal influence in their roles as herb doctors and "grannies," but men held all positions of formal political and religious authority. Ultimately, black people's "preferences" in the postwar period took shape within two overlapping caste systems—one based on race, the other on gender. Former slaves were "free" only in the sense that they created their own forms of masculine authority as a counter to poverty and racism.

The story of slave women's work encapsulates an important part of American history. For here in naked form, stripped free of the pieties often used in describing white women and free workers at the time, were the forces that shaped patriarchal capitalism—exploitation of the most vulnerable members of society, and a contempt for women that knew no ethical or physical bounds. And yet slave women demonstrated "true womanhood" in its truest sense. Like Janie Scott's mother who was "much of a woman," they revealed a physical and emotional strength that transcended gender and preached a great sermon about the human spirit.

Notes

Acknowledgments: The author would like to acknowledge the helpful suggestions and comments provided by Rosalind Petchesky and other members of the *Feminist Studies* editorial board and by Michael P. Johnson. Research for this project (part of a full-length study of black women, work, and the family in America, 1830–1980) was funded by a grant from the National Endowment for the Humanities.

1. On women's "productive-reproductive" functions and the relationship between patriarchy and capitalism, see Joan Kelly, "The Doubled Vision of Feminist Theory: A Postscript to the 'Women and Power' Conference," *Feminist Studies* 5, no. 1 (1979):216–27; Heidi Hartmann, "Capitalism, Patriarchy, and Job Segregation by Sex," and Zillah Eisenstein, "Developing a Theory of Capitalist Patriarchy and Socialist Feminism," and "Some Notes on the Relations of Capitalist Patriarchy," in Zillah R. Eisenstein (ed.), *Capitalist Patriarchy and the Case for Socialist Feminism* (New York: Monthly Review Press, 1979); Annette Kuhn and Ann Marie Wolpe, "Feminism and Materialism," and Veronica Beechey, "Women and Production: A Critical Analysis of Some Sociological Theories of Women's Work," both in Annette Kuhn and Ann Marie Wolpe (eds.), *Feminism and Materialism: Women and Modes of Production* (London: Routledge & Kegan Paul, 1978).

Several scholars argue that the last three decades of the antebellum period constituted a distinct phase in the history of slavery. Improved textile machinery and a rise in world demand for cotton led to a tremendous growth in the American slave economy, especially in the lower South. A marked increase in slave mortality rates and family breakups (a consequence of forced migration from upper to lower South) and a slight decline in female fertility rates indicate the heightened demands made upon slave labor during the years 1830–60. See Paul E. David et al., *Reckoning with Slavery: A Critical Study in Quantitative History of American Negro Slavery* (New York: Oxford University Press, 1976), pp. 99, 356–57; Jack Erickson Eblen, "New Estimates of the Vital Rates of the United States Black Population During the Nineteenth Century," *Demography* 11 (1974):307–13.

2. For example, see Kelly, "Doubled Vision," pp. 217–18, and Eisenstein, "Relations of Capitalist Patriarchy," pp. 48–52, on the regressive implications of family life for women. But Davis notes that the slave woman's "survival-oriented activities were themselves a form of resistance." Angela Davis, "Reflections on the Black Woman's Role in the Community of Slaves," *Black Scholar* 3 (Dec. 1971):7.

3. Interviews with former slaves have been published in various forms, including George P. Rawick, ed., *The American Slave: A Composite Autobiography,* 41 vols., series 1 and 2, supp. series 1 and 2 (Westport Conn.: Greenwood Press, 1972, 1978, 1979); Social Science Institute, Fisk University, *Unwritten History of Slavery: Autobiographical Accounts of Negro Ex-Slaves* (Washington, D.C.: Microcards Editions, 1968); Charles L. Perdue, Jr., Thomas E. Borden, and Robert K. Phillips, *Weevils in the Wheat: Interviews with Virginia Ex-Slaves* (Charlottesville: University Press of Virginia, 1976); John B. Cade, "Out of the Mouths of Ex-Slaves," *Journal of Negro History* 20 (1935):294–337.

The narratives as a historical source are evaluated in Paul D. Escott, *Slavery*

Remembered: A Record of Twentieth-Century Slave Narratives (Chapel Hill: University of North Carolina Press, 1978), pp. 3–18 ("the slave narratives offer the best evidence we will ever have on the feelings and attitudes of America's slaves"); Martia Graham Goodson, "An Introductory Essay and Subject Index to Selected Interviews from the Slave Narrative Collection" (Ph.D. dissertation, Union Graduate School, 1977); and C. Vann Woodward, "History from Slave Sources," *American Historical Review* 79 (1974): 470–81.

The Davidson quotation is from Rawick, ed., *American Slave,* Ohio Narrs., series 1, vol. 16, pp. 26–29. Hereafter, all references to this collection will include the name of the state, series number, volume, and page numbers. The other major source of slave interview material taken from the FWP collection for this paper—Perdue et al.—will be referred to as *Weevils in the Wheat.*

4. Joan Kelly-Gadol, "The Social Relations of the Sexes: Methodological Implications of Women's History," *Signs* 1 (1976):809–10, 819.

5. For discussions of women's work and the inadequacy of male-biased economic and social scientific theory to define and analyze it, see Joan Acker, "Issues in the Sociological Study of Women's Work," in Ann H. Stromberg and Shirley Harkess, eds. *Women Working: Theories and Facts in Perspective* (Palo Alto, Calif.: Mayfield, 1978), pp. 134–61; and Judith K. Brown, "A Note on the Division of Labor by Sex," *American Anthropologist* 72 (1970): 1073–78.

6. Miss. Narrs., supp. series 1, pt. 2, vol. 7, p. 350; Okla. Narrs., supp. series 1, vol. 12, p. 110; Davis, "Reflections on the Black Woman's Role," p. 8; Frances Anne Kemble, *Journal of a Residence on a Georgian Plantation in 1838 1839* (London: Longman, Green, 1863), pp. 60, 92.

7. Leslie Howard Owens, *This Species of Property: Slave Life and Culture in the Old South* (New York: Oxford University Press, 1976), pp. 8–20.

8. Kemble, *Journal of a Residence,* p. 28; Lewis Cecil Gray, *History of Agriculture in the Southern United States,* vol. 1 (Washington, D.C.: Carnegie Institution, 1933), pp. 533 48; *Weevils in the Wheat,* p. 199; Fla. Narrs., series 1, vol. 17, p. 305; Charles S. Sydnor, *Slavery in Mississippi* (Gloucester, Mass.: P. Smith, 1965), p. 20; Frederick Law Olmsted, *A Journey in the Seaboard Slave States* (New York: Dix and Edwards, 1856), p. 470; Frederick Law Olmsted, *A Journey in the Back Country* (New York: Mason Brothers, 1860), p. 59.

9. Olmsted, *Slave States,* p. 387; Ala. Narrs., series 1, vol. 6, p. 87. Work descriptions were gleaned from the FWP slave narrative collection (*American Slave* and *Weevils in the Wheat*) and Gray, *History of Agriculture.* Goodson ("Introductory Essay") has indexed a sample of the interviews with women by subject (for example, "candlemaking," "carding wool," "field work," "splitting rails").

10. *Weevils in the Wheat,* p. 26; Gray, *History of Agriculture,* p. 251; planter quoted in Owens, *This Species of Property,* p. 39.

11. Burke quoted in Gray, *History of Agriculture,* p. 549. Olmsted quoted in Sydnor, *Slavery in Mississippi,* p. 68; *Weevils in the Wheat,* p. 77. Of the women who worked in the South Carolina Sea Islands cotton fields, Harriet Ware (a northern teacher) wrote, "they walk off with their heavy hoes on their shoulders, as free, strong, and graceful as possible." Elizabeth Ware Pearson, ed., *Letters from Port Royal Written at the Time of the Civil War* (Boston: W. B. Clarke, 1906), p. 52.

12. Stuart Bruchey, ed., *Cotton and the Growth of the American Economy: 1790–1860* (New York: Harcourt, Brace & World, 1967), p. 174. See the documents under the heading "Making Cotton" and "The Routine of the Cotton Year," pp. 171–80. For examples of outstanding female pickers see Ala. Narrs., series 1, vol 6,

p. 275 ("Oncet I won a contest wid a man an' made 480 pounds"); *Weevils in the Wheat*, p. 199.

13. Texas Narrs., supp. series 2, pt. 1, vol. 2, pp. 93–94; Miss. Narrs., supp. series 1, pt. 1, vol. 6, pp. 235–36, and pt. 2, vol. 7, p. 404; Tex. Narrs., series 1, pt. 3, vol. 5, p. 231; Ind. Narrs., series 1, vol. 6, p. 25; Ga. Narrs., series 1, pt. 1, vol. 12, p. 113; Okla. Narrs., series 1, vol. 7, p. 314; Ala. Narrs., series 1, vol. 6, p. 338.

14. For a general discussion of slave artisans in the South see Gray, *History of Agriculture*, pp. 548, 565–67; Sydnor, *Slavery in Mississippi*, p. 9. Roger L. Ransom and Richard Sutch, in *One Kind of Freedom: The Economic Consequences of Emancipation* (Cambridge: Cambridge University Press, 1977), discuss "Occupational Distribution of Southern Blacks: 1860, 1870, 1890" in app. B, pp. 220–31. The works of Robert S. Starobin, *Industrial Slavery in the Old South* (New York: Oxford University Press, 1970), and James H. Brewer, *The Confederate Negro: Virginia's Craftsmen and Military Laborers, 1861–1865* (Durham: Duke University Press, 1969), focus almost exclusively on male slaves. See also Herbert Gutman and Richard Sutch, "Victorians All? The Sexual Mores and Conduct of Slaves and Their Masters," in David et al., *Reckoning with Slavery*, p. 160; Herbert G. Gutman, *The Black Family in Slavery and Freedom, 1790–1925* (New York: Pantheon, 1976), pp. 599–600. The "hiring out" of men and children frequently disrupted family life.

15. Ransom and Sutch, *One Kind of Freedom*, p. 233; Olmsted, *Slave States*, p. 388; Ohio Narrs., series 1, vol. 16, p. 28; Kemble, *Journal*, p. 121; S.C. Narrs., series 1, pt. 4, vol. 3, p. 78; *Weevils in the Wheat*, pp. 223–24. Eugene Genovese describes the plantation system as a "halfway house between peasant and factory cultures"; *Roll, Jordan, Roll: The World the Slaves Made* (New York: Random House, 1974), p. 286. For further discussion of the grueling pace of fieldwork see Herbert G. Gutman and Richard Sutch, "Sambo Makes Good, or Were Slaves Imbued with the Protestant Work Ethic?" in David et al., *Reckoning with Slavery*, pp. 55–93.

16. Ala. Narrs., series 1, vol. 6, p. 46; Fla. Narrs., series 1, vol. 17, p. 185; *Weevils in the Wheat*, pp. 259, 216; Va. Narrs., series 1, vol. 16, p. 51; Escott, *Slavery Remembered*, pp. 86–93. Escott includes an extensive discussion of resistance as revealed in the FWP slave narrative collection and provides data on the age, sex, and marital status of resisters and the purposes and forms of resistance. Gutman argues that the "typical runaway" was a male, aged sixteen to thirty-five years (*Black Family*, pp. 264–65). See also Mary Ellen Obitko, "Custodians of a House of Resistance: Black Women Respond to Slavery," in Dana V. Hiller and Robin Ann Sheets (eds.), *Women and Men: The Consequences of Power* (Cincinnati: Office of Women Studies, University of Cincinnati, 1977); Owens, *This Species of Property*, pp. 38, 88, 95.

17. *Weevils in the Wheat*, pp. 26, 282, 157. According to Gutman, plantation work patterns "apparently failed to take into account enlarged slave kin groups, and further study may show that a central tension between slaves and their owners had its origins in the separation of work and kinship obligations" (*Black Family*, p. 209).

18. Fla. Narrs., series 1, vol. 17, p. 191; Bennet H. Barrow, quoted in Gutman, *Black Family*, p. 263; Robert S. Starobin, ed., *Blacks in Bondage: Letters of American Slaves* (New York: New Viewpoints, 1974), p. 54.

In his recent study, *The Slave Drivers: Black Agricultural Labor Supervisors in the Antebellum South* (Westport, Conn.: Greenwood Press, 1979), William L. Van DeBurg examines the anomalous position of black (male) drivers in relation to the rest of the slave community.

19. Todd L. Savitt, *Medicine and Slavery: The Diseases and Health Care of Blacks in Antebellum Virginia* (Urbana: University of Illinois Press, 1978), pp. 115–20,

planter quoted in Owens, *This Species of Property,* pp. 38–40; planter quoted in Olmsted, *Slave States,* p. 190; Kemble, *Journal,* p. 121. Cf. Deborah G. White, " 'Ain't I a Woman?': Female Slaves in the Antebellum South" (Ph.D. Dissertation, University of Illinois–Chicago Circle, 1979), pp. 77–86, 101, 155–60.

20. Genovese, *Roll, Jordan, Roll,* pp. 328, 340; Ala. Narrs., series 1, vol. 6, p. 273; Miss. Narrs., supp. series 1, pt. 2, vol. 7, p. 400; Tex. Narrs., series 1, pt. 3, vol. 5, p. 45. Recent historians have emphasized that the distinction between housework and fieldwork was not always meaningful in terms of shaping a slave's personality and self-perception or defining her or his status. See Owens, *This Species of Property,* p. 113; Escott, *Slavery Remembered,* pp. 59–60.

21. Ala. Narrs., series 1, vol. 6, pp. 416–17. In her study of slave mistresses, Anne Firor Scott gives an accurate description of their numerous supervisory duties, but she ignores the fact that most of the actual manual labor was performed by slave women. See *The Southern Lady: From Pedestal to Politics, 1830–1930* (Chicago: University of Chicago Press, 1970), p. 31.

22. The FWP slave narrative collection provides these examples of children's work, and many more. Ala. Narrs., series 1, vol. 6, p. 157; Genovese, *Roll, Jordon, Roll,* pp. 502–19; Owens, *This Species of Property,* p. 202.

In early adolescence (ages ten to fourteen), a child would normally join the regular work force as a half-hand. At that time (or perhaps before), she or he received adult clothing. This *rite de passage* apparently made more of an impression on boys than girls, probably because pants offered more of a contrast to the infant's smock than did a dress. Willis Cofer attested to the significance of the change: "Boys jes' wore shirts what looked lak dresses 'til dey wuz 12 years old and big enough to wuk in de field . . . and all de boys wuz mighty proud when dey got big enough to wear pants and go to wuk in de fields wid grown folkses. When a boy got to be man enough to wear pants, he drawed rations and quit eatin' out of de trough [in the nursery]." Ga. Narrs., series 1, pt. 1, vol. 12, p. 203. For other examples of the significance of change from adults' to children's clothing, see Tex. Narrs., series 1, pt. 3, vol. 5, pp. 211, 275; pt. 4, pp. 109–10; Ga. Narrs., series 1, pt. 1, vol. 12, p. 277; Genovese, *Roll, Jordan, Roll,* p. 505.

23. Ga. Narrs., supp. series 1, pt. 1, vol. 3, p. 185; *Weevils in the Wheat,* pp. 264–65; S.C. Narrs., series 1, pt. 4, vol. 3, p. 257.

24. Okla. Narrs., series 1, vol. 7, p. 347; White, "Ain't I a Woman?" pp. 210–15; L. Maria Child, ed., *Incidents in the Life of a Slave Girl, Written By Herself* (Boston: L. Maria Child, 1861).

25. James Hugo Johnston, *Race Relations in Virginia and Miscegenation in the South, 1776–1860* (Amherst: University of Massachusetts Press, 1970), p. 247; Mary Boykin Chesnut, *A Diary from Dixie,* ed. Ben Ames Williams (Cambridge: Harvard University Press, 1980), p. 49.

26. Fla. Narrs., series 1, vol. 17, p. 35. For specific incidents illustrating these points, see *Weevils in the Wheat,* pp. 63, 199; Okla. Narrs., series 1, vol. 7, pp. 135, 165–66; Tenn. Narrs., series 1, vol. 16, p. 14. Slave punishment in general is discussed in Escott, *Slavery Remembered,* pp. 42–46; Owens, *This Species of Property,* p. 88; Savitt, *Medicine and Slavery,* pp. 65–69; Gutman and Sutch, "Sambo Makes Good," pp. 55–93; Frederick Douglass, *Narrative of the Life of Frederick Douglass, An American Slave* (Cambridge: Harvard University Press, 1960), pp. 60–61. These examples indicate that Anne Firor Scott is a bit sanguine in suggesting that although southern women were sensitive to the "depravity" of their husbands, "it may be significant that they did not blame black women, who might have provided convenient

scapegoats. The blame was squarely placed on men.'' See Anne Firor Scott, ''Women's Perspectives on the Patriarchy in the 1850s,'' *Journal of American History* 61 (1974): 52–64.

27. Genovese, *Roll, Jordan, Roll,* pp. 333–38. See, for example, the document entitled ''A Seamstress Is Punished,'' in Gerda Lerner (ed.), *Black Women in White America: A Documentary History* (New York: Random House, 1972), pp. 18–19.

28. Olmsted, *Slave States,* p. 421; S.C. Narrs., series 1, pt. 4, vol. 3, p. 126; Fla. Narrs., series 1, vol. 14, p. 356; Escott, *Slavery Remembered,* p. 64; Kemble, *Journal,* p. 98; Genovese, *Roll, Jordan, Roll,* pp. 346–47.

29. Fla. Narrs., series 1, vol. 17, p. 356; Gutman and Sutch, ''Sambo Makes Good,'' p. 74; Kemble, *Journal,* p. 153; Gray, *History of Agriculture,* p. 553; Owens, *This Species of Property,* p. 113.

30. Ga. Narrs., series 1, pt. 1, vol. 12, p. 243; Davis, ''Reflections on the Black Woman's Role,'' pp. 4–7. For general discussions of women's work as it related to slave communal life, see also Owens, *This Species of Property,* pp. 23, 225; and White, ''Ain't I a Woman?'' Polly Cancer recalled that when she was growing up on a Mississippi plantation, the master ''wudn't let de mammies whip dey own chillun [or ''do dey own cookin''] . . . , ef he cum 'cross a 'ooman whuppin' her chile he'd say, 'Git 'way 'ooman; dats my bizness.' '' Miss. Narrs., supp. series 1, pt. 2, vol. 7, pp. 340–41.

31. Gray, *History of Agriculture,* p. 563; Olmsted, *Slave States,* pp. 424–25, 697–98; Owens, *This Species of Property,* p. 47; Fla. Narrs., series 1, vol. 17, p. 175; Ala. Narrs., series 1, vol. 6, p. 216; Miss. Narrs., supp. series 1, pt. 1, vol. 6, pp. 10, 23, 25, 123; Ga. Narrs., supp. series 1, pt. 1, vol. 3, p. 27. Savitt, *Medicine and Slavery,* includes a section on ''Black Medicine'' (pp. 171–84) and confirms Rebecca Hook's recollection that ''on the plantation, the doctor was not nearly as popular as the 'granny' or midwife '': Fla. Narrs., series 1, vol. 17, p. 175.

32. The FWP slave narrative collection contains many descriptions of slaves engaged in household industry. Alice Morse Earle details comparable techniques used by white women in colonial New England in *Home Life in Colonial Days* (New York: Macmillan, 1935).

33. See, for example, S.C. Narrs., series 1, pt. 3, vol. 3, pp. 15, 218, 236; Tex. Narrs., series 1, pt. 3, vol. 5, pp. 20, 89, 108, 114, 171, 188, 220; Miss. Narrs., supp. series 1, pt. 1, vol. 6, p. 36.

34. Genovese, *Roll, Jordan, Roll,* p. 319.

35. Gutman, *Black Family,* p. 75. Escott points out that masters and slaves lived in ''different worlds'': *Slavery Remembered,* p. 20. This paragraph briefly summarizes Gutman's pioneering work.

36. Davis, ''Reflections on the Black Woman's Role,'' p. 7.

37. Gutman, *Black Family,* pp. 142, 67–68, 267–78; Genovese, *Roll, Jordan, Roll,* pp. 318, 482–94; S.C. Narrs., series 1, pt. 3, vol. 3, p. 192; Miss. Nars., supp. series 1, pt. 2, vol. 7, pp. 380–81.

38. Okla. Narrs., series 1, vol. 7, p. 210; Escott, *Slavery Remembered,* pp. 49–57, 87; Owens, *This Species of Property,* p. 201.

39. Unfortunately, much of the data about precolonial African work patterns must be extrapolated from recent findings of anthropologists. The author benefited from conversations with Dr. M. Jean Hay of the Boston University African Studies Center concerning women's work in precolonial Africa and methodological problems in studying this subject.

40. For a theoretical formulation of the sexual division of labor in preindustrial societies, see Brown, "A Note on the Division of Labor by Sex."

41. Peter Wood, *Black Majority: Negroes in Colonial South Carolina from 1670 Through the Stono Rebellion* (New York: Knopf, 1974), pp. 59–62; P. C. Lloyd, "Osi fakunde of Ijebu," in Philip D. Curtin (ed.), *Africa Remembered: Narratives by West Africans from the Era of the Slave Trade* (Madison: University of Wisconsin Press, 1967), p. 263; Marguerite Dupire, "The Position of Women in a Pastoral Society," in Denise Paulme (ed.), *Women of Tropical Africa* (Berkeley: University of California Press, 1963), pp. 76–80; Olaudah Equiano, "The Life of Olaudah Equiano or Gustavus Vassa the African Written by Himself," in Arna Bontemps (ed.), *Great Slave Narratives* (Boston: Beacon Press, 1969), pp. 7–10; Kemble, *Journal*, p. 42; Pearson, ed., *Letters from Port Royal*, pp. 58, 106.

42. Melville J. Herskovits, *The Myth of the Negro Past* (New York: Harper & Bros., 1941), pp. 33–85; Wood, *Black Majority*, pp. 179, 250; Hermann Baumann, "The Division of Work According to Sex in African Hoe Culture," *Africa* 1 (1928):289–319.

On the role of women in hoe agriculture, see also Leith Mullings, "Women and Economic Change in Africa," in Nancy J. Hafkin and Edna G. Bay (eds.), *Women in Africa: Studies in Social and Economic Change* (Stanford: Stanford University Press, 1976), pp. 239–64; Sylvia Leith-Ross, *African Women: A Study of the Ibo of Nigeria* (New York: Praeger, 1965), pp. 84–91; Ester Boserup, *Woman's Role in Economic Development* (New York: St. Martin's Press, 1970), pp. 15–36; Jack Goody and Joan Buckley, "Inheritance and Women's Labour in Africa," *Africa* 63 (1973); 108–21. No tribes in precolonial Africa used the plow.

43. Olmsted, *Slave States*, p. 433; Gray, *History of Agriculture*, p. 548; Kemble, *Journal*, pp. 164, 247; Douglass, *Narrative*, pp. 76–78. According to Genovese, the ability of these elderly slaves "to live decently and with self-respect depended primarily on the support of their younger fellow slaves" (*Roll, Jordan, Roll*, p. 523); White "Ain't I a Woman?" p. 49; Miss. Narrs., supp. series 1, pt. 1, vol. 6, p. 242.

44. Eblen, "New Estimates," p. 306; Pearson, *Letters from Port Royal*, p. 25; Genovese, *Roll, Jordan, Roll*, pp. 522–23; Eliza F. Andrews, *The War-Time Journal of a Georgia Girl, 1864–1865* (New York: D. Appleton, 1908), p. 101; Escott, *Slavery Remembered*, pp. 108–9; Owens, *This Species of Property*, p. 140; Gutman, *Black Family*, p. 218. For specific examples, see Ala. Narrs., supp. series 1, pt. 1, vol. 6, p. 217; pt. 2, vol. 7, pp. 369–73. See also White, "Ain't I a Woman?" pp. 107–12.

45. Miss. Narrs., supp. series 1, pt. 1, vol. 6, p. 217; pt. 2, vol. 7, pp. 369–73. See also White, "Ain't I a Woman?" pp. 107–12.

46. Ga. Narrs., series 1, pt. 1, vol. 12, p. 214; *Weevils In the Wheat*, p. 128.

47. Genovese, *Roll, Jordan, Roll*, p. 500. See also White, "Ain't I a Woman?" pp. 3–20, 51–54; and Davis, "Reflections on the Black Woman's Role," p. 7.

48. This section summarizes material in Chapter 2 of Jacqueline Jones, *Labor of Love, Labor of Sorrow: Black Women, Work and the Family From Slavery to the Present* (New York: Basic Books, 1985).

49. Robert Somers, *The Southern States Since the War, 1870–1* (London: Macmillan, 1871), p. 59; Ransom and Sutch, *One Kind of Freedom*, p. 233; Francis W. Loring and C. F. Atkinson, *Cotton Culture and the South Considered with Reference to Emigration* (Boston: A. Williams, 1869), pp. 4–23. Other primary works that include relevant information are Frances Butler Leigh, *Ten Years on a Georgia Plantation*

Since the War (London: R. Bentley, 1883); Charles Nordhoff, *The Cotton States in the Spring and Summer of 1875* (New York: D. Appleton, 1876); George Campbell, *White and Black: The Outcome of a Visit to the United States* (London: Chatto and Windus, 1879).

50. Freedmen's Bureau official quoted in Gutman, *Black Family,* p. 167.

51. The transition from wage labor to the sharecropping system is examined in Ralph Shlomowitz, "The Origins of Southern Sharecropping," *Agricultural History* 53 (1979):557–75, and his "The Transition from Slave to Freedman Labor Arrangements in Southern Agriculture, 1865–1870," *Journal of Economic History* 39 (1979):333–36; Jay R. Mandle, *The Roots of Black Poverty: The Southern Plantation Economy After the Civil War* (Durham, N.C.: Duke University Press, 1978); Joseph D. Reid, Jr., "White Land, Black Labor, and Agricultural Stagnation: The Causes and Effects of Sharecropping in the Postbellum South," *Explorations in Economic History* 16 (1979):31–55; Ransom and Sutch, *One Kind of Freedom.*

Jonathan Wiener suggests that blacks' rejection of gang labor and preference for family share units "represented a move away from classic capitalist organizations." See "Class Structure and Economic Development in the American South, 1865–1955," *American Historical Review* 84 (1979):984.

52. Elizabeth Hyde Botume, *First Days Amongst the Contrabands* (Boston: Lee & Shepard, 1893), p. 166; Campbell, *White and Black,* pp. 172, 344, 364; tale entitled "De Tiger an' de Nyung Lady," quoted in Owens, *This Species of Property,* p. 144. See Leon Litwack, *Been in the Storm So Long: The Aftermath of Slavery* (New York: Knopf, 1979), pp. 502–56, for a detailed discussion of various freedmen's conventions held throughout the South.

53. For an analysis of the ways in which the household responsibilities of women are defined and redefined to alter the supply of available wage-earners, see Louise A. Tilly and Joan W. Scott, *Women, Work, and Family* (New York: Holt, Rinehart & Winston, 1978).

4

The Historical Problem of the Family Wage: The Ford Motor Company and the Five Dollar Day

MARTHA MAY

One aspect of working-class family life that has been examined by theorists and historians in the past decade may be especially useful in analyzing the processes of reproduction and gender divisions within the family: the family wage. The ideology of the male-earned family wage, many suggest, became a powerful argument for women's domestic role and position as secondary wage-earner in the labor force. The family wage focuses our attention on the relationships among women, men, and children as they struggle to secure the means to survive. By analyzing the ideology of the family wage, its actual achievement by segments of the working class, and its impact on gender roles, we can begin to demystify the hidden relationships between sex, gender, and class.

The family wage as an ideology presented a particular arrangement of family work roles as socially desirable, articulating *both* demands for subsistence and survival of the working-class family as a unit *and* the notion of a dependent home-bound wife and children. The connection between these two elements of the family wage ideology has raised many questions for feminist scholars. Was the purpose of this wage form working-class survival, female subordination, or still other factors that had to do with capitalist control over the workplace? Or were these different aspects of class and gender conflict interconnected within the ideology and the reality of the family wage?

In this essay, I argue that in at least one case, that of the Ford Motor Company's Five Dollar Day, the family wage originated from the political conflicts between workers and their employer, not over wages or female subordination, but over the labor process. The Five Dollar Day operated to

Reprinted in abridged form from *Feminist Studies* 8, no. 2 (Summer 1982): 399–424, by permission of the publisher, Feminist Studies, Inc., c/o Women's Studies Program, University of Maryland, College Park, MD 20742.

turn a family wage into a subtle form of social control exercised by management over workers and the work process. At the same time, the rhetoric and
practice of the Ford family wage was used to the advantage of both classes
while it also reinforced gender divisions and a subordinate female role. To
place the family wage at Ford in a historical context, I will first examine the
development of the family wage ideology in America. The theoretical assess-
ments of this wage form are reviewed as they shape our understanding of the
family wage as a historical phenomenon. Finally, I examine the family wage
at the Ford Motor Company as an example of how ideology in this instance
became an actual achievement reflecting complex issues of class as well as
gender.

The Historical Development of the Ideology

The idea of the family wage appeared in America as early as the 1820s and
1830s and developed most clearly through the nineteenth century in the rhetoric of trade unionists and other agencies of the working class.[1] For its
working-class advocates, the family wage promised one solution to inadequate wages and marginal subsistence. The first premise of demands for a
family wage was survival: supporters of this wage form sought an increased
standard of living above what a single worker could achieve under existing
wage rates. Although they varied substantially among skilled and unskilled
laborers, most wages were sufficient only for the subsistence of one person.
Families depended upon the income contributions of children and women to
supplement male wages at different stages in the family life cycle.[2] A family
wage, it was hoped, would eliminate periods of hardship while ensuring a decent standard of living.

Less directly, the ideology of a family wage also confronted nineteenth-
century concepts of class and work. The common difficulty in making ends
meet brought workers face to face with the dominant ideologies of work and
wealth, which attributed poverty to individual causes, such as shiftlessness,
idleness, intemperance, and the lack of moral, virtuous character. Charitable
agencies might respond to need, but the ideology of work based on a laissez-
faire notion of industrial order held that the fault for indigence or unemployment lay with the working man.[3] The family wage challenged the ideology of
working-class poverty, invoking social justice and high wages in the name of
the family.

The second premise of the family wage was that a male should be the family breadwinner. Early demands for the family wage suggested that only
women, and not children, be withdrawn from the labor force. In 1836, for ex-

ample, the National Trades Union condemned female labor on the grounds that

the parent, the husband, or the brother is deprived of a sufficient subsistence to support himself and family, when without the auxiliary aid of the female, by his own labor alone he might have supported himself and family in decency and kept his wife or relative at home.[4]

In the latter half of the nineteenth century, demands for a family wage began to include support for children. As an increasingly prevalent goal of trade unions, the family wage took shape as an adult male prerogative. Workers predicated their notion of an adequate living wage upon a sum that would support an entire family: to meet emergency expenses, to have savings, to buy a home or rent sanitary living quarters, and to allow children access to education. Many working-class families relying on children's labor to improve their standard of living resented the necessity that forced their children to labor. One writer from Lynn, Massachusetts, complained in 1860 to shoemakers that "the parent finds the expenses of his household constantly increasing, while the wages of his labor are steadily diminishing," making him dependent upon his children's work.[5]

The inability of workers to provide necessities for their families throughout the family life cycle led to repeated and intensified arguments for a supporting "living wage."[6] The *Cripple Creek* (Colorado) *Daily Press* in 1902 expressed the opinion that male wages should allow the worker to "keep his wife and children out of competition with himself and give them the same opportunities for improvement and intellectual and moral training and comfortable living as are enjoyed by those who do not labor."[7] The *Shoe Workers' Journal* proposed in 1905: "Everything necessary to the life of a *normal man* must be included in the living wage: the right to marriage, the right to have children, and to educate them."[8]

Thus, the underlying premises of the family wage made a dependent family essential to a preferred standard *and* to the notion of "normal manhood." The ideology had special implications for women; the family "living wage" for male workers assumed that all women would, sooner or later, become wives, and thus it was legitimate to argue for the exclusion of women from the labor force. Working women were believed to devalue wages, making a "living wage" difficult to achieve and upsetting a natural sexual order.

In calling for subsistence and a dependent family, the family wage ideology linked concepts of class, poverty, generational reproduction, and domesticity. The response of more privileged classes to the family wage is less clear, and to a large extent commingled with the ideas of domesticity described by historians as the "cult of true womanhood" and later as "virtuous womanhood."[9] The separate spheres bought by the family wage paralleled those urged by a Utica, New York, author: ''the husband to go out into the world—the wife to superintend the domestic affairs of the household.'' [10] Both the ideology of the family wage and middle-class ideals of virtuous womanhood placed women in a privatized home sphere. Yet the two ideologies, while drawing upon the same concepts of an innate feminine predisposition for household life and labor, were not entirely identical. In the middle classes and among the bourgeoisie, there was no need for a companion demand for subsistence, and this difference suggests a critical divergence in class response to domesticity. Domesticity in the family wage arguments of the working class was tied to subsistence and an improved standard of living. Without the latter, female virtue had to be reflected in arduous domestic labor and, for a few married women, in waged work. The family wage argument, then, was composed of interrelated elements, and while domesticity was a central theme, it was not the sole determining definition of the struggle for a family wage. Family dependency, including children as well as women, held an even larger place in the family wage ideology, a distinction that resulted from class position and the need for subsistence.

The role of the dependent family in the ideology of the family wage gave this wage demand added acceptability outside the working class. By the turn of the century, the idea of the family wage extended far beyond union rhetoric. It became a central feature of analysis in the assessment of poverty and standards of living by Progressive reformers, and part of the works of sociologists, economists, and charity workers of the developing social survey movement.[11] Between 1890 and 1920, scientific examination of income and standards of living intensified; nearly three thousand surveys of individual and family budgets were completed by the 1930s.[12] These studies gradually changed from an investigation of the economic contribution of all family members to an emphasis on wages alone. Accompanying this concentration on wages was a special interest in the family wage.[13]

Unpaid domestic labor played an important role in the family's survival, according to early budget analysts. In the *Hull House Maps and Papers* of 1895, for example, settlement workers concluded that ''the theory that 'every man supports his own family' is as idle in a district like this as the fiction that 'everyone can get work if he wants it.' '' The Hull House investigators noted the importance of a family earning, recording not only the wages of working women and children, but also the domestic contributions of family members. But as budget studies became more quantified, an emphasis on wage contributions obscured the domestic role in a family's survival.

The ''living wage'' advocated by economists and social critics, like that of organized labor, criticized the labor-force participation of married women and supported the notion of a dependent family. If working mothers gave

effects of woman working

their families an extra edge toward physical survival, they did so at the price of their family's psychological welfare and comfort. Working mothers' neglect of the duties of nurturing and properly socializing their children was viewed as detrimental to the future of the human race, a social problem that could be addressed by adequate male wages.[14]

This assessment of the dangers inherent in female labor-force participation and of the superiority of male family wages also resulted in arguments for different minimum wage levels for women and men. Male minimum wages were based on the possibility of a dependent family at some point in the male wage-earner's life cycle. Studies of minimum wages for working women did not base minimum subsistence needs upon the possible presence of a family and rarely assumed women would be the financial heads of households. For example, Louise Bosworth's 1911 study of women workers in Boston found that $500 a year comprised a "living wage" for women.[15] In contrast, Robert C. Chapin's estimate for a family living wage in the New York City of 1909 had concluded that "an income under $800 is not enough to permit the maintenance of a normal standard."[16] Ironically, poverty studies completed in the same period revealed that an overwhelming proportion of destitute families were headed by women. The response to this seeming inequality was to propose charitable aid for women and children, not higher wages, thus perpetuating female dependency and poverty. One charity worker observed in 1909 that

relief should never be used as a substitute for fair wages. Ordinarily when a family contains an able-bodied man, on whom the responsibilities of its support should fall, philanthropy should not assume the burden.   When, however, a family is without male support, and consequently in want, this objection does not hold, and frequently relief extending through a period of years is the only proper solution of the difficulty.[17]

By the 1920s, standardized income levels were "absolutely necessary . . . for the guidance of the wage adjuster . . . and of domestic economists in suggesting changes in the consumption of families," said Royal Meeker, Commissioner of Labor Statistics.[18] For both trade unionists and economists in private agencies and the state, the family wage had become a standard convention.

Theoretical Assessments of the Family Wage

The potency of the family wage ideology in history raises the theoretical questions of how it operated as a restraint upon women and how it articulated a relationship between gender, work roles, and subsistence.[19] Two major perspectives emerge from the feminist literature, one emphasizing the role of patriarchy in the creation of family wages and the other identifying working-class resistance and family structure as the core of the demand.

Heidi Hartmann first examined the male-earned family wage and related this wage form, both as an ideology and as an actual achievement, to the creation of women's work roles. Hartmann claimed this wage form represented the patriarchal control of "men as men and men as capitalists" over women's paid labor, ensuring women's secondary role in the family's economy and lower wages in the work force.[20] This conclusion places gender at the heart of the family wage ideology, determining the struggle for subsistence through female subordination and linking patriarchal forces in the creation of the family wage with existing conditions of capitalist social relations. In this perspective, the family wage ideology appears as an intersection of these interrelated, yet autonomous, social systems.

Hartmann claims throughout her work that the family wage came to be a "norm" for "stable working-class families" at the turn of the century.[21] A significant ambiguity about ideology versus the actual achievement of the family wage results from this analysis, which may have important consequences for our theoretical understanding of the family wage. The implications of the family wage as an ideological construction are quite different depending upon whether the family wage was received by many or by few American working-class families. Had the American working class won a family wage?

To answer this, we must first distinguish between a male-earned wage which supports a family at a certain standard of living, allowing for their reproduction, and any male-earned wage. The former is a family wage, the key to its definition resting in a standard of living that allows for dependent women and children. The second formulation is not necessarily a family wage. If the male-earned wage will not purchase necessities, and the family compensates for this by sending other family members into the labor force, or by living in poverty or receiving charity, the family's economy is not based on a family wage.[22] We cannot say that simply because a male earns a wage which is a family's sole income it is a family wage. In the same manner, a family that receives a family wage may still choose to have more than one laborer in the work force.[23]

This proposition directs our attention to wage rates rather than to family structure in determining the presence of family wages as an achievement. Only in the skilled and unionized sectors of the labor force is there any convincing evidence of what may be family wages in the period under consideration. For example, masons received up to five dollars per day prior to 1900, at what was obviously a family wage level. Plumbers, plasterers, and stonecutters fared as well in some regions.[24] It seems likely that the family wage was won in some industries by a segment of male workers. But even for those workers who gained a family wage, the family standard was subject to many fluctuations over time. In the Ford Motor Company (FMC), for example, the family Five Dollar Day that became a family wage in 1914 could not provide the same family standard of living by 1919.[25] Changing costs of living required the high wage to be continually defended during general economic downturns and readjusted periodically. This readjustment depended upon such factors as the workers' level of organization, the employer's ability and desire to provide the wage, and the possibility of state intervention. Thus, the family wage probably appeared, disappeared, and reappeared in certain periods in specific industries. Based on research to date in several fields, it seems clear that the family wage was an isolated, rather than a national, achievement for male workers.[26]

If it is true that family wages were never received by the majority of male workers, we must then ask why the ideology of the family wage was so dominant in the United States in this period. A second major interpretation of the ideology provides some answer. Jane Humphries' work on English working-class demands in a somewhat earlier period suggests the ideology was strong because the working class advanced it in an attempt to raise wages. Humphries argues that the family wage was not simply a patriarchal tool, but may be seen as a material interest of the working class, allowing for the maintenance of supportive family structures in the absence of welfare agencies. The demand for the family wage was one moment of resistance to the initiatives of industrial capitalism. In the struggle to improve living conditions and meet reproductive needs, the working class sought to fulfill its requirements through a traditional social arrangement of kin, the family. Humphries argues that members of the English working class believed the presence of all family members in the labor force would lower the wages of each, reduce the family's ability to provide networks of support, and fail to meet the reproductive needs of each family member and succeeding generations.[27]

The absence of socially guaranteed reproduction formed one crucial aspect of the struggle for the family wage, the attempt to improve material conditions.[28] Without other means to guarantee a minimum standard of living, and without any widespread socialized forms of reproduction, the family was one of the few agencies that met these essential needs of its members. Yet this function of the family changed significantly as social welfare agencies developed to provide subsistence for some segments of the working class. Why did American trade unions nevertheless continue to support a family wage ideology during the Progressive era expansion of social services? Humphries's analysis cannot answer this question, for she ignores the obvious component of the family wage demand that has to do with maintaining gender divisions and keeping married working-class women in the home.

From both these theoretical treatments of historically specific moments in the family wage ideology spring new historical questions that refocus our attention on the *relationship* between gender and class components in that ideology. Hartmann and Humphries each develop an analysis of the family wage which is partial and reductive. For Hartmann, the patriarchal elements of capitalism shape the family wage demand, so that female subordination in both the family and the work force becomes the central issue. In Humphries's view, the working-class response to new social relations of production used traditional gender roles to gain wages in the interest of the entire class, which included the interest of women. The case of the FMC, however, provides us with another, more complicated reality.

Ford and the Family Wage

Henry Ford announced the profit-sharing plan for FMC workers at his Highland Park, Michigan, plant in 1914. The plan was to assure each male worker of the possibility of earning a minimum of five dollars per day. The self-congratulatory text of the Ford announcement said:

Our company has now doubled wages. . . . Our firm belief is that the division of earning between capital and labor is not fair, and that labor is entitled to a greater share. We desire to express our belief in some practical way, and we therefore adopted this plan. . . . it means in substance that no man over twenty-two years of age will receive less than five dollars for eight hours work. Others will be compensated in relation to their value, using the five dollar per day as a minimum.[29]

This profit-sharing plan was unique, not because it presented the FMC as sharing profits with workers, but because of the large payment to be made.[30] Closer examination of why the company chose to award this extraordinary sum to its workers, when the average daily pay for an unskilled male auto worker in Detroit was around two dollars and forty cents, reveals the plan as an inventive means of furthering the company's edge over its competitors in production and marketing, and of maintaining an open shop.[31] Ford's Five Dollar Day was an extension of his new methods of production and a response to labor struggles in Detroit. As Ford himself would later say, he was "not a reformer," and the Five Dollar Day was not motivated by purely humanitarian impulses.[32] An astute capitalist whose actions were frequently eccentric, Ford saw the Five Dollar Day as a means to deal with high labor turnover, union organizing efforts of the Industrial Workers of the World (IWW), and, most important, production changes in the FMC Highland Park plant.[33]

Ford attempted to link the lives of the workers in the factory with their lives at home, with a specific form of family structure. Ford was an important representative of a new awareness among some capitalists of the relationship between production and forms of social reproduction, and the Five Dollar Day as a family wage suggests that changes in the industrial structure of the United States at the turn of the century had significant impact upon family structures and family relationships. The Ford Five Dollar Day illustrates a crucial link between women's domestic role and class antagonism. The high Ford wage resulted from conflict between Ford workers and their employer, in unionizing attempts and in shop floor practices. The Five Dollar Day was obviously in the material interest of Ford workers and their families, yet the plan was also a useful tool in managerial terms, in keeping with Ford's productivity. Ford management attempted to manipulate the wage in the interest of the company, and did so through rhetoric and practice that linked workers in the shop with their families at home.

Ford's business strategy centered on producing an automobile that could be purchased by a large market through lowered production costs. This would in turn ensure high profits, which would recapitalize production, maintain profits, and, according to Ford, increase wages. In an industry with a failure rate of almost 74 percent, this bold concept enabled Ford to expand his share of the automobile market from 19.9 percent in 1911 to 55.7 percent in 1921.[34] By 1913 the company had grown from the small operation of 1903 at the Mack Avenue plant to the large Highland Park plant, with branch profit of $28 million and dividends of $15 million.[35]

By 1913, according to Ford's production supervisor Charles Sorenson, "the company was firmly established financially. Its problems were exclusively those of production and its expansion, of manufacturing and of supply."[36] The production problems included difficulties with labor. High turnover rates plagued the entire automobile industry; the average turnover was over 100 percent in the largest Detroit plants in 1914. The instability of the work force reduced efficiency in production. Unless an employer acted to lower this turnover rate, it remained high. Ford moved to solve his turnover problems in the Highland Park plant through implementing a reform program in 1913 which rationalized the labor process and simplified the management of labor. Lee, head of the employment office, introduced a three-pronged program that began by centralizing personnel decisions in one office and stripping shop foremen of their power to hire and fire new workers. Instead, workers at the Highland Park plant would be "moved" until they were placed in a job they could do efficiently.[37] As Lee said, "It is a great deal cheaper for us to take (a worker) from one department and transfer him to another than it is to discharge him."[38] Lee reduced the number of job classifications from sixty-nine to eight, with corresponding wage rates for each job. The work day was reduced from ten to nine hours, and new industrial safety standards were introduced. Under Lee's guidance, and with Ford's sanction, the company began to recognize the link between the "human element" and increased production, creating labor management policies to simplify its means of control over its workers.

As Lee rationalized the labor force, Ford instituted the rationalization of production. Beginning in 1912, he introduced the continuously moving assembly line at Highland Park. To function efficiently, the moving assembly ran at a rate that did not allow for "excess movements." Ford said, "The idea is that a man must not be hurried in his work—he must have every necessary second, but not a single unnecessary second."[39] This process allowed Highland Park workers to produce one thousand Model T's per day in 1914. It also meant that the labor process allowed the workers no creativity, limiting the need for skill or thought. As one worker put it, "The speed up had reached the point where a worker almost did not have time to catch his breath."[40]

This led to a new labor problem for the Ford management. In March 1913 organizers for the IWW began an effort to unionize Detroit's auto workers. The IWW was quick to criticize the moving assembly, nicknaming Ford the "Speed-Up King," and organizers chose to concentrate on the Ford plant because of the discontent of Ford workers.[41] By the winter of 1914, "it was common knowledge" that a strike at Ford was imminent. Then, on January 6, 1914, Ford announced the Five Dollar Day.[42]

Ford was able to resort to this high-wage "profit-sharing" plan for several reasons: the dominant position of the firm within the automobile industry, its strong overall position economically, and its business structure. Ford had the profits to gamble with new methods to increase productivity and the capital to avoid labor conflicts by responding to possible union efforts on his own terms. Within the industry, the company was remarkably healthy and successful between 1908 and 1921, while its competitors were not so fortunate. [43] The state of Detroit's labor movement further lessened the chance that other automotive firms would try a Five Dollar Day. The labor movement in the auto industry was not strong enough to press any advantage it held in these years in more than a random and individualistic way. The Employers Association of Detroit successfully maintained an open shop in the city throughout the decade, and most auto manufacturers suffered through whatever labor unrest occurred, tolerating the high turnover rates endemic to American industry. Even the IWW failed to consolidate any gains it made through 1913 and 1914 in Detroit, regardless of the fact that IWW activity had acted as a catalyst for the FMC Five Dollar Day by threatening both Ford's production strategy and Henry Ford's fiercely antiunion philosophy. [44]

Although Ford was alone in Detroit in engaging in a welfare program, many other corporations initiated some form of welfare on a large scale—

from stock-purchasing plans to company housing, schools, and stores, David Brody found that industrial relations departments, the administrative agencies of welfare in most firms, appeared in correlation to the size of the enterprise; over 50 percent of firms employing over two thousand workers had departments dealing with worker relations.[45] Many large firms discovered it was far more profitable over the long term to spend on worker relations than to risk interruptions in production by strikes.

By instituting a wage twice the amount available to unskilled workers in Detroit, Ford provided a strong stimulus for workers to tolerate the most stressful conditions in the factory. Although moving assembly processes and the rationalization of the labor force made working conditions in Highland Park monotonous and alienating, the high wages encouraged Ford workers to remain at their jobs and stifled overt demands for unionization. The Five Dollar Day reduced labor turnover rates dramatically. A contemporary magazine reported that "surplus labor from other places had been rushing there as if to a vacuum. At Ford's plant, a mob scene is enacted daily; thousands apply and few are hired." By 1918 Ford had reduced its turnover rate to 46 percent, the lowest in Detroit.[46]

The Five Dollar Day also operated to create divisions among Ford workers. Although Lee had reduced the number of job classifications in 1912, the Five Dollar Day established a wage differential among workers based on compliance with company policy. Ford claimed in 1915 that over 80 percent of FMC workers were earning a Five Dollar Day; historian Keith Sward has argued that many unskilled Ford workers never received the higher wage.[47] But even if the majority of Ford workers did earn the Five Dollar Day, differences between workers were created on the basis of pay, maintaining the ideal that good company men would one day merit the higher wage.

The administration of the Five Dollar Day showed the company's desire that workers maintain a stable family life, and linked the needs of production with family structure. A worker was eligible for the Five Dollar Day only after he had been at Ford for six months, and had to fall into one of three categories: "All married men living with and taking good care of their families" "all single men, over twenty-two years of age," of "proven thrifty habits" and men under the age of twenty-two years of age, and women "who are the sole support of some next of kin or blood relative."[48] Women were not initially included in the plan at all. Following Ford's announcement of the Five Dollar Day and his obvious exclusion of women workers, feminists such as Anna Howard Shaw and Jane Addams protested the discrimination.[49] Ford changed the wage qualifications, but later admitted that only 10 percent of the women employed at FMC earned a shared profit wage.[50] Moreover, Ford was explicit that the company did not hire married women "unless their husbands are unable to work."[51] As late as 1919, eighty-two women were discharged from Highland Park because it was discovered that their husbands were working.[52]

The Sociological Department at Ford policed the profit-sharing plan, and it was staffed by thirty to fifty male investigators whom Ford described as "good judges of human nature," whose job was to "point men to life and make them discontented with a mere living."[53] The investigator grouped employees applying for the plan into four categories: those "firmly established in the ways of thrift"; those "who never had a chance but were willing to grasp the opportunity in the way every man should"; those "who qualified but we were in doubt as to the strength of their character"; and those who did not qualify.[54] The Ford managers stipulated that "the man and his home had to come up to certain standards of cleanliness and citizenship."[55] Ford declared that

in order to receive the bonus married men should live with and take good care of their families. We had to break up the evil custom among foreign workers of taking in boarders—of regarding their homes as something to make money out of rather than as a place to live in.[56]

Ford believed that only a specific form of family relationship—one in which the husband provided for a non-income-earning wife—would ensure the stability of his labor force. The Five Dollar Day would encourage this type of family, in which a male wage supported a dependent family, who would then have no need to use their homes to make money. Ford appeared to sanction only the most "middle-class" form of family life, or what seemed to be the middle-class form of life to him, where a husband earned enough to protect the home as a sanctuary and a refuge.

The Ford management also wanted workers to own their own homes. In addition to raising wages for some workers, the company provided a lawyer to help workers secure credit and mortgages for new homes. As the result of the Five Dollar Day, Ford claimed, "eight thousand families have changed their place of residence. . . . The migration has been from poor and squalid to healthy, sanitary quarters, with environment conducive to health, happiness, and comfort."[57]

If this estimate was perhaps exaggerated, the FMC concern with family structure and family life remained apparent. Good, efficient, and happy workers, a stable work force and stable community, free from union threats and civil unrest, could only develop from a particular form of the family. And to ensure that optimal situation, the wage would have to be a family wage. By linking production, consumption, and family, the FMC under Henry Ford not only recognized the integral relationship between these elements, but also sought to manipulate them. Through the Sociological Department, the company promoted the belief that one wage, earned by a male worker, should be sufficient for the needs of an economically dependent family. According to Ford:

> If only the man himself were concerned, the cost of his maintenance, and the profit he ought to have would be a simple matter. But he is not just an individual. . . . How are you going to figure the contribution of the home to a day's work? . . . The man does the work in the shop, but his wife does the work in the home. *The shop must pay them both.* . . . Otherwise we have the hideous prospect of little children and their mothers being forced out to work.[58]

The Five Dollar Day accomplished two important management objectives: it successfully reduced turnover rates, and it destroyed the active threat of unionization for a period. The link between the family and factory, embodied in the form of a family wage, has a far greater importance for women's history. Not only were married women with working husbands directly excluded from employment, but the company provided both an economic and an ideological reinforcement for women's role in domestic labor. The company did so out of a primary motivation to increase its competitive advantages in production and marketing, and as a result of the increasing possibility of union activity. In other words, the Five Dollar Day was managerial strategy based on an understanding of inherent class conflict, a move to establish Ford's dominance within the automobile industry and control over Ford workers.[59] Yet it also embodied and reinforced a particular ideology—and social reality—of "family life" and gender division. Thus, it functioned as a form of social control both "in the shop" and "in the home."

Conclusion

The family wage as an actual achievement represents a concrete interaction between the reproductive needs of workers and their families, and the conditions of production. The high wage allowed working-class families to secure subsistence and attain a standard of living of "health and decency." Yet at the FMC, this family wage did not come as the result of workers' militant demands that their employer meet their reproductive needs. Nor did Ford workers call for the exclusion of women workers from the shop, for female laborers were already excluded. The main issue in workers' concerns appears to have been what is termed "workers' control," their ability to have input into the labor process.[60] Workers responded to the mass assembly line and to the efforts of the IWW in both organized and unorganized, individual forms.

The company reacted to worker discontent, reflected in turnover rates and incipient unionization, in a pragmatic manner: it granted a concession, an abnormally high wage. Ford managers made the concession fit with managerial strategy for high profits and improved productivity, in a recognition of the long-term benefits of stability in their labor force. They tied that stability to a particular family structure—not by accident, but *because* that structure was thought to be both stabilizing and profitable.

Ford's version of the family wage actively attempted to reshape the family, in the interests of profit and production, recognizing the possible benefits of working-class family life to the employer. Ford's rhetoric was similar to that of Progressive budget analysts who supported a family wage, but it marked a significant philosophical change in the attitudes of capitalists toward their employees. His was not the laissez-faire notion that workers could only receive the lowest rate of pay to ensure capitalist profits, a nineteenth-century commonplace. For Ford, productivity and, in turn, profits, came with a living wage offered as a family wage, with which male workers could earn better living conditions, a decent home life, and a dependent family. That family—or, more particularly, the wife at home—would provide for the worker, so the worker must provide for his family. And, in Ford's words, "the shop must pay them both."

Ford's family wage implicitly recognized the contribution of women's domestic labor to a stable and secure family life. In all likelihood, Ford believed that women's contribution was greatest in their emotional, nurturing, and motherly roles. This emphasis on psychological rather than material comfort parallels the arguments of many Progressive reformers, who saw the female emotional, affective role as a necessary aspect of family life which should be supported by adequate wages. Ford's family wage accomplished what budget analysts proposed: it provided some means to keep "little children and their mothers" out of the work force. However, Ford's primary goal was not female exclusion. The FMC family wage was offered as an incentive for workers to assume a stable home life, and the relegation of women to the role of domestic laborer was a secondary consideration, not a guiding motivation.

The Ford family wage illustrates that the creation of this wage form as practice and as ideology relied upon a complex cast of characters: workers, unions, managers, capitalists, and workers' families. The Ford family wage was not merely a case of men wanting to subordinate women, or of workers struggling only for subsistence needs, although both female subordination and adequate subsistence resulted from the family wage. I would argue that in this instance, the terms of the family wage were based on a political conflict between classes with substantially different interests. The political conflict at the FMC initiated the concession of a family wage; the interests of the employer for profits and productivity determined the framework of the awards. But gender categories played a role in this framework, in both its ideological aspects and in its immediate concrete goals. First, the family wage tied profits for the employer to a workers' family, in an indirect relationship based upon wage structure, which required a dependent female domestic laborer. Second, the ideology of the family wage used gender divisions to legitimate the benefit to the working class and the altruism of the employer. It was in the interests of society, according to the ideology, to keep women and children out of the labor force and at home where they belonged. Yet workers and employers brought different perspectives to this argument for the family wage. For the working class, the family wage, as Humphries suggests, operated as a real material benefit. The family wage provided one solution to the hard struggle for subsistence for many working-class families in a period in which poor working conditions and low wages predominated. Few married women, and probably many children, worked outside the home. In this context, it seems logical that both men and many women would argue that the wages of the adult male worker should support his family and allow children access to education. On these terms, subsistence was the primary goal of the family wage. To achieve this goal, the family wage ideology utilized and reinforced existing gender distinctions in work roles.

For the employer, the family wage ideology may have presented a different phenomenon. The ideology legitimated low female wages; women worked for "pin money" and required less compensation than family-supporting men. But for those employers aware of the benefits of a stable work force, and capable of taking advantage of them, the family wage awarded to eligible workers could increase long-term profits. And, as at the FMC, public recognition of a firm's benevolent family wage policy could have worldwide publicity value, an added bonus in an expanding marketplace. In the first and probably most prevalent case, the ideology works to a useful advantage for employers. In the latter instance, the ideology is transformed into an achievement, but both uses of the family wage serve the employers' interests.

What the Ford family wage suggests, if we move from this specific example to speculate about the more generalized nature of this ideology, is that the family wage as ideology became, and remained, important because it seemed advantageous to all participants in its creation. For the working class, it heralded the possibility of an adequate income. For employers, it meant lowered wages for some workers and stability in the labor force otherwise. We could also speculate that for the Progressive reformers who encouraged this ideology, the family wage seemed one solution to the "search for order" that marked this period.

The family wage benefited all segments of society, except those it excluded from the work force—women. By linking gender roles and subsistence, the family wage ideology successfully reinforced the notion that women should receive low wages or, preferably, remain at home. As Gwendolyn S. Hughes commented in 1925, the ideology of the family wage, which she argued was then widely accepted, presumed every man would provide for his family and that "women's place is in the home."[61] The consequences of the family wage ideology for women were serious constraints placed on work participation. And it was as ideology that the family wage remained strongest. By articulating the demand for subsistence in the form of family wages, the working class consented to a particular role for its women and children. Ironically, that family wage was not widespread or long-lived enough to benefit more than a small segment of the working class, and it dovetailed neatly with the concerns of employers for profits. In this sense, the family wage, as ideology, served to divide the working class for a temporary gain, at the great expense of its female members.

The family wage as ideology remains an important element in our culture and economy. The "middle-class" standard of living projected by the U.S. Department of Labor is based on a male worker, a dependent wife, and two children. And many women still work for single-person wages, a sum adequate to their own needs, but too low to meet the expenses of a family. As we frame our arguments for equal wages and comparable pay, as feminists we continue to face the ideology of the family wage—at the same time that the family wages of many unionized sectors of the labor force are threatened. Can the idea of the family wage be turned to the advantage of *both* working-class women and men, as we struggle to maintain recent gains? Or are the terms of the family wage, as ideology and as practice, dependent upon a certain vision of gender roles? Only by understanding how the family wage developed, and continues to operate, can we begin to answer these difficult and pressing questions.

Notes

Acknowledgments: The author would like to thank the many people who commented on successive drafts of this article, particularly Melvyn Dubofsky, Harold C. Livesay, Elizabeth Fox-Genovese, Joan Smith, Winifred Wandersee, Ronald Schatz, Anne Forsythe, and Stephen Burwood. Mary Ryan, Rosalind Petchesky, and the *Feminist Studies* editors have been especially helpful in suggesting both new directions and connections in the topic. Special thanks must go to Nancy Grey Osterud, who read every version of this paper and responded to all with supportive criticism, and Paul Garver, for his comments on current trade unionism.

1. The argument for a family wage has also been documented in England in a similar period of early industrial capitalism. See Jane Humphries, "The Working Class Family, Women's Liberation, and Class Struggle: The Case of Nineteenth Century British History," *Review of Radical Political Economy* 9 (Fall 1977):25–42, and her "Class Struggle and the Persistence of the Working Class Family," *Cambridge Journal of Economics* 1 (1977):241–58. See also Hillary Land, "The Family Wage,"

Feminist Review 6 (1980):55–77. For purposes of this analysis. I will consider only the American case.

2. David Montgomery, *Beyond Equality: Labor and the Radical Republicans, 1862–1872* (New York: Random House, 1967), p. 40; Alan Dawley, *Class and Community: The Industrial Revolution in Lynn* (Cambridge: Harvard University Press, 1976), p. 158–59; Stephen Thernstrom, *Poverty and Progress* (Cambridge: Harvard University Press, 1964), p. 22.

3. Thernstrom, *Poverty and Progress,* pp. 42–49; Thomas C. Cochran, *Business in American Life* (New York: McGraw Hill, 1972), pp. 170–71; Robert C. McCloskey, *American Conservatism in the Age of Enterprise, 1865–1910* (Cambridge: Harvard University Press, 1951).

4. Judith A. Baer, *The Chains of Protection: Judicial Response to Women's Labor Legislation* (Westport, Conn.: Greenwood, 1978), p. 35.

5. Quotation cited in Michael Katz, *The Irony of Early School Reform* (Cambridge: Harvard University Press, 1978), p. 83. See also Thernstrom, *Poverty and Progress,* and Dawley, *Class and Community,* pp. 131–48.

6. See, for example, Elizabeth Pleck, "A Mother's Wages: Income Earning Among Married Italian and Black Women, 1869–1911," in Nancy Cott and Elizabeth Pleck (eds.), *A Heritage of Her Own: Toward a New Social History of American Women* (New York: Simon and Schuster, 1979). See also Lawrence A. Glasco, "The Life Cycles and Household Structure of American Ethnic Groups," in Cott and Pleck, *A Heritage of Her Own.* Daniel Walkowitz provides an interesting look at the income of families of skilled workers in *Worker City, Company Town; Iron and Cotton Workers' Protests in Troy and Cohoes, New York, 1855–1884* (Urbana: University of Illinois Press, 1978).

7. Elizabeth Jameson, "Imperfect Unions: Class and Gender in Cripple Creek, 1890–1914," in Milton Cantor and Bruce Laurie (eds.), *Class, Sex, and the Woman Worker* (Westport, Conn.: Greenwood Press, 1977).

8. Anne Schofield, "The Rise of the Pig Headed Girl: An Analysis of the American Labor Press for Their Attitudes Toward Women, 1877–1920" (Ph.D. dissertation, State University of New York at Binghamton, 1980), p. 150.

9. See Nancy F. Cott, *The Bonds of Womanhood: "Women's Sphere" in New England, 1780–1835* (New Haven: Yale University Press, 1977); Carroll Smith-Rosenberg, "The Female World of Love and Ritual: Relations Between Women in Nineteenth-Century America," *Signs* 1 (1975): 1–29; Barbara Welter, *Dimity Convictions* (Columbus: Ohio University Press, 1976); Gerda Lerner, "The Lady and the Mill Girl: Changes in the Status of Women in the Age of Jackson," *Midcontinent American Studies Journal* 10 (Spring 1969):5–14; Mary P. Ryan, *The Cradle of the Middle Class: The Family in Oneida County, New York, 1790–1865* (New York: Cambridge University Press, 1981), p. 186–229; Sheila Rothman, *Woman's Proper Place: A History of Changing Ideals and Practices, 1870 to the Present* (New York: Basic Books, 1978).

10. Ryan, *Cradle of the Middle Class,* p. 190.

11. Discussion of the organized charity movement and the development of social surveys can be found in Daniel M. Fox, *Discovery of Abundance* (Ithaca, N.Y.: Cornell University Press, 1967); Roy Lubove, *The Professional Altruist: The Emergence of Social Work as a Profession* (Cambridge: Harvard University Press, 1965); Robert Bremer, *From the Depths: The Discovery of Poverty in the United States* (New York: New York University Press, 1956); Allen Davis, *Spearheads for Reform: Social Settlements and the Progressive Movement, 1890–1914* (New York: Oxford University

Press, 1967); James Leiby, *Carroll Wright and Labor Reform* (Cambridge: Harvard University Press, 1960).

12. Charles Y. Glock (ed.), *Survey Research in the Social Sciences* (New York: Russell Sage Foundation, 1967), p. 337.

13. A useful discussion of the growing interest in social reform and welfare by economists may be found in Sidney Fine, *Laissez-Faire and the General Welfare State: A Study of Conflict in American Thought, 1865–1900* (Ann Arbor: University of Michigan, 1956).

14. *Hull House Maps and Papers* (New York: Thomas Y. Crowell Co., 1895), p. 21. This point is expanded by Alice Kessler-Harris, "Women's Wage Work as Myth and History," *Labor History* 19 (1978):287–307; see also Anna Davin, "Imperialism and Motherhood," *History Workshop*, no. 5 (1978):9–66, for a provocative assessment of the importance of nationalism and racial ideology in the consideration of motherhood in this period.

15. Louise Bosworth, *The Living Wage of Women Workers* (New York: Longmans, Green, 1911), p. 11.

16. Robert C. Chapin, *The Standard of Living Among Workingmen's Families in New York City* (New York: Russell Sage Foundation, Charities Publication Committee, 1909), p. 245.

17. Mary Conyngton, *How to Help: A Manual of Practical Charity* (New York: Macmillan, 1909), p. 185.

18. Royal Meeker, "What Is the American Standard of Living?" *Monthly Labor Review* 7 (July 1919):8.

19. Many scholars have contributed to the analysis of the family wage and added to our knowledge of that wage form. See, for example, Land, "Family Wage"; Johanna Brenner, "Women's Self-Organization: A Marxist Justification," *Against the Current* 1 (1980):24–34; Mary McIntosh and Michelle Barrett, " 'The Family Wage': Some Problems for Socialists and Feminists," *Capital and Class*, no. 11 (1980):51–72; Mary McIntosh, "The State and the Oppression of Women," in Annette Kuhn and AnnMarie Wolpe (eds.), *Feminism and Materialism: Women and Modes of Production* (London: Routledge & Kegan Paul, 1978); Maxine Molyneux, "Beyond the Domestic Labor Debate," *New Left Review*, no. 116 (1979):3–28. Two collections dealing with issues pertinent to the family wage are Lydia Sargent (ed.), *Women and Revolution: A Discussion of the Unhappy Marriage of Marxism and Feminism* (Boston: South End Press, 1981); and Michelle Barrett, ed., *Women's Oppression Today* (London: New Left Books, 1981).

20. Heidi Hartmann, "The Unhappy Marriage of Marxism and Feminism: Towards a More Progressive Union," in Lydia Sargent (ed.), *Women and Revolution* (Boston, Mass.: South End, 1981); and her "Capitalism and Women's Work in the Home, 1900–1930" (Ph.D. dissertation, Yale University, 1974).

21. Hartmann, "Unhappy Marriage of Marxism and Feminism," p. 16.

22. A second indication that family wages were not common throughout American industry comes from the rise in female labor-force participation. The increasing number of women entering the labor force in this century suggests that many families required more than one income. Changes in children's labor-force participation suggest as well that the increase in female waged work may have compensated for the decrease in child labor. Nearly 20 percent of children worked in 1900, and the numbers increased throughout that decade. By 1930, however, only 4.7 percent of all children were *recorded* as working, as the movement to abolish child labor gained in strength.

See Winifred Wandersee, *Women's Work and Family Values, 1920–1940* (Cambridge: Harvard University Press, 1981).

23. We can speculate based on family budget studies that some families that received what appear to be family wages did send other family members into the labor force in order to further improve their standard of living.

24. Charles Bonnett, *History of Employers' Associations in the United States* (New York: Vantage Press, 1956), pp. 188–91; U.S. Department of Labor, *History of Wages in the United States from Colonial Times to 1928,* Publication Bulletin no. 604 (Washington, D.C.: Government Printing Office, 1934).

25. Keith Sward, *The Legend of Henry Ford* (New York: Rinehart, 1948), p. 55.

26. Several historians have studied industrial wage patterns without dealing specifically with the notion of a family wage. Their works indicated that family wages were achieved occasionally under a variety of conditions. See Robert Ozanne, *A Century of Labor Management Relations at McCormick and International Harvester* (Madison: University of Wisconsin Press, 1967); Peter Shergold, "Wage Differentials Based on Skill in the U.S., 1899–1914: A Case Study," *Labor History* 8 (1977):486–578; Paul Douglas, *Real Wages in the United States, 1890–1926* (Boston: Houghton Mifflin, 1930). Julian Skaggs and John Ehrlich present an intriguing account of the relationship between strike activity, wages, and paternalism in "Profits, Paternalism, and Rebellion: A Case Study in Industrial Strife," *Business History Review* 54 (Summer 1980):155–74.

27. Jane Humphries, "Working Class Family," pp. 25–42; and her "Class Struggle and the Persistence of the Working Class Family," pp. 241–58.

28. Humphries' argument also raises questions about the nature of wages and social reproduction. First, it is not clear that the presence of all family members in the labor force would in fact reduce the wages of all; wages could still remain high or adequate within the skilled sectors, for example, Humphries' position on wages here tends to minimize the skill divisions within the labor market. Second, the presence of workers' benevolent societies presents other questions about the demand for family wages which Humphries does not resolve.

29. "The Ford Melon for Labor," *Literary Digest,* January 12, 1914, p. 95.

30. See, for example, Ozanne, *Century of Labor Management;* Daniel Nelson, *Managers and Workers* (Madison: University of Wisconsin Press, 1975), pp. 105–6.

31. At $2.40 per day, a worker would make $750.00 per year if she or he worked six days per week the entire year. This would be less than Chapin's 1909 income for "health and decency," and barely above Ryan's 1906 $600 minimum for the nation.

32. Henry Ford, *My Life and Work* (New York: Doubleday, Page, 1925), p. 3.

33. Several historians have suggested that the Five Dollar Day was more the result of Ford's peculiar personality than a pragmatic business decision. From the accounts of Ford's decision, it is difficult to make an unqualified assessment of the Five Dollar Day decision. Charles Sorenson's version, for example, suggests more eccentricity than rationality on Ford's part. It seems unlikely, however, that the Five Dollar Day was the result of sheer caprice, because it remedied the most significant labor problems facing the company. If the Five Dollar Day was only the result of Ford's eccentricity, it was one of the luckiest strokes of caprice in business history.

34. Donald F. Davis, "Detroit's Automotive Revolution: A Case Study of Urban Enterprise, 1899–1933," manuscript, University of Ottawa, p. 7; Alfred Chandler, Jr., *Giant Enterprise: Ford, General Motors, and the Automobile Industry—Sources and Readings* (New York: Harcourt Brace and World, 1964), pp. 23–25.

35. Davis, "Detroit's Automotive Revolution," p. 7; Chandler, *Giant Enterprise*, pp. xi, 23.

36. Charles Sorenson, *My Forty Years with Ford* (New York: W. W. Norton, 1956), p. 138; Chandler, *Giant Enterprise*, p. 11; Nelson, *Managers and Workers*, pp. 23–24.

37. Nelson, *Managers and Workers*, p. 81; Allan Nevins (in collaboration with Frank Ernest Hill), *Ford: The Times, the Man, the Company* (New York: Scribner, 1954), p. 459.

38. Chandler, *Giant Enterprise*, p. 190.

39. Ford, *My Life and Work*, p. 82.

40. Philip Foner, *History of the Labor Movement in the United States*, vol. 4: *The Industrial Workers of the World, 1905–1917* (New York: International Publishers, 1965), p. 385.

41. Foner, *Industrial Workers of the World*, pp. 375–86; Nevins, *Ford*, p. 513.

42. Foner, *Industrial Workers of the World*, p. 386.

43. Ford netted $30 million after taxes in 1914, and the company's growth was remarkable. In 1917 the FMC sold 740,777 automobiles. Its closest competitor, General Motors, sold only 195,945. See Chandler, *Giant Enterprise;* Alfred D. Chandler, Jr., *The Visible Hand: Managerial Revolution in American Business* (Cambridge: Harvard University Press, 1977); Ralph Epstein, *The Automobile Industry* (New York: A. W. Shaw, 1928).

44. Melvyn Dubofsky, *We Shall Be All: A History of the Industrial Workers of the World* (Chicago: Quadrangle, 1969), pp. 267, 291; Foner, *Industrial Workers of the World*, pp. 385–86; Nevins, *Ford*, p. 513.

45. David Brody, "The Rise and Decline of Welfare Capitalism," in *Workers in Industrial America* (New York: Oxford University Press, 1980), p. 59.

46. "Unemployment in Detroit," *Literary Digest*, February 14, 1914, p. 358; Boris Emmet, "Labor Turnover in Cleveland and Detroit," *Monthly Labor Review* 7 (Jan. 1919): 12–13.

47. Sward, *Legend of Henry Ford*.

48. John R. Lee, cited in Chandler, *Giant Enterprise*, p. 191. This is also described by Ford, *My Life and Work*, and in Ford's testimony to the Committee on Industrial Relations in 1915: U.S. Congress, Senate, Committee on Industrial Relations, *Industrial Relations: Final Report and Testimony*, 1916, 64th Congress, 1st sess., p. 7626.

49. Nevins, *Ford*, p. 547.

50. Testimony of Henry Ford, p. 7636–37.

51. Henry Ford, *Today and Tomorrow* (London: William Heineman, 1926), p. 143.

52. Ford, *My Life and Work*, p. 111.

53. Testimony of Henry Ford, 1915, p. 7627.

54. Lee, cited in Chandler, *Giant Enterprise*, p. 192. Ford claimed the department employed fifty investigators; see Ford, *My Life and Work*, p. 129.

55. Ford, *My Life and Work*, p. 128.

56. Ibid., p. 129.

57. Testimony of Henry Ford, p. 7628.

58. Ford, *My Life and Work*, p. 111. Emphasis mine.

59. It should be emphasized that managerial strategy is also an essential part of class struggle—in this case, an offensive move by capitalists to maximize profits and minimize discontent within the labor force. I am not suggesting that managerial strategy should be viewed as the long arm of capital controlling every level of society. In-

stead, the relationship I am trying to suggest is one of conflicting and contradictory class interests, which, by the very nature and existence of struggle, create specific political, economic, and cultural structures. One class may achieve momentary or sustained dominance in the creation of a specific structure.

60. David Montgomery, *Workers' Control in America* (New York: Oxford University Press, 1980).

61. Gwendolyn S. Hughes, *Mothers in Industry* (New York: Arno Press, 1977), p. 9.

5

Gender, Race, and Class: The Impact of the State on the Family and the Economy, 1790–1945

EILEEN BORIS

PETER BARDAGLIO

The dismantling of the welfare state that first emerged during the New Deal has been a top priority of the Reagan administration. In response, feminists and other activists have rushed to the defense of the welfare state, arguing that its jobs, services, and income supports have been key resources for women. Indeed, as Frances Fox Piven insists in her essay in this volume (Chapter 26), "the state is turning out to be the main recourse of women." [1]

Recognizing the importance of the present welfare state as a resource for women does not mean, however, that one should overlook the ways in which state policies in the past have buttressed patriarchal social relations. Although the state cannot be viewed simply as an instrument of oppression—it serves rather as an arena of struggle between contending forces—it has played a crucial role in organizing patriarchy. By "patriarchy" we mean the system of male dominance in which men exercise control over women's labor power, reproduction, and sexuality, and in which some men control the access of other men to women. The central point here is that patriarchy has not been a static system of male dominance, but rather the historical product of a struggle for power. [2] This essay examines the impact of state policies on power relations within families and between families and the state, the historical process underlying these policies, and the ways in which their application and outcomes have varied by gender, race, and class.

In the United States, over the course of the nineteenth and early twentieth centuries, family relations became increasingly subject to judicial intervention. If at first the courts reinforced the status quo—the power of men over women and of adults over children—they gradually began to promote the rights of individual family members at the expense of the patriarchal father.

The contract became the primary metaphor for describing relations between members. This broke down the power of men within families, only to transfer male power to the courts and the structures of the larger society. At the same time, family law in nineteenth-century America reinforced the distinction between the public and private, between men and women, associating men with the world and women with the home. Judicial law on divorce, child custody, and family property applied primarily to the white middle class, while legislatures and government bureaucracies fashioned family policy for the destitute out of criminal and poor laws. For blacks, slave codes before the Civil War and Jim Crow laws after the war helped to set the context in which family life took place. Thus, there existed a civil law, housed in the courts and focused on the rights and responsibilities of family members, and also a penal law, subject to state and local agencies and controlled by legislative expenditures. Clearly, the overall impact of the law and public policy differed not only by gender but also by race and class.[3]

The growth of the twentieth-century welfare state incorporated gender and racial inequity even as it provided income supports for poor women and racial minorities. Such an outcome was not necessarily predictable from the struggle between reformers (mostly women) and government bureaucrats, trade unionists, and various sectors of capital. In hindsight, we can see that the reformers were politically weak and underfunded; the lack of influence of the Women's Bureau from its start in 1920 was symptomatic of sexual power relations within the state itself. Moreover, reformers shared the dominant values of their class—beliefs in domesticity, female biological weakness, and Anglo-Saxon racial superiority and these values generated contradictory policy goals and outcomes.[4]

The Nineteenth-Century Legacy: The Individualization of Women and Children

Nineteenth-century law functioned to sustain the public/private dichotomy that was central to liberal capitalistic society even as it provided women and children with their own legal personalities. Even as legal relations between family members appeared more egalitarian in the areas of divorce, child custody, and the property rights of married women, the state increased its power over family life, particularly when families strayed from the nuclear, male-dominated norm. With the father no longer mediating the impact of the state on family members, women and children came into direct contact with the state, gaining economic benefits while being restricted to behavior appropriate to their gender and age.

This transformation took place in two overlapping but distinct stages.[5] Between 1790 and the Civil War, individuals gained rights at the expense of the patriarchal family. Paternal superiority remained, however, not only because of the limited nature of reforms (which rarely gave women full control of their separate estates or children) but also because of the larger context in which legal changes occurred. After all, men's superior economic resources—as well as their strength—compelled most women to marry and generally accede to their husbands' wishes. As numerous nineteeenth-century commentators noted, marriage was the most important economic decision that a woman made; her survival and comfort depended on her choice.[6] Nonetheless, family law fell into line with bourgeois notions of individual rights; thus, the early women's movement won a victory that made women, like men, individual actors in a "free" market.[7]

During the second half of the nineteenth century, the law engaged in linking individual family members to the state. Laws and public policies, along with expanded government bureaucracies and new professional authorities (such as doctors, educators, and social workers), developed a larger support system to aid women in childbearing and -rearing. This system reproduced patriarchal social relations without individual patriarchs.[8] Consequently, male-dominated, even male-headed, families became less important in maintaining patriarchy in the larger social arena. Because men benefited from the structure of the labor market, the possibility remained for individual men to retain power in families through their economic prowess; certainly they gained from the unwaged (and devalued) labor power of wives and mothers.

Alterations in family property laws during the mid-1800s particularly reveal the individualization of women so crucial to the larger transformation of patriarchy, but they also show the limits of early judicial change for the middle-class family. Married women's property acts gave such women property rights for the first time, and husbands no longer automatically gained control over wives' land and other property. However, no antebellum statute clearly provided that the wife was entitled to money or property earned during the marriage, and none gave full legal equality. In fact, the major motive behind much of this legislation was to rationalize land transactions and protect family property from the husband's creditors. Moreover, badly written and ambiguous laws were subject to conservative judicial interpretation based on traditional sex roles.[9]

Yet nineteenth-century feminists had campaigned for married women's property acts out of the belief that "law and public opinion" made "the wife . . . subject to the husband." They attacked the state for not only making husbands sovereign within the family but upholding in the process those separate sexual spheres that denied women access to money, politics, and education. With Elizabeth Cady Stanton, they argued: "If you regard marriage as a civil contract, then let it be subject to the same laws which control all other contracts. Do not make it a kind of half-human, half-divine institution, which you may build up, but can not regulate.''[10] Feminists added their voices to the growing movement to democratize the American common law by seeking to replace the power of the head of the family with the equal standing of individual family members, an effort that ultimately produced a legal system in tune with an expanding market economy, but one that failed to make men and women equal even within the propertied middle class. Nevertheless, as Norma Basch contends, these changes in the law of family property recognized women as individuals within American families and brought married women into contractual relations with the state.[11]

This same process occurred in the reform of divorce laws. Before 1800 most states granted divorces only through private bills passed by legislatures, an expensive and time-consuming procedure. During the early part of the century, new general statutes gave most courts power to grant divorces. As women gained more individual rights, in William O'Neill's words, divorce became "the safety valve that [made] the system workable."[12] But it was a peculiar kind of safety valve, for it gave the state the power to determine the internal dynamics of families. Women did not always gain from expansion of divorce rights and often suffered a decline in economic status following divorce.[13]

The precariousness of divorce stemmed from its adversarial nature. The plaintiff not only had to prove the spouse's "guilt" but also show his or her own "innocence." For a woman to prove herself "worthy" of divorce, she had apparently to embody feminine virtue: domesticity, propriety, and submissiveness. Judges set standards against which women had to measure themselves, and those standards in turn justified women's subordinate place in public life. In general, divorce reform pictured women not as equals but as victims. As far as divorce was concerned, a paternalistic attitude and an image of wronged virtue undermined the notion of equality even as they strengthened women's individual legal rights. The patriarchal responsibility for women shifted from the male head of the family to male judges.[14]

This shift to what Michael Grossberg calls "judicial patriarchy" was most apparent in child custody.[15] Under English common law, and during the colonial period, the father possessed an almost unlimited right to the custody of his minor offspring. Custody law treated children as little more than pieces of property in which the unchallenged head of the family had a vested interest, rather than as individuals whose welfare and interests were legitimate legal issues. The outlines of a distinctively American law of child custody began to appear in the early 1800s as courts began to consider the welfare of the child, a concern closely linked to the concept of parental fitness. Paternal custody rights no longer stood unchallenged; courts exercised discretion based on "the best interests of the child" doctrine, which took into account such factors as age, gender, and health, as well as psychological and material considerations. During the second half of the century, courts also became more willing to acknowledge that the rights of biological parents were not always superior to those of third parties. [16]

Although some conservative jurists resisted the loss of the father's paramount custody right, by the late nineteenth century state courts had come to recognize the equal rights of mothers. This recognition stemmed in part from the growing woman's movement but more importantly from the cultural celebration of women as mothers, which the nineteenth-century women's rights movement shared. The judiciary increasingly considered women to be uniquely suited to childrearing, and it was this apparently natural maternal instinct, the courts agreed by the turn of the century, that most strongly supported women's claim to custody and would fulfill children's "best interests." As Grossberg explains, this judge-made law facilitated women's fulfillment of their domestic duties and expanded their presence in the law, "but in a way that ensured that women's domestic powers did not translate into extensive external political and economic authority." [17]

By the early twentieth century, women had gained superior rights in practice. Yet this shift took place at a time of profound change in the status of children. As industrial capitalism grew, children became less valued for their immediate, unskilled labor and more for their future potential as skilled workers. Compulsory education laws and child labor prohibitions, as well as the changing needs of the economy, meant that children were no longer property that men controlled. They became individuals who required a great deal of attention and training; thus, a new kind of labor, performed by mothers, was required to raise them. For the middle class, and increasingly for the whole of society, children became "priceless" or sacred resources. As Carol Brown has argued, when children lost their earning power and became an economic drain, mothers gained custody. [18]

While mothers and third parties gained rights at the expense of fathers and natural parents respectively, they all lost power to an increasingly powerful state. The state's recognition of married women's property rights, demands for divorce, and child custody laws favoring the wife and mother all arose out of the logic of domesticity itself and thus reinforced gender spheres. For middle-class women, the law elevated women's status only within the family, already considered to be her realm. However, middle-class women turned the "cult of domesticity" against itself. Acting on the belief that women were morally superior to men, they forged social movements to uplift and nurture the entire society. Their public activism, which often formed the basis for feminism, altered the outlines of the patriarchal family. [19]

Still, such women lost power in a key arena: control over reproduction. Before the Civil War, legislators and judges were noticeably reluctant to interfere with private control of the size of families and made only halting efforts to regulate childbirth. By the end of the century, however, most states had declared abortion and contraception obscene and illegal. This dramatic increase of state power stemmed from the same pronatalist conception of womanhood that had led to the individualization of women and children by the courts. Viewing the pregnant woman ''as the object of protection,'' new laws portrayed abortionists as criminals and women as victims. Banning birth control would, as the Massachusetts Chief Justice Samuel Ruggs stated in 1917, ''protect purity, . . . preserve chastity, . . . encourage continence and self-restraint, . . . defend the sanctity of the home, and thus engender in the state and nation a virile and virtuous race of men and women.'' Such pronouncements, however, could not stop the dissemination of birth control information or devices or the use of abortion by women determined to restrict reproduction.[20]

The Differential Impact of Class and Race

While women and children from economically self-sufficient families generally gained individual rights before the Civil War, those from indigent families found themselves subjected to harsher and more repressive legislation. The reluctance to interfere in family life rarely operated when it came to the lives of the poor or ethnic/racial minorities. Indeed, state policy could make it nearly impossible for such minorities to maintain a stable family life. The Chinese Exclusion Act of 1884, for example, prohibited further immigration to America and thus inhibited family formation among all but the most wealthy male migrants, who alone were permitted to bring over brides. Immigration laws governing the migrant labor of Mexicans similarly disrupted family relations.[21]

As Maxwell Bloomfield has noted, ''the law did not distinguish between 'nuclear' and 'extended' families; it recognized only one principle of classification—that which separated the poor household from the non-poor.'' In practice, this meant discrimination against those most likely to be poor: minorities, children of broken homes, the aged, and the disabled. Antebellum codes restricted the movements and options of poor families, subjecting them to public control. Legislatures and local governments denied or subordinated parental custody rights, imposed support obligations upon relatives, fanned concern over the paternity of bastards, and established the criminality of parental desertion—all with the goal of limiting public expense rather than reducing poverty.[22] In the name of child saving and humanitarianism, the family law of the poor regulated dependence.

Either poor women were not real mothers or motherhood lost its sacred quality in a poor-law system that separated parents from children. Even apprenticeship functioned in a punitive manner. Once it was a common educational strategy for all children, but in the nineteenth century it became a system that provided for poor children through their own labor. Poor children, thus, were still viewed as workers at a time when middle-class children had become "useless" objects of affection.[23]

A series of new asylums—penitentiaries, reformatories, mental hospitals, and orphanages—confined the dependent and "deviant" in factorylike environments. Many of these institutions began as private organizations, but the state soon took them over and thus played a major role in transferring responsibility for the poor and dependent from the family and community to itself. This was particularly true for specialized institutions that cared for, rehabilitated, and reformed children. State statutes incorporating childcare institutions granted them broad authority to intervene in families and, when contested, were generally supported by the courts.[24]

Juvenile courts provide a case in point. Developed in the early twentieth century, they strove to accommodate the delinquent—often immigrant—child to middle-class Protestant values. They represented the state's adoption of the goals of the child-saving movement, which, since the 1870s, had sought to aid abused or neglected children throughout the country. Along with legislators, judges, and professional experts, the child-savers sought to strengthen state controls over childrearing. But, as Linda Gordon has suggested, no simple model of social control explains why immigrant and poor women sought the services of societies for the prevention of cruelty to children. Child-savers may have hoped to reeducate the immigrant and poor, but the social control that they sought also freed women and children from the abusive behavior and lack of economic support of individual patriarchs, from familial patriarchy.[25] As with the application of family law to the middle class, however, the power of the state within family life increased without a corresponding growth in women's power in the larger society.

The ideal of separate spheres was outside the experience of large groups of women whose men would never earn a family wage (i.e., one high enough to support an unwaged wife and children). This was particularly true for racial/ethnic women, who, as Evelyn Nakano Glenn has argued, never experienced any split between the public and private. The dominant culture excluded them from domesticity, since "their definition as laborers in production took precedence over their domestic roles"; moreover, even their domestic work was never "private," because it encompassed a larger circle of kin and community. In this context, private and public merged as women's work for the family entered the world of the market. Thus, black mothers as sharecroppers maintained the family while contributing to the harvest, and Chinese mothers became unpaid laborers in family businesses. Indeed, public policy (e.g., the Jim Crow laws of the 1890s) curtailed the earning power of minority men, ensuring that minority women would have to engage in paid labor.[26]

From the start Afro-Americans faced a discriminatory legal system not of their own making. Under slave law, black men, women, and children were regarded as individual units of property, and marriage between slaves was not recognized. Since southern law denied slaves consensual ability, they were held, like children and the insane, to be incapable of forming legal relationships. Moreover, potential marital duties were seen as conflicting with their obligations to masters. Yet even though masters could terminate slave unions and spouses had no civil rights, slaves married anyway—sometimes in a religious ceremony, more often by consent, confirmed by jumping over the broomstick. Only insofar as a child's status derived from its mother's was any bond of kinship embodied in the law. Children belonged to their master, who was seen as having a custody of sorts over all his slave "children."[27]

The rights of free blacks who had married as slaves were precarious. The Louisiana Supreme Court recognized "dormant civil rights" in 1819 when it argued that "emancipation gives to the slave his civil rights, and a contract of marriage, legal and valid by the consent of the master and moral assent of the slave, from the moment of freedom, although dormant during the slavery, produces all the effects which result from such contract among free persons." However, later courts dismissed this opinion as a product of Louisiana's peculiar civil-law heritage and refused to recognize such marriages, especially when it came to intestate property settlements. Moreover, free blacks could not marry slaves or whites, so that demographic imbalances inhibited family formation, especially in the urban South. Manumission laws further interfered with family legalization, since they often required the emancipated person to leave the state within a year or else be sold back into slavery. Other laws, it should be noted, allowed former slaves to purchase members of their immediate families in order to free them.[28]

Free blacks faced poverty as well as discrimination. Freed women, who often were emancipated with their children, were less likely to receive adequate wages than white women or black men. In the North as well as the South, they worked primarily as servants, seamstresses, or laundresses. Suzanne Lebsock suggests that the inability of married women to retain their property may have played a role in the propensity of free black women to remain unmarried (in the eyes of the law). After all, a husband's creditors could seize the earnings that a woman saved to buy relatives out of slavery.

This unencumbered legal status could lead to unusual situations, especially when free women had slave spouses. For example, one woman had to bequeath to her slave husband boats she had purchased with his money as his agent and appoint, upon her death, a free black man as guardian to their child and agent to her husband. Her property went to her free child. [29]

Most free black children were not so fortunate. If courts, in the North as well as the South, determined that their parents could not support them, they could be bound out as apprentices. For female heads of household, apprenticeship of children was often the only option for economic survival in a society that often reserved poorhouses and outdoor relief for whites. But apprenticeship to a white could become another form of slavery. Harriet E. Wilson's autobiographical tale, *Our Nig,* clearly depicts the young black girl as a beast of burden, lugging and scrubbing beyond her strength, with only rudimentary schooling and sustenance in return. Apprenticeship orders reflected the sexual division of labor: boys were apprenticed to carpenters, coopers, painters, brickmasons, blacksmiths, and other skilled artisans, but girls usually found themselves bound to unspecified domestic duties. [30]

Such a division reflected the gender inequalities of the labor market, but it also mirrored the realities of Afro-American community life. Whether their common oppression made black men and women more equal than white men and women remains an open question. Masters viewed black women in the field as genderless, but prized them for their reproductive capacity and abused their sexuality. The slave community upheld gender differences, though separate spheres were conceived as complementary. One thing is certain: black family life hardly reproduced the dominant Victorian culture. Free blacks in the North developed their own cults of masculinity and domesticity, and yet such gender systems belonged to a larger community and kinship construction of ''the race'' that valued the contributions of both sexes in the struggle for freedom. [31]

Respect for black family life did not come easily with emancipation. Landowners attempted to employ black women and children as gang laborers, but black families withdrew the labor of their women and children. Sharecropping developed as a compromise: black families could decide how to allocate that labor, but the landowner still benefited from the labor power of women and children. Soon the southern legal system ratified sharecropping, tying debtors to the land in a form of peonage that appeared to many as a new form of slavery. Nonetheless, blacks forced the state to regard them as family units. [32]

Still, landowners, merchants, and Freedmen's Bureau agents differentiated family members by gender and age. They recognized husbands as heads of the family in labor contracts and provision accounts; the Freedmen's Bureau, established by the federal government to aid the former slaves in the transition to freedom, created wage guidelines that built in unequal compensation based on sex and at times provided less land to female- than to male-headed households. Its agents attempted to make husbands responsible for wives' actions. But when it came to parental rights to children, the right of contract and the need for labor usually took precedence. Nonrecognition of slave marriage and the separation of parents from children had the consequence after emancipation of making children subject to state-ordered apprenticeship, essentially a labor contract without wages or legal safeguards. Courts upheld former masters who claimed that apprenticeship would represent "the best interests of the child." When parents contested such contracts, bureau agents, like their judicial counterparts, judged the morality of the mother according to their own standards of purity and domesticity. Having children from different fathers, living together without marriage, and low income—all consequences of slavery—were evidence of "unfitness." In short, the state's definition of kinship and proper family life, rather than the freedmen's own, held sway after emancipation.[33]

Creating the Welfare State

By the late nineteenth century, changes in family law had loosened the power of fathers within families, yet public policies reinforced economic inequality through occupational segregation by sex. The family wage, along with protective legislation and mothers' pension laws, improved the conditions of working-class families but further limited women's options in the labor market. Child labor and compulsory education laws, however, made women's wages more necessary in many poor families, since the family wage was more of an ideal than a reality until World War II. The growth in female labor-force participation made it impossible to ignore the contradiction between women's roles as individual wage-earners and as moral bulwarks of the home.[34]

The major programs of the Progressive era (1900–1920) were intended to preserve domestic values. Workingmen's compensation, for one, allowed the disabled male breadwinner to receive a wage; federally supervised wage arbitrations sought to gain family wages. Tenement house reform, pure food and drug laws, and other health measures, such as visiting nurse programs, sought to permit mothers of the poor to fulfill their role in safe, clean domestic environments. Social purity legislation, antivice campaigns, censorship, and prohibition became the moral equivalent of tenement cleansing.[35]

The attempt to regulate tenement home work—bringing piece work into the home—particularly revealed the reformers' goals. According to one factory inspector, the "privacy of the home" must succumb to a "stronger duty," the public interest, which would "rescue . . . all homes, and make the necessary division between home and workplace." That is, state interference in the home violated a key component of liberalism in order to create a higher private life and save liberal capitalism from its own excesses. Similarly, when it came to child labor, reformers rejected the idea of "parental ownership" of children. If parents failed to provide proper care—that is, if they permitted children to work long hours and skip school—they argued, "the state is bound to enter and become the parent of that child." [36]

Child labor and tenement home-work regulations belonged to a larger class of protective legislation for women and children. At a time when unregulated industrial capitalism posed a serious threat to worker safety and health, female reformers, trade unionists, and much of the working class viewed such protective laws as a positive goal. Frustrated by the difficulty of organizing low-skilled women workers, reformers—notably the National Consumers' League and the Women's Trade Union League—turned to minimum-wage, maximum-hours, and other protective laws as a strategy for improving working conditions, first for women and then for all workers. The skilled craftsmen of the American Federation of Labor also supported such laws as a way to remove low-waged women from competition, justifying them on the basis of women's status as mothers and dependents. [37]

The courts shared this sentiment. Women were seen as a class apart from men; like children, they were "wards of the state," requiring state protection. This assumption permitted judges to uphold protective laws for women, as in the pioneer case *Commonwealth* v. *Hamilton Manufacturing* (1876), while rejecting them for men. Such legislation interfered with the so-called sanctity of contract, but, the judges reasoned, freedom of contract could hardly apply to dependent women. Since the courts recognized reasonable differences between classes of workers, sustaining state child labor laws and restrictions on dangerous trades, women reformers emphasized women's "specialness" to justify health and safety protections needed and wanted by working-class women. Thus, their defense of Oregon's ten-hour law for women contended that industrial conditions particularly weakened female health. The Supreme Court agreed and in its landmark 1908 decision, *Muller* v. *Oregon,* codified a new form of state paternalism: "as healthy mothers are essential to vigorous offspring, the physical well-being of woman becomes an object of public interest and care in order to preserve the strength and vigor of the race." [38]

Yet this decision also suggests the state as an arena of struggle. As Francis Olson points out, "*Muller* may be seen as part of an effort to make the marketplace responsive to human needs by 'delegitimating' certain forms of exploitation and limiting the free reign of market individualism." [39] As such, it improved the conditions of women workers in female-dominated industries, though it opened the door to exclusionary legislation under the guise of protecting future motherhood. Night laws and restrictions on the basis of women's health (as if hazardous substances failed to affect men) tended to maintain occupational segregation by sex. Since agricultural labor and domestic service—the two largest employers of women, particularly women of color—were not covered, such laws protected only the motherhood of some classes of women. Whatever the impetus behind the laws—whether to lessen competition, as male craftsmen would advocate during World War I, or to regulate and improve the workplace for unorganized women, as the female reformers in the Women's Bureau did during the 1920s—limiting women's work options confirmed that woman's anatomy determined her fate, confining her to the home.

This form of protection for potential motherhood aimed at working-class daughters had a counterpart in the movement for mothers' pensions. Pushed by women reformers, it too identified women with their role as bearers and rearers of children. By maintaining "half-orphans" with their mothers rather than institutionalizing them (a more expensive solution), by paying women to stay home instead of providing childcare so that they could go out and work, it also reflected the general commitment to the private family. Motherhood, in a sense, became a civic function. In some states only widows and not unwed or divorced mothers qualified for mothers' pensions because they alone were considered "physically, mentally, and morally fit," and in most states white women alone received funds. Eligibility rules and the meagerness of the grants actually forced many widows with small children to work. Rather than subsidizing motherhood, then, these pensions (like protective legislation) promoted female employment in the marginal labor market. Furthermore, the bureaucracy necessary to enforce the rules—inspectors to check on the number of days worked or whether male boarders resided in the home— enmeshed recipients in a net of state paternalism that carried over into the administration of the federal Aid for Dependent Children (ADC) program in the 1940s.[40]

Women reformers, as has already been noted, played a key role in obtaining these reforms. For them, the fight for better conditions for women and children was also a fight against the arbitrary power of the father in the family and his industrial surrogates. They assumed the moral superiority of women and gained strength from their knowledge of female difference. They would protect the uniqueness of womanhood just as they would save the special character of childhood, working to make it possible for immigrant and poor women to be true to woman's nature within a familial setting. Understanding that mothering is work, they looked at mothers' pensions not as charity but as payment "for doing [my] job." They promoted an alternative ethos based on their women's culture—on nurturing, selflessness, empathy, relatedness—

that used domesticity to critique industrial capitalism and improve the lives of working-class women. Yet their reforms fed into the constraints of the larger culture and, simultaneously, reinforced the gender-segmented labor market that was so detrimental to women's status.[41]

The ambiguous, often unintended consequences of reformers' actions are apparent in the social welfare programs that the New Deal network of women reformers fought so hard to achieve. New Deal measures codified sexual and racial divisions of labor, promoting motherhood without fundamentally altering power relations. A dual welfare system developed in which men received entitlements, such as public works jobs and unemployment compensation, while women with children were called unemployable and thus received direct relief, or welfare, if no man was present. The women of the Children's and Women's Bureaus were unable to convince Congress that raising children *was* work or that gender-based wages were unfair.[42] Blacks and Mexicans faced local discrimination in relief and government jobs; indeed, New Deal agricultural policy further impoverished rural black families in the South by disrupting the sharecropping system and encouraging mechanization, undermining the black family economic unit and encouraging northern migration. Similarly, the minimum wage mandated by the Fair Labor Standards Act (FLSA)—which did not include domestic service or agricultural labor—forced the repatriation of Mexicans when employers no longer found handwork profitable.[43] The framework of the current welfare state grew from these differentiations.

The domestic norm guided New Deal labor and relief policies, which either excluded women from benefits or reinforced the existing structure of the market. Wage codes under the National Recovery Administration (NRA) mandated differentials in a full quarter of the codes and exempted from coverage both "light and repetitious" or female work and major female occupations like domestic service and clerical work. Combined with regional differentials, the codes inherently discriminated against black and Chicana women, a pattern reinforced by lax enforcement.[44] The state provided jobs for women reluctantly and limited work relief to "female" occupations. Moreover, married women in the public sector were furloughed first under Section 213 of the 1932 Economy Act, "the married person clause," which dismissed married workers if their spouse also worked for the government. Not until 1937 did pressure from women's organizations push Congress to repeal this act, which was specifically intended to keep wives at home and reserve available jobs for male heads of households.[45]

Such ideas also governed relief programs. As one Texas administrator put it, "The general feeling in this part of the country is that her husband and father should earn the livelihood for the family." Thus, private organizations would not donate space for Works Progress Administration (WPA) programs—even those that trained women for traditional household work—if women recruits had potential male support. The eligibility requirements of the WPA—that the recipient be the principal breadwinner, that there be only one per family, and that the recipient prove that she or he was truly in the labor market—cut down the number of women to between 12 and 19 percent of all recipents. WPA nurseries, while providing work for unemployed women teachers, catered only to families on relief, so that once a mother found employment, she lacked the childcare necessary to maintain it. Their real purpose was to instill proper values in children from economically disrupted families, not to aid female employment. [46]

Nursery school teaching was among the better sex-linked jobs opened to women. Under the National Youth Administration, young men constructed highways and buildings; young women were clerical workers and assisted in nursery schools and libraries, performing services once associated with the home. Sewing projects employed the largest number of women. The WPA also sponsored canning and housekeeping aid projects. Women's jobs replicated the major areas of female employment, but did so by race. In San Antonio, for example, black women went to the household worker projects, Chicanas to unskilled work, and Anglo women to white-collar jobs. White and Chicana women in housekeeping aid projects worked under home economists and registered nurses; black women found themselves assigned to household drudgery in their own segregated projects. Because clerical work was the only expanding sector of women's work, and domestic service a declining occupation, such training further discriminated against black women. Moreover, black and Chicana women found it difficult to qualify in the first place: blacks were told to seek low-paying domestic service jobs, and Chicanas had to prove citizenship. [47]

White administrators throughout the South "Jim Crowed" the New Deal The Agricultural Adjustment Act (AAA), which paid farmers to limit crop production and attempted to raise the price of land, hastened the displacement of sharecropping families. Planters failed to pass on AAA funds to their tenants, using these funds instead to retire tenant debt. In some places landlords and government administrators divided black households into productive and incapacitated members: the former had to work at low wages for planters; the latter sometimes received relief. WPA reduced educated and skilled blacks to menial labor, devising "beautification" projects in which black women shoveled garbage in gangs. When the cotton crop came in, administrators closed black women's sewing projects so as to force them back to field labor at the going rate. Social workers in the North as well as the South reported greater tensions between black couples and an increase of paternal desertion among all racial and ethnic groups in the wake of male unemployment and state aid. It was as if relief undermined male authority within families without any corresponding increase in female power. [48]

The Social Security Act of 1935 most dramatically illustrates the dual welfare system. Its old-age insurance provisions gave more benefits to men than women; it left uncovered at least one-third of all married women workers and major areas of female employment. When in 1939 Social Security redefined the recipient as the worker and his family, it actually embodied the family wage and discriminated against wage-earning wives, who received the same amount as those wives not in the labor force unless their primary income benefit was more than half their husbands'. But other sections of Social Security expanded on the mothers' pension idea, so that the state truly played father for those families without a male breadwinner. Originally without a caretaker's grant, ADC was based not on wages, as unemployment and Social Security were, nor on an obvious inability to earn, like aid to the disabled and blind, but rather on the assumption that mothers were unemployable, an idea that would not change until the mid-1960s, and then only as a reaction to the growing number of black women on welfare. [49]

New Deal welfare programs and even labor standards legislation thus responded to the economic crisis in a manner shaped by the domestic ideal. Programs for children especially projected the state as a protective father. With child labor outlawed under the NRA and then the FLSA, more mothers had to enter the paid labor force. Their daughters left school on special work permits to care for the home. Yet a situation in which daughters acted as mothers and mothers as fathers was taken as an aberration of the Depression rather than a product of advanced capitalist patriarchy. [50] By maintaining the domestic ideal and keeping needy families together, New Deal welfare measures supplemented economic programs that helped to reorganize capital. But gender and race inequalities strained the seams of the American welfare state from the start.

Toward a Feminist Public Policy

What are the implications of this history? Should we despair of ever ending the oppression and inequality sustained by law and public policy? One goal of feminist theory has been to empower women by uncovering the past: to know the world in order to change it. The state, while incorporating existing power relations, still cannot be reduced to the hierarchies it reflects. In a liberal democracy, the state serves as an arena of struggle: its various branches and agencies bend not only to the demands of powerful economic and political blocs, but also to mass movements. The state in turn may try to coopt such movements or defuse or divert them. A continuous struggle results.

Thus, nineteenth-century feminists demanded suffrage in order to break down the distinction between public and private, world and family, and end the male monopoly on public power. But women's entrance into equal citizenship alone did not transform power relations within the family, especially since suffrage ultimately proved inadequate either to attack inequalities within the family or to keep the state from becoming the main force structuring patriarchy in the broader society. The second generation of women reformers, who fought for the family wage and the programs of the welfare state and who worked to alleviate the suffering of poor women and children, won significant victories but never challenged the existing arrangements of gender or race. Our agenda differs from theirs. We understand that the social relations of gender have a fundamental impact on all areas of existence, including the welfare state. At a minimum, feminists who intervene in current policy debates—over industrial policy, the military buildup, social service cutbacks, or equity issues—must ask what impact such policy has on power differences between the sexes and the generations and among different kinds of families. Otherwise, in attempting to restore the welfare state, we may replicate the inequalities which it has fostered.

The dismantling of social programs has inadvertently produced an opportunity to restructure them so to create a more just society. The details of that reformation, however, will be a product of struggle. At the least, its results should value unpaid as well as paid labor, break down the exclusive association of women with motherhood and mothers with the home, and provide social support for children—not merely childcare—that respects their needs and the needs of their parents. State support can more reasonably associate work and home, while preserving the distinction between them, and provide alternatives to the single-family dwelling that incorporates household services for employed parents. It can intervene in the structure of work so to fit work to parenting rather than the other way around. State policies can ensure that the family of the future will not consist of either impoverished mothers and their children or elderly women alone and in poverty.[51] Ultimately, a feminist public policy needs to recognize differences between women and between the sexes at the same time that it eliminates inequality. In this way the state will surely be transformed and patriarchy dismantled.

Notes

1. Steven P. Erie, Martin Rein, and Barbara Wiget, "Women and the Reagan Revolution: Thermidor for the Social Welfare Economy," in Irene Diamond (ed.), *Fami-*

lies, Politics, and Public Policy: A Feminist Dialogue on Women and the State (New York: Longman, 1983), pp. 94–119; and Chapter 26 in this volume.

2. Mary McIntosh, "The State and the Oppression of Women," in Annette Kuhn and Ann Marie Wolpe (eds.), *Feminism and Materialism: Women and Modes of Production* (London: Routledge & Kegan Paul, 1978); Heidi Hartmann, "The Unhappy Marriage of Marxism and Feminism: Towards a More Progressive Union," in Lydia Sargent (ed.), *Women and Revolution: A Discussion of the Unhappy Marriage of Marxism and Feminism* (Boston: South End Press, 1981); Ann Ferguson, "On Conceiving Motherhood and Sexuality: A Feminist Materialist Approach," in Joyce Trebilcot (ed.), *Mothering: Essays in Feminist Theory* (Totowa, N.J.: Rowman & Allanheld, 1984); Barbara Ehrenreich, "Life Without Father: Reconsidering Socialist-Feminist Theory," *Socialist Review* 73, no. 1 (1984): 48–57.

3. The most thorough examination of American family law to date is Michael C. Grossberg, "Law and the Family in Nineteenth Century America" (Ph.D. dissertation, Brandeis University, 1979), published as *Governing the Hearth: Law and Family in Nineteenth Century America* (Chapel Hill: University of North Carolina Press, 1985). See also Maxwell Bloomfield, *American Lawyers in a Changing Society, 1776–1876* (Cambridge: Harvard University Press, 1976), pp. 91–135, and Jacobus TenBroek, "California's Dual System of Family Law: Its Origin, Development, and Present Status," *Stanford Law Review* 16 (1963–64): 257–317, 900–981.

4. Eli Zaretsky, "The Place of the Family in the Origins of the Welfare State," in Barrie Thorne and Marilyn Yalom (eds.), *Rethinking the Family: Some Feminist Questions* (New York: Longman, 1982); Jacques Donzelot, *The Policing of Families* (New York: Pantheon, 1979); Judith Sealander, *As Minority Becomes Majority: Federal Reaction to the Phenomenon of Women in the Work Force, 1920–1963* (Westport, Conn.: Greenwood Press, 1983).

5. Grossberg, "Law and the Family," pp. iv, 18–19.

6. Frances E. Olson, "The Family and the Market: A Study of Ideology and Legal Reform," *Harvard Law Review* 96 (1983): 1523, 1532; Suzanne Lebsock, *The Free Women of Petersburg: Status and Culture in a Southern Town, 1784–1860* (New York: Norton, 1984), pp. 15–53.

7. Olson, "Family and Market," pp. 1531–33.

8. Christopher Lasch, *Haven in a Heartless World: The Family Besieged* (New York: Harper & Row, 1977); Carl Degler, *At Odds: Women and the Family in America from the Revolution to the Present* (New York: Oxford University Press, 1980), pp. 26–29, 144, 174–75, 279–327.

9. Norma Basch, *In the Eyes of the Law: Women, Marriage, and Property in Nineteenth Century New York* (Ithaca, N.Y.: Cornell University Press, 1982); Bloomfield, "American Lawyers," pp. 112–17; Lebsock, "Free Women of Petersburg," pp. 23, 53–86.

10. Lucretia Mott, as quoted in Olson, "Family and Market," p. 1511; Elizabeth Cady Stanton, "Address to the New York State Legislature," in Miriam Schneir (ed.), *Feminism: The Essential Historical Writings* (New York: Vintage, 1972), p. 113.

11. Norma Basch, "Invisible Women: The Legal Fiction of Marital Unity in Nineteenth-Century America," *Feminist Studies* 5, no. 2 (1979): 347–49.

12. William O'Neill, *Divorce in the Progressive Era* (New Haven: Yale University Press, 1967), p. 7; Bloomfield, "American Lawyers," pp. 97, 120–21.

13. Lebsock, "Free Women of Petersburg," pp. 68–72.

14. Jane Turner Censer, " 'Smiling Through Her Tears': Ante-Bellum Southern

Women and Divorce," *American Journal of Legal History* 25 (1981): 37; Christopher Lasch, "Divorce and the 'Decline of the Family' ", in *The World of Nations: Reflections on American History, Politics, and Culture* (New York: Knopf, 1973), pp. 39–40.

15. Michael Grossberg, "Who Gets the Child? Custody, Guardianship, and the Rise of a Judicial Patriarchy in Nineteenth-Century America," *Feminist Studies* 9, no. 2 (1983): 235–60.

16. Grossberg, *Governing the Hearth*, pp. 234–85; Jamil S. Zainaldin, "The Emergence of a Modern Family Law: Child Custody, Adoption, and the Courts, 1796–1851," *Northwestern University Law Review* 73 (1979):1052–74; Carol Brown, "Mothers, Fathers, and Children: From Private to Public Patriarchy," in Sargent, *Women and Revolution*, pp. 252–57.

17. Grossberg, "Who Gets the Child?" p. 237.

18. Viviana Z. Zelizer, *Pricing the Priceless Child: The Changing Social Value of Children* (New York: Basic Books, 1985), pp. 4–21, 54–112, 208–28; Brown, "Mothers, Fathers, and Children," pp. 242–47.

19. Nancy F. Cott, *The Bonds of Womanhood: "Women's Sphere" in New England, 1780–1835* (New Haven: Yale University Press, 1977), pp. 5–9, 194–206; Barbara Leslie Epstein, *The Politics of Domesticity: Women, Evangelism, and Temperance in Nineteenth-Century America* (Middletown, Conn.: Wesleyan University Press, 1981).

20. Grossberg, *Governing the Hearth*, pp. 155–95; James C. Mohr, *Abortion in America: The Origins and Evolution of National Policy* (New York: Oxford University Press, 1978), pp. 3–45, 119–46; Linda Gordon, *Woman's Body, Woman's Right* (New York: Penguin, 1977), pp. 95–115.

21. Evelyn Nakano Glenn, "Racial-Ethnic Women's Labor: The Intersection of Race, Gender and Class Oppression," *Review of Radical Political Economics* 17, no. 3 (1985): 89–95; Rosalinda M. Gonzalez, "Chicanas and Mexican Immigrant Families 1920–1940: Women's Subordination and Family Exploitation," in Lois Scharf and Joan M. Jensen (eds.), *Decades of Discontent: The Women's Movement. 1920–1940* (Westport, Conn.: Greenwood Press, 1983), pp. 59–84.

22. Bloomfield, "American Lawyers," p. 92; Jacobus TenBroeck, "California's Dual System," pp. 257–58, 900–981.

23. Zelizer, *Pricing the Priceless Child*, pp. 171–89; on apprenticeship, Edmund Morgan, *The Puritan Family* (New York: Harper & Row, 1966), pp. 75–77; Grace Abbott, *The Child and the State* Vol. 1 (Chicago: University of Chicago Press, 1938), pp. 189–94.

24. David Rothman, *The Discovery of the Asylum: Social Order and Disorder in the New Republic* (Boston: Little, Brown, 1971); Michael B. Katz, "Origins of the Institutional State," *Marxist Perspectives* 1, no. 4 (1978). 6–22.

25. Grossberg, *Governing the Hearth*, pp. 279, 303–4; Zaretsky, "Place of the Family," pp. 202–3; David J. Rothman, "The State as Parent: Social Policy in the Progressive Era," in Willard Gaylin (ed.), *Doing Good: The Limits of Benevolence* (New York: Pantheon, 1978), pp. 78–79; Linda Gordon, "Child Abuse, Gender, and the Myth of Family Independence: Thoughts on the History of Family Violence and Its Social Control 1880–1920," *New York University Review of Law and Social Change* 12 (1983–84): 523–37.

26. Glenn, "Racial-Ethnic Women's Labor," pp. 93, 96, 102; Jacqueline Jones, *Labor of Love, Labor of Sorrow: Black Women, Work, and the Family from Slavery to the Present* (New York: Basic Books, 1985), pp. 67, 91–92.

27. Eugene Genovese, *Roll, Jordan, Roll: The World the Slaves Made* (New York: Random House, 1974), discusses the patriarchal underpinning of the law. Also see, Grossberg, *Governing the Hearth,* pp. 126–40; Bloomfield, "American Lawyers," pp. 108–11.

28. Bloomfield, "American Lawyers," pp. 109–10; Grossberg, *Governing the Hearth,* p. 131; Lebsock, "Free Women of Petersburg," pp. 87–111.

29. Lebsock, "Free Women of Petersburg," esp. p. 109.

30. Ibid., pp. 101–2; Harriet E. Wilson, *Our Nig; or, Sketches from the Life of a Free Black* (reprint ed.; New York: Vintage, 1983).

31. For various interpretations, Jones, *Labor of Love,* pp. 3–35; Angela Davis, *Women, Race and Class* (New York: Random House, 1981), pp. 3–29; Deborah Gray White, *Ar'n't I a Woman? Female Slaves in the Plantation South* (New York: Norton, 1985); James Horton, "The Burden of Race and Sex," *Feminist Studies* 12, no. I (1986): 51–76.

32. Jones, *Labor of Love,* pp. 36–101.

33. Ibid., pp. 53–55; Rebecca J. Scott, "The Battle Over the Child: Child Apprenticeship and the Freedmen's Bureau in North Carolina," in N. Ray Hiner and Joseph M. Hawes (eds.), *Growing Up in America: Children in Historical Perspective* (Urbana: University of Illinois Press, 1985), pp. 193–207.

34. Alice Kessler-Harris, *Out to Work: A History of Wage Earning Women in the United States* (New York: Oxford University Press, 1982), esp. pp. 180–214; Martha May, "Bread Before Roses: American Workingmen, Labor Unions and the Family Wage," in Ruth Milkman (ed.), *Women, Work, and Protest: A Century of U.S. Women's Labor History* (Boston: Routledge & Kegan Paul, 1985), pp. 1–21.

35. Zaretsky, "Place of the Family," pp. 188–224, offers a good summary of these efforts.

36. Mary O'Reilly, "Sweat-Shop Life in Pennsylvania," in International Association of Factory Inspectors of North America, *Ninth Annual Convention* (Cleveland, Ohio: Forest City Printing House, 1895), p. 68; Owen Lovejoy, "Some Unsettled Questions About Child Labor," *Annals of the American Academy of Political and Social Science* 23, suppl. (March 1909): 58.

37. Ann Corinne Hill, "Protection of Women Workers and the Courts: A Legal Case History," *Feminist Studies* 5, no. 2 (1979): 247–73; Lynn Weiner, *From Working Girl to Working Mother: The Female Labor Force in the United States, 1820–1980* (Chapel Hill: University of North Carolina Press, 1985), pp. 68–78; Alice Kessler-Harris, "Where Are the Organized Women Workers?" *Feminist Studies* 3, nos. 1/2 (1975): 101.

38. As quoted by Hill, "Protection of Women Workers," p. 253; Alice Kessler-Harris, "Protection for Women: Trade Unions and Labor Laws," in Wendy Chavkin (ed.), *Double Exposure: Women's Health Hazards on the Job and at Home* (New York: Monthly Review Press, 1984), pp. 139–54; *Muller* v. *Oregon,* 208 U.S. (1908).

39. Olson, "Family and Market," pp. 1556–57.

40. Ann Vandepol, "Dependent Children, Child Custody, and the Mothers' Pensions: The Transformation of State-Family Relations in the Early Twentieth Century," *Social Problems* 29 (1982): 221–35; Weiner, *Working Girl,* pp. 128–32; on the last point, Melissa Skolfield, "From Widows' Pensions to Workfare: AFDC 1935–1985," manuscript, George Washington University, 1986.

41. Frederic C. and Marie Jenney Howe, "Pensioning the Widow and the Fatherless," *Good Housekeeping* 57, September 1913, p. 285; Kathryn Kish Sklar, "Hull

House in the 1890s: A Community of Women Reformers," *Signs* 10 (1985): 658–77; and Chapter 27 in this volume.

42. Susan Ware, *Beyond Suffrage: Women in the New Deal* (Cambridge: Harvard University Press, 1981); Diana M. Pearce, "Toil and Trouble: Women Workers and Unemployment Compensation," *Signs* 10 (1985): 439–59; Grace Abbott, Senate hearings on S. 1130, 74th Congress, 1st sess., pp. 1086–91, as quoted by Skolfield, "Widows' Pensions to Workfare," p. 5.

43. Jones, *Labor of Love,* pp. 174–77; Julia Kirk Blackwelder, *Women of the Depression: Caste and Culture in San Antonio, 1929–1939* (College Station: Texas A & M University Press, 1984), pp. 177–78.

44. Lois Scharf, *To Work and Wed: Female Employment, Feminism, and the Great Depression* (Westport, Conn.: Greenwood Press, 1980); Mary Elizabeth Pidgeon, "Employed Women Under N.R.A. Codes," *Bulletin of the Women's Bureau,* no. 130 (Washington: Government Printing Office, 1935), pp. 2–4; Gonzalez, "Chicanas and Mexican Immigrant Families," pp. 70–71.

45. Scharf, *To Work and Wed,* pp. 43–65.

46. Blackwelder, *Women of the Depression,* p. 126; Scharf, *To Work and Wed,* p. 123.

47. Scharf, *To Work and Wed,* pp. 110–38; Blackwelder, *Women of the Depression,* pp. 110–26, 171–72.

48. Jones, *Labor of Love,* pp. 177–78, 192–96, 200–207; "Family Life," in Rosalyn Baxandall, Linda Gordon, and Susan Reverby (eds.), *America's Working Women: A Documentary History—1600 to the Present* (New York: Vintage, 1976), pp. 241–45.

49. Scharf, *To Work and Wed,* pp. 128–30; Skolfield, "Widows' Pensions to Workfare," pp. 6–11; Sylvia Law, "Women, Work, Welfare, and the Preservation of Patriarchy," *University of Pennsylvania Law Review* 131 (1983): 1250–61.

50. Glen H. Elder, Jr., *Children of the Great Depression: Social Change in Life Experience* (Chicago: University of Chicago Press, 1974), pp. 281–83.

51. Dolores Hayden, *Redesigning the American Dream: The Future of Housing, Work, and Family Life* (New York: Norton, 1984); Wendy Sarvasy and Judith Van Allen, "Fighting the Feminization of Poverty: Socialist-Feminist Analysis and Strategy," *Review of Radical Political Economics* 16, no. 4 (1984): 89–110.

PART II

Work in and from the Contemporary Home

Introduction

Although the household was the site of most work at the beginning of the nineteenth century, over the course of that century the subsistence work done in families by both women and men became the domestic work of women and the waged work of men. As the essays in Part I imply, disconnecting job site and household led to an equation of "work" with paid employment. An ideology developed that made being a wife and mother an end in itself, a natural extension of womanhood. As a result, the modifier "house" (but not "real") attached itself to what women did in the home. And the home became a haven, a place for leisure and the expression of intimacy the very antithesis of work.

Until late in the twentieth century, sociologists too accepted uncritically this cultural equation: sociologists of work focused on the market economy and the waged work of men, while sociologists of the family focused on women, the home, and emotional life. Yet, especially since World War II, the availability of domestic services and products as salable commodities, the rising participation of married women in the paid labor force, and increased feminist analysis and protest have called into question the identification of the occupational system with men and work and the family with women and emotion.

The Analysis of Housework in the 1970s

In response to these new developments, two strands of feminist thought in the 1970s began to analyze housework as work. A number of quantitative researchers began to look at housework as a job and quite consciously applied to it the framework developed in the analyses of other jobs and occupations (calculating hours, prestige, and monetary worth).[1] This research showed conclusively that, despite the women's movement, housework remained women's work. Husbands "helped." But they did far less than their wives. Despite the rise of "labor-saving" devices, housewives in the 1970s spent as many hours on housework as did their counterparts at the turn of the century. Although contemporary employed women and women without children devoted fewer hours to housework than did housewives, they—no less than farm women—labored from dawn to dusk. Moreover, although these researchers were surprised to find that, on average, housework was ranked in the middle of occupational prestige scales, they found much variation. In particular, college-educated women and men gave housewives a prestige score far below the ranking the less educated assigned to it. Researchers who calculated the dollar value of housework, costing it at its equivalent market price, estimated that such compensation would increase the family's income by more than 60 percent.[2]

The largely quantitative research on housework was accompanied by the development of a far more theoretical (and sometimes overly abstract) socialist-feminist literature. Whereas the quantitative researchers attempted to count the amount of work women did, the socialist feminists struggled with its meaning and value for capitalism. They asked whether the unwaged work of women could be absorbed into the Marxist concept of "productive labor." In earlier Marxist theory, women's housework was as neglected as it was in conventional sociology. Though recognized as useful, housework was not considered "productive" or even "public," because it was not sold as labor power and therefore was not a source of profit.[3]

In contrast, socialist feminists argued that women's domestic work and exclusion from full-time paid labor was vital to the stability of the capitalist economy, just as it was central to the subordination of women. As part-time and occasional employees, women provided a "reserve army of labor," ready to move in and out of the labor market in response to changing economic demands. Moreover, housewives—as a frontline army of consumers—connected the products of the marketplace with the created needs of family members. And, perhaps most important, women's work in the home ensured the reproduction of labor power through raising children and sustaining husbands.[4] Through the analysis of housework, socialist feminists could elucidate the distinction between "public" and "private" as a feature of ideology under capitalism.

By conceiving of the beneficiaries of housework as not only husbands but the capitalist system, socialist feminists could see the value of concealing and trivializing women's domestic labor. Concealing the labor of the home ensures its removal from the cash nexus; it appears to come free as part of a "family wage" (see Chapter 4 by May). Because each women works alone in her private home and must buy her own "labor-saving devices," the market continues to expand. Whether or not ordinary men were instrumental in concealing domestic work, its trivialization is, at least partially, in their interest. Seen as doing the important work, husbands—often powerless on the job— lay claim to compensatory power at home, just as they benefit from the household services their economically dependent wives provide.

Both the quantitative and socialist-feminist analyses of the 1970s made valuable contributions. The quantitative researchers, by drawing an analogy between housework and other jobs, made visible the intensive effort required in the home. The socialist feminists' examination of its meaning and value revealed broader connections between housework and capitalism. Yet both sets of analyses have a number of limitations with which scholars are just beginning to grapple.

Unpaid Family Work in the Home:
New Understandings and New Questions

The early stages of industrial capitalism developed with—perhaps even depended on— women's labor at home. But the logic of capitalism is to extend markets into previously excluded areas. Women's exit from the home both provides a new source of cheap labor and generates demands for the products of new industries. As employed wives necessarily do less household labor, families must often purchase its equivalent. This expands the market for new prepared food, childcare, and cleaning services. The family's survival, or at least accustomed style of life, comes to depend upon her income as well as her husband's. At the same time, it continues to depend on her work at home. And although the development of capitalism moved some household products and services out of the household, into the market, such transference was selective.

In fact, one can see marked differences in the development of technologies and products associated with what had been women's and men's work in preindustrial households. Linking the historical trends discussed in Part I with our concern here for work in contemporary households, Ruth Schwartz Cowan analyzes these developments and their consequences in Chapter 6. She shows that industrialization relieved the burden of men's domestic labor considerably by providing substitutes for it. At the same time, what came to be known as women's household work (and after 1850 as "housework") was not so thoroughly replaced or superseded by developing technologies and services. These technologies—and thereby the persons who used them— continued to be anchored in households. Cowan's discussion shows how the development of household technologies contributed to, and at the same time was a response to, the growing ideological separation of women's and men's work and capitalist expansion. Bringing her analysis up to the present, she suggests that a contemporary consequence of the incomplete industrialization and specialization of women's domestic work is the twentieth-century's gender-stratified and inequitable labor force.

Capitalist expansion, then, produces contradictory developments that raise a number of new questions. Does the maintenance of old and the development of new domestic tasks threaten women's participation in the labor force at a time when families increasingly rely on their income? Does women's attachment to the market lead them to resent and resist household labor, or do they have a more ambivalent response? Does the availability of services in the market undermine marriage, pushing men to flee the "good-provider role," or does the reliance of families on women's earnings and services produce a heightened attachment to the privatized home? Finally, does the transformation in household tasks and women's waged work renew demands on children and produce new understandings of their labor at home?

Recent analyses suggest that women themselves have contradictory feelings about their continued responsibility for housework. On the one hand they resent being compelled to do the time-consuming, isolating, boring, and devalued chores that much housework involves. So, when they can afford to, many take advantage of alternatives available in the market. Since many discover that they cannot divide labor equally in the home, some middle-class women "subcontract" part of it out to poorer women (or to the growing number of organizations that employ such women). [5] So, too, newly created food services—from the caterers who serve the elite to the fast-food restaurants that serve the many—now provide a number of the meals once cooked at home. And, importantly, women finally seem to be lowering their standards for housework; one telling indicator is that the sale of paper plates has increased markedly in the last few years while the sale of floor waxes has declined. [6]

On the other hand, some women find satisfaction in some of the work they do for their families; it is both constituted and experienced as a "labor of love." Given the availability of commercial services and products, at least part of what was once experienced as compulsory has now become volitional and self-directed. Many women, for example, see sewing, cooking, and gardening as leisure activities, both pleasurable and freely chosen, enjoyable to themselves as well as to their husbands and children. [7] But there is more to such choices. In ministering to their families, wives and mothers are active agents who struggle to maintain autonomy and a sense of dignity for themselves and their families. To understand all family work as simply "social reproduction" or "oppressed labor" is to miss the ways wives and mothers make choices. To view women who chose to do housework as victims of false consciousness is to miss the point that some housework produces a sense of achievement as well as a measure of control over their families. And some are loath to relinquish (or even divide) that control. Indeed, recent studies show, often to the surprise of the researchers, that many women are reluctant to give up, or fully share, the housework.[8] Most still resist sharing childcare.[9] Thus, women resent their work in the home *and* resist forfeiting it.

Moreover, though feminist scholarship of the seventies showed us the ways in which housework resembled paid work, we must avoid overdrawing parallels. Indeed, much of the value of housework depends on its not being recognized as work. It is and must be understood at least in part—by both practitioners and recipients—as an act of love. Further, as Brown recently pointed out, "Purchased services usually do not reflect the kind of service the housewife provides because she intimately knows the family members she is serving and takes responsibility for organizing and providing the care that is needed."[10] Because of the diffuse and intermittent nature of their effort and their intimate relationship to its beneficiaries, housewives are not replaceable in the way occupants of other jobs are. More generally, conceptions of home and family (based on sharing and altruism) contrast with the principles of the market economy (based on competition and individual achievement). Valuing the former as well as the latter, women experience a certain ambivalence, for they sense "the tragic paradox that the bases of love, dependence and altruism in human life and the historical oppression of women have been found in the same matrix."[11]

Chapter 7 looks at the domestic work women continue to do and their response to it. Marjorie DeVault shows that women themselves still view meal preparation and planning as a labor of love and a natural extension of self in relation to family members. As important, she shows how this work helps create the social order we think of as family and how this order depends for its value on the invisibility of that effort. DeVault suggests that women feel oppressed because of the work they must do at home and that, at the same time, they want to do that work in order to create the family and self they value.

Contemporary men also face contradictory pressures that make them simultaneously resist and encourage their wives' labor-force participation. They gain financially from their wives' employment and may even benefit psychologically from reduced breadwinning responsibilities.[12] When both partners are employed, husbands obtain greater empathy and companionship from their wives.[13] Yet men may also resent the loss of unpaid household services that they expect will follow their wives' departure for jobs.[14] Chapter 8, by Janet Hunt and Larry Hunt, speaks to the contradictions in capitalism that contribute to the ambivalence of men. They locate the source of contemporary gender tensions, particularly men's resistance to symmetry in household work, in the antagonistic claims of the market for women's paid labor and of the family for women's unpaid labor.

Finally, by calling domestic work "women's work," feminist scholarship has all too often extended inadvertently the very invisibility they decry. In particular, this equation makes children's domestic work invisible. Although children today certainly do far less than they did in preindustrial settings and far less than their mothers, they still perform some household labor. Indeed, the development of capitalism, and the labor-force participation of women on which it relies, again makes necessary children's contributions to the work that still goes on in families.

In Chapter 9 Lynn White and David Brinkerhoff analyze the work that children do and the value that parents attribute to it. They find that parents themselves recognize both the importance and the noninstrumental nature of children's work when they say that it "builds character" and "teaches values." Many parents believe that the significance of children's domestic work lies in its contribution to the creation of family. Moreover, the study of children's housework shows that the devaluation of housework inheres in its association with women. Though trivialized when women do it, housework is imbued with value when children do it; though wives are not paid for doing housework, children often are.

Unpaid Family Work Outside the Home

Not all family work is based in the home. The second section of Part II turns to the unpaid family work that takes place outside the home. Feminist concentration on the connections between family work and the "external" world rekindled a longstanding intellectual tradition distinguishing public and private spheres. At first feminists attributed an ecological and gender-identified character to these spheres: the private sphere was located in the home and distinctive to women, and the public sphere was located outside the home and distinctive to men. But developing analysis revealed ambiguities in any such easy equation. Weinbaum and Bridges in a pioneering article showed that much of women's domestic labor has become "consumption work" that pulls women outside the home into shopping malls, supermarkets, and bank lines.[15] So, too, the development of the automobile in concert with the reorganization of merchandising—from house-to-house peddlers to mail order catalogues to centralized shopping malls—has shifted the burden of marketing and providing services from the seller to the buyer.[16] Moreover, mothers do "network building" and "kinkeeping" as they join and staff community organizations, drive their elderly relatives to doctors or provide lay care, and make phone calls to their parents and in-laws.[17] In doing so, they maintain resources for their children in the local community as well as the modern extended family. More generally, such unpaid work—most done by women, but some by men—moves back and forth, blurring the division between the public world of markets, government agencies, and community life and the private worlds of home and immediate family.

In doing volunteer work, helping relatives find jobs, making purchases, attending to hospitalized kin, families provide essential, though uncompensated, services on which the economy depends. Some of this unpaid work is voluntary, some involuntary; some is performed inside the home, some outside it. But however or wherever it is performed, family labor links family members not only to one another but also to those organizations that we conventionally think of as part of the public world. There are, then, no clear boundaries between private and public worlds and what boundaries there are constantly shift in response to changes in relations between the market and families.

The essays in the second section explore the permeability of boundaries between households and the worlds outside them. Each focuses on a different social class and examines different kinds of family work that go on outside the home. But both show how such work maintains the economy and how the success and failure of household members in the labor market and the community depend on unpaid labor performed out of family obligation.

Arlene Kaplan Daniels shows in Chapter 10 how the volunteer work of upper class wives maintains a system of class relations and contributes to their families' interests in the community. Yet volunteer work has mixed effects on the wives themselves. They must conceal the effort involved in their work if it is to have the desired effect; therefore, it cannot count as work. Thus, these upper-class women are caught in contradictions they perceive only dimly.

In Chapter 11 Nona Glazer shows how the pursuit of profit under capitalism increases women's involuntary, unpaid work—like self-service shopping. Such developments require more effort from poor and middle-class women, but no more from rich women, and substitute low-wage women's jobs for more costly men's jobs. Employed women are then pitted against unpaid women and paid men even as they remain dependent upon their husbands' "family wage." This article not only questions the equation of family work with the private sphere but shows that trends in capitalism intensify the obligations of women.

Notes

1. See Joann Vanek, "Housewives as Workers," in Ann H. Stromberg and Shirley Harkess (eds.), *Women Working: Theories and Facts in Perspective* (Palo Alto, Calif.: Mayfield, 1978); Helena Z. Lopata, *Occupation: Housewife* (New York: Oxford University Press, 1974); Richard Berk and Sarah Fenstermaker Berk, *Labor and Leisure at Home: Content and Organization of the Household Day* (Beverly Hills, Calif.: Sage, 1979). For a good review of literature estimating the dollar worth of housework, see Myra Marx Ferree, "Housework: Rethinking the Costs and Benefits," in Irene Diamond (ed.), *Families, Politics and Public Policy: A Feminist Dialogue on Women and the State* (New York: Longman, 1983).

2. R. L. Gronay, "Home Production—A Forgotten Industry," *Review of Economics and Statistics* 62 (1980): 408–16. Researchers have used a number of different techniques for assessing the dollar value of housework. Some economists use the "shadow wage" (or the value of hours put into housework that could be put into wage work). Others use the occupational components approach, in which the hours a housewife puts into particular jobs (e.g., her work as nurse, chauffeur, dietician, housecleaner, etc.) are multiplied by the wages for those particular jobs. Although each of these techniques has its own flaws (i.e., the shadow wage method pays highly educated women more than less educated women for the same job of housework; the occupational components method gives all women the same wage for similar tasks, although skill levels vary enormously). See R. K. Armey, "The Relative Income Shares of Homemakers," in Steven Bahr (ed.), *Economics and the Family* (Lexington, Mass.: Heath, 1980).

3. As Engels wrote of the rise of capitalism: "Household management lost its public character. It no longer concerned society. It became a private service; the wife became the head servant excluded from all participation in social production." Frederick Engels, *The Origin of the Family, Private Property and the State* (New York: International Publishers, 1972); p. 137.

4. See Wally Seccombe, "The Housewife and Her Labor Under Capitalism," *New Left Review,* no. 83 (1974):3–24. Margaret Benston, "Beyond the Domestic Labor Debate," *New Left Review,* no. 116 (1969):13–27. See also Nona Y. Glazer-Malbin, "Housework: A Review Essay," *Signs* 1 (1976):905–922, for a review of this work.

5. Rosanna Hertz, *More Equal Than Others* (Berkeley, Calif.: University of California Press, 1986).

6. Naomi Gerstel, "The New Superwoman," paper presented at Business and Professional Women's Annual Meeting, Boston, 1985.

7. As Ferree writes of housework: "While the competitive aspects of status production create productivity pressures on housewives, the cooperative aspect offers personal and social rewards not available in the market": "Housework," p. 155.

8. Although polls show that most women do not want more "help" in housework, increasing numbers of highly educated, younger women are more likely to want such help. As Pleck writes: "The increase in these groups may presage a challenge to the traditional division of household labor which will become more widespread in the future": (Joseph H. Pleck, "The Work-Family Role System," in Rachel Kahn-Hut, Arlene Kaplan Daniels, and Richard Colvard (eds.), *Women and Work: Problems and Perspectives* (New York: Oxford University Press, 1982), p. 105. For other discussions of women's resistance to asking husbands for more help, see Joann Vanek, "Household Work, Wage Work, and Sexual Equality," in A. S. Skolnick and J. H. Skolnick (eds.), *Family in Transition,* 4th ed. (Boston: Little, Brown, 1983), as well

as Sara Yogev, "Do Professional Women Have Egalitarian Marital Relationships?" *Journal of Marriage and the Family* 43 (1981): 865–72.

9. E. M. Hock, M. T. Gnezda, and S. L. McBride, "Mothers of Infants: Attitudes Towards Employment and Motherhood," *Journal of Marriage and the Family* 46 (1985):425–31.

10. C. Vickery Brown, "Home Production for Use in a Market Economy," in Barrie Thorne with Marilyn Yalom (eds.), *Rethinking the Family: Some Feminist Questions* (New York: Longman, 1982), p. 155.

11. Eli Zaretsky, "The Place of the Family in the Origins of the Welfare State," in Thorne and Yalom, *Rethinking the Family,* p. 193.

12. Indeed, recent research suggests that husbands whose wives are employed suffer no more psychological distress than those whose wives are not. See Michael Fendrich, "Wives' Employment and Husbands' Distress: A Meta-Analysis and Replication," *Journal of Marriage and the Family* 45 (1984):871–80.

13. I. H. Simpson and Paula England, "Conjugal Work Roles and Marital Solidarity," in J. Aldous (ed.), *Two Paychecks: Life in Dual-Earner Families* (Beverly Hills, Calif.: Sage, 1982).

14. In fact, studies show quite mixed results on the relationship between women's employment and husbands' marital satisfaction. Some find a positive correlation; others find a negative correlation; still others find no correlation. For a review of these findings, see Paula England and George Farkas, *Households, Employment, and Gender* (New York: Aldine, 1986), p. 72.

15. Datya Weinbaum and Amy Bridges, "The Other Side of the Paycheck: Monopoly Capital and the Structure of Consumption," *Monthly Review* 28 (July–Aug. 1976):88–103.

16. Ruth Schwartz Cowan, *More Work for Mother: The Ironies of Household Technology from the Open Hearth to the Microwave* (New York: Basic Books, 1983).

17. See Lydia N. O'Donnell, *The Unheralded Majority* (Lexington, Mass.: Lexington Books, 1984), pp. 117–27, for her discussion of the network building and kinkeeping of middle- and working-class women.

UNPAID FAMILY WORK IN THE HOME

6

Women's Work, Housework, and History: The Historical Roots of Inequality in Work-Force Participation

RUTH SCHWARTZ COWAN

Time's arrow makes a difference; the profound inequalities that we observe today in women's work-force participation have their roots in historical processes that have been unfolding for almost three hundred years. Sexual segregation in market labor and unequal rates of pay predate industrialization; they were economic facts of life even before the American economy was dominated by cash. The fact that they continue to plague us today—despite the profound transformations that have occurred since the colonial period—suggests a deep structural cause. Something there is which has persisted through political and economic upheaval, through the cataclysm of industrialization, through inflation and depression, through war and peace—something which has led (or pushed, or pulled) women's work down a very different historical path from men's.

Speaking socially, that "something" is the nuclear family; speaking demographically, it is the household; speaking technologically, it is the house. Some scholars and feminists believe that in this scenario the true culprits are capitalism and patriarchy. Perhaps so, but currently the methods of the social sciences provide us with no way to know for sure. On the other hand, as a result of nearly two decades of work on the part of social historians, historical demographers, and architectural historians, we now know a good deal more about the history of the family, the household, and the house than we once did. And what we now know suggests that the family, the household, and the house have been proximate causes of both social change and social stability in such a way as to implicate them heavily in the history of women's work-force inequality.

Prior to industrialization—which for the United States means roughly prior to 1840—most Americans worked "at home," and most homes were rural; the word "housework," which distinguishes work done "at home" from work done in other places, was not even part of the language until the middle of the nineteenth century.[1] The fuel supplied to most of these preindustrial homes was wood; water had to be carried into the house from wells and streams; food was by and large abundant, but the diet lacked variety and most foodstuffs were prepared, from start to finish, by members of the household. Clothing, linens (such as they were), and many household utensils were made at home, at least in some form: not all households spun and wove, but most sewed; not all households stripped and tanned leather, but shoes were made and repaired by many; not all households made cider or beer or bread, but most ground their own meal (or carried it to mill to be ground). The maintenance and sustenance of a family under such conditions was, to put it mildly, labor-intensive.[2]

In such a family economy, men and women performed different work, as indeed they do in all civilizations of which we have record. But the fact that they performed different work (and possessed different skills) did not mean either that they worked at great distances from each other or that they did not work in tandem to achieve any given goal. Stereotypically, for example, men worked in leather (shoes, vests, gloves, hats) and women worked in cloth, but the task of outfitting a family required the work of both sexes. Men were responsible for most of the tasks connected with wood, which was, of course, a central commodity not only in the family economy but also in the market economy; they cut down trees, stripped bark, sawed lumber, chopped firewood, whittled bowls and spoons, built houses. Women, on the other hand, were responsible for most of the tasks connected with the growing, gathering, and preserving of fruits and vegetables; they planted gardens, weeded and watered them through the growing season, harvested the crop, prepared the part of the crop that was to be eaten fresh and preserved the other part (in sugar, vinegar, brine, or whatever) for later consumption. They also collected and preserved the seed that would be used the following year. Men reaped wheat, but women threshed it. Men husked corn and stripped it from the cob, then ground it or carried it to the mill to be ground. Women cooked it into grits or baked it into bread. Men distilled it into liquor. Cooking was women's work, but the goal of getting any given meal to the table required the work and skills of both men and women, for the hearth had to be supplied with wood (men's work), the pig had to be butchered (men's work), the water had to be carried (androgynous work, frequently assigned to children), and the grain had to be reduced to meal or flour (men's work) before the bacon could be fried or the bread could be baked or the soup could be stirred. The stereotypical tasks and the special skills of both men and women were required to maintain a household even at a minimal standard of comfort and decency; small wonder then, as the demographers and family historians have demonstrated, that so many widows and widowers quickly remarried after the death of a spouse.

Two features of this economy are worth noting. Both men and women produced goods that were intended for sale in the market economy. Some women spun and wove cloth that they sold to their neighbors; some raised chickens and sold eggs to town and city dwellers. Some men chopped wood for sale; other men made cider or repaired their neighbors' shoes. But the vast majority of goods that were sold in the larger economy (which was, in the case of the American colonies, the international economy) were the products either of male labor or of male management: furs, pig iron, ships' stores, tobacco, flour, biscuits, rum. Women may have participated in the production of these goods as employees (or as slaves), but they were not regarded as "female" goods because, in general, they were not produced or owned by females. Women were involved principally in that part of the market economy that could be called the "local" economy.

Second, women had principal responsibility for two aspects of household labor that were extraordinarily time-consuming and in which men rarely shared: the care of infants and small children and the care of the sick. Demographic data on these matters are difficult to come by, but the little that we do know suggests that until the middle of the nineteenth century the birth rate on these shores was quite high and the infant mortality rate quite low (by European standards), which meant that an average woman could expect to be burdened with the care of an infant or a toddler for most of her adult life after marriage. Older children (especially girls) were expected to assist in carrying this burden.[3]

If we have little data about fertility patterns, we have even less about illnesses. Historians of medicine have as yet told us very little about the nature of the diseases that were prevalent in this period, and the impact of these diseases on the work that was done in households is not easy to assess, since the primary sources on which such an assessment might be built are scarce. Yet we do know (from recipe books, diaries, and letters) that the ill were nursed at home and that women performed most of the nursing functions: sitting at bedsides, swabbing foreheads, handling bedpans, changing bandages, preparing medications, cooking easily digestible foods.[4] If we extrapolate from our memories of the nature and duration of even so-called minor diseases prior to the advent of antibiotics and vaccinations, we have reasonable grounds for guessing that in the seventeenth and eighteenth centuries the task of caring for the victims of measles, smallpox, scarlet fever, pneumonia, and diphtheria must have been difficult and time-consuming. Even a woman whose own household was entirely healthy was expected to assist in the households of neighbors and friends who had been felled by disease.

Thus, the discovery that men and children participated in the work of the household prior to industrialization should not lead us to conclude that women were thereby freed from laborious or burdensome labor. Where small children were abundant and diseases rampant, where corn meal had to be cooked for hours on end in pots that weighed ten or twenty pounds when empty, and where the acquisition of a new shirt meant two or three weeks of labor, a woman's work was truly never done, whether or not her husband assisted by butchering hogs and her children by carding wool.

Industrialization changed this pattern of domestic life in many ways, not the least of which was the introduction of new products that profoundly affected the allocation of labor in the family. Merchant milling, for example, expanded enormously in the decades prior to the Civil War, spurred on by the opening of the Erie Canal, the expansion of wheat growing in the "old" Northwest, and increasing European demand for American wheat during the Napoleonic Wars. This growth of merchant milling (as distinguished from local or grist milling) turned us from a nation of corn-eaters into a nation of wheat-eaters and introduced "store-bought" flour in households across the land. The textile mills of Rhode Island and Pennsylvania provided yard goods, and factories in New York and Massachusetts provided shoes. Technological and structural changes in the iron industry combined with the advent of the railroads to lower the price and increase the durability of iron goods, which meant that Americans began bricking up their fireplaces and purchasing cast-iron stoves. After the Civil War even more changes occurred. Factories in Chicago and St. Louis began butchering the meat that had once been butchered at home; other factories began producing biscuits and cereals, soups and pickles, canned fruits and vegetables. By the end of the century most men's clothing was being purchased "ready made" and so were most of the remedies that had once been the staple of the pantry and the hearth.

Prior to 1870 industrialization relieved the burden of men's domestic labor considerably, but it had very little impact on the work of adult women. The growth of merchant milling meant that men no longer had to husk corn or grind it or take it to the mill to be ground, but women continued to bake and to cook. The introduction of factory-made shoes meant that men no longer had to make and maintain footwear for the family, but women continued to sew. The introduction of the stove markedly reduced the amount of wood that was required for heating and cooking, and therefore the amount of male labor that was required to keep a family comfortable; the introduction of coal reduced that labor still further. Factory-made textiles made women's work somewhat easier, but the baking and the cooking, the nursing and the tending, the cleaning and the laundering, still had not gone away—and the laundering, at least, was made *more* burdensome by the fact that factory-made cloth was washable, which its homespun predecessors had not been. In the earliest phases of industrialization, then, the someones who had previously chopped wood and ground the meal and spun the thread were no longer needed at home, but the someones who baked and cooked and washed and cleaned could not be spared without seriously threatening the health and the standard of living of the family.

The appearance of more and more products on the market (coal and gas, forks and spoons, brooms and brushes, mattresses and pillows, rugs and drapes) meant that more and more factories and offices were being built across the land, creating a demand for people who were willing to trade their labor for cash. At the same time, households were in need of more cash with which to make purchases. Fathers could be spared for these purposes because there were substitutes for the wood that they had once chopped; boys could be spared because there were now other ways of providing the grain that they had once ground; grown daughters could be spared because the spinning wheel had been put aside—but wives and mothers could not be spared (except in cases of extreme poverty) because there was still no substitute for the skills that only they possessed.

Not surprisingly a new ideology developed in the first decades of industrialization to rationalize the new familial relationships that were developing as a result of the divergence between men's and women's labor. This ideology historians have recently named the doctrine of separate spheres.[5] Woman's place was in the home; man's was in the world. Women were to be nurturant, religious, self-abnegating, demure—the better to fit themselves for their restricted but critically important domestic roles; men were to be strict, aggressive, calculating, realistic, expansive, bold—the better to fit themselves for the market. In the market it was dog-eat-dog, but home was where the heart was, a retreat to which the wounded could retire in order to refresh themselves for the battle that would begin the next day:

When our husbands and our sons go forth into the busy and turbulent world, we may feel secure that they will walk unhurt amid its snares and temptations. Their hearts will be at home, where their treasure is; and they will rejoice to return to its sanctuary of rest, there to refresh their wearied spirits, and revive their strength for the toils and conflicts of live. . . . If man's duties lie abroad, women's duties are within the quiet seclusion of home. It is in her home that a woman's strength lies; it is here that the gentle influence, which is the secret of her might, is most successfully employed; and this she loses as soon as she descends from her calm height into the world's arena.[6]

With both technology and ideology cooperating, it was scarcely surprising that married women were not usually tempted into the workplace, did not usually descend "into the world's arena," except under extreme duress. During the early years of industrialization, married women did not view themselves as likely candidates for employment, or as persons who were likely to be employed for long periods. Single women entered the work force (to tend machines in the textile mills, to tend customers in the department stores, to tend typewriters in offices) when their wages were needed to supplement the family economy, but they could reasonably expect (or at least hope) to leave it as soon as they were married, as soon as they too became the female adult head of a household. Contrarily, as industrialization proceeded apace, many men and boys found their social legitimation in the regularity of their market work and the size of their paychecks; for them the state of matrimony meant increased pressure to sustain work-force participation, since upon marriage they became (at least in theory) the sole producers of the family wage.

This situation handicapped women who were (for whatever reasons) actually employed in the labor force or who needed such employment. First, it positively discouraged them from undertaking work that had been stereotypically defined as male, for the ideology of separate spheres asserted that certain forms of work were ideally suited to members of each sex; even the *desire* to become a physician or a coal miner or a typesetter became proof positive of sexual deviancy and thus a desire that most women were unlikely to express. Second, women who expected to become full-time housewives had precious little reason to strive, when young, for the advanced training that would lead to labor-force mobility, and their parents had precious little reason to provide it. Since the chances were good that a woman would neither desire nor be rewarded with such mobility (witness what happened to the women who graduated with degrees in the sciences between 1880 and 1920), and that such mobility would preclude marriage and children, advanced training, in any form, was seen not only as a waste of time, but as a positive disability for a woman.[7] And finally, seeing themselves as only transient participants in the labor force (and as supplemental workers when they worked) there was little reason for women to engage in the kinds of militant activities that produced better paychecks and better working conditions for their male contemporaries. Simultaneously, there were many reasons for their male contemporaries to keep them out of labor unions, for working men apparently viewed women (even their own daughters and wives) as competitors for some other man's "family wage" or, worse yet, as strike-breakers, which women occasionally were.[8]

The net result of this complex of factors was that industrialization, at least in its earliest phases, did not provide any mechanism by which women could break out of the employment mode that had been set for them in preindustrial times: they continued to work for less when they worked, and they continued to occupy segregated places in the work force. The fact that they were willing to work for less was precisely why many employers hired them, and why other employers invested in new machinery that made it possible to switch from a male to a female labor force, as happened, for example, in cigar making and clerical work.[9] The entry of women into a field of work and the consequent lowering of wages were in fact sufficient to drive men out of that field within a generation or two—which is precisely what happened in teaching. [10]

Women were unreliable employees. Whether they were single or married, turnover rates were high. If they were single, they left the work force when they married. If they were married, they left the work force when their husbands returned to work, or when someone in the family became desperately ill, or when one or two of the children were earning enough to make mother's wage no longer necessary. As long as a family's standard of living depended upon the presence of someone "at home," every effort would be made to return that someone to the home whenever possible.

Even at the close of the first stage of industrialization (roughly the 1920s), a family's standard of living did indeed depend very much on the presence of some adult at home. Technological systems within the household had not yet produced effective substitutes for women's skills. Not surprisingly, then, as the nineteenth century turned into the twentieth, the dominant family form, for most Americans, was one in which a male traded his labor for cash (since he could be spared from the home and was likely to earn higher wages) and a female did the work that was necessary to turn that cash into the maintenance and the sustenance—the standard of living—of the family. [11] In such a technological and social system, the employment of married women and mothers was indeed a threat to families' standard of living, because the work that women did at home was essential work for which there were virtually no substitutes, and because men did not possess the skills to do it well. As long as this situation persisted, neither adult women nor girls had any particular reason to strive for anything other than low-skilled, low-paying, temporary and easily renounceable employment.

Were we to listen to social pundits and advertising copywriters, we would have every reason to believe that this situation changed markedly after 1920 and even more markedly after 1945, partly because the technologies (running hot and cold water, central heating, indoor plumbing, gas and electrical appliances, antibiotics, hospitals) either created substitutes for women's labor or made that labor unnecessary, and partly because the development of the "postindustrial" or "service" economy created expanded job opportunities in precisely those fields that had always been stereotypically assigned to females. Unfortunately, the persistence of both unequal pay and employment segregation suggests that the pundits and the copywriters are in some subtle way mistaken and that the cement in which our houses are built, our marriages are consummated, and our children are socialized resists the corrosive effects of attractive labor markets, persuasive political movements, and even apparently potent legislation.

Women continue to do housework today, lots of it—roughly thirty-five hours per week if they are employed full-time, fifty-five hours if they are not.

They do so because the modern technological systems in our households have neither created substitutes for women's labor nor made it unnecessary.[12] When the managers of electric utility companies and the creators of housing developments and the inventors of gas cooking stoves came to manage, create, and invent, they imagined (and rightly so) that the unit they were serving would be an individual household containing one nuclear family, itself managed and serviced by a woman who would (like their own wives and daughters) be "home" most of the time. Hot and cold running water, gas pipes, and telephone lines could have been run into communal households just as easily as they were in fact run into the individual households that now dominate the landscape (indeed, more easily)—but no one believed that Americans would want to live in communal households, and they were probably right. The same socio-technological organization that was capable of manufacturing small household washing machines or small household refrigerators could have manufactured large communal washing machines and refrigerators, capable of handling the wash and the perishable foods for a whole neighborhood instead of just one family—and, indeed, such washing machines and refrigerators *were* manufactured, but they were intended to be sold to "commercial" rather than "communal" establishments. Having started out as a nation of independent householders, Americans continued down the same road in the twentieth century, and built, as time went on, an infrastructure that is at once so complex (involving, for example, banks, post offices, and schools), so rooted in tradition, and so firmly cast in concrete, brass, copper, electric grids, and (soon) modems that nothing short of a nuclear holocaust is likely to dislodge it. This infrastructure assumes the existence of individual households and of individuals who will be available to answer those telephones, operate those washing machines, stock those refrigerators, and receive information from those modems. Needless to say, an infrastructure that is built on the assumption that people will behave in a certain fashion is likely to trap people into fulfilling its unspoken assumptions—a self-fulfilling technological prophecy in which (like the sorcerer's apprentice) the controller is subtly turned into the controlled.

What gas and electricity wrought in the twentieth century, the automobile solidified. The automobile created a task—transportation—that had only rarely accrued to households in the past. Before the advent of the automobile, transporting goods to the locale of the people who were to consume them had been the task either of the retailer (hence there were milkmen and baker's wagons, delivery boys, and peddlers) or—if the task had devolved upon the household—of men, for when wagons were horse-drawn, men were stereotypically assigned to drive them. The automobile brought with it the woman driver and the suburbs. The peddler disappeared and so did the milkman, replaced by the supermarket—and the women who drove there to shop. Men stopped walking to their offices and began patronizing the commuter railways—and women drove them there in "station wagons." Children stopped walking to school—and women started driving them there (as well as to friends' houses, football games, and music lessons). Doctors stopped making house calls—and ambulatory (a neat euphemism, that) patients were driven to their offices by women. Indeed, if an eighteenth- or nineteenth-century housewife was most likely to be found before the open hearth or cast-iron stove, her twentieth-century descendant is most likely to be inside an automobile.

And despite a good deal of hullabaloo in the press and some anecdotal evidence to the contrary, most of the hours spent in housework today are spent by women. Scattered across the land there may be an occasional "househusband" who has decided to stay home while his wife goes out to work (although usually he is a freelance writer, keeping a diary of his experiences for subsequent publication) or a helpful spouse who accompanies his working wife to the supermarket or volunteers to diaper the baby on weekends, but if national time studies as well as intensive sociological investigations are to be believed, women still do the bulk of the work at home—and still carry the bulk of the responsibility for organizing and managing it. [13] No one who has ever studied men's share of housework has ever estimated it at anything higher than one and a half hours a day, and then only when such chores as mowing the lawn and repairing household fixtures are included. Men whose wives are employed spend about ten more minutes a week on housework than men whose wives "stay home," and men who have small children add yet another ten—a grand total, for these particularly helpful and particularly stressed husbands, of eleven hours a week, compared with the forty or fifty (for women with small children) that their wives are putting in. The laundering, cleaning, cooking, feeding, clothing, bathing, shopping, and transporting that make up the bulk of the housework day are still being done by women—and, it seems, this is as true for young, cohabiting "career-minded" couples as it is for their staid, middle-aged counterparts in the suburbs. On top of this there is recent (and hardly surprising) evidence that pressure to "share" the housework is, if not a precipitating cause, then at least a contributing cause, of much marital tension. [14] Men simply do not want to do housework, and they have been extremely successful in avoiding it.

Thus, despite all the technological changes that have occurred inside our houses, the fundamental allocation of work within twentieth-century households remains similar to what it was in the nineteenth. Housework has become only incompletely industrialized, even with integrated circuits in our dishwashers and computer terminals in our dens. Most of the people who do housework still do not get paid for it, despite the fact that for many of them it is a full-time, or almost full-time, job. They do not have job descriptions or time clocks or contractual arrangements; indeed, they cannot fairly be said even to have employers. Over the years market labor has become increasingly specialized, and the division of labor has become increasingly more minute; but housework has not been affected by this process. The housewife is the last Jane-of-all-trades in a world from which the Jacks-of-all-trades have more or less disappeared; she is expected to perform work that ranges from the most menial physical labor (swabbing floors) to the most abstract of mental manipulations (deciding how to discipline an errant teenager)—and to do it all without specialized training.

Knowing that housework is likely to be the fate of most females (even if they combine housework in equal parts with market work), most parents and most educators have believed, until very recently, that girls require somewhat different socialization from boys. The president of a woman's college once optimistically predicted that

as women begin to make their distinctive wishes felt in curricular terms, not merely will every women's college and coeducational institution offer a firm nuclear course in the Family, but from it will radiate curricular series dealing with food and nutrition, textiles and clothing, health and nursing. . . . Why not study the theory and preparation of a Basque paella, of a well-marinated shish kebob . . . . Would it be impossible to present a beginning course in foods as exciting and difficult to work up after college as a course in post-Kantian philosophy would be?[15]

We may not all agree, but probably far too many of us would have to agree that it is still the case, as two students of developmental psychology asserted in the 1950s, that

the identity issue for the boy is primarily an occupational-vocational question, while self-definition for the girl depends more directly on marriage. . . . The girl's identity centers more exclusively on her sex-role [shades of separate spheres!]—whose wife will I be, what kind of family will we have; while the boy's self-definition forms about two nuclei; he will be a husband and father (his sex-role identity) but he will also and centrally be a worker.[16]

Lacking that central sense of themselves as workers, and trained from infancy to acquire the personality characteristics that will adapt them to the unspecialized and nurturant work-role "housewife," many (perhaps most) currently employed women do not possess the skills that are required to sustain long-term success in the work force. It is probably too soon to tell what the generation of female workers who have benefited from the rebirth of feminism will be like, because most of them are still in school. But vast quantities of recent literature on the attitudes and behavior of women who are currently in the work force suggests that like their nineteenth- and early twentieth-century predecessors, they still see themselves as both transient and supplemental workers, likely to leave employment when they marry (or, now, when they have children), or when the college tuition loans have been repaid. Women workers today are far more willing than their male colleagues to change jobs if their spouses are transferred or to give up employment if a relative needs nursing care. Women are also more likely to stay home from work if one of the children is sick, or the rugs are due to be cleaned—and they tend not to take on work that will interfere with their children's school vacation, or will require that they stay late in the office, or will need to be brought home on weekends. Many feminists will deny that this is true, but many employers, of course, either suspect it or know it to their sorrow—especially if the equal employment opportunity gun is being pointed at their heads. [17]

What twentieth-century household technologies *have* made possible is a marked improvement in the standard of living that can be obtained for a given number of hours spent in housework. A woman doing her wash in 1910 might spend eight or nine hours out of her week on the enterprise, and for her pains get eight or nine pounds of clean laundry (dry pounds, that is!), but if her grandaughter with a Bendix (or its descendants) puts in the same number of hours (carrying, folding, sorting, ironing), she and the members of her household will be able to change their underwear and outer clothing every single day, their sheets and towels every week—luxuries that in times past were permitted only to the rich (who employed laundresses). Similarly, the kind of cleaning that might have been accomplished in a week of work eighty years ago can be finished in a day at present, thanks to vacuum cleaners, electric brooms, floor waxers, and rug shampooers. Our houses are at once larger and cleaner (*markedly* cleaner) than the ones in which most of our parents and grandparents resided, our diet more varied, our meals served with more pomp, and our clothing changed more frequently and discarded more casually. This is a standard of living that intellectuals, energy-conservers, and rebellious teenagers are wont to denigrate, but apparently also one that most Americans (including a goodly number of intellectuals, energy-conservers, and rebellious teenagers) are unwilling to forsake.

What we have discovered since the end of World War II is that for the first time in our history, married women and mothers can manage full-time employment without forsaking or even threatening that standard of living. What the vacuum cleaner, the microwave oven, and the telephone have given women is the ability to maintain a middle-class standard of living on thirty-five hours' work a week, squeezed in (usually) on weekends, evenings, lunch hours, and an occasional day off from work. Modern technologies have not eliminated housework, but they have sufficiently eased the physical burden that housework can be combined with labor-force participation so as to maintain an appropriate level of comfort and decency, if rather inappropriate levels of exhaustion.

But the price that women continue to pay for their devotion to this standard of living (in addition to their exhaustion) is an unequal and segregated work force. A few imaginary scenarios can clarify how the demands of modern housework and the pattern of socialization that trains women to meet those demands lead inexorably to gender inequality in the labor force. Imagine a stereotypic couple who graduate from high school, go to work, marry, have children, and buy a house. Most likely the house is convenient to his place of work because he earned more than she did and she, in any event, stopped working for a few years when the children came. But then the children grew up, or her husband left, or his plant closed, and she had to find a job. In her immediate vicinity there turned out to be few opportunities for employment in the field in which she was trained, so she starts again at something else, but starts at the bottom, and her lifetime earnings will never catch up with his. Or suppose that she does find something in her line of work, and then a promotion looms, but with it comes a transfer, and the transfer means that they will have to move (which is impossible without terminating *his* employment), or she will have to commute (which means that he will have to fix dinner) or she will have more demanding responsibilities. So she forgoes the promotion and remains stationary on a career ladder along which her male contemporaries are advancing. Or suppose that they meet in graduate school and decide that neither will stop working when the babies come; so they hire a servant (or rather several servants, since the turnover rate is high), but he feels free to travel to sales conferences across the continent or to professional meetings in Europe, or to stay in his laboratory until all hours of the night, or to attend breakfast meetings—and she does not. Shortly she will decide to take a less demanding or less prestigious job than he, so that one of them will be free to prevent the centrifugal disintegration of their family; and before they know it, her career history has diverged considerably from his.

Each one of these scenarios, or something like it, is being played out in households across the land every day. Household technologies have developed in a pattern very different from market technologies, and housework has, consequently, developed a labor process that is very different from market work. Women have been assigned principal responsibility for this labor process since the earliest stages of industrialization, and consequently they have been socialized very differently from men. Had our households been communalized, for example, had housework been industrialized in exactly the same manner that market work was, then our housewives would not be trained to anticipate work that is essentially feudal—without paychecks and time clocks, without supervisors and job descriptions, without specialization and managerial control. If the care of the young and the ill had not been stereotypically assigned to women two hundred years ago, then we might have developed a socio-technical system that contained individual smithies in every backyard and communal kitchens in every neighborhood, or allowed for the manufacture of custom-made shoes in every kitchen and the laundering of all clothing by commercial agencies. Had we developed such a system, then we might see more equality in the labor force, since men as well as women would be at pains to ''get home,'' and both would be responsible for the essential work that converts wages into sustenance. Thus, the fact that housework and household technologies developed in the unique way that they did becomes the single most salient fact in explaining not only why unequal pay and sexual segregation persist in the labor force, but also why women continue to have so much difficulty defining themselves as workers in the same sense as men.

Notes

1. See the entry for ''housework'' in *A Supplement to the Oxford English Dictionary* (Oxford: Oxford University Press, 1976).

2. This sketch is derived from Mary Beth Norton, *Liberty's Daughters: The Revolutionary Experience of American Women, 1750–1800* (Boston: Little, Brown, 1980); Catherine Clinton, *The Plantation Mistress: Woman's World in the Old South* (New York: Pantheon, 1982); Laurel Thatcher Ulrich, *Goodwives: Images and Reality in the Lives of Women in Northern New England, 1650–1750* (New York: Knopf, 1982); Susan Strasser, *Never Done: A History of American Housework* (New York: Pantheon, 1982); and Ruth Schwartz Cowan, *More Work for Mother: The Ironies of Household Technology from the Open Hearth to the Microwave* (New York: Basic Books, 1983).

3. On birth rates see tables in Norton, *Liberty's Daughters,* and Clinton, *Plantation Mistress.* See also Daniel Scott Smith, ''The Demographic History of Colonial New England,'' in Michael Gordon (ed.), *The American Family in Social Historical Perspective* (New York: St. Martin's, 1973), pp. 397–415.

4. Gunter B. Risse, Ronald Numbers, and Judith Walzer Leavitt, *Medicine Without Doctors: Home Health Care in American History* (New York: Science History Publications, 1977).

5. Much has been written on the doctrine of separate spheres. For an introduction see Barbara Welter, ''The Cult of True Womanhood, 1820–1860,'' *American Quarterly* 17 (1966): 151–74, and Kathryn Kish Sklar, *Catherine Beecher: A Study in American Domesticity* (New Haven: Yale University Press, 1973).

6. Mrs. A. J. Gross, *Woman in America, Being an Examination Into the Moral and Intellectual Condition of American Female Society* (New York: Harper & Bros., 1841), as cited in Nancy Cott (ed.), *Roots of Bitterness: Documents in the Social History of American Women* (New York: Dutton, 1972), pp. 146–47.

7. Margaret Rossiter, *American Women Scientists: Struggles and Strategies to 1940* (Baltimore: Johns Hopkins University Press, 1982), and Roberta Frankfort, *Collegiate Women: Domesticity and Career in Turn-of-the Century America* (New York: New York University Press, 1977).

8. Alice Kessler-Harris, *Out to Work: A History of Wage Earning Women in the United States* (New York: Oxford University Press, 1982).

9. On cigar workers, see Edith Abbott, *Women in Industry: A Study in American Economic History* (New York: Appleton, 1910). On clerical workers, Margery W.

Davies, *A Woman's Place Is at the Typewriter: Office Work and Office Workers, 1870–1930* (Philadelphia: Temple University Press, 1982).

10. On teaching, Redding S. Sugg, *Motherteacher: The Feminization of American Education* (Charlottesville: University of Virginia Press, 1978).

11. This insight is drawn from the Marxist literature on women and the family. For an introduction see Bonnie Fox (ed.), *Hidden in the Household: Women's Domestic Labor Under Capitalism* (Ontario: Women's Press, 1980).

12. Joann Vanek, "Keeping Busy: Time Spent in Housework, United States, 1920–1970" (Ph.D. dissertation, University of Michigan, 1973); Kathryn Walker and Margaret Woods, *Time Use: A Measure of Household Production of Family Goods and Services* (Washington, D.C.: American Home Economics Association, 1976); Richard Berk and Sarah Fenstermaker Berk, *Labor and Leisure at Home: Content and Organization of the Household Day* (Beverly Hills, Calif.: Sage 1979); Cowan, *More Work for Mother,* chap. 7.

13. On men's share of housework, see Berk and Berk, *Labor and Leisure at Home:* William R. Beer, *Househusbands: Men and Housework in American Families* (New York: Praeger, 1983); Kathryn Walker, "Time Spent by Husbands in Household Work," *Family Economics Review* (June 1970): 8–11.

14. Philip Blumstein and Pepper Schwartz, *American Couples: Money, Work and Sex* (New York: Simon and Schuster, 1983), pp. 146–50.

15. Lynn White, *Educating Our Daughters: A Challenge to the Colleges* (New York: Harper, 1952), pp. 77–78.

16. Elizabeth Douvan and Carol Kaye, "Motivational Factors in College Entrance," in Nevitt Sanford (ed.), *The American College: A Psychological and Sociological Interpretation of the Higher Learning* (New York: John Wiley, 1962), p. 203.

17. For a survey of recent literature on women's work-force participation, see Mari anne A. Ferber, "Women and Work. Issues of the 1980's," *Signs* 8 (1982). 273–87.

7

Doing Housework:
Feeding and Family Life

MARJORIE L. DEVAULT

As recently as the turn of the century, housework was arduous and time-consuming. It required specialized skills—baking, canning, sewing, managing a wood stove—and a great deal of physical work (Strasser 1982). Now household tasks are physically easier, take less time, require fewer specialized skills, and can more easily be divided and accommodated to other activities. In spite of such changes, however, housework has not disappeared. In order to maintain small, nuclear family households, someone in each home must do the coordinative work that makes it possible for the individuals there to survive within a market economy. This coordinative work includes both the physical work of maintenance and also the work of "making meaningful patterns" of everyday life.[1] As the technical character of housework has changed, with more and more productive work (food processing, for instance) shifting to the market, the activity left in the household is increasingly the work of producing a social order, which has been largely invisible and therefore unlabeled. It has been easy to assume that there is little work left to do in modern homes, and we are often puzzled as we struggle to get it done.

Most studies of housework have been based on common-sense definitions of the work. Oakley (1974:49), for example, identified the "six core tasks" of housework as "cleaning, shopping, cooking, washing up, washing and ironing," and Berheide et al. (1976) studied "tasks" such as "meal preparation," "laundry," and "sewing/mending." Researchers have been guided by theoretical frameworks based on the organization of paid work. Economists, for example, have been concerned with establishing the time spent on housework, its value, and the determinants of resource allocations to the work (for a review, see Ferber 1982); sociologists have concentrated on issues such as the division of household labor, working conditions, and the work satisfaction of housewives (e.g., Berheide et al. 1976; Berk and Berk 1979; Oakley 1974). This kind of research has effectively called attention to previous neglect of household work. The significance attached to paid work—both in theory and in everyday life—has given force to the image of "housework as work." Ultimately, however, housework is not paid work, but a kind of "family work" organized quite differently. The translation of the activities of housework into the vocabulary of a paid job—to constitute "products" and "standards," for instance—has often resulted in limited definitions of housework and analyses confined to its most obvious, mechanical parts.

I will argue here that common-sense definitions leave out important parts of housework. I will report on a study based on intensive interviewing in thirty urban U.S. households,[2] in which I began with the accounts of those who do housework and used their own words to uncover and analyze the full range of their efforts.[3] Through close examination of the activities involved in feeding a family, I will show that beyond the material work necessary for physical maintenance, feeding involves connecting household members with the larger society and the day-to-day production of the kind of group life we know as "family."

"Work" or "Love"?

The apparently routine work that supports a household is complex and more meaningful than is typically acknowledged. We begin to see its significance in the language of those who do this work. As I talked with women (and some men)[4] about feeding their families, they often had trouble finding words to explain their experience. They talked about feeding as something other than work in the conventional sense, trying to explain how their activities are embedded in family relations. Some, for example, talked of this work in terms of family ties. They described feeding as part of being a parent: "I feel like, you know, when I decided to have children it was a commitment, and raising them includes feeding them." Or as part of being a wife: "I like to cook for him. That's what a wife is for, right?"

Women certainly recognize that feeding requires time, effort, and skill. But it is different somehow from paid work. One young mother who had quit her job as a social worker to stay home and take care of her children explained:

If you think of it as a job, you're not going to like it. I mean, believe me, I don't want to do this for the rest of my life. I mean, I worked before, and I enjoy working, but right now, this is something different for me.

Even though they recognize their effort, women have trouble equating their care for family members with paid employment; they describe their activity as "something different" from work.

These perceptions of housework as "not work" are reinforced by the fact that its results are somehow spoiled if it is thought of in purely instrumental terms. This effect was evident in the way that one woman talked about her mother's practices. By emphasizing the work involved in meal preparation, her mother had introduced an unpleasant "tone" into their meal:

We had Sunday dinner at noon. Her purpose of serving it then was, quote unquote, so I can relax the rest of the day, and it kind of put that moral obligation tone on it. You know, well, now that's over with. And my mother-in-law does the same thing. She'll cook a meal and then sit down and say, "Well, now that's over with." Which makes you feel like you've really imposed on her time.

By contrast, this woman explained that for her, cooking is "a way of saying I love you." Another woman, who also talked about cooking as an expression of love for family members, explained:

In preparing food—you know, there's a lot of work that goes into preparing food. Therefore, for one to commit himself to the work, that's love, that's shared with those people that the food was being prepared for. I think love has a lot to do with it.

Her comment, even though it labels feeding as "love," also reveals that it is not fully described as either "love" or "work" alone. She sees her activity in terms of love precisely because "there's a lot of work that goes into preparing food."

Vocabularies of work come from the model of paid employment; there are few words with which to express the kind of effort that so many women put into their family lives. Since they have no vocabulary for their own activity, these women talk of their work at home in terms of "love." Their talk suggests that we must look beyond the theoretical categories associated with paid employment if we are to understand the full character and significance of the work they do.

Family Meals

Changes in the organization of work and home have changed typical patterns of family meals. Even a few generations ago, when more households were involved in production as well as consumption, and when work was usually closer to home, families were more likely to eat together three times daily. They had little choice because there were few other places to be fed. Now family members who work for a wage often leave home early and work far away. They may do shift work that takes them from home at different times. Many children are at school or day care all day. In addition, cooking has become less and less necessary. Many technical skills have been marketized:

new products incorporate much of the work of food processing formerly done at home, and the growth of the restaurant trade and the tremendous expansion of fast-food franchising provide new options for purchasing meals. People are no longer forced to return to a household to be fed, so that family meals become less necessary and more a volitional social form.

Typically, in contemporary households, work and school schedules cut into meal times so that very few families eat even two meals together each day. Breakfast and lunch, especially, barely survive. In the households I studied, men and women who work outside their homes eat breakfast quickly, often before the rest of the household awakens. Some purchase something to eat at work. Even when all of the family is awake, the pressure of various schedules makes an elaborate meal unlikely. In almost half the households I studied, children are fed alone in the morning while parents are busy with other work.

At lunchtime almost a third of these households are empty; in several others, only the housewife is home. Even when women are home with children and prepare lunch, the meal is an attenuated ritual. In some households women sit down to eat with their children, but in an equal number they feed the children alone and either skip lunch or eat later by themselves.

Dinner is more consistently arranged as a well defined meal, but it too can be disrupted by the scheduling of outside activities. One man leaves the house for his night shift at 6:30, less than an hour after his wife returns from her secretarial job. Another, a professional worker, arrives home late in the evening, just as his children are going to bed. Evening activities—going to school or the gym, bowling or playing pool, working in church or community groups—may mean that men or women and their children miss dinner several times a week.

In the context of such changes, bringing a family together for any kind of regular meal requires a new kind of effort. Still, the parents I interviewed were concerned about establishing patterns of regular meals. They talked of strategizing about routines, and their comments revealed the importance of the concept "meal" as an organizer of family life. For example, the mother of an infant talked of pulling her high chair up to the dinner table so they could eat "as a family," and a single working mother explained that she has continued to cook every evening for her teenage daughter so as to provide "a dinner made by her mother." In addition, people arrange meals to mark the rhythms of family life, with regular dinners for extended family or "special" Sunday dinners designed "to enrich our family life."[5]

Meals do more than provide sustenance; they are also social events that bring family members together. Such rituals have been recognized as critical to the internal life of families, since they serve as a basis for establishing and maintaining family culture and creating a mutual recognition of the family as a group (Bossard and Boll 1950). Producing meals, then, has increasingly become work aimed at maintaining the kind of group life we think of as constituting a family.

Producing Meals

The work of feeding a family goes on and on; food must be provided again and again, every day. But the repetitiveness of the work can be deceiving. Far from a purely mechanical task, producing meals requires coordination and interpersonal work as well as the concrete activities of preparation. When I interviewed people about feeding, I wanted to elicit detailed reports that would display both aspects of the work and go beyond my respondents' conventional assumptions about their own work (for example, the common claim "I don't really do much housework"). I therefore asked for very specific accounts of the mundane business of producing everyday meals. Respondents sometimes stopped in mid-sentence to ask, "Is this really what you want to know?" as if surprised that these everyday activities could be a topic for research. I have used these detailed accounts to analyze parts of the work of feeding that are often ignored, not only by researchers but also by those who do housework. Planning and managing meals are examples of these invisible work activities.

PLANNING MEALS

I'll spend time in the morning thinking about what in the heck I'm going to fix.

Some women talk of planning meals as "enjoyable"; for others it is "a hassle." In any case, planning "what to put on the table" is an essential part of the work of feeding, and conceiving of a meal requires sensitivity to a variety of concerns.

The food provided for a family cannot be just any food, but must be food that will satisfy them. Family members may not eat if they do not like what is served, so women often restrict their planning to items that have been successful in the past. When I asked about typical dinners, most women responded by telling me about their families' likes and dislikes. For example:

Like for meats, let's see—he likes so many. Well, he doesn't like pork chops.

Let's see—well, beans are good. But my children aren't much on eating beans.

Responding to these individual preferences is not a personal favor, but a requirement of the work.

Mothers are often especially concerned that children eat the foods they need and work at devising menus that are both appropriate and appealing. Some cook special foods for their children in addition to the family's regular meal or invent techniques for encouraging children to eat, like the woman who "disguises" her daughter's meat in mashed potatoes and cuts cheese into amusing shapes.

The work of planning is rarely shared by those who only eat. In order to please family members, women must work at learning their husbands' and children's tastes. Children will sometimes respond if given a choice of foods, but husbands are typically more cryptic. Many women complained that they could not just ask their husbands what they wanted: "I'll call at the office and ask, 'Is there anything special you'd like for dinner?' And his standard answer is, 'Yes, something good.' " Women learn what their husbands like "just living with somebody," through "trial and error." They notice what gets eaten and what does not and which meals are special favorites. The active character of this learning process can be seen in one woman's comments: she explained that as a new bride she had not known what to cook for her husband, so she "started looking for things that he liked better."

When they plan meals, then, women respond to their husbands' and children's tastes. However, husbands' and children's tastes are often different, so that part of the planning must involve weighing and balancing people's contradictory desires. Again, some solve this problem by doing double cooking. Others make the balance a factor in their longer-range choices. For example:

If we've had a particularly good meal one night, and everyone enjoyed it, and everyone ate heartily, and they've eaten well, the next day I might make something that I know everyone—other than Richard and I—they're just not going to give a lick about. And I will try to have something else on the table, that they're going to—not another entree—but a vegetable that they like, or cheese, or something that will fill them up.

Planning means making sure that everyone gets "something that will fill them up."

Those who cook must consider their own tastes as well. However, in contrast to their responsiveness to the tastes of others, most women were scrupulously careful not to give their own preferences any special weight. One spoke of her care not to be "prejudiced one way or the other," and another explained, "One of us has to compromise, and it's going to end up being me."

In addition to pleasing individual family members, meals must be culturally appropriate. Anthropologists tell us that in any society food items become part of a cultural code, expressing the structure of social relations both within a household group and between household members and outsiders

(Douglas 1972). These cultural rules become part of the process of planning meals. Though not conscious of using food as a code, people talked about the essential elements in their meals (a meat entree, for example, or beans and tortillas), and the kinds of combinations of elements that make up proper meals. They spoke of rules for the combinations they can make. For example: "We Mexicans usually have rice with pork. And if you have steak, we would have, like, any kind of soup, with broth."

The importance of such categories can been seen in the fact that people referred to them as a sort of standard even when they described meals that deviated from the form that was typical for them. For example, this woman's description of a somewhat unusual dinner shows how she thinks of the meal as a set of "slots" to be filled:

Richard had been out for a business lunch, so I knew he wasn't going to be real hungry, and I'm on another diet, so I wasn't going to be eating the regular meal, so I didn't make, like, that slot that holds potatoes or noodles or something like that.

Family members respond to meals in terms of such patterns, insisting on "meat and potatoes," or rice with every meal. Some women reported that they were trying to change their families' ideas about meals—to encourage them to eat less meat or more vegetables, for instance. But they could only succeed if they were sensitive to household members' own ideas about what a meal should be. One woman reported that when she served a quiche, her husband told her, yes, it was very good, but he didn't want "breakfast for dinner."

And even though others respond to cultural patterns, those who are served are undoubtedly not as conscious of these codes as the women who actually work at designing meals. A man who had just begun to cook for his family explained some of the requirements of planning meals, and his problem: "There has to be a vegetable. And not two starches. The trouble is, I don't know what a starch is, I can't remember what a starch is, so sometimes I end up with two starches, sometimes I don't."

Beyond pleasing family members, and designing meals so that they conform to a cultural pattern, those who cook aim at making meals varied and interesting. Variety is more important in some households than in others, and it means different things in different households, but some notion of variety seems fundamental to meal planning. The women I interviewed reported that they decided to serve a particular meal because "we hadn't had it for a while," or "it was time to have fish again."

Concern with varied menus comes partly from contemporary U.S. health discourse, which links variety and nutrition. Food producers and nutritional scientists have promoted the idea that "all food is good food" and that the safest and healthiest diet is a varied one. Many people summarized "good eating habits'' with formulas like ''keep the variety up, and keep the sweets to a minimum.'' However, women also talked of variety as a part of their craft, important to producing meals that are not just adequate but interesting as well. Many expressed concern about ''getting into a rut'': they reported that it was ''boring'' to cook the same things, and that they talk with friends about ideas for different meals: ''Like, oh gosh, what am I going to do with the potato? There's only so many things you can do with it.''

Making these choices about meals is like solving a puzzle. There are special requirements stemming from individuals' tastes and preferences, and relationships within the household. There is a definite form to the problem, arising from shared cultural conventions. But variety is also important, so that the puzzle must be solved in relatively novel ways each day. The intersection of these different, sometimes contradictory concerns means that planning requires continual monitoring and adjustment. Planning is based on the overall form of each meal and also the way in which it fits into a pattern of surrounding meals. By solving this puzzle each day, the person who cooks for a family is continually creating one part of the reality of household life.

MANAGING MEALS

The details of meal patterns the times and places that families typically eat, the formal and informal rules that govern their behavior, and the kinds of interaction that are part of the meal—vary from one household to another. To some extent people's thoughts about meals reflect idealized versions of family life. One woman described her family's typical hurried breakfast and explained apologetically, ''It's not a Walton family breakfast, by any means.'' But even though actual events fall short of such ideals, people work at making their meals particular kinds of events. Those I interviewed reported that they tried to make meal time ''a calm time,'' ''a very social thing,'' or ''an important getting-together time.'' Such goals can only be accomplished through attention to the meal and efforts to orchestrate the event.

Talk is considered an important part of most family's meals, and is something that people work at. For example: ''At dinner we usually talk about the kind of day that Mark and I had. You know, you try to relate what cute thing, cute and wonderful thing the child did, and things of that nature. We try to talk during dinner.'' Sometimes, these norms are even more explicit: ''My son will sometimes be very grumpy and grouchy, because 'the whole day went wrong,' and he's told that that's simply not an excuse for not talking.'' One mother with five children, worried that they did not all have a chance to participate in the dinner talk, had tried to get each child to read a news item each day and report on it at the table. The system did not work, but it reveals this mother's attention to her family's meal-time conversation.

Children's behavior at the table must also be monitored and controlled. Sometimes this is relatively simple: "Now they're getting older they aggravate each other at the table. You know, 'She did this,' 'She's doing that.' So I have to sit there and kind of watch." In more difficult situations, when children are problem eaters, managing the meal can become a "project." One woman explained: "We give her real small portions and just try to encourage her, and praise her when she is cleaning her plate. It's a project for Richard and I to get going on."

Most parents are also conscious of monitoring their own behavior at the table, since their children learn from them; meal time is time for "setting an example": "I will always take the vegetable, even though I'm not much of a vegetable-eater. I don't make a big deal about it, but so that they at least see that that sort of thing is eaten." Thus, interpersonal relations, and even one's own eating, become a form of work that contributes to the production of a family meal.

I observed one family's dinner. The man who organized it clearly thought of this work of interaction as the essential part of the meal as event. After the family finished eating, the older son was to load the dishwasher; his father remained at the table, supervising him in this task. A younger son brought his book to the table, and his father looked through it, discussing the pictures with him. When they had finished, and the man had sent his older son off to do homework and was finally left alone in the kitchen, he turned to me and announced, "Well, that's dinner at our house." There was clearly more work to do—food to be put away, for example—and he went on to do it, but when the children left the room he felt the closure that marked the end of dinner as an interpersonal event.

The time and effort required to orchestrate family meals comes into focus when we examine the households in which family members do not come together for regular family meals. All of the women who reported that they rarely sat down to dinner as a group were women working outside their homes (although some working women did organize family meals). Conversely, of the women who were home full-time, only two reported that they sometimes did not eat as a family group. One woman, who works full-time as well as going to school, whose husband has two jobs, and whose teenage children are involved in their own activities, commented that sitting down to dinner every day is "just one of those luxuries that we have to give up." Thus, part of the reason for eliminating the dinner as a regular family event is the difficulty of coordinating many work schedules. However, it is also clear that arranging for family meals is itself work that takes time and energy and that is most easily accomplished when there is someone at home with time and energy to devote to the task.

One couple I interviewed talked eloquently about this problem. Their two

children were seven years and seven months old at the time of the interview.
Both parents had been working full-time throughout their marriage, though
their jobs had changed frequently because of cutbacks and layoffs. She was
going to school at night; they hoped that soon she would be able to earn
enough so that he could stay home as a househusband. For the present,
though, they described their routine as a "helter-skelter" one with no "set
patterns." She was usually late because of school or overtime work, so they
often ate at different times. In any case, supper was eaten in the living room,
in front of the television. She talked of how different their life is from the one
she grew up with, and her regrets:

My mom was home. And it really makes a world of difference. She always had good
meals on the table. . . . It was more of a family thing. You know, my dad got home
at a certain time, and we always ate dinner after he got home. . . . Now it's like a
helter-skelter routine. If we're all home, fine; if we're not, then we just work around
it. . . . There are a lot of times when I really regret it. I regret not having a family
routine. It feels like, you know, your kids are being shuffled around, and you're being
shuffled around.

It is the one thing that she would like to change about their eating habits; she
says that they talk about it "all the time." Her husband described the situation in much the same way. When I asked him why they did not have "set
patterns," his answer was ambiguous but reflected the time and effort involved in arranging meals:

It doesn't make any difference. Well, it does. But you're so damn tired. It's not the
time, because you could do it if you wanted to. It just gets to where you're so tired,
and fed up with the way the money situation is, and you just say, the hell with it.

In professional households, parents were more likely to work successfully
at arranging family meals, even if both were employed. However, in these
households, almost all the women who worked outside the home were working part-time, and they usually had jobs with flexible schedules. They had
fewer obstacles to overcome in arranging a regular meal-time routine, and
more time to devote to this work.

Single mothers were somewhat less likely than married women to arrange
regular meals together for their families. Some of these women reported that
their children ate together, but that they themselves ate alone, at another time.
A mother with six children, who is home all day, explained, "I'd rather wait
until it's quiet." And a single woman who works all day as a receptionist
said: "We usually sit down and eat. Or I have them in here and I'll—because,
you know, I've been working all day, and I might go in and sit in the living
room so I'll be by myself for a while." In these situations, there is only one
person to do all the family work, and no one to turn to for any relief, even
help in sustaining a conversation. Like the working couple described above,

these women need a respite. It is simply too much to keep working during their own meal times.

Invisible Work

The physical tasks of food preparation—essential as they are to the mainte-nance of individuals—are combined with another kind of coordinative work that produces group life within a market society. Those who do the work of feeding must adjust to the different schedules of household members and fun-nel resources from stores and service organizations into particular households for use by individuals. They plan meals, as I have shown here, so that they are appropriate for specific households and manage meals as part of a broader strategy for constructing family life. When they bring people together for meals, they are not only providing sustenance, but also producing family life itself.

The work of meal planning and management is invisible work. The meal patterns that families establish are often customary, copied from the house-holds of the parents' own parents. Practices seem natural, like "what every-body does," so that people fail to notice the work involved in maintaining them. And the unarticulated principles of meal planning can make the skills involved seem intuitive. Thus, a man who has just begun to cook attributes his wife's superior abilities not only to experience, but also to "personality." And a woman who has been married and cooking for over twenty years main-tains that her skills are "automatic"—"sort of like instinct."

Most analysts of women's "invisible work" have used the term to describe work that women are not given credit for, like volunteer work, work on a husband's career, or behind-the-scenes work in organizations (e.g., Kahn-Hut et al. 1982:137–43). The housework I have been discussing can be thought of as unacknowledged work in this sense; however, it is also literally invisible: much of the time, it cannot be seen. It is largely mental, spread over time and mixed in with other activities, and it can look like other things. For example, managing a meal looks like enjoying the companionship of one's family, and thinking about a menu can look like reading the newspaper, or just sitting and resting. The work is noticeable when it is not completed (when dinner is not ready on time, for instance) but disappears from view when it is done well.

Since feeding is embedded in relations with others and largely unrecog-nized as work, it often comes to be seen as an expression of personality and emotion. As women talked about their activities, several mentioned their "laziness'': for example, ''I really don't care much about making salad dressings. I think I'm a little lazy about things like that.'' One woman, who was running a business out of her home while caring for three children, told me that she tried to plan meals that were easy to cook: ''I really am stingy with my time.'' And the single mother with six children, who likes to save her own dinner until they are in bed, observed: ''That's a bad habit I have; I like peace and quiet.''

The widespread trivialization of housework and the invisibility of its most important parts lead women to feel that they ''don't really do much housework,'' or that the work is easy, and just ''goes by pretty good.'' But they are often ambivalent, anxious about ''making everything right,'' frustrated when their efforts fall short of their plans, and worried that they are not doing enough. The way they talk about housework provides clues to the kind of effort involved.

Although the work of feeding a family is not continuous, it requires attention to many different people and their needs and a continuing openness to new information of various sorts. As one woman explained, ''The antennas are always out.'' Those who do the work spend time thinking about what they will do and strategizing about how to get it done. This thought work is squeezed into the interstices of other activities. A busy mother with young twins explained: ''As soon as I get up in the morning or before I go to bed, I'm thinking of what we're going to eat tomorrow. Even though I know, but do I have this, and is this ready, and this ready?'' And another woman explained that she plans her son's lunch during ten minutes of ''kind of free time'' before she gets out of bed in the morning. At their paid jobs, or in odd moments, people think about what to have for dinner, what they need from the store, and how to fit all of the activities of food preparation into the time available to them.

Feeding also involves attention to the needs and tastes of others. Specific tasks and routines vary, but the heart of the work is serving and pleasing others, who have learned to expect that in the family they should get what they want. The houseworker has no one upon whom to make such claims; she learns to accommodate herself to others. Deference—the submersion of a woman's own needs—becomes a way of getting the work done.

Feeding is strongly gendered and, in spite of greater male interest and participation in some tasks, continues to be women's work. In a British study, for example, Murcott (1983) found that even when men did some cooking, wives were the ones who prepared ''cooked dinners,'' associated with home, health, and family. When adults—either men or women—were home without other family members, they tended not to cook, but to ''pick at'' food, or to ''snack.'' Some—husbands more often than wives—would go to eat with relatives, where they were fed by the women of other families. This alternative was one that men felt entitled to; by contrast, when women were served by someone else, they spoke of "being spoiled."

Much writing on housework is implicitly (if not explicitly) concerned with strategies for doing away with the burdens of housework. However, limited views of the work involved have often led to the notion that housework should be given up rather easily. The work is seen as so simple that its persistence is quite puzzling. What I have shown is that feeding, though certainly necessary, is neither trivial nor simply mechanical and that much of this work is not replaceable by labor-saving technology or purchased goods and services. The work, though invisible, has a logic; women have learned its principles and are disturbed when it is not done. I do not claim that feeding is inevitably women's work, nor that the organization of feeding cannot or should not change. However, the work as presently constituted is at the center of family life and sociability. In order to think about changing the organization of maintenance work, we must begin to uncover and articulate the principles that have traditionally organized housework and, through it, the family.

Notes

1. Davidoff (1976), from whom I have taken the phrase, reveals this aspect of housework in nineteenth-century households by examining upper-class homes, where the heavy work of maintenance was mostly done by paid domestic workers.

2. My study is based on interviews with those who do the work of feeding in thirty households (thirty women and three men). All of these households included children, but they were ethnically diverse and included single-parent and two-paycheck families, as well as families of different classes. Although there are important differences in the work of feeding, my analysis here focuses on those aspects of the work which were common to all households. For a more detailed discussion of methodology and sample, see DeVault 1984.

3. My approach is based on the method of doing "sociology for women" that is being developed by Dorothy E. Smith (1979). Smith calls for beginning with women's everyday experiences rather than a disciplinary agenda, and then seeking to explicate the broader social relations that shape those experiences.

4. Since I interviewed only a few men, I have not systematically analyzed gender differences in perspectives on the work of feeding. However, men who had taken on major responsibility for the work talked very much like the women in my sample; the differences I did notice seemed related to the different responsibilites of women and their husbands.

5. People in working-class and white-collar households, who usually lived closer to other members of their extended families, were more likely to gather with relatives for special meals; professional and managerial couples, lacking nearby kin, worked at creating special family occasions by preparing "elaborate" foods and serving them in "elegant" settings.

References

Berheide, Catherine White; Sarah Fenstermaker Berk; and Richard A. Berk. 1976. "Household Work in the Suburbs: The Job and Its Participants." *Pacific Sociological Review* 19 : 491–517.

Berk, Richard A., and Sarah Fenstermaker Berk. 1979. *Labor and Leisure at Home: Content and Organization of the Household Day*. Beverly Hills, Calif.: Sage.

Bossard, James H. S., and Eleanor S. Boll. 1950. *Ritual in Family Living*. Philadelphia: University of Pennsylvania Press.

Davidoff, Leonore. 1976. "The Rationalization of Housework." In Diana L. Barker and Sheila Allen (eds.), *Dependence and Exploitation in Work and Marriage*. London: Longman.

DeVault, Marjorie L. 1984. "Women and Food: Housework and the Production of Family Life." Ph.D. dissertation, Northwestern University.

Douglas, Mary. 1972. "Deciphering a Meal." *Daedalus* 101 : 61–81.

Ferber, Marianne A. 1982. "Women and Work: Issues of the 1980's." *Signs* 8 : 273–95.

Kahn-Hut, Rachel; Arlene Kaplan Daniels; and Richard Colvard. 1982. *Women and Work: Problems and Perspectives*. New York: Oxford University Press.

Murcott, Anne. 1983. " 'It's a Pleasure to Cook for Him': Food, Mealtimes, and Gender in Some South Wales Households." In Eva Garmarnikow, David H. J. Morgan, Jane Purvis, and Daphne Taylorson (eds.), *The Public and the Private*. London: Heinemann.

Oakley, Ann. 1974. *The Sociology of Housework*. New York: Pantheon.

Smith, Dorothy E. 1979. "A Sociology for Women." In Julia A. Sherman and Evelyn Torton Beck (eds.), *The Prism of Sex*. Madison: University of Wisconsin Press.

Strasser, Susan. 1982. *Never Done: A History of American Housework*. New York: Pantheon.

8

Male Resistance to Role Symmetry in Dual-Earner Households: Three Alternative Explanations

JANET G. HUNT
LARRY L. HUNT

The American family is changing, and men are dragging their feet. This is the message that emerges from the literature on domestic patterns and trends. The growth in dual-earner households has been the "subtle revolution" (Smith 1979) of the century, implying inevitable modification of the role division in marriage toward greater symmetry of responsibility for breadwinning and homemaking (Giele 1978; Goode 1982a; Matthaei 1982; Young and Willmott 1973). To date, however, women's lives have changed more than men's. Men have been reluctant to assume a greater share of responsibility for domestic chores and childcare and in fact do little more on the homefront when wives are employed than when they are not employed (Goode 1982b; Model 1982; Pleck 1977). They are, in general, less happy with the dual-earner arrangement than women and show more evidence of psychological distress (Bird 1979; Goode 1982b; Kessler and McRae 1982).

The news about men in dual-earner households, which has been out for some time, has inspired little intellectual curiosity. That women would more positively embrace the new roles and identities associated with symmetrical families, and that men would have to be prodded to accept their new status and responsibilities, has been treated as axiomatic. It has been thought important to check periodically into what the husbands in these households are doing, but not very important to ask why. Male resistance, in short, has been treated as basically not interesting and not legitimate. It has made social change, viewed as both inevitable and just, slower and more difficult for overburdened employed wives than it should be. For this, men are to be chided or tolerated, but not indulged by solicitous inquiry into their feelings.

A few men have attempted to explore the male crisis over role change, but in doing so they have stepped outside mainline thought and do not enjoy the level of attention and acceptance that feminist scholars have achieved.

This essay starts with the premise that the meaning of male resistance to role symmetry is neither obvious nor insignificant. We suggest three perspectives from which it might be understood, each with distinct implications for social policy and the future of the family.

Cultural Lag on the Road to Androgyny

The perspective on the domestic gender gap that we call the "cultural-lag view" derives from a cultural or normative understanding of gender roles. Gender roles are cultural constructs that emerge in particular social and historical contexts to organize human life. These constructs impose on physiological sex artificial dichotomies in personality and activity that deny both males and females opportunity to fully develop their human potential. The breadwinner/homemaker role division was a product of industrialization and the separation of most economic activity from the household. With this shift, the family was no longer a productive unit. Men followed the movement of work to the workplace to earn a living, and women largely remained in the household to care for children, maintain the home, and provide backstage supportive services for husbands. This role division gave men more power and independence than women but had oppressive implications for both genders. Women suffered from excessive domesticity and insufficient opportunity for personal achievement and public participation. Men suffered from excessive careerism (or work involvement) and were unable to develop their nurturing, caregiving, parental selves. Rapoport and Rapoport note a growing cultural recognition of the undesirability of radically polarized gender roles:

The contented helpmeet in the happy home and the tired warrior in the jungle outside were both blurring somewhat as representations of the real world, let alone the desirable one. If work was so bad, why did men want it so much for themselves? If the home was so good, why didn't men want to share more in its life? So a new balance has been in the making. (1976:345)

A series of interrelated trends in the twentieth century have shaped the new patterns and new consciousness that are rendering the breadwinner/homemaker conception of gender roles obsolete. Longer lives, smaller families, women's access to higher education, marital instability, growing demand for female labor, and expanding appetites for consumer goods and services have made labor-force participation for women an inevitable historical destiny. This means more symmetrical families and more androgynous personalities—free of negative and distorting personality characteristics and internal blocks to self-esteem (Ferguson 1977). It means men and women with more balanced and integrated lives and a more complete or whole sense of personhood. (For a thoughtful analysis of how the trends of the past two centuries are culminating in more symmetrical families and less sex-typed personalities, see Matthaei 1982).

This view stresses the benefits for men as well as women of gender role change. In a more symmetrical and androgynous world, men will be relieved of the achievement and performance pressures associated with their sole-breadwinner role; they will enjoy richer and more intimate marriages and family lives; and they will be freer to express and experience themselves authentically (Matthaei 1982; Pepitone-Rockwell 1980; Rapoport and Rapoport 1976). Given the male-supremacist themes in the old gender culture, however, men will be slower than women to discover the advantages of change. They will be threatened by a sense of erosion of traditional manly privileges and virtues (Filene 1975), suffer a loss of power and identity associated with their breadwinner role (Pleck 1977), and feel diminished by their "decreasing marginal utility"—the loss of claim to performance of indispensable, non-substitutable tasks in behalf of society (Goode 1982a, 1982b).

Until men "catch up," women will be overloaded in their double role of provider and homemaker, and there will be tension over the imbalances in marriage and men's and women's conflicting needs and expectations. Matthaei comments on the current disjuncture:

When this is a one-sided development, it upsets the stability of the marriage, necessitating a reassertion of the sexual difference, or bringing discord within the couple. However, the movement out of womanhood does bring the possibility of men moving out of manhood—and of replacing marriage based on difference and inequality with marriage based on similarity and equality. (1982:312)

This optimistic perspective assumes that eventually reequilibratation will bring about a less gendered society in which the quality of life is enhanced for women and men. "The most probable future," concludes Bird in her analysis of the two-paycheck marriage, is one of "better and happier people," and it will be "much, much more fun than the world we came into" (1979:265). All men need is a little more time and enlightenment.

The scenario sketched above represents a brand of liberalism that is particularly evident in the literature on dual-career families (e.g., Pepitone-Rockwell 1980; Rapoport and Rapoport 1976). This literature focuses on an elite segment of the population for whom the dual-earning arrangement has been highly voluntary, work has been "self-actualizing," the standard of living has been high, and domestic overload has been eased by hired help. It is, we submit, a very incomplete view of the experience of gender role change from women's and men's standpoint (Hunt and Hunt 1982). And it implies an agenda—education and androgynous socialization—that, at least by itself, will not solve the problems of living of the less advantaged and will not necessarily create a less gendered experience of the world, or one that is, if less gendered, more positive.

Sex Stratification (and the Hard Truth About Women's Work)

The "sex-stratification" interpretation of men's resistance to role symmetry emerges from a considerably less benign understanding of gender roles than the cultural lag view. It assumes that the social construction of gender has not oppressed men and women equally but has limited and constrained women particularly. The sex segregation of work in and outside the labor force has been associated with devaluation of women's work, regardless of its technical nature or social contribution. Women and women's work are consistently linked with lower power, prestige and material rewards than men and men's work. Although some (e.g., Bird 1979; Matthaei 1982) see sex segregation and devaluation of women's work primarily as a pattern of the past, others view it as a basic feature of contemporary gender roles. From this perspective, it is emphasized that women's growing labor-force participation has been largely within the female job sector and does not represent major movement into men's work roles (Almquist 1979; Hartmann 1979; Oppenheimer 1973). It has made women supplementary, not equal, providers in most married households and has not exempted them from primary responsibility for childcare and domestic chores (Hartmann 1979, Richardson 1981). Pleck summarizes the implications of sex segregation for male resistance to role symmetry:

As a result [of a sex-segregated dual market], changes in the level of female employment occur neither at the expense nor to the benefit of male employment. . . . This market mechanism is supported by ideology concerning the appropriate household activities of the two sexes as well as by differential training in family tasks. The result is that the husband's family role is generally unresponsive to changes in the wife's family role. (1977:423)

This interpretation says that women's greater satisfaction with the dual-earning arrangement, despite overload, reflects the objective status hierarchy of work: work outside the home (in the paid labor force) is worth more than work inside the home; men's work outside the home is worth more than women's work outside the home. For wives, simply being employed means some upward mobility (reflected in power, independence, prestige, and self-esteem) over being a housewife. For men, the movement of wives into the labor force means real status loss. They lose the power and privilege associated with being the sole provider and the services of a nonemployed wife. Their reluctance to assume domestic responsibilities, as well as their avoidance of "female jobs" in the occupational world, reflects the low-status and low-paid (or unpaid) nature of women's work.

Thus, in the old "his" and "her" marriage, his was better than hers (Bernard 1971). As his and hers become more equal, she gains and he loses. Men's resistance, therefore, is rational and rooted in real, not imagined, status interests that neither time nor education will alter. Whatever new opportunities men stand to gain from role change, they are not compelling enough to offset the losses, and most men will not change unless and until they are forced to. This will happen only insofar as women gain objective power to control their own destinies and the terms of marriage. "Men will not easily give up their rights, privileges, and power within the occupational and domestic spheres," concludes Scanzoni. "Only as women choose to press the conflict both at the group and individual levels will change eventually come about" (1972:164). And to press the conflict, in Scanzoni's view, women must gain access to forms of employment that will permit them to bring an equal share of the resources of "prestige" and "money" to marriage (1972:141).

It would be difficult to argue that the stratification perspective does not contribute to our understanding of male resistance and the necessary conditions for role symmetry. The finding that women's power in marriage is quite directly related to their economic contribution (Bahr 1974; Gillespie 1971; Hoffman 1963), and that men's participation in domestic and childcare activities is highest when spouses' incomes are similar (Model 1982; Scanzoni 1978), strongly suggests that there is an economic component to equity and symmetry in marriage that will not easily yield to normative pressures alone.

It is impossible, however, to understand the current state of marriage and gender roles—and their future—entirely through the lens of the stratification perspective. It presumes a highly cynical view of marriage as nothing more than a power arrangement in which economically dependent women serve the needs and interests of men, who, according to this logic, will not only refuse to relinquish power voluntarily but simply will abandon marriage if it ceases to be tilted to their advantage. Indeed, there is a strand of radical feminist thought that equates the liberation of women with the extinction of the institution of marriage and celebrates a society of individuals free to form whatever loose associations with others they find gratifying (e.g., Firestone 1970). But this construction, we would argue, fails to address the noneconomic and non-self-interested motivations for marriage and family, past, present, and future.

From the stratification standpoint alone, it is hard to explain the behavior of the many men who do not use their power resources to full advantage in marriage. Men at the top of the educational ladder, for example, have the greatest opportunity to maximize power in marriage and the most to lose in terms of their own success and earnings from a symmetrical marriage. Yet it is men from this category who are most likely to affirm the desirability of the arrangement (Rapoport and Rapoport 1977; Lopata et al. 1980). Even more to the point is the persistence of marriage and the proclivity for remarriage across class levels and income circumstances despite the tensions and imbalances in gender roles. People bring needs and values to this institution that transcend sex stratification. We must ask how gender role change affects these needs and values and whether men's resistance in any way reflects these concerns.

The Politics of Domination (Men and Women as Pawns in Larger Games)

To understand the current gender gap, we must examine the broader context in which gender roles have evolved and are being transformed. The "politics of domination" perspective draws on a radical analysis of this process, which assumes that gender roles reflect larger societal imperatives and interests than male-female power struggles. Real power has always tended to lie beyond ordinary men and women. Men's relative power over women provides incentives and vocabularies of motive for work roles that best serve the interests of power elites.

With industrialization came transformation of men's and women's work roles. Men had to be mobilized to leave home to toil on strange turf for little intrinsic reward. The concept of family breadwinner gave this new form of work its dignity. Coupling the male breadwinner with an economically dependent spouse and children (the future labor supply) gave men more power, independence, and prestige than women, but not without a price: men spent much of their time in alienating work roles and had relatively little time to experience the "comforts of home" and wifely services they had presumably earned through their work (Filene 1975; Lasch 1977).

Feminist theorists have examined the female side of this role allocation. Women, they observe, became captives of the home and were denied even the modicum of power and independence enjoyed by men (Benston 1969; Mitchell 1973). Further, the failure of the system to provide adequately for some women and households through male wages forced these women into forms of employment even more demeaning and devalued than men's. As women's labor-force participation has increased, it has remained largely channeled into the low-paid and low-esteemed female sector, adding more to women's workload than to their status (Richardson 1981). If men have had it bad, in other words, women have had it worse.

Articulated in this way, the radical perspective expands but does not contradict the stratification view. It suggests that gender inequality accommodates ordinary men to the status injuries they suffer in the service of other men. Men will not readily share power and roles with women as long as privilege in the home and power over women are experienced as compensations for exploitation and alienation in the public sphere (Richardson 1981). Pleck recognizes the "psychology," if not the economics, of this chain in his analysis of male power needs:

Men's patriarchal competition with each other makes use of women as symbols of success, as mediators, as refuges, and as an underclass. In each of these roles, women are dominated by men in ways that derive directly from men's struggle with each other. Men need to deal with the sexual politics of their relationships with each other if they are to deal fully with the sexual politics of their relationships with women. (1980:427)

Another less recognized variant of radical thought sees the family, even under industrialized capitalism, as more than a palliative and producer of labor. Despite the industrialization of most forms of productive work, there remains a "home economy" within which a variety of essential tasks and services including childrearing, food preparation, and maintenance of the household, clothing, and other personal possessions are performed (Brown 1982). Phrased alternatively, the family ensures the transgenerational continuity of human societies, not only through reproduction but by providing for the "varying needs of human beings over the span of their life cycle" (Elshtain 1982:446). Paramount is the provision of a nurturing environment for children:

We know—the evidence on this score is overwhelming—that children incur an assault to their humanity if they suffer from neglect, from the uprootedness that comes from being "cared for" by no one in particular. The evidence we have of what happens to children deprived of attachments to specific adults bears out that we are talking about a prerequisite for authentic human existence. (Elshtain 1982:448)

When these functions of home and family are recognized, the implications of the breadwinner/homemaker role division of the early stages of industrialization become more complex. Although the homemaker role denied women power, independence, and social recognition, it engaged them in activities that were potentially less alienating than men's extradomestic work roles. While men performed factory-paced or bureaucratically controlled jobs, women were involved in the essential care of children and production of domestic goods and services for people to whom they felt meaningfully connected. The lack of societal reward for this work and the isolation and dependence associated with it diminished women's own sense of worth and well-being. But the investment they made in their homemaking role often created a family life that was more humane and valuable to household members than the life outside. Women created homes that men could at least occasionally return to for comfort and retreat and to get in touch with their children.

Gender role change in the latter half of this century reflects the changing imperatives of postindustrial society. Corporate interests require ever-expanding appetites for and habits of consumption. Women in the labor force provide cheap labor for increased mass production of consumer goods and services and produce growth in household disposable income (to be channeled into consumption) and contraction of household time, generating the need for products and services (e.g., fast food and childcare) to replace what homemakers used to do for their families.

The consequences of women's movement out of the home and into the paid labor force are at the heart of feminists' contemporary "ambivalence" about the family (Thorne 1982) and, we shall argue, men's resistance to gender role change. Women have undeniably gained much from their expanded opportunities to work outside the home. Despite the routinization and bureaucratization of paid work, it nonetheless meets needs for accomplishment, service, and association that cannot otherwise be satisfied. Beyond this, employment is a requisite to being taken seriously and enjoying a measure of self-determination and, increasingly, basic economic security. The processes that have culminated in women's assimilation into market work have undermined the family to the point where women can less than ever look to it as a total source of identity and security.

As work outside the home becomes more accessible, more attractive, and more essential for women, they cannot afford to let reactionary threats or sentimental appeals force a retreat to old gender scripts. But this should not obscure the fact that women have been forced to trade gains in the market for losses in the social sphere that nurtures the needs and qualities that women have uniquely tended. Not only does labor-force work take time away from the household, but the consumption-oriented lifestyles associated with it are individuating rather than integrative. Consumption is an intrusion of market priorities into the home and tends to transform the "accidental" and nonutilitarian bonds of family into the limited, contingent and contractual relationships of the public sphere (Elshtain, 1982, 1983).

"It is a tragic paradox," writes Zaretsky (1982:193), "that the bases of love, dependence, and altruism in human life and the historical oppression of women have been found within the same matrix." Women's dilemma is to liberate themselves from oppressive social constructions of gender without permitting obliteration of the authentic and humane dimensions of their familial role in a world not designed to recognize the distinction. The profoundness of this tension is frequently glossed over with the rhetoric of symmetrical families and androgynous men and women. The synthesis of work and family extolled in most of these discussions accepts rather than challenges a redefinition of family to accommodate market imperatives (Elshtain 1982). It is a version of family that is divested of much of its time and function and blends easily into a smorgasbord of ad hoc living arrangements that bear little resemblance to stable, binding, caregiving worlds of kin that give moral purpose to people's lives and connect them to their past and to their future. There are, of course, many who welcome emancipation from just such family bonds. Freedom from all binding commitments is the ideal of classical liberalism and the essence of market individualism (Berman 1983; Ehrenreich 1983). But these are not the people among us who are troubled by gender role change. In a radically individuated society, gender is irrelevant. Those who care about gender care about families and what is happening to families as women cross gender barriers.

As women progressively disassociate themselves from any special or automatic responsibility for caregiving, men are left with a void and a sense of helplessness. The male experience from infancy on trains them to differentiate themselves from their caregivers and define self in terms of separation and individuation (Chodorow 1978; Gilligan, 1982; Hunt, 1980). The male culture supports this identity by focusing on public sphere events and processes and largely ignoring the supportive private substructure that frees and sustains public men and addresses the transgenerational concerns of society (Elshtain 1981; Gilligan 1982). Men thus have difficulty diagnosing and acknowledging the sense of loss that accompanies women's movement out of the private sphere. Their tendency is either to deny it or to try to understand it in terms of what has happened in their *public* rather than their private lives (e.g., the breadwinner role), or in terms of loss of power rather than loss of support, or in terms that would return women to an idealized version of their full- time homemaker role (Lasch 1977).

Men are responding, we suggest, to the same erosion of family life that worries women, but have even less control over the process. They have trouble articulating the problem, especially in ways that will not be construed as pressure to return to more conventional arrangements. And they find limited satisfaction in trying to share the homemaking role. They do not feel "natural" in the role, it does not provide them with the supports they have come to depend on, and it does not restore the social space the family has given over to market activities. This concern is not, we would stress, entirely—or even primarily—self-centered. The irreplaceable function of the family is to tend to the needs of people at vulnerable stages of the life cycle, especially infancy and childhood. Men in touch with their own familial origins sense these needs but cannot fulfill them, especially in the family of separate shifts and leftover time, competing with the electronic media for attention.

If this analysis is correct, men's resistance is in some measure a valid response to the situation in which they find themselves. For women to deny this is to be drawn into a form of gender politics that serves the interests of those political and economic structures that undermine the transgenerational and nonutilitarian forms of human connection. Corporate interests were first served by motivating men in terms that rendered women confined and subservient. These interests were then served by liberating women on terms that violate the integrity of family life. The resultant gender tensions place additional strain on fragile family bonds, further fragmenting and freeing family members for market absorption.

To short-circuit this cycle and get about the business of transforming family life into a more equitable and gender-integrated nurturing world, women and men must see their conflicts in broader perspective. Women must acknowledge what is oppressive about their *new* roles as well as the old for themselves and families. Men must acknowledge what was inadequate about *old* gender roles as well as current ones from the standpoint of family needs. And both must direct pressure at the public institutions that are dictating the terms of family life. Elshtain urges this agenda:

> Political thinkers, including feminists, devoted to the family reconstructive mode cannot carry out their supremely important tasks unless or until there are structural changes in American life. That is where the heart of "politics and the family" should lie—not in overpoliticizing our most intimate relations and turning the family into a war of all against all to be negotiated by contract, but in fighting the pressures at work from the outside which erode, impoverish, or preclude the flourishing of our most basic human ties. (1981:337)

In sum, the politics-of-domination interpretation of male resistance neither trivializes it nor denies its legitimacy but treats it as a symptom of larger forms of oppression. Diagnosing it as simply a misguided attachment to outdated role conceptions or a defense of male power and privilege vis-à-vis women plays into the ideological manipulation of gender by corporate interests. Properly understood and focused, it can help to energize the effort to create a more humane and equitable world for women, men, and families.

References

Almquist, Elizabeth M. 1979. *Minorities, Gender, and Work*. Lexington: Lexington Books.

Bahr, Stephen J. 1974. "Effects on Power and Division of Labor in the Family." In

L. W. Hoffman and F. I Nye (eds.), *Working Mothers*. San Francisco: Jossey Bass.

Benston, Margaret. 1969. "The Political Economy of Women's Liberation." *Monthly Review* 21:13–27.

Berman, Marshall. 1983. "Feminism, Community, Freedom." *Dissent* (Spring): 247–49.

Bernard, Jessie. 1971. "The Paradox of the Happy Marriage." In Vivian Gornick and Barbara K. Moran (eds.), *Women in Sexist Society: Studies in Power and Powerlessness*. New York: New American Library.

Bird, Caroline. 1979. *The Two-Paycheck Marriage*. New York: Rawson, Wade.

Brown, C. Vickery. 1982. "Home Production for Use in a Market Economy." In Barrie Thorne and Marilyn Yalom (eds.), *Rethinking the Family: Some Feminist Questions*. New York: Longman.

Chodorow, Nancy. 1978. *The Reproduction of Mothering: Psychoanalysis and the Sociology of Gender*. Berkeley: University of California Press.

Ehrenreich, Barbara. 1983. "On Feminism, Family and Community." *Dissent* (Winter): 103–6.

Elshtain, Jean Bethke. 1981. *Public Man, Private Woman*. Princeton: Princeton University Press.

———. 1982. "Feminism, Family, and Community." *Dissent* (Fall): 442–49.

———. 1983. "Jean Bethke Elshtain Replies." *Dissent* (Winter):106–9.

Ferguson, Ann. 1977. "Androgyny as an Ideal for Human Development." In Mary Vetterling-Braggin, Frederick A. Elliston, and J. English (eds.), *Feminism and Philosophy*. Totowa, N.J.: Littlefield, Adam.

Filene, Peter G. 1975. *Him/Her/Self: Sex Roles in Modern America*. New York: Mentor.

Firestone, Shulamith. 1970. *The Dialectic of Sex: The Case for Feminist Revolution*. New York: William Morrow.

Giele, Janet Zollinger. 1978. *Women and the Future*. New York: Free Press.

Gillespie, Dair L. 1971. "Who Has the Power? The Marital Struggle." *Journal of Marriage and the Family* 33 : 445–58.

Gilligan, Carol. 1982. *In a Different Voice: Psychological Theory and Women's Development*. Cambridge: Harvard University Press.

Goode, William J. 1982a. *The Family*. Englewood Cliffs, N.J.: Prentice-Hall.

———. 1982b. "Why Men Resist." In Barrie Thorne with Marilyn Yalom (eds.), *Rethinking the Family: Some Feminist Questions*. New York: Longman.

Hartmann, Heidi. 1979. "Capitalism, Patriarchy and Job Segregation by Sex." In Zillah R. Eisenstein (ed.), *Capitalist Patriarchy and the Case for Socialist Feminism*. New York: Monthly Review Press.

Hoffman, Lois W. 1963. "Parental Power Relations and the Division of Household Tasks." In F. I. Nye and L. W. Hoffman (eds.), *The Employed Mother in America*. Chicago: Rand McNally.

Hunt, Janet G. 1980. "Sex Stratification and Male Biography: From Deprivation to Ascendance." *Sociological Quarterly* 21 : 143–56.

Hunt, Janet G., and Larry L. Hunt. 1982. "The Dualities of Careers and Families: New Integrations or New Polarizations?" *Social Problems* 29:499–510.

Kessler, Ronald C., and James A. McRae, Jr. 1982. "The Effects of Wives' Employment on the Mental Health of Married Men and Women." *American Sociological Review* 47:216–77.

Lasch, Christopher. 1977. *Haven in a Heartless World: The Family Besieged*. New York: Basic Books.

Lopata, Helena Z.; Debra Barnewolt; and Kathleen Norr. 1980. "Spouses' Contributions to Each Other's Roles." In Fran Pepitone-Rockwell (ed.), *Dual-Career Couples*. Beverly Hills, Calif.: Sage.

Matthaei, Julie A. 1982. *An Economic History of Women in America: Women's Work, the Sexual Division of Labor, and the Development of Capitalism*. New York: Schocken Books.

Mitchell, Juliet. 1973. *Women's Estate*. New York: Vintage Books.

Model, Susanne. 1982. "Housework by Husbands: Determinants and Implications." In J. Aldous (ed.), *Two Paychecks: Life in Dual-Earner Families*. Beverly Hills, Calif.: Sage.

Oppenheimer, Karen. 1973. "Demographic Influence on Female Employment and the Status of Women." *American Journal of Sociology* 78:184–99.

Pepitone-Rockwell, Fran. 1980. *Dual-Career Couples*. Beverly Hills, Calif.: Sage.

Pleck, Joseph H. 1977. "The Work-Family Role System." *Social Problems* 24:417–27.

———. 1980. "Men's Power with Women, Other Men, and Society: A Men's Movement Analysis." In E. H. Pleck and Joseph H. Pleck (eds.), *The American Man*. Englewood Cliffs, N.J.: Prentice-Hall.

Rapoport, Rhona, and Robert Rapoport. 1976. *Dual-Career Families Re-Examined*. Norwich: Fletcher and Son.

Richardson, Laurel Walum. 1981. *The Dynamics of Sex and Gender*. Boston: Houghton Mifflin.

Scanzoni, John. 1972. *Sexual Bargaining*. Englewood Cliffs, N.J.: Prentice-Hall.

———. 1978. *Sex Roles, Women's Work, and Marital Conflict*. Lexington, Mass.: D.C. Heath.

Smith, Ralph E. (ed.) 1979. *The Subtle Revolution: Women at Work*. Washington, D.C.: Urban Institute.

Thorne, Barrie, and Marilyn Yalom (eds.). 1982. *Rethinking the Family: Some Feminist Questions*. New York: Longman.

Young, Michael, and Peter Willmott. 1973. *The Symmetrical Family*. New York: Pantheon.

Zaretsky, Eli. 1982. "The Place of the Family in the Origins of the Welfare State." In Barrie Thorne with Marilyn Yalom (eds.), *Rethinking the Family: Some Feminist Questions*. New York: Longman.

9

Children's Work in the Family: Its Significance and Meaning

LYNN K. WHITE

DAVID B. BRINKERHOFF

A prominent belief about the classic family of Western nostalgia is that "children used to work long and hard in the home, in the factory, on the farm" (Ingoldsby and Adams 1977:399). In contrast, most contemporary observers believe that today's children do not work—that outside of schoolwork, their primary obligation is to enjoy childhood. Boocock (1975:421) writes that "almost none do errands or chores or contribute in any other way to the running of the household." Similarly, Campbell (1969:824) argues that adolescents "possess only the shadow of significance and usefulness."

While some observers decry this state of affairs and compare it unfavorably with our nostalgic (but undocumented) picture of the past, there are others who clearly feel that work is a burden which children are well rid of and which, when present, represents neglect or exploitation of the child. There is, for example, a significant literature showing that children do more work around the house when their mother works outside the home (Hedges and Barnett 1972; Propper 1972). The interpretation of this finding has often been that this is a burden which inhibits the child from achievement in school or social life (Roy 1961). McClelland (1961), in his studies of childrearing practices related to achievement training, argues that making children do regular chores or pick up after themselves is a sign of rejection.

There thus is considerable ambivalence in the literature in regard to both the extent of children's work and its meaning. Almost universally, however, children's work has been a sidelight rather than a focus of research, and there is little accurate descriptive data on children's work in the family. Nor has

Adapted from *Journal of Marriage and the Family* 43 (1981). Copyrighted 1981 by the National Council on Family Relations, 1910 West County Road B, Suite 147, St. Paul, Minnesota 55113. Reprinted by permission.

there been any systematic consideration of the meaning of children's work for family organization and interaction.

This paper attempts to fill some of these gaps by reporting on a study of children's domestic work. It is concerned with the extent to which children work and the tasks they are given. Most important, it is concerned with the meanings families attach to children's work—that is, their rationales and interpretations. Finally, it is interested in integrating these findings with theoretical approaches within the social-psychological and sociological literature.

Children's Work: Literature and Conceptualization

With a few recent exceptions, children's work—or the lack of it—has been a concern of psychologists rather than sociologists.[1] Household chores as a means to individual development, particularly in regard to responsibility and morality, has been the major focus of the literature. Sociological concerns, such as the effect of children's work on the family, have been almost totally ignored. The existing research in children's work is briefly reviewed below, followed by a development of ideas drawn from the broader literature.

THE PSYCHOLOGICAL LITERATURE

A major research tradition in psychology has been the development of moral character in the child—that is, the development of responsibility, self-control, and service (Piaget 1948; Kohlberg 1964). As part of this concern, Harris et al. (1954) investigated the commonsense notion that children who are assigned home duties will be quicker to develop these notions of service and responsibility to others. They measured the extent of home duties by a simple checklist of chores that the children had ever done and responsibility by: (1) a teacher rating and (2) a student questionnaire on citizenship values. Data collected from 3,000 Minnesota schoolchildren showed no relationship between home duties and the development of responsibility. Although their measures can be faulted, in particular for using number of chores *ever* done as a measure of home responsibility, their research remains widely cited. For example, largely on the basis of their findings, Kohlberg (1964:425) concluded that "strong training demands which serve the parents' convenience (cleanliness, chores, neatness, [control of] aggression in the home) are, if anything, negatively related to moral response."

Elsewhere in the psychological literature, children's household chores have been investigated in terms of their relationship to the achievement syndrome. McClelland (1961) felt that requiring chores of children would reduce their opportunities to strive for excellence, and Smith (1969) noted that the skills and attitudes involved in doing routine chores may be actively contradictory to those demanded by a competitive drive for achievement. Nevertheless, Smith did find a significant correlation between having required chores and achievement motivation and concluded that chores may represent legitimate demands for independence and responsibility.

Apart from the above, the developmental literature has not included any theoretical or empirical work on the meaning of children's household chores. While the general tone of this literature is somewhat negative, the outstanding characteristic of the psychological literature on the developmental outcomes of children's contributions is the lack of research attention.

THE SOCIOLOGICAL LITERATURE

Sociological research on children's work is meager. An exception is the early work by Straus (1962), comparing work behavior of urban and farm boys. Straus included a thoughtful analysis of the implications of children's chores for development, noting that further research was badly needed in order to learn the values parents were trying to teach their children through work, the parental motivations behind asking children to work, and the importance of children's work in preparing them for adult roles.

These issues have not been addressed within sociology. Rather, sociological concern with children's work has been an empirical interest in the functional contributions of children's work to the family division of labor. Unfortunately, this interest in children's work has existed only to the extent that it has clarified the role of working mothers and their participation in the family division of labor. Generally, the research has shown that when wives work, children rather than husbands increase their involvement in housework to make up for wives' decreased availability (Hedges and Barnett 1972; Thrall 1978). In spite of some early concerns that this additional demand on children might negatively (and, it was implied, unfairly) affect children's social life, more recent studies suggest that housework has no adverse consequences for children's social or school life (Nye and Hoffman 1974).

THE SOCIOLOGICAL PERSPECTIVE

The literature that deals explicitly with children's work recognizes only a relatively narrow set of implications: psychological interest has focused on the developmental impact of work on the child and sociologists have concentrated on the functional impact of work on the family division of labor. A broader sociological perspective on the meaning of children's work, however, yields provocative insights.

First, picking up on Strauss's early ideas, one should consider the implications of children's work for adult roles. The work children do is not simply a practice exercise which may prepare them for real (i.e., paid) work, but rather consists of domestic chores that are likely to form part of their lifelong tasks. General socialization theory suggests that childhood experiences in this regard will have consequences for later roles in their own families. This expectation is supported by Thrall's (1978) finding that both men and women rely heavily on their childhood experiences when devising their own marital division of labor.

An additional perspective on children's work is drawn from the broader literature on the meaning of work. With reference to adult work, Menninger (1964:xiv) characterized the sociological approach as a recognition that "work is a method of relating meaningfully to the family and the community—a group process by which the individual becomes an entity, but, at the same time, is identified with the group." Application of this idea to children's work suggests that the coparticipation of children and adults in household tasks may contribute to increased family solidarity

If the literature on the meaning of adult work is any guide,[2] there are undoubtedly additional and more subtle meanings of children's work. The literature reviewed above, however, is sufficient to suggest that children's work may have important functional, integrative, and developmental implications, both for the child and for the family. Children's household work may have further outcomes for their performance in school, in the community, and on the job, but initially and intrinsically, it is a family matter.

Consequently, this paper concerns itself with the child's experiences with work in the family and the meanings of this work for the family. Because of the absence of any other holistic approaches to the role of children's work in the family, this research is necessarily exploratory. The preceding ideas, however, form a backdrop to the present exploration, and additional sociological research is drawn upon throughout the discussion in order to put the findings in context.

Study Design

Data for this study come from telephone interviews with parents collected as part of the Nebraska Annual Social Indicators Survey. Over 1,800 randomly selected adults from Nebraska were interviewed for this study in February–March 1979. This research reports on the 790 homes in which there was a child under age eighteen. In each household, a child was randomly selected to be the subject of the interview and the parent was asked whether the child was regularly required to do chores around the house or yard. Parents were also asked to provide some details about these activities and to give their reasons for requesting their children to work around the house. The rest of the questions in the interview consisted of general indicators of quality of life, including detailed background descriptions of family composition and history as well as information on the family's current situation.

Findings

This paper represents an exploratory study of the role of children's work in the family. As a preliminary step in this inquiry, the extent of children's involvement with household work is documented. The bulk of this paper, however, is concerned with exploring the meaning which children's work has for their families.

EXTENT OF CHILDREN'S WORK

Table 9-1 presents data on the extent to which children engage in regular chores, categorized by sex and age. These findings indicate clearly that being assigned chores around the house and yard is a developmental process. In some households it apparently begins very early and, by the time children are nine or ten, well over 90 percent are involved in regular chores. Participation tends to fall off slightly in the late teens as adolescents reduce their participation in all family activities, but chores remain a near universal. Although there is a consistent tendency for parents to report that their sons are more likely than their daughters to have chores, these differences are not statistically significant.

Table 9-1   Percentage of Children Regularly Required to Do Chores and Weekly Median Hours Spent on Chores by Age and Sex

| | % with Chores | | Of Those with Chores Median Hours | | |
Age Group	Boys	Girls	Boys	Girls	No.
Total	82	78	3.4	4.6	790
0–4	40	36	2.1	1.7	189
5–9	91	87	2.3	4.0	207
10–14	98	92	4.1	4.7	220
15–17	94	93	4.2	6.1	174

While these data indicate that children are increasingly involved with regular household chores as they get older, few of these children are required to put in grueling hours. The median number of hours spent by children on chores is 4.0 per week. Even for the hardest-working group, older girls, the median is only 6 hours per week. Still, on top of schoolwork, homework, and extracurricular activities, chores can add a significant additional demand on children.

Children begin their involvement in household chores by assuming responsibility for themselves: picking up their own toys, making their own beds, and cleaning up their own rooms. By the time they are ten year old, however, most children have moved beyond purely self-centered chores and are doing work for their family. As children grow older, they move from helping their parents—say, by setting the table or folding the clothes—to replacing their parents by assuming full responsibility for some tasks. [3]

THE MEANING OF CHILDREN'S WORK

The data reviewed above indicate that most parents assign regular chores to children and that this is a significant activity in terms of hours per week. The question remains, however, as to what this activity means for the child and the family. As Strauss (1962) noted over twenty years ago, it is frequently less trouble to do a task onself than to nag a child into doing it and then supervise and help. Until adolescence, children's chores probably represent more, rather than less, work for the parent. The following section empirically addresses some of the meanings parents attribute to assigning their children chores.

Parental responses to the question "Why do you ask your children to work?" are illuminating. The key word for most parents is "responsibility." In fact, over 25 percent of the parents surveyed spontaneously used the word "responsibility" in their reply. For example, parents made such remarks as:

[Work] gives them a sense of responsibility. Makes them appreciate what they have. I think it helps them grow into responsible adults. (Parent of eight-year-old girl)

I think it develops the character. Unless they do it, it won't get done. It builds their responsibility—his own responsibility toward others. (Parent of fourteen-year-old boy)

Regardless of the specific words used, the majority of parents gave character building as the primary reason for assigning their children chores. In fact, many parents reported that it was their duty to give children chores:

I feel children have to learn to work while young and it stays with them. We do them an injustice as a parent if we let them do nothing. (Parent of thirteen-year old boy)

Because he's a member of the family, because there's too much work for me to do it all. The main reason, he has to be responsible and I would be very derelict as a parent not to. (Parent of twelve-year-old boy)

Some parents also expressed a specific belief that household chores were a means to integrate the family and to provide greater cohesiveness among family members. A few of these parents sounded as if they had just finished reading Durkheim's classic treatise on the moral functions of the division of labor; they are clearly convinced that joint responsibility is positive and vital.

We think it makes them a part of the family; they're living at home. It makes them know they have their duties and share in making it a home. (Parent of six-year-old girl)

Their responsibility to help their family. A family becomes a family when we all take part and they have to learn that. (Parent of fourteen-year-old boy)

They need to know how to do some things. They need to help the family in their everyday living. They become a part of the family that way. (Parent of fifteen-year-old girl)

There are a few parents (22 out of 669) who gave purely extrinsic reasons for asking their children to work, such as, ''I need the help.'' A much larger number included remarks about wanting the help within a longer reply stressing character building. A few of these parents specifically noted that the work accomplished was a secondary consideration and that it was really for the children's benefit that they assigned them chores.

These verbatim responses from parents give an illuminating picture of the variety of meanings associated with children's work and an overall impression of concern with developmental outcomes. For a more careful analysis of the meaning of children's work, parental responses were coded into five categories of meaning corresponding roughly to the four a priori meanings developed above plus one residual category. These categories and some typical responses are:

1. *Developmental:* Doing chores builds character, develops responsibility, helps children learn.
2. *Reciprocal obligations:* It is their duty to help the family; working together is part of being a family; occasionally, more bluntly, ''They live here, don't they?''
3. *Extrinsic:* Parents need help.
4. *Task-learning:* Children need to learn how to do these tasks.
5. *Residual:* All other reasons, most often that child has to earn an allowance or needs something to do in order to keep busy.

Each response was coded twice by independent coders. Because many parents gave complex reasons, each answer was given as many as three codes. For example, the response for the fifteen-year-old girl cited above was

Table 9-2   Reasons Given for Assigning Children Chores, by Age and Sex of
Child

Reason	Total %	Age				Sex	
		0–4	5–9	19–14	15–17	Male	Female
Developmental	72.4	80.5	78.2	74.7	59.2	72.5	72.2
Reciprocal	24.8	12.2	19.9	24.7	36.8	27.2	22.0
Extrinsic	22.7	18.3	14.1	23.6	32.9	21.4	24.3
Task-learning	12.1	8.5	9.6	13.5	15.1	10.4	14.3
Other	9.2	6.1	6.4	12.4	9.9	10.4	7.7
N	568	82	156	178	152	309	259

Note: Percentages do not add to 100 because some parents gave more than one reason for
assigning children chores.

coded for both the second and fourth categories. Table 9-2 presents the distribution of the reasons given by parents for having their children work.

Clearly, most parents' responses fall into the developmental category. However, the age pattern for this meaning is in sharp contrast to the others: while the proportion assigning a developmental reason declines with the age of the child, the likelihood of giving all of the other reasons increases with age. While parents of older children still most commonly give a developmental reason, an increasing number report that they rely on the help of older children, see them as having some obligation to their family, or as needing to learn some basic domestic skills. There is a subtle change from "helping will build his responsibility" to "it is his responsibility to help" by late teens. [4] Note that compared with age the differences by sex are small and statistically insignificant.

The developmental response is so frequent across age and sex categories that it bear the characteristics of a normative or socially desirable response. It is suspected that most parents, without having given the matter a lot of thought, adhere to the conventional wisdom that chores are good for children. Or perhaps parents give this socially desirable response in order to rationalize more extrinsic or selfish reasons.

The approximately 45 percent of the sample who gave a nondevelopmental response express a view of the family as a working unit, not merely as a child-rearing agency. While this position is not always clearly articulated, the responses of many parents indicate a firm belief that "the family that works together, stays together," and a belief that children can be expected to contribute to the family regardless of developmental outcomes.

The strong moral tone that pervades many of these diverse replies suggests that the meanings of children's work may be part of a family ethos—what

Hess and Handel (1959) have called family themes. Conceiving of a family theme as a pattern comprising ''some fundamental view of reality and some way or ways for dealing with it,'' Hess and Handel (1959: 11) argue that families develop ''themes'' which then affect the way they, as a group, structure their environment, process new information, and perceive reality. These responses to children's work may be part of such a theme, providing significant insight into those family values surrounding the parent-child bond and the obligations that parents and children have to one another. A much broader study of family values and outcomes would be necessary to determine whether interpretations of children's work are part of such a theme. With data only on children, this larger interpretation must remain a speculation. It is possible, however, to explore the possibility that the different interpretations of children's work are products of different family environments. In the following section, the family characteristics that may affect assigned meanings are examined. In particular, the analysis attempts to determine whether the values assigned to children's work are simply another instance of social-class differentials or whether they are primarily reflective of structural differences among families.

THE DETERMINANTS OF MEANING

In order to answer these questions, multiple-classification analysis is used to investigate differentials related to the three major categories of meaning.[5] This form of analysis is well suited to this type of exploratory research: it is designed to evaluate the impact of categorical independent and control variables and offers a unique opportunity to examine the form of the relationships rather than just a measure of association (Andrews and Messenger 1973). This analysis is presented in two parts in Table 3. The first panel shows the independent effect of measures of family structure controlling for age and sex of child. The second panel shows the independent effect of each family background characteristic.

The results of the first panel indicate that there is no relationship between parents' assigning developmental meaning to children's work and family structure: all types of families appear to attribute this category of meaning to children's work. On the other hand, family structure shows some relationship to the other two categories of meaning. Urban families are significantly more likely than rural families to believe that children have an obligation to do chores; more predictably, families with working mothers or single parents are more likely to say that they ask their children to work because the work needs to be done and they need the help. While the B^2 does not reach significance, there is also a linear increase in the percentage saying they need help as household number rises. To a smaller extent, this same pattern appears between household size and a belief in reciprocal obligation.

In the next panel of Table 9-3 findings are presented on the effect of family background on the meaning of children's work, controlling for the structural variables previously found to have an impact: age of child, mother's work status, household type, and rural-urban residence. This analysis evaluates the independent effects of the four measures of family background: parent's education, family income, religion, and parental respondent's satisfaction with the family division of labor. The first two variables are routine measures of family's socioeconomic background. The measure of religion is included because earlier studies have found this to be related to work attitudes (Smith 1969). The measure of satisfaction with the marital division of labor is included in order to see the contextual effect of family attitudes toward household work on the meaning assigned to children's work.

The results again indicate that the developmental response is so standard that it is almost invariant across families. This strongly suggests the presence of a cultural norm. To the extent that this response is given as a socially desirable rather than an honest answer, the normative interpretation is strengthened. A nearly constant three-quarters of our sample believes or feels it ought to believe that chores are assigned to children for the benefit of the child.

The other two reasons, however, show some patterns. The belief that children have a duty to their family is significantly related to parents' education and positively, though not significantly, related to family income. The evidence is rather convincing that, for this sample, the ''work as duty'' ethic is positively associated with social class. Purely extrinsic meaning is significantly associated with only one variable: parental satisfaction with the marital division of labor. Parents who are dissatisfied with their own domestic share (presumably because they are over- rather than underworked) are more apt to demand work from their children for purely extrinsic reasons. There is also a linear relationship between extrinsic reasons and parental education, though this is not statistically significant.

In summary, there do appear to be some differences in the kinds of families that give one meaning for work as opposed to another. While approximately three-quarters of all kinds of families assign developmental reasons to children's work, higher-status and well-educated parents are more apt to attribute reciprocal obligations among family members as a reason and families with higher work loads—working mothers, single parents, or those with large households—are most apt to assign extrinsic meaning to children's work. It is important to bear in mind, however, that the meanings are not mutually exclusive: two-thirds of the parents who gave an extrinsic meaning to children's work also cited a developmental meaning.

Table 9-3   Determinants of Meaning Assigned to Children's Work

	Adjusted % Giving Each Meaning			
	Developmental	Reciprocal	Extrinsic	No.
Grand mean	72	25	23	548
Structural characteristics[a]				
Mother's employment				
Full-time	67	27	28	162
Part-time	76	23	28	133
Other	73	25	18	273
B^2	.0064	.0009	.0144*	
Number in household				
Two	74	16	8	13
Three	72	24	19	124
Four	70	25	22	209
Five	74	23	25	132
Six or more	74	31	30	90
B^2	.0009	.0049	.01	
Household type				
Husband-wife family	72	25	21	508
Single-parent family	70	21	52	43
Other	79	20	19	17
B^2	.0009	.0009	.04*	
Residence				
Rural farm	75	19	20	91
Rural nonfarm	70	19	26	116
Urban	72	29	23	361
B^2	.0016	.0121*	.0016	
Family background characteristics[b]				
Parental respondent's education				
0–11 years	70	18	17	
12 years	74	21	21	
13–15 years	71	31	24	
16 or more years	75	31	29	
B^2	.0025	.0169*	.0064	
Subjective family income				
Below average	73	21	20	106
Average	72	26	22	319
Above average	76	25	22	123
B^2	.0016	.0016	.0004	
Religion				
Catholic	73	24	25	157
Other	73	25	21	391
B^2	.0000	.0000	.0025	

Table 9-3   *(cont.)*

| | Adjusted % Giving Each Meaning | | | |
	Developmental	Reciprocal	Extrinsic	No.
Satisfaction with marital division of labor				
Completely satisfied	72	27	13	231
Fairly well satisfied	73	23	26	218
Somewhat dissatisfied	73	23	34	61
B^2	.0004	.0016	.0324*	

[a]Adjusted for age and sex of child plus the other three structural characteristics.
[b]Adjusted for age of child and structural characteristics shown to have a significant effect and other family background characteristics.
*Significant at the .05 level.

CONSEQUENCES OF MEANING

The previous analysis has demonstrated that there are some significant differences among families in assigning different meanings to children's work. Before attaching undue importance to this finding, however, it is important to evaluate whether these meanings have any significant consequences. Following Hess and Handel's (1959) lead, this study is concerned with whether these differences in meanings reflect underlying family values that have consequences for family organization. Specifically, do these differences in meaning affect what family members do?

This question can only be answered in terms of the consequences for children's labor—that is, how many hours children are asked to work each week and whether their parents pay them for work around the household. In the present study, children were regarded as being paid for their labor if their parents gave them an allowance and said that they thought of this primarily as payment for work around the household or if, aside from a regular allowance, parents paid their child for work done around the household.

In order to show the independent effect of family themes on children's behavior, multiple classification analysis was again used. This time the analysis looked at the effect of family theme on children's work hours and children's pay, controlling for the background factors found to be important in Table 9-3: parental education, mothers' employment, residence, family income, child's age, and satisfaction with family division of labor.[6]

The results in Table 9-4 show that family meaning has a small, but systematic, effect on the amount of work children do and their payment for this work. The data show that children whose work is given an extrinsic interpretation are likely to work the longest hours and the most likely to get paid for

Table 9-4   Adjusted Percentage of Children Who Get Paid for Their Work
Around the House and Mean Hours of Work per Week by Family Work Ethic

Family Work Ethic	% Paid[a]	Mean Hours/Week[a]	No.
Total	38	4.55	493
Developmental	38	4.40	295
Reciprocal	35	4.71	110
Extrinsic	42	4.86	88

[a]Controlling for age of child, parent's education, mother's employment, family income, residence, and parental satisfaction with marital division of labor.

their work. Similarly, those whose work is seen as part of a reciprocal obligation are, not surprisingly, least likely to get paid for their work. The number of hours this latter group works is a little above average, but not as high as the children who work for extrinsic reasons. Finally, the children whose work is assigned only a developmental meaning work the fewest hours.

While not significant, the pattern of results in Table 9-4 supports the idea that, controlling for family background and structure as well as child's characteristics, the way a family thinks about work has consequences for family organization.

Conclusions

The findings suggest that children's work around the house is an ubiquitous and value-laden feature of family life. And while there is only a limited literature to support it,[7] it is speculated that the parent-child division of labor (chores) may create almost as much family tension as does the husband-wife division of labor. Given the centrality of chores for the experiences of children and families, further research is necessary in order to document the vital role of work and work ethos in family life and the consequences (developmental and otherwise) of children's involvement in the family division of labor.

More generally, there should be an increased inclusion of children in studies of family structure and process. Whether the topic is the division of labor, power relationships, or family conflict, the role of children in the family has been neglected. Rather, family sociologists have largely been content to leave the subject of children to developmental scholars. Hopefully, this research on the integrative and functional, as well as developmental, significance of children's work will be a step in this direction.

Notes

1. A third area of research regarding children and work is not concerned with children's work at all, but with children's socialization into adult work roles. The best and most recent work in this tradition is Goldstein and Oldham's (1979) comprehensive study of the development of children's ideas about work and exchange, and, in particular, about specific occupations, occupational prestige, and occupations as intrinsic to a system of social inequality. Unique among such studies, the authors recognize that children do work themselves and that their own experiences, as well as other influences around them, may affect their work socialization.

2. These is a considerable amount of literature on the meaning of work for adults. Of particular interest are Berger's (1964) *The Human Shape of Work* and Tilgher's (1977) *Work: What It Has Meant to Man Through the Ages.*

3. A detailed analysis of age and sex differences in the content of children's work appears in White and Brinkerhoff 1981.

4. The first reason in this example would be coded as developmental and second as reciprocal obligation.

5. Task learning was dropped from further analysis, in part because of the smaller number of cases, but also from a conviction that this was the weakest coding category. Responses in this category were the most vague and the least likely to carry the moral overtone that characterizes the other three categories, an overtone which may represent a configuration of family values. When the analysis in Table 9-3 was performed for task learning, no significant relations were found.

6. It was necessary to make the categories of work meaning mutually exclusive for this analysis. In order to retain as many families as possible in the two smaller categories, parents who gave a reciprocal obligation or extrinsic reason as well as a developmental reason are coded only in the former categories. Families who gave both reciprocal obligation and extrinsic reasons ($N = 23$) were excluded from the analysis. This coding scheme produces three mutually exclusive categories: (1) families who see duty as a meaning ($N = 118$), (2) families who see extrinsic reasons for children's work ($N = 106$), and (3) families who see only developmental reasons ($N = 344$).

7. Griffiths (1954) found that in response to a question about what they could do that would please their parents most, the large majority of elementary school children responded that they could do their chores better.

References

Andrews, F. M., and R. C. Messenger. 1973. *Multivariate Nominal Scale Analysis.* Ann Arbor: Institute for Social Research.

Berger, P. L. 1964. *The Human Shape of Work.* New York: Macmillan.

Boocock, S. S. 1975. "The Social Context of Childhood." *Proceedings of the American Philosophical Society* 119:419–29.

Campbell, E. O. 1969. "Adolescent Socialization." In David Goslin (ed.), *Handbook of Socialization Theory and Research.* New York: Russell Sage Foundation.

Goldstein, B., and J. Oldham. 1979. *Children and Work: A Study of Socialization.* New Brunswick, N.J.: Transaction Books.

Griffiths, W. 1954. "Behavior Difficulties of Children as Perceived and Judged by Parents, Teachers, and the Children Themselves." Manuscript.

Harris, D. B.; K. E. Clark; A. M. Rose; and F. Valasek. 1954. "The Relationship of Children's Home Duties to an Attitude of Responsibility." *Child Development* 25 (March):29–33.

Hedges, J. N., and J. K. Barnett. 1972. "Working Women and the Division of Household Tasks." *Monthly Labor Review* 95 (Jan.):9–14.

Hess, Robert, and Gerald Handel. 1959. *Family Worlds: A Psychosocial Approach to Family Life*. Chicago: University of Chicago Press.

Ingoldsby, B. B., and G. R. Adams. 1977. "Adolescence and Work Experiences: A Brief Note." *Adolescence* 12:339–43.

Kohlberg, Lawrence. 1964. "Development of Moral Character and Moral Ideology." In L. W. Hoffman and M. L. Hoffman (eds.), *Review of Child Development Research,* vol 1. New York: Russell Sage Foundation.

McClelland, D. C. 1961. *The Achieving Society*. New York:Free Press.

Menninger, W. C. 1964. "The Meaning of Work in Western Society." In Henry Borow (ed.), *Man in a World at Work*. Boston: Houghton Mifflin.

Nye, F. I., and L. W. Hoffman. 1974. *Working Mothers*. San Francisco: Jossey-Bass.

Piaget, Jean. 1948. *The Moral Judgment of the Child*. Glencoe, Ill.: Free Press.

Propper, A. M. 1972. "The Relationship of Maternal Employment to Adolescent Roles, Activities, and Parental Relationships." *Journal of Marriage and the Family* 34:417–21.

Roy, Prodipto. 1961. "Maternal Employment and Adolescent Roles: Rural-Urban Differences." *Marriage and Family Living* 23:340–49.

Smith, C. P. 1969. "The Origin and Expression of Achievement-Related Motives in Children." In C. P. Smith (ed.), *Achievement-Related Motives in Children*. New York: Russell Sage Foundation.

Straus, M. A. 1962. "Work Roles and Financial Responsibility in the Socialization of Farm, Fringe, and Town Boys," *Rural Sociology* 27:257–74.

Thrall, C. A. 1978. "Who Does What? Role Stereotyping, Children's Work, and Continuity Between Generations in the Household Division of Labor." *Human Relations* 31:249–65.

Tilgher, A. 1977. *Work: What It Has Meant to Man Through the Ages*. Trans. Dorothy Fisher. New York: Harcourt, Brace.

White, Lynn K., and David B. Brinkerhoff. 1981 "The Sexual Division of Labor: Evidence from Childhood." *Social Forces* 60:170–81.

UNPAID FAMILY WORK OUTSIDE THE HOME

10

The Hidden Work of Constructing Class and Community: Women Volunteer Leaders in Social Philanthropy

ARLENE K. DANIELS

Introduction

Women who do full-time volunteer work are often placed in an ambiguous position by their status as unpaid workers. They are praised for their work in the community, but this praise often has a ritual aspect that underlines their marginal position in society. In hospitals and schools around the country, for example, administrators may set aside a time to express appreciation for the volunteers; luncheons provide the opportunity to give pins and flowers to commemorate and praise years of service. These ritual expressions, like those on Mothers' Day, underscore the ambiguity of the praise: once a year women receive accolades, but their contributions are not consistently rewarded or recognized in the remaining time. The unpaid work of women does not figure in the gross national product; the efforts of volunteers or housewives to transfer their skills into the paid market show the perils of assuming that any praised work can be turned into something valued in a cash-nexus economy.

Women who do not have to do paid work are thus seen as somehow outside the economy. They are not doing "real" work, and our society has developed no commonly understood categories to describe and evaluate any of the tasks in that amorphous area of nonpaid activity. Is volunteering work or leisure activity? Are the duties of housewives and mothers work or expressions of their caring for the family? Although social theorists have tried to explain the nature and importance of unwaged work for the family (Finch 1983; Fowlkes 1980; Lopata 1971; Oakley 1974; Strasser 1982) and for the economy generally (Kessler-Harris 1981; Luxton 1980), such ideas have not yet won general acceptance, particularly among traditionally oriented families where the division of labor between men and women is seen as clear and appropriate. This division is particularly strong in traditional middle- and upper-class families, where the preference for women's staying at home reflects general expectations and an ideology about family and work held by both men and women. Women clearly do not have to take paid work. Furthermore, why should they? Even with household help available, husbands, children, parents, and in-laws need the family services these women can provide. In addition, the community needs their services: various causes, philanthropies, and local services require organizing, staffing, fundraising, for the local, regional, and national governments do not take responsibility for these activities.

This paper is about women who stand at the intersection of "society" and philanthropy, who work for the community and for their families through their volunteer activity. They have the advantages of a comfortable, or even luxurious, lifestyle; they do not need salaried work and, in traditional families, would not wish to seek it. For a combination of practical and altruistic reasons (their husbands would disapprove of, or even feel threatened by, any public action suggesting that their wives needed a salaried position; their families need them; they wish to set their own schedules; they cannot expect to find work as varied, interesting, and challenging if they leave the volunteer world; they wish to make a contribution to society and community through volunteer work), these women make a long-term commitment to unpaid work.

This work, like that of women in other classes, has some disadvantages for those who do it—the character of the work and the skills and time it takes are not clearly understood; the importance is not widely recognized in society generally. Further, in the picture generated for the public through the mass media, the work of upper-class women carries a tinge of frivolity (aimless partying in the guise of sponsorhip of philanthropic benefits; social climbing) or condescension (lady bountifuls and do-gooders intruding into the lives of the less fortunate with judgments about who is worthy and unworthy to receive assistance).

I wish to go beyond this stereotype to show the significance of the work these women do in their volunteering. They serve as mediators between their families and the larger society; sometimes they further their husbands' careers. The ambiguity of their position, however, makes it difficult for even the most committed, able, and respected of these volunteer workers to receive the recognition and respect accorded to other, salaried, professional workers. The work of these women volunteers, then, highlights some of the problems many women face in modern American society. It is hard to gain recognition for work that is not waged, that contributes to community welfare but is performed collectively, that occurs in the interstices of modern capitalist society, where the "important" work is in profit maximization and work performed for community welfare falls into a residual category.

The benefits of the volunteer career—for the women, her family, and the larger society—are not without personal costs. Ambiguity about what is work and what is leisure, what is important and what is frivolous, create doubts about the value of volunteer work. And these doubts, no matter how often denied or repudiated by the workers themselves, affect women's self-esteem.

The Respondents

This study is based upon systematic interviews with seventy women in their homes or offices and additional interview-observations of them and their friends during a five-year period (1971–1976) at luncheons, social gatherings, and philanthropic events. After that period, and continuing to the present (1985), I have seen or phoned some of them, and gathered news of the rest, in occasional visits back to the research site, at least twice yearly. These are women who know each other through family and friendship connections, through community service, or both. They are volunteer community workers who have risen to community leadership in the major metropolitan area in and around what I shall call Pacific City, a large and relatively old, established community in the northwestern section of the United States. They were chosen through the reputational sampling method. Three women, acknowledged widely as volunteer community leaders (so identified in local media, holders of many distinguished local and national awards, officers and advisors on many prestigious boards) were the first interviewed and helped me to choose the remaining sample on the basis of their long experience in community service.

Focused interviews (Merton and Kendall 1946) permitted the discussion of selected topics (as opposed to adherence to a predetermined set of very specific questions). Interviews varied in length from one to four hours, sometimes requiring two or three appointments to complete. [1]

The resulting group presents a mixture of the upper and middle classes in Pacific City. Some of the women come from old families in this community or another; some are from newly prosperous families (new rich or solely dependent upon professional men's income for their affluence); and some are from ordinary middle-class homes that are financially secure but not notably prosperous.

These women are well-educated: 18 have had some college; 47 hold bachelors' degrees, and 15 of these have advanced degrees as well. They exhibit the lifestyle of the upper-middle or upper classes, living in comfortable, or even opulent, surroundings. Most (53) have never held a salaried job or else worked only for a year or two before marriage, although a few (3) have begun to work for pay after a long volunteer career. Six women in this group have worked some part of their lives at salaried positions, and 8 more have had paid careers in addition to their volunteer experience—after a husband's illness, widowhood, or divorce.

Acceptance of traditional values, suggested by these characteristics, is supported by other aspects of lifestyle. Virtually all (65) have either attended private schools themselves or sent their children to private schools. And about half (34) are listed in the *Social Register*. (Another 10 belong to wealthy and prominent Jewish families who are not listed in the register but who show their exclusivity by membership in a variety of other important social clubs.)

Every woman in the study has been married; 13 are divorced, and 21 have been widowed (6 of these 21 have remarried). Most of these women (63) have had children, ranging in number from one to ten, with an average of about three. The husbands of these women are mainly businessmen of various sorts: 7 are brokers in stocks, insurance, food, and merchandise; 5 are investment analysts or counselors; 33 are in business firms—generally a family firm—and many serve as chairmen of the board. But substantial numbers are doctors (14) or lawyers (11). This group is predominantly Protestant (40), but there are a number of Jews (18) and Catholics (12) among them.

The Responsibilities of Noblesse Oblige

The women in this study engage in charitable work out of noblesse oblige as practiced by an elite, for even when not wealthy, they consider themselves "fortunate." They are fortunate in that they do not have to work, because they are well provided for by husbands—even if widowed. Although a few women in this study have had to work after widowhood or divorce, they all meet the expectations for gender-related behavior common in traditional families. Many women meet the special expectations of upper-class families as well: to prepare a new generation of the elite for its responsibilities. These expectations are also consonant with community service, for women often have to build the institutions (schools and children's museums, for example) from which their own, as well as other, children will benefit.

The Maintenance of Class Across Generations

The upper-class women in this sample, like those described by Ostrander (1984), prepare their children for a place in the privileged class and are themselves active participants in upper-class society. But even when they are not upper-class, they reaffirm the significance of "society" and the social whirl through their acceptance of its importance in setting the stage for benefits, in attracting potential contributors. Though these women work seriously at philanthropy, (from the equivalent of half-time to more than full-time hours) and see themselves as different from those who are "only" socialites, many connections, sympathies, and interests are evident across these groups in the way women choose to meet family responsibilities. In addition to the traditional social expectation that women take responsibility for the care and socialization of children, these women uphold class expectations by sponsorship and active support of private schools and exclusive dancing classes where their children can socialize with appropriate peers. And some informants see to it that their daughters "come out" as debutantes in Pacific City's exclusive cotillion. All these activities are seen as part of women's community involvement.

They also indicate some of the dimensions of concern for the preparation of a new generation of the elite. Private schools and dancing classes provide some of the social skills required in elite circles—as well as opportunities to meet the right sort of people. Cotillions and debutante parties are signals to the elite circles that the participating young men and women are ready to accept some of the social responsibilities of those circles.

Women work hard to provide the context in which these educational and recreational activities can take place. One woman, for example, organized and raised funds for a new private school because she saw the existing one as too demanding:

There are an awful lot of pressures on the children at Lynley. But the kids who like music and need a good education and couldn't take the pressures could have another alternative. At Lynley they cheat and lie and crack up. The parents put a lot of outside pressures . . . into the children.

The assumption spurring her efforts, of course, was that children from her circle needed another private school. Good education would not be sought from the public system, although public schools were available to meet her requirements. The piece of the community that she helped to construct, then, bolsters the system by broadening the options for the children in her circle.

Others work hard to maintain the more clearly social activities of their children. This activity requires some oversight of the invitational dancing classes and social clubs the children attend. When women find the ambience or the management of these events unsatisfactory in any way (a dancing master seems too effeminate; a school's manager is rumored to be an alcoholic), they may organize a new set of activities as alternatives or replacements. Whether the current system of management is acceptable or not, the women realize that they must put time and energy into maintaining their children's interest in the activities as well as the activities themselves.

None of these social events requires more management and more infusions of energy, enthusiasm, and organizing ability than the yearly cotillion. A volunteer describes the arrangements:

In January and February we discuss what happened on the annual event [the previous month]. Then we go over the girls who are coming up. September [to] November are the three months of all-day meetings. . . . Thirty-six [girls] is absolutely tops. This year we will only have twenty-five. [It is a question of how many boys and girls are born each year. If there are more boys than girls, the number of debutantes decreases. Boys are only needed as partners; they do not "come out" themselves.] That's been a fun thing. There are eleven members, and we divide up the special jobs—like catering, decoration, membership.

Part of the implicit attraction of the event is that it is special, exclusive, and, of course, exclusionary. The participants (organizers, parents, debutantes, and escorts) make a symbolic statement about their membership in a closed circle by their attendance.

Of course, not all who are eligible care to participate. Some of the work of keeping these events successful is motivating the debutantes and escorts to appear. During the 1960s, when the youth rebellion against the established order reached some members of the upper classes, participation seemed less desirable to many than it did in other periods. Parents, accordingly, reported having to threaten, cajole, and bribe their children into attendance. This effort, like that of motivating younger children to attend dancing classes and social clubs, was accepted by the mothers as part of their work.

Preparing children for social responsibilities and participation in an elite society is only one part of the work women do in preparing the new generation to take its place in their class. Another part is teaching children how to engage in noblesse oblige activities. Some of what children learn can be inferred from women's reminiscences about how they themselves responded to external pressures. As one woman put it: "When I was a senior in college I joined the Junior League. It was really the determination of my mother" that sparked the decision. Another woman spoke of the constant direction offered by a parent: "I went to work as a member of [a special volunteer group] at the hospital in '46. And I was there about ten years. My mother got me in. It was the story of my life. My mother was a member of the board of directors for many years." Eventually this woman also became a director.

Not all women emphasize the pressures from parents. Some, even when young, wished to emulate their parents: "My mother was involved [in the community] and so was my father. I remember I was president of my high school sorority, and when I came home, I put my gavel next to that of my mother and father."

On the basis of their own training and, later, independent volunteer experience, women formulate expectations about what their children will do. Three women spoke specifically of their children as protégées and proudly mentioned their accomplishments in areas where the mother had trained them. In the course of one such statement, an older son of the house entered and explained how he had found enough benefactors to sit at twenty tables for a major event that his mother was sponsoring. He and his mother agreed that all the children of the house had learned to be great folders and envelope-stuffers. "We're quick on the staple," he said.

Six women spoke of taking young children along to help them in volunteer work. At first the help might be only docile assistance. A daughter who was listening to an interview volunteered that she was very involved. "What do you do?" I asked her. "Anything and everything I'm asked," she replied. Her mother added: "She's my good man Friday. She helped in [a conference I arranged] and helps at [an ongoing business operation to raise funds for the mother's main philanthropic interest]. She's part of the crew." Later, children may play an active part in a mother's political campaign or cooperate in organizing a new philanthropic service. One parent summarized the educational effect of this assistance: "My philosophy is that the impact from doing these things is invaluable. And it educates the children. They learn about the community when they help me. And they learn at an earlier age than otherwise."

The expected outcome of early training is that children become independently active in the community. Five women with grown children spoke with pride of what their children had accomplished for the community on their own. One woman explained her principle of encouraging initiative by avoiding any show of continued supervision once the children were trained:

Clara has done other things for me; [but] she had her first volunteer experience in [a local political] campaign. I really steered clear of her in that . . . because she was in the youth campaign on her own. . . . She did all kinds of really imaginative things. . . . [For example,] a fair for the aged [in the] south of Main Street [area], and [she] set up exhibits and manned them. . . . [She is] terribly well organized. . . . I think she'll be all right.

Other women in this group spoke with pride of children who were now on the boards of private schools that they had attended while their mothers were board members. And still others were proud of sons and daughters who had organized their own foundation and sat on the board of that organization, which gave money to unpopular but worthwhile causes.

From early apprenticeship through autonomous participation in the work of civic responsibility, then, these women guide their children and watch their growing independence and initiative with pride. The women volunteers see their successes as accomplishing a double purpose: providing a new generation of well-motivated workers for Pacific City, and also providing a new generation of responsible leaders to carry on the traditions of their families. The women generally do not, of course, stress the importance of maintaining their families' class position; that part is assumed. My impression was that they thought class an ungenteel matter for discussion. However, a woman who rose from the working class to a status that allowed her daughter the schooling and friends to consolidate her position in the upper class could see, and speak about, the importance of this work for class standing:

My daughter has this interest, not as strongly as I do, though. But she is Junior League and she belonged [to the exclusive club at her university]. . . . With my daughter, it is innate in her. She knows she has to donate her time. She has seen the way. It is in the family, like going to school. It was different for me, just starting out first generation. But I see for the others [who are well connected]. . . . Their daughters just naturally fall into it because it is part of what happens in the family.

What happens in the family is that parental efforts to teach social responsibility become mixed with a sense of noblesse oblige. This idea, no matter how soft-pedaled, is that "we" are different from and better than "they." [?] However, this idea is merely an undertone in the presentations made by the women in this study, and they seem to avoid it. Part of the work that these women do, then, is hidden by their own sense of what it is appropriate to claim in a democratic society. Their very real work of manufacturing class position is supposed to be ignored as they weave their volunteer activities around institutions that benefit their own children and prepare those children to participate in a world of civic beneficence and class standing. In fact, the maintenance of such conventions constitutes much of the work that these women do: to "ignore" successfully, to render invisible what is tangible and palpable, is also a product of someone's labor.

Contributions to Husbands' Careers

The same difficulty in seeing their work and laying claim to it arises when these women consider how volunteer leadership might affect their husbands' careers. Although volunteer work can support husbands' careers, most women in this study minimize the importance of their work for this purpose. They give little attention, for example, to the significance of their ability to use their community experience to organize business or professional conventions and parties at a husband's request. But what they do say reveals the use-fulness of their work. For example, the wives quoted below, active in power-ful and prestigious boards in Pacific City, are married to a doctor and a lawyer respectively. The women's board directorships give their husbands the oppor-tunity to make professional contacts and acquire "inside" information about future changes in community organization that can affect their practices—benefits that these women acknowledge only obliquely:

I was asked to be president, and I think it is one of the super boards of the city; I was flattered to be asked. My husband was anxious for me to be the president. He was ab-solutely great at helping me—listening to my speeches and [helping me do] my letters.

Last year when I was invited onto the trustee board, I was floored. My husband said: "Do it, do it!" He has gotten me into more things because I am not that aggressive a person.

Neither explains how her position might be useful in her husband's busi-ness or professional work. But one wife explicitly mentioned the helpful am-bience that she could create for her husband: "I loathed being president of the auxiliary, but I was a doctor's wife. I did it for my husband, of course. It wasn't unimportant, really, that men have the women create social connec-tions." Still another women earned her husband's gratitude by running a pro-fessional medical conference: "My husband said, 'They're going to ask you to be the women's chairman.' And I asked him if that's what he wanted me to do. He said, 'It would be very nice if you did it.' " One woman was quite ex-plicit about how a wife's honors are a credit to her husband: "My husband wanted me to be in volunteering. He felt it accrued to his prestige to have me president of the Junior League." Not only is it a form of conspicous con-sumption to have so prestigious a consort, but a wife may be able to improve the social status of her husband through her participation in prestigious com-munity welfare activity.

Some assignments undertaken specifically at a husband's request occur only when he—and she—are already in leadership positions. Prominent phy-sicians asked to host the convention of their professional society, for exam-ple, need their wives and their wives' friends and connections to make the ar-rangements that add luster to the substantive program.

It is difficult to assess the work women may do for their husbands through careers in volunteerism. First, the manipulation of philanthropic impulses to serve one's own materialistic ends runs counter to the ideology of altruism that pervades volunteer effort. Second, it is not "genteel" for traditional women to imply that their husbands need any help to be successful. Instead, women take the view that each spouse has a particular turf: if husbands live in a world of professions and business, then home, family, and the direction of their own volunteer efforts belong to the women. Here is how one women explained it: "I get a lot of satisfaction out of projects I'm into. I need something that's not medical. The symphony and museum are my own things. My husband is important in the medical world, and I need something that's my little area."

These respondents want to share actively in the American values of individual achievement and recognition, not just indirectly as the helper-facilitator to their families:

In volunteering, I gained personal esteem. I found out I could do something. I could get some self-identity and some confidence. Hubert was very popular, handsome, and personable. He had a big smile. And people would be attracted to him. "Oh, your husband is so marvelous," people would say. "What does Hubert think?" they would ask. It was never "What do you think?"

It is not surprising, then, that very few women in this study saw volunteer work as related to their husbands' interests. And, again, in not "seeing," they do the ideological work that makes any assistance to husbands disappear.

Attenuated Status:
The Consequences to Self of Contradictory Work

So far, I have suggested that these women develop their patterns of community service within the framework of traditional family relations. The consequence is that they work within and around their husbands' requirements and childcare responsibilities. Where husbands are busy with their own careers and childrearing burdens are eased by household help, women can create almost independent lives. And they may have to. Paradoxically, husbands may demand that their wives become independent. As early as the 1850s, commentators on the American scene reported that women were often neglected by their men, who "immersed in a whirl of business spend only short periods with their families" (Isabelle Bird, quoted in Douglas 1977:61). In modern-day professional families, this neglect may mean that the entire burden of household management falls to the woman (Fowlkes 1980). But it can also provide the impetus for a career of one's own, independent of a husband's name or fame. And further impetus comes from the social expectation that those with some free time should contribute their effort for the community welfare. These expectations have developed around the ideology of domesticity. As Sklar (1976) argues, the development of American culture in the nineteenth century increasingly polarized the ideal behavior of men and women. Males were to experience self-realization in independent activity; females were to find fulfillment in self-sacrifice and service to others. The activities involved in promoting community as well as family welfare were thus seen as appropriate to women. This career, then, is built in the interstices of family life.

Consequently, the ability that women show in their community service fulfills their obligation to represent the family and maintain social-class position, develop social connections, and show some individual initiative. For women in this social milieu, community service offers the best compromise between their personal ambitions and class and family demands and the best channel for their energies.

But the limitations of this choice should be noted. Whatever public acclaim an individual woman receives for her contribution (in awards and appointments), this career is not a recognized, prestigious one. The separation of women's work from the visible, income-producing sector of the society that accompanied the separation of the home and workplace in the nineteenth century (Kessler-Harris 1981) also lowered the estimation of that work. Women's work was visible when it had a direct relationship to the production of family income. Without that relationship, the social value of women's activities could be questioned and reassessed. The distinguishing characteristic of upper-class women became their use of leisure. They were expected to stay home and beautify, even ennoble, their surroundings. But this work, as well as the work of volunteer women who become civic leaders, has a faintly dubious image. This disesteem stems from the assumption that the work is in the main trivial or nonessential; it is marginal to the main productive work in the profit economy. And the women who make homemaking and volunteering their life's work are also marginal to that economy. These women are useful only as the agents who display, in their lifestyle, the wealth and culture that husbands and fathers can afford. Ironic commentaries on conspicuous consumption have been popular since Veblen used the term to describe the public display of wealth that captains of industry delegate to their wives as a symbol of male success and power. Women are expected to show, through their conspicuous consumption of the leisure required to become artistically cultivated, the vast quantities of vicarious leisure available to their husbands (Veblen 1953). It is men who gain status from women's activity, not the women themselves. The significance of this work in introducing the children to class values and reaffirming the family's place in the class structure is unacknowledged and, as we have seen, must remain so. In keeping it under wraps, these women create its value for their families, if not for themselves. However, both upper-class (Davidoff 1973) and middle-class families (Kohn 1959) depend upon the community work of women to place the family in the appropriate class context.

Even without an explicit appreciation of its significance for class maintenance, the importance of leisure time has been long recognized. The ability to
maintain women in leisure was an important asset for the family. As Douglas
(1977:55) says of the lady in mid-nineteenth-century America, even when she
was not idle, her leisure became the most interesting and significant thing
about her. This assessment hangs over the twentieth-century equivalent of
that lady. Much of the work that community volunteers do is seen as part of
leisure activity. Some of their comments suggest that they themselves accept
this view. They say, for example, that they do the work because they enjoy it,
not because they have to. Or they regard the expenses of volunteering, something they *like* to do, as an amusement rather than a work expense. But, for
many, the way they learn to be disciplined at their volunteer work and to
define it *as* work is part of an effort to resist the stereotypic definition of the
society matron, with its connotations of idleness and inconsequentiality.
Middle-class volunteers trying to avoid the label of "just" a housewife are
responding to the same stereotype (Lopata 1971). Women of both classes try
to escape the ambiguity of the catch-all title of "volunteer" and call themselves "citizen participants." Some use the terms "career" and "professional volunteer" to suggest the seriousness of their commitment.

One woman expressed the sentiments of many when she stoutly asserted
the professionalism of career volunteers:

I don't see the difference [between volunteers and other professionals]. That's what
I've been fighting for. The fact that volunteering is not paid is by the by. They are the
same or better than employed persons. . . . I feel we're upgrading the role of the
volunteer in America.

However, this woman adds a further comment that reveals another common
perspective—some abivalence about how the role of volunteer is carried out:

But I don't have the skills I should have learned. I should have learned to type, maybe.
We need exactly the same attitude as if you were paid. That's what it takes to do a
good job.

These doubts combine with the difficulties of resisting societal judgments and
the ambiguities inherent in their work. They are further complicated by resistance to seeing some of this activity as work to produce and maintain class
membership. All these doubts place many women in a quandary over what
they have accomplished. Have they been working seriously? Have they been
at work for family or community? Have they chosen independent fields of en-
deavor or only followed the guidance of a husband?

Questions of how their work should be regarded come to the fore when
volunteer women are around male professionals:

I consider myself a professional volunteer, but that's hard to explain to professional
people. I find myself rather intimidated by this group. What can I say, by God, that

can make them take notice when I'm not earning the almighty buck? And there is the lady bountiful image [to fight against]—the little rich girl who's never worked in her life.

Sometimes doubts can overwhelm women for a time. "The first year [on a city commission] was scary—I don't know why. Males dominate the groups, and I felt shaky. It takes a year to feel at home." And sometimes doubts keep recurring. These doubts about one's ability often center on public speaking:

It's hard for me to speak in public. I mastered it when I had to. But it was really difficult. The nervousness—I guess everybody has it, but some are able to do it without a crisis. In the lapses of time [since the last presidency] I got out of the habit. I won't make a speech for anyone now.

A few women accept their subordinate status as volunteer women and try harder to win the approval of men and salaried professionals: "On the women's committee I'm afraid I'm known as the late Mrs. Lathrop. But I'm careful [to be on time] when there are men on the committee."

Worries caused by the belief that the family comes first are a recurring theme. Women sometimes mention their guilt in a self-denigrating way ("I'm probably a lousy mother"). Yet even while experiencing guilt at not fulfilling their homemaker role better, women find themselves caught in conflicting expectations and wishes. And so they also express their sense of guilt about not doing more for themselves: "I have trouble recognizing my own talents and abilities. I still come at the tail end in the family situation and sometimes in a few others."

Inability to resolve the conflict between duties to family and duties to self are seen not as external, social problems but as internal signs of personal inadequacy. Women recognize that fragmentation and consequent inability to concentrate on intellectual matters are produced by myriad calls on their attention, although they do not see this as a problem produced by others—by family demands, for example. Nor do women see it as produced by traditional social expectations that ignore their need for, or right to, uninterrupted time in order to develop some kind of independent career:

I am mentally lazy, though not lazy about working. I know I have a good mind, and my husband is furious with me [for not developing it]. Improving your mind is difficult when there is always something to do . . . something in the garden to prune, or cooking and then one of the children calls and all you can do is listen. It seems I never have a minute when I feel I can sit down with a book and concentrate. [I would like to take a master's degree] but I feel guilty when I sit down and read.

Spontaneous comments during interviews occasionally seemed to go beyond conventional modesty. Women apologized for signs of clutter in beautiful, tidy homes; they peppered their discussion with questions and disclaimers ("Do I sound dictatorial?" "I have done nothing of any importance, really") and asked for reassurance about the quality of their responses ("I'm afraid that was a rather rambling answer." "I'm afraid I am giving you more than you asked").

Expectations that women will find their fulfillment in family responsibilities combine with other aspects of traditional upbringing to encourage modesty, reserve, and diffidence. This pattern may lead women to be thoughtful of and attentive to others, humble, cooperative, and pleasant, but it can also sap self-confidence and leach away the spirit of independence or assertiveness. The women in this study deal with the conflict between traditional expectations and the desire for self-assertion with considerable success; yet their reactions suggest that the dilemma is not always resolved.

Perhaps the difficulty lies, in part, in ambivalence about the value and prestige of volunteer work. The difficulty of assigning cash or salary equivalents to their work leaves many uncertain about how to assess its worth. The experiences of women who have to find salaried work following a husband's death or a divorce bring that difficulty home quite forcefully. Or the change in status to widow or divorcee may simply raise questions about one's worth that one has never had to face before. It is not surprising, then, that some to whom I spoke were anxious and uncertain about their potential for salaried employment after a change in their marital status. Doubts, anxieties, sadness, surrounded the question of their worth on the job market.

But something more than cash equivalence is at stake here. To the extent that their work is in part ideological, it carries with it an inherent contradiction. It must not be recognized for what it is. The work of these women is valuable to the extent that it is not explicitly recognized as having functional value.

Conclusions

Hidden work is difficult to assess. Both its nature and extent are necessarily amorphous. There may be many reasons to keep such activity unexamined. For example, it may concern problems that cannot be confronted directly. Women who do the work of maintaining class in a society with an aggressively democratic ethos are doing that kind of work. Similarly, women who have mixed motives for community service (altruism, but also a concern for a husband's career or the family's social position) are keeping some part of that work from observation and discussion. Some of the work is obscured, misunderstood, or dismissed through stereotyping of the workers and their work as inconsequential *because* it contains some of these elements within it.

Despite occasional symbolic gestures to the contrary, the lack of systematic attention to and respect for the work women do in family and community service is a sign to them that this work is regarded as having little value. At the same time, these women are caught in the paradoxical situation of wanting their work on class maintenance to be ignored or played down. They are not ready to want credit for *all* their efforts. Such dilemmas suggest some of the dynamics by which those who perform hidden work and the society in which they do it conspire to prevent any serious and systematic attention to that work. It is not surprising, then, that the evaluation of the hidden work of constructing class and community remains unresolved.

Notes

Acknowledgments: This paper is an offshoot of a larger study sponsored by the National Institute of Mental Health and by a Ford Foundation Faculty Fellowship 1975–1976). It is also part of a forthcoming book entitled *Invisible Careers* (University of Chicago Press).

1. In the quotations used from these interviews, all identifying charactersitics of the respondents or their city have been changed or removed.

2. In the work of Susan Ostrander (1984) and Robert Coles (1977), concepts of class position and class responsibility are more clearly expressed. Their respondents speak more openly of the importance of maintaining their own class through acts of charity and philanthropy.

References

Coles, Robert. 1977. *Privileged Ones*. Boston: Little, Brown.
Davidoff, Lenore. 1973. *The Best Circles*. Totowa, N. J.: Rowman and Littlefield.
Douglas, Ann. 1977. *The Feminization of American Culture*. New York: Knopf.
Finch, Janet. 1983. *Married to the Job: Wives' Incorporation in Men's Work*. London: Allen and Unwin.
Fowlkes, Martha R. 1980. *Behind Every Successful Man: Wives of Medicine and Academe*. New York: Columbia University Press.
Kessler-Harris, Alice. 1981. *Women Have Always Worked*. Westbury, N.Y: Feminist Press.
Kohn, Melvin. 1959. "Social Class and Parental Values." *American Journal of Sociology* 64:337–51.
Lopata, Helena Z. 1971. *Occupation Housewife*. New York: Oxford University Press.
Luxton, Meg. 1980. *More Than a Labour of Love*. Toronto: Women's Press.
Merton, Robert K., and Patricia L. Kendall. 1946. "The Focused Interview." *American Journal of Sociology* 51:541–57.
Oakley, Ann. 1974. *The Sociology of Housework*. New York: Pantheon.
Ostrander, Susan. 1984. *Women of the Upper Class*. Philadelphia: Temple University Press.

Sklar, Kathryn Kish. 1976. *Catherine Beecher: A Study in American Domesticity*. New York: W. W. Norton.

Strasser, Susan. 1982. *Never Done: A History of American Housework*. New York: Pantheon.

Veblen, Thorstein. 1953. *The Theory of the Leisure Class*. New York: New American Library.

11

Servants to Capital:
Unpaid Domestic Labor
and Paid Work

NONA Y. GLAZER

Introduction

I will argue in this essay for an interpretation of women's unpaid domestic labor that links the work *directly* to the everyday routines of the social relations of capitalism, far removed from the household. Unpaid domestic labor is seen usually (by those who do the work as well as those who theorize about it) as linked only in *indirect* ways to the reproduction of capitalism (e.g., Vogel 1973; Fee 1976; Molyneaux 1979). I argue, however, that domestic labor is integral to capitalism and the capitalist state in ways that are not recognized completely in theories about its indirect contribution to capitalism through social reproduction.

Social scientists have tended to adopt the view of a fundamental split between the family and other social relations rather uncritically, making it difficult to understand specific issues of domestic labor, such as the division of labor in the family.[1] Recently, the boundary as conceptualized in mainstream social science has been scrutinized more critically, and the questionable nature of seeing the family as more or less on the margins of "public" social life has come to be seen by many as a severe limit on understanding how capitalism shapes "private" life.[2]

I shift perspective and view domestic labor from outside the family, asking how social relationships outside the household (in capitalist firms or state agencies) require very particular forms of unpaid domestic labor from women. From the standpoint of capitalism and the state, women as consumers enter into definite social relationships—their labor enters into the work

Adapted from *Review of Radical Political Economics* 16, no. 1 (1984): 61–87. Copyright, *Review of Radical Political Economics*. Reprinted by permission of the Union for Radical Political Economics.

process,[3] but in the instances to be discussed here, they are exploited and their labor appropriated *without* their entering the wage relationship. Women's labor is appropriated (and women are exploited as domestic work ers) by corporations which are able to structure consumption in the commercial and service sectors (e.g., by the way in which goods and services are obtained in retail enterprises). Domestic labor thus includes some work which is part of both *social reproduction* and *production.*

Domestic labor's public face, it will be argued, is, as involuntary unpaid labor, part of how work is organized in the workplace and in state agencies. This unpaid domestic labor results from what is here called a *work transfer.* Work that may once have been done in the home and subsequently taken over by capitalism (or the state), as well as work that came into existence only because of capitalism, is reorganized. The reorganization takes the form of shifting once-paid work to consumers, making it part of consumption, and either eliminating or otherwise changing the work of paid workers.

Theories About Work

VIEWS OF UNPAID LABOR: IN AND OUTSIDE THE HOUSEHOLD

Mainstream and radical theories of unpaid domestic labor converge in several ways that are challenged by this paper. First, both approaches see women's unpaid domestic labor as private, performed by wives and mothers. Women's unpaid labor is seen as related to the world outside the family (i.e., to capitalism or to society) through the labor that they do for their families. Women are seen in Marxist feminist analyses as reproducing the working class materially and ideologically, and on a daily and generational basis, by caring for adult paid workers and rearing children (Dalla Costa 1972; Vogel 1973; Morton 1978). In mainstream social theory, the work that women do is seen only somewhat differently, with an emphasis on women's domestic work as being for "society" rather than for capitalism. Women are seen as maintaining the society and the culture by socializing the next generation into appropriate behaviors and beliefs, into readiness for school, and into other precursors of adult statuses (Parsons 1955; Lopata 1974; Oakley 1974).

Second, though consumption is seen by both mainstream and radical analysts as an important part of unpaid domestic labor, usually women's domestic labor is seen as centered basically in the household and done for the family. Among the social critics, only Seligman (1968: 229) sees that consumers (mostly women) may actually work directly for capitalists and that their work may be included literally in measures of productivity computed by managers for stores, banks, and other organizations. The sole theoretical challenge to conventional analyses of domestic labor has been the pioneer work of Batya Weinbaum and Amy Bridges (1976). They argue that part of women's domestic labor in capitalist society is consumption, that "capital organized consumption for women" and pulls women into the *work process* (Weinbaum and Bridges 1976: 88) in such disparate places as the supermarket, the doctor's office, and the laundromat (Weinbaum and Bridges 1976: 94–95).

This essay is complementary and yet emphasizes the logical and straightforward attempts by some capitalists to insert the consumer into the work process. It emphasizes how capitalism eliminates services in the struggle for markets, in an increasingly monopolylike sector, which, in turn, provides the condition for forcing most consumers into participating in the work process. This essay also emphasizes the impact of the work transfer on paid workers. The underlying theoretical concerns remain the issues of the dualist view of work, the inaccuracy of seeing only paid work as subject to appropriation, and the need to rethink the nature of the boundary between the private and public spheres.

THE PROBLEM OF CONCEPTUAL OPPOSITES

Most of the views summarized above see *work* as either *for* the household or *in* the workplace. Work itself is conceptualized as being one of two kinds.

Dualistic thinking about work seems to follow from observations of a particular historical process—the change from work for subsistence, concentrated in the household, to the emergence of a market economy where waged labor became critical to the survival of the working class. The analysis of the separation of much paid work from the household and the development of the marketplace as central to capitalism brings with it a whole set of categories reflecting an either/or view of work: exchange value versus use value;[4] productive versus nonproductive labor; market versus nonmarket work; the public realm of work outside the family versus the private realm of the family. Each pair reinforces the view that there is a sharp boundary between the economy and the workplace on the one side and the household economy and the family on the other. This conception may be accurate for describing critical changes in production that emerged from the late seventeenth century through the early twentieth century. Today, the use of these contrasts and the assumption of tight boundaries between domains of work prevent us from observing how work has been reorganized, pulling the consumer into the work process.[5] Within commercial capitalism, women as consumers substitute for once-waged workers; their work becomes a source of capital accumulation as their labor within the service sector is appropriated.

THE EXPLOITATION OF UNWAGED DOMESTIC LABOR

Commercial capital (e.g., the retail food industry) hires wage labor that does not itself add to surplus value, but is a way by which capitalists appropriate "a fraction of the sum total of surplus value accruing to the entire capitalist class" (Mandel 1981: 59). The *work transfer* to consumers means that commercial capitalists hire fewer workers: consumers work in their place, and the organization is altered to eliminate some steps in the work process (e.g., consumers locate and collect merchandise, while the prepacking of goods eliminates measuring and bagging). Thus, in place of the wage labor hired to appropriate a portion of surplus value belonging to the capitalist class, women as consumers do the necessary work. Women's unpaid domestic labor may still have only an indirect relation to increases in surplus value, but they now have a direct relation to attempts by commercial capitalists to appropriate a portion of surplus value. This analysis means not seeing the wage as the only connection to the appropriation of value and to exploitation. In a sense, women may be said to be even more exploited than paid workers, since their labor is appropriated without a wage.

The appropriation of women's work in the consumption of goods and services is essential to the particular form that distribution has taken over the last forty or so years. What may make it difficult to see the activity as work is that each individual woman does a trivial amount compared with paid workers in the organization and does so on an irregular basis—that is, once or twice a week, perhaps, for twenty-five minutes rather than five days a week for six hours each day. The work of the individual women, however, added together, substitutes for the work of many paid workers. It is this substitution that originally made the use of consumer work so attractive to capitalists, though other unexpected benefits continue to make it attractive. As will be discussed later, for the consumer there is no necessary *quid pro quo*, no price reduction that reflects the savings of the retailers on labor. In fact, in some cases of the transfer, the beneficiaries include those who do not even participate in it. [6]

DISENTANGLING CONCEPTS

The terms "service sector," "service worker," and "unpaid work" need discussion. The "service sector" contrasts with extractive and manufacturing sectors, which themselves actually also include "service workers." Many service workers and much of the service sector are part of the infrastructure of business and industry; they do not provide "service" to consumers: for example, most service workers maintain factories, offices, and stores, not private homes (Bureau of the Census 1973: 749).

The concept of "work" (paid and unpaid) also needs to be used with an awareness of the theoretical implications of various usages. Some social scientists have suggested that the word applies to just about any human activity that is not ''leisure.'' This obliterates two crucial points: that consumers are forced by capitalists into participating in the work process to further capital accumulation and that there are consequences of the work transfer for paid workers (Strauss et al. 1981: 404–12).[7]

Work cannot usefully be defined in universal terms, without a recognition of how one gender—women—is exploited by the social relations of capitalism outside the wage relation. The definition below recognizes activities socially assigned to women and also exploited by capitalism (Meiksens 1981: 32–42).[8] *Work* is here defined as those activities which produce goods and/or provide services and/or provide for the circulation of goods and services which are directly or indirectly for capitalism. Hence, this includes both paid work which is an indirect source of accumulation and unpaid work, inside and outside the home, which is organized by and for capitalism. This definition means that work for capital includes: (1) the commercial sector with its unproductive labor; and (2) unpaid domestic labor in the home and unpaid domestic labor outside the home, insofar as the labor is inserted into the work process in private firms.

The Emergence of Involuntary Unwaged Work: The Case of Retail Sales

This paper examines retailing in the United States to explore the issue of the boundary between paid and unpaid work and the changing nature of domestic labor, drawing on historical documents as well as secondary material and some interviews with retail workers.

The widespread adoption of self-service by retailers in the United States is one source of the expansion of women's unwaged domestic labor. Here, domestic labor takes the form of privatized labor, which is, at the same time, labor inserted into the public sphere. This privatized yet public labor grew side by side with expanding commercialization of domestic labor. For example, self-service emerged side by side with convenience foods. Perhaps it is these twin developments that make it relatively easy to overlook the appropriation of women's unwaged labor by commercial firms.

OVERVIEW

Self-service in capitalist society derives from the pursuit of profit and the social legitimacy of profit making at all costs, even the elimination of waged workers by pulling the consumer into the work process.[9] The reliance of consumers on the market for commodities, in turn, narrows options, making it difficult for them to find an alternative to self-service. Also, the development of monopolylike conditions (through the growth of chains, mergers of stores, and the vertical integration of much retailing) allows corporate control over the organization of work in retail stores with relatively little fear that consumers will shop elsewhere, seeking clerk-service. The mythology of consumer "convenience" and rewards to the customer in the form of reduced prices serves to legitimate the system for many consumers. Women, who are 60 percent of retail workers today, have had their jobs changed by self-service.

RETAIL SALES: THE EMERGENCE OF SELF-SERVICE

Prior to World War I, most food and other kinds of merchandise were sold in small, family-owned specialized shops. For example, meats were sold in butcher shops, and fabric in dry goods stores. Large food markets can be traced back to colonial days, to the public markets such as Faneuil Hall Market (Boston) and the Pike Street Market (Seattle) (Markin 1963; Bluestone et al. 1981). By the 1870s and 1880s, there were also larger, diversified dry goods stores such as Filene's (Boston) and Marshall Field (Chicago). Smaller, diversified stores often served neighborhoods and small communities, while the "general store" was traditional in rural market towns.

Typically, stores were organized on a clerk-service basis, meaning that the consumer had a variety of services available to her. Stores employed a staff (Mom and Pop stores used the unpaid labor of family members) whose jobs required knowledge of goods (and often of customer needs), and who also located and collected merchandise, totaled the cost, charged the account, and delivered the order to the customer's home. In contrast, self-service involves work for the customer. Some work begins before the shopping trip: reading customer education materials and advertising to familiarize oneself with the functions and quality of various products. The clerk-service store provided such information, though, no doubt, the clerk was encouraged to put the interest of the store before that of the buyer.

Today, shoppers themselves do work in the self-service store. In a food store, for example, the shopper locates the merchandise by following signs or by memorizing the location of goods and makes selections without consulting clerks, loads the cart, and pushes it to the checkout stand. Even at the checkout stand, the consumer often works by loading the goods onto the counter, placing purchases in bags, and portering them home.

Self-service was first introduced into food retailing in 1912 in southern California because of the relatively higher wages and the widespread use of the automobile there. The auto gave customers access to these innovating markets, which were often outside the inner city, away from public transportation (Schwartzmann 1971: 22, 144). Self-service was also introduced to chains in 1916 in Memphis by Clarence Saunder's Piggly Wiggly stores. Saunders introduced and patented the technology of the floor layout, the turnstile and checkout stand, and his advertising copy, and franchised his system nationwide. The Piggly Wiggly stores went bankrupt by 1924 because of manipulations on the New York Stock Exchange, and the firms (Kroger and Safeway) that took over Piggly Wiggly operations discontinued self-service (Zimmerman 1955: 22). During World War I, retailers, facing labor shortages and rising labor costs because of competition from war industries, extended self-service. Some stores tried a combination of self-service and clerk-service to attract new customers by cutting prices and yet keep the old customers who wanted an array of services (Zimmerman 1955: 24).

The rapid expansion of self-service occurred because of a combination of changes in capitalism that accelerated in the late 1930s: the increasing competitive advantage of chain stores in rivalry with independent and associated food stores, the development of supermarkets, which threatened specialty stores,[10] and the intense competition for customers during the Great Depression.[11]

Chain store organizations first became serious competitive threats to independent retailers in the 1920s. In 1890 there were only ten chains in the United States; by 1920 there were 808 chains, which grew to over double that in eight years, to 1,718 by 1928 (Haas 1939).

Some indications of why the independent retailers believed themselves so threatened by the chains is evident in the growth of the market share of chains during the first years of the Depression. In 1929 independents had about 89 percent of the retail stores and 78 percent of the sales. By 1933, independents decreased their share of stores by 1 percent but their share of sales to 71 percent. Though the chains also lost stores, they increased their share of sales from 20 percent in 1929 to 25 percent in 1933. Total retail sales decreased drastically and dramatically by nearly 50 percent between 1929 and 1933, from 49 million to 25 million, a reflection of massive unemployment and the loss of family income.

The chains are of particular importance in understanding the pressures under which the independent grocers found themselves and why they introduced self-service eventually and changed the gender of the work force, from men clerks to women cashiers. The chains began to develop about 1914 with a distinct advantage that came from quantity buying. They forced food wholesalers to give them sizable discounts that independents were refused. In the late 1920s, some grocers joined associations such as the Independent Grocers of America (IGA) and Red and White and buying groups that tried to get sizable discounts and carried on joint advertising campaigns. However, the chains maintained their competitive advantage legally until the passage of the Patman-Robinson Act of 1936,[12] which set "fair pricing practices" and outlawed different treatment of retailers by wholesalers. However, the Patman-Robinson Act was evaded and hurt small buyers (Bluestone et al. 1981). Independents attempted unsuccessfully to control competition from the chains with other legislation—for example, special local taxes. Independent grocers then adopted self-service, which decreased the labor costs that some retailers considered to be "too high" even in the 1920s (Harrington 1962: 2).

The supermarkets that boomed in the 1930s made self-service an integral part of their organization.[13] Eventually, supermarkets eliminated the clerk not only from the sale of goods that came to the store already packaged, but also from the sale of goods that grocers once thought demanded clerk-service, such as meats. The success of cash and carry self-service supermarkets encouraged chains and the associated grocers to convert from clerk-service to self-service as well as to eliminate other services such as credit and home delivery (Peak and Peak 1977).

By 1940 self-service was both sufficiently widespread in the United States and of sufficient interest to would-be adoptors that the national association of retail grocers did a nationwide study. The self-service store was described in the report as more profitable than comparable service stores, though some expenses were higher, such as advertising (used to "attain and hold a large volume") and the rent of a "more favorable location." But the explict recog nition of self-service as decreasing wages and of the consumer as doing work reveals the intentions of the retailers: "Wage expense, the biggest single item of operating costs, is as a rule lower in the grocery departments of self-service stores. Insofar as consumers wait on themselves in a store with a fairly good volume, clerk expense is smaller. Insofar as other services may be curtailed by self-service arrangement and operation, operating expense may be reduced" (Dipman and O'Brien: 266–67). In a follow-up report issued in 1946, the self-service operation was called "labor and expense saving." The increasing postwar activities of labor unions were noted as meaning higher wages for employees (Dipman et al. 1946: 5,8). Shorter working hours and higher wages made self-service desirable because, as the Progressive Grocer association stated, "by getting consumers to do some of the work now done by employees, . . . a merchant [can] make the greatest use of the fewer hours available to the store and employees" (Dipman et al. 1946: 9).

During and after World War II, the shortage of labor and goods speeded the adoption of self-service (Wingate 1942; Thompson 1942); stores had no problem in attracting goods-hungry customers. Unionization drives meant the possibility of a shorter work week and higher wages for clerks, making self-service attractive to department and variety stores, too (Dipman et al. 1946; Canfield 1948: 104).[14]

While the original reason for self-service was to lower labor costs, other changes in merchandizing and transportation help to explain its success. The wide use of the automobile, beginning in the 1920s, and increasing with suburban and highway development in the postwar years, made shopping-center construction with the self-service store a major form of investment for land developers.

Many services other than the clerk's help and knowledge of where the products are have been eliminated from stores. Retailers today rely on national manufacturers to provide services such as product information, guarantees, return and repair services, and quality control (Fuchs 1968). In addition, self-service is supported by national advertising and by national brands; in turn, the reliance of retailers on national brands is made possible—indeed, virtually forced—by other changes. These changes include vertical integration, mergers of stores and takeovers of family-owned, locally based stores by national chains and holding companies. This made it possible for national advertising to be an effective seller of national brands. By 1982 the concentration of capital in manufacturing and retailing, and the cooperation of supposed competitors, culminated in 28 major American department stores with a total of 353 branches and 17 affiliated overseas stores actually owning jointly the international Associated Merchandising Corporation (AMC). AMC advises its owners on all aspects of retailing, providing monopolylike conditions and homogeneity in the marketplace (Salmans 1982: 1).

Self-service began as a relatively small-scale attempt by food retailers to lower operating costs by shifting work to the consumer. It succeeded as retailing in the United States changed increasingly from local production, sales, and control to national control.

CLASS DIFFERENCES

Retailers have not been able to cut services identically across class lines. Reorganizations which require middle- and low-income consumers to substitute their own time and labor for those of once-waged workers have had less success among the rich and more affluent—except perhaps in grocery retailing. Retailers have responded to the wealthy by providing the services of sales clerks, locally available guarantees, free delivery, and special orders. The increased concentration in the retail industry may mean a loss of clerk-service and other services except for the very rich, or for those who buy in small, privately owned specialty shops.

Working-class consumers do not have the ready cash or credit necessary to pay the higher prices in the stores that give services to the more affluent. Though employed women, including working-class women, are advised by the mass media to turn to services in the marketplace to substitute for their own now-absent work in the household, low wages prevent this. Working-class women, especially those who are sole heads of families, are unlikely to have sufficient income to buy services or shop where services are available.

Self-service cannot automatically be interpreted as bad for consumers just because it is good for capital accumulation; nor is it automatically good because retailers and some customers say so. Certain aspects of self-service may be a convenience to the consumer; others may be an annoyance or set unsuspected limits. [15] Whatever benefits or losses there are for the consumer, the theoretical point about the insertion of the consumer into the work process remains: the consumer does work, unwaged, that was once done by a paid clerk.

The Reinforcement of Gender Subordination

WOMEN AS SELF-SERVICE CUSTOMERS

The following section will consider the gendered nature of the unpaid self-service workers and how advertisers and grocers view women as self service customers. In addition, the claim that self-service is an activity in which women customers are paid back for their work with lower prices and with benefits loosely called "convenience" will be examined.

Although not every self-service customer is a woman, the majority are. The customer is usually portrayed in the marketing literature as a woman. An economist in 1939 described why women used self-service: "There is one type of shopper whose importance is magnified by the feeling that she makes her own selections, serves herself, and gets the most for her money" (Haas 1939: 98–99). The implication was that the sense of importance rests on rather banal grounds, though it can be used to the retailer's advantage to reduce labor costs. Advertising aimed at encouraging women to shop in self-service stores played heavily on themes of choice, control, and freedom (Ladies Home Journal 1929: (Oct.): 185; (Dec.) 137).

Elaborate rationalizations were presented by marketing specialists from the 1920s onward to legitimate self-service. Distinctions between work and leisure were blurred in advertising self-service shopping—called an "adventure" (Ladies Home Journal 1929: (Dec.) 137) and described as a form of socializing for the housewife (which for some it was and may continue to be despite the few social contacts in self-service stores). One writer states that the reason merchants use self-service is to shift "much of the time-consuming unorderly marketing burden" from employees to customers and reduce "wasted [sic] time of employees waiting on each customer" (Cassady 1962: 101).

Most of the new "services" supplied by retailers are necessary or desirable exactly because other services, including clerk-service, have been eliminated. For example, "kiddie corrals" are "service" because self-service means that the customer with young children cannot telephone an order or drop off a list at the store and expect the clerk to do the work of assembling the goods. Retailers portrayed both the customers' opportunity to examine goods and standardized sizes and measures as "services." Yet prepackaging, recognized as a necessity by grocers and manufacturers if clerk-service was to be eliminated and goods successfully presold through advertising (Printers' Ink 1921a, 1921b), actually prevents most customer examination of goods.

Finally, the view that self-service means low prices to consumers is not supported by current retail pricing policies. When self-service was introduced widely in the 1930s, some of the reduction in labor costs was passed on to the customers as low prices (Haas 1939). According to business consultants, since World War II self-service retailers have been able to replace price competition (which cuts down on profit margins) with activities that do not. Loss leaders, for example, are used to attract customers, but as market consultants who advise about strategies for sales explain, these can be "used to create the general impression of over-all low prices" with the knowlege that customers cannot be aware of more of than a few prices among the thousands of items stocked in markets (Markin 1963: 82).[16]

WOMEN AS RETAIL WORKERS

Over the last fifty years, as self-service has become widespread in retailing, women have become the majority of paid workers.[17] In 1930, before the spurt in the adoption of self-service in food retailing, women were a minority (about 20 percent) of retail workers. Within a decade (by 1940), the proportion of women workers had jumped to 40 percent. By 1981, 60 percent of retail clerks and 85 percent of cashiers were women (Rytina 1982).[18]

There are no census data on cashiers before 1950, reflecting the relative lack of division of labor in retailing sales clerks handled the cashier work. However, in the 1940 census, "clerical workers" are included for the first time with sales clerks, showing the emergence of the "cashier" as a distinct occupation. Starting in 1950, the dominance of women in cashier jobs (80 percent) is evident. The relatively more powerful butchers' and teamsters' unions maintained male dominance in the food industry longer than in department and variety stores, where women moved rapidly into jobs, but where clerk unions were weaker. Also, women entered the retail industry as the overall proportion of cashiers was increasing relative to sales clerks. There were 50,000 cashiers in 1950, compared with 622,000 clerks. By 1970 a sharp shift had occurred: a majority of workers were cashiers—342,000, compared with 269,000 clerks.

Within food retailing, most jobs were done initially by men. As women entered, they tended to be hired for only certain jobs, so that sex segregation replaced sex exclusion. Thus, since 1940, the proportion of male sales clerks has declined; men have moved into management, while only a relative minority of them have become cashiers. Within twenty years, from 1950 to 1970, women workers (after their initial growth in sales work) were shifted to cashier work, not management. In 1950, 83 percent of women were sales clerks; by 1960, only 58 percent were. By 1970, only 35 percent of women sold and 60 percent were cashiers.

Women workers were in fact brought into food retailing as sales clerks, doing jobs once open to men, and not as cashiers. Until 1970, women in food retailing were more likely to be clerks than cashiers. As sales jobs were eliminated, men were not hired, but women were, and for the cashier job. Capital brought women into *paid* employment at the same time that women consumers were increasingly asked to do self-service. The result is a new division of labor: women shoppers so *some* of the work that men once did as sales clerks: women paid workers do *some* of that work as cashiers. Unpaid women were pitted against paid women only after paid women and men were pitted against each other. Hence, the *work shift* involves a further division of labor in which women were hired for jobs once held by men but now did parts of what had been a single job. The retail food industry is one among many in which cheaper female labor was substituted for more expensive male labor in the process of a detail division of work and a cheapening of labor.

The increase in women workers in retailing parallels the general economic expansion following World War II. Employers continued to divide the work of selling, reorganizing the job so that temporary workers could learn the tasks rapidly. Sales work changed to an intermittent source of income from a long-time, primary source of employment through management's eliminating commission sales and full-time and year-round work, and through a relative lowering of wages (Bluestone et al. 1981). In turn, women workers were increasingly hired (along with youths), brought in by employers instead of adult men who were entering other areas with higher earnings. The preselling of goods and services through advertising reduced the dependency of the retailer on the selling skill of the sales clerk; because of this, most clerks are no longer hired for their knowledge of products and of the psychology of selling. Therefore, commissions on sales are not used to encourage clerks to increase sales. A vastly expanded pool of workers whose skills do not have to include the product knowledge and sales skills once required allows wages to be lowered.

Today, women retail sales workers earn considerably less than men—sixty-seven cents for every dollar men earn—partly because of sex segregation within retailing (Rytina 1982). Women are segregated in the sales of less lucrative items, or "white goods," such as clothing, general merchandise, and in the smaller retail food stores, where hourly wages are typical. Male clerks dominate in the sales of "brown goods" such as motor vehicles, furniture, and home appliances, where commission sales increase earnings. Most important, self-service and, hence, lower wages characterize variety, department, and apparel stores, where women accounted for over two-thirds of workers in 1970 (U.S. Department of Commerce 1970: 798–800).

The tensions that once characterized the relations between the often working-class clerk and the wealthy customer were around interclass disdain and working-class resentment of the attempts of their employers and their customers to force them to conform in manners and deference to upper-class expectations (Benson 1982). Today, the tensions are more directly tied to the structure of selling: clerks are comparatively untrained in what might be called old-fashioned selling and often without much knowledge about product-use, let alone availability. Without systematic sales training and rewards in the form of commissions on sales and increases in wages, clerks have neither the knowledge nor the incentive to respond to customers' questions and demands for help in finding goods. Furthermore, the clerk-customer ratio is kept high by management as a way of keeping down the wage bill; cost-benefit analyses attempt to hit the highest ratio possible without driving away impatient customers.

The other side of the conditions of employment of women sales workers is the reinforcement of women's traditional economic dependency on their husbands and traditional responsibility for domestic work in the home. For women workers, the organization of retailing means that there is no job ladder, no increase in earnings with age, or a peak in earnings after years of work; in earlier decades, middle-aged women did earn more than younger or older workers (Bluestone et al. 1981: 103–4), but this is no longer typical.

Conclusions

The conventional view that women's domestic work is directly for the family and only indirectly for capitalism must be rejected as an artifact of sexism: a blindness to how women's domestic labor has been forced into the work process outside the home. Women as consumers must work in order to buy goods (and services too, though this has not been considered in the preceding analysis). The concept of "social reproduction" captures only the indirect contribution that women (as wives and mothers) make in their daily routines to the maintenance of capitalism. Most important, the view that the family and, hence, women's domestic work is *in* and *for* the private sphere, while only paid work is *in* the public sphere, can be rejected. Daily life is actually organized so that women's unpaid work *outside* the household is a critical aspect of the very basis of consuming in capitalist societies.

The ideology of convenience and the myth of cost-savings to consumers, used to make self-service palatable to women, has been questioned. The ideology and myth fit, in turn, with the ideology that applauds the housewife for frugality and good household financial management. These ideologies and supporting myths are important to examine, because capitalism and the state in capitalist societies, under cover of the continued "economic crisis," attempt to promote other *work transfers* (Glazer 1983). These are put forth as beneficial to family members, to the community, and to the unpaid workers themselves. Shifts in the responsibility for health, the funding problems of public schools, the threatened demise of the public law corporation, and the pretense that corporations can (and will) take over social programs eliminated from the federal budget make the social situation ripe for capitalists and the state arguing that women must do more unpaid work. What this means for women must be recognized: the work transfers are mainly to wives, mothers, and the other women with family responsibilities.

Work must be reconceptualized to recognize that the boundary between the family and other social relations is permeable, especially for working-class women. As defined by current social relations in capitalism, work includes the following:

1. *Domestic labor in the household:* unpaid, *directly* supportive of family life and indirectly supportive of the social reproduction of capitalism (of the present generation of workers and future workers). The extreme privatization of this labor appears to have been shaped by the emergence of industrial capitalism, supported by earlier forms of gender stratification and the later characteristics of capitalism.
2. *Paid labor:* work for wages or salary, done usually outside the home; a direct source of capital accumulation.
3. *Voluntary unpaid labor:* the labor voluntarily contributed to projects and activities that are attempts to solve problems thrown up by the social relations of capitalism.
4. *Involuntary unpaid labor:* labor that appears to be work *for* the family, done for the benefit of family members. The labor has the appearance of being privatized, the isolated work that is women's domestic labor. However, if one shifts perspective, a different interpretation is possible: our work can be seen as central to the distribution of goods in retailing and to

the performance of services. Women's unwaged work can be understood to be appropriated by capital.

Capitalism's emergence was a watershed for the oppression of women because of the resulting division of social life into, apparently, two spheres—the public sphere of social production and the private sphere of social reproduction. Value was attached to wage labor in the former; domestic labor was relatively devalued in comparison to wage labor; and the dominant ideology that emerged rejected more than a tenuous connection between the alleged "two spheres."

The trends in capitalism appear to intensify the pressures on women while weakening whatever relatively impermeable boundary may have existed between the public and private spheres of work. Our world is now firmly in both realms, and the belief in separate spheres of work is outdated imagery.

We must now (1) maintain our traditional responsibilities for the household (For there is little evidence of any significant shift in the gender division of labor in the home from women to men, whether in emotional or instrumental activities). But the double day is normalized because (2) we are increasingly expected to do paid labor outside the household, regardless of family responsibility. Also, we are (3) the backbone of the volunteer force in the United States, the source of the labor that does the work of running cultural institutions such as museums and symphonies, substituting for paid aides in the schools, and providing personal contact and nuturing in hospitals. To these widely recognized categories of our work in capitalist societies must be added (4) the exploitation of our labor in consumption.

Notes

Acknowledgments: Funds to support this work came from the Center for the Study, Education and Advancement of Women, University of California, Berkeley (Fellowship for 1982), and from the American Association of University Women.

1. Glazer-Malbin (1975) includes a methodological and empirical criticism of Parsons, who attempted to bridge the split by positing the employed male head of household as the link.

2. An excellent reference on the dialectic between domestic labor and the corporate development of technology for profit shows how capitalism shapes women's domestic work (Strasser 1982).

3. Women's domestic lives are also organized by the terms on which services are made available (Klein 1965). Interviews with German middle-class women conducted by the writer in 1979 confirm this. The women complain most about shopping and school hours as restricting their activities and complicating their doing paid work. In the Federal Republic of Germany, the extension of the hours of shops has been fought by the large department stores, who do not want to increase their labor costs; they view the smaller shops as competing unfairly, since the latter are run on unpaid family labor. Though some stores have changed their hours to accommodate the needs of em-

ployed women with family responsibilities, that change has been accompanied by the loss of services (e.g., of free delivery and knowledgeable clerks) that would make shopping easier.

4. Marx's use of exchange- and use-value does not, of course, divide the world into two realms but critiques how capitalism mystifies and appropriates exchange values. Ultimately, the dualism is rejected as part of the mystification of commodity production. In feminist analysis, the pair of terms does seem to be used in a way that lends itself to seeing women as devalued *because* their work does not enter into relations based on exchange value; see Benston (1977).

5. Many theorists have explored how capitalism and the state in capitalist society penetrate the family. For example, wage labor is seen to shape family dependence (Zaretsky 1973); the state regulates private life (Donzelot 1979); professionals dictate the terms of child care, marital relations, and other intimate parts of life and change how mothers educate children with the change from a peasant to a worker economy (Minge-Kalman 1977).

6. For example, a major medical center estimates that their "cooperative care unit" costs them 40 percent less than their traditional units. The cost reduction results both from reduced building costs (e.g., the absence of expensive medical equipment in each room) and from the labor of a cooperating, live-in family member who does the work usually done by nurses. However, the patients in the cooperative care unit are billed at exactly the same rate as the patients in the traditional nurse-supervised hospital units, and the 40 percent reduction in costs is shared out among all the units and all the patients. The special unit patients get some savings, but nothing commensurate with the savings from the labor of the family member. For the hospital, the use of unwaged family labor lowers costs without infringing on other lucrative sources of profit. (Source: Hospital Administrator Interview, January 1983, New York City.)

7. There is no doubt that patient cooperation is important for diagnosis and treatment. The question is whether or not "work" is the appropriate concept to use, Illich (1981: 100) broadens the concept of unpaid work, putting activities and emotional states together: for example, "housework, activities connected with shopping. . . . the stress of forced consumption, the tedious and regimented surrender to therapists, compliance with bureaucrats."

8. As Meiksins (1981) notes in discussing productive and unproductive labor, the crucial issue for an analysis is exploitation. The same should be said of analyses of work and domestic labor.

9. The rental of expensive equipment by the consumer is a somewhat borderline case in relating unpaid work outside the household to capital accumulation. People rent the use of washing machines and dryers in laundromats, grommet-applying machines in hardware stores, and photocopying machines in libraries and often do the work of once-paid workers. However, consumers who rent equipment such as carpet shampoo machines, steam cleaners for house exteriors, kits for installing door locks from locksmith shops, and chain saws to lower their own costs are not working for capitalism any more than when they add their labor to such goods as unassembled toys, unfinished furniture, fabrics and yarns, and, of course, raw foods.

10. Though it has been fifty years since retail food sales began to be dominated by the supermarkets, more than 30 percent of retail food stores are still run entirely by their owners and have no paid workers (Carey and Otto 1977).

11. The following definitions should help in following the social history of food retailing. In 1920 retailers were of several ownership types and sold varying products.

The *small independent* (often Mom and Pop) store operated with a minimum of investment and the unpaid labor of family members, selling usually an array of groceries, but no meat, or specializing in a single product such as food or clothing. *Independent* stores also were locally owned, had much larger inventories and investments than Mom and Pop stores, and some paid workers, though usually few. Among independent food retailers, some sold only groceries while others also sold meat. The *chains* included speciality shops each retailing such goods as electrical appliances, food, clothing, or shoes. Chains had many more stores than independents, often concentrated in a particular community or region, and were centrally owned and managed, though some local autonomy might be allowed to accommodate local tastes. The *supermarkets* were originally independents who sold a much wider variety of merchandise than either grocery or department stores and were organized on a self-service basis from their origin, even though some used clerk-service as an adjunct to self-service. There are different kinds of chains (local, regional, national) and various kinds of associations of independents (cooperatives, associated independents), but for this paper the broad categories are sufficient (Markin 1963; Haas 1939).

12. The Patman-Robinson Act of 1936 prohibited wholesalers from pricing the same merchandise differently for different retailers and from foregoing brokerage fees or giving other rebates (such as advertising) that would discriminate between different classes of buyers. Other legislation was eventually passed to set minimum or "fair trade prices," which effectively prevented discount houses from selling national brand merchandise until the 1960s (Bluestone et al. 1981).

13. The technology for self-service existed before the Depression: shopping baskets and basket carts, the turnstile, check-out stands, aisles for customers' circulation and open display counters were developed by the 1920s or before World War I.

14. Self-service was also adopted for the sale of goods in about the only area where men rather than women do the bulk of the buying—gasoline sales. The marketing of gasoline is also the history of competition between independents and monopolies, the smaller independent refineries and their retailers, and the big oil corporations and the brand dealers. Price subsidies for brand dealers (of gasoline sold by the giant companies) were used in the 1940s in a successful attempt to curtail competition from the independent refineries and dealers. The smaller self-service operators were closed down. Self-service was not adopted again until the late 1960s. Independent dealers were driven out of business by the major oil companies which withheld oil from the independent refineries during the so-called oil shortage of the early 1970s. The brand dealers then adopted self-service, so that by 1982 all but two states had self-service gas stations (Bluestone et al. 1981).

15. These points are made somewhat laboriously because American social scientists and humanists (mainly women) to whom this work has been presented sometimes react protectively and defensively about self-service. They point to the small European shop and the long hours of shopping by European women as the alternative, without connecting these to limited home refrigeration or to preferences for fresh foods. Open-air peasant markets also seem to leap to mind as another alternative. Why no alternative seems feasible that would combine quick service, home delivery, credit, and telephone orders for American women, especially the employed, says something about the success with which self-service has been promoted as "convenient" and about how this area of unpaid work is invisible to most social scientists.

16. During and for many years after World War II, goods shortages eliminated the need for much price competition. Later, monopolylike conditions—especially in food

retailing, but also in other manufacturing—made price competition much less important for marketing. Producers and distributors actually may raise prices when profits sag because consumers are not buying.

17. Retail workers also include stock persons, delivery persons, cleaners, and other miscellaneous occupations, but the majority of workers are managers, cashiers, and sales clerks, to whom this analysis is limited.

18. See Glazer 1986: 85, nn. 26–29, for sources of census data.

References

Benson, Susan Porter. 1982. "A Great Theater: Saleswomen, Customers, and Managers in American Department Stores, 1890–1940." Ph.D dissertation, Brown University.

Benston, Margaret. 1977. "The Political Economy of Women's Liberation." In Nona Y. Glazer and H. Waehrer (eds.), *Women in a Man-Made World*. Chicago: Rand McNally.

Bluestone, Barry; P. Hanna; S. Kuhn; and L. Moore. 1981. *The Retail Revolution*. Boston: Auburn House.

Bureau of the Census. 1970. Subject Reports, 1973. *Occupation by Industry,* PC (2)-7C. Washington, D.C.: Government Printing Office.

Canfield, Bertrand. 1948. "Unionization of Salesmen: An Outline of the Present Situation." *Printers' Ink* 239, no. 9 (May).

Carey, J. L.; and P. F. Otto. 1977. "Output Per Unit of Labor in the Retail Food Store Industry." *Monthly Labor Review* 100(1): 42–47.

Cassady, Ralph, Jr. 1962. *Competition and Price Making in Food Retailing*. New York: Ronald Press.

Dalla Costa, Mariarosa. 1972. "Women and the Subversion of Community." *Radical America* 6 (1972): 67–102.

Dipman, Carl W.; Robert W. Meuller; and Ralph E. Head. 1946. *Self-Service Food Stores*. New York: Butterick.

Dipman, Carl W., and John E. O'Brien. 1940. *Self Service and Semi-Self-Service Food Stores*. New York: Butterick.

Donzelot, Jacques. 1979. *The Policing of Families*. New York: Pantheon.

Fee, Terry. 1976. "Domestic Labor: An Analysis of Housework and Its Relation to the Production Process." *Review of Radical Political Economics* 8: 1:1–8.

Fuchs, Victor R. 1968. *The Service Economy*. New York: Columbia University Press.

Glazer, Nona. 1983. "Ideologies: Understanding the Legitimacy of Women's New Unpaid Work." Radcliffe Research Scholars Colloquium Series, Radcliffe College, May 19.

———. 1984. "Servants to Capital: Unpaid Domestic Labor and Paid Work." *Review of Radical Political Economics* 16, no. 1: 61–87.

Glazer-Malbin, Nona Y. 1975. "The Husband-Wife Relationship in the Division of Labor." Paper presented at the Ford Foundation Merrill-Palmer Institute. World Congress on Gender and Family Sociology.

Haas, Harold M. 1939. "Social and Economic Aspects of the Chain Store Movement." Ph.D. dissertation, University of Minnesota.

Harrington, Michael. 1962. *The Retail Clerk*. New York: Wiley.

Illich, Ivan. 1981. *Shadow Work*. Boston: Marion Boyers.

Klein, Viola, 1965. *Women Workers. Working Hours and Services*. Geneva: Organization for Economic Cooperation and Development.

Ladies Home Journal. 1929. Piggly Wiggly Stores advertisements. *Ladies Home Journal* (June): 144; (Oct.): 185; (Dec.): 137.

Lopata, Helena Z. 1974. *Occupation: Housewife*. New York: Oxford University Press.

Mandel, Ernest. 1981. Introduction. Karl Marx, *Capital*, vol. 2. New York: Vintage Books.

Markin, Rom J. 1963. *The Supermarket: An Analysis of Growth, Development and Change*. Pullman: Washington State University Press.

Meiksens, Peter. 1981. "Productive and Unproductive Labor and Marx's Theory of Class." *Review of Radical Political Economics* 13, no. 3: 32–42.

Minge-Kalman, Wanda. 1977. "Family Production and Reproduction in Industrial Society: A Field Study of Changes During the Peasant to Worker Transition in Europe." Ph.D. dissertation, Columbia University.

Molyneaux, Maxine. 1979. "Beyond the Domestic Labour Debates." *New Left Review*, no. 116: 3–28.

Morton, Peggy. 1978. "Reproduction of Labor Power: The Family." In Richard Edwards, Michael Reich, and Thomas Weisskopf (eds.), *The Capitalist System*. Englewood Cliffs, N.J.: Prentice-Hall.

Oakley, Ann. 1974. *The Sociology of Housework*. New York: Pantheon.

Parsons, Talcott, and R. F. Bales. 1955. *Family Socialization and Interaction Process*. Glencoe, Ill.: Free Press.

Peak, Hugh S. and Peak, Glen. 1977. *Supermarket Merchandising and Management*, Englewood Cliffs, N.J.: Prentice-Hall.

Printers' Ink. 1921a. "Piggly Wiggly in New Line of Merchandise." *Printers' Ink* 117, no. 1.

———. 1921b. "Piggly Wiggly Develops a Chain Store Copy Angle." *Printers' Ink* 117, no. 11.

Rytina, Nancy F. 1982. "Earnings of Men and Women: A Look at Specific Occupations." *Monthly Labor Review* 105, no. 4: 25–31.

Salmans, Sandra. 1982. "Seventh Avenue's Sharpest Eye." *New York Times*. May 23, section 3, p. 1 ff.

Schwartzmann, David. 1971. *The Decline of Service in Retail Trades*. Pullman: Washington State University.

Seligman, Ben. 1968. "The High Cost of Eating." In *Economics of Dissent*. Chicago: Quadrangle Press.

Strasser, Susan. 1982. *Never Done: A History of American Housework*. New York: Pantheon.

Strauss, Anselm L.; Shizuko Fagerhaugh; Barbara Suczek; and Carolyn Weiner. 1981. "Patient Work in the Technologized Hospital." *Nursing Outlook* 29: 404–12.

Thompson, Morris. 1942. "What About Self-Service? Is It an Answer to the Problem of Personnel Shortage?" *National Retail Dry Goods Association*

Vogel, Lise. 1973. "The Earthly Family." *Radical America* 7 (1973): 9–50.

Weinbaum, Batya, and Amy Bridges. 1976. "The Other Side of the Paycheck: Monopoly Capital and the Structure of Consumption," *Monthly Review* 28 (July–Aug.): 88–103.

Wingate, John W. 1942. "Wartime Personnel Problems in Department Stores." *Journal of Retailing* 19, no. 1 (Feb).

Zaretsky, Eli. 1973. "Capitalism, the Family and Personal Life." *Socialist Revolution* Pt. I, no. 13/14:69–119; Pt. II, no. 15: 19–123.

Zimmerman, M. N. 1955. *The Supermarket: A Revolution in Distribution*. New York: McGraw-Hill.

PART III

*Employment and Family
Life*

Introduction

Part II examined unpaid labor; Part III examines paid labor. It looks at the ways the economy and jobs shape family and the ways families shape occupational experiences. The essays in Part III are attentive to broad transformations of both family and economy in the twentieth century: the rise of the service sector as well the rise in the number of two earner families and female-headed households. But because the effect of such changes on individuals varies according to their location in the social structure, we must pay special attention to differences: between women and men, between parents and children, and among classes and occupations.

Women, Employment, and Family Life

Two oft-cited and connected demographic trends are particularly important for understanding the relationship between women's paid labor and family life. First, except for a brief period after World War II, the proportion of women in the labor force has increased steadily over this century. Up until the beginning of World War II, women in the labor force were primarily young and single. In the last few decades, not only has there been enormous growth in the employment of women—especially married women—but the pace of change has quickened dramatically. In 1985 over half of married women were employed (they now make up about half of all employed women), whereas only one-fifth of married women were employed in 1950 (when they made up only 24 percent of employed women). [1]

Second, since World War II the fastest-growing sector of the economy has consisted not of products but of services, including, for example, retail trade, personal and business services, and the food and health industries. Between

1970 and 1980 alone, the service sector grew by close to 14 million jobs, a 31 percent growth in its share of the labor market. This sector's growth relied upon a relatively large number of low-paid workers, many of whom were willing to work intermittently or part time, with limited benefits and chances for advancement. Significantly, it was women who took 75 percent of these new jobs.[2]

These two demographic trends are linked not only to one another but also to the family. Growth in the economy depended in large measure upon the characteristics of women's lives outside the labor market. As secondary breadwinners in the family's division of labor, women—economically dependent upon their husbands—became "natural" resources for the service sector's growth. Thus, the growth of this service-dominated economy—based on the inclusion of women—depended on those very features of family life created by the exclusion of married women from employment in the industrializing economy of the nineteenth century. In this sense, the twentieth century's economy inherited and made use of the nineteenth century's expectations about women's family lives and their identification with the "private" domain. In turn, the legacy of the family wage is that employed women remain ghettoized, often working in sex-segregated occupations for low pay.

Women's limited employment reinforces their dependence in and on the family. They rely on husbands for economic support. At the same time, the husband's wage alone no longer suffices. Inflation and the need to replace services once performed by wives with purchased services have increasingly made two-earner families necessary. Although wives now contribute, on average, an indispensable 29 percent of family income, they remain dependent on their husbands' larger paychecks.[3] Through these processes, women's subordination in the labor force and their subordination in the family remain mutually reinforcing.

As the labor force expanded, drawing on a supply of such economically dependent wives, families ceased to be a source of economic security for a growing number of women. High separation and divorce rates, accompanied by negligible alimony and unreliable child-support payments, have led an increasing number of women to rely on their own earnings.[4] Although neither marriage nor divorce has much effect on the economic status of male household heads, they are key events in accounting for the economic status of women.[5] Thus, changes in the family and the economy have produced what is now typically referred to as the "feminization of proverty": by 1983 two out of three adults whose income fell below the official federal poverty line were women, and more than one of three families maintained by women was poor, compared with one of thirteen other families.[6] That is, a feminization of the service economy and a feminization of the family (through female headship) has produced a feminization of poverty. This, in turn, has promoted a feminization of state subsidies to families: we have gone from the intrafamily income transfers of the family wage—from husbands to wives—to reliance on kin networks and public income transfers for women.[7]

During the same decade that produced the two-earner family and the feminization of poverty, political struggle and legislative breakthroughs allowed a growing (though still relatively small) elite corps of women to make inroads into prestigious and well-paying careers (e.g., 14.1 percent of lawyers and judges and 14.4 percent of physicians and dentists are now women, compared with 3 percent and 7 percent in 1960.)[8] For some women, these new career options provide alternatives to marital dependence.[9] It is true that better-educated and better-paid women are less likely to marry or have children and more likely to divorce than those with less education or personal income.[10] But we cannot conclude from these facts that families and professions are incompatible for women. Indeed, the involvement of a growing number of women in the professions has led to the social visibility of a new family structure: dual-career marriages that some celebrate as paving the way to the new symmetrical family.[11]

For those who do manage to combine career with wife- and motherhood, there are not only professional but personal, social, and economic advantages. Women with careers gain power at home, financial and social independence, and improvements in their self-esteem. Recent research suggests that married women are more successful in professional careers than unmarried ones. Whereas Cole suggests that the greater success of married women scientists is a result of the stability and routinization of work patterns associated with marriage, Epstein explains the success of married women lawyers by observing: "Married adults are simply considered more normal than single adults. They pose fewer problems socially to co-workers and clients." Moreover, married women are more likely than the unmarried to be integrated into networks of male colleagues and are able to make contacts through their husbands.[12]

Yet we cannot be too sanguine about the combination of career and marriage for women. Research makes clear that whereas the success of men's careers depends on incorporating their wives' labor, the success of wives' careers depends on containing their family's claims. Along with the career gains these married professional women obtain, they often feel the anxiety that accompanies high expectations and token status.[13] They often feel desperately pressed for time, giving up their own leisure and sleep to meet the demands of both employment and family.[14] Unlike men, these women discover that it is difficult to compartmentalize the different parts of their lives and that work and family constantly intrude on each other.[15] Notwithstanding the media's celebrated creation, the "superwoman," the woman who does it "all" is as unrealistic and pernicious an image as its predecessor, the "super-mom."

Finally, changes in women's participation in the labor force—be they poor, working-class, or elite—affect not only employed women but also the image and experiences of those who remain at home. Special praise now goes to the woman who does it all. The woman who works in the home becomes "just a housewife."[16]

The first three articles in this section examine women who have made different kinds of choices and are in different locations in the class structure. In Chapter 12, Kathleen Gerson compares women who have made the "hard choice" to follow a traditional domestic route (embracing full-time motherhood and homemaking) with those who have made a similarly "hard choice" to follow a non-domestic route. Each set of women faces a different series of unanticipated factors, all of which shape their choices—stable or unstable marriages, blocked versus expanding job opportunities, husbands' incomes that are adequate to support a family versus an economic squeeze, and a sense of greater rewards at home or, alternatively, on the job. These factors are themselves shaped by changes in the economy and family. Such contrasting experiences and choices vitiate the idea that either sex typing in socialization or an overarching dynamic of male oppression can account for the diversity in women's lives. This essay highlights the diversity and variation in women's experience among a generation caught at a critical moment in the changing relations between the economy and the family.

In the second essay in this section (Chapter 13), Myra Marx Ferree looks at employed working-class women. In a useful extension of research on working-class women in West Germany to her own research with such women in the United States, she suggests that much scholarship on work and family inappropriately generalizes to all women from a model based on a small number of dual-career couples. Though such a model might imply that working-class women are deficient in "work commitment" or "traditional" in family values, they are neither. Nor is the issue simply whether they are "forced" or "want" to work for pay. Ferree suggests that their individual struggles contradict characterizations of working-class women as "unliberated" or beset by false consciousness as they experience ambivalence yet draw satisfactions from (even resist relinquishing) both family work and low-paying jobs.

In Chapter 14, Marietta Morrissey turns to female-headed households, many of which are poor. We must recognize these female-headed households, especially when impoverished, as a social problem. But as Morrissey points out, we must also recognize that the growth of female-headed households may be the result and even, for some women, a source, of new independence. She argues that not only does female family headship lead to poverty, but both poverty and the relative increase in women's wages compared with men's create female headship. In other words, economic crises create family structure at the same time that family structure itself becomes a strategy for dealing with economic vicissitudes.

Men, Employment, and Family Life

Some argue that the very economic transformations that brought women into the labor force have pushed men out. [17] The rise of the service sector, composed primarily of women's jobs, occurred at the same time as the decline of the manufacturing and goods-producing sector, composed primarily of men's jobs. Yet it would be a mistake to exaggerate these developments. Men are still much more likely than women to be employed. And whereas unmarried women are more likely to be employed than married women, married men are more likely to be employed than unmarried men.

Just as some elite women have chosen careers over marriage, some writers suggest that men are now rejecting the responsibilities of husbandhood as they flee the good-provider role. [18] However, recent research clearly documents that married men, across class and occupation, share a common orientation: they believe that they work for their families, and their families keep them committed to their jobs. As in the nineteenth century (see Martha May in Chapter 4), the family continues to discipline the male labor force. At the same time, its gender-based division of labor helps men to justify and rationalize the job absorption that removes them from their families' daily life.

Yet men of different classes and occupations vary in the way they see and live out the relationship between work and family. Even a distinction between the working class and the middle class is not specific enough. For example, within the middle class, salaried white-collar workers and independent professionals experience a different relationship between work and family. The careers of the older middle class of independent professionals (most notably physicians and lawyers) and high-level executives incorporate their families. The very shape of these professions depends not simply on individual effort but on the multifaceted contributions of wives. At the same time, these upper-middle-class men find that their careers, their clients, and the organizations for which they work have become "greedy institutions," hoarding time and generally limiting their ability to meet family obligations. [19] In contrast, a recent national survey shows that salaried white-collar workers who do not work shifts or overtime and whose labor is not physically exhausting experience few conflicts between their jobs and family. [20]

Similarly, we must differentiate that large group of unionized, affluent blue-collar men who enjoy relatively stable work and family lives from those in the secondary labor market, who move in and out of both jobs and households.[21] Married men in the lower levels of blue-collar employment are more likely to experience what Piotrkowski calls "negative spillovers": irritations and boredom at work that make for irritability and boredom at home.[22] Some even suggest that there are greater differences between the family lives of skilled and unskilled blue-collar men than between those of skilled blue-collar and lower-level white-collar men.[23]

The articles in the second section of Part III, "Men's Employment and Family Life," answer the call to specify husbands' class and occupation in analyses of the varied consequences of work for family life. Examining the families of relatively affluent, unionized blue-collar men in Chapter 15, David Halle distinguishes those features of marriage specific to the working class and those shared with the lower levels of white-collar employment. Like men of other classes, the working-class men he studied believe that their marriages discipline them, keeping them at work and saving them from dissolute lives. But marriage also dampens protests that might transform the labor process. Whereas absorption in careers may pull professional husbands away from their families, it is work buddies who compete with the family ties of working-class men. And whereas professional husbands can justify their absorption in work and old-boy networks on the basis of the obvious payoff for family status and economic well-being, the lesser rewards of working-class men limit their ability to make such claims.

In Chapter 16, Robert Zussman, like Halle, presents a very different picture from that drawn in recent essays on men's flight from the good-provider role.[24] Zussman shows how the institutional separation of household and job help middle-level salaried employees and their employers maintain an ideological separation between work and family, while they maintain a commitment to both. On the one hand, because their families see little and know less about what they do on the job, and, on the other hand, because their jobs make few explicit demands on other family members, they are able to sustain the view that there is little conflict between their work and their families. This view, of course, requires inattention to the ways in which wives must adjust their own lives to make their husbands' careers possible.

In contrast to the groups Halle and Zussman studied, Martha Fowlkes (Chapter 17) shows that professionals—in this case professors and physicians—are manifestly greedy for their wives' labor. Fowlkes stresses that the character of this contribution varies from profession to profession. For both groups, however, wives' family work reinforces not only their husbands' careers but the whole structure of professional life under capitalism—including women's underrepresentation in it.

Children, Employment, and Family Life

Children's paid labor has been noticeably absent from sociological consideration of relations between work and family. To the extent that researchers have considered children at all in this context, they have done so primarily in terms of the effect of parents' employment on children. Even this research addressed only the negative impact of maternal employment on children's emotional and intellectual development or the effect of paternal employment on the intergenerational transmission of class.

The omission of children's labor from sociological analysis is both historically grounded and ideological. It reflects the history of children's wages. Together, the advance of industrialism, accompanied by protective labor laws, compulsory public schooling, and an extension of childhood, reduced the significance of whatever wages children might contribute to the family, just as it made invisible whatever work they did that was not waged. Children became increasingly viewed as "economically worthless but emotionally priceless."[25]

However, just as a service economy makes use of wives as a source of dependent and cheap labor, so too does it draw in children's labor, and for the same reasons. Children can take service jobs with low pay, no benefits, intermittent hours, and no chance for advancement because they are supported by families who view their labor as a temporary training ground for later, more serious jobs.

Young children, whether through newspaper routes and babysitting or street solicitation and drug dealing, gain a certain independence from families, yet they depend on their families for help with their jobs.[26] Adolescents in the service sector—employed in fast-food restaurants, shopping malls, and gas stations—enjoy an independent income, yet they continue to depend on their parents' financial support. Moreover, they depend on their parents, typically their mothers, to provide the help that makes their paid work possible. Mothers still chauffeur their children to work, forgo their own use of the family car, adjust meals to job schedules, clean uniforms, and take calls about work schedules.

Contemporary children are not expected to contribute their wages to the family. Still, their work has value in the family's eyes. Parents see their children's work not so much as a way to learn a particular skill as an opportunity to develop independence, discipline, and responsibility. To the contemporary parent, as well as the contemporary teenager, learning how to be a reliable worker and practical consumer is important training for adulthood as well as evidence of developmental progress. Twentieth-century parents look to wage work outside the home to accomplish characterologically what children's work in and for the family once produced automatically. There is a certain irony here. Contemporary parents support their children's work efforts because they think that these efforts will encourage independence and responsibility. Yet the actual work conditions of their children encourage subordination and passivity.

Two essays in the third section of Part III represent the two quite different sets of issues addressed in analyses of children, employment, and family. In Chapter 18 Lois Hoffman reviews research on how parents' occupations shape the home in which children are reared and produce varied modes of socialization. Unlike earlier approaches that focused exclusively on the negative impact of maternal employment, she specifies both the positive and the negative consequences for daughters and sons of both maternal and paternal employment. In Chapter 19 Ellen Greenberger takes the perspective of children themselves. In a historical overview, she discusses the changing meanings attached to children's paid labor. Although her analysis leaves implicit the ways in which the contemporary service-dominated economy capitalizes on the family dependence of teenage employees, she does explicate how parents and teenagers view adolescent employment and how that employment affects relationships among family members.

Employment and Changing Family Forms

The final section of Part III turns from individual members of families to the changing constellation of family forms. Studying the effects of employment on domestic life forces scholars to redefine what "family" is and to recognize the many forms it can and does take. The articles in this final section analyze the impact of employment in a variety of family forms.

Examining dual-career couples, Rosanna Hertz shows in Chapter 20 how the day-to-day complexities of juggling two careers shape the character of intimacy and create (rather than follow) an ideology of marital equality. Her couples are quite different from those studied in the 1970s, when researchers found far less commitment to equality.[27] Hertz draws our attention to the recent economic constraints that make couples believe that they need two salaries and the resultant internal processes that produce a commitment to equality among the most recent cohort of dual-career couples.

Hertz's work reminds us of something more: that the increasing need for two salaries in a family and the ideological support for that choice may overhaul the marriage contract as wives' job involvement enables both spouses to redefine the balance they strike in career and family commitments. "Modern" marriage, in which wives make significant contributions to household income, may allow men to reassess their own job commitment—to quit, to change jobs, to protest. As one study found, when wives earned 40 percent or more of the family income, the husbands were "extremely happy" that their wives worked, because "they no longer felt obligated to stick to jobs they hated."[28] Modern marriage, then, may disrupt social arrangements structured on the premise that men make a "family wage" and will keep going to work because they must support families.[29] At the very least, then, these marriages—like those Hertz studied—show that the family is not necessarily a passive recipient of market forces acting upon it: marriage may temper absorption in careers as well as buffer both husbands and wives against career reversals.

But not all dual-career couples are able to resist career absorption or undermining market forces. In Chapter 21 Naomi Gerstel and Harriet Gross examine commuter marriage—spouses who live apart in order to meet the dictates of professional life. Because the experiences in conventional marriage vary so clearly by gender and stage in the life course, the responses of these commuter couples can only be understood in comparative terms: women compared with men; older couples compared with younger ones. But all of the commuters, regardless of age or gender, defer to the intrusion of the market. Commuter marriage, then, does not so much resolve as give way to the conflicts between family and careers under capitalism.

In the final article in this section (Chapter 22), Kathleen Weston and Lisa Rofel analyze a lesbian work group and, in doing so, dramatically illuminate the difficulty of trying to create "family" kinds of relations at work in the context of capitalism. Community and loyalty—the early values and practice of this work group—proved incompatible with the requirements of a business bent on profit. Moreover, as this article makes clear, non-traditional family structures bring into relief tensions connected with public/private boundaries that might otherwise remain ideologically veiled. Because they operate in juxtaposition to mainstream cultural definitions of "family," such constellations highlight the ambiguities inherent in these boundaries. The issues Weston and Rofel wrestle with speak not only to the lesbian community's family-like bonds and its special concerns, but to all attempts to overcome employers' resistance to responding to problems construed as personal and private.

Notes

1. U.S. Department of Labor, Bureau of Labor Statistics, "Perspectives on Working Women: A Databook," Bulletin no. 2080 (Washington, D.C.: Government Printing Office, 1980); *Statistical Abstracts of the United States* (Washington, D.C.: Government Printing Office, 1984), p. 414.

2. Joan Smith, "The Paradox of Women's Power: Wage-Earning Women and Economic Transformation," *Signs* 2 (1984): 291–310.

3. "Contribution of Wives' Earnings to Family Income, 1983," in U.S. Bureau of the Census, Series P-60, *Current Population Reports* (Washington, D.C.: U.S. Government Printing Office).

4. As Weitzman found in her recent study, only 15 percent of divorced women in this country are awarded any alimony at all. The median child-support payment ordered by the courts covers less than half the actual cost of raising children. Moreover, in 53 percent of the cases, women do not receive the court-ordered payments. See Leonore Weitzman, *The Divorce Revolution* (New York: Basic Books, 1985).

5. G. J. Duncan, *Years of Poverty, Years of Plenty* (Ann Arbor: University of Michigan Institute of Social Research, Survey Research Center, 1984).

6. Barbara R. Bergmann, *The Economic Emergence of Women* (New York: Basic Books, 1986).

7. See Chapters 5 and 25 by Boris and Folbre in this volume and Eileen Boris and Peter Bardaglio, "The Transformation of Patriarchy: The Historic Role of the State," in Irene Diamond (ed.), *Families, Politics, and Public Policy: A Feminist Dialogue on Women and the State* (New York: Longman, 1983).

8. F. Linden and R. Marmon, *The Working Woman: A Progress Report* (New York: Conference Board, Consumer Research Center, 1985).

9. Andrew J. Cherlin, *Marriage, Divorce, Remarriage* (Cambridge: Harvard University Press, 1981).

10. S. K. Houseknecht, Sara Vaughn and A. S. Macke, "Marital Dissolution Among Professional Women: The Timing of Career and Family Events," *Social Problems* 31 (1984): 273–84.

11. Michael Young and Peter Willmott, *The Symmetrical Family* (New York: Pantheon, 1973); Julie A. Matthaei, *An Economic History of Women in America: Women's Work, the Sexual Division of Labor, and the Development of Capitalism* (New York: Schocken Books, 1983).

12. Jonathan Cole, *Fair Science: Women in the Scientific Community* (New York: Free Press, 1979); Cynthia F. Epstein, *Women in Law* (New York: Anchor Press, 1983). See also Debra Kaufman, "Associational Ties in Academe: Some Male and Female Differences," *Sex Roles* 4 (1978):9–12.

13. Rosabeth Moss Kanter, *Men and Women of the Corporation* (New York: Basic Books, 1977).

14. Rhona Rapoport and Robert Rapoport, *Dual-Career Families Re-Examined* (New York: Harper & Row, 1976).

15. Colleen Leahy Johnson and Frank A. Johnson, "Role Strain in High-Commitment Career Women," *Journal of American Academy of Psychoanalysts* 4 (1976):13–36.

16. See Kristin Luker, *Abortion and the Politics of Motherhood* (Berkeley: University of California Press, 1984); Naomi Gerstel, "Domestic Life: The New Right and the Family," in Barbara Haber (ed.), *The Woman's Annual* (New York: G. K. Hall, 1982).

17. Andrew Hacker, "Women vs. Men in the Work Force," *New York Times Magazine,* December 9, 1984, pp. 122–29.

18. See Jesse Bernard, "The Good Provider Role: Its Rise and Fall," in A. Skolnick and J. Skolnick, *Family in Transition* (Boston: Little, Brown, 1983), and Barbara Ehrenreich, *The Hearts of Men: American Dream and the Flight From Commitment* (New York: Anchor Press, 1984).

19. Diane Margolis, *The Managers: Corporate Life in America* (New York: Morrow, 1979); Kanter, *Men and Women of the Corporation*.

20. Joseph H. Pleck, Graham L. Staines, and Linda Lang, "Conflicts Between Work and Family," *Monthly Labor Review* 103 (March 1980):29–32.

21. For a useful discussion of the families of black men in the secondary labor market, see Elliot Liebow, *Tally's Corner: A Study of Negro Street Corner Men* (Boston: Little, Brown, 1967). For an interesting comparison, see Carol D. Stack, *All Our Kin: Strategies for Survival in a Black Community* (New York: Harper & Row, 1974), which tells about these men by focusing on their black women kin.

22. C. S. Piotrkowski, *Work and Family Systems* (New York: Macmillan, 1980).

23. See David Halle's review of the literature in Chapter 15 in this volume.

24. See Bernard, "The Good Provider Role," and Ehrenreich, *Hearts of Men*.

25. Viviana A. Zelizer, *Pricing the Priceless Child: The Changing Social Value of Children* (New York: Basic Books, 1985).

26. See Eleanor M. Miller's discussion of young women's street solicitation and their reliance on their families in *Street Woman* (Philadelphia: Temple University Press, 1986).

27. See Lynda Lytle Holmstrom, *The Two Career Family* (Cambridge, Mass.: Schenkman, 1972); Rhona Rapoport and Robert Rapoport, *Dual-Career Families* (Balitmore: Penguin Books, 1971); Margaret M. Poloma and T. Neal Garland, "The Myth of the Egalitarian Family," in Athena Theodore (ed.), *The Professional Woman* (Cambridge, Mass.: Schenkman, 1971).

28. Cited in Alice Kessler-Harris, *Women Have Always Worked* (Westbury, N.Y.: Feminist Press, 1981), p. 157.

29. See, for example, Maxine Atkinson and Jacqueline Boles, "WASP (Wives as Senior Partners)," *Journal of Marriage and the Family* 46 (1984): 861–70, who find that marriages in which women are the so-called senior partners, or in which wives' careers are considered more important than their husbands' by both spouses, reduce the pressure on the husbands. These husbands feel a particular reward from marriage: "the freedom and resources to pursue their own interests" (p. 866), even if those interests carry them away from jobs.

WOMEN'S EMPLOYMENT AND FAMILY LIFE

12

How Women Choose Between Employment and Family: A Developmental Perspective

KATHLEEN GERSON

How do women choose between the competing demands of employment and motherhood? Thirty years ago the answer to this question appeared straightforward: for most, commitments to marriage and childbearing took precedence over paid work or career. Those who did not or could not opt for domesticity were typically viewed with pity, disapproval, and even condemnation. Not so today. The homemaking wife who places motherhood above all other life pursuits persists, to be sure. But she coexists, and increasingly competes for social legitimacy, with a growing number of employed mothers, career-committed women, and permanently childless women. A close look at the people who have lived through this revolution in women's behavior, and have simultaneously helped to bring it about, can shed new light on the social, psychological, and ideological processes that structure "women's place."

Historical periods characterized by rapid social change are especially useful for social analysis because they make the hidden more obvious and call into question some of our most taken-for-granted assumptions about human society and human psychology. When the pace of historical change is slow, most are insulated from events that might shake up their views of the world or their proper place in it. Life appears preordained and rooted in the natural order of things. Periods of rapid social change, however, increase the likelihood of exposure to events that promote and even force individual change. At these times, many remain able to move stably along expected paths, but an in-

Adapted by permission of the University of California Press from *Hard Choices: How Women Decide About Work, Career, and Motherhood* (Berkeley: University of California Press, 1985), chap. 8. © 1985 The Regents of the University of California.

creasing proportion experience turning points at which they abandon old assumptions and confront new possibilities. These periods make it clear that stability, no less than change, is neither natural nor inevitable, but socially constructed and in need of explanation.

As other essays in this book attest, the decade of the 1970s was a watershed period in the history of American women. During this decade, female participation in the paid labor force rose above 50 percent for the first time in American history. Similarly, the birth rate dropped below the replacement rate to an unprecedented low.[1] The women most responsible for these dramatic changes in work and family patterns are those cohorts of young adults who came of age during this period. Although many of these women bore children and became homemakers, a historically high proportion entered the workplace, postponed marriage and childbearing, and forged new pathways for adult women. As members of a generation on the cutting edge of social change, these cohorts form a strategic group whose lives provide important clues about how and why women's social position is changing. Their lives can also tell us much about the more general process by which women choose between work and family commitments and about the role social arrangements play in structuring women's choices.[2]

To examine these issues, I conducted more than sixty in-depth life history interviews with a carefully selected group of college and high-school-educated women, all of whom entered and moved through young adulthood in the 1970s. Aside from their common historical location, however, they are a diverse group, representing a wide variety of class backgrounds and occupational positions. The group includes homemakers, employed mothers, and childless women as well as clerical and professional workers in both male- and female-dominated fields. By interviewing women of roughly similar ages who constructed a diverse set of resolutions to the conflict between employment and family commitments, I was able to compare those who became domestically oriented with those who developed nondomestic orientations in order to discover how and why their contrasting commitments emerged over time.[3]

Alternative Paths in Adult Development

The experiences of the respondents are best summarized in two words: diversity and change. As a group, they displayed a wide variety of orientations toward employment and motherhood. As individuals, most of them underwent significant change in orientation over the course of their lives. Although a minority enjoyed the luxury (or, viewed from a different perspective, the misfortune) of carrying through with the plans and expectations they took into adulthood, the more typical pattern involved encounters with new, unanticipated situations that deflected individuals from their early goals. Those who experienced change found themselves acting in ways they had not and could not have foreseen.

Amid the considerable diversity of these lives, four general patterns emerged, two involving stability and two involving change. First, about 20 percent of the sample followed a *traditional model* of female development, in which an adult woman chooses the domestic life for which she prepared emotionally and practically as a child. Although they had disparate class backgrounds, "traditional" women shared a similar life-course trajectory. Significantly, members of this group were insulated from events that might have caused them to veer off their expected paths. They were neither pushed out of the home by economic necessity or marital instability nor pulled into the workplace by expanding opportunities. Instead, they remained committed to the domestic path they assumed was a woman's proper and "natural" place.

A second group of women (just over 30 percent) followed a path that involved *rising employment aspirations and ambivalence toward motherhood*. Like their domestic counterparts, these women also grew up wanting and preparing for domesticity in adulthood. However, adult experiences prompted them to change their orientations and the direction of their lives. Compared with their domestic counterparts, members of this group were more likely to experience unstable relationships with men, unanticipated opportunities for job advancement, economic squeezes in their households, and disappointment with mothering and full-time homemaking. As a result, growing employment ambitions and increasing ambivalence toward full-time motherhood replaced early, home-centered aspirations.

A third group (slightly less than 20 percent) began from a notably different starting point. Even as children, these women viewed exclusive motherhood with apprehension and hoped for something different out of life. Like the first group, they were able to realize their early life goals and did not change significantly in adulthood. Because their early goals differed from those of traditional women, however, they rejected full-time homemaking, part-time or interrupted employment, and occasionally motherhood as well, in favor of permanent, committed employment. Circumstances pushed and pulled them down a *nontraditional path*.

A fourth group (about 30 percent) also developed nondomestic aspirations as children, but its members did not meet supportive circumstances as adults. Consequently, they turned away from career aspirations and toward home and children over time. These women experienced *falling employment aspirations* and *began to see the home as a haven*. They joined the labor force with high hopes, only to meet roadblocks to upward mobility and stifling work-place experiences. Over time, as career ambitions were thwarted and employ-ment commitments threatened to undermine a valued personal relationship, they came to view motherhood as their best hope for fulfillment and security and their only escape from alienating paid work.

These four patterns are based on two especially important dimensions of life-course development. First, whether they were born into the working or the middle class, women differed in their early childhood expectations. Exposed to a diverse, complex set of experiences as children, respondents formed a variety of conscious and unconscious aspirations long before they were able to test these wishes as adults. Once formed, these early orientations were subjected to the real constraints and opportunities encountered in adulthood, the second dimension that distinguishes groups of women. Although circumstances allowed, or forced, many to follow a stable developmental path and to realize childhood goals, most met unanticipated social circumstances that encouraged, and often required, significant personal change.

Explaining Divergent Pathways — *Structural Explanations 4*

When initial goals proved viable, both domestic and nondomestic women were able and motivated to follow a path consistent with childhood experiences. More often than not, however, social circumstances undermined original orientations. When this occurred, childhood orientations proved to be either uninviting or impossible to realize, and unanticipated events led both domestic and nondomestic women to reinterpret their past experiences, reevaluate their past assumptions, and reorient themselves toward a different future.

Whether pathways through adulthood followed or diverged from early baseline orientations was largely dependent on the set of structural constraints and opportunities a woman encountered. The respondents' diverse life paths developed out of and depended on how they negotiated four especially important aspects of their social environment.

First, whether she built or did not build a stable relationship with a male partner, together with this partner's orientations toward bearing and rearing children, had a powerful impact on a woman's choices. A stable, permanent marriage promoted a domestic orientation in a number of ways. It fostered a belief in marriage as a safe, secure place that both permits and rewards economic dependence; over time, it tended to narrow a woman's occupational options, as a wife's employment decisions were subordinated to those of her spouse; and it ultimately offered an attractive alternative to unsatisfying job

Structural Conditions — marriage, job opportunity, & income of men

experiences. Similarly, a stable marriage promoted a context in which child-bearing came to be seen as a natural outgrowth of the relationship. Stable marriage not only made female domesticity possible for many respondents; it also fostered an environment in which bearing children and withdrawing from the workplace to rear them seemed natural, inevitable, and desirable. Indeed, strong pressure or encouragement from a mate led some women to become mothers despite their own ambivalence and the dangers posed to their careers.

In contrast, when men were not a stable part of women's lives, when having children threatened a stable relationship, or when men rejected participatory fatherhood, women found convincing reasons to place commitments to employment over commitments to children and family. In these instances, women either curtailed or completely rejected childbearing in favor of strong, full- time, long-term participation in the paid work force.

Second, the experience of blocked versus expanding job opportunity had a similarly powerful impact on women's choices. Blocked mobility and constricted employment opportunities dampened expectations for future occupational accomplishment, imposed few costs for workplace withdrawal, and enhanced the pull of domestic life. In this context women tended to opt out of the workplace to embrace domesticity and motherhood as the preferred alternative to paid work.

On the other hand, expanding workplace opportunity, unexpected promotions, and the promise of a career ladder promoted the development of strong job commitment, even when employment had initially been seen as temporary. Upward job mobility competed directly with women's domestic pursuits. Rewarding jobs did more than provide economic independence outside marriage, although this alone expanded women's alternatives. They also provided another source of personal identity and social reward. The experience of workplace advancement increased the immediate social, economic, and emotional rewards of employment; it fostered a belief in future job rewards; and it raised the costs of quitting, even for a short time, to bear and care for a child.

Third, when the spouses of stably married women were able to provide an income that was perceived as adequate, women were not pushed out of the home. Male economic support both permitted respondents to withdraw from paid jobs to rear children and sheltered them from exposure to unexpected job opportunities that might have initiated a process of change.

Women who experienced economic squeezes in the household were likely to be pushed into the workplace, despite their earlier plans or preferences. When this occurred, it often triggered a chain reaction of events that ultimately altered employment and family decisions. Not only did the perceived need for a second income force some women out of the home; it also delayed childbearing decisions, limited the number of children parents felt that they could afford and the time a mother could devote to their care, and provided a period in which unanticipated job opportunities might initiate a reassessment of family as well as employment aspirations. Perceived economic squeezes thus led some stably married women to pursue nondomestic paths and to reconsider their commitments to motherhood as well as to paid work.

Finally, perceptions of the rewards and costs of domesticity shaped women's employment and family decisions. Some women found mothering and homemaking the fulfilling experience they had hoped it would be. Others were surprised to find that, contrary to their earlier expectations, life as a homemaker or full-time mother was decidedly disappointing. As growing numbers of their neighbors, friends, and peers took paid jobs, these women found the increasing isolation and devaluation of full-time mothering and houskeeping too costly to bear. This decline in the social supports for motherhood, together with the rise in supports for alternative choices, led many to reject the domestic patterns more typical of earlier generations.

Either alone or in combination, these four factors precipitated turning points for most respondents. At such times, unanticipated events intervened to reshape the course of their lives. For the individual experiencing them, these events seemed random and their effects idiosyncratic. From a broader perspective, this apparent randomness takes on an orderly form. No matter how fortuitous a divorce or a new job opportunity may have seemed to the woman confronted with change, these events are rooted in shifts taking place in the structure of American economic and family institutions.

Periods of rapid social change, when structural arrangements are undergoing transition, are especially likely to promote and be reflected in changes in individual lives. The fact of social change, however, did not determine a uniform outcome in all lives. Because women varied in the degree to which and ways in which they were exposed to changing structural arrangements, they consequently varied in the direction and shape of their developmental paths. These women faced dilemmas, not clear cut choices. The decision-making process was fraught with ambivalence and conflict. It involved development and negotiation in which women struggled with and against their employers and male partners to define and control their situations. In negotiating transitions through adulthood, these women veered in different directions, developed divergent orientations, and stressed different abilities, even when they started with similar goals, desires, and orientations. Change occurred, not because people wished it to, but because seemingly static, discrete, inconsequential decisions had only dimly perceived and usually unintended long-term consequences.[4]

If personal change is not only a persistent possibility but also a common occurrence, then the orientations, dispositions, and capacities these people brought to adult decisions could not have been irrevocably formed in the early years of life. Rather, individual abilities continued to develop as these women aged, moved into new life stages, and encountered critical choice points. Aging, by its nature, requires some kind of transition, as people move through a series of stages from one set of social and psychological tasks to the next.[5] These respondents, however, did not simply progress through a natural, predetermined, or uniform sequence of stages. Their adult development was instead variable, problematic, and subject to unanticipated change.

Neither chance circumstances nor psychological predispositions determined the paths these women took. Constraints and opportunities in the immediate social environment limited the range of possible options and motivated each woman to select one option from among this range. In this sense, the employment and family decisions of these women were active efforts to make sense of and respond to a set of socially structured alternatives. [6]

How do social arrangements structure women's choices? Women face a set of structures in which employment and family responsibilities are not only inextricably linked; they are also posed as competing, alternative commitments in which women are required to choose among a number of desired goals. It is difficult for women to build strong bases in both the domestic and the public spheres. Decisions in one sphere limit the range of options in the other and also depend on the opportunities and constraints that the other poses. Tradeoffs are thus built into the structure of choice: whether a woman opts for commitment to a job, to motherhood, or to some combination of the two, she must accept the costs of what is forgone as well as the benefits of what is chosen ("opportunity costs" in the language of economics).

These women responded to the dilemma of "packaged choices" in genuinely creative ways. Their struggles to create viable life paths often led to extensive personal growth. Taken together, their efforts are changing the social order as well as their own lives. Their individually creative responses have combined to create new social forms—forms springing from changes in social structures, but defined and implemented by individuals. As these women's biographies have collided with structures in transition, to some extent they have been the authors, and not just the passive receivers, of change.[7]

Not everyone, of course, is equally well situated to respond creatively to social change. As young adults, these women represent a group that plays an especially important role in the process of historical change, for they are young enough to take advantage of new opportunities, yet old enough to act independently. In early adulthood, employment and family options are still open, even if only to a limited degree and for a limited time. At this age people must form independent identities that reflect (but do not mimic) parental models and must make life commitments that will have fateful consequences for their future development and for the social institutions they join or reject.

These findings about the process by which women choose between employment and family commitments highlight the inadequacies of theories that posit either that early childhood experiences are the major determinant of women's adult choices or that women's behavior can be fully understood as the result of universal patterns of male domination. Instead, the extent, type, and permanence of change in women's social position must be located in the changing social order and in the process by which different groups of women develop different responses to variable social circumstances.

The Limits of Socialization, Personality, and Dominance Models

CHILDHOOD SOCIALIZATION

For the women in this study, childhood provided the first arena in which psychological orientations, capacities, and conflicts were formed. Taken alone, however, childhood messages, models, and relationships were not sufficient to explain women's adult decisions for three reasons.

First, to the extent that childhood socialization played a role in women's later life choices, it played a different role than gender socialization theories hypothesize.[8] These theories argue that parents, and especially mothers, consciously and unconsciously socialize their daughters to be feminine (that is, oriented toward nurturance and mothering) and not masculine (that is, oriented toward achievement in employment and lacking well-developed empathic capacities). Yet these women's childhood experiences were varied. The messages they received as children were often ambiguous and inconsistent. Not only did mothers present multifaceted models; children were also influenced by other figures in their social environment. As a result, these respondents could choose, both consciously and unconsciously, from a variety of messages, models, and experiences. In the long run, this variety alone led to ambivalence, resistance, and rejection, as well as to emulation.

Second, however parents, and especially mothers, treated their offspring, their behavior alone did not determine the child's reaction to it. Consciously and unconsciously, children responded to their childhood contexts in a variety of ways that were not determined by the context itself. In many cases parental messages actually backfired, triggering an opposite reaction in the child. The child's early orientations thus emerged from the interaction between early messages and her reaction to them—a response that was to some extent indeterminate from the perspective of childhood socialization taken alone.

Third, childhood influences were subject to later revision. Intervening events, especially in late adolescence and early adulthood, when the struggle to establish an independent identity began in earnest, often shook up old assumptions and led many respondents to reassess parental messages and the experiences of childhood. This process of reexamination was never guaranteed, but it was an abiding possibility. It was more likely to occur when the assumptions, orientations, and skills inherited from childhood left the respondent ill-prepared to deal with social arrangements encountered in adulthood.

Rapid social change increased the need for and the likelihood of personal change. The change process modified, and even diminished, the impact of early childhood experiences on adult choices. Women's orientations toward, decisions about, and capacities for parenting and achievement in employment are thus emergent, developmental, and subject to change over time.

In sum, childhood experiences set up the conflicts that formed the starting point from which these women's adult development proceeded. These experiences influenced how conflicts were *experienced* later in life, but they did not determine how conflicts were resolved—or whether they could be resolved at all. Women "used" their early childhood experiences in a variety of ways that were not wholly determined by the experiences themselves. [9]

PSYCHOLOGICAL VARIATION AND THE "FEMININE PERSONALITY"

Although the women analyzed here faced a number of similar dilemmas, they responded with a varied range of motives, aspirations, and choices. It is difficult, if not impossible, to extract from this variety a distinct "feminine personality" characterized by strong maternal desires or underdeveloped career ambitions. [10] The search to isolate some special psychological quality that binds all women together and distinguishes them from men thus obscures the differences among women and risks perpetuating the same stereotypes that have served historically to justify gender inequality. [11]

Similarly, at least in terms of these women's perceptions, men do not form a homogeneous group with uniformly undeveloped emotional capacities. The respondents became involved with male partners who held a wide range of orientations toward parenthood. Many men appeared to possess sufficient relational needs and capacities to parent successfully; as a group, they were perceived as neither significantly less equipped for nor less desirous of parenthood than their female partners.

Not only do there appear to be large differences among women in their orientations toward parenthood and employment; there also appear to be fewer sharp differences between women and men in these psychological attributes than theories that stress a feminine personality would lead us to believe. Women and men do experience different *conflicts*, not only because they are treated differently as children, but also because they confront different options as adults. But this does not imply that they have inherently different capacities, needs, or desires. Rather, they are offered different avenues for the expression, or thwarting, of these emotional possibilities.

Employment and parenthood are structurally difficult to integrate, but the emotional capacities to love and to work are not mutually exclusive. The dichotomy between "productive" labor that generates an income and "reproductive" labor that socializes new human beings—the so-called split between "instrumental" and "expressive" functions—is based not on inherent psychological antagonisms, but rather on malleable structural conflicts and social arrangements. Whatever their responses, women experience psychic conflict over the choice between family and paid work because structural arrangements make it a choice in the first place.

The psychological and behavioral variation among women dilutes the explanatory power of theories that postulate a distinct feminine personality as the cause of women's mothering behavior. Surely such variation in motives, needs, and capacities cannot explain the general uniformity and intractability of the social assignment of nurturing responsibilities to women. A more intriguing question asks why, if each gender displays such a variety of orientations toward employment and parenthood, is the sexual division of parenting tasks that assigns emotional duties to women and economic duties to men so persistent? The answer to that question lies more in the structuring of the alternatives open to women and men than in deep-seated gender differences in motivation or relational capacities.

Finally, regardless of women's personality traits, psychological attributes are linked to behavior in complex, problematic, and to some extent indeterminate ways. Most human beings experience a set of conflicting emotions, motives, and needs as they move through life. Because women are especially subject to structural conflict in which they must choose between incompatible goals, this multiplicity of emotional pushes and pulls does not produce any one specific response. Among the variety of emotional states women experience—from "fear of success" to "fear of failure," from the "need to nurture" to the "need to achieve"—no one emotion determines behavior. Rather, as women struggle with conflicting emotions, they will overcome some and act on others. Their choices are thus more likely to reflect the mix of structural constraints and opportunities available to them when major life decisions are made than to represent the preordained unfolding "feminine personalities" or the expression of a uniform and distinctly feminine voice.

MALE DOMINANCE AND PERCEIVED INTERESTS

If these women did not share a single orientation toward mothering, neither did they share a common, consistent set of interests. As a group, they occupied a variety of social positions, faced a set of ambiguous, often conflicting alternatives, and had unequal access to social resources. Their socially structured "interests" were variable, internally inconsistent, and hard to define, promoting a variety of ideological responses.

Most of these women faced conflicting pressures over the course of their lives that forced them to choose among a number of antagonistic interests. They found considerable difficulty in defining or locating their "true" interests. Although their responses to these contradictions may have appeared to reflect "false consciousness," it is more theoretically useful to analyze them as stances that make sense in terms of a person's perceived interests.

Domestic women, for example, not only chose to affirm a traditional division of labor between the sexes in their own lives; they also opposed the emerging life patterns developed by nondomestic women. It would be misleading, however, to interpret this response as mere powerlessness in the face of male domination or a passive, misguided acceptance of male privilege. Rather, it reflects an active attempt on the part of domestic women to protect their interests, as they defined and perceived them, from the incursions of social change. Domestic women felt threatened by the erosion of the structural supports for domesticity, however much these supports result from and reinforce male privilege and female subordination. Similarly, they concluded that they had little to gain and much to lose from social change, however much this change represents a challenge to male domination.

Under conducive circumstances, many women developed strategies of resistance to social oppression. Because the arrangements that subordinate women also depend on their participation, this resistance posed a challenge to the men and employers they confronted. This resistance may have produced opposition on the part of those who were challenged, but opposition alone did not and could not halt resistance that springs from underlying structural change. Some women thus acted as a force for change that reverberated throughout the social institutions that impinged on them.

Because their situations diverged, some women chose to defend traditional arrangements of gender inequality while others became involved in a struggled to overcome them. Whether they resisted or complied, all were nevertheless acting to protect what they perceived to be their interests. When people possessing different resources face different constraints, they are likely to disagree about where their best interests lie.

Men's relationships with women were also more complex and diverse than a pure dominance model suggests. Men, like women, possess conflicting, divergent, potentially malleable interests, some of which they are forced to affirm at the expense of others, and male and female interests are not uniformly and consistently opposed. A husband may have greeted his wife's paycheck with ambivalence, for example, because it undermined his authority at home, but he was also likely to welcome this easing of his economic burdens. Although some respondents had male partners who were hostile to their careers, other reported notable support from men who valued their wives' independence. Women's emergent independence thus does not represent an unqualified defeat to all men.

Moreover, although most men hold more structural power than most women, women are not uniformly and completely helpless in the face of male dominance. Because many men and women require some degree of mutual attachment beyond coercion, male-female relationships develop out of a negotiated process in which both struggle to define and meet their own needs while also trying to provide what the other wants and demands. When these demands are complementary, as was more often the case with domestic women, the sexual struggle is accordingly mild. When interests clash, however, as they were more likely to do between nondomestic women and their male partners, conflicting desires must be negotiated. When women bring increased economic, social, and emotional resources to this negotiation process, they are better positioned to achieve greater equality. Thus, nondomestic women who had gained economic and social independence through employment and had managed to build committed relationships with supportive partners were in a better position to resist male dominance and gain greater control in their relationships with men. [12]

Structural constraints, like patterns of socialization, define the limits of human action, but within these limits a range of responses is possible. Existing social arrangements can have unanticipated consequences and provoke unintended reactions, including resistance and conformity. The critical questions thus become: What conditions promote resistance rather than compliance to social inequality? When is resistance likely to succeed? To answer these questions, we must look to the larger social forces that are currently reshaping women's alternatives.

Economic and Family Structures in Transition

As a number of essays in this volume have demonstrated, the major institutional supports for women's domesticity have been transformed over the last several decades. Rising marital instability has undermined the economic and emotional safeguards marriage once provided; an erosion of the "family wage" has left a rising proportion of even intact families dependent on a second income; new opportunities for paid work have con fronted women with genuinely appealing alternatives to childrearing; and declining ideological supports for female domesticity have made it increasingly difficult for full-time mothers to maintain their once-revered place in American culture.

The cumulative impact of these changes has dramatically altered the balance of pushes and pulls women face inside and outside the home. Changes in economic and family structures have exposed an increasing proportion of women to nondomestic alternatives and led many of them, by either preference or necessity, to change the direction of their lives. These changes have also eroded the structural supports on which domestic women depend, placing them in a increasingly precarious and embattled social position. A brief examination of these changes, and their implications for women's lives, makes it clear how and why social change is restructuring the alternatives of women and inevitably changing the lives of men and children as well.

First, marriage no longer offers the promise of permanence on which women's domesticity depends. Over the last thirty years, rising rates of separation, divorce, postponed marriage, and permanent singlehood have combined to place an increasing proportion of women outside the structure of legal marriage.[13]

Young adult women cannot safely equate marital vows with lifetime economic security or assume that any children they might bear will grow up in a household with both parents. For those unwilling or unable to commit themselves to a permanent marital bond, which most still consider a precondition for parenthood, childbearing often appears out of reach. This changing context has encouraged, and even required, a growing proportion of women to eschew traditional domestic commitments in favor of fuller economic independence, stronger ties to paid employment, and higher job aspirations.

Second, economic strains, largely as a consequence of the decline of the family wage, have sent a growing proportion of even stably married women into the workplace, where social and emotional as well as economic rewards foster the development of committed job ties.[14]

Third, although the vast majority of women workers remain crowded into a narrow range of female-dominated occupations, where relatively low pay and constricted advancement opportunitites prevail (Barrett 1979; Blau 1979), two recent trends suggest that job opportunities for women have begun to change in ways that are changing the nature of women's commitment to paid work. The most dramatic change has occurred among college-educated women, who over the last several decades have entered male occupational preserves in unprecedented numbers.[15] Although the prospects for working-class women are less bright, a small but notable proportion of this group has also benefited from new employment opportunities. Even more important, as women have filled the growing pool of jobs in the rapidly expanding service sector, they have begun to recognize the permanent nature of their ties to paid work, and their aspirations and demands have risen accordingly.

Women's rising aspirations have also placed pressures on male-dominated institutions to open more highly rewarded male job categories to women and to reward female-dominated occupations with better working conditions, higher pay, and greater upward mobility. The gains thus far achieved are limited, but the pressures created by women's awakening aspirations are not likely to abate. As working women increasingly recognize that they cannot view paid work as an intermittent, secondary, or part-time commitment, their demands for upward mobility and occupational equality will mount.

Finally, all of these factors (declining marital stability, increasing economic squeezes, and expanding work opportunities have, as noted above, combined to erode the ideological supports for domesticity and to create deepening ideological schisms between domestic and nondomestic women across the class structure. As rising numbers of women have vacated the home for the workplace, those remaining at home have been left to defend an increasingly devalued way of life. No matter how intrinsically satisfying or valuable their work may be, full-time "career" mothers, no less than employed mothers and career-committed women, now find themselves embattled, forced to justify a position once considered sacrosanct.

To some extent, all women—including full-time mothers, employed mothers, and permanently childless women—face a set of alternatives that are inherently contradictory and ambiguous. Adherents to each pattern now have to struggle to legitimate their responses to the structural contradictions between employment and motherhood. This struggle between domestic and nondomestic women, whether it takes the form of battles over abortion rights, equal rights for women, affirmative action policies, or publicly provided day care, is likely to continue as long as the structural conditions that support it remain.[16]

Conclusion

Women's adult choices are neither the predetermined outcome of early childhood socialization nor mere reflections of static, purely coercive social structures, although each of these factors plays a role. Women's decisions for or against motherhood and for or against committed employment develop out of a negotiated process whereby they confront and respond to constraints and opportunities, often unanticipated, encountered over the course of their lives. The process is dynamic, not stable and fixed. It depends on how women perceive and define their situations as well as on the objective circumstances that structure these perceptions. Because the structural arrangements that shape women's perceptions, motivations, and behavior are ambiguous and contradictory, decision making involves an active, at times difficult, effort to identify, choose between, and act on situational interests that are rarley obvious, consistent, or straightforwardly "true."

Structural changes in the economy, the organization of the workplace, and the nature of private life have combined to create new avenues for women outside the home, to erode the supports for female domesticity, and to intensify the split between those reproducing old patterns and those riding the currents of social change. Women make different choices and develop differing orientations toward motherhood and employment, moreover, because some have been exposed to these changes while others have been relatively insulated from them. Experiences with economic and family structures in flux thus shaped these women's choices and prompted many of them to change the direction of their lives.

Many of the old contradictions between home and market work remain, but structural shifts have created new dilemmas, required new resolutions, and engendered new social cleavages and conflicts. Neither the type nor the extent of change is entirely clear or predictable. Changes across structures are nevertheless mutually reinforcing; change in one structure tends to promote a chain reaction of readjustments in the others. These patterns are thus likely to become more deeply anchored over time.

The combined effect of all these changes has a number of important implications for women's lives. Most obviously, a growing proportion of women—even among those reared to prepare themselves for full-time mothering—are likely to find their lives centered as much on the workplace as on the home. Many women will face no better alternative than the domestic path traveled by so many of their mothers and grandmothers, but this group is not likely to predominate as it did thirty years ago. In its place will rise a burgeoning group of employed mothers, childless women, and career-committed women from both the middle and working classes searching for new forms of intimacy outside traditional marriage.

Second, women, as well as men, are increasingly likely to experience change over the course of their lives. The rise in marital instability and nontraditional household forms, along with changes in the structure of workplace opportunities, means that women, and especially young women, have become increasingly likely to move in and out of a diversity of family and employment arrangements throughout adulthood. Among women coming of age today, there is no single, dominant pattern of adult development. The adult life course has become more fluid, more diverse, and less stable than it was thirty years ago, exposing a growing proportion of women to unanticipated events that are likely to promote and even require change. [17]

Interactive and reinforcing structural changes in economic and family institutions have thus created new alternatives for women; unless these changes are suddenly reversed, the new life patterns they promote are here to stay. Yet old patterns will persist—not only because many still find the structural support for them, but also because obstacles to progressive social change often make old patterns seem preferable to the new. Structural changes in the position of women have done more than create new options; when coupled with persistent gender inequality, they have also created new vulnerabilities and dilemmas for individual women and new social conflicts among women as a group.

Finally, as structural change produces individual change, it also increases many women's incentives to resist subordination and oppose inequality in the labor force and at home. Exactly how successful this pressure will be in achieving greater gender equality is much less clear. More likely, gender stratification in both public and private spheres will remain deeply entrenched, although the forms it takes and the dilemmas it poses will continue to become more variable and complex.

Notes

1. See Alonso (1980) and Sternlieb et al. (1982). The birth rate refers to the number of births per 1,000 members of the population.

2. The terms "domestic" and "nondomestic" are used here to distinguish between women whose primary adult commitments and orientations are to the family and women whose primary adult commitments include long-term, full-time employment outside the home. Domestically oriented women may or may not work outside the home for pay, but family responsibilities take precedence, and employment tends to be sporadic, part-time, and organized so as not to compete with mothering commitments. Similarly, nondomestic women may or may not bear children, but employment responsibilities command an equal, and in many instances superior, loyalty in their lives.

For an analysis of the relationship between young adult cohorts and the process of social change, see Ryder (1965).

3. See Gerson (1985; app. B) for a full description and explanation of the sampling and interview methods used in the study. Elder (1978) presents a lucid rationale for using life-course analysis to examine processes of social and especially family change.

4. For more on the long-run implications of short-run decisions, see Becker's (1964) analysis of building commitment through "side-bets" and Merton's (1957) discussion of the "unintended consequences" of human action.

5. See Erikson (1963) for the classic statement of the problem of psychological development through the life course and for a developmental schema based on psychoanalytic principles and assumptions. Gerth and Mills (1953) present an overview of competing theories of human development. For more recent studies of female and male adult development, see Rossi (1980), Smelser and Erikson (1980), and Gilligan (1982).

6. Sensible choices are not necessarily conscious choices. The forces that shape op-

tions and channel motives, actions, and beliefs are often hidden from conscious awareness. Unconscious motivation is not confined to psychodynamic processes, however; structural as well as psychological processes affect behavior in ways that the actor may not recognize. Indeed, structure may exert its most powerful influence by shaping one's perception of alternative options. Women respond in contextually sensible ways to their environment without full conscious awareness of the structural forces impinging on them or the overall logic of their choices, just as they may be unaware of psychodynamic pushes and pulls. The concept of "structured choice" thus does not refer to free will, but rather to decisions that are constrained by social circumstances and embedded in a social context.

7. Mills (1959) presents the classic discussion of the relationship between individual biography, historical context, and structural arrangements in social analysis.

8. Gerson (1985; chap. 2) presents an overview and analysis of competing theoretical approaches to the study of gender. For influential examples of the socialization approach, stressing psychoanalytic processes, see Chodorow (1978) and Parsons (1958). Gilligan (1982) focuses on gender differences in moral perception and reasoning. For analyses that stress structural factors such as "patriarchy" and capitalism, see Eisenstein (1979), Hartmann (1976), and Sokoloff (1980). For contrasting treatments of biological factors, see Rossi (1977) and Hrdy (1981).

9. Recent studies corroborate the finding that childhood socialization is linked in problematic and indeterminate ways to adult outcomes. Miller and Garrison (1982) report that the evidence linking parental behavior in the early years of life with "sex-typed" behavior in adults is inconclusive and weak. Kagan's (1984) and Mnookin's (1979) reviews of the long-term effects of socialization practices reach similar conclusions.

10. The finding that all women do not share a universal need to mother, whether rooted in biological predispositions or childhood socialization experiences, is confirmed by other recent studies. See, for example, Badinter's (1981) study of maternal indifference in eighteenth-century France.

11. This is so even when these approaches argue that women are morally or emotionally superior to men. Bringing women down from this pedestal facilitates analyzing how and why women, like men, construct their lives in contextually sensible ways. See also Epstein (1985).

12. Collins (1971) discusses how sex stratification in affluent market economies takes the form of negotiations between men and women. The outcome of these negotiations, he argues, depends on the relative balance of the various social and economic resources each brings to the relationship and is able to convert into power within it. Although most women command fewer social resources than most men, the more a woman brings to the negotiation process, the greater her ability to control the outcome.

13. For analyses of how and why patterns of marriage and divorce are changing, see Cherlin (1981), Glick and Norton (1977), and Weitzman (1985). Gerson (1985; chap. 8) presents a more detailed analysis of the scope and limits of the structural changes discussed in this section.

14. See Introduction to Part III of this volume as well as Blumberg (1980), Masnick and Bane (1980), Oppenheimer (1982), Sternlieb et al. (1982), and Vickery (1979).

15. See Introduction to this section and Gerson (1985).

16. Lo (1982) presents an overview of recent research on countermovements and conservative movements in the contemporary United States. Luker (1984) analyzes

the social-structural bases of "pro-life" and "pro-choice" abortion activism. For a more in-depth analysis of the likely political consequences of emerging social divisions between domestic and nondomestic women, see Gerson (1987).

17. For an analysis of the demographic contours of these changes, see Alonso (1980) and Cherlin (1981).

References

Alonso, William. 1980. "The Population Factor and Urban Structure." In Arthur P. Solomon (ed.), *The Prospective City*. Cambridge: MIT Press.

Badinter, Elizabeth. 1981. *Mother Love: Myth and Reality*. New York: Macmillan.

Barrett, Nancy S. 1979. "Women in the Job Market: Occupations, Earnings, and Career Opportunities." In Ralph E. Smith (ed.), *The Subtle Revolution: Women at Work*. Washington, D.C.: Urban Institute.

Becker, Howard S. 1964. "Personal Change in Adult Life." *Sociometry* 27:40–53.

Blau, Francine. 1984. "Women in the Labor Force: An Overview." In Jo Freeman (ed.), *Women: A Feminist Perspective*, 3d ed. Palo Alto, Calif.: Mayfield.

Blumberg, Paul. 1980. *Inequality in an Age of Decline*. New York: Oxford University Press.

Cherlin, Andrew J. 1981. *Marriage, Divorce, Remarriage*. Cambridge: Harvard University Press.

Chodorow, Nancy. 1978. *The Reproduction of Mothering: Psychoanalysis and the Sociology of Gender*. Berkeley and Los Angeles: University of California Press.

Collins, Randall. 1971. "A Conflict Theory of Sexual Stratification." *Social Problems* 19:3–21.

Eisenstein, Zillah R. 1979. "Developing a Theory of Capitalist Patriarchy and Socialist Feminism." In Zillah R. Eisenstein (ed.), *Capitalist Patriarchy and The Case for Socialist Feminism*. New York: Monthly Review Press.

Elder, Glen H., Jr. 1978. "Approaches to Social Change and the Family." In John Demos and Sarane S. Boocock (eds.), *Turning Points: Historical and Sociological Essays on the Family*. Chicago: University of Chicago Press.

Epstein, Cynthia F. 1985. "Ideal Roles and Real Roles, or the Fallacy of the Misplaced Dichotomy." *Research in Social Stratification and Mobility* 4:29–51.

Erikson, Erik H. 1963. *Childhood and Society*, 2d ed. New York: Norton.

Gerson, Kathleen. 1985. *Hard Choices: How Women Decide About Work, Career, and Motherhood*. Berkeley and Los Angeles: University of California Press.

————. 1987. "Emerging Social Divisions Among Women: Implications for Welfare State Politics." *Politics and Society* (forthcoming).

Gerth, Hans, and C. Wright Mills. 1953. *Character and Social Structure: The Psychology of Social Institutions*. New York: Harcourt, Brace and World.

Gilligan, Carol. 1982. *In a Different Voice: Psychological Theory and Women's Development*. Cambridge: Harvard University Press.

Glick, Paul C., and Arthur J. Norton. 1977. "Marrying, Divorcing, and Living Together in the U.S. Today." *Population Bulletin* 32 (Oct.):2–39.

Hartmann, Heidi 1976. "Capitalism, Patriarchy, and Job Segregation by Sex." *Signs* 1:137–69.

Hrdy, Sarah B. 1981. *The Woman That Never Evolved*. Cambridge: Harvard University Press.

Kagan, Jerome. 1984. *The Nature of the Child*. New York: Basic Books.

Lo, Clarence Y. H. 1982. "Countermovements and Conservative Movements in the Contemporary U.S." *Annual Review of Sociology* 8:107–34. Palo Alto, Calif.: Annual Reviews.

Luker, Kristin. 1984. *Abortion and the Politics of Motherhood.* Berkeley and Los Angeles: University of California Press.

Masnick, George, and Mary Jo Bane. 1980. *The Nation's Families: 1960–1990.* Cambridge: Joint Center for Urban Studies of MIT and Harvard University.

Merton, Robert K. 1957. *Social Theory and Social Structure.* New York: Free Press.

Miller, Joanne, and Howard H. Garrison. 1982. "Sex Roles: The Division of Labor at Home and in the Workplace." *Annual Review of Sociology* 8:237–62. Palo Alto, Calif.: Annual Reviews.

Mills, C. Wright. 1959. *The Sociological Imagination.* New York: Oxford University Press.

Mnookin, Robert H. 1979. "Foster Care—In Whose Best Interest?" In Onora O'Neill and William Ruddick (eds.), *Having Children: Philosophical and Legal Reflections on Parenthood.* New York: Oxford University Press.

Oppenheimer, Valerie K. 1982. *Work and Family: A Study in Social Demography.* New York: Academic Press.

Parsons, Talcott. 1958. "Social Structure and the Development of Personality: Freud's Contribution to the Integration of Psychology and Sociology." *Psychiatry* 21:321–40.

Rossi, Alice S. 1977. "A Biosocial Perspective on Parenting." *Daedalus* 106 (Spring): 1–31.

———. 1980. "Life-Span Theories and Women's Lives." *Signs* 6:4–32.

Ryder, Norman B. 1965. "The Cohort as a Concept in the Study of Social Change." *American Sociological Review* 30:843–61.

Smelser, Neil J., and Erik H. Erikson (eds.). 1980. *Themes of Work and Love in Adulthood.* Cambridge: Harvard University Press.

Sokoloff, Natalie J. 1980. *Between Money and Love: The Dialectics of Women's Home and Market Work.* New York: Praeger.

Sternlieb, George; James W. Hughes; and Connie O. Hughes. 1982. *Demographic Trends and Economic Reality: Planning and Markets in the '80's.* New Brunswick, N.J.: Rutgers Center for Urban Policy Research.

Vickery, Clair. 1979. "Women's Economic Contribution to the Family." In Ralph E. Smith (ed.), *The Subtle Revolution: Women at Work.* Washington, D.C.: Urban Institute.

Weitzman, Lenore J. 1985. *The Divorce Revolution: The Unintended Social and Economic Consequences for Women and Children.* New York: Free Press.

13

Family and Job for Working-Class Women: Gender and Class Systems Seen from Below

MYRA MARX FERREE

Despite the unmistakable increase in research on working-class women in the past decade, it remains a neglected stepchild among the thriving offspring of feminist inquiry. The expansion of research on women in contemporary society over the past two decades has been aptly characterized as "phenomenal" and "explosive," but the share of this growth that directly touches the world of the working class has been modest at best. Moreover, there has been remarkably little attention paid to the serious implications of this scholarship for our conceptions of women, work, and class. Theorizing rarely begins from the actual life experiences of working-class women, who experience the contradictions between capitalism and patriarchy and whose own insights into their workings might fruitfully be explored.

White working-class women, like black and other minority women, are still typically perceived in terms of stereotypes; it is easy and common to use them chiefly as a contrast with what are assumed to be the superior norms, values, and behavior of the white middle-class and professional elite (e.g., Harding 1981). Unlike these women, working-class women are presumed to be particularly "traditional"—that is, willing to accept patriarchal authority, reluctant to work outside the home, and prepared to sacrifice themselves endlessly to family demands.

In this paper, I look briefly at some of the distortions of perspective that arise from the widespread use of the dual-career model of women's employment and family relationships. Then I turn to a consideration of some alternative research on women and work done by feminist scholars in West Germany with a focus on working-class experience. Just as feminist research generally has made us sensitive to the ways in which male norms and male experience were inappropriately understood as universal, against which background women appeared deficient and backward, research *for* working-class women can lead us to appreciate the many ways in which middle-class norms and experience have been improperly generalized (cf. Smith 1979).

The Dual-Career Model

The implicit model of households used in much research on women and work is that of the "dual-career" family. This model pervades both the social sciences and the mass media, and it distorts our thinking about the meaning of paid employment for women (Benenson 1984). A research focus on women who are doctors, lawyers, college professors, and corporate managers leads to unrealistic perceptions of women in general (Harkess 1985). Such elite women are atypical not only of women, but even of women of their class, as most wives of such high-earning husbands are not in the labor force at all (Benenson 1984; Fowlkes 1980). Despite these facts, the dual-career model presents women in elite professions as exemplary of the nontraditional woman and assumes that the sharing of housework and childcare between husband and wife is the natural consequence of the marriage partners' shared commitment to egalitarian principles (e.g., Pepitone-Rockwell 1980; Rapoport and Rapoport 1971, 1976).

Since dual-career wives have husbands who are themselves good providers they are assumed to have purely noneconomic reasons for working. Such noneconomic motivations, along with the high level of education characteristic of elite couples, are then taken to be a prerequisite for an egalitarian relationship. Benenson points out that this model treats a nonconventional division of labor in the home as an elite innovation that might gradually diffuse downward, rather than as one possible response to wider trends of social change. Men's discontent with their own jobs and their individual capacity to enjoy closeness with their children are neglected variables in the model (Gerson, 1985; Hood, 1983).

Significantly, working-class men have typically placed family above job in survey ratings of importance and satisfaction, and they have fewer economic alternatives to doing a share of household chores (Pleck 1979). More affluent men can insist that their wives' income is unnecessary and that she should either stay home or hire others to replace her labor there; working-class families rely on two incomes. The larger the proportion of family income the wife contributes, the more likely it is that her husband will also contribute housework and childcare time to the family economy (Ferree 1987; Heer 1958; Hiller 1980).

Further, the dual-career model systematically misrepresents women's experiences with paid work and housework by putting "career commitment" in central position. This makes the conflicts women experience seem individual and psychological rather than structural because it compares working-class women, not with working class men, but with those women in the professions who most closely conform to male professionals in their career orientation and commitment. Working-class women's financial reasons for seeking employment are directly contrasted with the personal reasons given by dual-career professional women, and these two artificially separated orientations are seen as opposing each other. Financial need is often taken as excluding personal motivations; women who "have to" work for the money are seen as not wanting to work at all, rather than as disliking aspects of their present jobs (cf. Ferree 1984). Social policy is directed at ensuring women a "choice" and so protecting them from this presumably evil necessity, a formulation that perpetuates the notion that it is the male alone who is responsible for financial support, even if he does not much like his job either. Exploitation is assessed not from the characteristics of women's work itself, which are rarely studied, but from the simple fact of women's employment at all (Feldberg and Glenn 1979). Women stuck in bad jobs are not seen as entitled to better working conditions, but as needing to be "protected" from working for pay at all (e.g., Kreps 1972).

In fact, studies of working-class women in the United States conducted from the 1950s to the present consistently show not only high levels of actual employment but considerable interest in working for pay among women who are at home full time (e.g., Gavron, 1966; Berger, 1968; Ferree 1976; Komarovsky 1962; Rosen 1981). The problem is that other scholars are not sure how to interpret such findings. Awareness of how demanding and poorly paid these women's jobs are seems to demand a focus on financial need as the driving force behind women's interest in paid work, but the women's own more complex responses include mention of significant psychological rewards. Because the dual-career model conceptualizes noneconomic rewards only in terms of career commitment and a choice between work and family as the priority in one's life, evidence that a respondent finds psychological benefits in paid employment is often treated as a sign of lesser family commitment.

This is seriously misleading when applied to working-class women. However psychologically important it may be, a job is not a career. As Komarovsky puts it, "a good job is a means to a good living, but achievement in a specialized vocation is not the measure of a person's worth, not even for a man" (1962 : 57). Blue-collar women are proud of their accomplishments on the job, and they are proud of their role as family providers, alone or in conjunction with their husbands (Walshok 1981); this holds true not only for women who are "pioneering" in traditionally male craft jobs, but also for women in the pink-collar ghetto, as Walshok found to her surprise. Rosen's study of unemployment among blue-collar women found not only a sense of relief that there might finally be time to rest and catch up on housework, but also feelings of loss, anxiety, and disorientation that increased the longer women were out of work (1981). At the same time, working-class women are not committed to careers in the middle-class sense, and they are likely to change jobs, refuse promotions, and restrict their hours in order to carry out their domestic responsibilities.

The dual-career model also has difficulty dealing with women's apparent commitment to their unpaid "careers" as wives and mothers. From the perspective of the model, housework and childcare appear primarily as a burden. Although it is clear that women of all classes carry a disproportionate load of domestic labor even when they are employed full time (Berk 1985; Michelson 1985), there is a tendency to see this work as being imposed on women against their wills (e.g., Hartmann 1981). The ideal of the male professional who is almost completely divorced from daily household labor seems to shape the vision of what freedom for women would mean; the work involved in caring for a family is often seen as an *extra* burden handicapping women in their efforts to achieve economic success. This notion ignores the realities of a class system in which both men and women in working-class jobs labor *for* their families in jobs where advancement, achievement, and financial success are structurally limited, regardless of how committed one might be.

In sum, the dual-career model encourages us to see paid employment as the locus of rewards and housework as purely burdensome. At the same time, it tends to polarize our perceptions of women into those who receive psychological as well as economic rewards at work and those who are assumed to get little of either and so might as well stay home. There is also an assumption that people can and should make a choice between commitment to paid employment and involvement in their families. None of these premises fits the experience of working-class women very well, so the need for an alternative perspective is clear.

German Feminist Research

Some recent research in West Germany begins to develop an alternative to the dual-career model (see Ferree 1985). In particular, these researchers challenge the distinction between women who want to work and women who have to work; instead, they focus on the rewards and costs of both paid work and unpaid household labor. They do so by explicitly situating paid work and housework in the context of patriarchy and capitalism and then considering the interrelationships of these two systems.

Rather than facing merely a "double day" of housework and paid work, they argue, women are struggling with work that is organized according to two different and conflicting principles. Beck-Gernsheim (1980) and Ostner (1978) describe the distinctive qualities of housework as reflecting the fact that it is not done for pay in the market, but rather for the use of specific individuals. There are rewards as well as costs in meeting the needs of known others: doing a good job is more directly rewarding, the tasks are less specialized and abstract, and competition is unnecessary, but the time demands are also unbounded and the economic rewards precarious. Paid employment stands in contrast to this use-value type of work. In the market, the value of the job is primarily determined by the economic and social rewards it offers and its meaning is essentially impersonal and competitive. The market system, capitalism, is the dominant form of organization, however, and use-value work is necessarily marginal and dependent, as are the workers who do it. Neither type of work alone offers people a full and rewarding life.

Since each mode involves its own benefits and costs, many women find themselves struggling to maintain an involvement in both of these qualitatively different types of work, a struggle that Beck-Gernsheim designates the "divided life." She highlights the ways in which each makes demands on women that are incompatible with the demands of the other, but notes that each may also offer rewards that would not otherwise be available at all. This struggle is made especially clear in three empirical studies of working-class women and their work, both paid and unpaid.

Using a sample of seventy-one women who were pieceworkers in five firms in the electrotechnical and clothing industries, Eckart and her associates (1979) examined the ways in which housework and paid employment impinge on women's consciousness and life choices. These jobs are among the most onerous and poorly paid of any in the German economy, yet to describe these women as forced to work would distort their situation. The specific needs and goals met through work in the factory vary over the life course, but all revolve around what Eckart calls a "family-centered instrumental orientation" not unlike that usually ascribed to working-class men. This value system defines a job as important, but primarily as a means of earning money, carrying out one's family responsibilities, and trying to achieve the "good life." They differ from men chiefly in seeing marriage as another means by which they could achieve these goals. The two strategies are not entirely alternative either, as most women realize that their low-paying jobs will not release them from economic dependence on their parents or husbands and that marriage will not enable them to give up their jobs. The women described both dependencies as burdensome, yet also pointed to rewards offered by both family and job.

Few women seemed to see a life of full-time housework as meeting all their needs. Along with economic rewards, motives like the desire to expand areas of competence and to interact with people outside the family influenced women to take and keep paid jobs. These psychological rewards fitted within their general instrumental orientation, for in a market society competence is largely measured by earnings, and the more distanced and limited relationships of the workplace can be an emotional release from unceasing family demands for care and attention. When housework is romanticized as a good alternative for working-class women, its failure to satisfy certain needs and the insupportable demands it presents are overlooked. But women themselves are aware of these limits and value their paid jobs for supplying some of what they are missing at home.

Because women value paid employment, they do not want to appear constrained at work by their family commitments. They do not wish to admit to structural conflict between the two jobs and so tend to personalize their real limits as merely individual failings or to drive themselves to exhaustion to avoid falling short in either area. When conflicts are unavoidable (as when a child is suddenly taken sick), the women bargain individually with their husbands or employers to reach a solution that enables them to keep on with their jobs. When they are successful in obtaining concessions from one or the other, they then feel so grateful for having such an ''understanding'' husband or employer that they work harder to make it up to them and are unwilling to complain or demand change in any other area (cf. Freeman 1982). This paternalism seriously undercuts women's solidarity and resistance on the job.

On the other hand, housework is also valued, both in its own right as a source of intrinsic rewards and as a means of securing economic support. Thus, women have conflicting feelings about reducing their share of housework, despite the enormous burden it imposes. Returning to the job of full-time housewife is a potential route for escape from the factory, even if in practice it is more chimerical than not. Holding that alternative open by being the one who does the housework makes it possible to imagine ''someday'' being able to quit, and that dream may help to make the daily labor more endurable. Blue-collar men's dreams of early retirement, of winning the lottery, of opening their own business and being their own boss, may serve a similar function. Housework can also be a way for a woman to make amends to family members for the costs her job imposes on them. Especially if they disapprove of her working, she may feel that she owes them housework. Finally, women may not seek to reduce their share of housework because it gives them the chance to do work that they themselves control and where the only standards they have to meet are their own. When others share the work, they also have some say over how it is done, and this cost may outweigh the relief that their relatively minor contribution of labor provides.

A second study, by Lappe (1981) and Schöll-Schwinghammer (1979), focuses attention on the reconceptualization of women's work satisfaction. When researchers assume that housework and paid work form a single continuum of traditionality, they tend to presume that women's satisfaction with their paid work is caused by their attitude toward housework. Women who dislike their paid jobs, it is thought, would prefer full-time housework. Lappe and Schöll-Schwinghammer, in contrast, treat these as two separate dimensions and relate job dissatisfaction to the conditions in which women work rather than to attitudes about work and family roles.

They sampled factories in industries that employed a high proportion of women and interviewed a total of 500 women, two-thirds (372) in production work in a factory and the remainder in related clerical and retail sales jobs. They went into the factories and offices and actually measured the work conditions—the speed of the assembly line, the noise level, the temperature, and the like—as well as asking the women what they thought of their jobs. They are thus able to show that dissatisfaction is related to the work itself rather than a preference for so-called traditional roles at home. Even though managers rated the work as easy and unskilled, the researchers found conditions to be stressful and the work demanding. The extent to which women had to maintain a fixed posture, focus on fine detail, or work at a pace faster than a task a minute influenced the women's belief that their jobs were unendurable over the long run.

Unlike men, the women were generally in jobs that did not allow them to conserve their strength and to move around and made no allowances for the lesser physical capacities of aging workers. Also unlike men, the women thought that they could not endure a lifetime of work, and given the differences in their jobs, they were probably being realistic. However, despite the stress, nearly half the women found their work enjoyable in some respects. The most dissatisfied workers were those in low-level clerical jobs, like data entry, whose work demanded a high level of sustained attention to the task despite high noise levels, monotony, and a set posture. The image of clerical work as better than factory work was not confirmed here.

Housework increases the burden of the job. Women with exactly the same jobs reported them to be more tiring and stressful if they had children than if they did not, and being overburdened at home was the best predictor of a desire to quit paid work. Even so, the majority of the women did not see full-time housework as an acceptable alternative for themselves, and they were about evenly divided on whether the main advantage of paid work is the income or the social contacts and recognition it provides.

Because Lappe and Schöll-Schwinghammer measure discontent situationally, they avoid attributing women's unhappiness with their jobs to a traditional attitude. This suggests that women's jobs should be changed to make them more rewarding—not that social policy should drive women back to the kitchen in the name of making their lives more pleasant and enjoyable.

However, their study does not examine the rewards and conditions of housework in the same detail that it uses for paid employment and so does not recognize the ways in which housework, too, should be changed to make it also more bearable.

This close attention to both paid and unpaid labor is offered in a third study, conducted by Regina Becker-Schmidt and her colleagues at the University of Hanover (1984). They conducted sixty in-depth interviews, half with women presently employed in factories and half with women who had left such jobs for full-time housework; all sixty were also caring for small children. Their research offers a dialectical understanding of the burdens and rewards of housework and paid employment in terms of both the objective characteristics of the work and the subjective reality of the worker. They argue that women's attitudes cannot be reduced to a simple preference for one type of work or the other. Both positive and negative aspects of each type of work emerge through the comparisons women draw between them as they actively shift their perspective from one role to the other. Thus, women say that "as a mother" they find certain rewards and costs in their paid jobs, while "as a worker" they emphasize different aspects. The same dual perspective governs their reactions to their labors at home.

Because these working-class women describe both fulfillment and disappointment in paid work and housework, their responses are most aptly characterized as ambivalent. This ambivalence shows up in conflicting feelings, inconsistent opinions, and even the desire to be in two places at the same time. For example, at one moment they say that they are sure their jobs are good for their children, and at the next moment they say they feel guilty about their work.

Becker-Schmidt (1980) argues that this ambivalence is an appropriate response to real structural contradictions between and within the two very different forms of work. Ambivalence is not the only possible response, but to develop an unqualified preference for either paid work or housework would require the individual to deny the real problems in the one and the real rewards in the other. Such an unqualified preference for paid work is desirable "work commitment" in the eyes of an employer, but a costly form of psychological repression for the woman worker. Similarly, husbands may appreciate an unqualified preference for wife/mother roles, but women pay for their denial of the contradictions they experience.

Contradictions exist within both forms of work as well as between them, and these contradictions are structural rather than psychological. Contradictions in factory work, for example, include the simultaneous pressure to produce good, error-free work and to work as quickly as possible; to compete against co-workers to earn as much as possible and to cooperate with them to maintain a reasonable piece rate. Such contradictions generate the time pressure and nervous stress that make women want to quit, but they also give women the satisfaction and pride of knowing that they are skilled workers, able to meet the demands of a difficult job. Thus, objective recognition and a sense of being useful and important go hand in hand with physical exhaustion and a sense of being used up and exploited. The worker's pride in her own product and skill conflicts with her desire to protect herself and minimize the effort she must expend for a wage. She knows that there is a gap between what she can do and what she is expected and allowed to do on the job. This awareness can be a source of anger and of apathy.

There are contradictions in household labor also, and they are no less intense for being qualitatively different from those experienced in the factory. Personal relationships in the family are an important part of one's sense of self as unique, yet they are also a crucial force in demanding social conformity. Owning things like a house, car, or boat gives one some private space in which to feel free, but the burden of paying for them makes one feel that one is held hostage by the things themselves. The work of housework generates contradictory experiences: it is a "labor of love" done for known others who can directly experience and appreciate it, unlike alienated paid labor, but it is also not recognized or acknowledged as work because it is not alienated. It is identified with the relationships within which it occurs ("being a mother") rather than tied to a wage. The quantitative time demands of housework conflict with expectations for the quality of time expended at home: attempts to create schedules and have measurable output clash with efforts to respond to needs as they arise, to be sympathetic and patient. The defining tension in housework may be the conflict between the self, considered as a individual ego with unique limits and strengths, and the selflessness demanded as the "glue" that holds the family together by its conformability and responsiveness.

These separate contradictions in paid work and housework, Becker-Schmidt argues, are not resolved by women combining the two forms of labor. Some rewards and costs may be complementary. Some of the worst difficulties in full-time housework, such as isolation or lack of recognition, may be relieved by certain rewards in the work force, such as ties with co-workers and a paycheck, while some of the problems of paid employment, such as close supervision and fragmentation of the work, can be balanced by rewards at home, such as autonomy and an undivided work process. On the other hand, combining both types of work creates new contradictions. There are both the familiar problems of an excessive total work load, such as exhaustion, and the stresses that arise from moving back and forth between two qualitatively different types of work. Not only do women themselves have to mentally shift gears between work that demands clock-watching and work that requires one to be oblivious to the time spent, but they also experience the people with whom they work, both at home and on the job, as insufficiently aware of their skills and capacities in their other life of labor, and thus as unable to know them for who they really are.

In Becker-Schmidt's analysis neither housework nor paid employment is cast as the villain in women's double day because neither one is assumed to be a morally prior responsibility. Instead, she offers a theoretical perspective that is able to recognize these women as trying to transcend a purely one-sided existence, even at the cost of assuming additional burdens.

Conclusions and Policy Implications

When researchers try to fit working-class women into a dual-career model, such women tend to appear deficient in "work commitment" and traditional in "family values." Because this model places work and family at opposite ends of a single continuum, it cannot account for the balancing act in which these women are engaged, in which both forms of work are valued but for different reasons. The dual-career model is elitist because it assumes that everyone should aspire to what only the most fortunate can attain—namely, intrinsically rewarding and satisfying careers. It is also male-defined, for it sets as a standard of liberation the ability to minimize the burden of housework, reflecting the male perspective on what family life offers. For women, this is deeply problematic because women have always experienced the contradictions inherent in housework and childcare. They are indeed burdensome and costly but they are also rewarding and intrinsically valuable.

Working-class women, unlike more affluent women, are not offered the financial incentives to deny or minimize the experience of contradiction and so to express an unqualified preference for either paid work or housework. Thus, it is easier to examine and understand the ways in which these structural contradictions are played out in psychological experience when working-class women are studied. The theoretical model that is developed, however, can be seen as having application to all women's struggles with paid and unpaid work. Structural contradictions and psychological ambivalence may lie at the heart of efforts to come to terms with work that is fundamentally different in kind when it is performed in or out of the marketplace.

It is not hard to imagine policy alternatives that would be useful to women who are struggling to combine two contradictory and yet also complementary forms of work. Better pay and work conditions for all women workers, including part-time workers, greater availability of maternity leave and reliable out-of-home childcare, more schedule flexibility on the job and more limited demands at home would all make the burden easier to carry over the long run and increase the ratio of rewards to costs. It is harder to see how women will be able to achieve these policy goals when they are divided from each other into housewives and working women, traditionalists and feminists. These divisions between women may be the most damaging results of a dual-career model that places job and family—and the women who supposedly value each—at opposite ends of a single continuum.

Alternatively, the German feminist model suggests that women are really suffering from a divided life in which each of these valued dimensions is played off against the other. The denial and repression required for an unambivalent response to either paid work or housework may have not only psychological costs but also political ones, as women turn against each other trying to demonstrate that the choices they have made—and the renunciations society has demanded of them for those choices—are the only right ones. In contrast, the perspective of working-class women, which accepts ambivalence as an appropriate response to structural contradiction, may also be a vision that could encourage political alliances between women who have responded differently to similar situations. All women lack structural supports for domestic labor as well as for paid employment. The choices women face are between the devil and the deep blue sea, Hobson's choice—that is, no real choice at all.

The German studies suggest why and how women's struggles with the contradictions of housework and of paid work have failed to liberate women. Indeed, individual efforts to "have it all" have only succeeded in locking women as a group ever more tightly in the grip of patriarchy and capitalism. Women who seek to mitigate the strain of participating in two differently organized work systems tend to seek out positions that are structurally marginal to both, such as part-time jobs, occupations that utilize the use-value skills and relationships formed in domestic labor, temporary employment. These alternatives are all clustered at the bottom of the economic ladder. But for women to renounce their interest in these forms of work would be to accept the very values of capitalism that consign them to the lowest rungs regardless of their intrinsic merit. At the same time for women to give up their claims for equal pay, recognition, and opportunity in the work force would be to accept the values of patriarchy. While efforts to have it all are a form of resistance to confinement in a single role, such individual resistance simply perpetuates the collective marginality of women and does nothing to relieve the structural contradictions at the heart of women's oppression.

Working-class women's experiences of paid work and housework are thus not only valuable to study in their own right; they suggest as well that our prevailing model of work and family may do more to perpetuate women's disadvantage than to relieve it. By listening carefully to working-class women's accounts of their divided lives, these German researchers may have contributed a theoretical perspective that illuminates all women's experiences.

References

Beck-Gernsheim, Elisabeth. 1980. *Das halbierte Leben*. Frankfurt: Fischer Taschenburch Verlag.

Becker-Schmidt, Regina. 1980. "Widersprüchliche Realität und Ambivalenz: Arbeitserfahrungen von Frauen in Fabrik und Familie." *Kölner Zeitschrift für Soziologie und Sozialpsychologie* 32: 705–25.

Becker-Schmidt, Regina; G.-A. Knapp; B. Schmidt. 1984. *Eines ist zu wenig—Beides ist zu viel*. Bonn: Verlag Neue Gesellschaft.

Benenson, Harold. 1984. "Women's Occupational and Family Achievement in the U.S. Class System: A Critique of the Dual-Career Family Analysis." *British Journal of Sociology* 35: 19–41.

Berger, Bennett. 1968. *Working Class Suburb: A Study of Auto Workers in Suburbia*. Berkeley: University of California Press.

Berk, Sarah F. 1985. *The Gender Factory: The Apportionment of Work in American Households*. New York: Plenum.

Eckart, Christel; Ursula Jaerisch; and Helgard Kramer. 1979. *Frauenarbeit in Familie und Fabrik*. Frankfurt a/M.: Institut für Sozialforschung.

Feldberg, Roslyn, and Evelyn Nakano Glenn. 1979. "Male and Female: Job Versus Gender Models in the Sociology of Work." *Social Problems* 26: 524–38.

Ferree, Myra Marx. 1976. "Working-Class Jobs: Paid Work and Housework as Sources of Satisfaction." *Social Problems* 23: 431–41.

———. 1984. "Class, Housework and Happiness." *Sex Roles* 11: 1057–74.

———. 1985. "Between Two Worlds: German Feminist Approaches to Working-Class Women and Work." *Signs* 10: 517–36.

———. 1987. "The Struggles of Superwoman." In Christine Bose et al. (eds.), *Hidden Aspects of Women's Work*. New York: Praeger.

Fowlkes, Martha R. 1980. *Behind Every Successful Man: Wives of Medicine and Academe*. New York: Columbia University Press.

Freeman, Carolyn. 1982. "The 'Understanding' Employer." In Jackie West (ed.), *Work, Women and the Labour Market*. London: Routledge & Kegan Paul.

Gavron, Hannah. 1966. *The Captive Wife: Conflicts of Housebound Mothers*. London: Routledge & Kegan Paul.

Gerson, Kathleen. 1985. *Hard Choices: How Women Decide About Work, Career, and Motherhood*. Berkeley and Los Angeles: University of California Press.

Harding, Sandra. 1981. "Family Reform Movements: Recent Feminism and Its Opposition." *Feminist Studies* 7, no. 1: 57–76.

Harkess, Shirley. 1985. "Women's Occupational Experiences in the 1970s: Sociology and Economics." *Signs* 10: 495–516.

Hartmann, Heidi. 1981. "The Family as a Locus of Gender, Class and Political Struggle: The Example of Housework." *Signs* 6: 366–94.

Heer, David. 1958. "Dominance and the Working Wife." *Social Forces* 36: 341–47.

Hiller, Dana. 1980. "Determinants of Household and Childcare Task-Sharing." Paper presented at the meetings of the American Sociological Association, New York.

Hood, Jane. 1983. *Becoming a Two Job Family.* New York: Praeger.

Komarovsky, Mirra. 1962. *Blue-Collar Marriage.* New York: Random House.

Kreps, Juanita. 1972. "Do All Women Want to Work?" In L. K. Howe (ed.), *The Future of the Family.* New York: Simon and Schuster.

Lappe, Lothar. 1981. *Die Arbeitssituation erwerbstätiger Frauen: Geschlechtsspezifische Arbeitsmarktsegmentation und ihre Folgen.* Frankfurt a/M.: Campus Verlag.

Michelson, William. 1985. *From Sun to Sun: Daily Obligations and Community Structure in the Lives of Employed Women and Their Families.* Totowa, N.J.: Rowman and Allenheld.

Ostner, Ilona. 1978. *Beruf und Hausarbeit.* Frankfurt a/M.: Campus Verlag.

Pepitone-Rockwell, Fran. 1980. *Dual-Career Couples.* Beverly Hills, Calif.: Sage.

Pleck, Joseph H. 1979. "Men's Family Work: Three Perspectives and Some New Data." *Family Co-ordinator* 28: 481–88.

Rapoport, Rhona, and Rapoport, Robert. 1971. *Dual Career Families.* Baltimore: Penguin.

————. 1976. *Dual Career Families Reexamined.* New York: Harper & Row.

Rosen, Ellen. 1981. "Hobson's Choice: Employment and Unemployment Among Factory Workers in New England." Report to the U.S. Department of Labor.

Schöll-Schwinghammer, Ilse. 1979. *Frauen im Betrieb: Arbeitsbedingungen und Arbeitsbewusstsein.* Frankfurt a/M.: Campus Verlag.

Smith, Dorothy E. 1979. "A Sociology for Women." In Julia A. Sherman and Evelyn Torton Beck (eds.), *The Prism of Sex.* Madison: University of Wisconsin Press.

Walshok, Mary L. 1981. *Blue-Collar Women: Pioneers on the Male Frontier.* Garden City, N.Y.: Anchor.

14

Female-Headed Families:
Poor Women and Choice

MARIETTA MORRISSEY

Scholarly consideration of the conditions that lead to the formation of female-headed families is not new. In 1956 Smith attributed Caribbean female-led families to their African origins, and nearly a decade later Moynihan (1965) explained the dominance of females among U.S. black families in terms of the dissolution of conjugal ties in slavery. Rekindled interest in the topic has followed recent increases in the proportion of female-headed families in the United States and worldwide.[1] Female family headship is now commonly associated with poverty, but theorists posit different intervening variables. The link between economic deprivation and family form varies, too, for developing and industrial countries. In this essay I will explore the implications of contending theories of the formation of female-headed families for our understanding of women's material position and for the study of poverty. I will argue that female family headship represents a rational choice for some poor women.

The article is divided into three sections. The first reviews theoretical developments leading to the currently popular hypothesis that female headship is an economic strategy for managing resources that are limited but roughly equal to men's. Second, evidence pertinent to this hypothesis for Third World and industrial nations will be presented. Third, I will consider the implications of female family headship as an economic strategy.

Poverty and Female-Headed Families: The Theoretical Background

Smith (1956) and Moynihan (1965) first proposed the link between female-headed families and poverty, emphasizing the negative consequences for males of joblessness, their diminished economic role, and their consequent abandonment of familial obligations. They agreed that male demoralization, rooted in poverty, was the immediate precondition for the female-headed family.

A major challenge to Moynihan's and Smith's hypothesis was offered by Lewis' efforts to identify the universal characteristics of poverty. Lewis (1966 : xlii–lii) argued that mother-centered (and therefore unstable) family organization generally accompanied poverty, along with violence, fatalistic attitudes, and absence of political participation. Lewis associated the "culture of poverty" with large-scale cultural and technological transitions and a "cash economy, wage labor and production for profit" (1966: xliii), thus suggesting that the poverty of female-headed families is a consequence of a macro-social change, resulting from capitalism and accompanying proletarianization.

Others have pursued the relationship between proletarianization and the creation of female-headed families. Buvinić and Youssef (1978) review the literature on female-headed families and identify several key variables related to the proletarianization process: migration, urbanization, and marginalization of the work force. Yet the ensuing line of theory and research, while informative about the impact of social change on family organization at the aggregate level, tells us little of how proletarianization and its many dimensions affect individual families. In particular, we are left to wonder if males abandon families, as Moynihan and others have claimed, or if women are actors in the process as well, as some feminists and social scientists have recently argued.

Winch (1975) considered both proletarianization and the male response to explain the creation of female-led families:

Where it occurs, the absence of the husband-father seems usually to be associated with (a) economically depressed classes, (b) a situation wherein the unit of labor is the individual, (c) a situation where the man, if employed, is a migrant worker, and (d) where the man is not able to make a contribution to the family with respect to the position conferring function. (Winch 1977: 612)

Thus, with the first two conditions, Winch amplifies Lewis' theory that expansion of the wage-labor market is central to assumption of family headship by females. The last condition returns to Moynihan's and Smith's focus on the failure of the male to meet social expectations. Most important to the development of later, feminist approaches is condition *b*, by which Winch explains that proletarianization means not just a money economy, but individualized rather than group resource earning and accumulation.

The major theoretical shift implied by Winch is realized in Blumberg's assertion (1976; Blumberg with Garcia 1977) that *women's* individualized economic status contributes significantly to the formation of female-headed families. Thus, she argues that with proletarianization, a structural precondition for the emergence of female-led families develops in that women's subsistence opportunities are not drastically less than those of men of their class and are compatible with childcare (Blumberg 1975:109–10). Blumberg reminds us, then, that proletarianization has generally meant movement toward an equalization of individualized male and female earnings and earning opportunities. Only in wage-based societies do women have opportunities for economic independence from males with nearly equal resource-earning potential. She then introduces two theoretical innovations, suggesting that the unit of analysis at the individual level should be the female rather than, or as well as, the male and that motivation to establish a female-headed family may be materially based, rather than emotional or psychological. In other words, Blumberg implies that males do not simply fail in their economic roles and, psychologically bereft, leave home. Women, capable of relatively high levels of resource earning and accumulation, can and may choose to raise a family independent of husbands and lovers.

Alternative Hypotheses: Empirical Foundations

Let us pose, then, these hypotheses for the formation of female-headed families, allowing that they may not be mutually exclusive:

1. If he is poor, a male's earning capacity may be threatened, causing him to live apart from his family.
2. When male and female earning capacities are equal or nearly so, women will choose independence from males over unsatisfying conjugal relationships.

The first hypothesis, emphasizing male choice, has not been studied directly. There is, however, ethnographic evidence that unemployed or marginally employed males are unreliable partners (see, e.g., Slater 1977; Stack 1974).

The second hypothesis is somewhat more promising for direct study. If equalization of male and female incomes is associated at the aggregate level with growth in the proportion of female-headed families, we may infer female choice in family creation. For example, in the United States, women at the lowest income levels make more relative to men at their level than women at higher levels do. At the same time, divorce increases with women's wages, although women at high income levels actually make less relative to men than do other women. There are, then, more female-headed families as women enter the wage sector.

Blumberg offers other indirect evidence to support the second hypothesis. For U.S. families, she finds that divorce generally decreases with increased family income, and as the "sex gap in resources" increases. Moreover, the largest recent gains in real income have been among black females, for whom family leadership has increased dramatically in the last two decades. Comparing societies, Blumberg (1977) has found a high correlation between women's control over economic resources and lifestyle choices (e.g., divorce), along with some more direct evidence that female economic power generates female family leadership for specific societies. [2]

Recent ethnographic work adds further empirical support for the notion that women are key actors in the creation of female-headed families. Most influential is Stack's (1974) study of The Flats, a poor, urban, midwestern black community.

The women in Stack's study said that their relationships with men robbed them of dignity and self-respect. They left unions that seemed to humiliate them before the community. These women used "kin" to denote individuals with whom they exchanged resources. Stack concluded that biological and fictive kin compete with males for access to their female lovers' resources. The woman was viewed as a desired partner as well as kin in Stack's analysis because of her ability to contribute and exchange independent financial resources. Given the pressure from kin and the aids to survival that kin ties provide, the Flats women often "chose" family headship rather than conjugal ties.

Brown (1975:157) found a similar concern about diminished dignity and self-respect among Dominican women in both single and multiple mate unions. Among 916 women in a Dominican village characterized by a high incidence of matrifocality and female heads of household, those with a series of mates have an advantage in constructing many exchange relationships among kin and friends through which they can accumulate resources (Brown 1975:155). In contrast, a woman with one mate "becomes predominantly dependent upon her spouse, a situation little advantageous in the poverty sector" (Brown 1975:157). The women "verbalize the advantages of the more flexible free and visiting unions as follows: 'Once married, a woman is subject to her husband; not only can he dispose of his own resources as he sees fit, but also he has access to his wife's resources.' " [3]

Patterson (1982:158) makes a similar point about West Indian women, stressing their initiative in family formation. Although he argues that different socioeconomic factors explain "matrifocality" during each period in Jamaican history, "the extraordinary independence of West Indian women" has continued to be characteristic. Patterson attributes this "fully institutionalized continuity" to "the unusual status of women in traditional West Africa, a status which has no parallel in the premodern world."

Eugene Brody, a psychiatrist, treats another aspect of women's contribution to the creation of female-headed families: daughters' imitation of their mothers in assuming family leadership, thus contributing to an intergenerational tradition of matrifocality. In a study of fertility and contraceptive use among 150 Jamaican working-class women, Brody (1981) found that female family heads reared daughters in a conservative, sexually repressive way. Yet, argues Brody, Jamaican society identifies femaleness with motherhood. Female sexual expression and early motherhood become means of both expressing anger against apparently rigid mothers and achieving adulthood. But these experiences are seldom joyful, as the girl is generally left by her lover to bear the child alone, falling back on her disapproving mother for assistance. Brody's analysis captures, then, the psychological crises and transitions that are inseparable from sociological variables in explaining family creation and change.

It is possible, however, that female-headed families in the West and in Third World countries do not share the same structural bases. Let us examine variations in these two cases, and the apparent consequences for women and the families they maintain.

Female-Headed Families in Third World and Industrialized Countries

THIRD WORLD COUNTRIES

Urbanization, land alienation, and export expansion are key variables used to account for the tendency to encourage or discourage nuclear family formation in many Third World nations. Over the last twenty-five years, urbanization and land alienation occurred more rapidly in the Third World than they did in the West. Agriculture has been transformed into the large-scale production of export commodities, requiring unskilled labor, often only on a seasonal basis. These structural conditions have led to the rapid involvement of household members, especially males, in the wage-labor force. For example, Murray (1981) cites evidence of this pattern of family fragmentation in southern Africa with the expansion of monoculture and mining. Males migrate for work, leaving women behind to head families. Many marriages dissolve.

The focus on export expansion and its relation to female-headed family creation may also explain Clarke's (1957) finding that rural Jamaican female heads of households usually had ties to plantation workers. Smith (1956) found more visiting unions than consensual ones in plantation areas, and more formal unions and marriages in the towns and subsistence-based communities in British Guiana. Buvinić and Youssef (1978) suggest that landlessness in the Third World, highly related to export emphasis in production, has contributed to increases in female-headed families.[4]

But the hypothesis of export expansion as the dynamic behind the creation of female-headed families is unlikely to explain all cases, since evidence from other Third World nations suggests that impoverishment may deter marriage. Among members of the rural community in Martinique studied by Slater (1977), marriage is honored and cannot be undertaken until a couple is able to fulfill marital financial rights and obligations. Murray (1981) concludes that Lesotho's dependency has brought about a shortage of cattle and other resources used to complete the marriage contract, undermining the long-institutionalized way of legitimizing conjugal relationships and encouraging female family headship. Yet Smith's (1978) work with Guyanese families suggests that neither prosperity nor diminished resources alone can account for family forms, since new prosperity among the Guyanese black plantation workers did not increase marriage or nuclear family formation.

Other possible factors relevant to female headship among Third World nations involve women's marginalization and proletarianization. Third World women often work in the informal economy and thus are less often part of the paid labor force than their counterparts in developed nations. Children play a different role in Third World societies than in the developed world, more often contributing to family income in the former. Fertility and birth rates are, of course, much higher in the Third World than in industrialized nations. And public welfare is generally unavailable or meager in developing nations.

What, then, can we conclude about the relationship among the variables we have reviewed here and the possibility that women choose to head families in Third World nations? The diversity among nations indicates that there may be no single dynamic behind the creation of all female-headed families, and little evidence bearing directly on the issue of choice.

INDUSTRIALIZED COUNTRIES

We know surprisingly little about female-headed families in most industrial nations. However, here as well the available evidence does not point to any single dynamic leading to their creation. For twenty-six industrial nations I found no significant relationship between illegitimacy rate and welfare and social security as a proportion of national budget ($r = -0.186$), proportion of labor force female and illegitimacy ($r = 0.111$); labor force female and potential female-headed households as proportion of potential households ($r = -0.222$); and welfare and social security as proportion of national budget and potential female-headed households ($r = -0.019$) (World Bank 1968; United States 1977, 1982, 1984).[5]

The increase of factors associated with female headship confounds analysis, as does the variation in the amount and immediate causes of female family headship among ethnic groups in industrialized societies. It cautions as well against single causal explanations for as heterogeneous a category as "industrialized countries." Thus, divorce, separation, and illegitimacy have increased through much of the developed world, but with different relationships to female headship for different subgroups in industrialized nations. In a country like Sweden, with a relatively homogeneous population, extensive welfare benefits and increased social tolerance of illegitimacy, along with women's increased economic rights and resources, appear to contribute to the formation of female-headed families (Adams and Winston 1980:208). But in Britain, where about 10 percent of families are female-headed, and these are concentrated among the poor, some poor populations (e.g., West Indians) have a disproportionate share of female-led families, while others (e.g., Asians) have few. Elsewhere other unique factors may be operative. For example, Turkish women migrants to West Germany are often young women, commonly single mothers, who have been sent to make preparations for relatives who will follow later (Buvinić and Youssef 1978:77).

In the United States, too, dramatically different patterns of family organization prevail among ethnic groups. In 1983, 48.6 percent of black families had female heads, up from 30.6 percent in 1970 (U.S. Bureau of Census 1984:7).[6] Hispanics, also, have a large proportion of female-headed families; about 23 percent of Hispanic families were maintained by women in 1983, increasing from 15 percent in 1970 (U.S. Bureau of Census 1983:7). However, causation cannot be assigned to culture alone in either case. From 1970 to 1980 the rate of increase in female-headed families was greater among whites than among Hispanics or blacks. In 1970, 8.9 percent of white families were female-headed, but the proportion rose to 17.4 percent in 1983. The gap in the proportions of female-headed households among blacks, Hispanics, and whites can be almost wholly accounted for by relative poverty levels, and in particular by the comparative stability of male labor markets (Blumberg with García 1977; Ross and Sawhill 1975: 87; U.S. Commission on Civil Rights 1983).[7]

Ross and Sawhill's analysis of the influence of public welfare on the formation of female-headed families sheds some light on whether or not women's economic power may be a factor in family headship in the United States. They examined the relationship between female-headed households, the availability of welfare, and several other economic variables across states. For whites, women's earnings relative to men's were related significantly to the number of female-headed households, whereas the availability of welfare benefits was not. For nonwhites, access to welfare was associated strongly with number of female-headed households, but also contributed less to their formation than did earnings relative to men's. The authors conclude that there is little evidence that welfare and related programs created female-led families in any group.

Their work does support the hypothesis that, for the United States, relative economic power, whether through the labor market or through public assistance, enhances marital choice. But as the disparate findings reviewed above for other industrialized nations indicate, more society-specific explanations are needed, along with an understanding of the diverse experiences of ethnic groups within industrial societies.

A possible historical explanation derived from a modernization perspective should also be mentioned here. Some argue that First and Third World populations represent different stages in the absorption of women into the wage-labor force (see Tiano 1984 for a review of the literature). This contention assumes that proletarianization and marginalization of labor continue for centuries, eventually culminating in the equalization of male and female earning capacities. However, two important differences in the developmental histories of each group weaken the applicability of this "stage" hypothesis. Western industrialization did not produce large proportions of female-headed families, as industrialization has already done in some Third World countries.[8] Moreover, Third World development does not always produce female-headed families even among poor and apparently marginal populations (see Salaff 1981; Weekes-Vagliani 1976).

Given the diversity we have seen between and among developing and industrialized nations, we can only conclude that all female headed families may share little beyond that basic defining characteristic. Youssef and Hetler's (1983) charge that different family forms are mistakenly joined under this now-popular rubric may be on target. At the very least it appears that different concepts and theories may be necessary to account for cross-cultural variation among families maintained by women.

Female Headship as an Economic Strategy

UNDERSTANDING "CHOICE"

The hypothesis that female-led families among the poor are adaptive rests on an important assumption: that there are adequate resources available for survival, even if this is achieved only by pooling resources among several households. In some settings poor families do fail. There may be illness or death; children may be passed on to more financially stable relatives or to the state. It bears repetition that female-led families can be a choice adaptive to poverty only if such families manage to garner the resources they need. Current research offers few clues about when, and how often, failure occurs among such families.

Second, what women choose under conditions of economic hardship should not be confused with what they might do if the choices available to them were not few and narrow. Thus, women may claim to prefer to head a family when economic supports from kin and friends outweigh those available from a spouse or lover, but they might prefer other family forms under different conditions. Valentine's point is relevant here: commitment to cultural values "may often involve ambiguity, ambivalence, and the simultaneous holding of alternative or contradictory beliefs" (1968:120). The significance of the context of women's choice to be family heads is affirmed in Stack's (1974), Patterson's (1982), and Buvinić and Youssef's (1978) work. Stack's subjects, for example, wished to marry and form lasting unions but felt frustrated by economic realities and opposition from their own kin. The West Indian women claimed that their hopes for permanent unions were discouraged by what Patterson (1982:158) calls "pathetically sexist males." Buvinić and Youssef found a similar situation among Carribean women: with little education and high fertility, poor employment prospects, no public welfare, and little expectation of support from former lovers or the latters' families, the assistance of relatives and their children's employment constituted their principal means of support.[9]

Thus, women may choose to assume family leadership. But they seldom control the circumstances that make that choice necessary or salutary.

ISSUES FOR THE STUDY OF POVERTY

Locating women's motivation to form female-headed families in economic and social structural origins has significant implications for the study of poverty. First, although the impoverishment of proletarians predicted by Marx continues on a worldwide basis, neither Marx nor most later social scientists have considered whether proletarianization has different implications for males and females. Thus, while male proletarians may become fully independent economic actors, able to maximize their economic opportunities, the evidence we have reviewed here suggests otherwise for many poor women. Males' experience may better fit the traditional social science understanding of proletarianization and its cultural effects: atomization, alienation, and anomie. But women's experiences lead to strikingly different consequences. Since women, encumbered with children, most consolidate community ties to survive, community linkages conducive to political action may be increasingly female-based. This hypothesis dissociates, at least for many women, the tie suggested by Lewis (1966) and Valentine (1968) between poverty and political ineffectiveness.

Second, some mothers' preference for singleness calls for attention to economic strategies that should be seen as rational alternatives that vary by social class. Rapp (1982:81) speculates that poor and working-class families dispense material and economic resources, whereas middle-class people "invest lineally between parents, children, and grandchildren." Certainly among the families studied by Stack (1974), where resources were quickly distributed to needy friends and kin, saving was never possible. Brown (1975:157) found a similar pattern in the Dominican Republic. Poor women seemed to maximize resources most effectively through multiple male relationships, whereas among the affluent the single-male pattern was much more viable. Variation in economic strategy by social class, then, may be expressed in family form, individual goals, and community standards of sharing. This hypothesis is both intuitively acceptable and radically different from traditional social science images of poor people as irrational and emotionally motivated.

Conclusions

Poverty creates female-headed families. So do other social phenomena. Beyond this and the fact that we observe a great deal of variation among female-headed families, we know little that coheres into a theory of family origins, structure, or dynamics. Current thinking about female-headed families has not yet differentiated common characteristics of such families from those unique to specific cultural settings. Furthermore, we do not know the causal sequence among what we recognize to be key variables. Thus, we know that female-headed families are increasing throughout the world, along with several other trends: growth in women's labor-force participation, public expenditures on social services, proletarianization and marginalization. Any one, all, or some combination of these variables may explain the rise of female-headed families in specific settings, but we do not yet know how to specify the relationships among them.

Despite this present limitation, our knowledge about female headship is advancing. Our analysis reveals that processes of daily life thought to be highly specific to different cultural settings are surprisingly common among female-headed families in various world settings. These are rational patterns of survival among the poor, which social scientists, influenced by the sociological equivalence of poverty with pathology, have too often ignored. The important contribution of feminist thinking to the study of female-based families, then, may not be the hypothesized connection between women's economic independence and family headship—important as this appears to be in many settings. Instead, the lasting significance of the feminist-inspired attention to female headship as a family survival strategy may be its emphasis on women's capacity to act rationally toward the maximization of materially defined investments and opportunities.

Notes

1. Among U.S. whites, female-headed families with children have increased dramatically, from 8.9 percent of white families in 1970 to 17.4 percent in 1983 (U.S. Bureau of the Census 1984:7). Female-headed families have also increased throughout the Third World, particularly in urban areas (Buvinić and Youssef 1978; Tinker 1976; Youssef and Hetler 1983).

2. Blumberg's categories may be appropriate to the study of professional women as well as poor ones. Able to earn at the level of men, professionally employed women can buy services to assist them in combining careers and childcare and thus avoid emotionally constricting conjugal relationships. Havens (1973:218) found a "strong *direct* relation between economic attainment and unmarried status" among U.S. women around 1960. Ross and Sawhill's analysis of 5,000 families from the University of Michigan Panel Study of Income Dynamics suggests that as women contribute more economic resources to a marriage, the "cost of dissolution" declines and separation becomes more likely (1975:42).

3. Nevertheless, women in all these research settings do seek permanent unions and marriage, an apparent anomaly that will be discussed in a later section of this article.

4. Parts of nineteenth-century Latin America mirrored the Brazilian pattern: "Female-headed households were common in the period of modernization (at least 25 percent) in interior areas developed as frontiers where the expansion of exports was based on a single agricultural product grown on large estates" (Kuznesof 1979:607). These plantations drew men to work; women, alone, went to cities where domestic and other service jobs were available. Female-headed households were less frequent in rural than in urban areas, those that existed were commonly led by widows of plantation workers.

5. The indicator "potential female-headed households as a proportion of total potential households" is suggested by Buvinić and Youssef (1978). The category of "potential female-headed households" comprises all ever-married women, plus single mothers. "Total potential households" groups all ever-married males and females. The first figure, potential female-headed households, fails to capture de facto female family heads; moreover, single mothers are not included in calculations presented here, because their numbers are not reported by most nations. The figure for "potential households" is inflated, since most households are counted twice, but is used as a denominator in calculations to compensate for the "overestimation" of women heads (Buvinić and Youssef 1978:38). The relationship between illegitimacy rates for these twenty-six nations and the potential proportion of female-headed households is $r = 0.026$—not statistically significant.

6. In the United States black female-headed families have received much popular and academic attention but in fact have been common only since the migration of black families from the South to northern industrial jobs. Comparisons of U.S. black and other New World black families, based on presumed common origins in slavery, have been invalidated by the work of Gutman (1977) and others (see Blassingame 1972; Genovese 1976) establishing the high incidence of nuclear family formation among blacks during and immediately after slavery.

7. There are, of course, differences among female-headed families of different ethnicity. Rates of illegitimacy are higher among nonwhites than among whites. Nonwhites are also less likely to remarry after divorce than are whites and experience a longer interval between divorce and remarriage.

8. Although the character of family change in the West during the eighteenth and

nineteenth centuries remains in dispute and varies from region to region, female-led families were rare and apparently unpatterned. See Wall et al. (1983).

9. Buvinić and Youssef (1978:70) write: "While some of these women might 'choose' to leave common law unions in order to cope better with poverty, it is also likely (given their poor life-chances) that many others are forced out of these unions because of male marginality and desertion."

References

Adams, Carolyn Teich, and Kathryn Teich Winston. 1980. *Mothers at Work: Public Policies in the United States, Sweden and China*. New York: Longman.

Blassingame, John W. 1972. *The Slave Community*. New York: Oxford University Press.

Blumberg, Rae Lesser. 1975. "The Political Economy of the Mother-Child Family Revisited." In A. F. Marks and R. A. Römer (eds.), *Family and Kinship in Middle America and the Caribbean*. Leiden: Royal Institute of Linguistics and Anthropology.

———. 1976. "Fairy Tales and Facts: Economy, Fertility and the Female." Irene Tinker and M. B. Bramson (eds.) *Women and World Development*. Washington, D.C.: World Development Council.

———. 1977. *Stratification: Socioeconomic and Sexual Inequality*. Dubuque: W. C. Brown.

Blumberg, Rae Lesser, with María Pilar García. 1977. "The Political Economy of the Mother-Child Family: A Cross-Societal View." In Luis Leñero Otero (ed.), *Beyond the Nuclear Family Model: Cross-Cultural Perspectives*. London: Sage.

Brody, Eugene. 1981. *Sex, Contraception, and Motherhood in Jamaica*. Cambridge: Harvard University Press.

Brown, Susan. 1975. "Lower Economic Sector Mating Patterns in the Dominican Republic: A Comparative Analysis." In Ruby Rohrlich-Leavitt (eds.), *Women Cross-Culturally*. The Hague: Mouton.

Buvinić, Mayra, and Nadia H. Youssef, with Barbara Von Elm. 1978. *Women-Headed Households: The Ignored Factor in Devlopment*. Washington, D.C.: International Center for Research on Women.

Clarke, Edith. 1957. *My Mother Who Fathered Me*. London: Allen and Unwin.

Genovese, Eugene D. 1976. *Roll, Jordan, Roll. The World the Slaves Made*. New York: Vintage.

Gutman, Herbert. 1977. *The Black Family in Slavery and Freedom, 1750–1925*. New York: Vintage.

Havens, Elizabeth. 1973. "Women, Work and Wedlock: A Note on Female Marital Patterns in the United States." In Joan Huber (ed.), *Changing Women in a Changing Society*. Chicago: University of Chicago Press.

Kuznesof, Elizabeth Anne. 1979. "The Role of the Female-Headed Household in Brazilian Modernization: 1765 to 1836." *Journal of Social History* 13:589–614.

Lewis, Oscar. 1966. *La Vida*. New York: Random House.

Moynihan, Daniel Patrick. 1965. *The Negro Family: The Case for National Action*. Washington, D.C.: U.S. Department of Labor.

Murray, Colin. 1981. *Families Divided: The Impact of Migrant Labor in Lesotho*. Cambridge: Cambridge University Press.

Patterson, Orlando. 1982. "Persistence, Continuity and Change in the Jamaican Working Class Family." *Journal of Family History* 7:135–61.

Rapp, Rayna. 1982. "Family and Class in Contemporary America: Notes Toward an Understanding of Ideology." In Barrie Thorne with Marilyn Yalom (eds.), *Rethinking the Family: Some Feminist Questions*. New York: Longman.

Ross, Heather L., and Isabel V. Sawhill. 1975. *Time of Transition: The Growth of Female-Headed Households*. Washington, D.C.: Urban Institute.

Salaff, Janet W. 1981. *Working Daughters of Hong Kong*. Cambridge: Cambridge University Press.

Slater, Mariam. 1977. *The Caribbean Family: Legitimacy in Martinique*. New York: St. Martin's Press.

Smith, R. T. 1956. *The Negro Family in British Guiana*. London: Routledge & Kegan Paul.

———. 1978. "The Family and the Modern World System: Some Observations from the Caribbean." *Journal of Family History* 3:337–60.

Stack, Carol D. 1974. *All Our Kin: Strategies for Survival in a Black Community*. New York: Harper & Row.

Tiano, Susan. 1984. "The Public-Private Dichotomy: Theoretical Perspectives on 'Women and Development.'" *Social Science Journal* 21 (Oct.):11–28.

Tinker, Irene. 1976. "The Adverse Impact of Development on Women." In Irene Tinker and M. B. Bramson (eds.), *Women and World Development*. Washington, D.C.: Overseas Development Council.

United Nations. 1977. *Demographic Yearbook, 1976*. New York: United Nations.

———. 1982. *Demographic Yearbook, 1981*. New York: United Nations.

———. 1984. *Statistical Yearbook, 1983*. New York: United Nations.

U.S. Bureau of the Census. 1983. *Conditions of Hispanics in America Today*. Washington, D.C.: Government Printing Office.

———. 1984. *Household and Family Characteristics: March 1983*. Washington, D.C.: Current Population Reports, Series P-20, no. 388. Government Printing Office.

U.S. Commission on Civil Rights. 1983. *A Growing Crisis: Disadvantaged Women and Their Children*. Washington, D.C.: Government Printing Office.

Valentine, Charles A. 1968. *Culture and Poverty*. Chicago: University of Chicago Press.

Wall, Richard; Jean Robin; and Peter Laslett (eds.). 1983. *Family Forms in Historic Europe*. Cambridge: Cambridge University Press.

Weekes-Vagliani, Winifred. 1976. *Family Life and Structure in Southern Cameroon*. Paris: Organization for Economic Cooperation and Development.

Winch, Robert F. 1975. "Inferring Minimum Structure from Function; or, Did the Bureaucracy Create the Mother-Child Family?" In A. F. Marks and R. A. Römer (eds.), *Family and Kinship in Middle America and the Caribbean*. Leiden: Royal Institute of Linguistics and Anthropology.

World Bank. 1980. *World Tables*. Baltimore: Johns Hopkins University Press.

Youssef, Nadia H., and Carol B. Hetler. 1983. "Establishing the Economic Condition of Women-Headed Households in the Third World: A New Approach." In M. Buvinić, M. A. Lycette, W. P. McGreevey (eds.), *Women and Poverty in the Third World*. Baltimore: Johns Hopkins University Press.

MEN'S EMPLOYMENT
AND FAMILY LIFE

15

Marriage and Family Life of Blue-Collar Men

DAVID HALLE

Modern marriage is distinguished above all by the ideal that husband and wife should be each other's closest companion as well as sexual partner. As one study put it: "Among the many curious features of modern woman's life is one that would have thoroughly offended St. Paul, bewildered Tristan and amused Don Juan—namely the fact that she is her husband's best friend and he is hers."[1]

The contemporary view contains the expectation that the nuclear couple and their children should "be the object of a passionate and exclusive love," and that the family and home should be a "place of refuge," a warm shelter from the outside world. This places a heavy burden on the psychic resources of husband and wife.

At the same time, the American family has lost many of its material functions. Once, in an agricultural setting, its male and female members had important productive roles at home. Now paid labor ("work") typically takes place away from home, which has become the sphere of unpaid and therefore undervalued "housework." Once responsibility for educating the children lay mostly with parents. Now it lies with the school. Once care of the very sick took place within the family. Now it is the domain of the hospital and nursing home.

This is ironic. As the important material aspects of the lives of family members increasingly are handled outside the home, the expectation has grown that their deepest emotional relations should occur within it. As a result, the principle of the modern nuclear family can conflict with other principles of how to live interpersonal life—for instance, relations based on work and relations with friends of the same and of the opposite sex. This often causes problems for husbands and wives whatever their social class,

Adapted from *America's Working Man: Work, Home, and Politics Among Blue-Collar Property Owners,* by David Halle, by permission of The University of Chicago Press. © 1984 by The University of Chicago.

though occupation and education may influence the form such conflicts take.[2]

This perspective on the modern family implies some similarity between social classes—between marriages of blue- and white-collar workers. So does Komarovsky in her classic study, *Blue-Collar Marriage,* She points to differences, but also to similarities, as does Caplow's recent account of families in Middletown. The marriages of the blue-collar workers who are the subject of this article also fit such a view.[3]

Yet studies of the family life of American blue-collar workers stress the way in which their marriages are unlike those of the middle class. Rubin, for instance, argues that the marriages of blue-collar workers are distinct above all because of the misery that pervades them. They are, as she puts it, "worlds of pain."[4]

Such a view goes too far for the workers I studied. Certain characteristics of these blue-collar husbands do add a distinct flavor to their marriages. They have somewhat low status as "factory workers" and modest levels of formal education. And they have jobs, not careers. The impact of these features should not be ignored. Yet for a balanced picture it is important to place these distinguishing features in the context of the similarities between these marriages and those of the middle class.

The account that follows is based on research among the entire blue-collar labor force of a New Jersey chemical plant, owned by Imperium Oil and Chemicals (a pseudonym).[5] The research was designed to address a question that has long dominated discussion of the working class in advanced industrial societies. To what extent are blue-collar workers "middle-class" in the sense that their lives and beliefs overlap with those of white-collar workers? (The latter can be divided into an "upper-white-collar sector," composed of managers and professionals, and a "lower-white-collar sector," composed of clerical, secretarial, and sales workers.)

I chose to study a group of workers whose position is strategic for this debate, for if any blue-collar group is "middle-class," then these workers should be. Their wages and benefits are well above the average for blue collar workers in American, they are protected by a union, and the chemical complex where they are employed is typical of the kind of modern technological setting that is said to have transformed blue-collar work.

The research took place during a seven-year period, from late 1974 until late 1981. The total number of blue-collar workers fluctuated, from a high of 126 to a low of 115. All these workers are men, for blue-collar work is dominated by males.[6] I investigated their views through long and frequent informal conversations, individually and in groups, at and outside the workplace. I recorded these conversations as soon afterward as possible. During the long time I knew them, I talked with almost all these workers about marriage and family life. Seventy-nine were willing to discuss these questions at enough length for me to feel justified in including their views in the analysis that follows. Of this group, fifty-nine are currently married, and the rest are divorced, separated, or bachelors.

Most wives of Imperium workers are, like many women in America, in lower-white-collar occupations: secretaries, clerical workers, or salespeople. But an interesting and important minority of Imperium wives are professionals or managers. I knew the wives of most workers from the annual Christmas party and other social occasions. Although my discussion concentrates on blue-collar men, I have included data on their wives where it is pertinent and where I have enough information to justify doing so.

Marital Contentment and Discontent

Almost all the married men have in mind a general judgement about the quality of their marriages—the extent to which marriage is a source of satisfaction. The basic question underlying this judgment is whether they are glad or sorry to be married. This question naturally occurs to everyone, for the existence of divorced persons among their fellow workers, kin, or friends is a constant reminder that marriages can be terminated.[7]

Thirty-five percent say that they are glad to be married and speak with enthusiasm about their wives. Another 25 percent have mixed feelings. Some have gone through a long period of serious difficulty, often coming close to divorce. Others experience major problems, but also important satisfactions, in their marriages. The third and largest group, 40 percent of the husbands, are unhappily married. Relations with their wives are in general a source of considerable frustration and anger.

What reasons do those men give who do not, or did not, get along with their wives? What problems have they encountered?

THE PRINCIPLE OF THE MODERN NUCLEAR FAMILY VERSUS OTHER PRINCIPLES

The modern marital ideal of shared companionship as well as shared sex is one of which all these workers are aware and to which most subscribe. But in practice many find it hard to achieve. Thus, the most frequent problem in these marriages is conflict between spending leisure time with wives and spending it in other ways.

Leisure Relations with Male Friends

The main, but not the only, reason for conflict is the lack of common leisure interests. An important part of men's leisure activities are of a kind not easily shared with women. This motif touches most men's marriages, and for at least half it creates serious problems, constituting a recurring source of dispute, anger, and resentment.[8] Consider a worker in his mid-forties: "Susan [his wife] keeps saying, 'Why don't we go away together? Just you and I.' But that's boring. I like to go fishing and drink a few beers when I'm on vacation, but she doesn't want to do that."

The two most common joint leisure activities for husband and wife are eating at restaurants and visiting friends. But visiting friends is often a joint activity only in a formal sense. On such occasions the company tends to divide along gender lines. The men do talk with the women, but they spend far more time talking with each other.

Mindful of this dominant problem, those workers who are happily married commonly stress the importance of spending leisure time with their wives. This is widely viewed as the key to marital harmony:

I don't care what they [the other workers] say, marriage is a beautiful thing. But you have to work at it. You can't just leave your wife alone, like a lot of these guys.

I'll tell you what makes a good marriage. It's when you do things together. Like, my wife comes fishing.

Indeed, despite the difficulties just outlined, there is a sizable group of husbands (just under half) for whom the lack of share leisure time is not a serious problem. For some that is because the husbands have given up their contacts with the male leisure culture. They come home after work and, as they sometimes put it, "don't socialize with the other guys." Others develop leisure pursuits that they can share with their wives. Dancing is a common one.

The limited nature of their shared leisure pursuits is not a problem for some couples, because they are willing to allow each other considerable latitude. The wife does not mind if her husband spends several hours a day in the tavern, and the husband is content to let his wife spend time with her female friends or kin.

Some couples enjoy joint leisure activities and still allow each other room for their own interests, even tolerating extramarital affairs. One worker, who likes to go drinking and play cards with his friends, explained the understanding he had with his wife, and its limits:

We [his wife and he] do a lot together. We both bowl, and we go out to eat together, and go to parties. I'm happy.

My wife is very liberal. She doesn't bother if I'm out, and I don't bother if she's out. I know she's with her girl friends or something. She doesn't mind if I come home late unless it's very late, maybe two or three in the morning. Then the next day she'll say something like "Where were you?" And I'll say, "I have a right to stay out," and we'll argue. Maybe it'll last two days. I know she has a legal [he means moral] case, but I argue, and she does. It's like we're letting the other know we care.

Work and Workaholism

A desire to spend leisure time with male friends is not the only reason workers are not with their wives as much as the wives might like. Some men are "workaholics." They will repeatedly, over many years, spend as much extra time in the factory as they can. Many workers are tempted by the additional money overtime brings, but only a few will, throughout their lives, work overtime on every possible occasion.

Sexual Friendships with Other Women

Other men spend less time with their wives because they are having extramarital affairs. Given the geographic separation of work and home, this is not difficult. Also, as men get older, the gender ratio becomes increasingly favorable. For a worker in his forties and older, there is a plentiful supply of available women—divorced, widowed, or never married.

Thus, for many of these workers the principle of the nuclear family conflicts with the principle of male friendships, and for some it conflicts with the principle of work or the principle of sexual friendships with other women. The modern marital ideal that husband and wife should be each other's closest friend as well as sexual partner is hard to achieve regardless of occupation. As with leisure, occupation may make some difference to the way couples experience this ideal. But if it does, it does not separate working class from middle class, but those with jobs from those for whom work is a central interest, especially those with careers. And those with jobs include not only most blue-collar workers, but also most lower-white-collar workers and a portion of the upper-white-collar sector.

For these blue-collar workers, in jobs, not careers, friendships at work— "buddies"—are vital, for it is such camaraderie that makes a dull setting tolerable. And a work context involving cooperation and a union strengthens such ties. There is some tendency for this work-related culture to spill over into life outside work and to compete and interfere with wives' claims to a share of their husbands' leisure time. (This tendency should not be exaggerated. About half the married workers go straight home after work. And not all blue-collar settings involve cooperation and dense friendships at work.)

On the other hand, absorbing work and a career can intrude on marital life in a variety of ways that most of those in jobs are largely free of. Their husbands' lack of careers protects the wives of blue-collar workers from such difficulties.[9] Thus, the difference between a career and a job may change the likely order of conflict between the principle of the nuclear family and other principles. For those in careers it may be the principle of work that interferes most often with the principle of the nuclear family. For blue-collar workers in jobs, it may be the principle of male friendships.

THE SOCIAL STATUS OF THE HUSBAND

The second most common problem, cited by 30 percent of the married men, concerns the tendency of some wives to complain that their husbands' social status is too low. This complaint typically conveys a number of ideas. There is the obvious truth that blue-collar workers lack a college degree and whatever status this confers. There is the related notion that they lack the qualifications and aspirations for the kind of jobs that require college education and beyond, notably upper-white-collar jobs. One worker expressed this as follows: "You know, women are terrible. Here I am, just a working slob, and I've got a house and the mortgage all paid off. And still my wife says I should be looking higher. And *she* doesn't work. I hate work."

There is also the view that workers lack the social tastes, interests, and skills that education is supposed to confer. Particularly prone to give offense is men's earthy language and forthright manner. Tastes that wives perceive as unrefined are also a source of argument. A second-generation Italian worker in his early forties was angry about a recent incident. He and his wife had gone out to dinner at a New York restaurant with some friends. The others had ordered moderately exotic dishes, but he preferred simple Italian food and told the others so as he ordered spaghetti and meatballs. To his annoyance his wife publicly rebuked him, complaining that whenever he went out he embarrassed her. These issues are particularly explosive, since the overwhelming majority of workers are very sensitive about their lack of formal education.

This discussion illustrates again the interplay between themes that are distinctive to the marriages of blue-collar workers and themes that are not. Much blue-collar work carries less social status then upper-white-collar employment and, in some people's eyes, lower-white-collar work, which is at least performed in the clean surroundings of the "office." Imperium workers are well aware of the low status associated with "factory work," and there is a clear tendency for blue-collar workers to have less education than upper-white-collar workers. Given the high value attached to education in America, this often creates defensiveness and a feeling of inadequacy and failure.

Further, employed wives of blue-collar workers tend to have jobs that arguably carry higher status than their husbands' jobs. Most blue-collar workers' wives, if employed, are in clerical and secretarial jobs that, though typically poorly paid, are still "office jobs." And a minority are in upper-white-collar managerial or professional employment.

The impact of this is softened because the income of men at Imperium usually exceeds their wives'. Given the importance of income as a determinant of status in the United States, this clearly offsets any tendency of husbands to feel inferior, even if from other points of view their occupation carries lower status. Indeed, workers often pointedly contrast their income with that of white-collar occupations. Consider the mechanic with a ninth-grade education who said proudly: "My daughter told her teachers how much her father earned without an education! They didn't believe it so I Xeroxed a pay stub for her to show them!"

Still, in a society that has for so long stressed that occupation is of primary importance for the husband but only secondary importance for the wife, the relatively low status of factory work as compared with office work can create special problems for the marriages of blue-collar workers. [10]

Yet the difficulties created in these marriages by the tendency for wives' dissatisfaction with their husbands' job, education, or social demeanor should not be exaggerated. About a third of the married men find this a problem, but that leaves a larger group who do not. One worker's wife has a doctorate and is a college professor in New Jersey. Of all these marriages, this is the one where the educational and occupational imbalance between husband and wife is the greatest. Yet despite an occasional joke about the length and expense of his wife's education, this husband is obviously proud of her achievements. And though they allow each other freedom to conduct their own lives, they also move with a certain enjoyment in each other's social worlds. She sometimes spends time at the tavern where her husband does much of his drinking, and she is popular with his friends. To their delight she tells obscene jokes that any of the men would be proud to have originated. And he enjoys mixing with his wife's friends.

Their occupational imbalance is clearly exceptional, but their ability to prevent it from disrupting their marriage is not. This suggests that complaints about the husband's social demeanor, or his lack of education or occupational status, may have as much to do with psychological as sociological factors. In such cases the low status of factory work is clearly an excuse; spouses could, after all, focus on the husbands' superior income rather than the inferior status of factory work.

PROBLEM DRINKING

Heavy drinking that constitutes or verges on alcoholism is the third most frequent difficulty men cite in their marriages. Seventeen workers mentioned it as a problem.

These men commonly make a distinction between an alcoholic and a heavy drinker. An "alcoholic" is someone whose drinking persistently interferes with his ability to come to work or to perform minimally on the job. A "heavy drinker," on the other hand, enjoys spending time in the tavern and drinking beer at home but can usually still perform the routine activities of living and working. But this is a distinction that, some men believe, their wives do not always appreciate. As one worker complained: "Mary [his wife] reads a guy in the newspaper who says if you need a cocktail before dinner every night then you're an alcoholic, and she believes it. Then she yells at me because I have a beer before dinner."

Excessive drinking is, of course, likely to be a symptom of some other problem. But whatever its origin, it can become a serious and ugly difficulty in its own right. A worker in his early fifties:

Drunkenness is a big problem. I drank myself for a long time when I was working in the fasic plant [the process plant, which requires shift work]. It messed up my home life. My wife nearly left me. She said if I didn't stop drinking she would leave.

Mostly it is the men who drink too heavily (for their spouses' liking), but sometimes it is the women.

Workers who regularly drink beyond their capacity to control their behavior are fired fairly quickly. They are the ones who consistently fail to get to work on time or are consistently too drunk to make a contribution to the job. This leaves a group who sometimes (perhaps once a month) become dangerously drunk. Several years ago one such man, after an evening in the tavern, drove his car under a truck. His face had to be remodeled by a plastic surgeon.

Heavy drinking and problem drinking ("alcoholism") are obviously not confined to blue-collar workers, nor are they most concentrated among them. In a national sample, Don Cahalan and associates found that heavy drinking is about as widespread among managers and professionals as among blue-collar workers.[11] Beer and the tavern are part of traditional working-class culture, but the world of business and management also involves a considerable amount of drinking, though with differences of nuance—less beer in the tavern, more drinks over expense-account meals.

So far this article has explored the main difficulties that occur in these marriages. There are several reasons for this focus. First, more marriages have problems than do not. Second, workers tend to be more articulate about their troubles, for these provoke thought and reflection. Workers are less likely to be able to explain why their marriages are successful than why they are not.

Yet one theme persistently occurs when workers are discussing the benefits of being married—the idea that their wives rescued them from the wild life-style of the male culture, a lifestyle that they believe would in the end have been their downfall. A worker: "Marriage? Well, it's discipline. You know, a wife will straighten a guy out. She'll make sure he comes home instead of going out drinking every night, and he'll start to think of his responsibilities."

Wives

Imperium wives reflect the trend toward increased employment of women. Fewer than a third are not in paid jobs. Most of this group have young children. They remain at home because they believe that children in their early years need a mother's constant attention, or because they cannot find anyone else to care for their children during the day.

THE HOUSEWIVES

Only a very small number of wives of Imperium workers are committed housewives in the sense that they deliberately remain out of the labor market even after their children have grown up. And these women tend to be defensive, aware that they are a dwindling minority and feeling a need to explain and justify themselves. One, in her early forties with three grown children, commented:

I don't want to work. We were discussing it last night with some people, and two of the women said, "Don't you want to be something, to make something of yourself?" But I think they're deluding themselves. How are they "being something" [a reference to her friends' clerical and secretarial jobs]?

Some of these marriages provide satisfactions to both partners. But others illustrate all the problems such marriages bring among the "middle class" too—an excessively controlling husband and a depressed wife whose resentment against her husband appears in all kinds of ways.

THE EMPLOYED WIVES

Of those Imperium wives with full- or part-time jobs (more than two-thirds), the largest number work in lower-white-collar occupations, as secretaries or in clerical or retail settings (Table 15-1). A number of those in clerical jobs are bank tellers or enter data into computers. Retail jobs commonly involve selling in a store.

The second largest group of Imperium wives have upper-white-collar jobs as professionals or managers. Most are in the less-well-paid professions: four are schoolteachers, and four are nurses. There is one college professor, a social worker, and a middle-level manager in a hospital. The training and education of this group range from one or two years beyond high school for the nurses to a bachelor's degree (or more) for the teachers and a doctorate for the college professor. It is this group of wives of blue-collar workers, more likely than the others to possess a certain kind of energy and ambition, that is systematically overlooked by studies of working-class marriage that consider only couples where neither has more than a high-school education.

A small number of wives (six) are blue-collar workers with jobs that involve tending machines or packaging goods.

Census data make it possible to compare the occupations of Imperium wives with those of wives of men in a variety of occupations.[12] Women's jobs in America overlap in ways that transcend their husbands' occupations, especially in the middle range of the class structure. For instance, clerical work (including secretarial jobs) is strikingly common among wives. A third of the women married to professionals hold such jobs, as do 45 percent of the women married to better-paid managers.

Still, an important minority of wives are in professions, especially teaching, nursing, and social work (though far fewer are managers). Almost half of the better-paid professional men are married to other professionals, as are 23 percent of the better-paid managers. And 13 percent of wives of skilled blue-collar workers are professionals. Here it is important to remember that Imperium wives are likely to have education and jobs that are above the average

Table 15-1 Occupations of the Wives of Imperium Workers

Occupation[a]	No.
Professional or managerial (mostly teachers and nurses)	12
Clerical (includes secretarial) and sales	19
Blue-collar	6
Service workers	9
Housewives	19
Total	65

[a]Includes those who currently work in an occupation or have been employed in that occupation within the past two years.

for wives of blue-collar workers: This explains why upper-white-collar work is their second commonest occupation, whereas for wives of blue-collar workers in general, it ranks after blue-collar work.

There are, then, certain broad similarities in the labor-market positions of the wives of better-paid blue-collar workers and the wives of men in the lower and middle ranges of the managerial and professional sector. Certain forces tend, of course, to increase the differences between them. Studies of spouse selection point to the tendency for people to marry partners with similar social and educational backgrounds. Thus, wives of upper-white-collar workers are more likely to have upper-white-collar fathers than are wives of blue-collar workers (though it is not unusual for women from upper-white-collar families to marry blue-collar workers, especially the better-paid ones). [13] Professional men (but not managerial men) are as likely to marry women in professions as to marry women in lower-white-collar jobs. Further, studies suggest a strain toward "status consistency" within marriage. In particular, wives will be under pressure to avoid certain jobs that are incompatible with the status of their husbands' jobs. For instance, wives of upper-white-collar men are very unlikely to be blue-collar workers, in part because many such husbands would find it awkward to have a blue-collar wife. It is less appropriate for the wife of an engineer or a manager to work in a factory than for the wife of a factory worker to do so. [14]

Finally, marriage to a blue-collar worker involves certain concerns that wives of white-collar men are more likely to be free of. Much blue-collar work is dangerous, and this is certainly true of many of the jobs at Imperium. Wives of Imperium workers often express anxiety about their husbands' physical well-being. Some are resigned; others wish their husbands could find safer jobs.

Still, the preceding discussion suggests areas of overlap between the labor market positions of the wives of better-paid blue-collar workers and the wives of white-collar men in middle-level jobs. There are two reasons why this overlap is often ignored. First, the studies that stress differences between wives of blue-collar and upper-white-collar workers consider only those wives of blue-collar workers who have children and no more than a high school education. Focusing on women with young children ensures a disproportionately large number of housewives and women in part-time employment, and ruling out those with more than a high school education omits the interesting minority of blue-collar wives in upper-white-collar occupations.

Second, studies that stress the differences between blue-collar and middle-class marriages typically ignore the wife's occupation when defining the class character of the marriage. Marriages where the husband is a blue-collar worker are usually called blue-collar or working-class marriages regardless of the wife's occupation. And marriages where the husband has an upper-white-collar occupation are usually called middle-class marriages regardless of the wife's occupation. This practice avoids the complications, and the blurring of class lines, that result from taking the wife's occupation seriously.

It is hard to justify ignoring the wife's occupation in a period when women increasingly view themselves as serious contenders in the labor market. Ironically, these very studies that ignore the wife's occupation when defining the social class of the marriage tend to report that if she has a job, it is usually important to her. In any case, it is inconsistent to argue that the distinction between blue-collar and middle-class *occupations* is basic to an understanding of marriage in America and then to assume, before beginning the study, that the occupation of the husband is central while that of the wife is irrelevant to the class character of the marriage. [15]

The Children

What about the occupational attainment of the children of Imperium workers? Table 15-2 lists the occupations of those of the men's children who are no longer in school or college. The largest group of their sons are in blue-collar jobs (including six who work at Imperium). Most of the daughters are in clerical or retail jobs or are housewives looking after young children. A minority of the men's children are in professions or are managers. One son is a middle-level manager for Ford in England. Another graduated from the University of Wisconsin and works as a sports reporter for United Press International in Manhattan. Among the daughters, most of the professionals are,

Table 15-2   Occupations of the Children of Imperium Workers

Occupations	No. of Sons	No. of Daughters
Professional or managerial	9	11*
Clerical and sales	5	15
Blue-collar	24	0
Armed services	5	0
Own business	0	2
Housewives	0	12
Service workers	6†	7
Unemployed	4	0
Total	53	47

*Mostly teachers and nurses.
†Includes 3 policemen and firemen.

like the men's wives, schoolteachers and nurses. Two of the teachers have doctorates.

The symbolic importance of these occupations should not be underestimated. It is true that only a minority of the men's children are in professions (and none are lawyers or doctors, the goal of so many children of the white-collar professional sector). But workers talk to each other about their children. The UPI correspondent was covering the Olympic Games in Munich when the Israeli athletes were massacred. Through his father, most of the other chemical workers heard a detailed account of the dramatic events.

In such ways most workers come to believe that the class structure of America offers a degree of opportunity. They see that some men's children have attained significant advancement.[16] It is true that workers often comment on the difficulty they have, or will have, in paying for a college education for their children. But they know that students who do well in high school can attend inexpensive state or city colleges. I never heard a single worker suggest that his own occupation or modest education might seriously diminish the occupational chances of his children.

Marriage After the Children Leave Home

THE COMPANIONATE MARRIAGE

As men grow older, their marital and leisure lives enter a stage marked by a much-improved economic situation. Their children have grown up; their wives usually take jobs; and their mortgages are (or are almost) paid off. At work men have accumlated twenty or thirty years of seniority, which protects them against cutbacks in the labor force (though not against a plant closure) and entitles them to several weeks' annual vacation, as well as to a pension when they retire.

At the same time, workers begin to develop physical ailments that slow their mobility. By this time, too, everyone knows fellow workers who have died suddenly, and the lesson of life's brevity is not lost. As they enter their late forties, sometimes even earlier, workers often remark that they do not know how much longer they have to live—they might die tomorrow.

In this stage some of the married workers who once spent most of their leisure time with male friends now spend more time with their wives, either because physical ailments have curtailed their sporting activities, or because their buddies have died or moved away, or because they fear being alone in old age. The wife becomes more of a companion. Joint travel, in America and abroad, adds color to the marital relation. A worker in his mid-fifties commented on his own marriage and those of other older workers: "You know, with most of them [the older workers] it isn't even what you might call love. It's well, when you've been with someone for a long time you get like this" (locking his hands together).

Such marriages come to resemble those where husband and wife have always spent considerable time together, for there too the spouses tend to rely even more on each other for companionship as they grow older. One worker in his early fifties, whose marriage had always been happy, commented on this change. His younger son was in college:

You know, before we got married I used to like to go out with my wife. We'd eat and have a couple of drinks. Then after we got married we figured, "Why not stay home?" So we didn't bother to go out for drinks. We'd have our drinks at home. But we used to socialize. I couldn't imagine not going out Saturday night. My wife had four or five girl friends and I had my friends, and we'd do a lot in couples.

But then gradually it began to stop. You know, people got involved in their own families. One night you'd ask one couple and they'd be caught up with something with the kids, maybe something at school. And then they'd ask you and you'd be doing something and someone would get offended and you'd stop seeing each other. It happened to everyone I know. I don't know why, it's a pity. Like the last few years on Saturday evening we'll watch TV.

This tendency for husband and wife, as they grow older, to see each other increasingly as companions is not confined to the marriages of blue-collar workers. The "companionate" marriage is common among older couples regardless of social class. [17]

As these workers grow older, such differences as once existed between their marriages and those of the white-collar sector decrease further. Men's retirement removes a crucial factor that differentiates marriages the occupation of the husband. Both blue-and white-collar spouses become preoccupied with a similar series of problems concerning financial security, physical health, and making the most of their remaining years.

THE DISCONTENTED

On the other hand, some couples finally split up. With the children grown, an important reason for remaining in an unhappy marriage disappears. Whether happily or unhappily married, most men derive considerable pleasure from watching their young children develop. A divorce would risk loss, or considerable reduction, of this contact, since custody usually goes to the wife. Workers who are divorced often speak with regret about their inability to see their young children as much as they would like. Some have lost all contact except for occasional formal matters. Men who have stayed in unhappy marriages to enjoy their children have less incentive to remain after the children leave home.

The absence of young children also removes certain economic barriers to divorce. Wives no longer must stay home to care for them, so they can obtain full-time jobs, and thus some economic independence. The children's growing up frees the husband in a different way. He no longer has to fear heavy child-support payments if he quits the marriage.

Yet by no means all the workers who are unhappily married obtain a divorce when the children have left home. Forty percent of Imperium husbands are unhappily married, and the children of half this group are no longer in high school. These husbands consistently fail to get along with their wives. Why do they stay married?

For both husbands and wives there is a psychological dimension—fear of change, fear of independence. And there are still economic considerations. The wives doubt that they can maintain the same standard of living. As one wife commented about some of the Imperium wives who were unhappily married and did not have jobs:

They're scared. They don't know what they can do. You take a woman in her fifties, and she hasn't done anything [hasn't had a job] all her life. What's she going to do? And if they [husband and wife] break up, she *may* get something [alimony and property settlement], but she doesn't know, she can't be certain.

There is also an important economic reason why many of these men remain in unhappy marriages. They fear alimony payments and property division. In particular, men are very reluctant to lose their houses. In New Jersey property is usually divided equally between the husband and the wife after a divorce, and the husband must often pay alimony. And even though many men in America default on such payments after a few years, Imperium workers contemplating divorce face serious economic uncertainties. Ironically, the house, which represented economic independence, becomes a source of marital dependence.

Desertion, a traditional method of at least avoiding alimony payments, is not feasible, since men are to a large extent locked into their jobs. Unhappily married workers sometimes talk about disappearing out West as a way of freeing themselves without incurring crippling financial penalties. But loss of their relatively well-paying jobs and their seniority and pensions is a strong deterrent:

When you get married, you lose your freedom. And the divorce laws in New Jersey are brutal. Take Bill [a divorced worker in the plant]. He's still paying six years later [after the divorce], and if he doesn't, she sends the police around. And he lost his house. He can only afford a room in Elizabeth.

This motif illustrates a subtle way in which such men's position in the class structure and their level of income and wealth (but not their occupation) influence their married life. Since they have relatively well-paying jobs and usually houses, they have real assets to lose in any divorce settlement. Yet their income is not high enough for them to recover easily from a settlement. At their income level alimony and property division are severe economic blows.

Conclusion

There are three reasons for the divergence between these finding and studies that stress mainly differences between the marriages of blue- and white-collar workers. First, men at Imperium represent economically more privileged blue-collar workers. For the same reason their wives can be expected to have jobs and education above the average for wives of blue-collar workers. This study is designed to consider theories of possible overlap between blue- and white-collar workers, so that it is appropriate to consider a group of workers at a point in the class structure where overlap is most likely. However, care should be taken when generalizing from their marriages to those of blue-collar workers in inferior jobs.

Second, studies that stress the differences between "blue-collar" (or "working-class") and "middle-class" marriages contain three related features that lead them to understate certain overlaps. First, by focusing on couples with young children, they identify as the essence of working-class marriage characteristics that may be associated with only one stage of the marital cycle, a stage where leisure life is most curtailed, the wife is least likely to be employed, and economic problems are likely to be greatest. Second, they exclude couples with more than a high school education, thus overlooking an important minority of educated women who do not fit the stereotypes of the working-class wife. Third, they ignore the wife's occupation when defining the social class of the marriage. Thus, they define a "working-class" or "blue-collar" marriage as one where the *husband* is a blue-collar worker, regardless of the wife's occupation.[18] This implies that marriages in America can easily be divided by occupation into two main types, "blue-collar" and "middle-class." But the entry of a large number of wives into the labor market after World War II complicates this distinction. Indeed, the three selection criteria I have pointed to are mostly based on the assumption that paid employment of wives is of secondary importance. This assumption was more plausible in the past, so in part my findings reflect changes over time.

The lives of these blue-collar workers outside the workplace display several notable features. Because they often have jobs that are not absorbing, many stress friendships at and outside work and protect and enlarge their opportunities for leisure. In this sense they tend to be "person-oriented." They have less education and lower-status jobs than most upper-white-collar employees, which may produce a defensiveness about education, some sense of social inferiority, the absence of certain tastes and interests associated with a college education, and marital tension, especially if their wives have more education and are in good white-collar jobs.

Moreover, the class structure reproduces itself. Blue-collar workers are more likely than upper-white-collar workers to have blue-collar fathers. And their children are less likely than the children of upper-white-collar men to attain high-status jobs or to marry those with fathers in high-status jobs.

There are ways the class structure reinforces as well as reproduces itself. Many of the friends of Imperium workers are also blue-collar workers. And men in the pre–World War II industrial suburbs of Elizabeth and Linden inhabit areas where numbers of fellow workers from Imperium also live (although government and company insurance and welfare programs, and six-lane highways, have eroded an important part of the solidarity that once characterized these communities). Further, there are some pressures on people to select spouses from similiar backgrounds and to avoid incongruous occupational mixes.

These forces do affect the residential, marital, and leisure lives of blue-collar workers. If there is a "working-class culture" outside the workplace, then these are its ingredients, though a modest job, a modest level of education, an occupationally modest family of origin, and the absence of a career are not confined to blue-collar workers. Clearly some of these characteristics are often present in those who occupy lower-white-collar jobs and may, in a limited way, characterize some of those in upper-white-collar jobs.

Consider now the main overlaps between the lives of blue-collar and upper-white-collar employees outside the workplace. Better-paid blue-collar workers earn as much as or more than many white-collar workers. This enables workers at Imperium to move from older neighborhoods to areas that contain a greater occupational mix, especially to post–World War II suburbs in which their close neighbors are rarely other Imperium workers. And their income enables better-paid blue-collar workers to buy the same houses and consumer goods and services as many white-collar employees and to engage in many of the same leisure activities. There is no such thing in post–World War II America as a "blue-collar house," any more than there is a blue-collar car, stereo, or television. Instead, there are products that vary by size, quality, and price. Certainly inflation and high interest rates have eroded the standard of living of the blue-collar working class, but they also affect the white-collar sectors. Real income may fall in America, yet the overlap between classes remains. And if the suburban detached house becomes too expensive, effort will focus on more modest prizes, such as a suburban town house or a condominium. Goals may be trimmed, but they will be trimmed more or less uniformly.

Life outside work bears the mark of other forces, in addition to income level, that cut across collar color. Residential America is visibly divided by race, into black and Hispanic areas on the one hand and white areas on the other. This is potentially explosive. There are also differences of gender. For example, interest in sports such as football, baseball, hunting, and fishing is concentrated among males (though some women do follow such sports and though other sports, such as jogging and swimming, are less divided by gender). Gender operates in another way. Many wives in America share certain similarities that transcend their husbands' occupations. They are concentrated in unpaid housework, poorly paid clerical and service jobs, and certain professions such as teaching, nursing, and social work. And they, rather than their husbands, tend to be responsible for most of the housework and childcare. Finally, there are the effects of age and stage in the marital cycle. For example, the presence of young children often curtails the leisure lives of parents (though usually more for the mother than the father).

It is important to remember that Imperium workers are representative of neither extreme of the class structure outside the workplace. Their economic position is better than the average for blue-collar workers and well below that of the rich and the higher levels of the professional and managerial strata. Thus, poorer blue-collar workers are less likely to be able to live in occupationally mixed post–World War II suburbs, and their wives are less likely to have upper-white-collar jobs. On the other hand, the richer professionals and managers are more likely to live in architect-designed houses or houses on large expanses of land. And they are more likely to hire full-time help to handle the housework and childcare. Yet for blue- and white collar people between these extremes, overlaps outside work are numerous and important.

Finally, to mention such overlaps is not to imply that life outside work is integrated. For example, in their marriages both blue- and white-collar Americans face the task of reconciling the principle at the heart of the modern nuclear family—the idea of husband, wife, and children as each other's closest friends, a cohesive emotional unit based on relations of "love" rather than the often-exploitative relations seen as pervading the outside world—with other principles of interpersonal life. The principle of the modern nuclear family coexists uneasily with the principle of work and work relations (for those in careers, for example, leading to conflicts between absorbing work and home life; for those with jobs, perhaps leading to conflicts between friendships at work and home life; for anyone working shifts, leading to possible difficulties at home). It coexists uneasily with the principle of same-sex friendships, (leading to conflicts over how much leisure time spouses will spend together and how much separately with their own friends). And it coexists uneasily with the principle of friendships between men and women, including sexual relations.

If taken no further, the debate over the lives of blue-collar workers outside the workplace cannot be resolved. Some people will point to overlaps with the white-collar sectors and announce the disappearance of working-class culture. Others will stress differences and insist on its survival.

Yet the debate can be taken further. Most observers study the home, leisure, and marital relations of blue-collar workers less for their intrinsic interest than for their possible impact on working-class consciousness and political behavior. Now, Imperium workers seldom see their lives outside the workplace as distinctly "working-class." For example, those who live in post–World War II suburbs, and even those who inhabit pre–World War II areas, tend not to see themselves as living in "working-class areas." In reviewing the jobs of their own children or the children of their blue-collar friends, they notice the minority who have upper-white-collar jobs as much as the majority who do not. This point is generally true for other aspects of the lives of Imperium workers away from their jobs. They rarely see these as distinctly "working class." They are, of course, aware that above all their modest levels of education distinguish them from upper-white-collar people. But most are well aware of other features of their lives that overlap with those of many white-collar employees.

This should not be glossed over. There is a danger that snobbishness on the part of outside observers, many of whom come from the most privileged sections of American society, may lead them to overlook the way blue-collar workers view their achievements beyond the workplace. An outsider might examine the neighbors of workers in post–World War II suburbia and notice that none of them are lawyers or doctors. Most Imperium workers are aware of this, but they also notice that their neighbors include teachers or social workers or small business men. Outsiders may stress the fact that many Imperium workers spend time in occupational taverns with other blue-collar workers. Imperium workers are aware of this, but they also notice that when they go out to eat in certain restaurants, or visit New York City, or play golf, the context is occupationally mixed. Outsiders may classify their marriages as "blue-collar," but to most workers it is obvious that some of the successes and failures of their marital lives resemble those of white-collar people they know or hear about in the media.

Above all, most workers contrast what they see as a certain fluidity in their lives outside the workplace with their considerably more restricted lives at work. Nor is this necessarily the result of "false consciousness" or the "hegemony of ruling-class ideas," for it has some real basis. Most Imperium workers do not see the class structure outside the workplace as a graduated and benevolent hierarchy, but they do see it as having some fluidity in its middle range, as in fact it has.

Notes

1. Morton Hunt, *Her Infinite Variety: The American Woman as Lover, Mate and Rival* (New York: Harper & Row, 1962). For discussion of the modern marital ideal and the American family's loss of many of its material functions, see some of the other essays and references in this volume.

2. For a discussion of the emotional overload that the modern "companionate family" places on spouses and children by separating members from the community, see Philippe Ariès, "Family and the City," in Alice S. Rossi (ed.), *The Family* (New York: Norton, 1978); Lawrence Stone, *The Family, Sex and Marriage in England, 1500–1800* (New York: Harper & Row, 1977).

3. Mirra Komarovsky, *Blue-Collar Marriage* (New York: Random House, 1962), esp. pp. 22, 355; Theodore Caplow; H. M. Bahr; B. A. Chadwick; R. Hill; M. H. Williamson, *Middletown Families* (Minneapolis: University of Minnesota Press).

4. See Lee Rainwater, Richard Coleman, and Gerald Handel, *Workingman's Wife* (New York: Oceana Publications, 1959), p. 25, and Lillian Rubin, *Worlds of Pain: Life in the Working-Class Family* (New York: Basic Books, 1976), pp. 215 and passim. In later writings on the same topic, Rainwater and Handel present a picture more like Komarovsky's. See, for instance, Gerald Handel and Lee Rainwater, "Persistence and Change in Working-Class Life Style" and "Changing Family Roles in the Working Class," in Arthur B. Shostak and William Gomberg (eds.), *Blue-Collar World: Studies of the American Worker* (Englewood Cliffs, N.J.: Prentice-Hall, 1964).

5. For the entire study see David Halle, *America's Working Man* (Chicago: University of Chicago Press, 1984).

6. Men are concentrated in blue-collar craft and laboring jobs, whereas both sexes are about equally represented in blue-collar operative work. See Donald Treiman and Kermit Terrell, "Women, Work and Wages: Trends in the Female Occupational Structure Since 1940," in Kenneth Land and Seymour Spilerman (eds.), *Social Indicator Models* (New York: Russell Sage Foundation, 1974); Patricia Roos, *Gender and Work* (New York: State University of New York Press, 1985).

7. Thus, what most workers are reporting here is not quite the same as whether they have a psychological sense of well-being ("happiness") with their wives and children. Still, when workers ask themselves if they are glad or sorry to be married, the question whether the time they spend with wife and children brings about such a psychological state is important, for increasingly in America "happiness" in this sense is seen as the goal of marriage. Measuring "happiness" as a psychological state of well-being, akin to pleasure, is fraught with difficulties, as has often been pointed out. See, for instance, Edwin Lively, "Toward Concept Clarification," *Journal of Marriage and the Family* 31 (1969):108–14.

8. A number of works have discussed the struggle between the blue-collar husband and his wife, most intense at the start of the marriage, over whether the husband will continue to spend most of his leisure time with his friends or will now spend it with his wife. See Herbert Gans, *The Urban Villagers: Group and Class in the Life of Italian-Americans* (New York: Free Press, 1962), pp. 70–71, and Komarovsky, *Blue-Collar Marriage*, pp. 28–32.

9. For this point see also Komarovsky, *Blue-Collar Marriage,* p. 332.

10. The classic statement of the view that if the prestige of a wife's occupation approaches (or worse, equals or exceeds) her husband's, a destructively competitive element is likely to be injected into the marriage is Talcott Parsons, "The Kinship System of the United States," *American Anthropologist* 45 (1943): 22–38. A more recent theory also predicts marital trouble if the status of the wife's occupation, especially as measured in income, considerably exceeds that of the husband's. However, this theory suggests that a wife's occupation may approach, equal, or even moderately exceed that of her husband without causing marital problems so long as her occupation enhances rather than detracts from the status of the family as a whole. See Valerie Oppenheimer, "Sociology of Women's Economic Role in the Family," *American Sociological Review* 42 (1977): 387–406.

11. See Don Cahalan, Ira Cisin, and Helen Crossley, *American Drinking Practices: A National Study of Drinking Behavior and Attitudes* (New Brunswick, N.J.: Rutgers Center of Alcohol Studies, 1969); Don Cahalan, *Problem Drinkers* (San Francisco: Jossey-Bass, 1970); Don Cahalan and Robin Room, *Problem Drinking Among American Men* (New Brunswick, N.J.: Rutgers Center of Alcohol Studies, 1974).

12. The data are reported in Oppenheimer, "Sociology of Women's Economic Role in the Family." They are based on a sample of white couples drawn from the 1970 census.

13. Drawing on national survey data, Glenn and his co-workers stress this point. See Norval Glenn, Adreain Ross, and Judy Corder Tully, "Patterns of Intergenerational Mobility Through Marriage," *American Sociological Review* 39 (1974): 683–700.

14. On the tendency for people to marry persons of similar social and educational background, see Peter Blau and Otis Dudley Duncan, *The American Occupational Structure* (New York: John Wiley, 1967). For the strain toward status consistency within marriage, see Oppenheimer, "Sociology of Women's Economic Role in the Family."

15. For the observation that if wives work this is important to them, see Komarovsky, *Blue-Collar Marriage,* chap. 3, and Rubin, *Worlds of Pain,* chap. 9. For a general protest against the tendency for studies of stratification to ignore women, see Joan Acker, "Women and Social Stratification: A Case of Intellectual Sexism," *American Journal of Sociology* 78 (1973): 936–45.

A number of studies have challenged the idea that a wife's conception of her social status is derived exclusively from her husband's occupation and not at all from her own. See, for example, Dana Hiller and William Philliber, "The Derivation of Status Benefits from Occupational Attainments of Working Wives," *Journal of Marriage and the Family* 40 (1978): 63–69, and Kathleen Ritter and Lowell Hargens, "Occupational Positions and Class Identifications of Married Working Women: A Test of the Asymmetry Hypothesis," *American Journal of Sociology* 80 (1975):934–48.

The view that wives of blue-collar workers are a type distinct from wives of upper-white-collar workers rests only in part on the notion that they have a distinct position in the labor market. In part it also depends on the idea that they have a characteristic personality or psychology. For a critical discussion of this view, see Halle, *America's Working Man,* p. 318, n. 22.

16. See Halle, *America's Working Man,* chap. 7, for discussion of how workers have the same belief about their own occupational attainments, and chap. 7, n. 13, for studies that point out how widespread this belief is in America.

17. See Clifford Sager, *Marriage Contracts and Couple Therapy: Hidden Forces in Intimate Relationships* (New York: Brunner-Mazel, 1976), chap 6.

18. Komarovsky also concentrated on couples with these characteristics, which would explain most of the differences, not striking in any case, between her findings and mine. For the concentration on one stage in the marital cycle, couples with young children, see Rubin, *Worlds of Pain,* p. 9, Komarovsky, *Blue-Collar Marriage,* p. 9, and Rainwater et al., *Workingman's Wife,* p. 19. For the definition of a blue-collar or working-class marriage as one where the husband is a blue-collar worker regardless of the wife's occupation, see Rubin, p. 9, Komarovsky, p. 9 and 65, and Rainwater et al., p. 16.

16

Work and Family in the New Middle Class

ROBERT ZUSSMAN

Few developments have been so momentous for the ways in which we think about the relationship between work and family as the great transformation from an economy of farms and shops to one dominated by bureaucratic employment. For the old middle class of independent farmers, small shopkeepers, and fee-for-service professionals, a way of work was also a way of life. For the salaried employees of the new middle class—engineers, accountants, technicians, officials, administrators, and middle managers of all sorts—work may do little more than provide the wherewithal for a style of life. Only when work and family are distinct, as they are among salaried employees, does the relationship between them become problematic.

In the old middle class, the relationship between work and family was often intimate. Blending together in the form of unpaid family labor, the exercise of authority at work on the basis of parenthood or husbandhood, and the use of a single location as both residence and business, work and family formed a well-integrated whole. All this is captured neatly in terms like the "family farm" or "mom and pop grocery store." In such situations, there undoubtedly were—and, where such situations persist, undoubtedly still are—pervasive conflicts: between sons anxious to take over the family business and fathers holding on to parental authority; between husbands and wives; between brothers and brothers-in-law and cousins. Yet such conflicts were not between work and family: they were, put simply, all in the family.

For the new middle class the situation is different. Home and office are separated by time and space. If the salaried employee exercises authority over a subordinate, it is as a manager, not as a parent: and if he or she exercises authority over a child, it is as a parent, not as an employer. Where, for the old middle class, the relationship between work and family was diffuse and pervasive, for the new middle class it is specific and limited. [1]

It is precisely the separation between work and family in the salaried middle class that has led many sociologists to see a potential tension between them. Do one's obligations as a husband or wife or parent conflict with one's

338

obligations as an employee? Is work a "central life interest"? Or is the family? How is this tension experienced?

Certainly, for many members of the salaried middle class, the tension between work and family is both real and difficult, particularly for those women who have entered the labor force while maintaining the full burden of motherhood and domestic duties. Yet it is the contention of this paper that the men of the new middle class experience few tensions between work and family. Although work and family do not blend together as they did in the old middle class, these men see them as fitting together neatly, like the pieces of a carefully constructed jigsaw puzzle, as the obligations of fatherhood and husbandhood are met in the very course of meeting one's obligations as an employee.

Over a period of eight months in 1977, I studied engineers at two New England corporations, observing them at work, interviewing them, and, when invited, joining them for dinner or other casual social occasions. One of the companies ("Precision Metals") is in the metal-working industry. Founded just after the Civil War, it is still located in the small industrial town that was its original site. The other ("Contronics") is in consumer electronics. Founded after World War II, it is located in the suburb of a middle-sized city, roughly a twenty-minute drive from Precision Metals.[2]

Engineering is the prototypical occupation of the new middle class: in contrast to the old middle-class professions, engineering has from its very origins been characterized by salaried employment. It is also one of the most male-dominated occupations: according to the 1970 census, only 2 percent of American engineers were women, and even by 1980 that figure had risen only to 4 percent.[3] Engineers are well-paid: salaries for new college graduates started at an average of $26,000 in 1984 and, if the past is any guide, will continue to rise steadily (though in some cases slowly) over the remainder of a working life.[4] Engineering is also a secure occupation: although layoffs have been common in the more volatile advanced industries like aeronautics and electronics (and have affected a number of the engineers who worked at Contronics), extended unemployment is rare. Even during the much publicized aerospace cutbacks of the early 1970s, rates of unemployment in engineering have never reached even half that of the labor force as a whole.[5]

Families

Engineers' families are notable only for their conventionality. Sixty-five of the 80 engineers I interviewed were married; only 4 were divorced, and 1 widowed. Of the 70 engineers who had ever been married, 86 percent had at least one child. Only 2 of the married engineers lived in an extended house-hold, one sharing his home with his mother, the other with his mother-in-law. When the younger engineers, representing an earlier stage in the life cycle, are excluded, there is even less variation. Of the 61 engineers over thirty, only 2 had never been married, and only 3 were childless.

Roughly half of the engineers' wives work outside the home, and many more either have worked or probably will work over the course of their mar-riages. Most of the engineers support, and some actively encourage, their wives' employment, though typically only after their children are in school:

I love it for the extra income. She's not bored, and it gets her out. I didn't want her to work when the kids were younger. She agreed.

Terrific, as soon as the youngest is in school. I wouldn't want to deprive her. The em-phasis has changed in the last twenty years.

Thus, although most of the engineers' wives have had some experience in the labor force, only a few have had careers in the sense of continuous, full-time employment with orderly movement through a sequence of related positions. This, to the engineers, seemed as it should be.

The engineers themselves were their families' main providers. Although there are occasional hints of change, especially among the younger engineers, this, too, seemed to most as it should be. On the duties of husbands and wives, the engineers are still traditionalists. Virtually all mentioned love and companionship as essential to marriage. Many spoke of the relationship between husband and wife as a partnership. However, less than a third made no distinction between the ''partners' '' obligations. For the rest, love is ex-pressed and partnership realized through a division of labor. If some might see a tension in these ideas, the engineers themselves do not:

I believe in a marriage of equal partners with the man ruling the roost. Although I may be the primary breadwinner, I can use help and I can help around the house. My major responsibility is going to work every day and being a father to my children. I should be a companion to my wife, but we should be allowed to grow as individuals. She's responsible for the upbringing of the children, for the mundane chores of the house. She should be a companion to the children. She should have time to grow as an indi-vidual.

Most of the engineers expect their wives to care for their homes: ''she should cook and clean,'' do ''the mundane chores.'' But they also expect their wives to provide a home life: ''see the family runs smoothly''; ''provide an atmo-sphere I can come home to''; and ''create harmony.'' In return, almost all the engineers believe that it is their obligation to ''earn money to support a fam-ily,'' ''feed and clothe and take care of the family,'' ''provide a decent home and a decent income,'' and make sure that their children have ''bikes and food and education.'' In order to be reliable husbands and fathers, they must be reliable workers. But the emotional life of their families remains the primary responsibility of their wives. As one engineer put it, ''My job is to provide a home. Her job is to keep it happy.''

Work and Family

Beyond the income that it provides, however, the engineers' work has little to do with their family lives. ''It's a separate thing,'' said one engineer, ''There are no integral activities.'' Indeed, a formal separation between work life and family life is a striking, and distinguishing, characteristic of the salaried middle class: families play no official part either in finding work or in its practice.[6]

There is, of course, a considerable difference between the formal separation of work from family and the realities of corporate life. In fact, in the higher reaches of salaried employment, demands on families may be quite frequent: according to many reports, both scholarly and journalistic, a wife's willingness to share in her husband's career (for example, by entertaining business guests) is often an unspoken requirement of executive positions. So, too, many executive and professional positions require long hours of ''overtime'' and in some cases (particularly for employees in concerns dependent on public favor) participation in community service.[7]

But the engineers at Contronics and Precision Metals are largely free even of these demands. Work typically begins within a few minutes of the official opening time and ends within a few minutes of the official closing time. Only a few of the engineers take work home more than occasionally. Only in the manufacturing departments of the two companies, where production schedules are often tight, do any of the engineers come in on weekends. The entertainment of clients, rare in any event, is typically limited to lunch at restaurants close to the plant. Moreover, managers at both companies carefully avoid even the suggestion of imposing on private lives. This, like many policies, becomes clearest through its near violation. A personnel officer at Precision Metals found out, apparently quite by accident, that a newly hired, unmarried, young engineer was living with a woman friend. An older man, the personnel officer was taken aback by this arrangement. But he was also insistent on explaining that, whatever his personal feeling, he understood that the company had no legitimate concern in this area. In another case, two German engineers planning to visit Contronics asked to stay in private homes rather than in a hotel, in order to get a better feel for life in America. The appropriate manager called all his engineers into his office, explained the request, and asked for volunteers to put up the German guests—but only after apologizing and explaining, with great elaboration, that compliance was entirely voluntary and that neither he nor the company believed that any engineer should feel obligated to respond.

The separation of work and family is further reinforced by a pattern of residential dispersion that is particularly strong at Contronics. Of the 40 engineers I interviewed at Precision Metals, 16 lived in the town in which the company is located. The remaining 24 lived in a total of 13 towns within in a radius of roughly twenty miles from the worksite. At Contronics, located in a suburb and in this respect altogether typical of postwar industrial development, the pattern is more pronounced. Only 2 of the 40 engineers I interviewed lived in the suburb in which their company is headquartered, and only 4 more in the neighboring middle-sized city. The remaining 34 were scattered among no less than 24 towns and villages. This pattern has far-reaching consequences.

Most important, the engineers' work contributes little to a public identity. For the old middle class of shopkeepers, farmers, and fee-for-service professionals, this was not the case. Living and working in the same community, with diverse clients or customers, and often active in community affairs, they were known by what they did: their work became a way of life. But the engineers' work is hidden, invisible not only to neighbors, who may have only the vaguest conception of what an engineer is, but even to their own families. The engineers are known not by their work but as husbands and fathers, as homeowners, and as participants in a residential community.[8]

A few of the younger engineers at Contronics and Precision Metals do argue that who they are and what they do at work inevitably affected who they are and what they do at home. One told me, "It's made me think better and straighter—to slow down and take my time." Another said:

My job requires a certain amount of ability just like a lot of life situations. The practice I get here helps me out at home. Like, contrast it to the shop. I don't run around goosing everyone like they do down there. Everything here is on a more elite level, a more adult level. I try to treat everyone with respect and consideration.

This describes work's effect on personality, on an inner life, and on behavior. But such effects are largely a private matter, carrying none of the institutionalized obligations associated with the family life of the old middle class: they do not amount to a public identity.

To be sure, most of the engineers acknowledged that their work might have some effect on their family life—for example, the amount of time they have for their families: "It gets me home after eight hours." And: "The biggest thing is I don't have to spend a lot of time traveling.'' And work might affect their moods:

Compared to some other jobs I've had, this is a good one. At my other job I was ready to go home and punch the wall after work. This job doesn't detract as much. I've separated my career from my personal life.

The atmosphere here isn't depressing. I go home in a fair frame of mind. It's not bad financially, either, but the atmosphere's the most important thing. I don't have all that much to talk about when I go home. I'm not mad at my boss or anything like that, so I try to leave my work here.

Knowing that a man has some peace of mind, that he's accomplishing what he wants, I can talk about other things at home. I leave my problems at work so we can enjoy each other.

But these effects are transitory: they may last for a day or a week or even a month, but no longer than the duration of a particular situation. They may affect the family, but they are not fundamental to it. And they will not be integrated, in any permanent way, into a personality.

We should not, of course, read the engineers' claims as statements of fact. Undoubtedly, as Melvin Kohn and others have argued for many years, the kind of work that people do does affect their personalities, even if these effects are not recognized.[9] Yet even if the engineers' statements cannot be read as literal descriptions, they can be read profitably for the values implicit in them. In this sense, they are an ideology of family life.

Above all, the engineers see the relationship between work and family as an exchange in which they give time in return for income to support their families. This exchange is seen as altogether fair and appropriate so long as the demands of work are limited to a "normal" working day of eight hours, five days a week. This image of an exchange excludes the idea that work may influence the quality of family life in any but a material sense: work and family are linked by what a husband takes from and brings to the family, not by what he does within the family itself.

Insofar as the engineers do see any effects of work on the internal life of their families, they see it negatively. When work is going well, the employee does not bring it home with him ("I can talk about other things than work at home"); when work is not going well, and only then, bad moods may spill over into family time ("If I was unhappy, it would come home with me"). Whereas the bad job generates tensions that cannot be contained within the workplace, the good job is marked merely by the absence of any effect. Thus, the separation of work from family becomes a virtue, and the statement that "I've never brought my problems home" becomes a mark of pride. In short, the best situation, as the engineers see it, is one in which the relationship between work and family is limited to an exchange of resources; in all other respects, particularly in regard to emotional life, they should be kept separate.

The engineers see themselves as having successfully contained work within its proper boundaries. They are satisfied with the terms of exchange they have established: very few say that their income is insufficient to meet their families' needs; more are pleased that work does not make excessive demands on family time than complain that it does; considerably more are satisfied that work creates no problems at home than are concerned about the tensions it might generate. [10]

Conclusion

The rebirth of feminism over the last two decades and the concomitant entrance of large numbers of married women into the labor force have been widely announced as sources of new tensions between work life and family life. Perhaps, for women, this has been the case. Yet among the men of the American middle class, these tensions are not apparent. Shaped by the structure of salaried employment, the values of the engineers at Contronics and Precision Metals have proven surprisingly resistant to change: possible tensions between work and family continue to be resolved by a conception of the "good provider" that has been a familiar presence in American life at least since the rise of a corporate economy. [11]

For the engineers at Contronics and Precision Metals—and perhaps for middle-level male employees more generally—there is a rather easy harmony between the demands of work and the demands of family. Salaried employees do not face the strains on family lives created by either an insufficiency of income or difficult working conditions, both frequently reported as endemic to contemporary working-class life. [12] Nor do they, as a rule, face the strains associated with excessive demands on their time, strains quite common in the lives of many professionals and upper-level managers. This harmony, though, is based on a strict compartmentalization of work and family: each is a distinct sphere of experience, with its own satisfactions and its own logic.

At the same time, however, work and family are part of a single whole. Work and family are not competing "central life interests." [13] Rather, the engineers meet what they see as the obligations of husbandhood and fatherhood precisely by meeting their obligations as employees.

But harmony is rarely achieved without cost or compromise. The engineers keep a distance from their work. They do not see it as a source of identity, and certainly not as a source of public identity. They work so that they can support their families. But what are the consequences for their lives in those families in whose name they work? The engineers' work is hidden from their families. And whether by choice or necessity elevated to principle, they prefer to keep it hidden. They are good providers but abdicate full participation in the emotional life of their families to their wives. The engineers themselves express contentment with this arrangement, and we have no reason to doubt them. Yet we may well wonder if they have not become strangers in their own homes.

Notes

1. For discussions of the relationship between work and family in a number of settings, see Rosabeth Moss Kanter, *Work and Family in the United States: A Critical Review and Agenda for Research and Policy* (New York: Russell Sage Foundation, 1977), and Stanley R. Parker, *The Future of Work and Leisure* (New York: Praeger, 1971).

2. For a full discussion of this research, see my *Mechanics of the Middle Class: Work and Politics Among American Engineers* (Berkeley: University of California Press, 1985).

3. U.S. Bureau of the Census, *1980 Census of Population, Supplementary Reports* (PC80-S1-15) (Washington, D.C.: Government Printing Office).

4. Engineers Joint Council, Engineering Manpower Commission, *Professional Income of Engineers* (New York: Engineers Joint Council, 1984).

5. U.S. National Science Foundation, *Unemployment Rates and Employment Characteristics for Scientists and Engineers, 1971* (Washington, D.C.: Government Printing Office, 1971).

6. Although a father and a son both work as engineers at Precision Metals, engineering is among the occupations in which formal qualifications are likeliest to count more than family connections in finding employment. See Mark Granovetter, *Getting a Job* (Cambridge: Harvard University Press, 1974)

7. On executives, see, for example, Rosabeth Moss Kanter, *Men and Women of the Corporation* (New York: Basic Books, 1977), and Diane Margolis, *The Managers: Corporate Life in America* (New York: Morrow, 1977). On professionals, see, for example, Martha R. Fowlkes, *Behind Every Successful Man: Wives of Medicine and Academe* (New York: Columbia University Press, 1980), as well as her essay in this volume (Chapter 17), and Jerome Carlin, *Lawyers on Their Own* (New Brunswick, N.J.: Rutgers University Press, 1962).

8. For a more general discussion of this issue, see John Alt, "Beyond Class: The Decline of Industrial Labor and Leisure," *Telos*, no. 28 (1976): 55–82, and Christopher Lasch, *Haven in a Heartless World: The Family Besieged* (New York: Basic Books, 1977).

9. Melvin Kohn, *Class and Conformity*, 2d ed. (Chicago: University of Chicago Press, 1977). See the review of related research in Lois Hoffman's essay in this volume (Chapter 18).

10. For discussion of what happens to engineers and their families when the accustomed income and security are disrupted, see Paula Goldman Leventman, *Professionals Out of Work* (Glencoe, Ill.: Free Press, 1981).

11. On the history of the conception of the good provider, see Jessie Bernard, "The Good-Provider Role: Its Rise and Fall," *American Psychologist* 36 (1981):1–12.

12. See, for example, Lillian Breslow Rubin, *Worlds of Pain: Life in the Working-Class Family* (New York: Basic Books, 1976).

13. For discussions of "central life interests," see Robert Dubin, "Industrial Workers' Worlds: A Study of the Central Life Interests of Industrial Workers," *Social Problems* 3 (1956):3–42, and Robert Dubin, R. Alan Hedley, and Thomas C. Taveggia, "Attachment to Work," in Robert Dubin (ed.), *Handbook of Work, Organization, and Society* (Chicago: Rand McNally, 1976).

17

The Myth of Merit and Male Professional Careers: The Roles of Wives

MARTHA R. FOWLKES

Family and work, particularly professional work, are the "greedy institutions" (L. Coser 1974) of modern society. Although women frequently forgo or foreshorten work commitments in order to sustain allegiance to family life and responsibilities, male professionals do not do without families in order to sustain the expectations and requirements of work. Indeed, the overwhelming majority of male professionals are married, and for them family life itself functions both to serve and preserve their career commitments. An examination of the work-family system as it pertains to male professional careers reveals a pattern of subordination of family life to professional life that works to the advantage of the male professional. In particular, the wives of professional men make invaluable contributions to their husbands' careers through the integration of their roles with the requirements of male professional life. The extent to which the wife role functions as a resource in a husband's quest for career success poses a fundamental challenge to the view that male professional achievement is solely the product of individual merit.

The idea that women's roles in the family make possible male's careers is not a new one. Bernard (1971) and Slater (1970) have each called attention to the ways in which wives provide the emotional support necessary to enable men to meet their own set standards of professional work. Papanek (1973:93) identified the "two-person" career as a distinctively middle-class career pattern involving "the induction of the wife into the husband's work orbit." By now quite a sizable literature has accumulated that deals with the ways in which specific features of the wife role are linked to the enhancement of male careers in particular occupational settings. Douglas (1965) describes the high demands placed on wives of clergymen. More than any other profession, the ministry embodies the notion of a "calling," and parishioners look for this to be demonstrated and reflected in the behavior and activities of the minister's family as well as the minister himself. Politicians' wives, of course, are subject to the scrutiny and approval of a much wider public and are expected to

347

display active support for their husbands' views and to contribute positively to their husbands' images (MacPherson 1975). In another kind of political career, the ambassador's wife plays a unique role in her political decoding of seemingly superficial social small talk as she participates in the highly ritualized and obligatory events of the diplomatic social world (Gotlieb 1985; Hochschild 1969). In each of these occupations—politics, diplomacy, and the ministry—the values and beliefs that are central to a husband's career set clear limits on the wife as a person in her own right. Thus, we cannot conceive of a minister whose wife is an atheist or of a Republican politician married to a Democrat.

The relationship of wives to male careers is especially well documented for the corporate managerial and executive ranks (Grieff and Munter 1980; Helfrich 1965; Kanter 1977; Pahl and Pahl 1971; Seidenberg 1975; Whyte 1971). Taken together, these studies show what is required by a man in his climb up the corporate ladder, and how these requirements in turn affect and/or incorporate his wife along the way. Above all, a corporate wife accommodates to the high geographic mobility that is associated with organizational mobility. Sometimes this geographic mobility takes the form of a husband's frequent and extended work-related travel, in which case the family is left behind with the wife as sole caretaker. In other instances frequent relocation is required, in which case the whole family goes along and it falls to the wife to reestablish family life in all of its myriad detail and to forge the new social connections relevant to her husband's career as well.

Finch (1983) has usefully extended the discussion of the interdependence of men at work and women at home to encompass work across the occupational and class structure. She describes the twofold effect of men's work on their wives: how women are constrained temporally and spatially in the home as well as geographically by the work their husbands do; how wives contribute directly and indirectly to their husbands' productivity. Although she demonstrates that these patterns of wives' engagement in their husbands' work are not solely the province of high-status occupations, the features of work with which they are associated are nonetheless most commonly the features of high-status work.

Male Careers and the Roles of Wives

The study reported on here (cf. Fowlkes 1980) explores the many and varied ways in which a wife's contributions conform to and reinforce the structure and values of her husband's professional commitment. The resultant intricate tailoring of family life to professional life stands out most clearly when the wife role for one profession is compared with that for another. Here the comparison involves husband-wife relationships among couples where the husband is either a physician or an academic. Forty wives of successful professional men were selected to study the interdependence of male careers and women's roles and to put to empirical test the popular but light-hearted proposition that "behind every successful man is a woman." Twenty of these women are wives of board-certified practicing physicians, and the other twenty are wives of high-ranking university professors in the scientific and humanistic disciplines.

These two professions exhibit contrasting features of professional life. The practice of medicine can be characterized as a quintessentially male role—dominant, individualistic, entrepreneurial, and authoritative. Mastery and control and the application of knowledge are the prevailing values of medical work, and inequality is structured into almost all of the doctor's working relationships (cf. Freidson 1970). Academic life, on the other hand, occurs in an organizational setting that is less formally hierarchical in its division of labor and less concerned with differences in authority among its roles. Communication and cooperation are essential to collegial relationships among academics and students alike (cf. Lipset and Ladd 1975). The work of the academic is the production of knowledge, and the central values of academic life are intellectual, which supposedly discourages expressions of overt dominance. Thus, although males predominate numerically, the collegial, expressive, analytic orientation of academe represents a deviation from traditional male norms, especially those of the medical profession.

The husbands of the women studied represent typical academic and medical careers. That is, they are successful in ordinary (rather than extraordinary or elite) ways in the mainstream career tracks of their professions. Their careers are located in analogously middle-range settings, not at the most prestigious centers of university teaching and medical practice. Most of these men are in their early forties (their wives just a few years younger), their careers a proven success in terms of their accomplishments and reputations. The average marriage in each professional group is now sixteen years old and has run a parallel course to the husband's career, beginning with the period of career education and training.

Women were selected for study solely on the basis of their being wives, regardless of their own educational and work histories. This was done in order to maximize the variation in the wife role so as not to predetermine its character. Over three-quarters of the forty wives have bachelors' (or registered nursing) degrees or higher. One medical wife is herself a physician, and five academic wives hold doctorates. At the time they were interviewed, all of the academic wives were either employed to some extent or were studying for credit. Only one academic wife with her own doctorate holds a regular, tenure-track academic appointment, and she is as yet untenured in the department where her husband is a full professor. In contrast, three-quarters of the medical wives had no work or study commitments. However, no wife worked (either part time or full time) without interruption throughout her marriage. These patterns of wives' educational achievements in conjunction with their attenuated occupational achievements are preliminary clues to the patterns of their accommodation to their husbands' careers.

As he goes about the business of establishing and maintaining a successful professional career, a man has at least three distinctly different kinds of needs. For each of these there is a counterpart in the wife role. In the first place, there is the need to do the work of his profession in a way that will establish him in a favorable position vis-à-vis those who are positioned to influence the direction of his professional life. Second, there is the need for a sustained achievement drive, which implies the opportunity to put a premium on his career and the ability to cope with the particular stresses of his career commitment. Finally, there is the absolutely crucial need for time in which to accomplish the work at hand. The three counterparts to these needs are the (1) adjunct, (2) support, and (3) double-duty roles of wives, each of which will be discussed in turn.

In response to the first need—the establishment of a husband's career worthiness—a wife may play an adjunct role in which she makes an active contribution to the status or content of her husband's work. Both the medical and the academic wives studied encountered a wide range of obligations and expectations in this area. However, the adjunct role of the medical wife is noticeably more rigidly sex-typed and subordinate than that of the academic wife. Like the services performed in the highly stratified medical division of labor, the adjunct tasks of the medical wife flow upward toward the top to support and reflect the work and status of the physician. The medical wife contributes to the content of her husband's work primarily as a ''girl Friday,'' functioning variously as office decorator, office manager, or receptionist. She also serves as human relations consultant to her husband when problems arise in the working relationships among the ''girls'' in the office. In these capacities the medical wife lends the ''woman's touch'' or perspective to her husband's work.

Furthermore, the private practice of medicine is competitive and locally based. It is therefore very difficult for a doctor's wife to escape a substantial social and public claim on her time and energy as an aspect of the adjunct role. Almost every medical wife invests quite heavily in some combination of medical or hospital auxiliary work, community volunteer service, and social life, all of which serve to promote or maintain her husband's status (cf. Chapter 10 in this volume): —

I think I felt it would have looked bad if I had not been in the auxiliary.

To some extent I helped him get known. I joined things to help him get known. Otherwise you are a name in the phone book.

The adjunct role of the academic wife is more akin to that of a junior colleague. Her social role is tied to the more limited departmental base. It does not entail elaborate or frequent obligations unless her husband is serving as department chair, in which case she may have to assume more responsibility for welcoming new faculty members and for planning social life on behalf of the entire department. It is primarily as typist, research assistant, and, more substantively, as professional critic, editor, and collaborator, that the academic wife contributes directly to the content of her husband's work: "I typed his M.A. thesis and his Ph.D. and also did some research for him." Not infrequently, such contributions make use of the wife's own training or advanced degree in the same discipline as her husband's or a closely related one. Whereas the adjunct role of the doctor's wife is similar to a nurse's and is organized around traditionally feminine attributes, the adjunct role of the academic wife is shaped by her intellectual attributes, reflecting the differences between medical and academic values and the organization of work in the two professions. In both cases, though, the traditional concept of wife as helpmate underlies each one's particular expression of the adjunct role.

In response to the second need—the need for a sustained achievement drive—a wife offers her husband the kinds of support that not only nurture and revitalize his career ambitions, but also ensure that he is untroubled and unhampered in his quest for career success. Unlike the adjunct role, the supportive role is diffuse and pervasive. It inheres less in specific tasks than in a generalized stance with accompanying attitudes and responses. Moreover, a wife supports her husband both actively and passively; as she reaches out to sympathize and encourage, she must submerge her own emotions and needs in the service of his.

The medical wife's support for her husband's career consists, in essence, of her subordination to that career and to her husband's personal and professional dominance and authority. The doctor's wife accommodates to the high status of the physician by accepting a nonintrusive, even secondary, place for herself in marriage. This is conveyed by the frequently expressed vocabulary of sexual rivalry in which the physician's career is described as his "first love." In her support role, the doctor's wife relates to both the stress and the status dimensions of her husband's work as well. A practitioner's work is likely to leave him feeling pressured, preoccupied, and uncertain at the day's end, and he returns home needing recognition and appreciation. Whatever the appropriate mode of response on the wife's part, be it brow-soothing, bolstering, passively listening, or not intruding, it has the effect of relegating her own concerns and her day to second place, if it does not eclipse them altogether. It is quite common for a doctor's wife to describe the content of her own day (and her children's) as "trivial" in comparison with her husband's.

The academic work role (and the person in it) is less comprehensively authoritative than the physician role, and its time demands, though pervasive, are less consistently rigid. The theme of playing emotional "second fiddle" to her husband's career is largely absent from the academic wife's account of her relationship to her husband's work, although she is not unaffected by its pressures: "This year I haven't seen him since April. He's been writing and is very involved in this translation. We spent the summer together but I was really all by myself."

In her support role the academic wife responds more collegially than the doctor's wife and may often engage in actual debate with her husband around troublesome issues of academic or departmental politics. In any event, she feels less called upon to support her husband's career by explicit subordination to it. The faculty wife has more chance to express her own ideas and opinions as she reacts to the content of her husband's day; end-of-the-day information sharing is more likely to flow both ways among academic than among medical couples.

It is nevertheless true that the academic wives, as much as the doctors' wives, acquiesce to the time and mobility requirements of their husbands' careers by not pursuing their own work in any way that would interfere with those requirements. Although geographic mobility is rarely an issue once a doctor has established his practice, it is a likely feature of the quest for academic success and recognition. Most of the academic wives are prepared to relocate when and as necessary to attest to the primacy of their husbands' careers. Finally, wherever the academic family makes its home, the academic wife has a unique responsibility for providing her husband with a home base for his work that is undisturbed by domestic demands and routines: "I feel somewhat restricted as to what I can do in the house when he works here. . . . My husband's work needs define our routines here."

As a wife responds to her husband's need for time by doing double duty as parent, homemaker, and organizer of family life, she leaves her husband free from the interruptions and distractions of home-based responsibilities and routines. Among the wives studied, double duty is at the center of the wife role. In medical and academic families alike, the task of planning and organizing childrearing responsibilities each day belongs to wives, so that a wife's own day is neither distinct from nor independent of her children's day. Similarly, the division of labor in household management follows sex-typed lines, and both academic and medical wives accept primary responsibility for the daily, repetitive, and routine chores of housekeeping and homemaking.

The medical wife does her work as a parent in response to the way her husband does his work as a physician. Emotional distance and absence from home are bred into the doctor by a profession that officially leaves the business of nurturing to women (nurses at work and wives at home); that removes men almost entirely from family life and from opportunities for personal growth throughout a very long and demanding training period; that jealously safeguards its autonomy, with the result that the doctor hoards patients who then hoard his time. Consequently, the medical wife is not only the primary manager of childrearing, but the emotional mainstay in the lives of her children as well—so much so that she runs the risk of deserting her children emotionally if she chooses to have substantial commitments of her own outside the home (cf. Gerber 1983):

He's had very little of a father role. When they were small there would be days that he would go without seeing them. In those days he was on every other weekend. He would leave before they awoke and get home after they were asleep. . . . I feel I've carried a lot of bringing up the kids. He knows it and has been appreciative.

The effort to maintain an elaborate home at a standard that makes it a suitable domestic statement of the husband's professional life constrains the medical wife. More important, however, the dominance of the physician's role and personality is matched by a dominance in the home setting. The doctor's unfailing nonparticipation in housework, further attests to his control over the household: "He's demanding of me. He expects the house to be running smoothly and not to have any problems with the kids."

For the many medical wives who receive household allowances to run their homes, not even the illusion of independence or self-sufficiency in their domestic roles is possible. Furthermore, the doctor's social standing and his family's add civic responsibilities to the double duty role of the medical wife.

The double-duty role of the academic wife is typically less elaborate and less confining. The academic husband's professional commitment has been no more constrained than the doctor's by family and household responsibilities. Over time, though, he has made some contributions to childcare and household work insofar as those could be made to conform to his professional schedule. The academic husband is also more predisposed by his professional role at least to share occupancy in his home with his family than is the medical husband, who so often seems like a visiting dignitary there. The structure and values, and possibly even the content, of academic life encourage an emphasis on process, communication, collegiality, and cooperation that are similar to the way in which a teaching-committed academic husband lives with his family. Even though he may not participate much in the work and schedules of childrearing, he does build relationships with his children. Often this consists of acquainting them with the subject matter of his own discipline:

Our children are fully versed in the *Odyssey* and in tales of ancient Greece.

My husband has gone into the school and talked about genetics, and he does try to interest them in his field.

And he is far less inclined than the doctor to leave the stamp of male dominance on the household division of labor, in terms of his own expectations, his patterns of participation, or his willingness to tolerate some rearrangement in those patterns. In any case, housekeeping in the academic home is a less demanding undertaking than in the doctor's home, which is usually larger, more highly decorated, and meticulously maintained. In the academic household, maintenance is geared more toward amenities than status and is not, therefore, the major occupation or preoccupation for either spouse.

Consequently, more doors open outward for the academic wife than the medical wife in her double-duty role. No doubt this difference helps account for the higher proportion of academic wives who have done some paid work or gone to school during their marriages. Relative to the medical wives in the study, academic wives show a rather impressive record of accomplishments. Relative to the accomplishments of their high-ranking, well-published academic husbands, however, their achievements are slight. The double-duty role falls to academic and medical wives alike, and for both the freedom to achieve has to be found *within* that role, not outside it. Although the academic wife has indeed found greater freedom inside the double-duty role than the doctor's wife, her record of accomplishments is also a record of deferments, holding actions, interruptions, substitutions, dead-ends, and making do in the interests of being true to the domestic role as she finds it necessary and desirable.

The career ambitions and accomplishments of every wife in this study have been secondary to her husband's. No doubt the picture of the greater collegiality of the academic marriage and the relatively flexible and participatory academic husband and father is more reassuring to well-meaning humanistic liberals—including academics themselves—than the picture of the hierarchical medical marriage and the authoritarian and remote physician husband. However, the wives in both professional groups have integrated their roles with the requirements of their husbands' careers. The career success of the professors in the study reflects the accommodation, effort, and input of their wives no less than the career success of the physicians.

Patterns of variation in the shape and content of the wife roles are related to variations in the structure and roles of professional careers and most likely as well to variations in the personalities of the people who choose to have, or marry into, those careers. The roles of doctors' wives tend to be highly sex-typed and subordinate and are tailored to their husbands' dominant, conventionally male, personal and professional roles and the local setting of the medical practice. Academic wives develop their roles in more collegial ways and relate less to the status of their husbands' work than to its content. In keeping with the organization and values of academic work, the roles of professors' wives are more flexible and less traditionally female than the roles of doctors' wives. In short, the roles of wives are professionalized in ways that render them highly serviceable to the particular career commitments of their husbands.

Male Careers and the Ideology of Merit

Sociological "truths" about the nature of society and the arrangement of social institutions have not infrequently been the "truths" of male experience. This is well illustrated in the traditional separation of the study of work and the study of the family, which, as this volume attests, must be conjoined if sociology is to contend with the real world (cf. Mortimer and London 1984; Pleck 1977). In large part the immediate impetus for the new attention to work-family connections derives from the personal experiences of women (and men) with an investment in enhancing women's opportunities for successful careers in academic disciplines as well as in the professions generally. Ironically, the experiential underpinning of much feminist scholarship often serves to render it suspect in terms of orthodox judgments of what constitutes "real" scholarship, which is supposed to emanate from sources loftier than the "merely personal."

Yet it would appear that it is not so much the association of personal concerns per se with scholarship that demeans it as the association of personal concerns with female concerns and those, in turn, with scholarship. The designation of the worth, and therefore the prestige, of one or another area of scholarly inquiry has always been both arbitrary and highly personalized. As Rossi has noted, the current generation of senior male sociologists "built their careers on topics which had their deepest roots in these men's personal histories" (1973:127). Social value attaches to male experiences, and, by extension, academic value to studies based on those experiences—on social mobility, social stratification, anti Semitism, bureaucracy, and military service, to name a few. This is not to say that these topics are unworthy of investigation but, rather, to illustrate the ease with which subjective male concerns convert to objective professional accomplishments.

Nonetheless, the prevailing ideology of professionalism is an ideology of individual merit. Indeed, the cultural ideal of the male good-provider role is best expressed by the man who "makes it" into the high reaches of occupational life as, variously, a doctor, lawyer, university professor, scientist, engineer, or corporate executive (cf. Bernard 1981). This is the "heroic male professional'' (Laws 1976:36) whose achievements are viewed as representing a uniquely high level of competence and dedication to his work. The successful professional is the embodiment of the successful man. Similarly, the sociological analysis of professional career lines focuses on the processes by which professionals emerge successfully and on the strength of their own abilities (these more diffusely defined by Becker et al. 1961 and Hughes 1971 than by Merton et al. 1957 or Parsons 1951, 1954b) as products of career systems.

These perspectives beg the more important question: namely, to what extent are career systems themselves the products of their incumbents—that is to say, men? Men have created the conditions of professional participation and professional success, and it is not surprising that these are the conditions that work best for men. Insofar as high-ranking occupational careers—law, medicine, university teaching, science, engineering, corporate executive positions—are male-intensive and male-dominated, the standards for career training, mobility, and success contain a host of assumptions about what is primary and what is secondary in the pursuit of the professional career. As Hochschild (1974:22) has noted, professional structures have developed to ''suit half the population in the first place.''

The fundamental expectations of professional life are that a career is the major source of one's personal and social identity; that the career has priority over and, when necessary, subordinates all other life involvements; that the career is the major determinant of the chronology and geography of one's life and the central organizing feature of a given day; that, in short, commitment to a professional career is the central commitment in a person's life. When viewed in light of these expectations, it is obvious that professional life is neither incidentally nor coincidentally a male way of life. It is intrinsically and ideologically a male way of life, an occupational extension of the male role (Epstein 1971).

By the same token, the domestic roles of women as housewives and mothers are rarely analyzed from the sociological perspective of their functional contributions to male careers, though Parson's (1954a) suggestion that family solidarity maintained by women is a necessary complement to men's occupational achievement is, of course, well known. In the typically segregationist approach to the sociological study of work and family, the domestic roles of women just *are;* they exist as a given. The operative assumption is that because women bear children, they must naturally rear them; because women rear children, they are naturally in the home; because women are in the home, they must naturally manage the home. Another way of looking at this, however, is that the shape of women's domestic roles in the home is the historical by-product of the emergence of the specifically male ''breadwinner'' role and the need for men to have time and person free and flexible for the pursuit of a career (Epstein 1976; Harris 1978; Oakley 1974).

Prospects for the Two-Career Family

In light of the contributions made by the wives in this study to the careers of their academic and medical husbands, it is clear that the view of male professional achievements as meritocratic and independent is a half-truth. The organization of professional work and rewards is far from a rational development of efficiency and universalism; rather, it is a socially constructed phenomenon that reflects the predominantly male incumbency of professional life. And central to the traditional system of male careers is a traditional wife at home, whose support and services are major building blocks of modern professional structures. Yet those structures stand as the virtually unalterable givens of professional life and dictate the terms of professional participation for men and women alike. What, then, are the prospects for the success of the two-career family, by definition a form that does not function on behalf of its careerists? In the one-career family the work of the wife at home is a resource for her husband's work. The model of the two-career family assumes that each partner can and will add the work of home and family to the work of a professional career, while managing at the same time with little by way of the sustained encouragement and assistance that an available spouse could provide.

Although admirable as an egalitarian ideal, in its reality the two-career family most often results in a surfeit of work and a deficit of support and opportunities for revitalization for its members. As Hunt and Hunt (1977:409) observe, "The problem of how to survive without a wive . . . is not simply a logistical one of covering the workload, but also a social-psychological one of sustaining the careerist's personal and social identity." Studies of two-career families document the stresses that result from role overload, emotional and recreational deprivation, and social isolation (Holmstrom, 1973; Rapoport and Rapoport 1971). In an autobiographical piece, the sociologist S. M. Miller (1971) admits to his own resentment that his responsibilities as husband and father in a two-career family curtailed his professional productivity and placed him at a competitive disadvantage relative to other men whose work and family roles were divided along more traditional lines. Although it is difficult enough to accomplish the ordinary work of a professional career within the framework of a two-career family, the extraordinary demands and crises of professional life often prove nearly impossible for the two-career family to accommodate (Rice 1979). And just as careers do not thrive without wives attached to them, neither do nuclear families, which are organized to require the same kind of commitment and devotion on the part of a woman that a career requires of a man (R. Coser and Rokoff 1971).

The prospects for the actualization of the two-career family—one in which both partners achieve career success in the mainstream of professional life—are best understood, then, not in terms of wishes about what might be, but in terms of the fundamental incompatibility of professional and family life when both spouses attempt simultaneous and equal participation in both of these spheres. It is very difficult to imagine how, as a generalized social pattern, couples will be able to combine family and career, when the structures of career participation, which have been built by men on the basis of being family-free, are applied to people who are not family-free. Historically, such freedom for women has most often been achieved only by remaining outside marriage and family roles altogether. Even now it is not difficult to find aspiring professional women who regard the affective commitment and role demands of family life as major liabilities to career success. The result of any of these choices—to remain unmarried or childless or to give up one's professional aspirations—is, of course, not a two-career family at all.

For those who do choose the life of the two-career family, sooner or later either career or family is likely to be compromised, most commonly through an attenuation of the wife's career (Holmstrom 1973; Poloma and Garland 1971). For what this study of male careers and the roles of wives demonstrates empirically and unequivocally is that traditionally successful male professional careers are propped up at every turn by the roles of the wives of professional men. We may well ask who and what structures will function in a similar fashion to prop up the members of the two-career family. It is not with a light but with a heavy heart that women who are now trying to travel the road to professional success that men before them have laid down are so often heard to say that what they really need is a good wife. Under the circumstances, the prospects for the success of the two-career family and the eradication of the prevailing patterns of male dominance in the professions appear very dim indeed.

References

Acknowledgments: This chapter is dedicated to Alice S. Rossi. As mentor and friend, she has contributed much to my professional development generally and to my thinking concerning the integrated study of family and work specifically. I gratefully and proudly acknowledge these contributions.

Becker, Howard S.; Blanche Geer; Everett C. Hughes; and Anselm L. Shauss. 1961. *Boys in White*. Chicago: University of Chicago Press.

Bernard, Jessie. 1971. *Women and the Public Interest*. Chicago: Aldine-Atherton.

———. 1981. "The Good-Provider Role: Its Rise and Fall." *American Psychologist* 36:1–12.

Coser, Lewis A. 1974. *Greedy Institutions: Patterns of Undivided Commitment*. New York: Free Press.

Coser, Rose, and Gerald Rokoff. 1971. "Women in the Occupational World: Social Disruption and Conflict." *Social Problems* 18: 535–54.

Douglas, W. 1965. *Ministers' Wives*. New York: Harper & Row.

Epstein, Barbara. 1976. "Industrialization and Femininity: A Case Study of Nineteenth Century New England." *Social Problems* 23: 389–401.

Epstein, Cynthia Fuchs. 1971. *Women's Place: Options and Limits in Professional Careers*. Berkeley: University of California Press.

Finch, Janet. 1983. *Married to the Job: Wives' Incorporation in Men's Work*. London: Allen and Unwin.

Fowlkes, Martha. 1980. *Behind Every Successful Man: Wives of Medicine and Academe*. New York: Columbia University Press.

Freidson, Eliot. 1970. *Professional Dominance*. New York: Atherton Press.

Gerber, Lane. 1983. *Married to Their Careers: Career and Family Dilemmas in Doctors' Lives*. London: Tavistock.

Gotlieb, Sondra. 1985. *Wife of——*. Washington, D.C.: Acropolis Books.

Grieff, B. S., and P. K. Munter. 1980. *Tradeoffs: Executive, Family and Organizational Life*. New York: Mentor.

Harris, Barbara J. 1978. *Beyond Her Sphere: Women and the Professions in American History*. Westport, Conn.: Greenwood Press.

Helfrich, M. L. 1965. *The Social Role of the Executive's Wife*. Columbus: Ohio State University, Bureau of Business Research, 1965.

Hochschild, Arlie Russell. 1969. "The Role of the Ambassador's Wife." *Journal of Marriage and the Family* 31:73–87.

——. 1974. "Making It or Making It Better: Notes on Women in the Clockwork of Male Careers." Manuscript produced for the Carnegie Commission on Higher Education.

Holmstrom, Lynda Lytle. 1973. *The Two Career Family*. Cambridge, Mass.: Schenkman.

Hughes, Everett C. 1971. *The Sociological Eye: Selected Papers on Work, Self and the Study of Society*. Chicago: Aldine-Atherton.

Hunt, Janet G., and Larry L. Hunt. 1977. "Dilemmas and Contradictions of Status: The Case of the Dual-Career Family." *Social Problems* 24:407–16.

Kanter, Rosabeth Moss. 1977. *Men and Women of the Corporation*. New York: Basic Books.

Laws, Judith Long. 1976. "Work Aspirations of Women: False Leads and New Starts." In Martha Blaxall and Barbara Reagan (eds.), *Women and the Workplace*. Chicago: University of Chicago Press.

Lipset, Seymour Martin, and Everett Carll Ladd, Jr. 1975. *The Divided Academy: Professors and Politics*. New York: McGraw-Hill.

MacPherson, Myra. 1975. *The Power Lovers: An Intimate Look at Politicians and Their Marriages*. New York: G. P. Putnam's Sons.

Merton, Robert K; George Reader; Patricia L. Kendall (eds.). 1957. *The Student Physician: Introductory Studies in the Sociology of Medical Education*. Cambridge: Harvard University Press.

Miller, S. M. 1971. "The Making of a Confused Middle-Aged Husband." *Social Policy* 2, no. 2:33–39.

Mortimer, Jeylan T., and Jayne London. 1984. "The Varying Linkages of Work and Family." In Patricia Voydanoff (ed.) *Work and Family: Changing Roles of Men and Women*. Palo Alto: Mayfield.

Oakley, Ann. 1974. *Women's Work: The Housewife Past and Present*. New York: Random House.

Pahl, J. M., and R. E. Pahl. 1971. *Managers and Their Wives*. Baltimore: Penguin Books.

Papanek, Hanna. 1973. "Men, Women, and Work: Reflections on the Two-Person Career." In Joan Huber (ed.), *Changing Women in a Changing Society*. Chicago: University of Chicago Press.

Parsons, Talcott. 1951. *The Social System*. New York: Free Press.

———. 1954a. "Age and Sex in the Social Structure of the United States." In *Essays in Sociological Theory*. New York: Free Press.

———. 1954b. "The Professions and Social Structure." In *Essays in Sociological Theory*. New York: Free Press.

Pleck, Joseph H. 1977. "The Work-Family Role System." *Social Problems* 24:417–27.

Poloma, Margaret M. and T. Neal Garland. 1971. "The Married Professional Woman: A Study of the Tolerance of Domestication." *Journal of Marriage and the Family* 33:531–40.

Rapoport, Rhona, and Robert Rapoport. 1971. *Dual Career Families*. Baltimore: Penguin Books.

Rice, David G. 1979. *Dual Career Marriage: Conflict and Treatment*. New York: Free Press.

Rossi, Alice. 1973. Comments on "Minorities and Women in Sociology," *American Sociologist* 8:126–128.

Seidenberg, Robert. 1975. *Corporate Wives—Corporate Casualties?* Garden City, N.Y.: Doubleday.

Slater, Philip E. 1970. *The Pursuit of Loneliness*. Boston: Beacon Press.

Whyte, William H., Jr. 1971. "The Wife Problem." In Cynthia Fuchs Epstein and William J. Goode (eds.), *The Other Half*. Englewood Cliffs, N.J.: Prentice-Hall.

CHILDREN:
THE EFFECT OF THEIR
OWN AND THEIR
PARENTS'
EMPLOYMENT

18

The Effects on Children of Maternal and Paternal Employment

LOIS HOFFMAN

At least three research foci in the social science literature of work-family connections are relevant to children's socialization experiences. At the most
global level, there is research about how general economic conditions and the
organization of work affect the home environment in which children are
reared. At a somewhat less global level, there is research about how socialization experiences vary for children in different classes. A third, more focused
level, consists of research about how particular features of parental occupations might impinge upon children's experiences. The review that follows
concentrates on the third category.[1] How does the parent's particular job affect the family? This question is not concerned with the money the job brings,
or its impact on the family's position in the social status system, but rather on
the job as it is experienced by the worker and, in turn, his or her children.

A consideration of three dimensions of each parent's occupation organizes
our discussion. In terms of the father's and then the mother's occupation, we
consider how employment (1) shapes family values, (2) influences the
worker's psychological state, and (3) imposes time schedules and demands.

The Father's Job

Almost all of the research that has focused on the effects of parents' jobs on
the family has considered only the father's employment. The father's job has
been considered from a number of standpoints. One group of studies suggests
that the parent comes to value the traits that are required for success in his
work and to encourage these qualities in his children. A second group of stud-

Adapted from *Review of Child Development Research* 7, edited by Ross Parke, R. Emde,
H. McAdoo, and G. Sackett, by permission of The University of Chicago Press. © 1985 by The
Society for Research in Child Development, Inc.

ies views the link between occupation and family in terms of the father's psychological state. Certain needs, habits, or satisfactions are created on the job, and these affect the father's behavior in the family. A third group of studies to be considered here defines the work in terms of time demands and explores how the father's availability affects the family.

FATHER'S WORK AS A SHAPER OF VALUES

In a study of social class (rather than of specific job effects), Kohn (1963, 1980) hypothesizes that the structure and content of activities in the father's job affect his value orientations and childrearing practices. According to Kohn, middle-class, or white-collar, occupations involve manipulating ideas, symbols, and interpersonal relations and require flexibility, thought, and judgment. Lower-class, or blue-collar, occupations require the manipulation of physical objects and are more standardized, less complex, and more supervised. Because of these differences, middle-class fathers would be expected to value self-direction and independence in their children—qualities demanded by their own occupations—whereas lower-class fathers would value obedience and conformity. Kohn's data supported this prediction, and more or less corresponding differences in reported childrearing practices were also found: lower-class parents used more physical punishment and judged the child's misbehavior in terms of the consequences, whereas middle-class parents used more "psychological" discipline (such as "love-withdrawal") and judged misbehavior in terms of the child's intent. Further, when the father's job involved autonomy and working with people, the parents were more likely to stress achievement, independence, and self-reliance to their children (Pearlin and Kohn 1966). Many of the differences predicted by Kohn's theory have been found in other studies (Gecas and Nye 1974; Pearlin 1970), but whether these differences are a function of the father's job is not clear. Even in Kohn's work, education seemed to have an effect independent of the job per se, and the work of Lueptow et al. (1979) suggests that education is the more potent variable and, further, that the data supporting Kohn's hypothesis were not controlled adequately on the related extrinsic aspects of the father's occupation. The real test of this specific hypothesis requires an examination of differences among occupations within the same general socioeconomic class and education category, but it is very difficult to untangle the independent effects of these highly interrelated variables.

Little research of this sort has been carried out. The idea that specific occupations can become shapers of values that extend into the family was developed by the sociologist Everett Hughes (1958), but the accompanying research focused on the community of workers in specific occupations, not on family effects. A few small studies have tried to relate specific within-class occupations to parental discipline techniques (Steinmetz 1974) and at-home leisure patterns (Gerstl 1961). These show certain consistencies between job patterns and family behavior, but it is difficult to unravel the causal connections. If, for example, a college professor values education for his children more than a businessman does, is it because he is a professor, or is he a professor because he values education?

In a study of college students, Mortimer (1974, 1976) demonstrated that sons tended to choose their father's occupations or to pick jobs involving similar occupational experiences and rewards, a pattern that has been seen as reflecting the communication of values from father to son. The findings also indicated that the most effective transmission of vocational values from father to son occurred when there was a close father-son relationship with a prestigious father, the combination that in several previous studies has been associated with sons' identification with and modeling on the fathers' achievements (Hetherington 1979; Hoffman 1961).

It is important to note such conditioning factors—that is, other aspects of the situation that may influence whether or not parent-child similarity in occupational outlook is likely to develop. In fact, under some conditions effects can be reversed. The parent's work can be experienced negatively by the parent, or perceived negatively by the child, and thus affect the child's occupational choice in a different direction. Immigrant parents, for example, have been described as pushing their children toward education so that they can escape their parents' occupational roles (Howe 1976; Sarason 1973).

THE FATHER'S PSYCHOLOGICAL STATE

A psychological process commonly assumed to link the father's occupation with his family role is a frustration-aggression model: the job creates frustration, which the father takes out in the family. A man may be on the bottom of the power hierarchy at work, but he is on the top at home; aggression engendered on the job, which cannot be expressed there for fear of negative sanctions, is displaced to the safer target, the family. The idea of parental authority over children as a compensation for power frustration at work comes up in the work of Blau and Duncan (1967) and Hoffman and Manis (1979) and some empirical support comes from research by McKinley (1964). Particularly at the higher socioeconomic levels, McKinley found that fathers low in autonomy in their work were more likely to be hostile to and severe with their sons. Rainwater (1965), in a study of the lower-income family, presents data suggesting that the occupationally frustrated father may take out his frustrations on his wife, and Hoffman's data (M. Hoffman 1960) suggest that the assertion of power by the father over the wife leads to assertiveness by the mother over the child in what is interpreted as a pecking order.

The idea of the family as fulfilling complementary needs—needs that are unsatisfied or aroused at work— does not have to imply a negative effect, as in the frustration-aggression hypothesis. In my work on the value of children to parents (Hoffman and Hoffman 1973; Hoffman and Manis 1979; Hoffman et al. 1978), children are seen as satisfying those psychological needs that are not met by other aspects of life. Although these may be power needs, they may also be needs for morality or self-esteem, for a sense of accomplishment, for affiliative satisfaction, for fun and stimulation. An implication of this work is that to the extent that these needs are not satisfied on the job, the man may seek to satisfy them in the family. Energy, effort, warm interaction, high performance standards, enthusiasm, and joy may thus go into parenting because the job is not an alternative source of gratification.

To see the family as a place to express the frustrations of the job, or as a way of gratifying needs not satisfied on the job, or as a source of compensation of any sort, is to expect a difference in the man's behavior in these two worlds. An alternative hypothesis predicts a carry-over of style. Although there are data consistent with this view (Gerstl 1961; Steinmetz 1974), it is very difficult to know whether the similarity of behavior is a matter of habit, or a reflection of values formed on the job (as discussed above), or a correlation without causality, a function of self-selection. Several studies have tried to show that certain personalities are attracted to certain occupations (Roe 1956), and thus it is possible that some of the similarity in behavior in the two settings reflects the qualities of the person and not the effects of one setting on the other. The idea of the preacher who preaches to his family, the salesman who "sells" the behaviors he wants his children to follow, the professor who answers his children's questions with a lecture, is popularly accepted but rarely researched. The two hypotheses—compensation and carry-over—are not really incompatible. It is quite possible that gratifying behaviors are replicated in the family while needs generated or left unsatisfied on the job lead to compensatory gratification seeking there.

Another theory of carry-over—mood carry-over—has been seen as the link between occupation and family (Dyer 1964; Hammond 1954; Sennett and Cobb 1972). This theory is most recently represented by the work of Piotrkowski (1979). Piotrkowski has conducted a small-scale clinical-style investigation of the interface between occupations and family life among young blue-collar families. She sees the linkage more in terms of morale than in terms of specific mechanisms and identifies three interface patterns: positive carry-over, negative carry-over, and energy deficit. According to Piotrkowski, positive carry-over, in which a kind of good feeling from work carries over into the home, can come from the positive qualities of the job, or simply because a job is not stressful or totally absorbing. She finds little evidence that the family provides compensatory gratification for unsatisfying employment; instead, a job that leaves the man feeling assaulted and depleted leads to a kind of depression and low involvement in the family. A very satisfying and absorbing job can also lead to decreased involvement in the family, but, perhaps because of her lower-class sample, such cases are not prominent in her discussion. The implicit focus in this investigation is on the mood and energy level of the man as he comes into the house from his work.

Certain occupations have been singled out as particular sources of negative carry-over for family life. For example, a number of problems associated with family disorganization and personal stress—divorce, family violence, and alcoholism—are particularly common in the families of urban policemen. Although it is not impossible that selective factors are involved, the source of these problems seems to lie to a considerable extent in the tension-producing conditions of work. The exposure to the seamier side of life, intimacy with violence, the temptations of bribery, the presence of personal danger, and the hostility of the neighborhoods in which one works all combine to make urban police work particularly stressful. The high rate of personal and family difficulties among the police seems to reflect this situation (Kroes and Hurrell 1975; Lewis 1973; Nordlicht 1979; Symonds 1970). Military families have also been studied because of their high rates of wife and child abuse (Myers 1979).

On the other hand, some occupations have been singled out because they lure and involve the worker, pulling him away from his family. Although two national sample investigations have reported that most Americans see their family roles as more satisfying than their occupational roles (Hoffman and Manis 1978; Veroff et al. 1981), and Piotrkowski did not encounter the seductive-job pattern in her lower-class sample, investigations of executive and professional occupations have noted that the man may focus his involvements and satisfactions on his occupation to the detriment of his family roles. This pattern may develop because the work is more attractive and satisfying, because it is particularly relevant to the person's dominant needs, or because it compensates for family difficulties. It might also develop because adequate performance in a particular occupation is objectively very demanding. However, the theme of the father who invests so much of himself in his work that his family life is diminished is a common one in the mass media and in studies of men (and women) in the higher-status occupations (Elliot 1978; Heath 1977; Kanter 1977; Rapoport and Rapoport 1965; Whyte 1956). In a recent national sample study (Veroff et al. 1981), over half of the college-educated men reported that work interfered with their family life, whereas only 21 percent of the grade-school-educated men did.

Four different routes by which the father's job-engendered psychological state affects his family have been noted here. Two assume that his behavior is different at home and at work: the father expresses needs aroused at work that cannot be expressed there, or he seeks satisfactions from his family that his work does not provide. Two assume that his behavior is similar in both places: accustomed or satisfying behaviors on the job are replicated at home, or the mood and morale of the job carry over into the family situation. In most of the work in this area, the investigator has put all of his or her chips on one of these patterns, found an instance of it, and pulled out of the game. It seems reasonable to assume that all four patterns exist, and a more valuable approach to the father's state as a link between the job and the family would be to try to discover when each pattern operates. Furthermore, a fuller understanding of these processes might require considering not only the occupational situation, but also the family situation, because the effects on the family probably involve a more complex interaction than is implied by the unidimensional models discussed here.

WORK TIME

The man's availability to his family is affected by the hours he works—both the number of hours plus commuting time and his particular schedule. In general, men in higher occupational groups, especially executives and independent professionals, work longer hours on the job (Riesman 1958; Wilensky 1961), but blue-collar workers are more likely to hold down more than one job. It has been suggested, in fact, that the shorter work week in the United States may have diminished the working hours only for white-collar occupations such as clerical work and low-level administration (Kanter 1977; Willmott 1971). Most data indicate that a father is less likely to have two jobs when his wife is employed. However, Pleck and associates (1980) report an opposite trend for parents of preschool children: fathers of preschool children whose wives are employed spend about two and a half more hours per week in paid employment than comparable fathers whose wives are not employed.

Perhaps because the range of working hours for men is limited, there have been few studies of this variable. The fact that the father is out of the house at work while the mother is more likely to be at home is important in a number of child development theories (e.g., Lynn 1974), but the number of hours the father works has rarely been considered. When this variable has been studied, it has been more often in relation to the marital than the parental relationship. Clark and his associates (1978), for example, investigated but found no relationship between husband's job time and marital satisfaction. Clark and Gecas (1977) also report, however, no relationship between the number of hours the father works and his parental role as reported by his wife. There are studies that indicate that fathers who spend long hours at work report more work-family conflict, and, interestingly, their hours of work also predict their wives' work-family conflict. Wives' work hours, on the other hand, predict only their own role strain, not their husbands' (Greenhaus and Kopelman 1981; Keith and Schafer 1980).

Data are, however, available on men's seasonal work schedules — specifically the effects of the long absences from home of Norwegian fishermen—as well as shift work and flexible work schedules. Studies of families in Norwegian fishing villages revealed a pattern much like that found among fatherless families and the families of war-absent fathers. The most often-noted effect on children of the permanent, temporary, or repeated absence of the father is "dependency" in sons. Because of the absence of the male model, the absence of the father's influence, or the effects of the father's absence on the mother-son relationship, the sons have often been seen as dependent, or nonassertive, or less masculine in some way (Herzog and Sudia 1973; Lynn and Sawrey 1959; Tiller 1958). As Herzog and Sudia (1973) have noted, however, it is not at all clear that this effect is a negative one, for the indices of masculinity used are questionable.

Several exploratory studies have considered the effects of shift work on the family (Aldous 1969; Landy et al. 1969; Lein et al. 1974; Mott et al. 1965). Night-shift work tends to increase the amount of father-child contact if the children are preschoolers, but to diminish it if they are school-aged. In fact, one study found that daughters whose fathers worked night shifts when they were between five and nine years of age had lower quantitative scores on college-entrance tests than a group whose fathers had similar occupations but did not work night shifts (Landy et al. 1969). The researchers suggest that night-shift work be considered as a point on a father-absence continuum. There is evidence that afternoon shifts interfere even more with the parental role than night shifts do (Mott et al. 1965).

Effects of shift work have also been noted on the marital relationship, many of them attributable to the atypicality of the pattern. The couple's social life is diminished, and the wives sometimes resent the husbands' obtrusive presence during the day. In fact, although it has sometimes been suggested that the ideal way of working out childcare arrangements when the mother is employed is for the parents to work different shifts, Lein and her colleagues (1974) note that some of the wives in their research sought shifts at the same time as their husbands, even though it made childcare arrangements more difficult, because it was less of a strain on the marital relationship. A similar pattern has been observed in the flexitime studies: although the assumption is that dual-wage couples will use the opportunity to extend the hours of parental supervision, they often use it instead to extend their precious time alone.

The Mother's Job

As Bronfenbrenner and Crouter have pointed out (1982), the unemployment of the father and the employment of the mother have both been presumed to be disrupting of the family and damaging to the child. The former assumption is not totally accurate, as Elder's work suggests, and the latter is almost totally inaccurate, as fifty years of research attest (Hoffman 1963, 1974c; Maccoby 1958; Mathews 1934; Stolz 1960). The myth of the negative effects of maternal employment has persisted despite this research because it is based on the assumption that the employed-mother family is just like the "typical" traditional family of twenty or more years ago. The stereotype of the traditional family may have been apt for some families in past generations, but it did not fit the employed-mother family even then: the employed mother had fewer children, older children, outside relatives living in the household, more education, or greater economic need, and probably more energy and better health (Nye and Hoffman 1963). And the image of the traditional family of past generations does not fit the modern family at all: families are smaller, modern technology has enormously diminished the amount of housework and food preparation necessary, women are better educated, marriages are less stable, life expectancy is greater, youthfulness has been extended, expecta tions for personal fulfillment have expanded, and traditional sex roles are no longer fully accepted (Hoffman 1977). These two points—(1) that employed mothers are different from nonemployed mothers in many ways besides employment status, and (2) that new social conditions require a reconsideration of maternal employment effects—are basic to an understanding of the role of maternal employment in the socialization process.

GENERAL ISSUES IN MATERNAL EMPLOYMENT STUDIES

Selective Factors

The fact that employed mothers are different from nonemployed ones with respect to motivational factors and facilitating conditions, and that these differences need to be controlled in studying the effects of maternal employment, has been so often repeated and is so thoroughly documented that it seems trite to mention it again. Unfortunately, there is ample evidence that the point needs repeating. Most researchers have learned that employed mothers are more likely to be poor and husbandless, and so social class and family intactness are usually controlled. On the other hand, studies often fail to control for the number of children or their ages, even when such controls are obviously essential. Time-use studies, in which subjects are asked to keep daily records of how they spend their time, provide a good example. Since employed-mother families include fewer children in general, and fewer preschoolers and infants in particular, there are fewer childcare tasks to perform. Researchers using time-use data based on heterogeneous samples have often reported no differences between the husbands of employed and the husbands of nonemployed women in participation in household tasks. But studies that fail to control for family size and the ages of the children, obscure the higher participation of fathers in employed-mother families, which shows up in comparisons where the number and ages of the children are matched (Hoffman 1977, 1983; Pleck et al. 1980; Robinson 1978; Walker and Woods 1976).

Other, comparable problems are more subtle. For example, researchers often study the effects of maternal employment on preschoolers by obtaining a sample of children in full-time day care and exploring the differences between the children of the employed and the nonemployed mothers. Typically, these studies find that if there are differences, they favor the employed mothers' children, who show higher scores on various measures of adjustment or cognitive development. However, even when the two groups are matched on variables such as family size and ordinal position, the design cannot escape the fact that there are different reasons for sending each group to a day-care center. The children of employed mothers are typically there because of a need for childcare during the mother's working hours, but the nonemployed mothers' children may be there because of some disturbance in the home or the mother's attitude toward the child. Thus, the selective factors operating are different for the two groups, and this might introduce a bias that affects the other differences in adjustment or development. What are assumed to be differences resulting from maternal employment status may be differences resulting from different sets of selective factors.

Here is another example—also not obvious. As society moves from a situation in which maternal employment is atypical to one in which it is the norm, there may be new selective factors to consider that explain why some mothers *resist* employment. I have suggested (Hoffman 1980b) that the repeated finding in studies of poverty groups of higher social and cognitive development scores for the children of *employed* women may represent an effect of maternal employment, or it may represent selective factors. Specifically, in circumstances where maternal employment seems particularly appropriate, the employment resisters may represent a more troubled or less competent group, and it may be these problems, rather than employment status itself, that the differences reflect.

New Social Conditions

Perhaps the most eloquent testimony to the point that maternal employment effects cannot be considered as though the mother's employment had been laid on the traditional family of the past is presented in Table 18-1.

Table 18-1   Labor-Force Participation Rates of Mothers with Children Under Eighteen, 1940–80

Year	% of Mothers
1980	56.6
1978	53.0
1976	48.8
1974	45.7
1972	42.9
1970	42.0
1968	39.4
1966	35.8
1964	34.5
1962	32.9
1960	30.4
1958	29.5
1956	27.5
1954	25.6
1952	23.8
1950	21.6
1948	20.2
1946	18.2
1940	8.6

Sources: U.S. Department of Commerce 1979; U.S. Department of Labor 1977, 1981.

These data indicate first that maternal employment has gone from being a rare pattern to being the modal one. This shift alone means that the selective factors will be different—as already indicated. It is not "going to work" that selects "special" mothers, but rather "not going." It also means that the significance of maternal employment for the family will be different—for example, mothers are less likely to feel guilty or unusual, husbands are less likely to feel that it is a mark of their failure, children are less likely to feel special, neighboring families will be having similar experiences, the employed-mother family is more likely to be similar to the families the children will form when they are adults. And, on the other side, nonemployed mothers are more likely to feel pressure to justify their own nonemployment.

Moreover, since the change is so great, the trend so steady, there must be other accompanying social changes. Such a change does not happen in a vacuum. The increased maternal employment rates are a response to some new events, are accompanied by several other responses to these events, and are the cause of still other changes. Such is the nature of social systems: a change in one part involves a change in others. It is important to understand these social changes to see how maternal employment fits into the picture.

The events that contributed to the high maternal employment rates depicted in Table 18-1 can be classified into four general categories. One set of changes occurred on the macro-economic level. Well before 1940, industrialization had developed to the point at which outside-the-home production was economically advantageous—that is, it became more economically efficient to earn wages and buy a loaf of bread than to stay home and bake it. Other changes at a broad social level affect the demand for female labor, including changes in the jobs themselves such that they are seen as appropriate for women as well as men, the general economic expansion, and such demographic factors as the low birth rate in the 1930s, which created a labor scarcity in the 1950s (Hoffman and Nye 1974; Oppenheimer 1975).

A second group of changes altered the housewife-mother role. These changes, like those in the first set, were largely a response to technological and scientific advances: whereas the first group operated to pull women into the labor force, these made it more feasible for mothers to work. Modern household appliances; advanced food processing, storage, and delivery systems; and such time-saving products as no-iron fabrics have enormously diminished the amount of work required for operating a household. Smaller family size, facilitated by improved contraception, has meant fewer children to care for and a shorter period with preschoolers.

It is important to emphasize that it was *necessary* housework that diminished because, as one study indicates, nonemployed mothers commonly report a great deal of time spent on housework that was unnecessary (Hoffman 1974b). Until recently, time-use studies indicated that nonemployed wives put in as many hours on domestic tasks as wives in the 1920s (Hall and Schroeder 1970; University of Michigan 1973; Walker 1969). More recent time-use data, however, show substantial reductions in household task hours. Robinson (1977, 1980) found a considerable decrease in housework time for all women between 1965 and 1975, and Pleck et al. (1980) reported that the same period showed a shift from a heavy work overload among employed wives to a pattern in which employed wives looked very much like the husbands in total number of work hours—at home and on the job—while nonemployed wives stood out as "uniquely low."

Third, these changes in the household, along with other, related events, have made the role of full-time housewife and mother less psychologically satisfying. Satisfaction with the housewife role decreased markedly between the mid-fifties and the mid-seventies, as evidenced in the replication of a national survey entitled "Americans View Their Mental Health" (Veroff et al. 1981). The new feminist ideology may have augmented this discontent, but much of it is also a response to the changed nature of the role itself. The decrease in required homemaking time and in the number of children may make the role of full-time homemaker seem an insufficient contribution and an inadequate use of the woman's ability, particularly when she knows that she could use her time to earn money for the family. An additional factor is the upswing in women's educational levels that began in the sixties (Hoffman 1974a), which may have increased the housewife's discontent as well as her ability to obtain more satisfying employment. If the first group of changes pulled women into the labor force and the second operated as facilitators, this group might be seen as providing a push out of the full-time housewife role.

Finally, a fourth group of changes has to do with economic insecurity. Mothers' incentives for seeking employment and establishing occupational competence have increased because of rising divorce rates, the increased number of female-headed households, and economic circumstances that make it necessary for wives to be employed in order to maintain an acceptable (objectively or subjectively) standard of living (see Chapter 20 by Hertz in this volume).

Simply focusing on the changes that have led to the increase in maternal employment reveals how family life has changed and indicates the fallacy of analyzing the effects of maternal employment as though it were occurring in the traditional family of generations ago. Nor is the present-day *nonemployed* mother like the *nonemployed* mother of that time. In view of the social changes that have occurred over the years, the role of the present-day nonemployed mothers may be as new as the role of the *majority* of present day mothers who are employed. In considering now how the mother's employment affects the child's socialization in the family, it is important to keep this new social situation in mind.

MOTHER'S WORK AS A SHAPER OF VALUES

We have noted in the preceding section a group of studies that explore the idea that the traits required for success in the father's occupation are valued and passed on to the child. Some support for this hypothesis as applied to the mother's job is provided in a recent study of lower-class employed mothers of preadolescent children (Piotrkowski and Katz 1982). The extent to which the mother's job allowed for autonomy and the utilization of skill predicted the child's performance in an academic summer program, high autonomy going with the child's more frequent absence from classes and high skill utilization going with the child's higher academic performance. For the most part, however, studies that view the mother's work as shaping the child's values differ from studies of fathers' work in a number of respects. First, by and large it is not the mother's particular occupation that is considered but her employment status per se. Second, the activities of the job receive less attention than the roles and activities in the family that mediate employment effects. To describe the research on the mother's employment as shaping values, then, it is necessary first to consider effects on family roles and activities.

When the mother is employed, the division of labor between the husband and wife is less traditional. Though the woman maintains the larger share, the husband of an employed woman participates more in housework and childcare (Bahr 1974; Baruch and Barnett 1981; Gold and Andres 1978c; Hill and Stafford 1978; Hoffman 1974b, 1977, 1983; Pleck et al. 1980; Robinson, 1978). Recent data, as well as a reanalysis of the 1950s data from the Blood and Wolfe study (1960), do not support the idea that employed wives have more decision-making power generally in the household but, rather, suggest that working increases the wife's say in money matters and the husband's say in household routines in proportion to their respective participation patterns (Hoffman and Manis 1978; Quarm 1977). School-aged children are more likely to have household responsibilities and to participate in tasks. The data suggest that the employed mother, except when guilt intervenes, is more likely to encourage independence in her children. Studies of lower socioeconomic populations and one-parent families have found that employed mothers are more likely to have structured rules for their children and consistency between theory and practice (Hoffman 1974c, 1977). All of these differences between the families of employed and nonemployed women can be seen as functional adaptations. The greater participation of the father and children in household tasks helps to compensate for the wife's outside employment. The independence training of the children and the rule-governed households also diminish the need for steady maternal surveillance.

One effect of the mother's employment, then, is to diminish the traditional sex-based division of labor and to encourage the two parents to share the breadwinner, housekeeping, and childcare functions. This difference is reflected in the children's conception of what adult men and women are like, what roles are appropriate, and, for a girl, what her own life will be like as an adult. Both sons and daughters of employed mothers are less stereotyped in their views of men and women, and this has been demonstrated even among preschool children (Gold and Andres 1978c; Hartley 1960; Miller 1975). They do not see the sharp distinctions that the children of nonemployed women see, and, specifically, they are not as likely to see competence as a peculiarly male trait nor warmth as a peculiarly female trait. Both sons and daughters of employed mothers are more likely to approve of maternal employment, and the daughters are more likely to expect to be employed themselves when they are mothers. Further, the adolescent daughters of employed mothers are more likely to be already employed (Hoffman 1974c; Marantz and Mansfield 1977; Romer and Cherry 1978; Vogel et al. 1970).

As I have pointed out in previous reviews (Hoffman 1974c, 1979, 1980b), many characteristics of the employed-mother family function to increase the academic-occupational competence of daughters and to contribute to positive adjustment generally. Academic-occupational competence in women is respected in the working-mother family. Further, the mothers provide models for their daughters more consistent with occupational roles and achievement orientations, and the daughters of employed mothers are more likely to indicate that they want to be like their mothers (Baruch 1972b; Douvan 1963). Diminished sex-role stereotyping, according to Bem's work (1975), is associated with a better sociopsychological adjustment generally.

Furthermore, the two childrearing patterns most often associated with employed-mother families (which can be seen both as functionally adaptive and as reflecting the values implicit in the maternal employment situation) also contribute positively to the daughters' development. In the traditional family, dependency is encouraged in daughters. This pattern has been seen as a source of excessive affiliative concerns and as a block to high achievement and the development of independent coping skills (Block 1979; Hoffman 1972, 1977). Thus, the encouragement of independence in the employed-mother family is a boon to daughters. It is not clear whether it is an advantage or a disadvantage to sons, however. Sons generally receive more independence training than daughters, and although this seems to provide them with an advantage in the nonemployed-mother family, it may be excessive in the employed-mother family (Bronfenbrenner and Crouter, 1982; Hoffman 1980b). The other childrearing pattern commonly associated with maternal employment is the higher level of household responsibilities required of children. Though it can obviously be overdone, the relationship of this pattern to ego development and self-esteem for both sons and daughters has already been noted (Elder 1978; Medrich 1981; Smokler 1975).

THE MOTHER'S PSYCHOLOGICAL STATE

We have noted hypotheses suggesting a reciprocality or complementarity between fathers' jobs and family life and others suggesting a commonality of behavior. These same patterns could be applied to the mother's work.

Complementary Need Satisfaction

The needs expressed in parenting will be affected by whether or not they are satisfied through other routes (Hoffman and Hoffman 1973; Hoffman and Manis 1978; Hoffman et al. 1978). Research focuses on nine (later eight) basic needs: the needs for love, fun and stimulation, adult status and social identity, achievement, a sense of morality or feeling good about oneself, power or influence, economic security, and "expansion of self"—that is, a sense of significance or perception of meaning in life. Parenting is one of several ways of satisfying these needs. If the need is strong and there is no alternative way of satisfying it, parenting may become the major means, and both fertility behavior and parenting style will be affected. The data support the hypothesis that women who are employed are less likely to cite as a major advantage of having children that it gives them a sense of identity or feeling of attaining adulthood. They are also less likely to indicate that children are a source of stimulation. These particular needs can be satisfied, at least in part, by employment. Employed women are *not* less likely to indicate that children are a major source of love or any of the other, less work-relevant needs, nor do they indicate any less enthusiasm for motherhood.

This research, as well as other studies, however, found a link between mothering attitudes and the extent to which employment provides achievement satisfaction. The data indicate that women who held high-status occupations before motherhood but are currently not employed are the most likely to see children as a source of achievement satisfaction (Hoffman and Manis 1978). Whether they express this through excessive achievement demands on their children, through wanting to mother a great many children, or through excellence in mothering was not explored in that study, but the first two patterns have been demonstrated in other research. Birnbaum (1975) found that women who had shown high achievement in college but did not work after marriage were excessively involved in their children's achievement, and more so than a comparable group who were professionally employed. Livson and Day (1977) analyzed longitudinal data from the Berkeley Growth Study and found that women who showed high academic achievement before marriage but did not pursue careers were the ones particularly likely to have larger families during the baby boom years of the 1950s, expressing achievement needs through numbers.[2] Thus, there is evidence from several quarters that high achievement needs that are not satisfied through employment may affect mothering attitudes and behavior.

The complexities of this connection are further illustrated by a longitudinal study of women who were college students in 1965. Women who showed a pattern of high achievement in college but were anxious about too much academic-occupational success—the pattern known as "fear of success"—

later became pregnant when they were on the verge of success, particularly one that threatened to surpass their husbands'. The data support the hypothesis that for women with "fear of success," occupational- academic success vis-à-vis the important man in their lives would be seen as threatening to the relationship or to their sense of femininity. The pregnancy, though unconsciously motivated, was a means of strengthening the relationship and reaffirming femininity (Hoffman 1977).

Morale

The link between the mother's occupation and family-based socialization patterns has often been considered in terms of morale. Although some writers expect employed women to have higher morale because of the satisfactions of outside employment, and others expect them to be stressed because of work overload, there is agreement that satisfaction with one's employment status—whether one is an employee or a full-time homemaker—will have a positive effect on family relations, mothering behavior, and child outcomes. A number of studies support this prediction (Birnbaum 1975; Farel 1980; Kappel and Lambert 1972; Woods 1972; Yarrow et al. 1962). As has often been pointed out, however, the causal direction involved in these studies is not clear, for satisfaction could be the consequence of the happy outcome as well as the antecedent. Attempts to deal with this problem have not been entirely successful. In a study that linked job satisfaction to childrearing patterns (Hoffman 1961), I tried to show that a woman's measure of satisfaction was closely related to her occupation and thus a consequence of the particular job, not the family variables.

Measures of satisfaction vary a great deal from study to study. For example, I used attitude toward the job; Yarrow and her colleagues (1962), like most researchers in this area, used attitude toward the combined mother-worker role. The outcomes predicted in these two studies are accordingly different. Yarrow, like most investigators, was operating from a morale hypothesis, with morale seen not as job engendered, but as based on dual-role satisfaction. The prediction, borne out by the data, was that satisfied mothers, whether employed or not, would be more "adequate" as mothers. My own study, focusing on work attitude, predicted that employed mothers who enjoyed work were more likely to feel guilty and to overcompensate; a different pattern was predicted for the employed mothers who saw their jobs as more functional than pleasant.

Two other studies that also compared the mother's intrinsic job satisfaction with a functional orientation found the former to have positive effects. In an early study by Kliger (1954), women who worked because of their interest in the job were more likely than those who worked for financial reasons to feel that there was improvement in the child's behavior as a result of employment. Kappel and Lambert (1972), in a study that, like my 1961 study, obtained independent measures from parents and children, found that the nine- to sixteen-year-old daughters of full-time employed mothers who were working for self-oriented reasons had higher self-esteem and evaluated both parents more highly than did either the daughters of full-time employed mothers who were working for family-oriented reasons or the daughters of nonemployed mothers.

However, the simple hypothesis that a generally satisfying occupation leads to positive family interaction has not been applied much to women. An oversimplification for men, it is even more obviously one for women because of traditional ideology and the prevailing dual-role pattern. Employed women still maintain the major responsibility for housework and childcare, and this influences the occupation-family relationship. Nevertheless, there is increasing attention to the idea that employment, in the absence of dual-role stress, may provide a valuable morale boost to mothers. Although complaints about the dual-role problems are common in surveys, complaints about the full-time housewife-mother role are at least as common (Veroff et al. 1981). Employed mothers, most notably in the recent studies, are more likely to indicate overall satisfaction with their lives than the nonemployed (Gold and Andres 1978a, 1978b, 1978c). In studies using mental health indices, employed women generally indicate more positive adjustment, although for mothers this effect is more apparent when their husbands also provide some childcare assistance (Kessler and McRae 1981). Furthermore, both national sample data and class-specific studies show that the psychological satisfaction that employment provides is not peculiar to the middle class (Kessler and McRae 1981). For blue-collar working women as well, employment provides evidence of self-worth, an opportunity for adult companionship, challenge, stimulation, and a sense of achievement that they do not experience as full-time homemakers, as indicated specifically in the data reported by Walshok (1978) and also by Ferree (1976) and Rubin (1976). National sample data indicate also that women's work commitment is increasing. A larger percentage of employed women in the United States state that they would continue working even if there were no monetary need—76 percent in 1976; more nonemployed mothers say that they would like to work and plan to soon; and, as already indicated, housework has diminished over the years as a source of satisfaction (Veroff et al. 1981).

Thus, although it obviously depends on many aspects of the situation, there is increasing evidence of a growing morale problem among *nonemployed* mothers (Birnbaum 1975; Gold and Andres 1978a, 1978b, 1978c). Birnbaum's study of educated women is particularly salient. The nonemployed mothers, in comparison with the professionally employed, had lower self-esteem, less of a sense of competence, felt less attractive, expressed greater concern over identity issues, and more often indicated feelings of loneliness. They described parenthood more in terms of the sacrifices it entailed and less in terms of enrichment and self-fulfillment. They voiced more anxiety about the children, and they expressed ambivalence and regret about their children's movement toward independence as they matured. It was noted earlier that employed mothers generally place greater stress on independence than nonemployed ones and that this pattern was consistent with the functional needs of their situation. The *psychological* needs of the nonemployed mother may also operate to extend and encourage dependency. In view of the changes in the housewife-mother role already discussed, the full-time homemaker may be unintentionally nurturing dependency in her children as she seeks to enhance, prolong, and justify her role.

On the other hand, there is also evidence that excessive strains resulting from the difficulty of juggling maternal and work roles may be disruptive for the family and the child. For example, studies of black families in poverty have generally found that the children of employed mothers have higher scores on cognitive, social, and personal-adjustment tests *except* where there is particular strain, as when substitute supervision is not adequate or the family includes six or more children (Cherry and Eaton 1977; Woods 1972). Several studies across social class have associated more positive child outcomes with part-time than full-time employment, a finding that has also been interpreted in terms of differences in role strain (Hoffman 1974c; Kappel and Lambert 1972). Further, the perception by college-aged daughters that their mothers are under stress from employment affects their own aspirations. Under these conditions, the tendency, indicated earlier, for daughters of employed women to seek dual roles themselves is reversed (Baruch 1972b).

Interest in the mother's morale as the linkage between her employment status and the child's socialization in the family has been given a boost by the recent rapid increase in employment rates for mothers of preschoolers. In 1980, 45 percent of the mothers of preschool children in families with the father present were employed, as were 59 percent of mothers of preschoolers in father-absent households. For families with children under three, the comparable figures were 41 and 47 percent (U.S. Department of Labor 1981). Although the prevalent maternal employment pattern can be seen as adaptive and functional to the school-aged child's development for the reasons noted above, the only nonmonetary advantage that maternal employment is seen as offering the very young child is the mother's improved morale: some mothers are happier when employed and thus more effective as mothers. Accordingly, studies of maternal employment during the early years have been particularly interested in this issue, and much of the recent research showing positive morale among employed mothers with carry-over for the child looks at employment during the early years (Farel 1980; Gold and Andres 1978a; Gold, Andres, and Glorieux 1979; Hock 1980).

WORK TIME

The mother's availability to her family is affected by the hours she is employed—both the number of hours plus commuting time and the particular schedule. These hours vary more widely for women than for men. Forty-three percent of the mothers in America were not employed at all in 1980, and of the 57 percent who were, 29 percent were employed less than thirty-five hours per week (U.S. Department of Labor 1981). Furthermore, more women than men are employed for less than twelve months a year, and their employment is often discontinuous—that is, they enter and leave the labor force more often. There is such variation in the hours of employment for women that Goldberg (personal communication) has suggested that it be operationalized as a continuous variable. Three recent studies of married women consider the number of hours of work as a continuous variable in relation to family adjustment and time patterns. Staines and Pleck (1983) found a negative relationship between the time women spend in employment and the time they spend in family roles, but Robinson (1977) did not. Piotrkowski and Crits-Christop (1981) found no relationship to self-reported measures of family adjustment. None of these studies, however, were focused on the child, and not all subjects were parents. Studies of *maternal* employment usually measure work status as a dichotomous variable, with all women who are employed more than a certain number of hours called employed, and all others called nonemployed. Sometimes there is a distinction between full-time and part-time employment; sometimes the middle group is excluded from the study. Despite these imprecisions, however, researchers have at least been more interested in studying how the family is affected by the mother's than the father's time out of the home, on the job.

Nevertheless, there is inadequate information on how the mother's employment affects her availability to her family, and particularly her children. The time-use studies in which subjects are asked to keep daily records of how they spend their time should have such information, but these data have generally been obtained for other purposes. One problem already noted is that inadequate attention is given to selective factors that differentiate employed from nonemployed women, and thus one cannot tell whether differences in time use reflect employment effects or other aspects of their lives. A second problem is that the descriptions of household activity have been too crude. For example, until recently, "childcare" might mean laundering diapers or closely interacting with the child: they were not differentiated. Recent research, however, has attempted to remedy this situation by distinguishing between "primary childcare'' and ''child contact'' (Robinson 1978), or among ''direct,'' ''indirect,'' and ''available'' child contact (Goldberg 1978).

In general the data indicate that the employed mother spends less time with each child, but this differs by social class and the definition of child contact. Hill and Stafford (1978), for example, include as childcare physical care, teaching, reading, talking, playing, and providing medical care. They report that women employed more than twenty hours a week spend less time in per-child care whether the child is a baby, preschooler, grade-schooler, or high-schooler. They also note that the differences vary with the education of the mother and that the difference between employed and nonemployed is considerably less for college-educated women. Employed college-educated women reduce mainly ''personal-care time,'' which is primarily sleep, and ''passive leisure,'' which is primarily television watching. These authors still report, however, a 25 percent deficit in childcare time for the employed, college-educated mothers of preschoolers. On the other hand, Goldberg (1978), in a study of middle-class preschool children enrolled in a nursery school, found no difference in the amount of direct one-to-one interaction between the mother and the child, although the mothers employed full time did have less ''available'' time with the child (when the mother was within calling distance) and less ''indirect'' time (when the two were in the same room but engaged in separate activities).

At best, these data leave a number of questions unanswered. One is probably unanswerable: how do children today compare with yesterday's children with respect to maternal contact time? It is possible that employment fills in time previously consumed by greater household burdens and more children. If so, differences between employed-mother and nonemployed-mother families may reflect an unprecedented amount of mother-child interaction in the nonemployed-mother family. As noted in previous publications, the amount of maternal attention a child receives is not infinitely valuable. The optimum level varies with the child's age. Whether maternal employment today facilitates or hinders the achievement of this level is a complicated and interesting issue (Hoffman 1979, 1980b).

Nature of the Mother-Child Interaction

The mother's time on the job may affect the quality of mother-child interaction as well as its quantity. The time spent at work might improve the mother's morale or contribute to a feeling of work overload. Or the employed mother might consciously decide to compensate for her absence by setting up special times for nondiverted interaction and special activities. Employed women report this pattern in several studies (Hoffman 1980b). Furthermore, recent behavioral observations of mother-infant interaction reveal a more intense interaction for the employed mothers (Pederson et al. 1981; Schubert et al. 1980). Employed mothers were highly interactive, specifically in social play and verbal interaction. The data reported by Pederson and his colleagues were collected in the evening, after a work day, and may reflect efforts to compensate for absence during the day or enthusiasm for interaction that is less intense in mothers who are with their infants all day. These researchers note that the employed mother's interaction style is one that typically characterizes fathers, including social play and a physically robust way of handling the infant. They suggest that the often-noted differences in parenting style between fathers and mothers might be a function of work roles, representing a form of greeting and renewing contact after absence.

The Pederson data are also interesting in their implications for the effects of the mother's employment on the father's family behavior. Though maternal employment is typically seen as increasing father-child interaction, these data showed fathers as less interactive when their wives are employed than when they are not. It may be that the after-work hours in the dual-wage family are devoted to mother-infant interaction, whereas in the single-wage family this is the father's special time. The possibility that maternal employment during the child's infancy squeezes the father out is consistent with the fact that the studies of middle-class families find no employment-status differences for mother-infant attachment (Chase-Lansdale 1981; Hock 1980), but the one study that looked at father-infant attachment found more insecurity in the dual-career families, though only for sons (Chase-Lansdale 1981).

Care in the Mother's Absence

As important as the questions of how the mother's time at work affects the quantity and quality of her interaction with the child are the questions of how the child is being cared for in her absence. Although the mother's employment may sometimes coincide with the child's public school hours, this is not possible with the preschool child and is usually imperfectly achieved with the school-aged child.

A common public concern is that many of these children go unsupervised. Data on this issue are grossly inadequate. Those that exist suggest that the children of employed mothers have more unsupervised hours per day than the children of nonemployed ones (Glueck and Glueck 1957; Gold and Andres 1978b), but no study has investigated whether the unsupervised time is excessive, extensive, inappropriate for the child's age, or monitored by telephone contact. Further, there are no adequate data on how this unsupervised time is used by the child. Bronfenbrenner and Crouter (1982) suggest that lack of supervision may increase the socialization impact of the peer group, diminishing that of the family, a pattern that might provide a link between maternal employment in the middle class and the sometimes-observed lower academic performance of sons. A related theory (Hoffman 1980a) asks whether there are differences between sons and daughters in both the amount of unsupervised time and its significance for development. This is a rich area for study. Depending on the age of the child and the circumstances, it cannot be assumed without investigation that periods without supervision have a negative impact on the child.

For the most part, however, substitute care is provided by other members of the family, relatives, friends, babysitters, home-based day care, day-care centers, and after-school programs. All of these affect the family and the child. Exposure to outside socialization agents may diminish the intensity and relative exclusivity of the family influence; family help may bring about changes in the family structure and organization. The differences in family structure between dual- and single-wage families have already been described, and, as indicated, many can be seen as functional shifts to accommodate to the mother's absence, with considerable impact on the child. The increase in the father's participation in household tasks and childcare and the reduction of the sex-based division of labor in the family are particularly important links between the mother's employment and the child's socialization (Hoffman 1979).

Part-Time Employment

A few studies differentiate part-time maternal employment from full-time. The results were summarized a decade ago (Hoffman and Nye 1974: 228). The studies

found part-time employment an unusually successful adaptation to the conflict between the difficulties of being a full-time housewife and the strain of combining this role with full-time employment. These mothers seem to be physically and psychologically healthy, positive toward their maternal roles, and active in recreational and community activities. Their children compare favorably to the other groups with respect to self-esteem, social adjustment, and attitudes toward their parents; scattered findings suggest that their marital satisfaction is the highest of the three groups

Yet part-time employment is difficult to find, pays less, often excludes employee benefits, and may be inappropriate for career advancement. Perhaps because of these difficulties, and perhaps because it has been accepted that part-time employment does not disrupt family life, little subsequent research on this pattern was conducted until recently. The new interest in maternal employment and the preschool child has brought with it renewed attention to part-time employment. The "part-time" pattern is more common for employed mothers with preschool children than for mothers with only school-aged children: about one-third of the former were employed part time. Recent studies of these younger families are consistent with the pattern noted earlier. In a particularly interesting study of three-year-olds, Bronfenbrenner and his colleagues found that mothers employed part time had the most positive attitudes toward their children (Bronfenbrenner and Crouter 1982). This study also found interesting differences between boys and girls: sons were viewed most positively by mothers who worked part time, least positively by mothers who worked full time. Both employed-mother groups expressed more positive attitudes toward daughters than did the full-time homemakers. These results may be relevant to the previously noted differences in the apparent effects of maternal employment on sons and daughters. It is possible that the higher activity level of boys (Hoffman 1977) makes part-time employment a particularly satisfying compromise for their mothers, at least when the children are young.

Duration, Timing, and Long-Term Effects

Here, as in most research, family life is considered contemporaneously. No attention has been given to the duration of employment or to the timing of changes in employment status in relation to the stage of the family, the child's age, or such specific events as divorce, although these are important ways to consider the "time" aspect of the woman's employment.

Furthermore, studies that look only at the correlations with maternal employment at one point in time can be misleading in at least three ways: (1) the effects of employment at one stage in the child's life may only show up later; (2) a contemporaneous effect may disappear with time; (3) the traits that seem maladaptive at one age may develop into strengths as the child matures, or the converse pattern may emerge. Studies that show no differences between infants of mothers employed full time and nonemployed mothers (e.g., Hock 1980) are an example of the first problem. The second possibility (an observed effect that disappears with time) can be seen in the parallel studies by Gold and Andres (1978a, 1978b) of children of different ages. None of the negative symptoms correlated with maternal employment in the ten-year-old sample was found in the adolescent sample. This could indicate that maternal employment effects are different for ten-year-olds than for adolescents, but since most of the employed mothers of adolescents in their sample had also been employed when the children were ten, it may also mean that effects observed at ten will wash away by adolescence. The third possibility (a trait that changes its manifestation as the child matures) has been demonstrated generally in the longitudinal work of Kagan and Moss (1962). In the case of maternal employment research, I have suggested elsewhere (Hoffman 1980b) that the pattern of better school performance by the middle-class sons of nonemployed mothers may reflect cognitive ability or simply conformity to adult standards, a distinction that would affect the prognosis for later development. If it is based on conformity, the manifestation at older ages and higher academic levels might be considerably less positive.

The duration, timing, and long-term effects of maternal employment have not been totally ignored by researchers, however. Burchinal (1963) used retrospective reports of the mother's employment history to see how employment at different periods in the child's development affected the child in adolescence. Romer and Cherry (1978) used a similar technique with subjects at several different ages to see whether sex-role attitudes were more affected by the child's age at the time of the mother's employment or the child's age at the time of measurement. Gold and Andres (1978b, 1978c) examined the duration of maternal employment as a variable as well as current status (in all of their research, it should be noted, even "current status" involved continuous employment for a specified number of years). The retrospective studies, however, have turned out to be more complicated than might be anticipated. A common problem has to do with the ever-intrusive selective factors. Researchers who carefully match their samples with respect to current maternal employment status ignore this issue when introducing previous employment history (Hoffman 1981).

Both short-term and long-term longitudinal designs have also been employed to investigate some of the issues raised here (Cherry and Eaton 1977; Hetherington 1979; Moore 1975). The Moore study, begun in England in the 1950s, is particularly interesting. Children who received full-time mothering during their preschool years were compared with a group whose mothers were out of the home for regular periods, usually because of maternal employment. The development of these children was followed through adolescence and is, in fact, currently being reassessed (T. W. Moore, personal communication). The pattern revealed at adolescence would not have been easily foreseen earlier. One of the particularly interesting outcomes was that boys who received full-time mothering during their preschool years were good students but also more conforming, fearful, and inhibited as adolescents. This combination of qualities is consistent with the suggestion (noted above) that the academic performance of the sons of nonemployed mothers may reflect conformity with adult standards rather than cognitive ability per se—that is, it may reflect a pattern of oversocialization. If so, the performance advantage might be lost at higher intellectual tasks, where conformity is less advantageous than in the public schools. The common response to the finding that one group shows better school performance is that it must have had superior socialization. Yet that performance might be achieved at a cost in mental health and self-fulfillment. It is probably not irrelevant that Moore's data were collected in England, where families were smaller than they were in America during the 1950s. One of the problems with long-term longitudinal research is that one often learns a great deal about a pattern that no longer exists. Moore's English data may be more relevant to the situation in the United States today, at least with respect to family size, than similar data collected in America in the 1950s would be.

The Hetherington study, a short-term longitudinal one, is the only study that looks at the timing of employment status with respect to other significant events in the family when evaluating its impact on the child. In a study of the effects of divorce on four-year-olds, Hetherington found that adverse effects were diminished when the mother had been employed before the divorce. The mother's job helped her to cope more effectively, both psychologically and economically. A particularly difficult situation, on the other hand, occurred when the mother started work at the time of the divorce. The new job helped the mother in some ways, such as providing self-esteem and new social contacts, but it increased the disruption in routines and thus added to the child's sense of loss.

RESOURCES

An important way in which the mother's job affects the family and the child's socialization is through the money it brings in. Cherry and Eaton (1977) examined the relationship between maternal employment during the first three years of the child's life and various indices of cognitive and physical development at ages four, seven, and eight. The generally positive associations between maternal employment and scores on the Illinois Test of Psycholinguistic Ability and the Wechsler Preschool and Primary Scale of Intelligence, as well as positive findings on the children's physical development, were in part mediated by the higher per capita income. Maternal employment related to higher per capita income; higher per capita income related to higher cognitive and physical development scores, at least for this sample of low-income families.

The effect of the mother's wages on the middle-class family is not as clearly documented. Several studies examined the relationship between the mother's employment status and the children's college plans, but no clear pattern emerged (Hoffman 1974c). Where the range of income is wider, as in the "middle class," it is difficult to demonstrate the effects of an increment.

A popular theory in sociology is that the woman's occupation and the wages she contributes to the family provide a resource that increases her family power (Blood and Wolfe 1960; Goode 1964). As noted above, maternal employment does seem to increase the woman's say in economic decisions and thus may increase her status in the family and contribute to the children's greater respect for female competence.

Conclusion: The Father's and the Mother's Jobs

We have observed both parallels and divergences in considering the effects on the family of the mother's and the father's employment. Four general processes involved in employment—shaping family values, influencing the worker's psychological state, imposing time and schedule demands, and providing resources—have served to organize both discussions. The independent variable in the discussion of the mother's occupation, however, has typically been employment versus nonemployment. Unemployment per se has not been studied, though some research has considered nonemployed women who would prefer to work. Furthermore, studies that consider the effects on the family of the mother's particular job have been rare. There has been research on women in selected occupations—such as engineering (Perrucci 1970), medicine (Cartwright 1972; Walsh 1977), management (Hennig and Jardim 1977)—but the focus of these investigations has not been on family effects. The father's occupation, on the other hand, has been considered in its more specific aspects—his capacity for authority, for example—and there has been some research on the family impact of the father's involuntary unemployment.[3] These differences are not, of course, capricious. Fathers are not voluntarily "nonemployed." The mother is more likely to have childcare and household responsibilities with which work time competes. There is a wider variety of male occupations for specification. Many studies of unemployment were conducted in the 1930s, when maternal employment was uncommon.

Furthermore, and for similar reasons, the dependent variables have been different. The studies of the father's occupation, since they look at a more specific independent variable, have also looked for more specific effects, and these studies have not been burdened by the "social problem" label. The dependent variables in the maternal employment studies, on the other hand, have often been too broad and evaluative to be meaningful. It seems likely that both maternal employment and nonemployment produce certain strengths and vulnerabilities in the child, as well as influences not capable of evaluation, and the social as well as scientific value of these studies will be enhanced when this is more widely appreciated.

In view of these divergences between the studies of maternal and paternal employment, it is not surprising that few research endeavors have examined the effects of both simultaneously. Some qualitative investigations of dual-wage couples have considered the mutual accommodations and adjustments that are involved when both parents work (Garland 1972; Holmstrom 1972; Lein et al. 1974; Poloma 1972; Rapoport and Rapoport 1971). And several studies have reconsidered the Parsonian hypothesis that the division of functions between spouses, and particularly the unilateral occupational commitment that circumvents competition between spouses, is functional to marriage. The possibility that a woman's superior occupational status is disturbing to the marital relationship has been investigated in several studies. Both Garland (1972) and Safilios-Rothschild (1976) suggest that there is a problem, but it can be tolerated if the husband's income is higher; as already indicated (Hoffman 1977), some women get pregnant in order to cope with this problem. But Richardson (1979) found no marital difficulty associated with the woman's greater occupational prestige, and several studies suggest that when the husband's occupation leads to new experiences and growth, the marital relationship does better if the wife has a comparable kind of occupation (Dizard 1968; Levinson 1964; Seidenberg 1973).

None of the studies dealing with the possible threat of occupational competition examined effects on the child's socialization experiences, though these might be expected. I have suggested elsewhere (Hoffman 1979), for example, that the strained relationship sometimes observed between fathers and sons when mothers are employed in blue-collar occupations is a function of the perception that maternal employment undermines the father's prestige. This perception does not typically prevail in the middle class, but it might under conditions of occupational competition. Social scientists have not yet dared to tackle the complex task of analyzing the interactions among the occupations of both parents, family patterns, and the child's socialization.

Notes

1. The first two categories are covered in the original publication from which this chapter is derived (Hoffman 1985).
2. The complicated tradeoff between women's employment and fertility is discussed more fully in a previous publication (Hoffman 1974b).
3. The effects of the father's unemployment are discussed in the original version of this paper (Hoffman 1985).

References

Aldous, Joan. 1969. "Wives' Employment Status and Lower-Class Men as Husband-Fathers: Support for the Moynihan Thesis." *Journal of Marriage and the Family* 31:469–76.

Bahr, S. J. 1974. "Effects on Power and Division of Labor in the Family." In L. W. Hoffman and F. I. Nye (eds.), *Working Mothers*. San Francisco, Calif.: Jossey-Bass.

Baruch, G. K. 1972a. "Maternal Influences Upon College Women's Attitudes Toward Women and Work." *Developmental Psychology* 6:32–37.

———. 1972b. "Maternal Role Pattern as Related to Self-Esteem and Parental

Identification in College Women.'' Paper presented at the meeting of the Eastern Psychological Association, Boston.

Baruch, G. K., and R. C. Barnett. 1981. ''Father's Participation in the Care of Their Preschool Children.'' *Sex Roles* 10:1043–56.

Bem, S. I. 1975. ''Sex-Role Adaptability: One Consequence of Psychological Androgyny.'' *Journal of Personality and Social Psychology* 31:634–43.

Birnbaum, J. A. 1975. ''Life Patterns and Self-Esteem in Gifted Family Oriented and Career Committed Women.'' In M. S. Mednick, S. S. Tangri, and L. W. Hoffman (eds.), *Women and Achievement*. Washington, D.C.: Hemisphere.

Blau, P. M., and O. D. Duncan. 1967. *The American Occupational Structure*. New York: Wiley.

Block, J. H. 1979. ''Personality Development in Males and Females: The Influence of Differential Socialization.'' Master Series Lecture, annual meeting of the American Psychological Association, New York.

Blood, R. O., Jr., and D. M. Wolfe. 1960. *Husbands and Wives*. Glencoe, Ill.: Free Press.

Bronfenbrenner, Uri, and A. Crouter. 1982. ''Work and Family Through Time and Space.'' In S. B. Kamerman and C. D. Hayes (eds.), *Families That Work: Children in a Changing World*. Washington, D.C.: National Academy Press.

Burchinal, L. G. 1963. ''Personality Characteristics of Children,'' In F. I. Nye and L. W. Hoffman (eds.), *The Employed Mother in America*. Chicago: Rand McNally.

Cartwright, L. K. 1972. ''Conscious Factors Entering Into Decisions of Women to Study Medicine.'' *Journal of Social Issues* 28:201–16.

Chase-Lansdale, P. L. 1981. ''Effects of Maternal Employment on Mother-Infant and Father-Infant Attachment.'' Ph.D. dissertation, University of Michigan.

Cherry, R. R., and E. L. Eaton. 1977. ''Physical and Cognitive Development in Children of Low-Income Mothers Working in the Child's Early Years.'' *Child Development* 48:158–66.

Clark, R. A., and V. Gecas. 1977. ''The Employed Father in America: A Role Competition Analysis.'' Paper presented at the annual meeting of the Pacific Sociological Association.

Clark, R. A.; F. I. Nye; and V. Gecas. 1978. ''Work Involvement and Marital Role Performance.'' *Journal of Marriage and the Family* 40:9–22.

Dizard, J. 1968. *Social Change in the Family*. Chicago: Community and Family Study Center, University of Chicago.

Douvan, E. 1963. ''Employment and the Adolescent.'' In F. I. Nye and L. W. Hoffman (eds.), *The Employed Mother in America*. Chicago: Rand McNally.

Dyer, W. G. 1964. ''Family Reactions to the Father's Job.'' In A. Shostak and W. Gomberg (eds.), *Blue-Collar World: Studies of the American Worker*. Englewood Cliffs, N.J.: Prentice-Hall.

Elder, G. H., Jr. 1978. ''Approaches to Social Change and the Family.'' *American Journal of Sociology* 84: special supplement.

Elliot, F. R. 1978. ''Occupational Commitments and Paternal Deprivation.'' *Child Care, Health, and Development* 4: 305–15.

Farel, A. N. 1980. ''Effects of Preferred Maternal Roles, Maternal Employment, and Sociographic Status on School Adjustment and Competence.'' *Child Development* 50: 1179–86.

Ferree, Myra Marx. 1976. ''Working Class Jobs: Housework and Paid Work as Sources of Satisfaction.'' *Social Problems* 23:431–41.

Garland, T. N. 1972. "The Better Half? The Male in the Dual Professional Family." In C. Safilios-Rothschild (ed.), *Toward a Sociology of Women*. Lexington, Mass.: Xerox College Publishing.

Gecas, V., and F. I. Nye. 1974. "Sex and Class Differences in Parent-Child Interaction: A Test of Kohn's Hypothesis." *Journal of Marriage and the Family* 36: 742–49.

Gerstl, J. E. 1961. "Leisure, Taste, and Occupational Milieu." *Social Problems* 9: 56–68.

Glueck, S., and E. Glueck. 1957. "Working Mothers and Delinquency." *Mental Hygiene* 41: 327–52.

Gold, D., and D. Andres. 1978a. "Developmental Comparisons Between Adolescent Children with Employed and Nonemployed Mothers." *Merrill-Palmer Quarterly* 24: 243–54.

———. 1978b. "Developmental Comparisons Between Ten-Year-Old Children with Employed and Nonemployed Mothers." *Child Development* 49: 75–84.

———. 1978c. "Relations Between Maternal Employment and Development of Nursery School Children." *Canadian Journal of Behavioral Science* 10: 116–29.

Gold, D.; D. Andres; and J. Glorieux. 1979. "The Development of Francophone Nursery School Children with Employed and Nonemployed Mothers." *Canadian Journal of Behavioral Science* 11: 169–73.

Goldberg, R. J. 1978. *Development in the Family and School Context: Who Is Responsible for the Education of Young Children in America?* Paper presented at the annual conference of the National Association for the Education of Young Children, New York.

Goode, W. J. 1964. *The Family*. Englewood Cliffs, N.J.: Prentice-Hall.

Greenhaus, J. H., and R. E. Kopelman. 1981. "Conflict Between Work and Nonwork Roles: Implications for the Career Planning Process." *Human Resources Planning* 4: 1–10.

Hall, F. T., and M. P. Schroeder. 1970. "Time Spent on Household Tasks." *Journal of Home Economics* 62: 34–46.

Hammond, S. B. 1954. "Class and Family." In O. A. Oeser and S. B. Hannond (eds.), *Social Structure and Personality in a City*. London: Routledge & Kegan Paul.

Hartley, R. E. 1960. "Children's Concepts of Male and Female Roles." *Merrill-Palmer Quarterly* 6: 83–91.

Heath, D. B. 1977. "Some Possible Effects of Occupation on the Maturing of Professional Men." *Journal of Vocational Behavior* 11: 263–81.

Hennig, M., and A. Jardim. 1977. *The Managerial Woman*. Garden City, N.Y.: Anchor Press/Doubleday.

Herzog, E., and C. Sudia. 1973. "Children in Fatherless Families." In B. M. Caldwell and H. N. Ricciuti (eds.), *Review of Child Development Research*, vol. 3. Chicago: University of Chicago Press.

Hetherington, E. M. 1979. "Divorce: A Child's Perspective." *American Psychologist* 34, no. 10: 851–58.

Hill, C. R., and F. P. Stafford. 1978. *Parental Care of Children: Time Diary Estimates of Quantity Predictability and Variety*. Working paper series. Ann Arbor: Institute for Social Research, University of Michigan.

Hock, E. 1980. "Working and Nonworking Mothers and Their Infants: A Comparative Study of Maternal Care-Giving Characteristics and Infant Social Behavior." *Merrill-Palmer Quarterly* 26: 79–101.

Hoffman, L. W. 1961. "Effects of Maternal Employment on the Child." *Child Development* 32: 187–97.

———. 1963. "Effects on Children: Summary and Discussion." In F. I. Nye and L. W. Hoffman (eds.), *The Employed Mother in America*. Chicago: Rand McNally.

———. 1972. "Early Childhood Experiences and Women's Achievement Motives." *Journal of Social Issues* 28: 129–56.

———. 1974a. "The Employment of Women and Fertility." *Merrill-Palmer Quarterly* 20: 99–119.

———. 1974b. "Psychological Factors." In L. W. Hoffman and F. I. Nye (eds.), *Working Mothers*. San Francisco: Jossey-Bass.

———. 1974c. "Effects of Maternal Employment on the Child—A Review of the Research." *Developmental Psychology* 10: 204–28.

———. 1977. "Changes in Family Roles, Socialization, and Sex Differences." *American Psychologist* 32: 644–57.

———. 1979. "Maternal Employment: 1979." *American Psychologist* 34: 859–65.

———. 1980a. "The Effects of Maternal Employment on the Academic Attitudes and Performance of School-Aged Children." Report prepared for the National Institute for Education, Washington, D.C.

———. 1980b. "The Effects of Maternal Employment on the Academic Attitudes and Performance of School-Aged Children." *School Psychology Review* 9: 319–36.

———. 1981. "Dual-Wage Family and the Preschool Child." Paper presented at Yale University, Bush Center in Child Development.

———. 1983. "Increased Fathering: Effects on the Mother." In M. Lamb and A. Sagi (eds.), *Social Policies and Legal Issues Pertaining to Fatherhood*. Hillsdale, N.J.: Erlbaum Press.

———. 1985. "Work and the Family." In R. Parke, R. Emde, H. McAdoo, and G. Sackett (eds.), *Review of Child Development Research*, vol. 7. Chicago: University of Chicago Press.

Hoffman, L. W., and M. L. Hoffman. 1973. "The Value of Children to Parents." In J. T. Fawcett (ed.), *Psychological Perspectives on Fertility*. New York: Basic Books.

Hoffman, L. W., and J. D. Manis. 1978. "Influences of Children on Marital Interaction and Parental Satisfactions and Dissatisfactions." In R. Lerner and G. Spanier (eds.), *Child Influences on Marital and Family Interaction: A Life-Span Perspective*. New York: Academic Press.

———. 1979. "The Value of Children in the United States: A New Approach to the Study of Fertility." *Marriage and the Family* 41: 583–96.

Hoffman, L. W., and F. I. Nye (eds.). 1974. *Working Mothers*. San Francisco: Jossey-Bass.

Hoffman, L. W.; A. Thornton; and J. D. Manis. 1978. "The Value of Children to Parents in the United States." *Population: Behavioral, Social, and Environmental Issues* 1: 91–131.

Hoffman, M. L. 1960. "Power Assertion by the Parent and Its Impact on the Child." *Child Development* 31: 129–43.

Holmstrom, Lynda Lytle. 1972. *The Two-Career Family*. Cambridge, Mass.: Schenkman.

Howe, Irving. 1976. *World of Our Fathers*. New York: Harcourt Brace Jovanovich.

Hughes, Everett C. 1958. *Men and Their Work*. Glencoe, Ill.: Free Press.

Kagan, J., and H. A. Moss. 1962. *Birth to Maturity*. New York: Wiley.

Kanter, Rosabeth Moss. 1977. *Work and Family in the United States: A Critical Review and Agenda for Research and Policy*. New York: Russell Sage Foundation.

Kappel, B. E., and R. D. Lambert. 1972. "Self-Worth Among the Children of Working Mothers." Manuscript. University of Waterloo, Ontario.

Keith, P. M., and R. B. Schafer. 1980. "Role Strain and Depression in Two-Job Families." *Family Relations* 29: 483–88.

Kessler, R. C., and J. A. McRae, Jr. 1981. "Trends in the Relationship Between Sex and Psychological Distress: 1957–1976." *American Sociological Review* 46: 443–52.

Kessler, R. C., and J. A. McRae, Jr. In press. "The Effects of Wives' Employment on the Mental Health of Married Men and Women." *American Sociological Review*.

Kliger, D. 1954. "The Effects of Employment of Married Women on Husband and Wife Roles: A Study in Cultural Change." Ph.D. dissertation, Yale University.

Kohn, M. L. 1963. "Social Class and Parent-Child Relationships: An Interpretation." *American Journal of Sociology* 68: 471–80.

———. 1980. "Personlichkeit, Beruf, und soziale Schichtung: Ein Bezugsrahmen." Klett-Cotta.

Kroes, W. H., and A. Z. Hurrell. 1975. "Job Stress and the Police Officer: Identifying Stress Reduction Techniques." Washington, D.C.: Department of Health, Education and Welfare, Public Health Service.

Landy, F.; B. G. Rosenberg, and Brian Sutton-Smith. 1969. "The Effects of Limited Father Absence on Cognitive Development." *Child Development* 40: 941–44.

Lein, L., et al. 1974. "Work and Family Life." Final report to the National Institute of Education. Cambridge, Mass.: Center for the Study of Public Policy.

Levinson, H. 1964. *Emotional Problems in the World of Work*. New York: Harper & Row.

Lewis, R. 1973. "Toward an Understanding of Police Anomie." *Journal of Police Science and Administration* 1: 484–90.

Livson, N., and D. Day. 1977. "Adolescent Personality Antecedents of Completed Family Size: A Longitudinal Study." *Journal of Youth and Adolescence* 6: 311–24.

Lueptow, L.; M. McClendon; and J. McKeon. 1979. "Father's Occupation and Son's Personality: Findings and Questions for the Emerging Linkage Hypothesis." *Sociological Quarterly* 20: 463–75.

Lynn, D. 1974. *The Father: His Role in Child Development*. Monterey, Calif.: Brooks/Cole.

Lynn, D., and W. L. Sawrey. 1959. "The Effects of Father-Absence on Norwegian Boys and Girls." *Journal of Abnormal and Social Psychology* 59: 258–62.

Maccoby, E. E. 1958. "Children and Working Mothers." *Children* 5, no. 3: 83–89.

Marantz, S. A., and A. F. Mansfield. 1977. "Maternal Employment and the Development of Sex-Role Stereotyping in Five- to Eleven-Year-Old Girls." *Child Development* 48: 668–73.

Mathews, S. M. 1934. "The Effects of the Mothers' Out-of-Home Employment Upon Children's Ideas and Attitudes." *Journal of Applied Psychology* 18: 116–36.

McKinley, D. G. 1964. *Social Class and Family Life*. New York: Free Press.

Medrich, Elliot, and J. A. Rozien. In press. *The Serious Business of Growing Up: A Study of Children's Lives Outside of School*. Berkeley: University of California Press.

Miller, S. M. 1975. "Effects of Maternal Employment on Sex-Role Perception, Interests, and Self-Esteem in Kindergarten Girls." *Developmental Psychology* 11: 405–6.

Moore, T. W. 1975. "Exclusive Early Mothering and Its Alternatives." *Scandinavian Journal of Psychology* 16: 256–72.

Mortimer, J. T. 1974. "Patterns of Intergenerational Occupational Movements: A Smallest-Space Analysis." *American Journal of Sociology* 79: 1278–99.

———. 1976. Social Class, Work, and the Family: Some Implications of the Father's Occupation for Familial Relationships and Son's Career Decisions." *Journal of Marriage and the Family* 38: 241–56.

Mott, P. E., et al. 1965. *Shift Work: The Social Psychology and Physical Consequences*. Ann Arbor: University of Michigan Press.

Myers, S. S. 1979. "Child Abuse and the Military Community." *Military Medicine* 144: 23–25.

Nordlicht, S. 1979. "Effects of Stress on the Police Officer and Family." *New York State Journal of Medicine* 79: 400–401.

Nye, F. I., and L. W. Hoffman. 1963. *The Employed Mother in America*. Chicago: Rand McNally.

Oppenheimer, V. K. 1973. "Demographic Influence on Female Employment and the Status of Women." *American Journal of Sociology* 78: 946–61.

Pearlin, L. I. 1970. *Class Context and Family Relations: A Cross National Study*. Boston: Little, Brown.

Pearlin, L. I., and M. L. Kohn. 1966. "Social Class, Occupation, and Parental Values: A Cross National Study." *American Sociological Review* 31: 466–79.

Pederson, F. A.; R. Cain; M. Zaslow; and B. Anderson. 1981. "Variation in Infant Experience Associated with Alternative Family Role Organization." In L. Lacsa and I. Sigel (eds.), *Families as Learning Environment for Children*. New York: Plenum.

Perrucci, C. C. 1970. "Minority Status and the Pursuit of Professional Careers: Women in Sciences and Engineering." *Social Forces* 49: 245–58.

Piotrkowski, C. S. 1979. *Work and the Family System: A Naturalistic Study of Working-Class and Lower-Middle-Class Families*. New York: Free Press.

Piotrkowski, C. S., and P. Crits-Christop. 1981. "Occupational Life and Women's Family Adjustment." *Journal of Family Issues* 2: 126–47.

Piotrkowski, C. S., and M. H. Katz. 1982. "Indirect Socialization of Children: The Effects of Mothers' Jobs on Academic Behaviors." *Child Development* 53: 1520–29.

Pleck, Joseph H.; Linda Lang; and M. Rustad. 1980. "Men's Family Work, Involvement, and Satisfaction." Manuscript. Wellesley College Center for Research on Women, Wellesley, Mass.

Poloma, Margaret M. 1972. "Role Conflict and the Married Professional Woman." In C. Safilios-Rothschild (ed.), *Toward a Sociology of Women*. Lexington, Mass.: Xerox College Publishing.

Quarm, D. E. A. 1977. *The Measurement of Marital Powers*. Ph.D. dissertation, University of Michigan. University Microfilms, no. 7726339.

Rainwater, Lee. 1965. *Family Design: Marital Sexuality, Family Size, and Contraception*. Chicago: Aldine.

Rapoport, Rhona and Robert Rapoport. 1965. "Work and Family in Contemporary Society." *American Sociological Review* 30: 381–94.

———. 1971. *Dual-Career Families*. Baltimore: Penguin.

Richardson, J. G. 1979. "Wife Occupational Superiority and Marital Troubles: An Examination of the Hypothesis." *Journal of Marriage and the Family* 41: 63–72.

Riesman, David. 1958. "Work and Leisure in Post-Industrial Society." In E. Larrabee and R. Meyersohn (eds.), *Mass Leisure*. Glencoe, Ill.: Free Press.

Robinson, J. P. 1977. "Change in Americans' Use of Time: 1965–1975." Manuscript. Cleveland Communications Research Center, Cleveland State University.

———. 1978. *How Americans Use Time: A Sociological Perspective*. New York: Praeger.

———. 1980. "Household Technology and Household Work." In S. F. Berk, (ed.), *Women and Household Labor*. Beverly Hills, Calif.: Sage.

Roe, A. 1956. *The Psychology of Occupations*. New York: Wiley.

Romer, N., and D. Cherry. 1978. "Developmental Effects of Preschool and School Age Maternal Employment on Children's Sex-Role Concepts." Manuscript. Brooklyn College of the City University of New York.

Rubin, Lillian Breslow. 1976. *Worlds of Pain: Life in the Working Class Family*. New York: Basic Books.

Safilios-Rothschild, C. 1976. "Dual Linkages Between the Occupational and Family Systems: A Macrosociological Analysis." *Signs* 1: 51–60.

Sarason, S. B. 1973. "Jewishness, Blackishness, and the Nature-Nurture Controversy." *American Psychologist* 28: 962–71.

Schubert, J. B.; S. Bradley-Johnson; and J. Nuttal. 1980. "Mother-Infant Communication and Maternal Employment." *Child Development* 51: 246–49.

Seidenberg, Robert. 1973. *Corporate Wives—Corporate Casualties?* New York: AMACOM.

Sennett, R., and J. Cobb. 1972. *The Hidden Injuries of Class*. New York: Knopf.

Smokler, C. S. 1975. "Self-Esteem in Pre-Adolescent and Adolescent Females." Ph.D. dissertation, University of Michigan, 1975. University Microfilms, no. TS2 75-00, 813.

Staines, G. L., and J. H. Pleck. 1983. *The Impact of Work Schedules On the Family*. Ann Arbor: Institute For Social Research.

Steinmetz, S. K. 1974. "Occupational Environment in Relation to Physical Punishment and Dogmatism." In S. K. Steinmetz and M. A. Strauss (eds.), *Violence in the Family*. New York: Dodd, Mead.

Stolz, L. M. 1960. "Effects of Maternal Employment on Children: Evidence from Research." *Child Development* 31: 749–83.

Symonds, M. 1970. "Emotional Hazards of Police Work." *American Journal of Psychoanalysis* 2: 155–60.

Tiller, P. O. 1958. "Father Absence and Personality Development in Children of Sailor Families." Nordick Psykologi's Monograph series, no. 9. Oslo: Bokhjrnet.

U.S. Department of Labor, Bureau of Labor Statistics. 1981. *Marital and Family*

Characteristics of Labor Force. Special Labor Force Report, no. 237, pp. 3–79. Washington, D.C.: Department of Labor.

University of Michigan, Office of Research Administration. 1973. "Household Work, 1926–1965." *Research News* 22, no. 12: 6–7.

Veroff, J.; E. Douvan; and R. Kulka. 1981. *The Inner American: A Self-Portrait from 1957 to 1976.* New York: Basic Books.

Vogel, S. R.; I. K. Broverman; D. M. Broverman; F. Clarkson; and P. Rosenkrantz. 1970. "Maternal Employment and Perception of Sex Roles Among College Students." *Developmental Psychology* 3: 384–91.

Walker, K. E. 1969. "Homemaking Still Takes Time." *Journal of Home Economics* 61: 621–24.

Walker, Kathryn, and Margaret Woods. 1976. *Time Use: A Measure of Household Production of Family Goods and Services.* Washington, D.C.: American Home Economics Association.

Walsh, M. R. 1977. *Doctors Wanted: No Women Need Apply.* New Haven: Yale University Press.

Walshok, M. L. 1978. "Occupational Values and Family Roles: A Descriptive Study of Women Working in Blue-Collar and Service Occupations." *Urban and Social Change Review* 11: 12–20.

Whyte, William H. 1956. *The Organization Man.* New York: Doubleday.

Wilensky, H. L. 1961. "The Uneven Distribution of Leisure: The Impact of Economic Growth on 'free time.' " *Social Problems* 9: 107–45.

Willmott, Peter. 1971. "Family, Work, and Leisure Conflicts Among Male Employees: Some Preliminary Findings." *Human Relations* 24: 575–84.

Woods, M. B. 1972. "The Supervised Child of the Working Mother." *Developmental Psychology* 6: 14–25.

Yarrow, M. R., P. S. Scott, L. M. DeLeeuw, and C. S. Heinig. 1962. "Childrearing in Families of Working and Non-working Mothers." *Sociometry* 25: 122–40.

19

Children's Employment
and Families

ELLEN GREENBERGER

An enormous literature documents the rising labor-force participation of married women—especially mothers of minor children—over the last two decades and the consequences of their employment for them and their families (e.g., Ferber and Birnbaum 1982; Johnson and Waldman 1981; Kamerman and Hayes 1982; Levitan and Belous 1981). During this same period, however, comparatively little attention has focused on the rising employment rates among another group of family members: high-school-age children. Because research documents the substantial impact of adults' employment on their mental health and their families' social and economic well-being, it is important to determine whether the work of adolescents is similarly consequential. In the following brief analysis, I present an historical overview of the functions of children's work and describe what is known about the effects of adolescents' employment on their relations with family members.

An Historical Overview of Children's Work

Viewed from the perspective of our own society, at least three major periods distinguish the history of children's work: a preindustrial era when children's work benefited the family unit; an intermediate phase when children's paid labor was actively discouraged; and the current period, when older children again are employed, but with consequences accruing more to themselves as individuals than to the family unit.

THE PREINDUSTRIAL ERA

In the longest and historically most distant period, the preindustrial era, children's work figured prominently in the economy of both family and community. At this time, when the family was the productive unit of society, children's unpaid work, such as tending animals and harvesting crops, directly affected their families' economic output. Children also performed unpaid work that affected household output indirectly. Older children in the family took care of their younger siblings, thus enabling parents to concentrate their efforts on more economically productive work. As well, families benefited directly from the additional income brought in by older children who went to work outside the home. In short, all family members worked to the degree that they were able, and children's work contributed to the cohesion and economic well-being of the family unit. It is worth underscoring the fact that the contribution of children's work to the family was sanctioned by English common law: in return for the duty of support, the father was entitled to both the services and the earnings of his minor children. The rights of the father to children's labor were eventually expanded to the mother (Vernier 1936).

Although the advent of the industrial revolution subsequently removed most work for the home, children's work in the early stages of industrialization remained important to the family economy. Not only their mothers and fathers, but poor children themselves, went to work in the factories. In fact, the early demand for children's cheap labor gave them a competitive advantage that adversely affected the employment opportunities of adult males. The result was that children's earnings, in affected families, became essential to their families' survival.

THE DEMISE OF CHILD LABOR

The conditions of work in turn-of-the-century America are well known. Together, humanitarians (chiefly women) who fought to remove children from the harsh conditions that prevailed in the workplace, and labor organizers (mainly men), who sought to protect adults' jobs from the inroads of cheap labor, won the legal victories that removed children from the work force.[1] These developments, alongside the changing nature of the workplace and the concomitant enactment of compulsory education laws, transformed the workplace, so that children's labor-force participation steadily declined between 1900 and 1950.[2]

THE RISE OF A SERVICE ECONOMY AND TEENAGE EMPLOYMENT

Although we cannot explore in detail all of the factors that have contributed to a renewed demand, since the close of World War II, for older children's labor-force participation, we can highlight significant features of this growing trend. These features include both economic and social changes. The most important economic change entailed the celebrated shift from an industrial economy that manufactured products to our present economy, which delivers a wide variety of personal and business services (Ginzberg 1977). One feature of a service economy is the proliferation of part-time jobs, many of which require little skill, necessitate work at "off" hours (evenings and weekends); and carry low wages.[3] These jobs, "bad" for adults, are in some ways well suited to teenagers, who have not developed a high level of job skills; whose regular work hours are committed to school-going; and whose wage requirements are lower than those of self-supporting adults. In terms of social changes, increased consumerism among teenagers and their parents (Levitan and Belous 1981; Yovovich 1982) and a less protectionist orientation toward children (Winn 1984) seem to have encouraged the return of youngsters to the workforce.[4]

This brief historical overview has sketched important changes in the nature of children's work and the places where it is performed. We have yet to mention, however, a major change that has occurred in the meaning of children's work for their families. Today the family's subsistence needs no longer consume most teenagers' earnings, nor is most youngsters' chief motivation for work the family's financial need. In fact, the benefits of teenagers' employment redound mainly to themselves: they spend their earnings to underwrite a level of personal consumption that their family cannot, or will not, provide.

Two characteristics of teenage workers, their demographic base and the target of their earnings, explain much of the impetus behind the labor-force presence of teenagers. Demographically, it is a white, middle-class, suburban youngster, rather than a black, Hispanic, or poor urban youth, who is most likely to work during the high school years (Lewin-Epstein 1981). And his or her earnings are most likely to be put toward the acquisition of discretionary items, not necessities: that is, cars, stereos, "extra" clothing, concert tickets, and drugs (Johnston et al. 1982). Consistent with this picture, which emerges from ongoing national surveys, Bachman observes that teenage employment has produced the phenomenon of "premature affluence" (see Morgan 1981).

In sum, we can characterize the shift over the three periods we have distinguished as a transformation of children's work from activities performed for the benefit of others to those performed largely for themselves.

Adolescent Work: Repercussions on Family Relations

Deeply rooted religious and philosophical traditions regarding the presumed character-building effects of work underlie our cultural conviction that work is good for children. Viewed as unproblematic, youngster's work has received little attention from researchers. Yet the few empirical studies that have examined correlates or consequences of adolescents' work have identified possible costs, as well as benefits, to young people and their families. [5]

In a previous examination of teenagers' psychosocial development, I stressed the importance of autonomy and social integration as standards of healthy behavior against which to measure the effects of teenage employment (Greenberger 1984). More research has addressed the implications of adolescent work for the development of independence than for the development of feelings of community with others, as this brief review will indicate.

WORKING AND ADOLESCENT DEVELOPMENT

Greenberger and Steinberg (1986) have examined the relations between working and several attributes that might facilitate the development of autonomy from the family of origin. These attributes include self-reliance, good work habits, knowledge of business and money matters, and financial self-sufficiency. The subjects for these studies were 212 youngsters who were currently holding their first part-time job and 319 students who had never worked. All attended one of four high schools in Orange County, California. They came from families with diverse socioeconomic backgrounds (Greenberger and Steinberg, 1986).

Longitudinal data from this project revealed an interesting sex difference on a self-report measure of self-reliance (see also Steinberg, et al. 1982). The measure, which is a subscale of the Psychosocial Maturity Inventory, taps willingness to take the initiative, feelings of personal control, and freedom from excessive need for social validation (Greenberger and Bond 1976; Greenberger et al. 1975). Among girls, but not boys, self-reliance increased with work experience. Girls who had more extensive labor-force experience, moreover, showed greater gains than others, while effects for boys ran in the opposite direction. Since there were no reported differences between boys and girls in *opportunities* to exercise autonomy on the job, the effort to explain this finding focused on differences in the *meaning* of work to the two sexes. We argued that because employment is less expected of girls than boys, the former may be more likely to view their work as an expression of independence and, consequently, to draw from their experiences on the job affirmation of their ability to function on their own (cf. Bronfenbrenner 1961; Elder 1974).

Evidence concerning the impact of employment on work habits is somewhat mixed. On the one hand, youngsters who work—and especially those who have worked for a longer time—show a slight but significant gain on a measure of work orientation. This self-report measure (also from the Psychosocial Maturity Inventory) assesses the disposition to work persistently and to obtain satisfaction from completing tasks competently. On the other hand, interviews with 100 working youths raise some doubts about the translation of this disposition into performance. Over half of the interview sample admitted to ''goofing off'' and neglecting duties, and only a handful spontaneously described incidents of performance beyond the call of duty (Greenberger and Steinberg 1981).

Results also are mixed for working youngsters' presumed knowledge of economic and business matters. Working adolescents did score higher than their nonworking peers in a cross-sectional analysis of workers and nonworkers (Steinberg, Greenberger, Garduque, and McAuliffe 1982). (The research instrument was a timed test of practical knowledge that included consumer arithmetic problems and the definition of terms such as ''overhead,'' ''gross income,'' and ''interest.'' Social class and grade-point average were controlled in the analyses.) Longitudinal analysis of the same measure of practical knowledge, however, raised questions about whether the observed difference between workers and nonworkers is due to factors related to initial selection for work, or to the actual experience of working itself (Steinberg, Greenberger, Garduque, Ruggiero, and Vaux 1982).

At least two other outcomes of work experience conceivably might contribute to working youngsters' long-range autonomy. One has to do with the skills acquired in the work setting, which might be transferrable to subsequent, adult jobs and thus enhance young people's prospects for self-sufficiency. The other has to do with the ways in which earnings from work might lead to lessened dependence on the family of origin. Research from several sources is relevant to these issues.

For most youngsters, it is probably the case that specific job skills, useful in later-life jobs, are not acquired during their school-year, part-time employment. Adolescents' jobs typically require only rudimentary skills and involve little training. Half the teenage workers in the Greenberger and Steinberg study judged that individuals with less than a grade-school education could perform their job satisfactorily (Greenberg, Steinberg, and Ruggiero 1982). Nonetheless, there is compelling evidence that youngsters who have worked during high school earn higher hourly wages, and experience fewer weeks of unemployment, in the first several years after school completion (Freeman and Wise 1982). Presumably, general work experience, if not the particular skills acquired, pays off. The unanswered question is whether this early labor-market advantage persists. Tradeoffs between intensive work experience early in life and investment in education may undermine the positive effects of working on young people's long-run prospects for autonomy (Mortimer and Finch 1986).

The fact that teenagers who work earn significant sums of money creates substantial opportunities for exercising autonomy in the realm of money management. In 1981, for example, the average working sophomore earned $143 per month; the average senior, $273 (based on the figures from Lewin-Epstein 1981). Nationwide, 56 percent of high school seniors with jobs spent between half and all of their earnings on what they described as their "own needs and activities" (Johnston et al. 1982). Compared to nonworkers, adolescents who work report less parental control over how they deploy their money. Parents seem to view the money children earn as their own to do with as they choose—more so than money that is not earned. As well, youngsters who work pay for more of their own expenses than nonworkers (Greenberger et al. 1980). This shift in financial responsibility amounts to an indirect income transfer between adolescents and their parents and thus reduces youngsters' financial dependence on their families. The size of this income transfer should not be overestimated, however. Many of the items teenagers buy with their earnings are things that their parents would not have purchased for them.

There is another way in which adolescents' earnings conceivably could enhance their prospects for autonomy. Youngsters who work might accumulate savings that are used to offset the costs of establishing an independent residence or obtaining postsecondary education in the ensuing years. But data about the uses to which adolescents put their earnings do not lend much support to this possibility. Over 80 percent of high school seniors in a national sample said that they saved "none" or "only a little" of their earnings for long-range purposes (Johnston et al. 1982). In short, adolescent workers make some short-term gains in economic independence from the family, but do not make a substantial investment in reducing their potential long-term financial dependence on others.

One other aspect of autonomy merits attention here. White and Brinkerhoff (Chapter 9) have documented the fact that work assignments in the home are strongly sex-typed. This is also true of adolescents' first formal jobs. Current and retrospective data from more than three thousand tenth and eleventh graders indicate not only that boys and girls work in different types of jobs—the result, most likely, of both differential selection to work and differential opportunity—but that boys earn higher hourly wages and work more hours per week (Greenberger and Steinberg 1983). These findings mirror well-known sex differences in adults' labor-force activity. An interesting consequence of sex differences in wages and hours of employment is that teenage girls who work achieve less economic power than boys. This fact may help support traditional dominance relations between the sexes during adolescence and reinforce expectations for future family roles in which men's work is more valuable than women's.

WORKING AND FAMILY RELATIONS

We have just speculated that several features of teenagers' employment may aid and abet socialization for traditional family roles in the future. Very little information exists, however, about actual responses to teenagers' employment in the family of origin. Greenberger and Steinberg's study suggests that the reaction is favorable: by far the majority of parents approve of their youngsters' working (Greenberger and Steinberg, 1986).

Because a teenager's success in getting and keeping a job may be viewed as evidence of growing maturity, parents might be expected to decrease surveillance of working children. Apparently, however, parents do not make this adjustment. Working adolescents report as many rules as nonworkers in such areas as curfews, peer associations, and homework obligations. They also do not play a larger role in decision making that affects the family as a group (Greenberger et al. 1980).

Several findings do point to subtle changes in family relations. The most difficult finding to interpret concerns the effect of teenagers' employment on emotional ties to their parents. Boys who work intensively show increased feelings of closeness to their parents, whereas comparable girls show a decline in closeness (Steinberg, Greenberger, Garduque, Ruggiero, and Vaux 1982). A possible interpretation of this sex difference rests on the degree of boys' and girls' attachment to parents prior to employment. Since girls generally report much greater closeness and self-disclosure to parents (especially mothers) than same-age boys (Douvan and Adelson 1966; Kandel and Lesser 1972), the apparent reduction in intimacy may not indicate a worsening of relations with parents. Rather, for girls reduced closeness may mean an age-appropriate lessening of their earlier dependence. Such a view is consistent with the increased self-reliance reported above for girls who spend considerable time at work. On the other hand, boys' increased closeness to parents as a result of work experience may reflect an age-appropriate recognition of, and empathy for, parents who themselves play the role of worker. In view of the fact that the worker role is a more central component of the male sex role, working may draw boys selectively closer to their fathers.

It is also clear that working reduces dinnertime contact between adolescents and their families, largely as a result of adolescents' work schedules. This is not a trivial issue: dinnertime is one of the few times of day that many families can count on seeing and talking to one another. And although teenagers who work do not, as a group, report lower involvement in household chores, an appreciable number do: one in three working youngsters reports doing ''a little less'' around the house than before; another 14 percent, ''a lot less'' (Greenberger and Steinberg 1986). An unanswered question is whether the departure of adolescents for paying jobs in the formal labor force has left younger siblings at home without adequate supervision and care.

Summary and Conclusions

Although researchers have shown increased interest over the last few years in the consequences of adolescents' labor-force participation, few studies have paid close attention to the effects of teenagers' work on family functioning. The research reviewed here provides only a first step in this direction.

Earlier, I noted that two criteria of healthy development during adolescence are improvements in the capacity for autonomy and for socially integrative, or socially responsible, behavior. That is, socialization should prepare young people to function competently on their own and to contribute to the well-being of others. On balance, the family impacts of adolescent work seem to be more noticeable in the first domain than the second.

Several lines of evidence suggest that working increases youngsters' autonomy in certain respects. On the one hand, both boys and girls who work seem to develop more effective work habits—a potential resource for achieving independence of the family of origin. Girls also become more self-reliant and less emotionally close to their parents. For boys, on the other hand, the opposite effects seem to occur: there is some evidence that working may lead to lower self-reliance; and working increases boys' closeness to their parents. Insofar as girls typically have greater problems with individuation, and boys with "connecting" emotionally to others (Douvan and Adelson 1966), these effects of employment may be constructive for both sexes. Perhaps the most obvious increase in autonomy, however, occurs in the realm of money. Youngsters who work have more freedom to do as they wish with money than youngsters who do not work. As well, working youths pay for more of their own expenses. Nonetheless, this work-related increase in autonomy is not so great as it might be. Youngsters who work save only a small fraction of their earnings to defray the potential costs of the transition to adulthood and thus do not seem likely to reduce their long-term dependence on their parents.

Children's work in the past constituted early training in social responsibility: their labor contributed to the economic well-being of the family. Today's working teenagers, in contrast, typically do not work to help their families but, instead, to achieve a higher standard of living *for themselves*. It is interesting to ponder this and related facts in light of the common-law entitlement of parents to the earnings and services of their minor children. Not only do children now keep their earnings, but many reduce their services to the family as well. One of the services that families may be forgoing is the time-honored responsibility of older children for the care of their younger siblings. At a time when so many mothers, as well as fathers, work outside the home, this may be an unaccounted social cost of adolescents' labor-force participation.

Notes

1. The initial site of legislative reform was the states. By 1860 eight states had laws that restricted the number of hours per day that children could work. By 1930 most states had set minimum age requirements for employment and had reduced permissible working hours to eight per day. Federal legislation, first attempted in 1916 but declared unconstitutional, came to fruition in 1938, when Congress enacted the Fair Labor Standards Act (Mnookin 1978).

2. For example, 60.1 percent of all white males between fourteen and nineteen were employed, or had tried unsuccessfully to find employment, in 1900, in comparison with 39.5 percent of similar youngsters fifty years later. Figures for other population groups showed the same trend (Lewin-Epstein 1981).

3. Among the most common jobs are counter worker (food service), boxboy/bagger, sales clerk, busboy, cashier, assembler, waitress, cleaner (janitor), vehicle washer, typist, service station attendant.

4. On the basis of a national survey of high school youths, Lewin-Epstein (1981) estimates that 63 percent of high school seniors and 42 percent of sophomores are working at any given time during the school year. Census data indicate that between 1947 and 1980, the labor-force participation of school-going sixteen- and seventeen-year-olds increased by 65 percent among boys; by 240 percent among girls. The proportion of fourteen- and fifteen-year-old students in the labor force has remained fairly stable, with some increase among girls but not boys. Winn (1984) argues that children's experiences today threaten the "loss of childhood." The notion that children should be allowed to savor a protected period of life seems to be giving way to acceptance of early exposure to the "realities" of life. Early sexual experimentation and substance use—and, perhaps, early commitment to working—seem to fulfill this prophecy.

5. For a more comprehensive review of the effects of teenage employment than fits our purposes here, see Greenberger and Steinberg (1986).

References

Bronfenbrenner, Urie. 1961. "Some Familial Antecedents of Responsibility and Leadership in Adolescents." In Lewis Petrullo and Bernard Bass (eds.), *Leadership and Interpersonal Behavior*. New York: Holt, Rinehart & Winston.

Douvan, Elizabeth, and Joseph Adelson. 1966. *The Adolescent Experience*. New York: Wiley.

Elder, Glen H., Jr. 1974. *Children of the Great Depression: Social Change in Life Experience*. Chicago: University of Chicago Press.

Ferber, Marianne, and Bonnie Birnbaum. 1982. "The Impact of Mother's Work on the Family as an Economic System." In Sheila Kamerman and Cheryl D. Hayes (eds.), *Families That Work: Children in a Changing World*. Washington, D. C.: National Academy Press.

Freeman, Richard, and David Wise. 1982. *The Youth Labor Market Problem: Its Nature, Causes and Consequences*. Chicago: University of Chicago Press.

Ginzberg, Eli. 1977. The Job Problem. *Scientific American* 237: 43–51.

Greenberger, Ellen. 1984. "Children, Families, and Work." In N. D. Reppucci, L. A. Weithorn, E. P. Mulvey, and J. Monahan (eds.), *Mental Health, Law and Children*. Beverly Hills, Calif.: Sage.

Greenberger, Ellen, and Lloyd Bond. 1976. "User's Manual for the Psychosocial Maturity Inventory." Mimeographed. University of California, Irvine.

Greenberger, Ellen; Ruthellen Josselson; Claramae Knerr; and Bruce Knerr. 1975. The Measurement and Structure of Psychosocial Maturity." *Journal of Youth and Adolescence* 4: 127–43.

Greenberger, Ellen, and Lawrence Steinberg. 1981. "The Workplace as a Context for the Socialization of Youth." *Journal of Youth and Adolescence* 10: 185–210.

———. 1983. "Sex Differences in Early Labor Force Experience: Harbinger of Things to Come." *Social Forces* 62: 467–86.

———. 1986. *When Teenagers Work: The Psychological and Emotional Costs of Adolescent Employment*. New York: Basic Books.

Greenberger, Ellen; Lawrence Steinberg; and Mary Ruggiero. 1982. "A Job Is a Job Is a Job . . . or Is It? Behavioral Observations in the Adolescent Workplace." *Work and Occupations* 9:79–96.

Greenberger, Ellen; Lawrence Steinberg; Allan Vaux; and Sharon McAuliffe. 1980. "Adolescents Who Work: Effects of Part-Time Employment on Family and Peer Relations." *Journal of Youth and Adolescence* 9: 189–202.

Johnson, B. M., and Elizabeth Waldman. 1981. "Marital and Family Patterns of the Labor Force." *Monthly Labor Review* 194, no 10: 36–38.

Johnston, Lloyd; Jerold Bachman; and Patrick O'Malley. 1982. *Monitoring the Future: Questionnaire Responses from the Nation's High School Seniors, 1981*. Ann Arbor, Mich.: Institute for Social Research.

Kamerman, Sheila B., and Cheryl D. Hayes (eds.) 1982. *Families That Work: Children in a Changing World*. Washington, D. C.: National Academy Press.

Kandel, Denise B., and Gerald S. Lesser. 1972. *Youth in Two Worlds*. San Francisco: Jossey-Bass.

Levitan, Sar, and Richard Belous. 1981. "Working Wives and Mothers: What Happens to Family Life?" *Monthly Labor Review* 104, no. 9:26–30.

Lewin Epstein, Noah. 1981. *Youth Employment During High School*. Washington, D.C.: National Center for Education Statistics.

Mnookin, Robert. 1978. *Child, Family and State: Cases and Materials on Children and the Law*. Boston: Little, Brown.

Morgan, Dan. 1981. "Coming of Age in the '80's, Part II—Security Versus Fulfillment: Caught in Conflicting Values." *Washington Post*, December 28.

Mortimer, Jeylan, and Michael D. Finch. 1986. The Effects of Part-Time Work on Adolescent Self-Concept and Achievement." In Kathryn Borman and Jane Reisman (eds.), *Becoming a Worker*. Norwood, N.J.: Ablex.

Steinberg, Lawrence; Ellen Greenberger; Laurie Garduque; and Sharon McAuliffe. 1982. "High School Students in the Labor Force: Some Costs and Benefits to

Schooling and Learning.'' *Educational Evaluation and Policy Analysis* 4: 363–72.

Steinberg, Lawrence; Ellen Greenberger; Laurie Garduque; Mary Ruggiero; and Allan Vaux. 1982. ''Effects of Early Work Experience on Adolescent Development.'' *Developmental Psychology* 18: 385–95.

Vernier, C. G. 1936. *American Family Laws*. Stanford, Calif.: Stanford University Press. (Reprinted by Greenwood Press, Westport, Conn., 1971.)

Winn, Marie. 1984. *Children Without Childhood*. New York: Penguin.

Yovovich, B. C. 1982. ''A Game of Hide-and-Seek.'' *Advertising Age,* August 2, pp. 17ff.

EMPLOYMENT AND CHANGING FAMILY FORMS

20

Three Careers: His, Hers, and Theirs

ROSANNA HERTZ

The dual-career marriage challenges a number of principles of traditional marriage. Employment and its rewards still shape a couple's life chances; but instead of a single career or job defining marital roles, there are two careers, qualifying each spouse as a "breadwinner." Many dual-career couples live better than their more traditional counterparts, but ambiguity and confusion surround the marriage of two careers. No one partner can claim authority in the household based on "bringing home the bacon." Questions as to whose career and time commitments should take precedence are befuddled by similar (and competing) employer demands. Arriving at a division of labor for household tasks is complicated by both spouses' daytime absence from the home. Traditional corporate careers required that the husband (as employee) and the wife (as his aide) join forces in what Papanek (1975) referred to as the "two-person career." (See Chapter 17 in this volume.) Dual-career marriages have, in this sense, two husbands and no wife.

Ambiguity and confusion about social roles are common among people experiencing social change. New expectations about behavior are only dimly perceived as new practices emerge. Marital roles are no exception. What makes the experience of the couples in this study[1] important is that their efforts to define a new set of roles did not precede the marriage but, rather, occurred only after the practical aspects of change began to emerge. Not unlike a picture slowly brought into focus, the practical implications of change in their situations took time to appear as something comprehensible: a marriage, but a relationship apart from, yet dependent on, their individual careers.

The dual-career marriage consolidates three careers: his, her, and theirs. The marriage, the "third career," bears remarkable similarities to the career one makes in work, especially in a new industry. That is, everyone knows what the title "manager" is, but few have a clear sense when they embark on

For a lengthier discussion of dual-career couples and methods used in this study, see Rosanna Hertz, *More Equal than Others: Women and Men in Dual-Career Marriages* (Berkeley and Los Angeles: University of California Press, 1986).

a career just where they will end up—though, of course, everyone has plans. Career marriages are similar, but in addition to wanting to be a "husband" or "wife," each has to comprehend and work at that role as it emerges over time.

Without many models to use as benchmarks, couples tend to measure themselves against the roles of the traditional husband and wife, a model that provides insufficient and contradictory advice. The third career (marriage) is "made," not imitated or automatic, and therefore involves confusion and uncertainty. Thus, their unease in dealing with an ambiguous situation leads to frustration in trying to make a new reality fit an old model. Far from being the avant-garde of a social movement with an articulate vision of something they wanted to create, one is struck by their lack of ideological prescriptions about equality of marital roles. Instead, they simply practice it. Though rough edges remain to be smoothed, marital roles have been shaped in the direction of the objectives espoused by many feminist theorists, but largely without a prior indoctrination of either spouse in the ideology of equality. In this paper, I will discuss the process through which dual-career couples "make" their third career.

Career Beginnings: His Career

The men in this study grew up in the 1940s and early 1950s. For them working was expected, not a matter of choice. Their lives reflect the prototypical middle-class male career pattern: college, graduate training, and then a series of jobs. Their lives followed a neat, orderly sequence as they moved directly from one stage to the next. Fifty-two percent of the men went directly from college to graduate school. Another 24 percent went to the military after college graduation before proceeding to graduate school. Many men prepared for careers through their choice of undergraduate majors. Unlike women, whose undergraduate majors are a bit more evenly distributed, almost two-thirds of the men majored in social science (specifically economics), and only a quarter majored in the humanities (specifically history).

Forty-three percent of the men married when they graduated from college; in the majority of these cases, wives supported husbands while the latter earned advanced degrees. However, 48 percent of the men married after completing graduate education, when their wives typically were just completing college. In the former group, husbands and wives went through graduate school in turn-taking fashion and in the latter group it was the husbands who supported their wives through advanced training. Table 20-1 details the positions the men occupy.

Table 20-1   Organizational Positions and Activities for Dual-Career Husbands

Position/Title	Number	Associated Activities
Vice-president	5	Personnel
		Commercial lending
		Marketing and communications
Manager	8	Financial
		Sales
		Loans
		Advertising
		Marketing
Professional	5	Corporate lawyer
		Doctor—health administration and health policy
Self-employed	3	Law
		Consulting
Total	21	

The early part of men's careers did not involve a change in attitude about their role as breadwinners. Change took place more subtly as a result of their wives' entry into the labor market. The issue of how men's careers developed in tandem with their wives' and how that altered the social roles of husband and wife will be discussed in a later section.

Career Beginnings: Her Career

''Caught in the middle''—between an old dream and a new reality—best captures the story of the lives of these women. The last issue to emerge out of the turbulent sixties was the question of women's rights. Most of these women graduated from college before 1972, the year in which the Senate passed the Equal Rights Amendment; few really had plans or thoughts about careers. Rather, they dreamt of traditional roles as wives and mothers. Work was a waystation to fulfilling that dream. These women were neither visionaries, activists in the women's movement, nor adherents to its ideology even when it became visible. Instead, they were the beneficiaries of labor-market openings. They were in the right place at the right time. For many, this meant that early job experiences after college provided them with sufficient training to move into managerial positions. For others, employment backgrounds allowed them to join the first large group of women to enter advanced degree programs, and obtain credentials that were later translated into corporate careers.

Although both groups of women drifted into the work force, at some point something changed that placed them in career tracks instead of more peripheral occupations. At the time these interviews were conducted, these wives, as well as their husbands, occupied a fairly varied array of management or management-level positions (Table 20-2). Each foresees a reasonable probability of promotion. None sees herself locked into the position that she presently occupies. However, some do foresee corporate moves (within Chicago) as critical for their career advancement. Their dreams of career success today match those of their husbands and their male colleagues.

How is it that these women came to acquire and invest in corporate careers at variance with traditional expectations? To answer this question, it is necessary to analyze the process through which they made career investments. The decision to work was eased by the fact that most of these women had acquired college degrees in disciplines that qualified them for starting salaried positions in corporate settings (see Table 20-3). Despite the apparent applicability of many of these degrees to a white-collar job market, the majority of these women did not consciously decide to major in fields that would qualify them for salaried positions. Most thought that their degrees and college job experience would transfer into employment, but they had no initial goals for "business careers" of the sort for which they saw men being trained. One woman, typical of this group, describes her thoughts about her "career start":

Table 20-2 Organizational Positions and Activities for Dual-Career Wives

Position/Title	Number	Associated Activities
Vice-president	5	International business Planning
Director	2	Public relations Personnel
Manager	9	Advertising and marketing Tax accounting Communications Special projects
Professional	3	Corporate lawyer Doctor and professor of medicine Corporate accountant
Consultant	2	Marketing Strategic planning
Total	21	

Table 20-3   Marriage and Undergraduate Majors for Women

Undergraduate Majors	Married Before Career Began	Married After Career Began	%
Business	2	2	19%
Journalism	1	2	14%
Social science	6	—	29%
Humanities	4	2	29%
Sciences	1	1	10%
Total	14	7	100%

Note: Numbers do not sum to 100% due to effect of rounding.

So I was somewhat directionless and unfocused at that point. Chicago seemed as good a place to be as any, and my boyfriend was here. In 1966 it was relatively easy for women with math and philosophy degrees to get good-paying jobs in data processing. The whole career start was accidental.

Moveover, fully two-thirds did not begin to pursue careers until some time after they were married. In order to avoid confusion over the process of career investment, I will analyze these two groups separately, drawing them together toward the end of the section to discuss general issues.

The women who married before beginning careers married either before they finished college or shortly after receiving their college degrees. They married under the middle-class "rules" of the old dream, thinking that once their grooms had completed their graduate studies, they would assume their place beside them as homemakers and wives. As one woman explained:

At that point I really didn't have any long-term career goals. My goals had stopped when I graduated from college and I hadn't really thought through what I intended to do after that . . . . Here I was with the thought that I was going to obviously get married and have children at a young age and do all those nice things that my mother did.

The initial employment histories of these women are simply not based on long-term career goals for themselves; instead, they are directly linked to husbands' future career prospects:

We both had degrees in journalism but I followed him—his career. Every six months they would send him someplace else. His first job was in Georgia, and I worked as a news editor for the Dublin Herald. . . . Six months later he got transferred to Chicago, and I followed him here and I got a job as a secretary at a TV studio, and six months later he got transferred to Philadelphia . . . and I worked as an assistant director for an advertising agency. . . . He was pursuing his career, and I was picking up whatever I could.

So, although the majority of these women were not thinking in terms of careers or career goals, they were gaining job experience and skills as they followed their husbands' leads.

Until this point they are pursuing one career—his. How is it that these women came to have careers of their own? Even though they expressed satisfaction with their work and feelings of self-confidence about their early employment histories, it is unclear that labor-force participation by itself explains a shift in thinking about careers. Similarly, even though these women recall their traditional aspirations prior to marriage, marriage itself allowed their career goals to take hold. Both employment opportunities and husbands' encouragement appear critical. However, it is difficult to assess the relative contributions of employment opportunities and the marital relationship, especially since these data was gathered in the context of reconstructing history.

Once these women began to consider themselves in a career path, they sought to acquire the additional training or certification necessary to enhance their chances of promotion. Fully 71 percent of the women earned a postgraduate degree in a career-related field. The percentage of women who earned postgraduate degrees is the same for those married before and after they began their careers.

For the one-third of the women who married in their mid- to late twenties, employment was an assumed part of their marital relationship. Although their lives did not include following a husband from one position to the next, career beginnings for half this group were incremental as well. Regardless of which route they took to their careers, women's career decisions became intertwined with their husbands'.

CHANGING GENDER ROLES: THE CHOICE TO WORK OUTSIDE THE HOME

Although employment prior to marriage or at the beginning of marriage, to help husbands financially, has always been part of the traditional female role, all the women talked about having chosen to seek a job beyond these early years. There are two dimensions to this choice: a gender role decision and an economic decision. One woman compared male and female expectations about employment:

I made a choice to work and I like it. And I do it because I like it. I mean I wasn't socialized to think I'm a bad person if I didn't work, when most men never really had that choice. They've always known they were going to work. They were going to support a family, and they never were able to make a choice. But I did. It's very important to me, or I wouldn't have made the choice.

Although this may sound like a personal and idiosyncratic choice, it is in fact a gender-role decision. Implicit in the choice to work outside the home is not only a comparison of women's and men's roles but a confrontation between traditional values for women and their new desires. The choice to work outside the home constitutes a decision *not* to pursue a traditional role as homemaker. This decision has been eased by the fact that few encountered direct opposition in their choices—for example, from a husband who insisted on his wife's occupying a traditional role.

Employment was conceived of as something they should do because "we had to have more money." Almost from the very beginning of their marriage, her earnings constituted a significant contribution to their shared lifestyle. They did not just live on his salary, banking hers. Instead, they lived on both incomes, and their lifestyles expanded accordingly—including their rent or mortgage, their bills, the places they chose to go to, and so on. They became dependent upon their dual earnings. Put differently, their joint earnings determine their standard of living while, at the same time, their standard of living determines how much money they need to earn. Both husbands and wives made comments like: "We could live on one salary. We could adjust. But we couldn't live today the way we live on two salaries."

These women cannot choose to opt out of the labor force and give up their "choice to work outside the home." Without planning to do so, they have accrued financial obligations and debts. Women, then, come to experience the same kind of career pressure as men.

At the time when many of these women took their jobs, no real decisions had to be made about *future* investments in careers. These women assumed that, in the early stages of a career, the opportunity costs were relatively low: since little investment had been made, little cost would be incurred if they left the workplace. Questions concerning her career only became salient when children became an issue. Decisions thus appeared much less significant at an earlier time. In fact, earlier behavior came to be recognized as decision making only as time passed and career investments grew to the point where couples faced fairly significant costs if she forsook her career.

Making the Marriage

It's two separate lives in some ways. It's like a dual carriageway, and we are both going down those carriageways at more or less the same speed, I would say. While those carriageways don't cross one another, if something happens on one of them, something necessarily happens on the other one.

Because *both* husbands and wives have careers, the marriage can no longer respond entirely to the demands of only one spouse (or spouse's career). Marriage can no longer serve to define a division of labor between "breadwinner'' and ''homemaker'' and, with that division of labor, a relative priority or valuation of the different activities. If two careers are to be nourished, they must also be constrained by a set of rules for how competing career demands are to be balanced *and* how the ''homemaking'' or reproductive activities of the marriage are to be organized. Among the couples I interviewed, the predominant mechanism for negotiating individual careers is based upon marriage as a third career. For these couples marriage represents *both* the social contract entered into by a man and a woman for purposes of gaining intimacy, love, children, and all the other intangibles of such a union *and* the conjoining of two careers.

This conception of a shared career infuses marriage with a different meaning than the traditional pattern. Couples do not always articulate a clear statement about the equity of careers and the equality of spouses. Yet the practice of balancing the demands of two careers produces an outcome in which, if both careers are to survive, some vision of mutual benefit must be invoked on a daily basis. This criterion serves to distribute or accomplish reproductive/homemaking tasks (both broadly and narrowly conceived) and is referred to as a guide when either spouse confronts a situation that challenges or potentially affects the other spouse's career. Marital equity is not taken for granted; it is worked at. As one typical husband put it: ''I certainly don't think this is a gloriously equal marriage marching off into the sunset. I think we struggle for equality all the time. And we remind each other when we are not getting it.''

Put differently, it is not an ideology of marital equality that determines careers; instead, it is because of the two careers that equality becomes an issue. Indeed, couples rarely spoke directly about equality. They spoke instead of trying to strike a balance between careers and family commitments by keeping each other in check, so that neither spouse could tip the scale in favor of his or her own career. Although symmetry may produce feelings of equity, attempts to maintain symmetry provide a constant source of conflict within dual-career marriages.[2] One husband explains how individual career involvement is a catalyst for assessing family involvement.

There is this constant pressure of trying to balance things, constantly reassessing how much time we spend in family and careers. [Could you give me an example?] Sure. Every day. Every week. Trying to figure out how much time to spend—whether you should be with the kids, or with Ann, or working. . . . You make definite tradeoffs. You *both* make a tradeoff. It's also hard because we both frequently talk about it. How much of a tradeoff each one of us should be making—whether we are both making the same amount or whether the other one feels that one of us is spending too much time on the job.

Although couples do not keep ledgers, most have instituted rules over job choices and moves. One couple decided to establish a rule to prevent recurrent disagreements surrounding job moves. The wife explained how this a priori rule reflected their sense of marital equity:

What we have tried to do is set the groundrules before we are faced with a specific decision. [Why?] To give it some neutrality . . . whoever did not have the offer made the basic decision to move. If he had an offer, I had first crack at rejecting the city. It's really a veto power.

Other couples had different mechanisms for achieving parity, including rules about lateral moves as well as promotions.

The marriage thus comes to operate as a constraint on the unbridled pursuit of one career to the possible disadvantage of the other. But it also operates as a buffer, cushioning the negative impact of failures or reversals in one or the other career. The unpredictability of careers and responses to them demands such an arrangement, and, paradoxically, it forges an emphasis on equity and symmetry for each career. Were it not for the fact that marriage is so elevated in importance that it can constrain as well as buffer, then one might refer to the relationship merely as a convenience. But the marital tie operates as a legitimate constraint on careers, and it stimulates a review of the gender roles associated with marriage. Again, as is the case with marital roles, it is the practice of combining two careers, not the articulation of a nonsexist ideology, that shapes decisions and informs change.

A STEP OUT OF TRADITIONAL GENDER ROLES

I was a product of a family where the mother didn't work ever and whose job, in her mind, and her responsibility, in that marriage, was the maintenance of the household, the parenting function, cooking meals and keeping things organized. So that when my Dad got home he didn't have to put up with anything. . . . Joan [his wife] says, "I'm not going to scurry around here at 10 to 6 and clean up the house so it looks neat and clean when you get home, so you can think that's the way it's been all day. You can help clean it up." But that was not the way my mother was. I guess I wouldn't enjoy it as much if someone with a broom was dusting a path in front of me as I walked.

First-hand knowledge about the organization of family life comes from what we observed our parents doing. Even if couples had friends in dual-career marriages, they were more likely to compare themselves with their parents, not friends. Like the husband quoted, the majority of men and women in this study came from families that had clearly defined roles and expectations for husbands and wives. Gender roles continue to play a part in determining the form of marital relations, and it takes a constant struggle not to fall back on the old ways of marriage—the old rules and roles—that these individuals witnessed as children in their parents' homes.

Yet things have changed for these couples. Again, there was no ideological underpinning to their marriages that caused the roles of husband and wife to be dramatically altered. The break with their traditional upbringing is simple to explain: as women's careers became as demanding as their husbands', there was no time for a wife to be a "wife." The initial change, then, was in the wife's role. Thus, as wives and husbands became "duplicates" of one another (at least as workers outside the home), her "new" role altered his. The invisible work of the home is now in plain view, and although couples do hire household labor (cf. Hertz 1986), many chores remain to be done around the home. One husband explains how this change came about for him and his wife: "We don't consciously say that we're going to share, but it just turns out with both people working you can't have one do everything. If one of us were relying on the other to fix meals, we'd both starve."

Her career alters not only the meaning of wife but, in the process, his role as husband. This role expansion is fundamentally different for men and women: she has moved outward, discovering the world of making a living, and he has moved inward, discovering the intricacies of running a home. However, lingering ambivalences are connected with "giving up" clearly defined husband-wife patterns. These stem from the couple's failure to fulfill what are conceived of as traditional gender roles. For example, women worry about emasculating their husbands by asking them to do more around the house, even when they employ full-time housekeepers. As a result, they retain some aspect of household work as their exclusive turf. One woman reserves one chore for herself, despite her husband's insistence: "I don't like the way he looks doing the laundry. Well, to me it's something that women do. It represents a nurturing activity to me—something very feminine. Maybe it's my way of showing him I still have that." This was typical: remnants of a "traditional" division of labor was defended by the wives as much as, or more than, the husbands.

It is in the emotional arena that men feel most slighted. The attention wives once showered on their husbands is reduced because they no longer have the time, or energy, or perhaps even the need to do so. Further, although men are involved in the domestic arena, their feelings are not necessarily aligned with their actions. As one man put it:

You know, I don't consider myself the ultimate liberated man. In terms of the pendulum swing, I'm pretty far in that direction [left]. But, you know, when she's had to work on Saturdays or Sundays to finish a big project, I take care of the kids, and I'm not overly thrilled about it. But I do it.

CAREER DEVELOPMENT AND CHOICE

Even if the "steps" out of traditional gender roles are somewhat tentative and cause some discomfort, the conjoining of two careers does open some real possibilities for change in careers and job relationships. In most cases, the development of careers is "alternating" in character. His career comes first and makes possible hers or investments leading to hers. Her career makes possible shifts in his career. Perhaps more important than the alternation of investments is the fact that the large and stable portion of family income coming from the wife's career makes possible career shifts for him. Because the dual-career marriage frees men from sole economic responsibility, the men can be less obsessed by work, less aggressive, and even less motivated because the weight of this responsibility is shared. One man explains how this has made a difference in his life:

I'm not a workaholic. I'm pretty comfortable at what I'm doing. I probably could make more money if I was interested in working a lot harder, but I would have to sacrifice a lot of things for that—like time with my family, personal time, a lot of things. I'm just not willing to do that, and in part I don't have to do that because my wife works.

A woman describes the freedom she feels her career gives her husband:

The woman who works and makes as much as the man gives the man flexibility and freedom in his job. He doesn't have to worry incessantly: "What if something happens—what if I die or what if I get fired or what if I hate this career and I'd rather refinish furniture and start my own business." He has more flexibility because of the economic freedom.

Men did not just fantasize about a career change: several enacted one; for others a career shift was in the talking stages. In all cases the wives encouraged such moves. In this regard the career marriage paves the way for career choice. One man, after having a disagreement with the president of his company, made good on his intention to "strike out on his own" in the consulting field. He explains how this was possible:

We [he and his partner] went into business with virtually no clients. The fact that Susan was working and making a good income was significant. The decision would have been different if that had not been the case. We couldn't have afforded it. She and I talked about my leaving the company, and she agreed with me.

But the business was not on a solid footing, and this started to affect their marriage:

It's good we started to make money when we did. It took a bit longer than we expected. We'd both reached a point where, if we hadn't started being more successful within a year, I probably would have gone back into the job market. If I hadn't, she would have been pretty unhappy about it. She was feeling the pressure of carrying the financial responsibility and feeling the sacrifice that we were making collectively was beginning to add up.

Shared economic responsibility is these couples' goal, and it is only for brief periods that either spouse is willing to assume full economic responsibility.

In short, the career marriage offers husbands a freedom to explore career alternatives and career shifts much like the "choice" reserved for middle-class women in a more traditional pattern. Women in this study have not yet done the same, but that may be because their careers are newer (both in terms of their thinking of their employment as a career and in terms of the number of years they have actually spent in their chosen fields). His career change may eventually make possible alternatives in her career trajectory.

COMMUNICATION AND SUPPORT

Despite moments of doubt, ambivalence, and conflict, dual-career couples often develop a style of communication that they believe is quite different from that which characterizes traditional marriages. Husbands and wives with careers spend the bulk of their time engaged in similar activities, which, while often drawing on different kinds of expertise, share a rhythm and a structure; this situation is far different from the chasm that separates paid employment and housework. Thus, these spouses understand each other's lives and experience a high degree of empathy: "She has a sense of what I'm doing 'cause she's out there doing the same damn thing every day."

One woman explains how a shared understanding makes her relationship with her husband different from that of traditional husbands and wives:

Another aspect of my traveling and his traveling is that each of us understands what travel is to the other and is not sitting at home thinking that it's glamorous or exciting and that I'm being left out, as a lot of wives who are very resentful of their husband's traveling. We don't give each other hassles about traveling.

Most couples talk about the day's events over dinner or in bed, whether there is one earner or two. But what is striking in these cases is the similarity of the talk. She talks finance and he talks marketing. It is the content of her end of the conversation that has changed.

Although they can "support" one another through similar organizational experiences, they are not conduits linking one firm to the next. The majority talk about personal problems, office politics, and unusual events. Unless couples are in the same field, they do not talk about the details of their jobs because of the specialized knowledge needed to understand the finer points. Even when they are in the same field, they do not necessarily talk about the specifics of the work, especially when issues are confidential. The similarity of their employers' organizational structure, however, provides a basis for shared understanding and communication:

We talk a lot about common problems in respect to interrelating to the other associates. Her study teams are like my study teams. Her problems of having a junior associate who doesn't seem to be able to get his or her game together is the same as my problems, and we are a resource to each other in saying "have you tried this or that?"

These couples, then, have the quintessential modern marriage—theirs is truly a "companion" marriage.

Yet there is also the potential for competition for status between spouses. Sometimes spouses pointed out that their talk leads to disagreement about "who knows best" and who is really the expert. Couples try to resolve this problem by carving out distinct areas of expertise. One man explains how this operates in his marriage:

Our work coincidentally overlaps an awful lot. . . . But we each have a reasonable working knowledge of where the other person is stronger. There's some recognition that I know more about certain things and she knows more about other things. . . . Sometimes we interrupt each other when we are talking about things, but if it is my area that I know more about, she backs off, and vice versa.

The carving out of distinct areas of professional turf allows each partner to avoid getting too close to the world the other occupies outside the home. It is one way in which the marriage buffers the careers and keeps husbands and wives from developing the petty jealousies and conflict characteristic of co-workers in the same office.

Conclusion

At the outset, I suggested that the dual-career couple represented a situation with two husbands and no wife. However, that epigram ignores synchronous movements in other directions, including that of limiting the career aspirations and goals of husbands and wives and opening new avenues of expression for each. This combination of new limits and new openings marks a fundamental departure from traditional marital arrangements for those couples who are willing to undertake the challenge of negotiation. And the terrain of negotiation included not just two parties or areas of interest—his and hers—but a third: theirs. "Their career," the marriage, is both a set of shifting boundaries that define mutual interests in careers *and* a relationship that, more than the traditional marriage, poses a potential counterweight to the influence of employment.

The third career forces a clearer set of limits on the demands of the other two, offering the possibility that marriage and family could exert some influence on what employers can ask of their employees. But because dual-career marriages are few and far between, and careerists tend to be located in organizations that are capable of resisting collective demands from managerial workers, the influence of marriage on work organizations tends to be reduced to selective incidents of individual resistance or, more commonly, individual opportunities forgone in order to sustain the balance between his career and hers. This fact makes even more important the definition of a set of principles that can guide the pursuit of two careers and permit an acceptable union between them and family. In this sense, norms of equity and reciprocity must be made much more open to discussion and debate. Since neither husband nor wife can claim sole authority on the basis of "breadwinning," rules of conduct and a division of labor must be created to service the equally compelling demands of two careers. But, as I have attempted to show, concerns with "equity" between husbands and wives rarely precede the construction of the dual-career marriage. Rather, those concerns commonly *follow* investments in two careers.

Notes

1. Data were collected in semistructured depth interviews with twenty-one dual-career couples. Each spouse was interviewed individually about his or her attitudes regarding work and family, work histories, work relationships, family and personal finances, and household issues. Participants in this study were selected from a pool of couples identified by informants in corporations located in the Chicago metropolitan area. The median age for males was thirty-six and for females thirty-four. The median number of years married was nine; 65 percent of the couples had children. Because they were corporate dual-career couples, they were quite affluent: the median joint income was $90,250 in 1981–82. Wives' median income was $40,200; husbands' median income was $47,500.

2. Although it is difficult to directly assess equality in the household division of labor and in marital roles, these couples exhibit a greater degree of symmetry than has been reported by research on traditional families. Whether these couples are more egalitarian than those studied in previous research—which suggested that dual career marriages do not always lead to equality—is difficult to discern (see Holmstrom 1973; Garland and Poloma 1971; and Pleck 1977). The findings from prior research and this study are not strictly comparable, and definitions of equality remain to be tightened.

References

Hertz, Rosanna. 1986. *More Equal than Others: Women and Men in Dual-Career Marriages,* Berkeley and Los Angeles: University of California Press.

Holmstrom, Lynda Lytle. 1973. *The Two-Career Family.* Cambridge, Mass.: Schenkman.

Papanek, Hanna. 1975. "Men, Women, and Work: Reflections on the Two-Person Career." *American Journal of Sociology* 78:852–872.

Poloma, Margaret M., and T. Neal Garland. 1971. "The Married Professional Woman: A Study in the Tolerance of Domestication." *Journal of Marriage and the Family* 33, no. 3 (August): 531–540.

Pleck, Joseph H. 1977. "The Work-Family Role System." *Social Problems* 24: 417–427.

21

Commuter Marriage: A Microcosm of Career and Family Conflict

NAOMI GERSTEL

HARRIET GROSS

Resenting terribly the imputation that their families are not as important to them as their jobs, commuters—married couples who live apart in order to pursue their careers—are at pains to underscore the effort it takes to live this way.[1] "It's a potlatch," one husband said, attempting to convey how many resources—money, time, energy—he and his wife used to affirm to each other (and to others) just how important preservation of a marriage can be to these dual-career spouses.[2]

Yet these couples do not seem to have agonized over their decision to commute or even to have seen it as a matter of choice:

We fell into it. Not a conscious thing to do it.

No real discussion. It was the only logical thing to do.

It happened.

It was not a decision. It was not one spot where one pulls oneself together and says, "Let's face up to it."

"Deciding" to commute is, for these couples, logical, even unconscious, a necessary choice emerging out of a long series of earlier decisions, commitments, and experiences. They had pursued high levels of education consistent with their ambitions. They had tried living together and often faced the unemployment of one spouse. They slowly came to recognize that the sacrifices necessary for pursuing two careers, over which they have little control, produced dislocations in their families. As a consequence, they endure a way of life that reflects one of the most intrusive effects of the marketplace on the family. They learn to adjust, hoping that it will be temporary. And they accept its costs, trying to convince themselves that to do so is the only way to have the families and career they value equally.

Nonetheless, many of these couples have nagging doubts. They know that this is not the way they learned to do marriage. And they worry about what living this way means about them—as individuals and spouses. These doubts and worries are shaped by particular combinations of career and family stages as well as gender. Here, we will analyze family stages in concert with career stages to see which combinations are associated with couples' distress. Then we look at husband and wife separately to see the effects of gender. Having done so, we will be in a position to consider the issues commuting raises for our culture's current understanding of the connection between jobs and families.

Family and Career Stages:
Commuting Among Three Types of Couples

Career and family characteristics interact to influence couples' experience of commuting because the family characteristics that matter most—length of time married and presence of children—tend to converge with particular career stages. These family-career composites reveal three types of couples—"adjusting," "balancing," and "established"—who experience commuting quite differently.

Although all of these couples have common concerns, there are important variations in their experiences. The youngest wives and husbands (most likely to be childless) grapple more with conflicts about whose career needs should predominate—what we call career politics or career ascendancy conflict. Compared with the older couples, they expend a good deal of effort "adjusting." Although more advanced in their careers, older couples, with children at home, contend more with conflict over the increased childcare and domestic responsibilities of the spouse who stays with the children. They must strike a balance between the demands of their jobs and those of their families. Finally, the "established" couples—those whose children are no longer at home—have cemented their marital relationships and face neither the guilt nor the anxiety associated with parenting in separate homes. At the same time, they face fewer conflicts over the priority of careers because at least one spouse (typically the husband) is likely to be advanced in his career. Though not without difficulty, these couples' commuting lives are the least stressed because they are the most "established" in both their work and their family lives.

ADJUSTING COUPLES: YOUTH AND CAREER POLITICS

Among young couples, the likelihood is great that the marriage is relatively new (less than ten years old) and also that they are both in the beginning stages of their careers—a time for laying the groundwork on which later advancement and promotion depend. That is, not only are they in the process of establishing a sense of "we-ness" as a couple, but they have also not yet firmly established professional identities in which they can experience confirmed competence. At the same time that they are adjusting to marriage, then, they must simultaneously deal with the issue of career ascendancy, asking themselves whose career concerns should predominate.

In this situation, the young wife and husband struggle with conflicting emotions generated by the career opportunities commuting promises and the stress it imposes on their relationship. Husbands especially chafe at these conflicting emotions. Although intellectually they want their wives to achieve as much career success as they want for themselves, they feel simultaneously bereft (and guilty for this, too) because their wives are not beside them to affirm the masculine marital prerogative that puts a premium on their careers. Husbands both yearn for these prerogatives and castigate themselves for wanting them, because they realize that such a stance flies in the face of their other standards for marriage. As one young husband put it:

I thought her getting the degree was going to finish it. She went up there to be a potter, she got the M.A. and got seduced into high art and wanted to be a sculptor. Intellectually, I was very supportive of that; emotionally, it was something I couldn't handle easily. I feel deprived.

Young wives also wrestle with the antagonistic pulls of family and career that living apart implies. For the young wife, to have her professional identity given such attention, for it to be a factor causing the difficulty separation entails, means that she is getting a benefit denied the "traditional" wife. She is thus "special," and she knows it. Yet she sometimes feels guilty because she feels that her husband is giving up so much and that her marriage is not exactly as it "should be." While subscribing to an egalitarian model of marriage, she nonetheless finds herself heir to traditional models. Separation denies her husband the ministrations of a supportive wife that marriage and living together had promised.

In this situation, the concern husbands and wives share with other dual-career couples—"Is my marriage as important as my career?"—is not yet counteracted by a sense of the marriage as one that can, in fact, endure the tensions they see beleaguering it. Because they have not yet created a long-standing marital unit involving two professional careers, they are not at all convinced that they can. Hence the inner nagging: "What kind of emotional freak am I? Why is my career as important to me as my marriage is?" As one husband, married two years, put it:

We know that neither of us is willing to give up the course we are going on, so we can't ask the other to. Yet implicit in that is the realization that somehow you are making the statement that at least some aspect of your career is more important than being together. I get really angry and feel like, why do I even have to make the choice, one against the other. It doesn't seem right. There's obviously still a lot of pain.

BALANCING COUPLES

Clashes resulting from the antagonistic claims of marriage and career are less disturbing to older couples married for a longer time (typically ten to twenty years). Older spouses are very much aware of the importance of a backlog of experience for coping with separation:

We had enough of a base beforehand. I think if we had done this when we were married two or three years, we never would have made it. We have a lot invested emotionally in one another and I think we had a strong enough reserve and had enough smooth times before to make it.

Still another factor related to length of marriage mutes any career ascendancy conflict among these couples. Older couples often sense that the wives are correcting an imbalance in the marital relationship. Since they have been married longer, the past usually includes more time when the husband's career came first, and the wife stayed home to raise the children or worked a "job" to enable him to succeed. Now that the wife finally has decided to pursue her own career, they both look forward to the results. In fact, in these instances the husbands explicitly say: "It's her turn now!"—a sentiment the wives clearly share. Each feels a sense of accomplishment because the decision to live apart gives the wife her turn. The husbands in these marriages are most likely to say that the best thing about living apart is the opportunity it affords the wife to measure up to her potential, to "fulfill herself," "to be the person she's capable of being." These older husbands are able to respond to the difficulties of commuting as returns for the advantages they previously enjoyed. Although we shall see in the next section that most husbands dislike commuting more than most wives, the older husbands' sense of burden is tempered somewhat by the real satisfaction they get from seeing their wives develop.

Yet despite their common reservoir of experience and their sense that they are correcting a previous imbalance, these older couples are still not free of pain. Parental responsibilities trouble this group of older mates. Husbands who keep the children with them (about one-third of commuting parents) are proud of their wives' accomplishments but still resent the increased childcare and household maintenance burdens:

There are chores and running of errands and I feel the anger and the frustration of the needs and demands placed on me by the three kids. More than anything else, the need to be at a piano lesson, to go to the doctor. I'm not sure I am angry at her as much as I am just angry that the need is there, that I can't share that.

These wives, in their turn, miss their children and worry about their lessened input into their lives. Given the tenacity of the equation between parenting and mothering in our culture, these mothers find it especially painful to leave the family home and to relinquish day-to-day responsibilities: "I don't know how you balance it. I don't know how to balance two or three years of wanting to stay and watch my kids against twenty years of my life."

Whether the children stay with the father or the mother, both parents feel guilty. Away from his wife and daughter, one father spoke of parenting apart as the greatest cost of commuting:

There are times when our daughter's behavior will cause me to have some questions about whether we are doing the right thing. I'm perhaps more conscious of what I consider atypical behavior that doesn't seem to be quite the way I wanted it and, you know, that shakes me up. I think: I should be there, not here.

Parents fear that their young children will have trouble with "rejection," with "anxiety," with "insecurity." These words appear repeatedly in mother's and father's discussions. Not only did these parents have to deal with their own sense of guilt, but some faced pressures from others. A few mothers recounted how their children came home from school, saying that they were teased or questioned by the other children about the absence of their fathers: "One problem has been dealing with the children's remarks. Junie, the little one [nine years old] has had kids say to her: 'Oh, you don't have a father.' "

These greater domestic and childcare costs are, for "balancing" couples, the counterpart to the career ascendancy conflict that troubles younger couples. However, the tradeoffs are not equally painful. Older couples acknowledge more sources of satisfaction: the solidity of their relationship, faith that they can endure the demands of living apart, and the recognition that they are compensating for the wife's past efforts on her husband's behalf.

ESTABLISHED COUPLES

Couples established in their marital, parenting, and career lives experience the fewest strains while commuting. They already have a long marital history, which sustains them during their separations. One commuter who had lived with his wife for twenty-five years and whose only daughter was now in college put it this way:

Time means a lot to me. It's partly a clue to my attitude to my wife. I don't understand how someone at the age of fifty can pick up and go off and make another relationship.

I mean, you know them so well; the relationship has been cemented by the time we've already lived together.

More important, the children of these "established" couples are grown and out of the home, which leaves their commuter parents with a sense of accomplishment and freedom. As they see it, the spouses can now optimize their career involvement. However, even these established couples—precisely because they have shared so much—experience some regret because they live apart. The very fact that their lives are more connected, that they have built up a common identity, makes the separation that much more of a trial: "I don't relate intimately to a lot of people, but by now I do to her, so I've lost a great deal when she's gone." And: "I really don't handle aloneness well because I'm so used to having someone to come home to."

Overall, then, it is this group of older couples, without any children at home, who see the greatest advantage to commuting. Yet despite these compensations, their accounts suggest that even they cope with commuting more than they enjoy it. For each type (and for each spouse) a compromise has been fashioned, but it is "no bargain" either.

HUSBANDS AND WIVES: WHO LOSES LESS?

Commuting is a solution to the incompatible demands of career and family, but it does not end the need to wrestle with the conflicts between these two spheres. In fact, it ushers in new problems, albeit different ones, depending, as we saw above, on the couple's stage of family life and career. Yet, although commuters as a group view their adaptation as a complex mixture of costs and benefits, women tend, in general, to evaluate the overall arrangement less negatively. Why this should be so becomes apparent as we listen to how members of each sex evaluate the consequences—for them as individuals—of living apart.

To these strongly career-committed individuals, one of the most keenly felt advantages of living separately is the simplification of their daily lives and the intensification of professional work that it allows. Both spouses are freed from the constraints of having to coordinate their schedules with each other's, and both luxuriate in the freedom to work as hard as they wish without interruption: "There is a great luxury in coming home whenever you want and then doing just what you want to do." But the fact of having less to distract them (e.g., regularly scheduled meals and other communal living responsibilities) and being able to work without interruption is valued more by wives than by husbands:

I was really unprepared for the fierce joy I have felt at being my own woman, being able to concentrate on my own activities, my own thoughts, and my own desires. It's a completely selfish, self-centered existence. It's almost a religious experience when you're fifty years old and have never felt that before.

The key phrase here is "have never felt this before," which is much more likely to be true for a woman who has reached fifty in our culture than for a man, given expectations that assign the bulk of domestic and family responsibilities to wives and not husbands. That women are more likely to regard positively the release from daily family demands should come as no surprise. Because in a shared residence women are still more likely to be responsible for family demands (Robinson 1980; Yogev 1981; and Cowan (Chapter 6) and Hunt and Hunt (Chapter 8) in this volume), they are also more likely to experience separation as freedom, just because separation removes them from those demands:

Every night I bring work home. If he was here, I'd have to let it go. I would have prepared real meals, made sure the house was neat, had more laundry to do. Oh, you know, the whole list. But, being alone, it's just easy to do my work. I'm kinda lured into it.

For most men, by contrast, the time saved and obligations avoided do not free a significant amount of time for professional work. In fact, many echoed the man who stated simply: "It's had no effect on the amount of work that I do. I thought that I would spend more time working living apart, but I don't think that I do."

Not only were women able to increase the amount of time they spent on professional work, but they could focus better with fewer interruptions when alone: "I love my work, and here apart I can really enjoy the freedom to put as much into it as I want to. If I were with him and wanted to put in extra time, I would run into real conflict."

If a reduction in the ability to work was mentioned, it was typically a man who noted this effect. Some men made statements like: "I might work less now." These husbands' professions set the parameters of their daily existence when they shared a single home with their wives. For them, the single-residence family did not intrude on, but instead supported, their professional lives. Some men explicitly stated that because living in a family relieves strain, it simultaneously promotes intense career involvement: "I probably work less now. I think I spend more time moping around. Maybe a bit more drinking. Not excessive, but a bit more escapist." Marriage provides for these men a sense of order that makes productive work possible; marriage, that is, provides the moorings for purposeful action. Yet the inability to concentrate, to work productively in the absence of the spouse, was far less characteristic of commuter wives.

In fact, for many wives the husband's loss was their gain. Women spoke enthusiastically about the redistribution of domestic work that commuting brought about:

Before, I did the breakfasts, the dinners—often he did the dishes. But I ran the place. I was the person in charge of saying: "This needs to be done." Now, there is just much less with him away from this place, and when I go there, it's just not as clean as I'd keep it, but I do very little housework. So he has to do more.

And her husband, like most others, agreed: "Here, alone, I'm not as neat, but she isn't around to get things done. I do have to clean up; I do have to eat." Commuting equalizes the division of domestic labor: women do less than they had done in the past; men do more.

Another benefit recognized by both sexes is also valued more by wives than by husbands. Separation brings the need, but also the opportunity, to increase independence and autonomy. As a husband put it: "We've both discovered that we have some resources that we may not have used for a while. One of the things that worried me to begin with was that I was going to get uptight at the idea of being alone. I have proved to myself that I can." But women went much further in their analysis of how separation afforded them an opportunity to grow as individuals and to achieve heights previously denied them. Women who had, in the single home, faced job losses because they followed their husbands instead of their own careers could now obtain the sense of self-worth and autonomy associated with career development:[3]

Last year, I was thinking to myself that I am all washed up and had nothing to offer. He was the one person who made our world. Now, I am much more secure. I regard myself up here, having a job, as a neater person.

I guess the best way to explain it is that I am an individual in my own right. And partly because I am not playing the role of wife. I like the idea that other people will like me, or they don't like me, but for my own characteristics, not because I am my husband's wife.

Further support for the conclusion that wives gained more as individuals from commuting than did husbands comes from analysis of their overall evaluations of the arrangement. In nearly two-thirds (62 percent) of the couples, it was the husband who disliked commuter marriage more than his wife, whereas wives disliked the situation overall more than their husbands in only 16 percent of the couples. (Spouses shared the same overall evaluation in 22 percent of the couples.) In most cases the commuters themselves were aware of this difference but did not attribute it to gender. Rather, they accounted for the husband's greater dissatisfaction in terms of their particular circumstances—which spouse traveled more, which spouse kept the children. But even when we controlled for these circumstances, we still found greater dissatisfaction among husbands. That is, no matter what the situation, wives typically evaluated commuting less negatively than their husbands. Thus, we would argue that it is the culturally prescribed operation of gender in the conventional family, and its dislocation in a commuter marriage, that shapes the assessment of either family form.

Conclusion

Commuters have to contend with, if not acknowledge, an intrusion of jobs on family that may more easily escape single-residence employed couples. Yet commuters do not question the legitimacy of the relationship between jobs and families that has caused so much dislocation in their lives—figuratively and literally. Instead, they complain and adjust, some better than others, and point to (even focus on) not only costs, but limited benefits as well. And they hope that the tenure of the arrangement will be short.

As we have seen, commuters find some benefits in being forced to establish two separate homes, although even for most of the women, these are islands of benefits in a sea of costs. Residential separation may equalize the division of labor at home, yet at the same time provoke a sense of guilt and threaten the sense of what a marriage "should be." Residential separation may provide the time for increased professional productivity, yet—especially for men—diminish the sense of security and order that makes continued productivity possible. Most generally, residential separation may open new opportunities for the career advancement of both spouses, but at the expense of shared space and time that are equally valued. Commuters recognize these consequences—both positive and negative. Yet whatever their overall assessment, they would prefer to share a home. They recognize that they have made a forced choice necessitated by the "misfit" between demands rooted in dual careers and needs whose fulfillment depends on a shared family life.

Because they adjust as individuals, they cannot realize how the experience of commuting itself reflects interacting social characteristics and conditions: those rooted in gender, in career stage, and family life course. That is, the conditions that determine the impact of commuting are themselves based on the way jobs and families have been constituted in our society.

We have seen that an important determinant of the costliness of the arrangement is the couple's particular family/career constellation. Here the number of years they previously shared a residence and the presence of children are key factors. The longer the marital history, the easier the commuting. Even though they, too, typically miss the daily interaction, "established" and even "balancing" couples have developed a strong, stable bond of trust that eases living apart. Then, too, the fact that they are older means that at least one is likely to be advanced in his or her career and not as anxious about achievement as a younger person might be. This difficulty is greater for couples married only a short time, when both may be just beginning to receive professional recognition. Those married only a few years must develop a "habit system" and focus on their marital relationship. So, too, the presence of children not only overloads parents but limits their ability to provide each other with the necessary emotional support during their short periods together. When children must be included, the marital relationship itself cannot be the central focus.

We have also seen the influence of gender: wives gain more and give up less than husbands do, with the result that they tend to view the overall arrangement less negatively. This difference provides additional evidence that the typical nuclear family restricts women more and rewards them less than it does men (a finding now substantiated by much literature on more conventional families: see, for example, Bernard 1972; Locksley 1980; Schafer and Keith 1981). In the traditional family unit, demands emanating from the husband's career, such as the need for geographic mobility, receive priority. Consequently, the wife is required to be the more dependent family member. It is she who suffers professional setbacks, losses of self-esteem, and consignment to relative invisibility even when she attempts to pursue a career (Gerstel and Gross 1984: chap. 6). When a woman is employed (as some of these commuters were before they lived apart), she typically continues to perform more than half of the domestic work. When the partners are apart, the domestic tasks are necessarily redistributed and equalized. Consequently, a woman's professional work output increases when she is living in a separate home, whereas her husband's is less likely to do so. In addition, it is typically the woman who makes greater marital adjustments, acting as the flexible and supportive family member. When away from her husband, she may simplify her daily life, paying more attention to her own needs and priorities.

What we think this analysis shows is that commuter marriage is both a laboratory for viewing enduring issues in family life and a microcosm of changes in the larger society. In the last decades, changes in the labor market and attacks on gender-based obligations in the home, as well as changes in ideology, have rendered obsolete older models of the relationship, or "fit" (Parsons 1955, 1965), between the family and economy. More and more married women are employed, and more are becoming professionals. A growing number of married women committed to careers that bring them income and status are likely to face the costs—both occupational and psychological—of subordinating their interests. Two earners per family are increasingly necessary as inflationary pressures mount. A tight job market, characteristic of many professions today, reduces the ease of finding two jobs in a single locale. Moreover, these developments are occurring in an ideological context that supports alternative marital structures like commuter marriage. The woman's movement has, in some measure, legitimated women's demands for independence within and outside the home. Commuter marriage is a structure spawned by this ideology of individualism, which emphasizes that each spouse's worth depends on individual achievements rather than on family membership. This American ideology has a long history of application to husbands; what is new is its application to wives.

The application of this principle to women forces our attention back to the family life behind the employee. Commuters, like a growing number of couples, act on their conviction that for women, as for men, fulfillment in the family depends upon their identities away from home. Believing this, these men and women take both spouses' careers into account in determining how they shall live. And though they know that they are nontraditional in this sense, they do not regard themselves as such in any other way. Quite the contrary: they are ambitious, family-oriented people for whom marriage and work are the bedrock of mature, adult achievement. Their attachment to the institution of marriage as well as their striving for success in careers keeps commuters in the mainstream of American values. And precisely because they participate in that mainstream, they are witness and victim of the structural "misfit" between the family and the economy that grows out of women's full and equal participation in the labor force. Yet, as heirs to an ideology that gives priority to career absorption as it simultaneously sets in place the myth that work and family are separate worlds, the commuters blame and sometimes praise themselves as they struggle to adjust.

Notes

1. Analysis in this paper was based on in-depth interviews with 121 commuters who resided in seventeen states (50 couples in which we interviewed both husband and wife, 16 additional wives, and 5 additional husbands.) In those cases in which we interviewed both husband and wife, we interviewed each spouse separately. Interviews ranged in length from one to five hours, with most lasting two and one-half to three hours. For a full discussion of our research methods and of the characteristics of the commuters, see Gerstel and Gross (1984).

2. "Potlatch" is a ceremonial feast or festival of North American Indians of the northwest coast given for the display of wealth to validate or advance position and marked by the host's lavish destruction of personal property.

3. We asked commuters about the mobility decisions they made before they began to commute: their decision to remain in one place when job possibilities existed elsewhere as well as their relocations in response to job offers. Even in this vanguard population, the husband's career was the determining factor in 80 percent of the joint-mobility decisions; both spouse's careers were given equal weight in only 8 percent of the decisions; in only another 8 percent of the cases was the wife's career the determining factor. (The other 4 percent of the mobility decisions were not determined by careers; for example, couples moved to be near kin or to achieve the lifestyles associ-

ated with particular cities.) In these earlier decisions, commuter couples resembled the "conventional" intact marriage. That is, even highly trained, skilled women tend to follow their husbands when they move to take a new job (Duncan and Perucci 1976; Yohalem 1979). And both sets of wives—the conventional and the commuter—face occupational losses because they follow their husbands', rather than their own, careers. See Gerstel and Gross (1984: chap. 2) for a fuller review of this literature on the mobility of professional wives and for an analysis of the consequences of that prior mobility for commuters.

References

Bernard, Jessie. 1972. *The Future of Marriage*. New York: Bantam.

Duncan, R. P., and Perucci, C. C. 1976. "Dual Occupation Families and Migration." *American Sociological Review* 41:252–61.

Gerstel, Naomi, and Harriet Gross. 1984. *Commuter Marriage*. New York: Guilford Press.

Locksley, Anne. 1980. "On the Effects of Wives' Employment on Marital Adjustment and Companionship." *Journal of Marriage and the Family* 42:337 46.

Parsons, Talcot. 1955. *Family, Socialization and Interaction Process*. Glencoe, Ill.: Free Press.

———. 1965. "The Normal American Family." In S. M. Farber, P. Mustacchi, and R. H. L. Wilson (eds.), *Man and Civilization*. New York: McGraw-Hill.

Robinson, J. N. 1980. "Household Technology and Household Work." In S. F. Berk (ed.), *Women and Household Labor*. Beverly Hills, Calif.: Sage, 1980.

Schafer, R., and Keith, P. M. 1982. "Equity in Marital Roles Across the Life Cycle." *Journal of Marriage and the Family* 43:359–68.

Yogev, Sava. 1981. "Do Professional Women Have Egalitarian Marital Relationships?" *Journal of Marriage and the Family* 43:865–72.

Yohalem, A. M. 1979. *The Careers of Professional Women*. Montclair, N. J.: Allanheld Osmun.

22

Sexuality, Class, and Conflict in a Lesbian Workplace

KATHLEEN M. WESTON
LISA B. ROFEL

History of the Conflict

Amazon Auto Repair was founded in 1978 by two lesbian auto mechanics, Carol and Lauren, with $1,400 in capital from personal savings.* Within the first two years, their financial success led them to hire several more mechanics, who were paid on a commission basis of 50 percent. In the summer of 1981, the owners embarked on a major expansion, raising the total number of employees to eleven. When their clerical worker left in August of that year, both owners went into the office, discontinuing the practice of one owner's supervising on the shop floor at all times.

The first overt incident in the conflict occurred about this time when Mary, the parts runner at the bottom of the job hierarchy, refused to stop working on a car in order to get lunch for everyone, as had been her custom. The owners not only insisted that this task was one of her job responsibilities but also added office filing to her duties, a change she resisted. In Mary's view, they also reneged on their earlier promise to make her an apprentice.

When the owners responded to new problems and pressures associated with expansion by tightening shop discipline, conflicts with other employees seemed to escalate as well. Tensions erupted at Christmas when the owners gave each employee a small gift that included a nailbrush and chocolate-

*Editor's Note: This case study of events, antecedent and consequent to a strike in an auto repair shop owned and staffed by lesbians, is based on participant observation and in-depth interviews with eight of the ten women (including the owners) who worked in the shop at the time of the strike.

Adapted from *Signs* 9, no. 4, by permission of The University of Chicago Press. © 1984 by The University of Chicago.

covered almonds. The workers, insulted by what they regarded as insignificant gifts in place of bonuses, presented the owners with a list of issues and demands calling for continued commission with a guaranteed base pay of $200 per week, paid sick leave and a paid vacation, and a salaried shop manager. On February 2, 1982, the owners distributed statements rejecting the employees' demands, accompanied by nonnegotiable job descriptions that put everyone on an hourly wage effective the following week. That Friday, the workers asked the owners to postpone implementation of the descriptions and to meet with them in order to discuss salaries, the apprenticeship promised Mary, and other issues.

At this meeting the owners informed their employees they could no longer work at Amazon if they did not sign the job descriptions by 8 A.M. that day. Employees refused and, claiming they felt sick, left the shop. While the owners insist the employees walked out on their jobs, the workers say they were essentially locked out. The workers promptly filed charges of unfair labor practices with the National Labor Relations Board and set up a picket line, successfully turning away much of Amazon's business.

On February 24 the owners offered immediate and unconditional reinstatement under the old working conditions if the workers would drop all charges. But contrary to their stated intentions, the owners instituted speedups, set up procedures for signing in and out, and fired Mary for refusing to do filing. Two days later the workers went on strike. After picketing for several weeks with no sign of negotiations resuming, the workers reluctantly decided to join the Machinists Union and sought other employment. The owners continue to operate the business with a reduced staff of new employees. Technically the Amazon conflict still has not been resolved, but a year after the strike workers have given up hope of reaching a settlement.

Bridging the Public and Private

The establishment of Amazon as a lesbian workplace challenged one of the deepest cultural divisions in American society: the split between private and public life. The very categories "lesbian" and "work" mirror this dichotomy, since lesbian identity has historically been defined in terms of the sexual and the personal,[1] whereas wage work in a capitalist context constitutes the public activity par excellence. In a homophobic society, any attempt to establish an institution that links lesbian identity and productive activity entails—not as a matter of ideological principle but by definition—a renegotiation of the culturally constructed boundary that differentiates public and private spheres. To the degree that Amazon integrated these spheres by hiring lesbians and bringing them into an environment that encouraged them to be "out" on the job, it not only provided a space sheltered from the heterosexism of the wider society but also undermined the compartmentalization of lives and self characteristic of most workplaces. Out of this radical potential to create a nonalienating work environment emerged an atmosphere of involvement, excitement, and commitment at Amazon during its early years. An analysis of the reconciliation of private and public inherent in the project of a lesbian workplace cannot explain Amazon's ultimate failure to realize this radical potential. But because sexual and class politics meet at the boundary between personal and public life,[2] such an analysis is crucial for understanding aspects of the Amazon case that resemble conflicts in other lesbian institutions and that distinguish it from more traditional labor disputes.

The measure of what made Amazon a specifically lesbian workplace was not the sexuality of individual employees or the women's music played on the shop floor but the extent to which sexual identity received public affirmation in a place where being a lesbian was the rule rather than the exception.[3] Being out at Amazon was different from "coming out" at a straight workplace because, as one mechanic put it, workers "didn't *have* to talk about being dykes. It was pretty obvious!" Yet, as another women said, "You could go in and when you're sitting around having lunch you could talk about your family, you could talk about your lover, you could talk about what you did last night. It's real nice to get that out and share that." Conversations at work led to friendships that carried over into the evenings and weekends. Women went to flea markets together, carpooled to work, cooked dinner for one another, and attended each other's sporting events. Lovers were treated as members of the extended Amazon "family" and welcomed into the shop during business hours. One woman's lover acknowledged: "There's nothing like walking into a women's[4] business and being able to walk right up to my lover and kiss her and have lunch with her and have my kids behind me, our kids. But you can't do that in the straight world, you know? It was a real valuable place to be." Friendships spanned all levels of the job hierarchy, weaving together employees' lives inside and outside work.

In a sense, Amazon resembled other small and alternative businesses that foster the development of multiplex ties among employees. Although such businesses often promote an integration of personal and work relationships, the size of an enterprise does not necessarily contribute to a breakdown of the private/public split within the self. The compartmentalization of life in Western industrial societies often leads individuals in public situations to withhold full expression of their feelings, sexuality, and other central aspects of identity regarded as private.[5] One decisive difference between Amazon and the "straight" businesses employees mentioned in contrast was the way public and private aspects of the self were united once lesbian identity became linked to productive activity. In attempting to elucidate how lesbian identity shaped social relations at Amazon, we are not asserting that the reconciliation of the cultural dichotomy between public and private is characteristic of lesbian institutions alone. A similar integration may occur in any organization of an oppressed group that explicitly invokes racial, ethnic, gender, or sexual identity to set the institution and its members apart from the dominant society. At the same time, we believe there are factors unique to lesbian institutions that affect the way conflicts are generated and negotiated but that cannot be explored here. These include the effect of same-sex romantic and sexual involvements on work relationships; the possibility that lesbian institutions foster what Audre Lorde calls "the power of the erotic," which may contribute to the tranformation of alienated labor;[6] and the ways in which lesbian-feminist ideology, the organization of production, and systems of meaning originating in the wider lesbian community interact in the formation of lesbian workplace culture.

A principal effect of structuring Amazon so that lesbians could "be themselves" at work was the integration of emotions into workplace dynamics. "There was far more feeling than there ever is when it's just a cold business situation with men," remembered one owner. The reason was not simply, as she surmised, that women are socialized to express their feelings more freely than are men. Most former Amazon employees emphasized that their present work situations in straight businesses are not as emotional for them. But as a lesbian identified workplace, Amazon encouraged the women who worked there to bring with them onto the shop floor the entire range of emotions and personal attributes associated with identity in American culture.[7]

Despite the lesbian-feminist principles of Amazon's owners, it is important to remember that this integration of public and private was not the product of a shared ideology. The commitment workers felt to Amazon was developed on the job, not brought to the workplace from other contexts. Some started their jobs with a nine-to-five attitude, only to find themselves becoming increasingly involved in what happened during business hours. It would therefore be a mistake to portray the Amazon conflict as a case in which women's unrealistically high expectations for an alternative institution led to disappointment when those expectations could not be met.

When she first came to Amazon from her job in a straight repair shop, one women said, "I didn't *have* different expectations." But within a month, she was "like a kid in a candy store." It was precisely because working at Amazon had been such a positive, fulfilling experience, said another, that the rift between owners and workers came as such a shock and a loss: "That's why [leaving Amazon] feels like death. It was a part of my life—it was a part of our [family's] life—that would have gone on and on." By December 1981 the excitement of earlier years had given way to feelings of anger and betrayal, feelings so intense that the women involved in the dispute still dream about Amazon a year after the strike. "It hurts more with lesbians," concluded one mechanic, recalling that it had felt as though her whole being were under attack. The hurt was as much a product of the integration of private and public as the fulfillment that preceded it. In most work situations, the compartmentalization of life and self that accompanies alienation also protects individuals from the destructive effects of fixed power inequities.[8] Without that protection, the women at Amazon found themselves particularly vulnerable as tensions began to explode.

When Mary refused to get the mechanics' lunches, her intention was to defend herself against what she regarded as the owners' arbitrary exercise of power. Because she refused on the grounds that this task was a personal favor rather than a job duty, she tacitly reinvoked the private/public split. As the conflict deepened, attempts to reaffirm this distinction assumed a key position in the strategies of both parties. Workers called for a "businesslike" handling of affairs and tried to put their emotions aside. The owners took steps to distance themselves from workers by curtailing friendships and adopting written rules. By the time women were called back to work, the employee phone had been disconnected, giving symbolic emphasis to the new segregation of work from personal life.

Even as Amazon's radical potential to provide a nonalienating work environment was being undermined, its distinctive characteristics as a lesbian workplace continued to shape the course of the conflict by focusing the struggle on the division between the private and the public. But with the reaffirmation of the private/public split, many of the special qualities that distinguished Amazon from straight repair shops seemed to disappear. "I'm not in business to be a machine, to be a man, to be something I don't want to be," protested one owner. "This wasn't what we wanted to create," insisted the other. Both sides were left wondering how the conflict could have escalated so quickly, destroying relationships of trust and cooperation built up over three and one-half years.

The Politics of Trust

In the eyes of everyone who worked there, Amazon was built on trust. The owners trace this trust to their political commitment to lesbian feminism, which fostered a sense that a common lesbian identity would override other differences.[9] Before the February 8 walkout/lockout, neither seriously believed a strike could occur at Amazon. They displayed a similar degree of confidence in each other when they elected to go into business without a partnership agreement. For the workers, trust was not so much an outgrowth of ideology as a consequence of the multiplex ties that developed in the workplace. Not all employees identified strongly as feminists or saw themselves engaged in the project of creating a feminist business. But for workers and owners alike, trust was underpinned by friendships and the support Amazon provided for being openly and proudly lesbian.

From the beginning Lauren and Carol stressed that they were the owners, that Amazon was not a collective, and that they reserved the right to make all business decisions. Beyond these ground rules, however, they assumed a basic compatibility between their needs and those of their employees. In accordance with a feminist ideology that valued being ''nurturing'' and ''supportive,'' the owners installed a separate phone for employees' use and agreed to flexible scheduling around women's extrawork commitments. The lack of set policy and formalized rules, combined with the owners' efforts not to ''act like bosses,'' made it easy to believe that everyone was equal at Amazon and that trust grounded in the integration of public and private life would constitute a sufficiently radical solution to the problems of oppression women face in other workplaces. But in the absence of a clearly defined business structure, this trust became politicized when owners and workers had to rely on interpersonal relationships to negotiate labor relations from day to day. The emergence of a politics of trust at Amazon points to a conclusion the owners never reached and the workers only gradually realized: the personal can be political, even among lesbians, whenever the personalization of work relations obscures power differentials structured through property relations and the division of labor.

As managers, the owners had the authority to define and evaluate other's needs, transforming what would otherwise have been examples of mutual agreement into instances of benevolence. Even if they had been able to satisfy every request or concede every point raised by employees, control of the business altered the meaning of their actions. What the owners perceived as gifts or favors the workers often saw as customs or rights. It is not surprising, then, that the owners began to get angry when workers stopped asking permission for routine procedures such as leaving early when work was finished for the day. Conversely, the workers' mistrust of the owners developed when Lauren and Carol chose to assert their covert power—for example, when they forced Mary to get lunches or do filing. For some workers the strike came to be seen as a fight to create a work environment in which the owners ''would not have the power to say one thing and do another thing and change things around'' when their decisions could have a major impact on employees' livelihoods.

It was not coincidental that the politics of trust fragmented along class lines, pitting owners/managers against workers. But because such a politics was grounded in interpersonal relationships, it tended to personalize the issues for the women involved, leading them away from a relationally defined class analysis. The politics of trust, rooted in the liberal conception of autonomous selves interacting on a basis of equality, supported interpretations that reduced the conflict to a matter of individual actions, intentions, and capabilities.

The analysis of the conflict favored by the owners was built on a personality/provocateur theory, which held that the strike was instigated either by chronically dissatisfied workers or by someone in league with outside forces interested in destroying a "growing, thriving lesbian business." The owners alternately portrayed the workers as lazy, irresponsible, resentful because of unrequited love, or consciously determined to undermine the business. Power enters into this analysis only in the owners' focus on the individual psychology of certain employees who allegedly were not comfortable accepting authority and so created a strike situation in order to feel some measure of control.[10]

Explanations that ascribe the conflict to static personality traits fail to account for the workers' movement from enthusiasm to anger over time. The provocateur theory provides no better explanation, since it discounts the solidarity maintained by the workers throughout the struggle.[11] To speak of the "mob mentality" that held workers together, or the weakness of character that prevented individuals from standing apart from the group, implies that the workers followed one another like sheep, without legitimate grievances and a clear understanding of their own actions. The owners' preoccupation with the personality/provocateur theory also draws attention away from the possibility that they too might be implicated in the conflict.

The workers were less inclined to reduce the conflict to personalities, insisting instead that "nobody [at Amazon] was a good guy or a bad guy." They learned to distinguish between an individual's particular attitudes or competencies and her standing in the job hierarchy. Rather than defending Mary's actions, they identified broader problems with training and apprenticeship. Rather than attacking Carol's decision to side with Lauren about the lunches, they criticized the division of labor that induced the owners to take the same position. However, this growing awareness of structural factors underlying the conflict existed alongside, and in contradiction to, a set of liberal presuppositions evident in the workers' two most popular explanations for the dispute: the miscommunication theory and the mismanagement theory.

The miscommunication theory represents the women of Amazon as equal, rational, independent individuals who came into conflict only because they misunderstood one another. Individual interviews clearly show, however, that both sides in the dispute can accurately reproduce the other's point of view. In addition, the premises of this theory are invalidated by the power differential that allowed the owners to set the terms for communication and to refuse to negotiate with their employees.

The mismanagement theory depicts the owners as incompetent managers; presumably, if Lauren and Carol had taken a few business courses or had acquired more experience running a shop, the conflict could have been avoided. Although this analysis recognizes the power differential at Amazon, it does not call for a redistribution or redefinition of power, because it shares the owners' basic assumption that the needs of employers and employees can always be reconciled. But if we consider needs as historical products tied to a changing division of labor,[12] it becomes apparent that merely substituting more competent actors or rectifying individual "mistakes" would not have been sufficient to prevent these needs from coming into conflict.

We believe that a class analysis is essential for comprehending the social, historical, and structural factors shaping the conflict that these theories ignore. By class we mean the relations of property and production mediated by the division of labor that separated the women of Amazon into owners/managers and workers, adding a dimension of power to personal relationships that politicized bonds of mutual trust. In our view, material factors like ownership, the division of labor, and the organization of production are dynamically interrelated with the production of needs, culture, perceptions, and feelings. Obviously, then, we disagree with those who interpret class in a narrowly economistic or deterministic sense. The way in which the public/private split is bridged by linking lesbian identity to productive activity demonstrates that class relations alone cannot explain events at Amazon. But without an understanding of class relations, lesbian feminism remains grounded in the same liberal, individualistic assumptions that originally led the women of Amazon to expect the bonds of trust to prevail over any dissension that could arise.

Class Relations and the Organization of Production

Class relations at Amazon, based on a hierarchical division of labor that enabled two individuals to own the business and maintain the power to define the conditions under which the others would work, shaped the tensions that eventually led to the strike. From the beginning, these tensions were inherent in the organization of production at Amazon, particularly in four key areas: the commission system, job allocations, apprenticeships, and informal job definitions.[13] They surfaced and became the focus of overt conflict only after the owners decided to expand the business and work in the office, creating a dichotomy between mental and manual labor that sharply distinguished owners from workers. In the face of these changes, Lauren and Carol found themselves struggling to defend their prerogatives as owners as their needs increasingly came into contradiction with the needs of their employees.

Carol and Lauren certainly never aspired to be bosses. In establishing Amazon they were motivated not by the desire for profit or the will to exercise power for power's sake but by the vision of working independently and determining the conditions of their own labor. Like many entrepreneurs who open small businesses, they initially hoped to escape the alienation [14] they had experienced in other work situations: "Do we want to work for those creepy lawyers and doctors for the rest of our lives? [Or] do we want to try to set up something that's ours? It may be a lot of things, but it will at least be ours." The connection Lauren and Carol drew between ownership and self-determination lay behind their insistence on maintaing control as tensions heightened during the months prior to the strike.

When Carol and Lauren first began to hire mechanics to work under them, they decided to pay them by commission rather than salary to ensure that the fledging business would not go in the red. The commission system allowed mechanics a degree of control over their work, an arrangement that neither owner initially regarded as problematic but that later became a key issue in the struggle. Because mechanics were paid not by the hour but for jobs actually completed, they came to feel, as one mechanic phrased it, "the time we worked there was our time." Some saw themselves more as subcontractors than employees, insisting, "All we were doing, really, is using [the owners'] space and giving them half the money we made." Workers felt not so much a time obligation to Amazon as an obligation to get the work done.

The commission system also tended to give employees a clearer picture of how Amazon made its profit and how much of that profit came from their labor: "We could see how much money they made off of our labor. . . . You doubled everybody's wages and they got it, plus the money they made on parts." This perception of the relation between their work and the business's prosperity fed the workers' sense of outrage when the owners refused to negotiate the terms of the February job descriptions.

The owners' control of job allocations constituted another potential source of conflict. A mechanic's commission-based income was contingent on the availability of work and on whether or not she received time-efficient jobs that matched her skill level. Several workers recalled being the "star" or the "fave" when they first arrived at Amazon, only to become the recipients of time-consuming "shit jobs" as newer employees were given preferred assignments. Although not all the mechanics at Amazon experienced favoritism, concentration of the power to allocate jobs in the hands of the owners made the workers equally dependent on Carol and Lauren's continued good will.

Training and apprenticeship were vital under commission, since specialization in only a few tasks left an apprentice-level mechanic particularly vulnerable to job-allocation decisions. Without adequate supervision and opportunitites to learn new skills, a novice assigned an unfamiliar task—and the more experienced mechanics she turned to for help—lost time and money. At Amazon apprenticeship was not a formal program but a loosely structured arrangement in which employees were told an owner would be available to assist them when necessary. After the owners moved into the office, apprentices were largely left to fend for themselves in what became an increasingly untenable position.

Finally, the informality of job definitions under the politics of trust highlighted the inconsistencies between the owners' feminist ideals and Amazon's actual business structure. The owners promised their parts runner, Mary, that she could become an apprentice as part of their commitment to helping women enter the auto-repair trade. At the same time, however, the owners expected her to continue to make herself generally available to meet their needs because she was the only salaried worker below them in the job hierarchy. Without reorganizing the division of labor, the owners never provided the conditions that would have made it possible for Mary to become a mechanic. Nor were the owners willing to relinquish their control over defining the content of workers' jobs, as Mary discovered when she confronted them on this issue.

Because capitalist culture values conceptual work over the "mere" execution of ideas,[15] the mental/manual division between owners and employees that arose in the late summer of 1981 reinforced the owners' power to set the terms for the other women's labor. In practice, this separation meant that the two owners' needs and perceptions became more congruent and more opposed to those of their employees. One owner noted, "There's always been a kind of an 'us' and a 'them' between the office and the shop," a division that separated even the two owners when they worked in different spheres. "You're in the shop and you see everything from the mechanics' side. You're in the office and you see everything from the customers' side." For Carol, "the one thing that was a big pull for me about both of us being in [the office] was that we were going to be on the same side."

The way the owners chose to expand the shop and the creation of a mental/manual split deepened class divisions at Amazon and brought underlying tensions to the fore. A heavier work load, tighter scheduling, and a greater number of mechanics meant an increase in work pressures and a decrease in the time available to resolve conflicts as they emerged. As the owners perceived a need to cut overhead and raise productivity, they began to contest accustomed areas of worker self-determination in a general move to tighten up the shop.

Control over mechanics' hours became a matter of controversy once the owners decided to adhere to a strict 8:30 to 5:30 rule. When workers resisted rigid scheduling by arguing that their time was their own under commission, the owners interpreted their defiance as laziness and a lack of commitment to Amazon's success. In their proposed job descriptions, the owners finally decided to replace the commission system with salaries "because that was the only way . . . we could know we were going to get eight hours of work from people." Many mechanics opposed the change because their new salaries were based on individual averages of their previous years' wages, which meant that they would receive the same amount of money annually for working longer hours.

Meanwhile, the owners' preoccupation with office work meant a decline in income for apprentice-level mechanics, who lacked regular supervision. Although the more experienced mechanics were willing to offer their assistance, they nonetheless resented these costly intrusions on their time. The owners rebuffed the workers' suggestion to pay a mechanic to be a lead worker or supervisor, even though the owners previously had compensated themselves for the same responsibility. Problems involving novice mechanics' limited training and narrow specialization were compounded when the owners allocated simple but money-making jobs to a new employee hired in the fall of 1981, who turned out to be on an apprectice level. The other less experienced mechanic in the shop promptly witnessed a sharp drop in her weekly paycheck as she lost most of the jobs she knew how to do well. Such actions incensed many workers, ultimately leading to their demand for a steady base pay.

Carol and Lauren found themselves in the middle of yet another struggle when what they saw as a need for greater efficiency with expansion led them to oppose Mary's efforts to renegotiate the definition of her job to meet her need for an apprenticeship. By insisting Mary get the lunches and do the filing, the owners invoked tasks especially symbolic of female subordination. The other workers, disturbed by the way the owners were "jerking Mary around," made her right to an apprenticeship a major issue as the strike developed.

With tensions mounting, workers saw their Christmas presents as the "last straw." The owners still find it incomprehensible that the workers organized over such a seemingly trivial issue because they fail to recognize the symbolic meaning of those presents. Since Christmas bonuses traditionally serve as a statement of evaluation from employers, these token gifts were taken as a "slap in the face" of the workers' commitment to Amazon. The gifts had economic as well as ideological significance, since they were associated with the owners' decision to close the shop for a week, leaving the workers with no income, no Christmas bonus, and, according to employees, no respect.

Because the owners were now so clearly treating the other women not as friends and equals but as employees, the Christmas presents symbolized the demise of the politics of trust by marking the class division that later would separate the two sides in the dispute.

Paradigm Shifting: From the Politics of Trust to the Politics of Contract

As the politics of trust began to disintegrate, the women of Amazon adopted an opposing symbolic paradigm, what we term the politics of contract. It represented an alternative mode of negotiating labor relations in which owners and workers ideally would bargain to agree on a business structure made explicit through written job descriptions and set policies. Although this formulation appears neutral from the standpoint of gender and sexual identity, the women at Amazon came to favor it precisely because the two paradigms of contract and trust were relationally defined by incorporating popular—and opposed—notions of male and female.[16] Although the women at Amazon did not consciously define themselves in relation to men, their understanding of a lesbian business as an "all-giving, all-nurturing, endlessly supportive" institution carried an implicit contrast with the "cold, unfeeling" world of heterosexual male businesses where decisions were held to be determined legalistically without regard for workers' needs.[17] Because the categories female and male exhaust the range of possible gender attributes in American society, the link between these categories and the two contrasting paradigms made those paradigms appear to be the only conceivable options for conducting labor relations. When the politics of trust proved inadequate, the politics of contract provided a readily available model sanctioned by the dominant society for attempting to settle the growing differences between workers and owners.

Both paradigms obscured class relations within Amazon. Under the politics of trust, the owners had asserted that Amazon was a nonoppressive environment by definition because it provided a haven from the "real world" where women have to "put up with crap from men." This belief allowed them to argue that any woman dissatisfied with working conditions should "go be with the boys," which had the double effect of augmenting their power and suppressing worker initiatives for change. At the same time, industry standards implicit in the contrast between Amazon and the straight male business world could be selectively invoked to justify practices such as paying the parts runner a minimal salary.

The owners' shift toward a politics of contract came in the wake of expansion. In light of their new concern with raising productivity and decreasing overhead, the owners began to perceive their employees as taking advantage of Amazon's loose structure. The institution of a written policy in October marked the owner's first attempt to establish a more structured work environment. To the owners, this deliberate decision to "act like bosses" meant abandoning the ideals of nurturance and sensitivity they associated with lesbian-feminist entrepreneurs to assume the straight male-identified role of a "wrist-slapping disciplinarian." By the time they handed out job descriptions in the form of ultimatums, they had come to see themselves as "behaving maybe the ways the boys do when . . . they say, 'This is it. Either you do it or you're not here.' "

The workers also came to accept the framework of the politics of contract in their interactions with the owners, but for very different reasons. Workers began to press for job descriptions, monthly shop meetings, and more specific policies in order to protect themselves against what they regarded as arbitrary assertions of managerial power. The formal presentation of a list of issues and demands represented their attempt to "depersonalize [the situation at Amazon] and make it a business thing."

Because the politics of contract was identified with a combination of formality and male gender attributes, the women of Amazon began to belittle emotional reactions to the growing conflict as responses typical of women but inappropriate to businesslike conduct. In the process, they unknowingly rejected one of the most positive aspects of lesbian workplace culture: the integration of public and private that encourages bringing the whole self, including feelings, into work. Workers criticized the owners for responding "on this real emotional level to our demands, about how we were insulting their intelligence and honor." Meanwhile, the owners dismissed the strike as lacking substantive issues by referring to the emotional weight behind workers' actions. Maintaining the bridge between the private and public would have allowed both sides to acknowledge the intensity of feeling surrounding the dispute without separating emotions from more tangible bread-and-butter issues. Instead, the women at Amazon redrew the private/public boundary by shifting to a paradigm identified solely with the public sphere.

No one at Amazon was satisfied with the character of labor relations under the politics of contract, but the dualistic definition of the two paradigms made contractual relations seem to be the only possible substitute for relations based on friendship and trust. Since both sides viewed the loose structure and informal managerial style associated with the politics of trust as the source of the conflicts at Amazon, both initially expected a shift to a more formalized business structure to solve their differences. While some workers continued to hope for a consensual settlement, others began to understand the conflict as a power struggle rooted in the division of labor that would not be resolved by the establishment of a set policy. Implicit in the struggle over job descriptions was the recognition that measures intended to protect workers could also be used by the owners to maintain control. Workers who once had argued against the commission system opposed conversion to salary on the grounds that an hourly wage would "give [the owners] too much power" by allowing them to regulate employees' hours and subject workers to arbitrary requests.

Despite their growing awareness of the implications of the power differential at Amazon, workers believed the dispute could be resolved within the existing class structure. Yet the issues they raised posed a tacit challenge to relations of production that concentrated decision-making power in the owner's hands. This seeming paradox rests on the fact that to the degree the workers' stand encompassed a claim to self-determination, their concerns could not have been adequately addressed while class relations at Amazon remained unaltered. Ownership never became an articulated issue largely because workers were tactically and philosophically committed to a politics of contract that limited their proposals to discrete, point-by-point demands.

Frustration with the restrictions of a bargaining procedure derived from male trade unionism led the workers to search for a "different way" to approach the owners, but their efforts to break through the paradigms that framed their struggle were unsuccessful. They failed in part because the shift from a politics of trust to a politics of contract focused discussions on questions of work discipline and managerial style. The deeper questions concerning ownership and the division of labor at Amazon, which were not mediated by notions of gender and sexual identity, could not be addressed within the terms of either paradigm. The final irony was that the configuration of class relations at the heart of the Amazon conflict was never questioned as being incongruous in a lesbian institution but was instead uncritically adopted from the straight male world.

Lesbian Identity in the Formation of a Workers' Alliance

The radical potential created with the bridging of the private and public was not completely destroyed by the elaboration of class relations and the emergence of open conflict at Amazon. The commitment that accompanied the integration of personal and work life had the radicalizing effect of motivating workers to struggle against what they perceived to be unfair labor practices. The unusually high degree of solidarity maintained by the workers throughout this struggle also had its roots in the kind of workplace Amazon was before the strike. Solidarity among workers was not a deterministic consequence of their being lesbians per se, but an outgrowth of a social context that allowed them to be out on the job in a lesbian-identified institution. Any analysis that reduced events at Amazon to a class conflict without taking these distinguishing features into consideration would miss the dynamics that turned a situation of contention and contradiction into a full-blown labor dispute.

The workers' radicalization was gradual. In the beginning, one mechanic commented, "We weren't a political force; we were just a bunch of women working." Concern about working conditions led them to meet as a group, but class and politics were not explicit topics at these initial meetings. At first women simply compared their reactions to incidents at work, breaking through the silence surrounding grievances that had kept individuals believing they were the only ones angered and confused by the owner's actions. As workers found their personal experiences confirmed by the experiences of others, they began to discuss the possibility of collective action.

Paradoxically, the same bonds of trust and friendship that made it difficult for many workers to break with the owners also stimulated their willingness to challenge the owner's position. Because the politics of trust masked power inequalities at Amazon, it had encouraged workers to consider all points negotiable and to believe they could ask for whatever seemed "fair" and "reasonable" according to their own needs. When the owners met their list of issues with a sct of nonnegotiable job descriptions, the workers' fundamental point of unity became an agreement not to accept the job descriptions in the form of ultimatums.

The workers' ability to achieve and maintain such solidarity is all the more remarkable given the diversity of the group and the differences in their politics. But the foundation for the collective structure that enabled them to mediate their disagreements had already been laid by the patterns of cooperation and strong emotional ties the women had developed working together in the shop. Workers referred to this sense of camaraderie and closeness to explain what differentiated Amazon from a shop employing straight women, suggesting that these patterns were a product of lesbian workplace culture rather than a composite of individuated ties: "Everybody was a tight group at Amazon. . . . You've got all these dykes! [The owners] used to be a part of that when we were smaller, but then we started getting bigger and everybody had different needs, and so it was 'us' and 'them.' Unfortunately it had to come to that. But we were all pretty grouped emotionally before this stuff came up, so that we were all grouped in battle."

The workers' alliance was based on the synthesis of lesbian identity and a growing awareness of class divisions tied to the division of labor. On the one hand, the women clearly interpreted the conflict as a labor dispute and took a stand based on their needs as workers. On the other hand, they directed their appeals primarily to other lesbians and selected their tactics with the aim of keeping the struggle within the lesbian community.

Sensitivity to stereotypes about lesbians' pugnacity and women's alleged incompetence in business affairs made the workers deliberately protective of Amazon at the gay/straight boundary. Workers consistently refused to address the general public or what they considered the "straight media." They turned to the National Labor Relations Board as a last resort in order to keep the owners' job proposals from taking effect as contracts. Workers reluctantly agreed to bring in the "big boys" from the union only after they felt they had exhausted alternatives within the lesbian community and faced the possibility of having to abandon the strike effort altogether. Today, the union's failure to make progress toward a settlement seems to confirm the workers' original skepticism about the union's commitment to the Amazon struggle and its ability to comprehend the concerns of a lesbian shop.

Stanley Aronowitz has argued that the most significant innovations in recent social theory have come from movements like feminism that have grown up outside the traditional boundaries of Marxist and trade unionist politics. Because strictly economic disputes appear to have lost their subversive potential under advanced capitalist conditions, Aronowitz predicts that questions raised by what he calls "cultural movements" will become the new focus of historical change.[18] Events at Amazon seem to corroborate both hypotheses. However, Aronowitz's thesis is qualified by the fact that lesbian workplaces represent a historically unprecedented form of organizing productive relations that cannot be adequately comprehended by a notion of culture set apart from economic factors. The culture that has emerged in institutions like Amazon is not a simple reflection of lesbian-feminist principles but results in part from the bridge between the public and private spheres created by bringing together in practice the hitherto ideologically opposed categories of labor and sexuality. In the Amazon case, the development of a lesbian workplace culture united workers in a struggle that encompassed both economic and cultural concerns. In this sense the Amazon conflict challenges socialist-feminist theory to grapple with issues of sexuality, and urges lesbian-feminist theory to move beyond its focus on sexuality and its legacy of liberal assumptions, in order to develop an analysis of class relations in the lesbian context.

Conclusion: Class and Sexuality

Why has a dialogue about class comparable to the current discussion of race and racism failed to emerge within lesbian feminism? The Amazon case draws attention to several contributing factors: (1) the limited interpretation of class as class background favored by lesbian feminists; (2) liberal strains in lesbian-feminist theory that discourage a relational analysis of class focusing on social structure; (3) the institutional hegemony of an entrepreneurial and professional stratum within the lesbian community; and (4) the heterosexual bias of socialist and socialist-feminist approaches to class theory, which limits their applicability to lesbians.

Information on individuals' class backgrounds clearly cannot explain events at Amazon, for women from both middle-class and working-class backgrounds allied on opposite sides of the dispute. "It would be so much easier, in a way," observed the owner who grew up in a working-class household, "if Lauren and I were both upper-class and my father gave me $50,000 and her father gave her $60,000, and we plunked it into a bank and started the business. . . . But it's not that simple." To claim that class background does not determine present behavior does not mean it did not influence decisions made and strategies adopted during the conflict. For example, the limited resources available to workers from certain class backgrounds made it more difficult for them to remain out on strike. In general, however, Amazon's employees had a clear sense that their current position in the relations of production outweighed their varied class backgrounds: "We all knew where we came from, but we all were working, and we knew how hard we worked, and we knew how we were getting treated. When you're a worker, you're a worker."

A background interpretation of class has led most lesbian feminists to define class according to individualized criteria like occupation, income level, education, values, attitudes, and other indicators of socioeconomic status. While these attributes may be linked to class, they do not define class, unless one accepts the liberal view of society as an amalgam of autonomous actors fixed in absolute class positions. On the basis of occupation, all the women at Amazon could be labeled working-class because of their blue-collar trade. If a combination of income and educational attainment were used as a gauge, some workers might be assigned a higher class position than the owners. Aside from the mutual inconsistency of these evaluations, neither offers any insight into the relations of class and power that actively shaped the Amazon conflict.[19] In contrast, placing the owners within the context of the job hierarchy at Amazon and the division of labor that structures ownership in society at large allowed us to explore the power differential that put Lauren and Carol in a position of dominance over other women working in the shop.

A relational analysis of events at Amazon supports the conclusion that since property relations and the division of labor continuously generate class divisions, tactics of consciousness raising and moral exhortations to eliminate classism will be insufficient to keep conflicts from emerging in lesbian and feminist institutions. The expectation that "feminist morality" or a principled politics can mitigate class differences rests on a notion of politics as an individualized, ideological stance adopted at will, independent of material circumstances and capable of transcending them. But at Amazon, differences in the values and political commitments of the owners did not prevent them from taking the same side in the dispute once lines were drawn. Lauren felt "morally justified" in presenting the workers with nonnegotiable job descriptions, never realizing the extent to which she defined morality and "responsible action" with regard to the needs of the business. Carol, on the other hand, found it "bizarre to be on the side of the owner. It's much easier for me to think of it from the workers' standpoint." Yet she held to her position.

The owners both supported the principle of solving Amazon's problems through dialogue rather than firing dissenting employees, yet in the end their power as owners and managers allowed them to abandon this ideal. In Carol's words, "Somebody reached the point where they put their foot down and said, 'That's it.' And you can only do that when you are in the powered position, which we were." Both owners admitted having discussed strategy about the possibility of an employee walkout in response to their job descriptions: "We did discuss it. We said, 'If that happens, the two of us built this from nothing. Now we have the books, we have the diagnostic equipment, we have the customers, we got the building, we're way ahead.' "

In the workers' eyes, control of the property associated with the business gave the owners a decisive advantage during the struggle. When economic necessity forced the workers to drop the picket line to look for other jobs, the prospect of negotiation receded as the owners continued production in the building all ten women had shared before the strike. Since the owners established Amazon with minimal capital investment and took out few loans in succeeding years, the property and equipment that helped them win the struggle actually came from surplus value created by the combined efforts of Amazon's employees and nonpartisan support from the women's community. The owners' exclusive claim to this property was based solely on a legal concept of ownership backed by a patriarchal state. The same principle of ownership underpinned the dominant class position that structured the owners' moral stance, neutralized their well-meaning intentions, and superseded their lesbian-feminist politics at the point of conflict.

It is true that Amazon is "not Bechtel"—a major multinational corporation—as the owners were quick to point out, but this fact obviously did not prevent class relations and a class-linked conflict from emerging in the shop. Although the lesbian community lies well outside the mainstream of American capitalism, it does include a stratum of entrepreneurs, professionals, and small capitalists like Carol and Lauren who own or control many of the institutions serving and symbolizing that community. We suggest that in practice such control allows this group of women to maintain an institutional hegemony[20] that mediates the relation of lesbian identity to community in ways that alternately support and oppress lesbians who stand in different relations to the social division of labor.[21]

The concern with self-reliance and independence that originally led Carol and Lauren to become entrepreneurs also informed their argument that dissatisfied workers should open their own enterprises rather than challenge the owners' right to make unilateral decisions in matters affecting employees.[22] Yet what might otherwise be dismissed as regressive, petit-bourgeois values in the tradition of nineteenth-century entrepreneurial capitalism has a different meaning, origin, and political significance in this lesbian context. For Lauren and Carol, self-sufficiency represented a liberating ideology that signified autonomy from men in the area of skills, training, and the ability to earn an equitable income. The same ideology became oppressive only when, as owners and employers, they confused self-determination with the need to control the labor of women they hired.

The coincidence of entrepreneurial values with aspects of lesbian identity in the ideology of self-sufficiency is one more example of the recurrent theme in this study: there is no justification at the level of concrete analysis for abstracting class from sexuality or for treating heterosexism and class hegemony as two distinct types of oppression operating along separate axes. The strike at Amazon cannot be analyzed as a textbook labor conflict precisely because the male and heterosexist bias of most scholarly texts renders them incapable of grasping this integration. While a critique of the bias in class theory is beyond the scope of this paper, the Amazon case indicates why such an integration is necesary.

Lesbians are not simply exceptions to the rule who defy categorization as "nonattached" or "single" (but presumably self-supporting) women or as women residing in households with men.[23] Since self-identified lesbians in American society share an ideology of self-sufficiency rather than the ideological expectation not to work traditionally held by many heterosexual women, the question of derived class becomes largely irrelevant in speaking of lesbian relationships.[24] None of the women in the Amazon study even suggested the possibility of defining her class position through her lover, though several were in relationships of long standing. Lesbians also fall outside the theoretical focus of most debates in socialist feminism, which tend to center on the sexual division of labor.[25] Although the sexual division of labor and job segregation by sex influence all women's experience, for most lesbians gender distinctions do not coincide with the split between home and work life or with the allocation of tasks within the home. When the split between personal and work life is linked to sexuality with the bridging of the private/public split in lesbian workplaces, socialist feminism proffers no theory capable of grasping the significance of what happens once lesbian identity is joined to productive activity.

At Amazon we saw how the reconciliation of the public and private created the potential for a nonalienating work environment where women were able to develop close ties with co-workers as well as to bring into the shop emotions and other ostensibly personal aspects of the self. After the walkout/lockout this integration shaped the dispute by placing emotions at the center of the struggle so that at various points the struggle itself involved drawing and redrawing the boundary between elements of public and private life. While the bridging of the private/public split could not defuse class relations at Amazon, it generated the conditions for overcoming class divisions by fostering a lesbian workplace culture that promoted solidarity among the workers and motivated them to defend their needs in a situation where the owners held the balance of power.

One of Amazon's owners ended her interview with a plea that lesbians learn to "put aside personal feelings and vested interests" or risk the destruction of community institutions. A careful analysis of the Amazon dispute points to the importance of taking personal feelings into account rather than putting them aside and remaining within the limitations of the contrasting paradigms of trust and contract. The effect of suppressing or ignoring the personal will be to reinvoke the division between the private and public, when the ability to bridge that gap constitutes one of the greatest strengths of lesbian institutions. In this sense, the experience of the women of Amazon Auto Repair challenges both lesbian feminism and socialist feminism to break through old paradigms, to recognize that separating sexuality and class in theory merely replicates the segregation of the private from the public, and the personal from the political, in the realm of everyday life.

As for vested interests, they cannot simply be discarded at will, since they have material roots in socially constructed needs mediated by property relations and the division of labor. Yet there exist options for restructuring lesbian workplaces that reject ownership while providing leadership roles, job rotation, procedures for delegating responsibility, shared decision-making processes, and a division of labor that does not rest on a fixed power differential. The radical potential for nonalienated labor created in lesbian workplaces invites us to explore these alternatives as a means of redefining power as energy, skill, and capacity rather than as domination.[26] By drawing attention to the ongoing reproduction of class relations within the lesbian community, the struggle at Amazon advances the possibility of self-determination inside and outside the labor process for all lesbians, not just for the few who formally or informally control lesbian institutions.

Notes

1. Regardless of where one stands in the definitional debate on lesbian identity (see Ann Ferguson et al., "On 'Compulsory Heterosexuality and Lesbian Existence': Defining the Issues," *Signs* 7 [1981]: 158–99), it is clear that competing usages of the

term "lesbian" all rest on criteria such as friendship, sexuality, and feeling, which historically have been assigned to the realm of the personal.

2. See Annette Kuhn and AnnMarie Wolpe (eds.), *Feminism and Materialism: Women and Modes of Production* (London: Routledge & Kegan Paul, 1978); Iris Young, "Beyond the Unhappy Marriage: A Critique of Dual Systems Theory," in Lydia Sargent (ed.), *Women and Revolution: A Discussion of the Unhappy Marriage of Marxism and Feminism* (Boston: South End Press, 1981), pp. 43–69.

3. Lesbian identity then becomes a defining element of a distinctive type of workplace culture, making Amazon something more than an aggregation of isolated employees who "happened" to be lesbians or a repository for the piecemeal importation of artifacts from lesbian feminism.

4. In our heterosexist society, "woman" and "feminist" often function as code words among lesbians for "lesbian" and "lesbian feminist," in much the same way as sexism encourages the substitution of "people" or "men" as generic terms for "women."

5. Nancy Hartsock, "Political Change: Two Perspectives on Power," in *Building Feminist Theory,* edited by the *Quest* staff (New York: Longman, 1981), pp. 3–19.

6. Audre Lorde, *Uses of the Erotic: The Erotic as Power* (New York: Out & Out Books, 1978).

7. The bridging of the private/public split provides a mechanism to explain the high levels of commitment often noted as characteristic of lesbian institutions. See Barbara Ponse, *Identities in the Lesbian World: The Social Construction of Self* (Westport, Conn: Greenwood Press, 1978). Contrary to Ponse's findings, no significant association between commitment and conformity appeared in the Amazon case.

8. Hartsock, "Political Change."

9. An assumption widely criticized in recent years in the discussion on race and difference within the women's community. See Cherríe Moraga and Gloria Anzaldúa (eds.), *This Bridge Called My Back: Writings by Radical Women of Color* (Watertown, Mass: Persephone Press, 1981).

10. Compare Sherry McCoy and Maureen Hicks, "A Psychological Retrospective on Power in the Contemporary Lesbian-Feminist Community," *Frontiers: A Journal of Women Studies* 4, no. 3 (1979) 65–69. Their exclusively personal conception of power ignores the possibility that both power and needs may be shaped by social relations like class that divide the lesbian community.

11. We do not mean to imply that the owners' fears for the survival of lesbian businesses are groundless; we do question the allegation that the workers acted as agents of reactionary forces.

12. Agnes Heller, *The Theory of Need in Marx* (London: Allison & Busby, 1976), p. 25.

13. On the links between the changing organization of production and class relations under industrial capitalism, see Harry Braverman, *Labor and Monopoly Capital* (New York: Monthly Review Press, 1974); Richard Edwards, *Contested Terrain: The Transformation of the Workplace in the Twentieth Century* (New York: Basic Books, 1979).

14. Bertell Ollman, *Alienation* (London: Cambridge University Press, 1971), pp. 133–34. Following Ollman, we take alienation to mean a separation of the individual from her life activity, the products of her labor, and other human beings within the labor process.

15. Karl Marx and Frederick Engels, *The German Ideology* (New York: International Publishers, 1978), pp. 51–52.

16. For cross-cultural discussions of relationally defined gender constructs, see Carol MacCormack and Marilyn Strathern (eds.), *Nature, Culture and Gender* (London: Cambridge University Press, 1980); Sherry B. Ortner and Harriet Whitehead (eds.), *Sexual Meanings: The Cultural Construction of Gender and Sexuality* (New York: Cambridge University Press, 1981).

17. On the owners' side this understanding reflected lesbian-feminist ideology, but for most workers it developed through an appeal to notions of gender and sexuality to explain differences in their work experience at Amazon and at other businesses.

18. Stanley Aronowitz, *The Crisis in Historical Materialism* (New York: Praeger, 1981), pp. 105–6, 133.

19. Anthony Giddens, "Class Structuration and Class Consciousness," in Anthony Giddens and David Held (eds.), *Classes, Power, and Conflict* (Berkeley and Los Angeles: University of California Press, 1982), p. 158.

20. On the concept of hegemony, see Antonio Gramsci, *Selections from the Prison Notebooks* (New York: International Publishers, 1980), p. 12; Raymond Williams, *Marxism and Literature* (Oxford: Oxford University Press, 1977), pp. 108 14.

21. Introducing power as a variable challenges Susan Krieger's static view of lesbian communities as either supportive or coercive to individuals: "Lesbian Identity and Community: Recent Social Science Literature," *Signs* 8, (1982): 91–108.

22. Clearly it would be impractical for every lesbian auto mechanic to open her own repair shop. This admonition also avoids dealing with the source of divisions in the lesbian community by deprecating worker struggles and initiatives.

23. Elizabeth Garnsey advances these categories in an attempt to correct the androcentrism of such theories: "Women's Work and Theories of Class and Stratification," *Sociology* 12 (1978): 223–43.

24. Jackie West, "Women, Sex, and Class," in Kuhn and Wolpe, *Feminism and Materialism*.

25. The isolated attempts to apply socialist-feminist analysis to lesbians ignore class relations within the lesbian community, directing their attention instead to the origins of women's oppression or to relations at the gay/straight boundary. In addition to Christine Riddiough, "Socialism, Feminism and Gay Liberation" in Sargent, *Women and Revolution*, see Susan Williams, "Lesbianism: A Socialist Feminist Perspective," in Pam Mitchell (ed.), *Pink Triangles: Radical Perspectives on Gay Liberation* (Boston: Alyson Publications, 1980), pp. 107 16.

26. Hartsock, "Political Change," draws a useful distinction between power understood as domination and power understood as energy, capacity, and initiative.

PART IV

State Policy and Employers' Policy

Introduction

In the late 1960s and early 1970s, younger feminists promoted the idea that "the personal is political" and used consciousness raising as a political tool to overcome gender inequality in the division of labor and hierarchy in intimate relations. Although the understanding that the "personal is political" had enormous significance for women's lives, a narrow interpretation of the idea led to a focus on "interpersonal politics" that eclipsed the larger economic and political organization undergirding gender inequality. So, too, much of the research on work and family has focused on individual adaptations (often reduced to "coping mechanisms") without addressing the collective efforts and structural solutions that might reduce individuals' need to adapt. In contrast, this last section turns to the policies of employers and government—to the larger political context within which solutions are sought.

Family Policy

While many European nations—notably Sweden, France, and Germany—have an explicit family policy, and most European nations negotiate industrial benefits at the national level, the United States does neither. Indeed, some suggest that a coherent American policy is impossible because "the meaning of profamily cannot be agreed upon," and consequently "our intangible sentiments that are the foundation of strong family relations can neither be legislated nor set forth in executive order or court decree." [1]

In this view, the combination of pluralism in family life, persistent diversity from state to state, and an ideology of the family as a bastion of privacy make futile any attempt to develop an explicit national family policy. [2]

Nonetheless, Kamerman and Kahn suggest in their description of government and families in fourteen nations that the absence of a federal policy does not mean that there is no family policy in the United States. As they write: "True, there is no comprehensive, overall national policy. Yet . . . there is a rich tradition of state programs and laws which may certainly be described as embodying relatively extensive and quite explicit family policy."[3] In this formulation, many government initiatives bearing on economic well-being—including tax and social security plans, welfare and work-incentive programs, childcare and child-support systems—are part of this "family policy."

To accept the idea that the United States has a family policy is not to minimize its many inconsistencies and contradictions. Federal laws vary from administration to administration and contain contradictory agendas, especially for those in different social classes. Thus, for example, while the federal "marriage tax penalty" and Social Security laws penalize a dual-earner couple for marrying (or a married woman for her employment), many welfare laws and work-incentive programs have made it increasingly difficult for single mothers to stay home. Though Aid to Dependent Children was designed during the Great Depression to keep single mothers (typically widows) out of the paid labor force,[4] legislative programs in the mid-1960s introduced an "income-disregard"[5] policy for recipients of Aid to Families with Dependent Children (AFDC)—now primarily single and divorced—to encourage their employment. In the late 1960s Congress enacted a mandatory work registration and training program for adult welfare recipients.[6] In 1971, for the first time, federal AFDC policy required women whose children were under six to enter the labor force.[7] Since 1980 the Reagan administration has reduced the income disregard, put a new and lower ceiling on work-related expenses, and developed a mandatory workfare scheme for welfare recipients to eliminate the use of AFDC as a supplement to low wages.[8] These policies essentially reversed the tactics of his predecessors but still insisted that single mothers—in contrast to married mothers—belonged in the labor force even if that ensured that they and their children would remain poor.[9]

Moreover, states implement federal policy in vastly different ways, producing uneven benefits (a single mother living in Alabama, Mississippi, or Texas will receive far lower AFDC payments than one living in Alaska or New York) and different requirements for aid (e.g., only about half the states have chosen to provide AFDC welfare benefits to families with an unemployed father at home.)[10]

Finally, most employee benefits are negotiated between particular unions and their employers or, in some cases, even between individuals and their bosses. Employers vary enormously in the family benefits they provide: small firms provide far less than large ones; the public sector provides somewhat more than the private. Consequently, individuals who live in different places or work for different employers enjoy significantly different benefits relevant to family support.

In this section, we look at the consequences of this incoherent "family policy." First, we look at the policies of employers that are now the loci of struggles to make jobs more responsive to familial concerns. Second, we turn to state policy to assess the role it plays, has played, and can play in generating, or alleviating, gender inequality in the labor market and in families.

Employer Policy

The entry of increasing numbers of married women with young children and single mothers into the labor force put pressure on employers to implement policies at the job site responsive to employees' domestic obligations. Many such policies were widely heralded: corporate childcare, maternity and paternity leaves, relocation policies, flexitime and flexiplace. For the most part, however, researchers have found that these changes fell short of their anticipated outcomes.

Although pressured to provide childcare, few employers are doing so. A range of business supports have been proposed: regular on-site care; care for sick children; subsidies or vouchers; discounts at selected childcare programs; or even information or referral centers. But in 1984, only 2,000 businesses (out of 6 million) provided any of these types of support.[11] In fact, the number of industry-sponsored centers has declined since 1970.[12]

The 1970s did see a major development in corporate maternity policy: short leaves (typically less than three months) at the time of childbirth became available to most employed women. However, most maternity leaves are not paid leaves. Paid maternity leaves included (under disability policies) in employee benefit packages were available to only 40 percent of employed women in 1984.[13] Even those plans that do provide paid leaves tend to do so for only a brief period (less than half of all firms offer more than a few weeks of paid leave).[14] Moreover, only a handful of companies have formal policies relating to paternity leaves. In fact, only a minority even allow new fathers a few days off as sick leave.[15]

As more employees refuse to move because of their spouses' job commitments, some U.S. corporations have reduced their transfer requirements.[16] But only 4 percent of corporations assist the spouses of relocating employees at all.[17] The policies that do exist are typically minimal, like providing referrals to employment agencies. Few companies have removed antinepotism rules in order to accommodate both transferred partners.[18]

The first two essays in this part analyze two other much discussed innovations—flexitime and flexiplace—which have been heralded as a means for both men and women to overcome the difficulties arising from the separation of employment and household. In Chapter 23, Sheila Rothman and Emily Marks analyze the growing use of flexitime and the compressed work week. They show that these adaptations are of limited value, especially for those engaged in professional careers. Moreover, they show that alternative work schedules may actually serve to reinforce gender inequality rather than reduce it: whereas these schedules promote men's satisfaction and attachment to a particular job, they encourage women to concentrate on meeting family obligations.

Kathleen Christensen's analysis of home-based employment (Chapter 24) comes to quite similar conclusions. Though it is widely celebrated by the media and the federal government as a panacea for employed mothers attempting to transcend the split between worksite and household, women's actual response to this adaptation suggests otherwise. Christensen shows that while home-based employment is increasing, it offers advantages to corporations but less clear benefits to the isolated and stressed women who try to care for their home and children at the same time as they try to do their jobs.[19] And, like Rothman and Marks, she finds that what benefits there are accrue more to women in low-paying clerical jobs. She cautions against "solutions" that may further ghettoize women and contribute to gender inequality.

Overall, most employers have managed to remain indifferent to workers' personal concerns and, in doing so, have affirmed the ideology that separates jobs from families. By and large they have not been pressed too hard. Though goaded by some women activists, unions—whose membership has been dropping in recent years—have been unable, and typically unwilling, to press employers for these policies.[20] Although unions increasingly rely on female membership (in 1980 women made up 30 percent of union membership, compared with 23 percent in 1973), the basic economic threats and "give-backs" of a conservative political climate discourage new demands responsive to women's familial obligations.[21] While some public sector unions make demands for childcare and flexitime, they are unwilling to give priority to these issues in actual negotiations. And unions, along with management, maintain the idea that childcare is women's work and have "a deep rooted ambivalence toward making it easier for mothers to work."[22] Individuals are often left to negotiate their own distinctive packages, which may only serve to divide workers and reinforce employers' control and resistance to change.

Consequently, the job policies that exist bolster gender inequality by limiting women's economic independence at the same time that they undergird their primary responsibility for childcare. Although employers recognize their increasing dependence on the labor of mothers, they maintain that domestic work is either a private family's (or, more specifically, mother's) responsibility or an issue for the state.

State Policy

Over the course of this century, government has increasingly come to be viewed as the appropriate instrument for redress of economic inequality. Since World War II, government outlays for social welfare purposes have grown dramatically. Much of the current discussion of government family policy centers on issues of economic inequality. How do state policies shape the relationship of employment and families and women's and men's positions in both? To what extent do state policies undermine—or reinforce—a division of labor and stratification by gender?

STATE INTERVENTION, THE PRIVATIZED FAMILY, AND GENDER INEQUALITY

Ronald Reagan was elected to the presidency with the aid of the New Right on a platform that promised to oppose state intrusion into family life. However, many scholars—from diverse theoretical and political perspectives— now suggest that the American ideology of a self sufficient, autonomous family (which extends far beyond the New Right) is contradicted by the practices of the modern state, whether administered by the right or the center. Some argue that American policy makers "have shown an uncharacteristic willingness to intervene in the lives of welfare families,"[23] who are viewed as "deviant" or "failures."[24] But many now insist that since the early part of this century, families—"normal" and "deviant" alike—have become increasingly subject to "policing by the state."[25] Indeed, Christopher Lasch writes: "Today the state controls not merely . . . the public realm but the darkest corners of private life, formerly inaccessible to political domination."[26] Domesticity and privatization did not just diffuse; they were imposed by agents of the state—public health and police officers, social workers and educational reformers, judges and court-appointed doctors—on an often reluctant working class.[27] As Lasch shows, the private family and individual freedom that this culture values are created and sustained by these "intrusive" relations between state and family.

Whereas Lasch mourns these intrusive relations because they imply the decline of husbands' and fathers' authority, many feminists now argue that state intervention imposes and sustains a gender hierarchy characterized by women's isolation in and dependence on the privatized family and a subordinate position (if any) in the labor market.[28] Government policies, including both social insurance programs (e.g., unemployment compensation and Social Security) and means-tested or welfare programs (e.g., AFDC, food stamps, Medicaid) operate to maintain men's and women's unequal positions at home and on the job. To be sure, women are the overwhelming majority of recipients of means-tested income-maintenance programs, such as AFDC (81.1 percent are women), food stamps (73.3 percent), and Medicaid (71.9 percent), as well as most insurance programs, including Social Security benefits (61.6 percent) and Medicare (64.8 percent).[29] However, the social insurance and means-tested programs produce a two-tiered benefit system that reinforces gender inequality.

Although they no longer practice de jure discrimination against women, the higher-paying, less-stigmatizing unemployment compensation programs were designed for regularly employed male heads of households. Women, who constitute a disproportionate share of the unemployed, are disqualified as claimants or allotted reduced unemployment benefits more often than men.[30] If a woman quits her job for domestic reasons (i.e., unavailability of childcare or inappropriate hours), she is unlikely to obtain unemployment compensation.[31] Similarly, Social Security retirement programs were established to respond to the needs of male workers and have a long-standing bias in favor of homemaking and against employed wives.[32] In contrast, women have constituted a larger proportion of the beneficiaries of the welfare programs than of the insurance programs. Significantly, current cutbacks now center on the former category, where women are the primary beneficiaries. Most importantly, women can only lay claim to these reduced welfare benefits on the basis of their positions as mothers or wives.[33]

By failing to provide adequate childcare that would allow mothers to hold jobs and earn an independent income, state policies commit women to mothering.[34] Because mothers are still primarily responsible for parenting (see Part II of this volume), the provison of day care is central to women's ability to seek and maintain employment.[35] It is also an indicator of our society's willingness (or reluctance) to see children as a public rather than a private good and childcare as a social, rather than maternal, responsibility. Since Reagan entered office, direct government funding for childcare services has been sharply reduced. Moreover, state policies, in the current conservative climate, reinforce class advantage: while the middle class can now take an increased tax deduction for childcare, the poor have lost the few existing public facilities available to them.[36]

Finally, because the state provides a level of benefits inadequate to ensure women's full independence (at the same time that it upholds their obligation to children), it forces women to relay on husbands. In contrast to many other Western nations, not a single state's AFDC program offers cash grants and nonincome transfers that bring its recipient's total income above the official poverty line's austere standard of living.[37] Workfare programs, in combination with levels of benefits adjusted to be lower than prevailing wage rates, are also used to ensure that welfare recipients will remain in low-paying jobs.[38] Thus, employers in the low-wage sectors gain a captive labor force and in effect secure a government subsidy while they can pay wages based on the premise (often false) that women share in a family (that is, man's) wage. In fact, the primary way poor women can improve their economic situation is through remarriage.[39]

Many feminists now argue that these policies and programs reinforce the husband's position as household head and primary breadwinner while they uphold women's position as homemaker and parent. The net effect is to maintain a primary identification of women with domestic and family concerns that all too often hampers them when they move into the labor force and renders them financially dependent on men. In addition, these policies propel men to concentrate on jobs while they depend on their wives for creating and maintaining a home.

Some feminists go further. They suggest that the development of laws and public poicies transferred the power of men within families to the power of men through the state. Men continue to rule, not so much as individual husbands or, more clearly, as individual fathers, but through law and public policy.[40] But individual men are still the beneficiaries: "Public patriarchy benefits individual men in enabling them to shift the financial and labor burden of their children onto mothers while retaining access to women's services through the formal organizations, both governmental and industrial, of capitalist patriarchy."[41] According to this view women cannot—and should not—rely on the state as a lever to unhinge the relations between the economy and the family that support their subordinate position in both.[42]

In Chapter 25, Nancy Folbre presents this perspective through an overview of state policy bearing on families and the labor market. She picks up where Boris and Bardaglio, in Part I, left off. Folbre analyzes how twentieth-century state policies have served the interests of men while disadvantaging women, especially mothers. Reviewing maternity-leave and child-support laws, childcare and tax policies, as well as AFDC programs, she argues that patriarchal assumptions have produced policies that refuse to recognize mothering as work while they assign to women a disproportionate share of the costs involved in raising the next generation. Such public policies, she contends, have contributed significantly to the pauperization, and therefore dependence, of mothers.

THE STATE AND LIBERATION

Although state policies have served to reinforce gender inequality, we should not forget that they also have the partially realized potential to liberate or emancipate. It is this potential that is currently being threatened by Reagan's budget cuts. Not only are women the majority of welfare recipients, but the expanding social welfare economy has also been an important source of job opportunities for them. In the 1970s government employed about one-quarter of all women and about half of women professionals.[43] These opportunities provide an economic base outside marriage. Eisenstein suggests that "to the degree that it played an active role in providing opportunities to women, the welfare state itself, like liberal democracy, has become a subversive force challenging the patriarchal ordering of the marketplace."[44]

As Piven and Cloward have shown, earlier increases in state subsidies and public relief were a direct consequence of social unrest and protest.[45] Recipients of benefits (whether means-tested or insurance programs) are considerably more likely to evaluate negatively Reagan's performance in office.[46] The dismantling of the welfare state helps explain the growing alienation of women from the Reagan administration.[47] Rather than seeing government welfare programs as reflecting simply a state-imposed politics of domination, Frances Fox Piven reminds us in Chapter 26 that state policies give women an alternative, albeit a limited one, to dependence on the family. She argues that the "public patriarchy" thesis does not recognize how the apparatus of the welfare state, by bringing women together, helps to generate political resources among both the professionals who administer it and the beneficiaries who depend upon it. This creates the potential for cross-class alliances among women.

In Chapter 27, Alice Kessler-Harris raises the possibility of even more far-reaching alliances among women, and between women and men, that would allow all workers to enjoy the advantages of both families and jobs. She argues that we must advocate state and employer policies that recognize— indeed, celebrate—what women's employment has made visible: the societal importance of families.

Her historical overview of concepts and policies developed to overcome women's disadvantaged place in the labor force asks the general questions with which much of this book has been implicitly concerned: Is gender equality compatible with gender difference? Can women move toward equality without negating their special family commitments and obligations? It presents historically specific answers. Tracing the development of nineteenth- and early twentieth-century theories of "separate spheres," Alice Kessler-Harris argues in Chapter 27 that these informed past social policies, like protective legislation, that many feminists supported. Though developed to advance women's rights, such notions often served to deprive women of employment opportunities and, by the 1960s, were abandoned. But, she suggests, these "lessons of history" deserve a new look today: within a corporate capitalist economy, ignoring women's special family obligations (one basis of their difference) may perpetuate gender inequality. Recognizing gender differences, by promoting policies such as comparable worth, may now speed movements toward gender equality just as it may challenge the individualism and competition characteristic of the economy. Hers is a compelling, though certainly controversial, case for the way making public our previously privatized obligations will assist not only women, but also men, families, communities, and the social fabric more generally.

We have come full circle in this book. The question is not whether we have a "family policy," for, in effect, we do. The question is whose interests it serves: the interests of business, or, more broadly, capitalism; the interests of men, or, more broadly, "state patriarchy?" These policies, like all others, do not simply happen. Those who are affected respond to their substance and implementation with struggle. Whether these policies are favorable or unfavorable to the diverse needs of women, and the families in which they live, depends upon historical context and the historically specific ability of women to unite and organize on their own behalf. As this book makes clear, such organization today must decry the ideology that separates work and family just as it must, at least for a time, acknowledge the significance of gender differences in both spheres.

Notes

1. Gilbert Steiner, *The Futility of Family Policy* (Washington, D.C.: Brookings Institute, 1981), pp. 26 and 215.
2. Steiner, *Futility of Family Policy*.
3. S. B. Kamerman and A. J. Kahn (eds.), *Family Policy, Government and Families in Fourteen Countries* (New York: Columbia University Press, 1978), p. 432.
4. In 1962 the Aid to Dependent Children program was renamed Aid to Families with Dependent Children, marking a shift in policy objective from long-term provision of cash assistance to needy children to provision of social services to needy families, with the goal of getting them off the public dole.
5. Welfare mothers were encouraged to mix work and welfare by the "thirty dollars and one-third rule," whereby a recipient could retain the first thirty dollars she earned and one-third of additonal earnings without a proportionate reduction in welfare payments.
6. L. E. Lynn, "A Decade of Policy Developments in the Income Maintenance System," in R. H. Haveman (ed.), *A Decade of Federal Antipoverty Programs* (New York: Academic Press, 1977).
7. M. N. Ozawa, *Income Maintenance and Work Incentives* (New York: Praeger, 1982).

8. Inconsistent political agendas coexist with inconsistent research findings. In line with Reagan's view, some studies suggest that increases in welfare benefits lead to family instability (e.g., fathers desert, mothers choose to remain unmarried). Others find no major effects of welfare payments on family composition decisions. Still others find that payments, depending on their size, produce contradictory effects: low levels of support produce greater marital dissolution; high levels encourage family members to stay together. The same inconsistency is apparent in investigations into whether changes in welfare payments and income disregards reduce attachment to the labor force: evidence can be marshalled for both sides. Administrations, then, can obtain "expert" evidence supporting their contradictory positions. For reviews of such studies, see M. McDonald and Isabel Sawhill, "Welfare Policy and the Family," *Public Policy* 26 (1978):89–119; G. J. Duncan, *Years of Poverty, Years of Plenty* (Ann Arbor: University of Michigan Institute for Social Research, Survey Research Center, 1984); W. A. Darity and S. L. Myers, "Does Welfare Dependency Cause Female Headship? The Case for the Black Family," *Journal of Marriage and the Family* 46 (1984): 765–90; Charles Murray, *Losing Ground: American Family Policy, 1950–1980* (New York: Basic Books, 1984).

9. Deborah K. Zinn and Rosemary C. Sarri, "Turning Back the Clock on Public Welfare" *Signs* 10 (1984):355–70.

10. Barbara R. Bergmann, *The Economic Emergence of Women* (New York: Basic Books, 1986), pp. 227–254.

11. "Child Care Factsheet" (Washington, D.C.: National Commission on Working Women, 1986).

12. Carol Joffe, "Why the United States Has No Child Care Policy," in Irene Diamond (ed.), *Families, Politics and Public Policy: A Feminist Dialogue on Women and the State* (New York: Longman, 1983); Sheila Kamerman, "The Child Care Debate: Working Mothers Vs. America," *Working Woman,* November 1983, pp. 131–36.

13. "Child Care Factsheet."

14. Sheila B. Kamerman, Alfred J. Kahn, and Paul Kingston, *Maternity Policies and Working Women* (New York: Columbia University Press, 1983).

15. "Catalyst Career and Family Bulletin" (New York: Catalyst, 1981).

16. H. H. Bohen, "Gender Equality in Work and Family: An Elusive Goal," *Journal of Family Issues* 5 (1984):254–72.

17. From a national study, *Corporations and Two-Career Families: Directions for Change* (New York: Catalyst, 1983).

18. Sheila B. Kamerman, "Employer Responses to the Family Responsibilities of Employees," in Sheila B. Kamerman and C. D. Hayes (eds.), *Families That Work: Children in a Changing World* (Washington, D.C.: National Academy Press, 1982).

19. In contrast, Judith Gerson and Robert Kraut ("How Well Off Are Home Workers," paper presented at the annual meeting of the American Sociological Association, September 1986, New York) compared secretaries who work at home to those who do not and found that home workers feel they have greater flexibility, do not feel isolated, and experience less psychological distress.

20. Bettina Berch, *The Endless Day: The Political Economy of Women and Work* (New York: Harcourt Brace Jovanovich, 1982).

21. As Ruth Milkman points out, even feminist organizational efforts within the labor unions have not pressed for these issues: "While taking account of the fact that women have 'family responsibilities' that obstruct their union activity, CLUW [Coalition of Labor Union Women] does not view this as the basis for a critique of established organizational forms within the labor movement but rather as an additional han-

dicap which women must somehow overcome"; "Women Workers, Feminism and the Labor Movement Since the 1960s," in Ruth Milkman (ed.), *Women, Work and Protest: A Century of U.S. Women's Labor History* (Boston: Routledge & Kegan Paul, 1985), p. 313.

22. Dianne Bell, "Unionized Women in State and Local Government," in Milkman, *Women, Work and Protest*, p. 291.

23. Carolyn Teich Adams and Kathryn Teich Winston, *Mothers at Work: Public Policies in the United States, Sweden and China* (New York; Longman, 1980), p. 253.

24. Mary C. Blehar, "Families and Public Policy," in A. S. Skolnick and J. H. Skolnick (eds.), *Family in Transition*, 4th ed. (Boston: Little, Brown, 1983).

25. This phrase is from Jacques Donzelot, *The Policing of Families* (New York: Pantheon, 1979). Though this book deals with French families, its ideas have been widely applied to the United States.

26. Christopher Lasch, *Haven in a Heartless World: The Family Besieged* (New York: Basic Books, 1977), p. 189.

27. Ibid.

28. For good summaries of this point of view, see B. C. Gelpi, N. C. Hartsock, and C. C. Novack, "Introduction," *Signs* (1984): 206–98; N. D. Hunter, "Women and Child Support," in Diamond, *Families, Politics and Public Policy*, p. 215.

29. Barbara J. Nelson, "Women's Poverty and Women's Citizenship: Some Political Consequences of Economic Marginality," *Signs* 10 (1984):209–31.

30. D. M. Pearce, "Toil and Trouble: Women Workers and Unemployment Compensation," *Signs* 10 (1985):439–59.

31. Pearce, "Toil and Trouble."

32. M. Derthick, *Policymaking for Social Security* (Washington, D.C.: Brookings Institute, 1979).

33. Nelson, "Women's Poverty and Women's Citizenship."

34. Kamerman. "The Child Care Debate."

35. Most mothers rely primarily on relatives to provide day care while they are away from home; group day-care centers provide only a small proportion of such care: A. Clarke Stewart, *Day Care* (Cambridge: Harvard University Press, 1983). However, women—when offered free day care in centers—seem to prefer it to care provided by relatives. Recent research shows that about one-fifth of nonemployed women say that they would be looking for work if satisfactory childcare were available at reasonable cost. Among employed women, another one-fifth said they would work more hours if additional childcare were available. See H. B. Presser and Wendy Baldwin, "Child Care Constraints on Employment," *American Journal of Sociology* 85 (1980):1202 13.

36. Rosemary C. Sarri, "Federal Policy Changes and the Feminization of Poverty," *Child Welfare* 65 (1985):235–47.

37. U. S. Commission on Civil Rights, *A Growing Crisis: Disadvantaged Women and Their Children* (Washington, D.C.: Government Printing Office, 1983), pp 5–7; see also Adams and Winston, *Mothers at Work*, who compare the low levels of payment in the United States with the higher levels in Sweden and China.

38. Frances Fox Piven and R. Cloward, *Regulating the Poor* (New York: Pantheon, 1971).

39. Duncan, *Years of Poverty*.

40. See Chapter 5, and note 16 in the Introduction to Part I.

41. Carol Brown, "Mothers, Fathers and Children: From Private to Public Patriar-

chy'' in Lydia Sargent (ed.), *Women and Revolution: A Discussion of the Unhappy Marriage of Marxism and Feminism* (Boston: South End Press, 1981), p. 249.

42. See also Jean Bethke Elshtain, ''Antigone's Daughters: Reflections on Female Identity and the State,'' in Diamond, *Families, Politics and Public Policy*.

43. Lester Thurow, *The Zero-Sum Society* (New York: Penguin Books, 1980). Steven P. Erie, Martin Rein, and Barbara Wiget suggest that even these figures underestimate the number of women employed, directly or indirectly, by federal, state, and local governments. See their ''Women and the Reagan Revolution: Thermidor for the Social Welfare Economy,'' in Diamond, *Families, Politics and Public Policy*.

44. Zillah Eisenstein, ''The Patriarchal Relations of the Reagan State,'' *Signs* 10 (1984):329–37.

45. Piven and Cloward, *Regulating the Poor*.

46. Nelson, ''Women's Poverty.''

47. Erie, Rein, and Wiget, ''Women and the Reagan Revolution.''

23

Adjusting Work and Family Life: Flexible Work Schedules and Family Policy

S H E I L A M. R O T H M A N
E M I L Y M E N L O M A R K S

Over the past several years there has been a growing interest in implementing flexible work schedules to help employees balance the conflicting demands of work and family life. A coalition of family policy advocates and management and labor leaders are persuaded that flexible schedules both provide employers with a tool for increasing worker satisfaction and productivity and afford employees the opportunity to manage dual obligations more effectively. This paper will examine how flexible work schedules became a family-oriented personnel policy and explore their potential for increasing opportunities for workers in different social classes.

History of Flexible Work Schedules

The idea of work schedule redesign is highly innovative. The impetus for the development of new schedules comes most frequently from low morale, poor productivity, or an insufficient labor supply. It also requires an economic system that already guarantees some prerogatives to individual workers: it could not occur under an earlier industrial-labor model that viewed the worker as an extension of the machine.[1] The evolution of typing as woman's work illustrates the earlier perspective. Remington, the first company to develop the typewriter (in the 1870s) realized that to market its product it would have to train operators; only when typists, like spare parts, were available on demand would businesses invest in the machine. The company opened typewriting schools, established an employment bureau as an adjunct to each of them, and called both its operators and their machines "typewriters." This link between the worker and the machine made fixed hours of labor a necessity: a worker might have a choice of shifts, but not a choice of time within a shift. The industrial-labor model also ignored non-workplace considerations affecting the laborer.[2] The occasional exception, such as a company town's ban on taverns within its jurisdiction, might be presented as a measure in the best interest of employees and their families, but it primarily reflected management's determination to maximize social control rather than promote workers' contentment or convenience.[3] So too, labor union negotiations under this model focused on the number of hours to be worked, not their allocation across the work day or week. The unions' rallying cry in the Progressive era was to reduce the hours of labor for all employees, and to prohibit women's (and children's) employment in sectors that seemed physically overdemanding or dangerous.[4]

The first departure from the industrial-labor model came as a response to emergency conditions. During World War II the federal government instructed civilian employees to stagger their arrival and departure times to ease the burden on public utilities. It was also during the war, with men on the front lines and war supplies in acute demand, that women, including married women with young children, for the first time gained access to male jobs and were permitted to work male hours. The War Manpower Commission did instruct employers to hire women with children only "at such hours and on such shifts that will cause the least disruption in family life." Given wartime conditions, however, hard-pressed manufacturers were not likely to ask women about their household responsibilities or do much to tide them over during what was assumed to be a war emergency. After the war, the traditional occupational patterns and hours of labor for women returned. But the rapid growth of service industries dramatically expanded the number of white-collar jobs for both sexes. In short order, more and more women, including those with children, joined and remained in the labor force.[5]

In the postwar decades, the economy expanded, particularly in the service-oriented sectors. More employees began to commute from suburban residences to jobs in the central city. Soon, congestion on subways, railroads, and highways became oppressive and costly to employees. Some corporations and government agencies decided to space out the arrival and departure times of groups of employees in predetermined and inflexible intervals of fifteen to thirty minutes.[6] These "staggered-hours schedules" were a minor departure from traditional hours of labor and represented a collective response to commuting delays, not to employees' nonwork obligations.

Not until the 1970s did managers begin to experiment with a variety of flexible schedules for offices and factories. They had become aware of high levels of discontent, particularly in jobs that were rigidly suspervised and offered little opportunity for advancement. Managers had learned that low employee morale frequently correlated with reduced productivity, high absenteeism, and poor quality of work. European employers, notably the West Germans, first used flexible schedules to counter worker alienation. Such schedules were then introduced into the United States to offer employees greater control over their daily responsibilities.[7]

The desire to help employees manage dual obligations was a secondary motive. Worker surveys revealed a growing concern about the difficulties inherent in combining work and family demands. When a Gallup poll asked employees to indicate which of several programs would help them most in coping with the "conflicting demands of work and family responsibilities," the largest number of respondents (54 percent) selected more flexible schedules. The next largest group (37 percent) wanted more flexible sick leave; only 28 percent cited day care.[8]

The identification of flexible schedules as a family-oriented personnel policy has achieved increasing consensus. Ninety-two percent of the delegates to the White House Conference on Families in 1980 joined in "a call for family-oriented personnel policies," such as flexitime, flexible leave policies, shared and part-time jobs, and job sharing programs.[9] The link between better performance on the job and satisfaction in the home has for the first time become an issue for the personnel officer as well as the family counselor.

Types and Prevalence of Flexible Schedules

Two kinds of flexible schedules have been widely introduced: flexitime and the compressed work week. Under flexitime, employees may vary their arrival and departure times each day, generally over a two-hour band at either end, provided that they work a core period of four to six hours. By 1977 about 30 million employees were using a flexitime schedule. In the compressed work week, a five-day schedule is reduced to three or four days by lengthening the hours worked each day. Although the compressed work week has had more limited use, the number of employees using this schedule has slowly risen nationwide to 2.7 percent of all full-time wage and salary employees.[10]

By 1980, 12 percent of all American corporations were offering some form of flexible hours for their employees, and several of them had added other types of scheduling innovations. Some companies, for example, have experimented with flexible leave policies. One allows employees with fifteen years experience to take three months of paid leave to pursue personal goals. Permanent part-time employment has also become more common among clerical workers, particularly those in civil service positions. In some corporations and state government agencies job-sharing is also provided. A few firms offer "flexiplace" schedules, which allow employees to work out of their homes, often using a computer hookup to the office. In fact, flexible work schedules are becoming so widespread that some analysts estimate that in 1990 one-fourth of all full-time workers will be on a flexible schedule. [11]

Flexible Schedule, Women's Work, and an Altered Feminist Agenda

The use of flexible schedules to help coordinate workplace and family demands requires not only new business orientations but also new assumptions about women's place in the labor force and in the home. The male familial roles of husband and father are totally compatible with their public roles as breadwinner and provider. It is only when women added to their roles of wife and mother that of breadwinner and provider that a potential conflict was recognized. Thus, as large numbers of women have defined themselves as permanent employees, the redesign of work schedules has emerged as a way of helping them manage dual obligations.

Although women have long been a permanent part of the labor force, it was not until the emergence of the women's movement in the mid-1960s that feminists challenged inherited notions of woman's proper place in it. The major goals of the movement aimed at facilitating women's entry into all areas of the labor force by ending discrimination in the public sector, in universities, corporations, and the professions. They were built on a model that emplasized first and foremost the similarities between the sexes. Feminists were convinced that by taking the male role as a model for female advancement, women would gain access to new positions. At the same time, they insisted that the enhancement of opportunities for women in the workplace, the promotion of participation identical to that of males, would not disrupt family life. These new assumptions were accompanied by an increasing awareness that the women who most successfully resolved the tension between domestic and public roles stood the best chance for advancement in the labor force. This recognition has recently made the redesign of work schedules a feminist issue. To be sure, feminists have only recently recognized the centrality of work schedule redesign to women's lives. Initially, they were so eager to facilitate women's entry into the labor force that they failed to realize some of the dilemmas the male model might pose for women throughout their life cycles.

Through the 1970s feminists perceived only one major obstacle to equality of opportunity: distribution of domestic and childcare responsibilities. Accordingly, they sought to redistribute parental responsibility, joining with family policy advocates to promote the establishment of a federally funded network of childcare centers for children from all social classes [12] and pressing for individual families to reorganize household chores. However, the expectation that day care and sharing household responsibilities would solve the problem has not often been realized. The duties remain disproportionately with women, regardless of social class or economic position. As other articles in this volume make clear, women have, in effect, two jobs instead of one, adding work at home to work at the office. The combination of workplace and family responsibilities has made coping with the demands of children, spouses, and the household more troublesome than anyone predicted. Moreover, the focus on day care has obscured the fact that workers have obligations that do not end when children enter school. Responsibilities continue for school-aged children, for aging parents, or for kin in need of help. Thus, even an excellent network of childcare centers would only begin to resolve the conflicts families face in balancing private and public responsibilities. Rather, policies are needed that recognize the ongoing responsibilities of workers as family members even after their children enter school. [13]

Implementation of Flexible Schedules

Most studies evaluating flexible schedules have focused on the benefits to employees, in part to encourage broader implementation. For example, in 1978 the American Management Association surveyed 196 corporations using flexible schedule programs to learn the extent of the innovations and their value for managers. They reported that 97 percent of the corporations indicated an improvement in employee morale for workers in flexitime programs. They also noted that the new schedules frequently reduced tardiness, assisted in the recruiting of new employees, reduced employee turnover, and in some instances (48 percent), increased productivity. The studies attributed these increases to an improvement in morale, an ability to select more convenient hours, and a more efficient use of capital equipment and space in customer services. The report did note that these advantages were not always present. Forty-eight percent of the firms reported productivity increased, but another 48 percent reported that it remained unchanged. [14]

Yet flexitime schedules also present some disadvantages for management. Varying arrival and departure times may create problems in scheduling work tasks. Communication between supervisors and employees, or among employees, or with the public may be delayed. Timekeeping, especially where manual time-recording systems are used, often becomes burdensome. In workplaces where automatic equipment was installed after the schedule was implemented, employees accustomed to sign-in sheets saw this equipment as a punitive symbol or an indication of a lower status.

In 1983 we evaluated a pilot project on alternative work schedules implemented by New York City for some of its employees. Our report focused on the obstacles and opportunities flexible schedules posed for both managers and employees in a large municipal bureaucracy. To understand the expectations and experiences of employees, we interviewed twenty workers from two agencies, one employing primarily women for clerical and administrative tasks, the other primarily men for a variety of construction and maintenance services. The interviews revealed that although employees of both sexes joined the program, it fulfilled different expectations for each gender. For example, women employees often requested a specific schedule to help resolve a particular family obligation. Most often they used the schedule to coordinate childcare or transportation with their husbands (one parent took responsibility in the morning, the other in the evening; or the couple now traveled to and from work together). One woman with a mother in a nursing home had a flexible schedule that gave her time to visit more often and yet not arrive home too late.

The interviews underscored a tension between work and leisure that the women could not resolve. Most of these long-time employees looked forward to retirement, yet described their jobs as the focal point of their lives. To them the program was a way of having more time for informal activities, such as shopping or volunteer work, but it did not provide the blocks of time they desired.

Although the male employees generally did not request schedule changes, they did join the programs in their units. With the flexitime schedule they often reported a release from the rigidity of the time clock that made them feel "more professional." In ways that they had not anticipated, the new schedules gave them an increased sense of autonomy. Only one man we interviewed had childcare responsibilities. He reported that he had frequently been late because the day-care center did not always open on time. After this happened several times, he would take the day off instead of going to work late. Under the new schedule he missed far fewer days and was rarely late. Thus, in ways that were totally unanticipated, the flexible schedules tended to further job satisfaction for men and enabled women to meet family obligations.[15]

Bohen and Viveros-Long's study of several hundred federal employees using a flexitime schedule found that the program was most useful to those who had the fewest work-family conflicts. Women who had primary responsibility for childcare reported that the program did not give them enough latitude to reduce conflicts significantly. Parents with less demanding jobs and fewer work-home conflicts saw work and family life as two separate worlds and sought logistical solutions to schedule conflicts. But for parents who wanted both to sustain the challenge of work and to remain deeply involved in child-rearing, the flexible schedules were of little value. The study concluded that it was necessary "to look further than flexitime to help such families."[16]

Flexible schedules may be most useful to employees who work in positions where the hours are fixed. In these situations the shift from a standard schedule to a flexible schedule does not appear to result in opportunity costs for the employee. Flexible schedules may be more problematic for those pursuing professional careers. Predetermined hours and flexible schedules may be so antithetical to professional advancement that they put the employees using them on a separate track.

For example, there is growing evidence that many young women still plan their careers with the assumption that they will be the ones to fulfill dual obligations. Thus women physicians are entering not only traditional fields like pediatrics and psychiatry, but also specialties like radiology and anesthesiology, where the time allotments are known in advance and responsibility is well defined. By the same token, one finds more younger women working in medical research because laboratories allow for a fixed schedule. Women are also entering group practice, where the duties are bounded and household obligations can be juggled to fit them. Similar patterns appear in law. More women are becoming attorneys, and some are entering corporate practices, but most tend to remain crowded in family and governmental law positions, opting for set hours and well-defined responsibilities.[17]

Moreover, there is little reason to believe that flexible schedules will expand professional options for women. In academe, there are proposals for longer tenure tracks for women, and part-time residences exist in a few places, but if only women use them, they may create new dilemmas. It was one thing to work part time when it was assumed that woman's proper place was in the home, but it is quite another thing to work part time when it is assumed that women have the same opportunities as men.[18] The new programs become sidetracks. To choose part-time work in a profession that places a premium on commitment without attention to a time clock is to invite and receive second-class citizenship.

Conclusion

Although it is primarily professional women who are demanding flexible schedules, it is doubtful that these programs can meet their expectations.

Rather, flexible schedules may well be the first feminist policy whose primary beneficiaries are nonprofessional women. An awareness of this diversity of interest among women with different career goals should encourage feminists both to advocate family-oriented personnel policies and at the same time explore the effects that an adherence to a traditional professional ethos has had on both sexes. There is mounting evidence that traditional patterns may be not only limiting women's options but also depriving men as well as women of opportunities for family interaction. To help some men and women strike a better balance, feminists should encourage the implementation of flexible schedules. At the same time, aware that this program cannot solve the problems of all workers in balancing work and family obligations, they should search for policies that will give as high a priority to family satisfaction as to job satisfaction.

Notes

Acknowledgment: The research for this article was conducted under grants from the Foundation for Child Development and the Fund for the City of New York.

1. For a fine historical analysis of this complicated issue see Herbert G. Gutman, *Work, Culture and Society in Industrializing America* (New York: Random House, 1976).

2. Sheila M. Rothman, *Woman's Proper Place: A History of Changing Ideals and Practices, 1870 to the Present* (New York: Basic Books, 1978), pp. 48–52.

3. Stanley Buder, *Pullman: An Experiment in Industrial Order and Community Planning 1880–1930* (New York: Oxford University Press, 1967), pp. 94–97.

4. Rothman, *Woman's Proper Place,* pp. 154–65.

5. For an excellent discussion of women in the labor force during World War II, see William H. Chafe, *The American Woman* (New York: Oxford University Press, 1972), pp. 166–72. A discussion of staggered-hour schedules during the war can be found in Work in America Institute, Inc., *New Work Schedules for a Changing Society* (Scarsdale, N.Y., 1981), pp. 75–87.

6. The Port of New Jersey and New York actively promoted flexible schedules among Manhattan organizations to reduce rush-hour congestion and set up a flexible-schedule program for its own agency. For its experience see the Port Authority of New York and New Jersey, "Flexible Work Hours Experiment at the Port Authority of New York and New Jersey, 1974–75" (mimeographed).

7. George Strauss, "Workers: Attitudes and Adjustments," in Jerome M. Rosow (ed.), *The Worker and the Job* (Englewood Cliffs, N.J.: Prentice-Hall, 1974), pp. 73–98. For a summary of the German experience see Alvar Elbing, Herman Gordon, and John R. M. Goundon, "Flexible Working Hours: It's About Time," *Harvard Business Review,* January–February 1974, pp. 18–34.

8. Gallup Organization, "American Families—1980," mimeographed (Princeton: Gallup Organization, 1980), p. 34.

9. White House Conference on Families, *Listening to America's Families: Action for the 1980's* (Washington, D.C.: Government Printing Office, 1980), p. 18.

10. Stanley D. Nollen and Virginia Martin, *Alternative Work Schedules, Flexitime,*

Permanent Part-Time Employment and the Compressed Work Week (New York: Amacom, 1978), discuss these innovations. See also Work in America Institute, *New Work Schedules,* p. 4.

11. Maureen E. McCarthy and Gail S. Rosenberg, *Worksharing Case Studies* (Kalamazoo, Mich.: W. E. Upjohn Institute for Employer Research, 1981), pp. 205–30. See also Work in America Institute, *New Work Schedules,* p. 4.

12. Rothman, *Woman's Proper Place,* p. 235, and Larry Hunt and Janet Hunt "The Dualities of Careers & Families: New Integrations or New Polarizations?" *Social Problems* 29 (1982): 499–509.

13. Colleen Leahy Johnson and Frank A. Johnson, "Attitudes Toward Parenting in Dual-Career Families," *American Journal of Psychiatry* (April 1977): 391–95. Joseph H. Pleck, Graham L. Staines, and Linda Lang, "Conflicts Between Work and Family Life," *Monthly Labor Review* (Sept. 1981): 26–30; Chafe, *American Woman* pp. 166–73. Emily Stopper, "Alternative Work Patterns and the Double Life," in Ellen Boneparte (ed.), *Women, Power and Policy* (New York: Pergamon Press, 1982), pp. 90–107, is also convinced that alternative work schedules should be part of a feminist agenda but argues for a partnership between feminists and union members to achieve this goal. Stopper, to be sure, is aware of the impediments to this alliance but feels that it is necesssary for broad structural changes to occur.

14. See Robert T. Golembiewski and Carl W. Proehl, Jr., "Public Sector Application of Flexible Work Hours: A Review of Available Experience," *Public Administration Review* (Jan.–Feb. 1980): 72–85; Simcha Ronen, *Flexible Working Hours: An Innovation in the Quality of Work Life* (New York: McGraw Hill, 1981). See also R. A. Winnett and M. S. Neale, "Results of an Experimental Study on Flexitime: A Survey of Three Industries," *Personnel* (April 1985). 40–44, which reports similar findings.

15. Emily Menlo Marks and Shella M. Rothman, "New Options in the Workplace: an Examination of a New York City Pilot Program on Alternative Work Schedules" (mimeographed, 1983).

16. Halcyone H. Bohen and Anamaria Viveros-Long, *Balancing Jobs and Family Life: Do Flexible Schedules Help?* (Philadelphia: Temple University Press, 1981) p. 198.

17. Marjorie P. Wilson and Amber B. Jones, "Career Patterns of Women in Medicine," in Carolyn Spieler (ed.), *Women in Medicine: 1976* (New York: Josiah Macy Foundation, 1977), pp. 89–103. See also Marilyn Heins et al., "A Profile of the Woman Physician," *Journal of the American Medical Women's Association* (Nov. 1977): 421–27. Sidney P. Gardner and Flora P. Parisky, *Job Sharing in New York State: An Assessment of Implementation and Participants' Experience* (mimeographed, 1981); New York State Council on Children and Families, *Part-Time Employment: Implications for Families and the Workplace* (mimeographed, 1983).

18. Some of the problems that arise when part-time work becomes institutionalized as women's work can be found in Ruth Nielsen, "Family Responsibilities as a Labor Market Issue: A Scandinavian Perspective," in Irene Diamond (ed.), *Families, Politics, and Public Policy: A Feminist Dialogue on Women and the State* (New York: Longman, 1983), pp. 295–99. The ways in which earlier generations handled this dilemma can be found in Sheila M. Rothman, "Going Public: Historical Perspectives on Working Women," *American Journal of Psychoanalysis* 45 (1985): 167–75.

24

Women, Families, and Home-Based Employment

KATHLEEN E. CHRISTENSEN

The electronic cottage of the 1980s certainly differs from the sweatshops of the early 1900s. Professional and clerical workers seated at home computers in suburban comfort are a far cry from immigrant women hunched over sewing machines in the crowded tenements of New York City. It is this difference in image that is apparently behind both the media's and the federal government's celebration of home-based employment as an ideal arrangement allowing women to combine employment and family commitments. Much press coverage stresses the advantage of working at home for mothers and their families (Brooks 1984; Churchman 1983; Gillette 1983; Langway et al. 1984; Somerson 1983; Vicker 1983). And the federal government, through congressional and departmental activity, is also promoting home-based employment, which will clearly affect women more than men, given their different responsibilities in the home.

But what is now known about the actual effect of home-based employment on working mothers—how they themselves value the experience—suggests that this celebration may be premature. This article will examine factors in the late twentieth century that encourage the development of gainful employment within the confines of the home. It will then review the findings that exist to date about the effects of this employment and suggest policy considerations that stem from these findings.

Factors Affecting the Growth of Home-Based Employment

As Part 1 of this book makes clear, the notion of employment and family as separate and relatively autonomous behavioral spheres grew out of the physical separation of centralized workplace and household. Until the industrial revolution agriculture and cottage industries dominated the economy, and throughout history certain groups, such as scholars, writers, craftsmen, and artists, have worked at home. But with the growth of industrialization, a need

478

for increased supervision, communication, and the cooperative use of resources and equipment led to the centralization of workplaces, first in factories, then in offices. More recently, with the rapid advances in computer and telecommunication technologies, many white-collar workers can be employed in their homes and yet remain in immediate contact with their supervisors, colleagues, and clients. At least three technological trends are responsible for this decentralization of white-collar work.

TECHNOLOGICAL FACTORS

Increasing numbers of offices and office jobs are automated, meaning that they are supported by computer and communication technologies, including word processors, electronic filing and scheduling, electronic mail services, and teleconferencing services. The degree to which the technologies are integrated with one another varies from office to office, but the growth of office automation is great. It has been estimated by the computer industry that by 1985 there was a word processor for every three clerical workers in the United States.

Probably the most significant technological potential for home-based work is offered by the personal computer. The advent of the silicon chip has made this technology affordable and easy to use. According to Jack Nilles, a futurist at the University of Southern California, 89 percent of all American households will own a personal computer by 1990 (National Academy of Sciences 1983). This technology has fueled the imagination of the futurist Alvin Toffler, whose vision of an American economy based on electronic cottages depends on the availability of home computers (Toffler 1980). But, more important, personal computers can be invaluable to self-employed professionals and clericals. The former can substitute them for secretaries, and the latter can use them to start word-processing business, which are more lucrative than typing services (Christensen 1985b).

Electronic communication services, the third emerging technology, can transmit information from one location to another. Electronic mail and teleconferencing are examples. Several commercial communication networks exist, including The Source, CompuServe, and Plato. At a cost, they offer electronic mail, bulletin boards, special interest newspapers, and various databases.

The combination of automated offices, personal computers, and electronic communication services has led to increased decentralization of employment, including home-based work. As offices automate, valued employees increase their opportunities for flexible work alternatives, whereas full-time clericals face a shrinking job market (Leontief and Duchin 1986). Both trends promote home-based employment: valued professional employees may enjoy the luxury of working at home on their computer terminals; clerical employees may find fewer full-time salaried positions, but more opportunities as home-based independent contractors paid by piece rates.

Computer-mediated home-based employment is frequently referred to as "telecommuting"—that is, computer technology replaces the daily commute to work (Nilles et al. 1976). Several studies measure the energy saved by using the computer rather than the car to go to work (Harkness 1977; Kraemer 1981; Nilles 1976). But research on the effects of telecommuting on families is only beginning (Christensen 1985a, 1985b; McClintock 1984; Pratt 1984).

Although no one knows exactly how many people currently work at home on the computer, *Business Week* reports that 15 million current information-processing jobs could be done at home (1982). It must be stressed, however, that despite the importance of computer technology as a facilitator of home employment, it is not a cause. The decision to be employed at home is driven by values, not by technology (Christensen 1986, 1987). Certain other conditions, such as the corpofate and business climate, also play a major role.

CORPORATE RESPONSIVENESS

At least two hundred corporations now have some type of home-based employment arrangement for their professional and/or clerical employees (Gil Gordon, personal communication, 1985). Others show interest in the possibility. For example, a New York–based consulting firm, Electronic Services Unlimited (ESU), recently conducted a proprietary study of current corporate activity in home-based employment and sold it to such clients as J. C. Penney, Digital Equipment Corp., Citibank, AT&T, Xerox, General Motors, and Hartford Insurance Group.

Several of the better-known existing home-based programs include those sponsored by Control Data Corporation (CDC), New York Telephone, Blue Cross/Blue Shield of South Carolina, Mountain Bell, and Shearson-American Express. These corporate programs vary across four dimensions: structure of work done at home (professional or clerical); type of payment (salary or piece rate); amount of time spent at home vis-à-vis time spent in a central office (full time at home or part time); and availability of health or pension benefits to employees (available or not available). Some of these variations can be illustrated by examining three corporate home-based programs.

CDC's Alternate Work Site (AWS) program had, at its peak, twenty-three full-time salaried professionals working at home, from one to five days a week. An in-house evaluation of the AWS program found that the employees, who were known as high performers prior to starting the program, increased their productivity by an average of 35 percent (National Academy of Sciences 1983). CDC management rated the AWS program a success because it allowed the company to retain good employees and increase productivity at minimal cost.

Blue Cross/Blue Shield of South Carolina has a program entitled "Cottage Coders and Keyers," which involves fourteen claims-coders and data-entry operators (Blueprint 1983). All of these clerical employees are women who work part time, get no benefits, and are paid on a piece-rate basis for each claim processed. They usually operate on a quota of 1,000 claims per week. Management expresses pleasure with this program, citing shorter turn-around time in processing the claims and lower error rates (Olson 1983). This program has been the target of much criticism for its treatment of employees (Mattera 1983).

Mountain Bell's program in Denver employed, at its peak, eight technically oriented, salaried professionals who worked at home four days a week and in the office one. An in-house evaluation found that productivity increased under this program (National Academy of Sciences 1983).

Overall, corporate management has expressed satisfaction with home-based work in all its variations. Corporations stand to gain in other ways besides productivity. They can employ people who would otherwise have been unavailable, reduce their turnover of personnel, and cut costs through off-hour utilization of their computer and decreased needs for office space (Olson 1983). Yet caution has been expressed about the long range receptiveness of corporations to decentralization because of difficulties in managing workers and socializing them to the company's culture (Margrethe Olson, personal communication, 1985).

THE RISE IN SMALL BUSINESS

Probably the strongest business force accounting for home-based work is the increasing number of small businesses. From 1977 to 1982 the total number of sole proprietorships increased 21 percent, whereas the number of women increased 46 percent.

Women-owned sole proprietorships are the fastest-growing segment of American small businesses. Women are more apt than ever before to start their own businesses. They have more job experience and are better educated, making them able to handle the varied aspects of running a business. Moreover, at certain life junctures they often find themselves in situations in which it is easier to be self-employed than to work within the routines of a corporation.

Tax advantages and limited overhead expenses make the home a desirable place in which to start a business. In a recent survey I conducted of over 7,000 women who work at home, 71 percent of the white-collar women were self-employed (Christensen 1985c; see also Hirshey 1985). They can limit overhead expenses, take advantage of tax writeoffs, and minimize startup costs. In effect, the home allows them to be sheltered entrepreneurs.

THE POLITICAL CLIMATE

In addition to this favorable business climate, at least three federal activities currently support work at home: the proposed Family Opportunity Act, the 1984 Department of Labor ruling that lifted the ban on home knitting, and the proposed Freedom of the Workplace Bill (S. 655), now before the U.S. Senate.

The Family Opportunity Act (H.R. 2531) was first introduced into the 97th Congress, was reintroduced into the 98th, and is intended to be introduced yet again into the 99th by Rep. Newt Gingrich (R.-Georgia). One of its purposes is to "restore the family setting by allowing families to learn and earn together at home." It would achieve this purpose by granting tax credits for home computers purchased for educational or work purposes. By granting such tax credits, this bill would promote the full-scale development of home-based work. Although Gingrich has not directed his proposed legislation exclusively to women, it is clear that any legislative push for home-based work will affect women differently than men, given their current social roles and responsibilities.

In the fall of 1984, the Department of Labor lifted its forty-two-year-old ban on the home production of women's knitted outerwear, opening up the possibility for federal support of other types of home-based work, including computer-mediated employment. Sen. Orrin Hatch (R.-Utah) followed up by introducing his Freedom of the Workplace Bill (S. 665), which would repeal all prohibitions on home work so long as minimum-wage laws, overtime standards, and child labor laws, as established in the Fair Labor Standards Act (1942), were upheld. In the summer of 1986, Secretary of Labor William Brock proposed the repeal of bans on home production in the remaining six industries: women's apparel, gloves and mittens, jewelry, embroidery, belts and buckles, and handkerchiefs. These actions have sparked a controversy with labor unions, particularly the International Ladies Garment Workers Union (ILGWU), which opposes industrial home work on the grounds of potentially unsafe work conditions and possible violations to minimum-wage, overtime, and child labor laws. The AFL-CIO and the Service Employees International Union (SEIU) have extended their opposition to computer-based home employment, having passed resolutions in 1983 calling for its ban.

Despite the unions' opposition, however, the federal government has been intent on expanding opportunities for people to work at home, particularly women. Evidence of where the government intends to go over the next four years can be found in the 1984 platform of the Republican party, which states: "We demand repeal of prohibitions against household manufacturing. Restrictions on work in the home are intolerable intrusions into our private lives and limit economic opportunity, especially for women and the home-bound" (1984: 9).

Collectively, therefore, technological conditions, economic incentives, and political support are converging to create a climate in the United States that is highly conducive to home employment. At the same time, the social realities faced by working mothers are forcing them to look for viable work-family arrangements.

The Social Realities of Working Mothers

Women have entered the labor force in record numbers over the last several decades. The most dramatic increase has been in the participation of mothers. As of 1986, six out of every ten women with children under eighteen were gainfully employed.

The rapid introduction of women into the labor force has resulted in functional adaptations by family members. As Hoffman notes in Chapter 18, husbands of employed wives participate more in housework and childcare than the husbands of the nonemployed. Moreover, children of employed mothers are more likely to be encouraged to be independent and to be given more household responsibilities than are children of nonemployed mothers. Hoffman further shows that the effects of maternal employment are reflected in how children conceive of adults. They engage in less gender stereotyping, and daughters have a clearer notion of what their lives will be like as adults.

Our society is rapidly changing from one in which the norm is for mothers not to be employed to one in which the prevailing norm is employment. But the day-care opportunities for pre-school-aged children have not kept pace with this changing norm. It was recently estimated that of the approximately 13 million children under the age of thirteen who are in need of childcare services, over 7 million are known to have them, leaving over 5 million children in this country without any known childcare arrangements (Children's Defense Fund 1982). A major factor in this gap is simple lack of services. Additional problems are related to the quality, accessibility, and affordability of available services. The costs cannot be underestimated. A 1985 National Academy of Science paper reports that the average cost of day care for two children is $4,000 a year—nearly one-third of the average working woman's income (cited in U.S. Department of Labor 1985). Finding affordable childcare services is a major concern of employed mothers of preschool children.

Home employment has been promoted as an ideal childcare arrangement for these women. They can be employed and care for their children at the same time and in the same place. Yet the evidence calls for caution.

Employed Mothers and Home-Based Employment

Several studies have examined the experiences of diverse home-based workers (Christensen 1985b, 1985c; McLaughlin 1981; Olson 1983; Pratt 1984). From their findings we can begin to evaluate how women who are employed at home view the experience.

In 1985 I surveyed over 7,000 women who were employed at home (Christensen 1985c). The sample included women of diverse occupations, including professionals and clericals as well as those engaged in services, sales, and handcrafts. I also conducted in-depth in-person interviews with one hundred employed and self-employed professional and clerical women engaged in home-based work (Christensen 1987). Olson (1983) focused on thirty-two home-based employees in seven corporations, including the ones discussed earlier. Pratt's study (1984) examined thirty-five home-based workers, male and female, including professionals, managers, and clericals. McLaughlin (1981) studied forty-five women with office-type jobs and forty-six women with sales-type jobs, all of whom work out of their homes. With these studies we can profile the employment arrangements of these women and then examine the impacts of such arrangements on the women and their families.

EMPLOYMENT STATUS

Despite all the public attention to telecommuters, those company employees who substitute the computer for the commute, the vast majority (71 percent) of white-collar women who are employed at home are self-employed and do not use computers (Christensen 1985c). Only one-third of the entire white-collar sample used computer technology, and the use varied by occupations. Although 38 percent of the professionals used computers, only slightly over a quarter (27 percent) of the clericals used them. Clearly, the attention to telecommuting masks the reality of home employment. Furthermore, companies that hire women to work at home are much more apt to hire them as independent contractors than as salaried employees with benefits (Christensen 1985b). This is as true for professionals as it is for clerical workers.

As independent contractors, women professionals typically are paid by the hour and clericals by a piece rate (Christensen 1985c). Both professionals and clericals are paid only for the work they do, not for lag times between projects. They are not given benefits, nor are they provided with advancement opportunities. These independent contractors are entirely out of the mainstream of their companies. Although companies could hire homeworkers as salaried employees and could prorate health and pension benefits, they typically do neither (Christensen 1985b; Costello 1985). The implications of this arrangement will be examined later, but it is important to note that independent contractors typically end up receiving markedly less than their salaried counterparts (Christensen 1985b; Costello 1985).

MOTIVATIONS FOR HOME EMPLOYMENT

When a woman has children, she typically seeks home employment as an employment-family tradeoff. In the national survey, the most frequently cited reasons given by mothers for home employment were "to take care of my family" and to "earn extra money" (Christensen 1985c; Hirshey 1985). Yet they do not see the arrangement as perfect.

These women would rather work at home than not work at all. They repeatedly claim that they are better off than full-time homemakers who do not work (Christensen 1985b; Olson 1983; Pratt 1984). As we move toward a society in which mothers are more often employed than not, the pressure is on these women to earn money. I repeatedly found (1985c) that both professional and clerical women, especially those who had worked outside the home prior to having children, held full time homemakers in low esteem. They did not want to see themselves or be seen as housewives. Home employment allowed them to be home with their children but not to be identified as housewives. Yet the situation does not necessarily preclude such an identification (Christensen 1985c).

Career-oriented women report that home-based work is detrimental to career advancement. They believe that home employment provides more career options than nonemployment, but certainly not as many as would be provided by working outside the home (Christensen 1985b; Olson 1983; Pratt 1984). In fact, one programmer who worked as an independent contractor for an insurance company said that if it were not for her son, there would be no advantages to home employment (Christensen 1985b). The overriding reality for most women is that home employment leads to isolation and decreased credibility as a professional or clerical.

IMPACTS ON WOMEN

Women who are employed at home report more social isolation than men who do so (Olson 1983). This appears to be due to the fact that young mothers are employed at home as a work-family tradeoff, whereas young fathers are not (Olson 1983).

Lack of credibility as a wage-earner is cited as one of the most serious disadvantages of working at home. Women find that because they are home, friends, family members, and institutions think of them first as wife and mother and second as wage-earner. They do not believe that they or their efforts are taken as seriously as they were taken when they were employed outside. Since she is home, it is assumed that she can handle housework and children (Christensen 1985b).

The result is stress, mentioned as a major cost by those women who have primary responsibility for childcare and housework in addition to employment demands (Christensen 1985b; Olson 1983). The more household responsibilities the wage-earner has, the more stress she reports. The stress is tied to the fact that the house is not designed to support her role as wage-earner: the house expects the women to tend it, not earn money in it. As one home-employed mother said, ''When I worked in an office and got up to get a drink, the water cooler didn't say clean me; at home the refrigerator does'' (Hirshey 1985). The house talks back, and the language it speaks has far more to do with household tasks than wage-earning ones.

HOME EMPLOYMENT AS A CHILDCARE ARRANGEMENT

Contrary to many popular notions, home employment does not solve the childcare problems faced by all working mothers. I found (1985c) that nearly two-thirds of the home-working professionals (61 percent) and over a third of the clericals (36 percent) relied on supplemental childcare for their preschool children. Professionals, however, were more likely to pay for the supplemental childcare than were clerical workers. This research confirms earlier work done by Pratt (1984), which shows that professionals are more apt than clericals to rely on additional assistance to fulfill their employment responsibilities.

SATISFACTION

Although McLaughlin (1981) found that satisfaction with home employment was a function of separate workspace and supplemental childcare, I found (Christensen 1987) that satisfaction has more to do with attitude and motivation. Women who see home employment as the ideal and who are motivated to work at home for job-related reasons are more satisfied than those who do not. In fact, when women are motivated to work at home as a way to earn extra money, they are less satisfied than when motivated for other reasons. Family motivation does not appear to affect satisfaction one way of another.

In the light of such findings, one may wonder whether current efforts to promote home-based employment for professional and clerical women is premised on faulty assumptions. It is worth spelling out these assumptions.

Critique of Assumptions

One common assumption is that women can simultaneously care for their children and work. In fact, most women can't, don't, and won't. They either use supplemental childcare or work when their children are out of the house or asleep. Professional women are more likely than clerical to use paid supplemental childcare, but *only* when there is a dependable, steady flow to their work. Furthermore, when women do not use other forms of childcare, they extend their days to accommodate work. By rising well before their children are awake, or by working deep into the night, these women get their work done in the quiet and isolation they need.

The image of the woman at her kitchen computer terminal with her baby playing quietly behind her is more fiction than fact and entirely underestimates the amount of time and attention women want and need to give to both their children and their work.

A second assumption is that they like working at home. They do like working there better than not working. But when these women have primary responsibility for childcare, they report the combination as stressful. If they are career-oriented, they report that working at home hurts their career options. Finally, their satisfaction with the arrangement has more to do with work-related factors than with family ones.

A third assumption is that home employees have the same status as office ones. Several, although certainly not all, corporations assign a different status to professional and clerical women employed at home (Christensen 1985b; Costello 1985). Full-time employees are switched to the status of independent contractors, who trade a dependable salary for an undependable hourly or piece rate, often with no guarantee as to the number of hours they will work or the number of projects they will receive. They make less than they got for doing the same work in the office. And they lose all employee benefits, including health care, pension plans, paid sick leaves, and vacations. Finally, they are taken out of the pool of employees considered for promotion. Such arrangements threaten to turn home-based independent contractors into second-class corporate citizens, denied the rights and benefits of full-time employees. Insofar as more women than men accept this arrangement, and evidence indicates that more women do, then they run the further risk of becoming a disadvantaged corporate community, denied access to pools for advancement or skill upgrading.

Although the data are limited, it is clear that professional and clerical home contractors view the arrangement as less than ideal but nonetheless a win-win situation for themselves and their employers. These women get to earn money, and the company gets a relatively cheap labor pool. The women more often than not are very well aware that the company benefits, but they see home employment as the best alternative they have, given their full-time responsibilities at home and the limited options for part-time employment outside it. Men with primary family responsibilities would face the same constraints.

Conclusions

Given what we know so far about the drawbacks of home-based employment as an alternative to traditional work-site employment, any public or corporate policy regarding employees who work at home should safeguard the following principles:

1. Home-based employment as only one type of childcare: people employed at home should have access to other forms of childcare so that they can give full attention to work and family, but not both at the same time.
2. Home-based employment as only one type of flexible work-family arrangement: other options, such as job sharing, part-time work with benefits, or flexitime, should be available to working parents so that home employment is a choice, not an option forced by limited alternatives.
3. Equal pay for equal work, regardless of place: if paid an hourly wage or piece rate, people who work at home should receive what their counterparts get in the office.
4. Minimum work, not just minimum wage: people working at home as independent contractors with sole-source contracts should be guaranteed a steady, dependable flow of work to ensure a dependable income.
5. Equal status: workers at home should be afforded the same benefits as those in an office or comparable ones, including the benefit of career advancement.
6. An explicit definition of employee: people who are expected to perform as employees for companies should be defined and recompensed as employees, not as independent contractors.

Home-based employment is an alternative for older mothers who spent their twenties and thirties advancing their careers and who are now ready to start childrearing, as well as for younger women, who are now more apt to begin married life attempting to combine careers and childrearing. But it is far from ideal. Although it solves some problems, it may lead to others: increased stress, social isolation, and career sacrifices, especially for those professional women who by staying home become less visible and less enmeshed in the professional networks so critical to future career advances.

Furthermore, powerful interests stand to gain from women's widespread use of this option. The current technology could allow millions of information-based jobs to be done outside a central office, at home or elsewhere. Corporate management finds home-based work good for business: it increaes productivity, decreases office costs and staff turnover, and attracts desirable employees. The federal government is throwing its supsport behind home-based work options. These forces are converging to create a climate favorable to working at home.

In view of these forces, it is important to insist that women who choose this option should do so freely. They should not have to do so under the constraints of limited childcare, hostility to employed mothers, and the sheer momentum created by the convergence of technology, economics, and politics.

References

Blueprint. 1983. "Cottage Coders and Keyers." *Blueprint* (South Carolina), October.

Brooks, Andre. 1984. "When Her Office Is at Home." *New York Times*, February 27.

Business Week. 1982. "If Home Is Where the Worker Is," *Business Week*, May 3.

Children's Defense Fund. 1982, *Employers, Parents and Their Children: A Data Book*. Washington, D.C.: Children's Defense Fund.

Christensen, Kathleen. 1985a. "Women and Home-Based Work." *Social Policy* (Winter): 54–57.

————. 1985b. "Impacts of Computer Mediated Home-Based Work on Women and Their Families." Contract report for Automation of America's Offices, Office of Technology Assessment, U.S. Congress. New York: Center for Human Environments, City University of New York's Graduate Center.

————. 1985c. "Women Work at Home: An Invisible Labor Force." Working paper no. 90-PD-1. New York: Center for Human Environments, City University of New York Graduate Center.

————. 1986. Testimony before the Employment and Housing Subcommittee, Committee on Government Operations, U.S. House of Representatives Hearing on the Pros and Cons of Home-Based Clerical Work (February 26). Washington, D.C.: Government Printing Office.

————. 1987 *The Unspoken Contract: Women and Home-Based Work*. New York: Henry Holt and Company.

Churchman, D. M. 1983. "Welcome Home—Fresh, Vocal Support for At-Home Mother." *Christian Science Monitor*, November 21.

Costello, Cynthia. 1985. "All the Top Brass Are Men." In "On the Front: Class, Gender, and Conflict in the Insurance Workplace." Ph.D. dissertation, University of Wisconsin.

Gillette, A. 1983. "Cottage Trade Could Fill Directory—and Does." *Detroit News*, November 24.

Harkness, R. C. 1977. *Technology Assessment of Telecommunications— Transportation Interactions*. Menlo Park, Calif.: Stanford Research Institute.

Hirshey, Gerri. 1985. "How Women Feel About Working at Home." *Family Circle Magazine*, November 5, pp. 70–73.

Kraemer, Kenneth. 1981. "Telecommunications—Transportation Substitution and Energy Productivity: A Re-Examination." Public Policy Research Organization, University of California, Irvine.

Kraut, Robert. 1984. "Telework: Cautious Pessimism." Murray Hill, N.J.: Bell Communications Research.

Langway, L. 1984. " 'Worksteaders' Clean Up." *Newsweek,* January 9, pp. 86–87.

Leontief, Wassily, and Duchin, Faye. 1986. *The Future of Automation on Workers,* New York: Oxford University Press.

Mattera, Paul. 1983. "Home Computer Sweatshops." *Nation,* April 2, pp. 390–92.

McClintock, Charles. 1984. "Working Alone Together: Managing Telecommuting." Cornell University, Department of Human Service Studies.

McLaughlin, Mary Ann M. 1981. "Physical and Social Support Systems Used by Women Engaged in Home-Base Work." Master's thesis, Cornell University.

National Academy of Sciences. 1983. Office Workstations in the Home. Washington, D.C.: National Executive Forum.

Nilles, Jack; S. Carlson; P. Gray; and G. Hanneman. 1976. The *Telecommunications-Transportation Tradeoff.* New York: Wiley.

Olson, M. H. 1983. "Remote Office Work: Changing Work Patterns in Space and Time." *Communications of the ACM.* [Association for Computing Machinery] 26 (3): 182–87.

Pollack, Andrew. 1981. "Rising Trend of the Computer Age: Employees Who Work at Home." *New York Times,* March 12.

Pratt, JoAnn. 1984. "Home Teleworking: A Story of Its Pioneers." *Technological Forecasting and Social Change* 25 : 1–14.

Somerson, Paul. 1983. "There's No (Work) Place Like Home." *PC Magazine,* December, pp. 106–33.

Toffler, Alvin. 1980. *The Third Wave.* New York: Morrow.

U.S. Department of Labor, Bureau of Labor Statistics. 1980. *Perspectives on Working Women: A Databook.* Washington, D.C.: Department of Labor.

U.S. Department of Labor, Women's Bureau. 1985. "Women and Office Automation: Issues for the Decade Ahead." Washington, D.C.

Vicker, R. 1983. "To Work at Home Instead of Commuting." *Wall Street Journal,* August 4.

25

The Pauperization of
Motherhood:
Patriarchy and Public
Policy in the United States

NANCY FOLBRE

Introduction

In recent years, demographers have devoted increasing attention to analyses of the net cost of children in different social and economic settings, including the United States (Lindert 1978; Espenshade 1973). There has been relatively little research on the distribution of the costs of children between men and women. Several studies, however, show that even where parents share a common standard of living, the time costs of children are distributed very unequally between mothers and fathers (Hartmann 1981a; Folbre 1983). It seems likely that the continuing growth in the percentage of households headed by women is exacerbating inequalities in the cost of parenthood to men and women.

Between 1960 and 1981 the number of poor persons in families headed by women increased 48 percent, while the number of poor persons in all other families decreased 45 percent. Over the same time period, the percentage of all families below the poverty line headed by a woman, with no husband present, increased from 20 percent to 40 percent (Bureau of the Census 1976:fig. 1; 1981a:table 17; New York Times 1981).

The number and age of children in a female-headed household are primary determinants of its economic welfare. In 1981, 68 percent of mothers heading households with children under six and between six and seventeen years were poor. By contrast, female householders without either husband or children in 1981 actually had a higher average per capita income than husband/wife fami-

From *Review of Radical Political Economics* 16, no. 4 (1984). Copyright, *Review of Radical Political Economics*. Reprinted by permission of the Union for Radical Political Economics.

lies without children (Bureau of the Census 1981b:table 29). These comparisons suggest that the feminization of poverty reflects, at least in part, a certain pauperization of motherhood.

Why are mothers so vulnerable to the threat of poverty? Some neoclassical economists suggest that the increase in the percentage of families headed by women simply reflects the utility-maximizing choices of individuals responding to a decrease in the economic benefits of marriage (Becker 1981; Fuchs 1983). But the fact that such choices have more negative economic consequences for women than for men suggests their outcome is largely determined by preexisting inequalities. Many serious efforts to explain and analyze such inequalities utilize the concept of patriarchy, and this concept promises some important insights into the distribution of the costs of childrearing in the United States.

In this paper, I focus on one aspect of the relationship between patriarchy and parenthood: the impact of public policy. Specifically, I show that state policies toward motherhood in the United States have consistently benefited men and disadvantaged women and children. In the first section, I conceptualize the relationship between patriarchy, parenthood, and the state, emphasizing the distribution of the social costs and benefits of children. In the next three sections, I provide historical illustrations of patriarchal bias in three separate arenas: family policy, labor market policy, and the welfare system.

Patriarchy, Parenthood, and the State

The concept of patriarchy is often used to describe systematic inequalities between men, women, and children that cannot be explained simply as a result of capitalist relations of production (Hartmann 1981b). Some critics argue that it is an inherently ahistorical concept; others find it confusing to place control over children and control over women under the same rubric (Barrett 1980). Partly in response to these criticisms, there have been a number of recent efforts to distinguish between different historical "stages" of patriarchy and to clarify the changing relationship between gender- and age-based inequalities (Brown 1981; Ferguson 1984). A brief review of these efforts provides a good starting place for further analysis of the political economy of parenthood and sets the stage for an analysis of aspects of state policy that cannot be explained purely in terms of class interests.

Numerous historical and contemporary studies of societies that have not moved beyond the early stages of a transition to capitalism show that male parents wield considerable economic power over their adult children (Greven

1970; Cheung 1972; Quadagno 1982). Much of the recent demographic literature focuses on the relationship between patriarchal power over children and economic incentives to high fertility (Caldwell 1982; Mosk 1983). Mothers, as well as fathers, may enjoy certain economic benefits, such as support from their children in old age. But mothers almost certainly pay a larger share of the physical risks and time costs of rearing children.

The legal and economic structures that often bolster high fertility suggest that the economic benefits of children can provide a material incentive for certain types of control over women (Folbre 1983). "Coercive pronatalism" (Blake 1974) may help men accumulate large numbers of children. It may also help explain the severe sanctions many societies impose on homosexuality and other nonreproductive sexual activities. Furthermore, guaranteed legitimacy of descent in the male line may strengthen a man's authority over his children and his claim on their labor, providing a rationale for a sexual double standard.

Ann Ferguson (1984) uses the term "father patriarchy" to describe social relations that enable men to garner direct economic benefits from their children as well as their wives. A synonymous term is "paternal patriarchy." Whichever nomenclature is used, the term implies a particular stage, rather than merely a type or a variant of patriarchy, because the expansion of capitalist relations of production tends to weaken patriarchal authority over children. Indeed, many contemporary demographers argue that a reversal of traditional intergenerational income flows increases the costs of rearing children and contributes to the decline in fertility that accompanies economic development (Caldwell 1982; Folbre 1983; Mosk 1983).

Changes in intergenerational relations can be traced through changes in state laws and policies. For instance, parents in early capitalist societies tend to have strong legal rights vis-à-vis their children, including a right to support in old age (Handel 1982:6; Quadagno 1982). The expansion of capitalist rela tions of production often leads to child labor laws and public education requirements that directly limit paternal authority over children. In more mature capitalist economies, social security programs often emerge, partly in response to the increased uncertainty of intergenerational support. These systems provide more security for the elderly and probably also relieve the younger generation's personal financial responsibilities for parents (Patterson 1981).

State policies toward women's rights have seldom been changed without a struggle. But some feminist successes reflect a diminished resistance to reproductive choice that was partly motivated by a recognition of the growing cost of children (Gordon 1977). In both the United States and England, there was an important historical relationship between feminism and family planning (Banks and Banks 1964; Smith 1973). The causality could be reciprocal: as women gain new political and legal rights, they may shift some of the costs of children toward men, motivating further fertility decline. Historically, however, women have not been particularly successful in this regard. While the weakening of paternal patriarchy benefited women in some respects, the motives for patriarchal control over women remain quite strong.

Both men and employers in general may benefit directly from the low economic value placed on women's work. And even when children no longer provide economic benefits, men have an interest in enjoying the pleasures of fatherhood at a relatively low cost. Ann Ferguson (1984) uses the term "husband patriarchy" to describe the stage at which men begin to benefit from patriarchy more as husbands than as fathers. Carol Brown (1981) uses the term "public patriarchy," arguing that the power of individual fathers is replaced by the power of men who use the state to dictate family laws that help preserve patriarchal privilege.

Patriarchy has always benefited husbands and has always been bolstered by a patriarchal state. A more important difference between stages of patriarchy lies in the way women's work as mothers is exploited. When paternal patriarchy is strong, individual fathers are likely to enjoy economic benefits from their children. When children provide primarily personal and emotional benefits (Zelizer 1985), mothers are likely to pay a disproportionate share of the economic costs. When the state takes control over intergenerational transfers, the economic benefits of children become "public" benefits. The Social Security system distributes the earnings of the younger generation to the older generation largely on the basis of wages, without taking the unpaid labor of childrearing into account.

For instance, a male wage-earner who divorces his wife and contributes a negligible amount to the expenses of raising his own children will receive far more income in old age through the Social Security system than a single mother who remained largely unemployed, or employed at a low wage, because she devoted her time to raising those children. Mothers may receive the emotional and personal benefits, but they are largely denied the economic benefits of children. On the other hand, men who minimize their own expenditures on children, as well as nonparents in general, are rewarded not only by their own tax contributions, but also by the unpaid labor embodied in the younger generation whose wages are the actual source of Social Security funds. These individuals may not live in traditional patriarchal households. But they enjoy a traditional patriarchal privilege.

Most economists simply assume that children are "luxury goods" for whom women, in particular, have a taste. Some economists treat children as consumer durables (Becker 1960) or as producer goods (Edlefson 1984). But apart from the many other tangible and intangible ways that children contribute to society as a whole as they mature, the Social Security taxes they pay are literally "nonexcludable" to retired wage-earners. Children are *public goods*. And in the United States Social Security system today, nonparents and many fathers are free riders—they enjoy economic benefits for which they have not paid.

The United States government acknowledges the public value of children's education in schools by assuming a share of financial responsibility. It does not acknowledge the public value of the time mothers (and, to a lesser extent, fathers) spend caring for and educating their children. As some observers have noted, such acknowledgment would prove extremely costly (Schorr 1979:465). The theoretical perspective laid out above suggests an additional motive for neglect: recognition of childrearing as highly productive labor would currently entail considerable redistribution of income from wage-earners to homeworkers and from men to women.

The following discussion of public policies in the United States in the twentieth century illustrates some of the more important economic implications of defining childrearing as a personal indulgence rather than a social contribution.

Family Policy

In the contemporary United States, one occasionally hears the argument that feminists have contributed to the rise of female-headed households by promoting state interference in family life (Gilder 1981). Yet the state interfered in family life from the very outset of United States history, not to strengthen the family per se, but to strengthen the power of elder men (with the exception of black men) within it. Up until the latter half of the nineteenth century, most aspects of family law in the United States reinforced the coercive pronatalism characteristic of paternal patriarchy (Folbre 1979). As social and economic changes wrought a decline in desired family size, policies toward divorce, child custody, contraception, and abortion gradually changed. But these policies continued to disadvantage mothers by restricting public funding for reproductive health and failing to enforce father's child-support responsibilities.

The latter third of the nineteenth century witnessed changes in family law that were emblematic of the transition from paternal to public patriarchy. Child-labor and compulsory-education laws brought working-class children alongside their middle-class counterparts into a new "nonproductive world of childhood" (Zelizer 1981:1039). Divorce laws were liberalized, and the divorce rate soared (Wright 1891). Traditionally, fathers had an automatic right to the custody, earnings, and services of their children in the event of divorce.

But as children became more expensive and divorce became more common, the doctrine of "father right" was replaced by what Carol Brown has termed the doctrine of "mother obligation" (1981:260). Between 1900 and 1930 mothers' responsibility for child custody was written into many state divorce statutes.

Official state sanctions against contraception, formalized by the 1873 Comstock Law, continued well into the twentieth century, partly because the new technologies promised women a new and somewhat threatening sexual autonomy (Blake 1984). As many scholars have noted, the campaign for reproductive rights proved most successful when it aroused the economic self-interest of the white population as a whole. Margaret Sanger, among other advocates of contraception, played on the white population's fears of an immigrant "population explosion" (Kennedy 1970:40). In 1938, amidst widespread concern over the high fertility of the population on relief, particularly in the South, a legal decision lifted the stigma of criminality from birth control. Prophylactics had been widely known, and widely used, since World War I. But it was not until 1958 that federal and state policies stopped making it difficult for health professionals to dispense contraceptives designed explicitly for women (Gould 1979:453).

Furthermore, expenditures on reproductive health were strictly limited. None of the Maternal and Child Health Funds made available through Title V of the Social Security Act of 1940 were used to promote contraception. In the 1950s President Eisenhower declared that birth control was a private problem rather than a public concern. This particular definition of public concern exacted a heavy toll. Surveys of white mothers in the 1950s revealed that nearly one out of every five births was unplanned and unwanted (Adams and Winston 1980:44). The putative privacy of birth control did, however, prove weaker than racist ideology: during the same period, the federal government turned a blind eye to policies implemented in a number of southern states to virtually force sterilization on large numbers of black women, assuaging fears that the fertility of the black population was getting out of control (Davis 1983).

Despite the fact that federal laws and policies have been generally supportive of family planning since the late 1960s, family planning programs, administered primarily by states, remain extremely uneven in their coverage (Gould 1979). In 1981 the Reagan administration cut federal expenditures on family planning by 22 percent; in 1984, for the fourth year in a row, it proposed repeal of the family planning program, which would place family planning services entirely at the discretion of the states (Coalition on Women and the Budget 1984).

State policies toward abortion have also been characterized by a legal concession followed by a budgetary decision restricting economic access. In

1973 the Supreme Court gave women the legal right to abortion in the first trimester of pregnancy. In 1976, at a time when approximately 75 percent of all abortions were Medicaid-financed, Congress passed the Hyde Amendment, making it legal for states to deny Medicaid financing for abortions. As of 1980 all but seventeen states and the District of Columbia had ceased providing assistance for abortions requested by indigent women (Mendelson and Domolky 1980:124). This policy was not successful in reducing abortions, as abortion rates increased among white women from 172 per 1,000 births in 1972 to 373 per 1,000 births in 1979 and, among Black women, from 223 to 625 abortions per 1,000 births over the same period (Statistical Abstract 1984:Table 98, p. 71). But the policy was successful in slowing the growth of Medicaid expenditures and forcing women and their families to assume the burden of expense.

While the state proved reluctant to assume any of the costs of reproduction, women increasingly had to pay them on their own. Perhaps as a response to the declining economic benefits of family life, partly in response to women's increased bargaining power within the home, there was a sharp decline in the percentage of women married in the postwar period (McCrate 1985). Divorce, separation, and illegitimacy rates all rose substantially between 1960 and 1980; divorces alone from 9.2 per 1,000 married women to 22.6 (Statistical Abstract 1984:table 120). Largely as a result, the percentage of female-headed households increased from 28.7 percent to 44.4 percent for blacks and from 17 percent to 24.9 percent for whites between 1960 and 1982 (Statistical Abstract 1984:table 61).

Relatively few of the women heading these households received any economic assistance from the fathers of their children. In 1975, the earliest year for which data are available, only 25 percent of the 4.9 million divorced, separated, remarried, or never married women with a child or children in the home received the child support they were due. The figures for 1981 were remarkably similar—59 percent of such women were awarded child-support payments; only 47 percent of these received the full amount awarded, meaning that only 28 percent of the total received the amount they were due (Bureau of the Census 1983:1). Furthermore, child support awards have not kept pace with inflation. According to a recent study based on Current Population Survey data, the average amount due in 1981 was about 21 percent less in real terms than the amount due in 1978 (Beller and Graham 1985). As Diana Pearce points out, "It is as though a husband's economic support is in 'payment' for the wife's housekeeping, emotional support, and sexual access, not for her childrearing activities" (Pearce 1979:122).

A study based on Michigan Panel Survey data shows that separation and divorce brought about a reduction of income for women in every income category, the reduction being greatest (about 50 percent) where married income was greatest. These income reductions are relatively permanent—female single parents are very unlikely to regain levels of income even approaching those of married household income (Weiss 1984). Other longitudinal studies show that divorce, desertion, or the birth of a child significantly increase the probability that a woman will go on welfare (Hampton 1975; Dickenson 1975).

The Child Support Enforcement Act of 1975 required recipients of Aid to Families with Dependent Children (AFDC) to cooperate in establishing paternity and locating an absent father for the purposes of child-support enforcement or risk losing their benefits. It was passed in large part because it promised to reduce net expenditures on AFDC (Steiner 1981). In August of 1984, after an extended lobbying effort, both the House of Representatives and the Senate approved a bill that would require states to withhold money from the paychecks of parents in arrears on child-support payments and to establish similar procedures for withholding state income tax refunds (Congressional Quarterly 1984:992). The efficacy of this legislation remains to be seen.

Andrew Cherlin's (1981) recent study is one of many that show that most of the supposed deficiencies of "broken homes" are related not to the absence of a father but to the absence of a father's income. But the economic aspects of family policy are often obscured by patriarchal rhetoric. Gilbert Steiner, for instance, writes that "a broken family supported in part by a reluctant father is no stronger than a broken family supported by public assistance" (1981:128). He never questions the extent of support that either reluctant fathers or a reluctant state provides, because he defines broken families as families without fathers rather than as families unable to meet their basic economic needs. George Gilder simple carries this reasoning one step further when he glorifies the demand for further cuts in welfare spending (1981).

Many European countries provide family allowances that defray at least a portion of the direct costs of childrearing and improve children's standard of living. In the absence of such policies in the United States, the costs of rearing children will continue to mount. Women will continue to shoulder a disproportionate share of the costs, a cost imposed on them in the workplace as well as in the home.

Policies Toward Mothers in the Labor Market

Women's work as mothers has always constrained their participation in wage labor. Public policies could serve to make these limitations less binding, but they have seldom done so, largely because this would entail transferring more of the costs of children to employers and/or taxpayers. The lack of any consistent policies to help working families accommodate childrearing responsibilities or to help mothers make transitions between work in the home and work in the market has contributed significantly to the pauperization of motherhood.

The responsibilities of motherhood have been defined in ways that have benefited both men and employers. Married women began to enter the labor force in the United States only in the last decades of the nineteenth century. Those who opposed their participation asserted that it would conflict with the putative demands of motherhood (Bartlett 1841). Forms of protective legislation that contributed to occupational segregation were justified by reference to women's unique vulnerability as mothers (Kessler-Harris 1982). As women were gradually pulled into employment, however, motherhood was increasingly used as a rationale for making the supply of women's labor conform more closely to the specific needs of employers.

When employment rates increased during the Great Depression, for instance, efforts to provide jobs for men were enhanced by explicit discrimination against married women. The federal government set an example for private industry by placing employees with a spouse employed by the government at the top of the layoff list, a policy that legitimated widespread layoffs of married women. The National Educational Association Survey of 1930–31 revealed that 77 percent of some municipal governments would not employ married women as new teachers, and more than 50 percent of those cities dismissed women teachers when they married. Government relief programs put into effect in the later 1930s virtually ignored the female unemployed, while the National Recovery Act set a lower minimum wage for women than for men (Humphries 1976).

When labor became scarce during World War II, however, the federal government not only established work and training programs for women in industrial skills such as welding, but authorized federal support for the day care of the children of women defense workers through the Lanham Act of 1941. Despite the fact that this program cared for only a small proportion of the children whose mothers were working, it served 1.5 million children at its peak, more than were in all day-care programs combined in 1974 (Adams and Winston, 1980). After the war the putative demands of motherhood were invoked again to dismantle both training and childcare programs.

Still, female labor-force participation grew rapidly throughout the postwar period. By the 1970s an increasing number of mothers of young children were participating in wage labor, and Congress responded to substantial political pressure by proposing federal support for day care. President Nixon vetoed the legislation, explaining that "for the Federal Government to plunge headlong financially into supporting child development would commit the vast moral authority of the National Government to the side of communal approaches to childrearing over the family centered approach'' (Adams and Winston 1980:40).

Such rhetoric both protected the state from any further expenditure and provided a market for the expansion of private profit-oriented facilities. Between 1958 and 1978 the percentage of children of mothers employed full time enrolled in group care centers increased from 4.5 percent to 14.6 percent (Bureau of the Census 1982:16). Between 1967 and 1981 the proportion of children between the ages of three and six attending nurseries or kindergartens increased from 31.6 percent to 57 percent. Mothers not working in the formal labor force full time were almost as likely as women working full time to enroll their children in such programs; the relative proportions enrolled were 47 percent and 55 percent, respectively (Statistical Abstract 1982–1983:table 102).

While motherhood is idealized as the most fulfilling work a woman can perform, public policy continues to define it as though it were not really work at all. Pregnancy is at best considered a disability. The Equal Employment Opportunities Commission, set up as a result of the Civil Rights Act of 1964, argued that denial of maternity leave represented a form of sex discrimination. The Supreme Court ruled against this interpretation in 1974. In 1978 an amendment to Title VII of the 1964 Civil Rights Act required employers to treat pregnancy and pregnancy-related conditions (with the exception of medical coverage and sick leave for abortions) exactly as they treat other physical disabilities (Adams and Winston 1980:40). This regulation pertains only to women employed by firms covered by collective bargaining agreements. According to one recent estimate, only about 40 percent of working women are covered (Kamerman, Kahn, and Kingston 1983).

In the late 1970s California passed legislation guaranteeing a woman up to four months' unpaid maternity leave with job security. Recently a Federal District court overturned this legislation, ruling it inconsistent with the Civil Rights Act of 1964, which stipulates that pregnant women may not be treated differently from other employees (New York Times 1984b). The United States remains the only Western industrialized country lacking both national health insurance and some form of maternity leave policy guaranteeing seniority and pension rights (Cook 1978).[1]

The lack of maternity leave and publicly subsidized day care has limited the labor-force experience of women with young children, and the long-run effects of time taken out of the labor market to care for young children comprise the most significant indirect costs of motherhood. In 1981, 65 percent of mothers with children under eighteen worked in the wage-labor force. But only 25 percent of mothers worked full year full time (Statistical Abstract 1982–83:table 102). The majority of working mothers were concentrated in part-time jobs that are typically low-paying and occupationally segregated. Lower levels of labor-market experience are associated with lower levels of earnings, and though differences in experience do not account for the large and persistent wage differential between men and women, they do have a significant impact (Corcoran and Duncan 1979; Hill 1979).

Rather than alleviating this problem, state policy toward mothers exacerbates it. The structure of the United States tax system hurts women's long-run prospects in the labor market by discouraging transitions from family work to market work.[2] In the short run, full-time homemakers and their families benefit from the tax-exempt status of nonmarket labor as well as deductions for dependents and childcare payments. The gains vanish in the long run, however, for women who experience divorce or separation. As Michael Boskin concluded in 1974, "the net effect of the tax system is clearly to drive female labor out of the market into the home and to reduce the (market oriented) human capital accumulation of women relative to men" (1974:256). These policies reinforce the effects of the persistent sexual wage differential and significantly increase the "economic risks of being a housewife" (Bergmann 1982).

The lack of any positive efforts to help mothers in the labor market has a particularly serious impact on women already in poverty. Many women lack marketable skills, but even at the height of the War on Poverty, the Women's Job Corps was given short shrift (Zelman 1982:88) In 1979 only 25 percent of all mothers receiving AFDC were in the labor force, largely because of their limited earning capacity combined with their responsibility for young children (Sawhill 1976; U.S. Department of Labor 1979). An estimated one-half of all mothers with children under six who wanted to participate in the Work Incentive Program were unable to do so because of childcare responsibilities (Rein 1974; U.S. Department of Labor 1979). At least one state-funded job-training program that provides AFDC mothers with childcare assistance has proved highly successful. But policy-makers question whether these programs are "worth the investment" (Business Week 1985).

In 1982 the National Advisory Council on Equal Employment concluded that public programs toward the working poor do not meet the "special needs of women workers" (1982). It might better be said that they fail to recognize the economic contribution of time devoted to childrearing, a contribution that patriarchy has always undervalued. An equitable parenthood leave policy and increased public spending on job-training and day-care programs, in conjunction with lower unemployment rates, could ameliorate the problem.[3] Until such a public commitment is made, motherhood will continue to provide a rationale for using women as a uniquely flexible reserve army of labor. And mothers will remain uniquely disadvantaged members of the labor force.

Policies Toward Mothers in the Welfare System

Mothers who receive little financial support from men and who do not earn sufficient income to support their families adequately can apply to the United States government for assistance. But the public transfers that women and children receive are low both in relative and in absolute terms. A brief history of the AFDC program in the context of the larger transfer system clearly reveals the devaluation of women's work as mothers and shows how this devaluation has helped minimize social welfare expenditures on women with incomes below the poverty level, many of whom are women of color.

The Social Security system set up in the 1930s promised to ameliorate the welfare problems of women and children but allocated far fewer resources to them than to the elderly. The "categorical aid" programs of the Social Security Act provided one dollar of federal money for every one dollar spent by the states for the needy, aged, and blind but only one dollar for every two dollars spent on Aid to Dependent Children (ADC). The total maximum payment for an aged person was set at $30 per month, relative to only $18 for a mother and her dependent children (Patterson 1981:68).

Social Security quickly came to be seen as a program for the "deserving poor," and amendments to the Social Security Act in 1939 shifted responsibility for divorced or deserted women and their dependent children to the AFDC program (widows continued to be covered by Social Security). Many AFDC recipients were women of color, and as they increased in numbers and visibility, they became politically vulnerable. States with large black populations devised a patriarchal justification for limiting public expenditures.

Strict restrictions on women's personal lives were designed both to reinforce the patriarchal family and to reduce eligibility. Arkansas unilaterally cut off aid to mothers engaged in a "nonstable illegal union," and Texas to "pseudo–common law marriages." Michigan was somewhat more euphemistic—families with "male boarders" were excluded (Patterson 1981). Legal challenges by welfare rights activists ultimately led to the lifting of these restrictions, and there was a sharp increase in the number of eligible families that applied for aid (Steiner 1981). Real increases in AFDC payments actually exceeded increases in real spendable earnings between 1963 and 1971.

During the same period there were serious discussions of welfare reform. But efforts to implement a carefully designed negative income tax system that would streamline the welfare system and provide benefits to all poor families (regardless of gender of household head) were unsuccessful, not only because of a growing resistance to increases in social welfare spending, but also because the program threatened to weaken the families that patriarchal ideology deemed strong. Empirical studies of the experimental Negative Income Tax program put into effect in several cities showed that moderate income transfers to husband-wife families increased the probability of marital dissolution (Pechman and Timpane 1975).

The social scientists involved in the NIT experiments had a particularly sophisticated understanding of their implications for the patriarchal family. Robert Spiegel, project leader of the Seattle-Denver experiment, attributed the increase in marital dissolution to a reduction in wives' financial dependence on their husbands, labeling this the "independence" effect. John Bishop of the University of Wisconsin's Poverty Institute argued that relief payments caused a decline in the morale of the male head of household and went so far as to suggest that transfers should be added onto the husband's paycheck so that he personally could bring them home (Steiner 1981:109).

One of the advantages of maintaining the existing AFDC program, perhaps not unanticipated, was that its decentralized structure left it extremely vulnerable to cutbacks. AFDC levels had always varied substantially among states. Since 1971 many states, with the tacit support of the federal government, successfully pursued a variety of strategies for lowering AFDC costs. Federal law requires states to set a Standard of Need reflecting the amount of money a state determines essential to meet a minimum standard of living in that state for a family of specified size. The federal government has not overseen or enforced this requirement.

States simply neglected to revise the real standard of need to adjust for the rapid inflation of the 1970s, and as a result the amount of money states deemed necessary to meet a minimum standard of living declined an average of 26 percent between 1969 and 1979 (Urban Systems Research 1980). The maximum payment or amount of money a state guarantees to families with no other income declined by 19 percent over the same period (Urban Systems Research 1980). Any pretence that AFDC is designed to keep families out of poverty has been dropped. By 1979 only two states had a standard of need that exceeded the poverty line for a family of four. The average payment across states was $327 per month, or only 53 percent of the federal poverty line (U.S. Department of Health and Human Services 1980; Solomon 1981).

Changes in AFDC alone do not provide an accurate picture, because in-kind transfers such as food stamps, medicaid, and housing assistance have become increasingly important. Food stamps cushioned the decline in AFDC real benefit levels during the 1970s and reduced interstate differentials in total benefits. But in 1981 even combined AFDC and food stamp benefits were below 75 percent of the poverty line in twenty-six states (Center on Social Welfare Policy and Law 1982). By October 1983 combined benefits for a family of three or four were below 75 percent of the poverty level in thirty-nine states (Coalition on Women and the Budget 1984:9). By comparison, a minimum-wage worker retiring in 1978 received levels of support from public programs that amounted to almost 110 percent of the poverty level (Bane et al. 1983:135).

Women who receive public transfers by virtue of their relationship to a deceased husband or a paying job have been and remain far better off than women who receive transfers because they are indigent mothers. The average payment to an AFDC recipient relative to a widow or dependent receiving Social Security diminished from 58 percent in 1970 to 40 percent in 1980 (see Table 25-1). As can also be seen in Table 25-1, the difference between average monthly benefits from AFDC and unemployment insurance (UI) has also widened steadily since 1970. By 1980 the average unemployment monthly benefit was $395.68 relative to $287.77 for AFDC. UI benefits are typically available for only six months (though they have occasionally been extended by law to longer periods), and no time limit is set on AFDC payments. But AFDC represents a form of social insurance for women denied any payment for their work as mothers, directly analogous to UI for workers who lose access to wages. Studies show that approximately half of all AFDC families leave the program within two years (Coalition on Women and the Budget 1984:9).

Black female-headed families are particularly disadvantaged by low AFDC benefit levels. Although they comprise approximately one-half of the AFDC case load nationwide, they are concentrated in states with the lowest benefits. In 1981 in the thirteen states where black families comprise at least 60 percent of the case load, the average total monthly disposable income from AFDC, food stamps, and energy assistance was $354, or 60 percent of the federally established poverty standard. In those states where black families comprise 10 percent or less of the AFDC case load, the average income is considerably higher: $451, or 78 percent of the poverty level (Joe 1982:11).

AFDC and Child Support Enforcement bore the brunt of the Reagan administration's cuts in social spending (Coalition on Women and the Budget 1984). Between 1981 and 1982, actual expenditures on these programs fell about 12 percent in real terms, and the AFDC case load fell by 8 percent, despite increased unemployment among mothers because of the recession (Budget of the U.S. 1982, 1983, 1984). In January 1984 the Congressional Budget Office estimated that the 1981 and 1982 changes will shave federal family aid expenditures by more than $3.6 billion through 1986. Because the states normally match federal spending on AFDC, the final reductions will come to nearly twice that amount. Many of the families excluded from AFDC will lose Medicaid coverage. Black and Hispanic families will be disproportionately affected.

Women and children comprise 85 percent of all food stamp recipients. In 1982 and 1983 food stamp funding was cut by $5 billion. WIC, a supplemental food program for pregnant mothers and children under five, now reaches

Table 25-1 Average Monthly Payments Aid to Families with Dependent Children (AFDC), Old Age Security and Disability Insurance (OASDI), and Unemployment Insurance (UI)

Year	AFDC Average Monthly Payment per Recipient[1]	OASDI—Average Monthly Payment[2]		AFDC Average Payment per Family[1]	UI Average Monthly Benefit[3]
		Widowed Mothers	Child Survivors of Deceased Workers		
1940	9.85	19.60	12.22	32.40	42.24
1950	20.85	34.24	28.43	71.45	83.04
1960	28.85	59.29	51.37	108.35	131.48
1965	32.85	65.45	61.26	136.95	148.76
1970	50.30	86.51	82.23	190.40	201.36
1975	71.58	147.25	139.40	228.81	280.92
1976	77.29	159.78	152.12	241.48	300.64
1977	82.29	173.69	165.68	250.03	315.16
1978	86.15	190.36	182.12	255.53	334.68
1979	92.86	212.55	205.53	270.74	358.68
1980	99.61	246.20	239.52	287.77	395.68

Source: *Social Security Bulletin* 44, no. 11 (November 1981).
[1]Table M28.
[2]Table M13.
[3]Average weekly benefit × 4 (Table M37).

only one-third of those eligible for it, but the administration has proposed a 15 percent cut in funding (New York Times 1984a). According to a study cited in the *New York Times,* cuts in welfare might have been twice as large and those in food stamps might have been nearly four times as large if Congress had passed everything the Reagan administration proposed (New York Times 1985).

In the words of the National Advisory Council on Equal Employment (1982), the welfare system has "reinforced gender inequality." They attribute the failure to reduce or even to prevent increases in the poverty of female-headed households to a tendency to apply a "male pauper" solution to female poverty. Samuel Preston (1984) points out that most voters hope to join the ranks of the elderly someday, whereas a far smaller proportion of voters live with dependent children. But the inequity has other roots as well, roots that lie in the patriarchal assumption that childrearing is not really work and that AFDC mothers are not among the "deserving poor."

Conclusion

Children no longer provide significant economic benefits to parents, but they do provide significant economic benefits to the elder generation as a whole. Mothers, single mothers in particular, pay a disproportionate share of the costs of rearing the next generation, and public policies exacerbate this inequality. Patriarchy has gone "public" in the sense that employers and the state have proved as reluctant as individual fathers, if not more reluctant, to help out with the kids.

It could well be the case, as Victor Fuchs (1983:158) suggests, that women have a greater personal "taste" for children than men do and willingly choose to pay a larger share of the costs. It could also be that women's choices have been shaped by a patriarchal ideology that cheapens motherhood even as it pretends to glorify it. Economists seem prone to the same patriarchal influence; much as they study the pecuniary costs and benefits of children, they seldom ask who pays the costs or who enjoys the benefits. It seems the question, as well as its answer, can only arise from an understanding of patriarchy as a system.

Notes

Acknowledgments: I would like to acknowledge Melissa Roderick's important contributions to this paper, both as motivating force and as coauthor of an earlier draft.

Staff and participants at the Center for Popular Economics provided considerable intellectual and personal support. Thanks also to Cyndi Auburn, Lourdes Benería, Ann Ferguson, Michael Jacobs, Elaine McCrate, Laurie Nisonoff, and Tom Riddell for their thoughtful comments and criticisms.

1. Even in the most generous situations in the United States, "no firm and no State provides for a paid maternity leave that lasts more than an absolute maximum of 12 weeks and most provide far less or none at all; no country in Europe, even the least generous, provides less than 14 weeks, and most provide more" (Kamerman et al. 1983:140).

2. The 1983 Report of the National Commission on Social Security apologetically describes several "unintended inequities" that they have been as yet unable to address. A secondary earner, in most cases a wife, gets little if any return on Social Security taxes, and two-earner couples receive less in benefits than one-earner couples with the same earnings. The current income tax code taxes married women's earnings at a rate determined by the sum of their own and their husband's income. Thus, a woman earning as little as $5,000 a year often propels her husband and herself into a higher tax bracket.

3. See, for instance, the proposals in Bowles et al. (1983:290–92, 369–70).

References

Adams, Carolyn Teich, and Kathryn Teich Winston. 1980. *Mothers at Work: Public Policies in the United States, Sweden, and China*. New York: Longman.

Bane, Mary Jo; Julie B. Wilson; and Neal Baer. 1983. "Trends in Public Spending on Children and Their Families." In Richard R. Nelson and Felicity Skidmore (ed.), *American Families: The High Costs of Living*. Washington, D.C.: National Academy Press.

Banks, J. A., and Olive Banks. 1964. *Feminism and Family Planning*. New York: Schocken Books.

Barrett, Michele (ed.). 1980. *Women's Oppression Today*. London: Verso Editions.

Bartlett, Elisha. 1841. "A Vindication of the Character and Condition of the Females Employed in the Lowell Mills." In *Women of Industry*. New York: Arno Press.

Becker, Gary. 1960. "An Economic Analysis of Fertility." In National Bureau of Economic Research, *Demographic and Economic Change in the Developed Countries*. Princeton: Princeton University Press.

———. 1981. *A Treatise on the Family*. Cambridge: Harvard University Press

Beller, Andrea H., and John W. Graham. 1985. "Child Support Awards: Differentials and Trends by Race and Marital Status." Faculty Working Paper no. 1124. University of Illinois at Urbana-Champaign.

Bergmann, Barbara. 1982. "The Economic Risks of Being a Housewife." *American Economic Review* 71, no. 2: 81–86.

Blake, Judith. 1974. "Coercive Pronatalism and American Population Policy." In Ellen Peck and Judith Senderowitz (eds.), *Pronatalism: The Myth of Mom and Apple Pie*. New York: Crowell.

Boskin, Michael. 1974. "The Effects of Government Expenditures and Taxes on Female Labor." *American Economic Review* 64: 251–56.

Bowles, Sam; David M. Gordon; and Thomas E. Weisskopf. 1983. *Beyond the Waste Land: A Democratic Alternative to Economic Decline*. New York: Doubleday.

Brown, Carol. 1981. "Mothers, Fathers and Children: From Private to Public Patriarchy." In Lydia Sargent (ed.), *Women and Revolution: A Discussion of the Unhappy Marriage of Marxism and Feminism.* Boston: South End Press.

Budget of the U.S. 1982, 1983. Executive Office of the President, Office of Management and Budget. Washington, D.C.: Government Printing Office.

Bureau of the Census. 1976. *Characteristics of the Population Below the Poverty Level.* Current Population Reports, Series P-60, no. 115. Washington, D.C.: Government Printing Office.

―――. 1981a. *Characteristics of the Population Below the Poverty Level: 1981.* Current Population Reports, Series P-60, no. 138. Washington, D.C.: Government Printing Office.

―――. 1981b. *Money Income of Households, Families and Persons in the U.S.: 1981.* Current Population Reports, Series P-60, no. 137. Washington, D.C.: Government Printing Office.

―――. 1982. *Trends in Child Care Arrangements of Working Mothers.* Current Population Reports, Series P-23, no. 117. Washington, D.C.: Government Printing Office.

―――. 1983. *Child Support and Alimony: 1981.* Advance report. Current Population Reports, Series P-23, no. 124. Washington, D.C.: Government Printing Office.

Business Week. 1985. January 28, p. 85.

Caldwell, John. 1982. *The Theory of Fertility Decline.* New York: Academic Press.

Center on Social Welfare Policy and Law. 1982. Report on AFDC Benefit Levels. New York.

Cherlin, Andrew. 1981. *Marriage, Divorce, Remarriage.* Cambridge: Harvard University Press.

Cheung, S. 1972. "The Enforcement of Property Rights in Children and the Marriage Contract." *Economic Journal* 82, no. 326: 641–57.

Coalition on Women and the Budget. 1984. *Inequality of Sacrifice: The Impact of the Reagan Budget Cuts on Women and Children.* Washington, D.C.: Coalition on Women and the Budget.

Congressional Quarterly. 1984. "Senate Child Support Vote Unanimous." *Congressional Quarterly* 42, no. 17.

Cook, Alice. 1978. *The Working Mother: A Survey of Problems and Programs in Nine Countries.* Ithaca; N.Y.: New York State School of Industrial and Labor Relations.

Corcoran, Mary, and Greg J. Duncan. 1979. "Work History, Labor Force Attachment, and Earnings Differences Between the Races and Sexes." *Journal of Human Resources* 14: 1–20.

Davis, Angela. 1983. *Women, Race and Class.* New York: Random House.

Dickenson, Katherine. 1975. "Transfer Income." In *Five Thousand Families: Patterns of Economic Progress,* vol. 1. Ann Arbor: University of Michigan Survey Research Center.

Edlefson, Lee. 1984. "Children as Investment Goods." Paper presented at the meeting of the American Economic Association, Dallas.

Espenshade, Thomas. 1973. *The Cost of Children in Urban United States.* Berkeley: Institute of International Studies, University of California.

Ferguson, Ann. 1984. "On Conceiving Motherhood and Sexuality: A Feminist Materialist Approach." In Joyce Trebilcot (ed.), *Mothering: Essays in Feminist Theory.* Totowa, N.J.: Rowman Allenheld.

Folbre, Nancy. 1980. "Patriarchy in Colonial New England." *Review of Radical Political Economics* 12, no. 2: 4–13.

———. 1983. "Of Patriarchy Born: The Political Economy of Fertility Decisions." *Feminist Studies* 9, no. 2: 261–84.

Fuchs, Victor. 1983. *How We Live: An Economic Perspective on Americans from Birth to Death.* Cambridge: Harvard University Press.

Gilder, George. 1981. *Wealth and Poverty.* New York: Basic Books.

Gordon, Linda. 1977. *Woman's Body, Woman's Right.* New York: Penguin.

Goudreau, Karen W., and Robert E. March. 1982. "Aid to Families with Dependent Children: Characteristics of Recipients in 1979." *Social Security Bulletin* 45, no. 4: 3–9.

Gould, Ketayun. 1979. "Family Planning and Abortion Policy in the U.S." *Social Service Review* 53: 452–63.

Greven, Philip. 1970. *Four Generations: Population, Land, and Family in Colonial Andover, Massachusetts.* Ithaca, N.Y.: Cornell University Press.

Hampton, Robert. 1975. "Marital Dissolution: Some Social and Economic Consequences. In *Five Thousand Families: Patterns of Economic Progress,* vol. 3. Ann Arbor: University of Michigan Survey Research Center.

Handel, Gerald. 1982. *Social Welfare in Western Society.* New York: Random House.

Hartmann, Heidi. 1981a. "The Family as the Locus of Gender, Class, and Political Struggle: The Case of Housework." *Signs* 6: 366–94.

———. 1981b. "The Unhappy Marriage of Marxism and Feminism: Towards a More Progressive Union." In Lydia Sargent (ed.), *Women and Revolution: A Discussion of the Unhappy Marriage of Marxism and Feminism.* Boston: South End Press.

Hill, Martha. 1979. "The Wage Effects of Marital Status and Children." *Journal of Human Resources* 14: 529–54.

Humphries, Jane. 1976. "Scapegoats and Safety Valves: Women in the Great Depression." *Review of Radical Political Economics* 8, no. 1: 98–121.

Joe, Tom. 1982. "Profiles of Families in Poverty: Effects of the FY 1983 Budget Proposals on the Poor." Washington, D.C.: Center for the Study of Social Policy.

Kamerman, Sheila B.; Alfred J. Kahn; and Paul Kingston. 1983. *Maternity Policies and Working Women.* New York: Columbia University Press.

Kennedy, David M. 1970. *Birth Control in America: The Career of Margaret Sanger.* New Haven: Yale University Press.

Kessler-Harris, Alice. 1982. *Out to Work: A History of Wage Earning Women in the United States.* New York: Oxford University Press.

Lindert, Peter. 1978. *Fertility and Scarcity in America.* Princeton: Princeton University Press.

McCrate, Elaine. 1985. "The Growth of Non-Marriage in the U.S." Ph.D. dissertation, University of Massachusetts.

Mendelson, June, and Serena Domolky. 1980. "The Courts and Elective Abortions Under Medicaid." *Social Service Review* 54: 124–34.

Mosk, Carl. 1983. *Patriarchy and Fertility: Japan and Sweden, 1880–1960.* New York: Academic Press.

National Advisory Council on Equal Employment. 1982. Final report. Washington, D.C.: Government Printing Office.

New York Times. 1984a. "Female Sacrifice." *New York Times,* April 14.

———. 1984b. "Maternity Leave Legislation Overruled." *New York Times,* August 22.

————. 1985. "Extensive Cutbacks in Health Aid Subsidies," *New York Times,* February 5.

North, Douglas. 1981. *Structure and Change in Economic History.* New York: Norton.

Patterson, James T. 1981. *America's Struggle Against Poverty, 1900–1980.* Cambridge: Harvard University Press.

Pearce, Diana. 1979. "Women, Work and Welfare: The Feminization of Poverty." In Karen Wolk Feinstein (ed.), *Working Women and Their Families.* London: Sage.

Pechman, Joseph, and P. Michael Timpane (eds.). 1975. *Work Incentives and Income Guarantees: The New Jersey Negative Income Tax Experiment.* Washington: Brookings Institute.

Preston, Samuel. 1984. "Children and the Elderly: Divergent Paths for America's Dependents." *Demography* 21: 435–57.

Quadagno, Jill. 1982. *Aging in Early Industrial Society: Work, Family, and Social Policy in Nineteenth Century England.* New York: Academic Press.

Rein, Mildred. 1974. *Work or Welfare.* New York: Praeger.

Sawhill, Isabel. 1976. "Discrimination and Poverty Among Women Who Head Families." In Martha Blaxall and Barbara Reagan (eds.), *Women in the Workplace.* Chicago: University of Chicago Press.

Schorr, Alvin. 1979. "Views of Family Policy." *Journal of Marriage and the Family* 41, no. 3: 464.

Smith, Daniel Scott. 1973. "Family Limitation, Sexual Control and Domestic Feminism in Victorian America." *Feminist Studies* 1, nos. 3–4: 40–57.

Solomon, Carmen C. 1981. "Benefit Adjustments in the Aid to Families with Dependent Children Program." In Congressional Research Service, *Indexation of Federal Programs.* Washington, D.C.: Government Printing Office.

Statistical Abstract of the United States. 1982–84. U.S.Department of Commerce, Bureau of the Census, Washington, D.C.

Steiner, Gilbert. 1981. *The Futility of Family Policy.* Washington, D.C.: Brookings Institute.

Urban Systems Research and Engineering. 1980. *AFDC Standards of Need.* Cambridge, Mass.: USR and E.

U.S. Department of Health and Human Services. 1979. "Aid to Families with Dependent Children, 1979 Recipient Study, Part I." Demography and Program Statistics, Social Security Administration, Office of Policy, Office of Research and Statistics. Washington, D.C.

————. 1980. "AFDC Standards for Basic Needs: 1979." Office of Research and Statistics, Washington, D.C.

U.S. Department of Labor and U.S. Department of Health, Education and Welfare. 1979. *WIN:1968–1978: A Report at 10 Years.* Washington, D.C.: Department of Labor.

Weiss, Robert S. 1984. "The Impact of Marital Dissolution on Income and Consumption in Single-Parent Households." *Journal of Marriage and the Family* 46, no. 1: 115–27.

Wright, Carroll. 1891. *A Report on Marriage and Divorce in the U.S.* Washington, D.C.: Commissioner of Labor.

Zelman, Patricia. 1982. *Women, Work and National Policy: The Kennedy-Johnson Years.* Ann Arbor: University of Michigan Research Press.

Zelizer, Viviana A. 1981. "The Price and Value of Children: The Case of Children's Insurance." *American Journal of Sociology* 86: 1036–56.
———. 1985. *Pricing the Priceless Child: The Changing Social Value of Children.* New York: Basic Books.

26

Women and the State:
Ideology, Power, and the
Welfare State

FRANCES FOX PIVEN

There is reason to think a mass movement of women is emerging in the United States. The movement is broad and multifaceted; it includes women from all classes and takes diverse political forms reflecting the very different social locations of its constituents. Nevertheless, it is unified in raising a credible challenge to current policy on the military, the economy, social welfare, and the environment. I believe the emergence of women as active political subjects on a mass scale is due to the new consciousness and new capacities yielded women by their expanding relationships to state institutions. There is, however, little in left feminist theorizing about the state to prepare us to understand or contribute to this development.

To the contrary, much of the socialist-feminist literature reveals a categorical antipathy to the state, recognizable in the use of terms such as "social patriarchy" or "public patriarchy" to describe state policies that bear on the lives of women.[1] Or the antipathy takes form in the nostalgic evocation of the private world of women in an era before state programs intruded on the family.[2] This negative assessment is punctuated and justified with the oft-made characterization of the relationship of women to the state as "dependence."

The irony is that the animus toward the state expressed by women intellectuals flies in the face of the political attitudes of the mass of American women as evident in the survey data. True, the opposition of women to the military buildup is presumably opposition to the military aspects of state power. But in domestic policy areas women evidently believe in a large measure of state responsibility for economic and social well-being, suggesting they believe in the strong and interventionist state that some feminist intellectuals abjure.[3] These attitudes, and the demands for "big government" they imply, are in

Reprinted from *Socialist Review* No. 74 (March–April 1984), 3202 Adeline St., Berkeley, CA 94703.

512

turn increasingly reflected in the positions and activities of women's organizations.

Of course, popular attitudes, including the attitudes of women, can be wrong. But in this instance, I think it is an undiscriminating antipathy to the state that is wrong. Arguments that contrast social control by the state to women's power, or dependence on the state to autonomy, are so naively desirous of social relationships outside of "social control" or without "dependence" as to be entirely misleading in their characterizations of the nature of the relationship of women to the state. In fact, I think the main opportunities for women to exercise power in the United States today reside precisely in women's relationship to the government.

Explaining the Gender Gap

The new attitudes revealed in recent public opinion surveys are a reflection of the changing institutional relationship of women to the state. But other and very different explanations will come quickly to mind. The media, for example, attribute the cleavage in the opinions and voting behavior of men and women to the policies of the Reagan administration.[4] Media commentators consistently see the main significance of the gap in the effects it is likely to have on the outcome of the 1984 election. This is not wrong. But while I think the Reagan policies may well have had a catalytic effect on the expression of women's political attitudes, a development of this scale is likely to have deeper roots.

I do not think the gap can be attributed solely to the influence of an organized women's movement either, although the movement may have contributed to it. There is not much correlation between the largely middle-class constituency of the movement and the cross-class constituency of the gap, or between the issues emphasized by the movement and the issues highlighted by the gap. In fact, attitudes toward the reproductive and legal rights of women, which have been the central issues of the movement, do not differentiate male and female respondents in the surveys.[5] But attitudes toward war and peace, government's management of the economy, and its responsibility for social welfare, do.

The emphasis on peace, economic equality, and social needs associated with the gender gap suggests the imprint of what are usually taken as traditional female values. This frequently made observation suggests that the gender gap is not a fleeting response to particular current events, but that it has deep and authentic roots in the longstanding beliefs of women. The experience of women within the patriarchal family of the past generated distinctive values and interpretations of the world with lasting effect. Women valued the family; they celebrated maternity and the nurturing services they provided their children and their men, and they honored the family bonds which seemed to guarantee them and their children a measure of security in exchange for their services.

Still, traditional values themselves cannot account for the emergence of the gender gap. The caretaking values of women are old, but the sharp divergence between women and men is entirely new. However much tradition may color the politics of women, the fact that traditional values associated with the family are now being asserted as public values is a large transformation. The beliefs associated with the gender gap, in fact, are about the obligations of government to protect these values. Through their votes women are asserting that the state should represent women in their terms.

The ideological transformation suggested by this assertion is, in part, a reflection of large changes in the circumstances of American women, and the new oportunities and constraints that result. Women are losing their old rights and their limited forms of power in the family. In the marketplace their position is weak; they are not likely to gain new forms of mass power in production, and prospects for advancement through market processes are dim. As a consequence, women have turned to the state and especially to the expanding programs of the welfare state. Income supports, services, and government employment have compensated somewhat for the deteriorating position of women in the family and economy, and have even given them some measure of protection and hence power in these institutions. Therefore, the state is turning out to be the main recourse of women.

The relationship of women to the welfare state hardly needs documenting. Women with children are the overwhelming majority among the beneficiaries of the main "means-tested" income-maintenance programs, such as AFDC, food stamps, and Medicaid.[6] Moreover, the numbers of women whose life circumstances are affected by these programs are far greater than the numbers of beneficiaries at any one time, for women in the low-wage service and clerical sectors of the labor force turn to welfare-state programs to tide them over during family emergencies or their frequent periods of unemployment. Older women receive the largest part of Social Security and Medicare benefits.[7] Without them, most would be desperately poor. These programs benefit women for the obvious reason that they moderate the extremes of poverty and insecurity, however inadequate the income or services may in fact be. The availability of these benefits also reduces the dependence of younger women on male breadwinners, as it reduces the dependence of older women on adult children, and thus gives both groups some protection from the power of others in family relations.

The same is true in the relations of working women with employers. Most women work in situations where there are few protections from the terror of being fired if they do not concede to employer demands. Social welfare programs provide some protection; the knowledge that they and their children will not starve reduces the terror.

Women have also developed a large and important relationship to the welfare state in the sense that it is women who are the overwhelming majority of the employees of welfare programs. In 1980 fully 70 percent of the 17.3 million social service jobs on all levels of government, including education, were held by women. This accounted for fully a quarter of all female employment.

In these different ways, the welfare state has become critical in determining the lives and livelihood of women. The belief in a responsible state, which I believe underlies the gender gap, is partly a reflection of this institutional reality. But will this new institutional context yield women the resources to participate in the creation of their own lives as historical actors? Can it, in a word, yield them power?

Women's Power Through the Welfare State

Very little that has been written about the relationship of women to the state suggests we look to it for sources of power. To the contrary, the main characterization made by socialist feminists is of a state that exercises social control over women, supplanting the eroding patriarchal relations of the family with a patriarchal relationship of the state.[8] In my opinion, the determination to confirm this assessment is generally much stronger than the evidence for it. From widow's pensions and laws regulating female labor in the nineteenth century, to AFDC today, state programs that provide income to women and children, or that regulate their treatment in the marketplace, are condemned as new forms of patriarchal social control.

Now, there is surely reason for not celebrating widow's pensions or AFDC as emancipation. These programs never reach all of the women who need support (widow's pensions reach hardly any); the benefits they provide are meager, and those who receive them are made to pay a heavy price in pride. Similarly, government regulation of family and market relations has never overcome economic and social discrimination, and in some instances reinforces it. But perhaps because some income would seem to be better than none, and even weak regulations can be a beginning, feminist opponents of the welfare state cannot simply argue that it is weak and insufficient, but that involvement with government exacts the price of dependence, somehow robbing women of the capacities for political action. From this argument it follows that the massive expansion of welfare programs in the past two decades, and the massive involvement of women and their children in them, is cause for great pessimism about the prospects for women exerting power, and surely for pessimism about the prospects for women exerting power on the state.

In general, I think this mode of argument is a reflection of the eagerness with which we have embraced a simplistic "social control" perspective, straining to interpret every institutional change as functional for the maintenance of a system of hierarchical relations. Of course, ruling groups do have power; they do try to exercise social control, and they usually succeed, at least for a time. But they are not all-powerful. They do not rule entirely on their terms, and they do not exercise social control without accommodations. The institutional arrangements of social control are never entirely secure, for people discover new resources and evolve new ideas which can be generated by the very arrangements that, for a time, seemed to ensure their repression.

Thus far, women's involvement in the welfare state is not generating the acquiescence many socialist feminists would predict. To the contrary, the expectations of government revealed by the gender gap, as well as the indignation and activism of women's organizations in reaction to the policies of the Reagan administration, are not the attitudes of people who feel themselves helpless. They suggest that women think they have rights vis-à-vis the state, and some power to realize those rights. If, however, the wide involvement of women in the welfare state as beneficiaries and workers erodes their capacities for political action, as the social control perspective argues, then what we are witnessing is a deluded flurry of activity that will soon pass. But perhaps not. Perhaps this is the beginning of women's politics that draws both ideological strength and political resources from the existence of the welfare state.

When middle-class women reformers in the nineteenth-century United States tried to "bring homelike nurturing into public life," they were pitted against the still very vigorous doctrines of American laissez faire. Not only were their causes largely lost, but their movement remained small, failing to secure much popular support even from women. The situation is vastly different today. The women reformers who are mobilizing now in defense of social welfare programs are not isolated voices challenging a dominant doctrine. The existence of the welfare state has contributed to the creation of an ideological context that has given them substantial influence in Congress, as well as mass support from other women.

Women have also gained political resources from their relationship with the state. One critical resource would appear to be of very long standing. It is, quite simply, the vote, and the potential electoral influence of women, given their large numbers. Of course, that resource is not new, and it is not owed to the welfare state. Women have been enfranchised for over six decades, but the promise of the franchise was never realized, for the reason that women followed men in the voting booth as in much of their public life.

Only as women are at least partially liberated from the overweening power of men by the "breakdown" of the family has the possibility of electoral power become real. The scale of the gender gap, and the fact that it has persisted and widened in the face of the Reagan administration's ideological campaign, suggests the enormous electoral potential of women. This, of course, is the media's preoccupation, and the preoccupation of contenders in the 1984 election as well. But its importance extends beyond 1984. Women have moved into the forefront of electoral calculations because they are an enormous constituency that is showing an unprecedented coherence and conviction about the key issues of our time, a coherence and conviction which I have argued owes much to the existence of the welfare state. This electorate could change American politics.

The welfare state has generated other political resources which, it seems fair to say, are mainly women's resources. The expansion of social welfare programs has created a far-flung and complex infrastructure of agencies and organizations that are proving to be resources in the defense of the welfare state and that may have larger potential. The historic involvement of women in social welfare, and their concentration in social welfare employment now, have combined to make women preponderant in this infrastructure and its leadership positions. The political potential of these agencies cannot be dismissed because they are part of the state apparatus. The byzantine complexity of welfare-state organization, reflecting the fragmented and decentralized character of American government generally, as well as the historical bias in favor of private implementation of public programs, may afford the agencies and organizations a considerable degree of autonomy. That so many of these organizations have lobbied as hard as they have against Reagan's budget cuts is testimony to this measure of autonomy. They did not win, of course, but mounting federal deficits are evidence they did not lose either.

The welfare state also brings together millions of poor women who depend on welfare-state programs. These constituencies do not represent simply atomized and therefore helpless people, as is often thought. Rather the structure of the welfare state itself has helped to create new solidarities and generate the political issues that continue to cement and galvanize them. We can see evidence of this in the welfare rights movement of the 1960s, where people were brought together in welfare waiting rooms, and where they acted together in terms of common grievances generated by welfare practices. We can see it again today, most dramatically in the mobilization of the aged to defend Social Security. The solidarities and issues generated by the welfare state, of course, are different from the solidarities and issues generated in the workplace. But because they are different does not mean they are insignificant as sources of power, especially for women who have small hope of following the path of industrial workers.

The infrastructure of the welfare state also creates the basis for cross-class alliances among women. The infrastructure is dominated by better-educated and middle-class women. But these women are firmly linked by organizational self-interest to the poor women who depend on welfare-state programs. It is poor women who give the welfare state its *raison d'être* and who are ultimately its most reliable source of political support. Of course the alliance between the organizational infrastructure and the beneficiaries of the welfare state is uneasy and difficult. Nevertheless, the welfare state has generated powerful cross-class ties between the different groups of women who have stakes in protecting it.

The future of these women—workers and beneficiaries alike—hangs on the future of welfare programs. They need to defend the programs, expand them, and reform them. In short, they need to exert political power. The determined and concerted opposition to welfare-state programs that has emerged among corporate leaders and their Republican allies, and the weak defense offered by the Democratic Party, suggests that a formidable political mobilization will be required. The programs of the welfare state were won when movements of mass protest forced the hand of political leaders by raising issues that galvanized an electoral following. The defense and reform of the welfare state is not likely to be accomplished by less. There is this difference, however: the growing politicization of American women suggests that the electoral and organizational support needed to nourish and sustain movements, and to yield them victories, is potentially enormous.

Notes

1. See Eileen Boris and Peter Bardaglio, "The Transformation of Patriarchy: The Historic Role of the State," in Irene Diamond (ed.), *Families, Politics, and Public Policy: A Feminist Dialogue on Women and the State* (New York: Longman, 1983); Carol Brown, "Mothers, Fathers, and Children: From Private to Public Patriarchy," in Lydia Sargent (ed.), *Women and Revolution: A Discussion of the Unhappy Marriage of Marxism and Feminism* (Boston: South End Press, 1980); Mary McIntosh, "The State and the Oppression of Women," in Annette Kuhn and AnnMarie Wolpe (eds.), *Feminism and Materialism: Women and Modes of Production* (London: Routledge & Kegan Paul, 1978).

2. See Jean Bethke Elshtain, "Feminism, Family, and Community," *Dissent* (1982):442–49, and "Antigone's Daughters: Reflections on Female Identity and the State," in Diamond, *Families, Politics, and Public Policy*.

3. Attitudes toward defense spending accounted for a good part of the difference between male and female preferences in the 1980 election. This pattern persisted into 1982, when increased defense spending was favored by 40 percent of men but only 25

percent of women. However, by 1982 women had come to place concerns about defense secondary to their concerns about the economy.

4. Exit poll data after the 1980 election showed an unprecedented 9 percent spread in the voting choices of men and women. By the summer of 1983, according to both Gallup and New York Times–CBS News polls, this spread had substantially widened to an 18 percentage point difference between men and women in their approval of Reagan's handling of the presidency. Moreover, while the ratings of men fluctuated with the upturn in economic indicators, the unfavorable rating by women remained virtually unchanged.

5. Single women, however, are much more likely than men to support the "women's rights" issues.

6. Over one-third of female-headed families, or 3.3 million, received AFDC in 1979 (Census Bureau). An almost equal number received Medicaid, and 2.6 million were enrolled in the food stamp program.

7. Women receive 54 per cent of Social Security benefits, despite the fact that the average benefit paid to women is almost one-third lower than that paid to men ($215.80 a month compared to $308.70).

8. See, for example, Zillah Eisenstein, *The Radical Future of Liberal Feminism* (New York: Longman, 1981).

27

The Debate Over Equality
for Women in the
Workplace:
Recognizing Differences

ALICE KESSLER-HARRIS

What constitutes a "special" group in the work force? Why is it that after all these years of striving for equality, we still refer to women workers as "special"? The familiar statistics belie any such categorization. Fifty-three percent of all women work for a living—more than 70 percent of them full time. Whereas the proportion of white women working for wages has expanded recently, black women have worked at these rates for most of this century. Currently more than four of every ten workers is female. And women have demonstrated that they no longer fit the old stereotypes. Relatively fewer women than in the past quit when they have babies; their absenteeism and turnover rates are no higher than those of men holding the same kinds of jobs; and they are not more temperamental on the job.

What is it, then, that makes this large group of workers "special"? That separates them from male workers? That enables most of us without a second thought to cast them into an apologetic place in relation to work? This chapter argues that women's continuing "special" position derives in part from our historical failure to come to terms with whether in fact women are different from men. It seeks to explore how dominant perceptions about women's nature have conditioned past and present strategies for achieving equality in the labor force. Finally, it argues that for a variety of historical reasons, a strategy that accepts women as different might enhance the speed with which they can move toward equality.

At the core of the consensus that has shaped women's labor-market position is the family. To most historians it seemed self-evident that women's re-

Adapted from Alice Kessler-Harris, "The Debate Over Equality for Women in the Work Place: Recognizing Differences," pp. 141–61, in *Women and Work: An Annual Review,* Vol. 1, edited by Laurie Larwood, Ann H. Stromberg, and Barbara A. Gutek. Copyright © 1985 by Sage Publications. Reprinted by permission of Sage Publications, Inc.

lationship to their families accounted for their unique labor-force position. Whatever our own predilections and lifestyles, historians of women understood that most women bore children, were responsible at some level for rearing them, and that they perpetuated the value systems of their communities in the home. Beyond this, the sheer physical demands of these tasks, as well as the special abilities developed to do them well, inhibited successful labor-force roles. Given the realities of work in the home and the nurturing and self-sacrificing qualities most people believed were required to sustain a household, women could not be expected to perform effectively in the labor force. For when they entered it, they brought with them not the competitive and achievement-oriented attitudes required for success in that sphere, but the more cooperative and relational spirit said to be cultivated in the home (Gilligan 1982; Welter 1966; Kessler-Harris 1975).[1] The attribution of family-related goals and norms to women thus constituted problematic, or even negative, features in the labor force.

To say that women have historically remained a "special" group, then, is to say that in the past, by and large, they did not act like male workers, choose the same responsibilities, make the same commitments, compete as effectively, or expect the same rewards. In the words of one recent historian of women and the family, "Women are still the primary child rearers, even when they work, and the purpose of their work in the main is to support and advance the family, not to realize themselves as individuals" (Degler 1980: 452–53). If this can be said to be true of men also, an important distinction remains. The popular mind saw women as primarily responsible for the family's emotional and physical well-being—a function that conflicted with that of success in the workplace. For men, in contrast, responsibility for the family's financial needs fostered a search for more options in the labor force, and this, in turn, enhanced the possibility of individual fulfillment.

Economists, too, have tended to rely on some notion of women's social place to explain their currently disadvantaged places in the labor force. Traditional or neoclassical economists argue that women's decisions as to when and how to enter wage work are based on their present or anticipated responsibilities for household care and childrearing. They argue further that investment in human capital determines how far and how quickly workers will be upwardly mobile and conclude that women occupy low-paying jobs because their family orientations and responsibilities discourage them from investing in their own skills or in human capital. And those who resort to the notion that employers simply have a "taste for discrimination" believe that, rightly or wrongly, people in charge of hiring attribute certain qualities to women that have emerged from their natural or culturally assigned roles.

The more radical perspective of labor-market segmentation theory seems to suggest at first that inequality is a function of the job and not the home. And yet segmentation theorists argue that income and rewards (especially in the lower primary sector) come largely from job training and socialization. To cite Michael Piore, "a good deal of what is required to perform effectively on the job and is involved in the improvement of productivity during the 'training' period is the understanding of the norms of the group and of the requirements of the various roles which are played within it and conformity to the generalized norms and to the specialized requirements of the particular role or roles to which one is assigned" (Piore 1979:135). But if learning on the job is a process in which custom and skill are handed down, it is also one that reinforces old roles: the more skilled teach the newcomers, and men tend to resist learning from women. Female workers cannot therefore be advanced beyond the point at which they are accepted by co-workers. The traditional values of the home are reinforced, in this schema, by the demands of production.

For feminists attempting to develop a theory of labor-force patterns that both explains women's historically disadvantaged position and offers some hope for future equality, the notion that women derive their identity, self-esteem, and workplace personas primarily in families has constituted a central and precarious dilemma. Short of challenging the structure of work itself, and by implication the individualistic nature of work in the United States, it places women in the awkward position of either defending or rejecting the family in order to enter work on an equal footing with men. Some have insisted that the search for equality requires women to abandon traditional notions in regard to their family roles and to adopt the competitive and achievement-oriented hierarchy of the work sphere (Sokoloff 1980; Epstein 1971; Kanter 1977). But assuming that work lives remain demanding, that path also requires women to give up many of the comforting values associated with home and childcare. Resistance to this direction is familiar, visible, for example, in the current concern for the family and its value. And troubling questions about the nature and scope of parenting remain even for those of us who accept these new work-force roles.

An alternative is to adopt what the philosopher Iris Young calls a "gyno-centric" or woman-centered view of feminism—a view that accepts women's differences from men and argues that women bring to the workplace something of their traditional, socially and culturally inculcated behavior patterns (Young, in press). This position, however, seems to return women to the beliefs of an earlier period when acknowledging family roles placed them in the position of perpetual outsiders in a labor force that bowed to their special needs only under legislative duress. And it carries with it the danger that insisting on recognition of such qualities as cooperation or sharing above competition, and on such legitimate needs as childcare, flexitime, extended parental leave, personal days and so on, assigns to women the sometimes unspoken designation of "special" with all of its potentially discriminatory consequences. Either way, equality for women becomes a distant goal.

Can women move toward equality without either negating family roles or reifying them? One way, of course, is to revalue these roles. If men did them too, they would no longer be negative attributes in the work force, but simply part of the baggage all workers brought with them to the workplace. And there would then be a greater likelihood that jobs would alter to accommodate family roles. Is this plausible? I want to suggest in this chapter that it becomes more likely if we rethink social policy in regard to women wage-earners anew, recognizing some of the lessons of history. The apparent lesson of the past was that paying attention to the characteristics of one group of workers can overemphasize their special needs and result in discrimination. A second, and now overlooked, lesson is that ignoring difference tends to perpetuate existing inequalities. The bridge between these two lessons first conceptualizes difference as a broadly social phenomenon—one that touches all workers at some point—and, based on this understanding, proposes a pluralistic solution to broadly address difference. Second, it insists on sharing some of the social costs of family and childrearing that historically have been borne by women and have made them "special." We can more easily understand how such a strategy might work if we look back at the history, the assumptions, and the legacies of an earlier search for equality.

We must begin, if only briefly, with a sympathetic understanding of the plight of most working women in the late nineteenth and early twentieth centuries. Limited by widely accepted practice to relatively few occupations and paid little because it was assumed that they had homes in which husbands or fathers were the primary breadwinners, women's real or imagined attachment to home and family led to their widespread abuse as workers. While wage-earning women struggled to organize in order to combat the resulting problems of unemployment, overwork, malnutrition, and inadequate care for children, reformers and feminists developed two alternative and sometimes competing theories to inform social policy.

The first theory, which, following Iris Young, I have labeled "humanist," traces its roots back to the early campaigns for women's rights and beyond. It derives from the belief that women, by virtue of their common humanity with men, are entitled to all the same rights and privileges. They share with men, the theory argues, a set of human rights that transcend biological/gender differences (Fuller 1971). This tradition spawned Alice Paul's militant battle for suffrage in the early twentieth century and continued into the National Women's Party in the 1920s. Governed by a belief that women were more like men than different from them, members of the NWP believed that dropping barriers to work for women would yield eventual work-force equality.

They shared with other groups the slogan "Give a woman a man's chance—industrially." And they sponsored the first Equal Rights Amendment, introduced into Congress in 1923. Its friends called it the Lucy Stone amendment after the nineteenth-century women's rights advocate, and its enemies labeled it simply the "blanket amendment" because, they said, it covered such an enormous variety of sins. The key phrase of that very first ERA stated simply, "Men and women should have equal rights throughout the United States and every place subject to its jurisdiction" (Woloch 1984:383). The language has changed since then, but the assumption that human rights transcended any biological difference remains much the same. Current arguments from this humanist feminism assert women's capacity to participate in the work force as equals, demanding only that barriers to fair competition be dropped.

In sharp contrast, the second, or "women-centered," position emerged from the belief that women were inherently different from men. In the nineteenth century such differences were commonly seen as spiritual or moral, and, in the interpretation of today's historians, provided women with the strength and influence from which they could look after community welfare (Ryan 1983; Smith-Rosenberg 1971). Doing good works, an extension of women's duty to guard national virtue, became a springboard for women's civic clubs and charitable and welfare acts, as well as for legislative lobbying and municipal reform. The same kind of argument—that women had special insights and special needs whose representation in the polity would uplift public debate—is widely credited for persuading a largely male electorate to give women the vote in 1919.

The goal of this group of women's rights advocates was not so much equality as a place in the public sphere for their own form of moral influence. Their position achieved public support partly because it did not explicitly violate commonly held views of men's and women's separate spheres and partly because it seemed to offer some moderate and sensible solutions to the social and economic problems produced by women's increasing wage-earning roles. But a position that contained the potential for obtaining equity for women in the political sphere proved to be more constraining when it came to economic issues. Those who believed in women's special attachment to the home and her more refined spiritual sensibilities deplored the idea of paid work for women as depriving the home of her guidance.

Applied to the workplace, difference arguments insisted that women required special protection. Their natural sensibilities, their greater delicacy, as well as the morality and spirituality they were destined to uphold, were incompatible with the coarseness and competitiveness of the marketplace. And more realistically, excessive and poorly paid work might lead to fatigue, ill health, inadequate housekeeping, and neglected children. Faced with the need to work like men, so the argument went, women would be crushed, their capacity for uplift drained, their virtue tempted, and their bodies so weakened as to incapacitate them for healthy future motherhood. This argument, supported by social and scientific findings, researched by Josephine Goldmark of the National Consumers League, was incorporated in the 1908 Brandeis brief. It persuaded the U.S. Supreme Court to sanction special labor legislation for female workers on the grounds that the state had a legitimate interest in protecting the mothers of the race. The principle adopted mirrored the Supreme Court's rationale for denying protection to male workers. The Court would not sanction labor legislation that protected workers per se, but it could and did sustain laws that regulated working conditions for those whose safety or good health could be construed as in the public interest (Baker 1969). In the case of women, the public or state interest involved what the Court understood as a permanent or biological difference—women's childbearing capacity and its concomitant childrearing function.

Given the Court's repeated and consistent refusals to sustain labor legislation on other grounds, most female activists, working- and middle-class alike, accepted this difference argument and agreed that women ought indeed to constitute a special group or "class" in the work force. They took this position, as one proponent argued, not "because we want to get anything for women which we do not desire for men, but since protective legislation for men has been declared unconstitutional, the best means of aiding both men and women is to secure laws for women" (Shuler 1923,12).

The legislation that emerged from this widely shared understanding took a variety of forms. It limited the hours per day and days per week during which women could work, regulated night work, prohibited women from lifting heavy weights, and outlawed their employment in certain jobs altogether. Despite the attempts of fifteen states to establish minimum wages for women or to create a minimum-wage commission, protagonists of special legislation never succeeded in compensating for reduced hours through an adequate floor under women's wages. Efforts to do so were effectively stymied until the New Deal by a 1923 Supreme Court decision that invalidated a Washington, D.C., minimum-wage law for women, calling it a "wage-fixing law, pure and simple."

Most historians now agree that whatever the short-term benefits, the consequences of protective labor legislation were in the long run negative for women, rigidifying separate niches in the labor market and depriving women of opportunities they might otherwise have had. Reading back into the past, they argue that the critical mistake of early social feminists was to accept, as the basis of legislation, the assumption that women's work-force roles rested on their biological differences from men (Baker 1964; Baer 1978; Hill 1979; Kessler-Harris 1982). But it is important to remember that in the teens and the early 1920s, hard-fought battles for special legislation were treated as important victories by wage-earning women and reformers alike. So widely accepted was the notion that women occupied a separate sphere that the idea that they could win protection for their differences seemed like triumph indeed. And in the same years, other groups from railroad workers to government employees eagerly sought protected status. Advocates of protection urged the few working women who suffered from new laws to sacrifice their own interests to what the Women's Bureau concluded in 1926 was the well-being of the vast majority. Drawing a distinction between industrial equality and legal equality, Mary Anderson, head of the newly created Women's Bureau of the Department of Labor, defended her position in favor of special legislation by arguing, ''I consider myself a good feminist, but I believe I am a practical one'' (Anderson 1925:4).

The debate over strategy ushered in by this early twentieth-century conflict has continued in one form or another up until the present. Those who advocated social legislation to ameliorate women's family and work roles, usually called social feminists, have shared the notion of women's differences. Eleanor Roosevelt is a useful example. From the early 1920s, as her membership in such groups as the National Women's Trade Union League (NWTUL) and the League of Women Voters indicates, she supported the notion that women were in fact different from men. Like other social feminists who belonged to these groups, she vigorously opposed the Equal Rights Amendment, fearing that its passage would eliminate all special protection for female workers. In doing so, she rejected the arguments of what was then the more radical wing of the women's movement, the National Women's Party, which believed in women's rights as a matter of justice and humanity. To Eleanor Roosevelt and the social feminists, career and job satisfaction were as important as to the Women's Party. But the notion that a married woman could value individual achievement and personal aspiration above the welfare of her family was inconceivable. ''I never like to think of this subject of a woman's career and a woman's home as being a controversy,'' she wrote in 1933. ''It seems to me perfectly obvious that if a woman falls in love and marries, of course her first interest and her first duty is to her home, but her duty to her home does not of necessity preclude her having another occupation'' (Roosevelt 1933:145).

In the 1920s, short of women placing jobs first (that is, short of rejecting differences), possibilities for improving the working conditions and opportunities of even well-educated women seemed negligible. Even the trade unions conceded that among poor women improved conditions depended on legislation, a lesson learned from the unenviable position of most black women, whose work in domestic service and in agriculture all but excluded them from protection.

The depression proved to be a watershed in which opinions began to change. It challenged an array of assumptions about women's difference, shaking the assurance that had surrounded three decades of mostly successful work for protective labor legislation and extending its benefits to many more workers (Kessler-Harris 1982: chap. 8; Milkman 1976). As in the war that followed, New Deal policy-makers introduced solutions to labor problems that undermined earlier certainties about the importance of difference. Together, depression and war, and the social policies they spawned, revealed that male and female workers shared more than they realized. Despite their differences, they could be equally protected.

To begin with, widespread economic privation destroyed the always tenuous illusion that families could be securely supported by a single male breadwinner. Among broader sectors of the population than had ever been true before, economic collapse meant that wives, as well as grown children, needed to earn wages and that more and more families were dividing the task of sustaining themselves among their members. As wives became more frequent and sometimes more permanent wage workers, they raised questions as to whether some of work's rewards could not also be theirs. Did personal aspiration in fact conflict with family values? "Was work," as some asked, "an exclusive prerogative of the male portion of humanity," or was it "a fundamental right of every human being?" These questions were to reemerge in the 1950s. Despite desperate attempts to drive them out of the work force, married women worked in ever-larger numbers, accounting for 35 percent of all women workers by 1940. And though they were abused in the public press and attacked by unmarried women, these new workers stood their ground. Some, like the San Antonio woman whose wages were deeply cut, did so because her job provided free meals, relieving her family of the need to feed her (Blackwelder 1983: chaps. 4–5). Others simply found work gratifying. Male and female workers experienced other commonalities. Unemployment and homelessness, for example, crossed gender lines.

The solutions of the New Deal summed up the similarities among workers. The same National Recovery Administration (NRA) codes that discriminated against women acknowledged that male workers needed protection too, and extended the arms of the state to them. Eleanor Roosevelt, Frances Perkins, and other social feminists fought consistently to defend the right of married women to work, to ensure equal pay for equal work, and to provide equal treatment for women on work relief. Partly as a result of this, public policy that at first treated women as if they always had somewhere to go was altered, and the New Deal made some crude attempts to find jobs and relief for women. Finally, the Supreme Court opened the possibility of general labor legislation. After decades of rejecting the idea that the state had any interest in the hours and wages of most male workers, the Supreme Court upheld the 1938 Fair Labor Standards Act, which for the first time legislated a minimum wage for many workers and successfully gave to men the kinds of legal protections against excessive hours from which women had benefited. Only twelve short years before, Mary Anderson had mocked what she called the "ultrafeminist" position for holding that such laws could be extended beyond women (Anderson 1925).

Perhaps most important, notions of sturdy individualism suffered a severe blow as even the best competitive energies of male workers could not alter the bleak prospect of unemployment. A trade union movement that had been at best ambivalent about recruiting women revitalized itself by relying at least in part on the energies of female workers as well as on the wives of male workers to sustain its expansion. Willingly or not, male unionists evoked the values of community, the virtues of cooperation, and family at its best as women turned their tradition and experience into mechanisms for survival. In significant ways, the depression experience meant reduced differences. New laws or regulations extended the protections of women to working men and in everyday life demonstrated the unforgettable lesson that family survival and wage work were an inseparable whole.

By the end of the decade these changes had revitalized the movement for an equal rights amendment and reduced opposition to it among some women's groups. To many, equality now seemed a plausible as well as desirable goal (Becker 1981). The notion of difference, which in the 1920s had been largely reduced to biology as two groups of feminists adopted competing positions, was now broadened to include some notion of socially defined roles. Its champions responded to the challenge of women's new stature by drawing up what they called a Women's Charter. Conceived in 1936 by social feminists led by the Women's Bureau's Mary Anderson, the charter claimed to offer an alternative to constitutional amendment by declaring the desirability of equality while acknowledging the need for protective labor legislation. Differences that earlier had been asserted as a means for women to achieve a place in public life were now claimed not to inhibit the goal of equality. But the difference argument itself was not abandoned. The argument put its proponents in the unwieldly position of asking for equal treatment and pay on the one hand and protected status on the other. One protagonist commented that it asked for "full responsibility and special privilege" at one and the same time (Becker 1981:180). But though the issue tore the group apart, social feminists were not yet ready to assert equality if it meant abandoning their notion of womanhood. As one businesswoman put it, "There are hundreds and thousands of the group I represent who are muddled by the whole thing" (Becker 1981:179).

Like other social feminists, Eleanor Roosevelt found herself changing. Her concern and that of others increased during World War II as challenges against notions of difference multiplied. During the war years, women demonstrated their capacity to work at the same jobs and as effectively as men. To support needed female workers, industry and government adopted new and imaginative policies for housing women and for feeding and caring for their children. What reasons now could be adduced for treating women as outsiders? For arguing that their positions as "mothers of the race" demanded special treatment? Toward the end of the war, Eleanor Roosevelt, although still opposed to the ERA, thought that the new circumstances warranted some compromise. "We must do a lot more than just be opposed to an amendment," she wrote to her friend Rose Schneiderman. "I believe we should initiate through the Labor Department a complete survey of the laws that discriminate against women and the laws that are protective; that we should then go to work in every state in the Union to get rid of the discriminatory ones and to strengthen the protective ones; and if the time has come when some of them are obsolete, we should get rid of them even though they were once needed as protective" (Roosevelt 1944).

Mrs. Roosevelt had touched a historical nerve ending. She understood that the notion of difference, having emerged from a particular historical context, had taken on a shape appropriate to its time. As circumstances changed, the idea that men and women were different appeared to be undermining the equal opportunity that had been its goal. Further change was hidden below the placid surface of the 1950s. Public education expanded dramatically, offering new opportunities to men and women, and though women gave birth to more children, soon the need to educate them and to provide them with the benefits of a consumer society led mothers back into the work force. Tempting possibilities of upward mobility in an expanding economy fostered a meritocratic ethic posing a challenge to which women were not immune. Ideas of personal progress on the basis of individual merit nestled into an egalitarian framework. It was not only that some would make it; if ideology were to be believed, everyone who tried would do so. A decade of relative prosperity, shorter hours for everyone, and reasonable working conditions provided unusual optimism about the present and future possibilities of work. Although most activists still clung to the belief that women were not like men, pressures for equality mounted.

For women, new job-related opportunities still competed with notions that kept them tied to the family. Married women entered the work force in unprecedented numbers. Although most would have argued that wage work was only a means to some other family end, the pressures of opportunity and mobility exercised their own influence. Old defenders of protection for women began to see it as no longer necessary. As Alice Hamilton wrote to one critic of her new position, "I have seen so great a change in the position of women workers in the last fifteen years or so that it seemed to me there was no longer any need to oppose the formal granting of equality'' (Hamilton 1953).

But arguments from difference were rooted not merely in an understanding of women's historical exploitation in the labor force. They had come as well out of a set of shared understandings about women's relationship to the home. And they persisted in the 1950s, despite new protections for all workers, because to abandon them was to leave questions about home and family unanswered. Short of arguing for an abstract equality or a humanist feminist position that most men and women in the 1950s did not support, solutions to women's disadvantaged labor-force position lay in addressing particular issues. In 1951, for example, the heirs of social feminism tried for three years to pass a ''Women's Status Bill'' that would have declared in national legislation that there be ''NO DISTINCTION on the basis of sex, except such as are reasonably justified by differences in physical structure, or by maternal function'' (''Reasons for opposing the Equal Rights Amendment,'' n.d.). The draft bill also recommended a presidential commission to review discrimination against women. Without confronting the fundamental problem of family-care responsibilities, the bill, like earlier demands for equal pay, simply insisted that women be treated equally in the labor force. But equal treatment for different people seemed hard to achieve, as a staff writer for the labor movement's *American Federationist* discovered in 1957. Vehemently opposed to the ''misnamed Equal Rights Amendment,'' she argued that ''an intelligent approach to women workers takes into account differences between men and women workers. On the other hand, these social differences in employment patterns should not be used to rationalize wage discrimination where women are doing the same jobs as men'' (Pratt 1957:8). The author did not explain how, if differences were taken into account, women could obtain the ''same jobs as men.''

Very much weakened, the old idea that women required special protection because they were different suffered its mortal wound at the hands of President Kennedy's Commission on the Status of Women. The commission, which Eleanor Roosevelt headed until her death in 1962, was recommended to Kennedy by, among others, Esther Peterson, then head of the Women's Bureau. It took an ambiguous stance, calling for more attention to preparing young women for motherhood at the same time as it explored job-related issues like training, selection, advancement, and equal pay in women's jobs. At the same time, the commission issued the first quasi-official public calls for ''necessary supportive services by private or public agencies'' to women in gainful employment. Here, at last, was a peacetime statement of social policy that acknowledged the double-sided nature of the dilemma of difference. Could women ask for equality at work without compromising their family roles? If they asserted a claim to motherhood, how, then, could they justify demands for equal opportunity in the workplace?

In the context of the 1960s, the fight to acknowledge women's difference, still tarnished by biological notions and those of the centrality of motherhood, took on a defensive posture. The idea that women had family lives in need of protection had seemed a great and humane breakthrough in 1920 and 1930. By 1940 and 1950, women who wanted to advance in the sphere of work were willing to assign the issue of family lives to the private sphere. By 1960, to argue that women were different from men was tantamount to believing that little could be done to allow full work lives and quickly became a position largely held by those who preferred dependent roles. The old belief system was held responsible for limiting personal aspiration and for creating discrimination by fostering among employers the notion that women were not genuinely committed to wage work.

Simultaneously, the competing notion that women, not merely as equals to men, but like them, could and should be permitted to function as individuals at work—which had seemed to many in the 1920s at best as an invitation to exploitation and at worst as a threat to the separation of the sexes—had become by the 1950s more attractive to millions of women who now saw family lives as parallel to paid work. By the 1960s, the argument for equality seemed to those concerned with women's labor force roles the only viable way to create job options for women and had certainly replaced notions of difference as the operative factor in the wage labor force.

By the end of the 1960s, attempts to achieve special treatment for women in the work force had come to an end. Most feminists, seeing what they took to be the consequences of "special protection," rejected the assumption that women were somehow different from men and argued instead that as far as the work force was concerned, they were more like them than not. This humanist feminism insisted that it was because women had been treated as a special group that they continued to be disadvantaged. From their perspective, if women were to achieve equal status, they would have to give up the traditional attributes of their gender as well as the special treatments that were attached to them. Only by adopting the competitive and achievement-oriented values of the work sphere could women achieve equality. Informed by a new faith in more egalitarian household relationships that were thought to make possible job-related aspirations for women at work, new feminists believed that separating women's two roles would enable the married as well as the single to compete effectively for wages, promotions, and new opportunities. The result, as we know, was the spate of legislation that started with the Equal Pay Act of 1963, continued with Title VII of the Civil Rights Act of 1964, ran through Title IX of the Higher Education Act of 1972, and culminated the same year in the passage by Congress of an Equal Rights Amendment. Each of these bills attempted to remove some barriers to equality. And yet together they have had little discernible impact for women as a whole. [2]

The current movement has relied heavily on a strategy of dropping barriers to work and encouraging women, their opportunities purportedly equal, to fend for themselves. Even the addition of affirmative action has not brought anticipated gains. [3] Real advances have occurred for a few women in such professional and business areas as pharmacy, law, medicine, personnel management, banking, and accounting. And real alternatives have been created among women in intact two-income professional families—families that can afford to replace the services of the homemaker and childrearer—as well as among some who postponed childbearing or marriage until their thirties. In blue-collar jobs, women have made modest gains as bus drivers and repair persons, but in general equality has floundered. Fearful that demands for modified working conditions and benefits will be seen by male co-workers as coming out of their pockets and will leave them wondering whether such essentials as maternity leaves, day care, and flexitime will be used by employers as excuses to lay off women or reduce their chances for promotion, women have only reluctantly asked for them. Nor have trade unions actively pushed such issues. Instead, employers have taken advantage of women's assertion of equality to treat them more like men than as people with different needs. Since the early 1970s, we have seen a relative increase in the amount of female poverty, little reduction of unemployment in poorly paid workforce sectors, a rather small narrowing in the wage gap (the ratio of female to male pay), and only selective relief from occupational segregation. [4]

In short, for all its euphoric and insistent tone, the notion of dropping barriers to equality for women at work has not prevented women from becoming poorer and has only marginally increased opportunities for genuine mobility. Nor have affirmative action programs brought about any deep transformation of women's position in the work force. Clerical jobs, always female-dominated in the modern period, have become even more so. And clerical jobs continue to be those held by the largest number of women. Women remain a disadvantaged group.

How then should we integrate this group into the work force? At least one current strategy holds some promise. It revolves around two areas, each of which has, to some degree, abandoned the notion that women should adapt to male structures and returned to the idea that their differences require accommodation. Both represent what we have earlier called woman-centered or gynocentric feminism in that they recall the assumptions, if not the strategies, of the social feminists.

The first is best illustrated by the current strategy of the Women's Rights Project of the American Civil Liberties Union (ACLU). In a July 1984 amicus brief, the ACLU opposed the constitutionality of Montana's Maternity Leave Act—an act that entitled pregnant women to extended unpaid leave before and for several weeks after the birth of a child. Arguing that the effect of such a law would be to place women in a "special" category and citing the history of past discrimination that had "perpetuated destructive stereotypes about women's proper roles and operated to deny them benefits enjoyed by men," the ACLU proposed that the law be extended to permit health-connected unpaid leaves for all workers. The discriminatory effects of the act would be mitigated, the brief argued, and its "ultimate goals and purposes" supported if the court tied the act to Title VII of the Civil Rights Act of 1964, which forbade distinctions on the basis of gender. The effect of such a link would be to extend leaves to all workers unable to work for reasons of health.

Here the ACLU argues that the law, while acknowledging gender-based differences, can encompass them instead of isolating or ignoring them. By extending rights granted to some workers to all, invidious discrimination is turned into a potential gain for everyone. The pluralism of the work force is given its due, and each group of workers has access to the special treatment it needs.

A second example of current strategy emerges from the issue of comparable worth. The proponents of this effort to equalize pay acknowledge the existence of occupational segregation on the basis both of prior discrimination and of structural barriers. They insist, however, that the social roles that account for women's segmentation not be penalized. Instead, they demand that some objective scale be devised to evaluate the education, training, responsibility, and initiative required for a range of jobs within firms and that pay be granted accordingly. Such a strategy promises to protect women's social needs even when they emerge as job preferences because it avoids the assumption that equality can be achieved only by dropping barriers, challenges the notion of the market as the fairest determinant of the value of work, and substitutes instead the idea that women's goals are as legitimate as those of men and deserve equal rewards.

Such strategies emerge from an understanding of differences that acknowledges the social importance of familial roles and insists on the necessity of integrating them into a demand for equality. Insofar as these roles are traditionally preferred by women, sharing their immediate and opportunity costs by encouraging workplace compromises to accommodate them reduces the penalty women pay for engaging in them. At the same time, the workplace that accommodates family roles will exact fewer sacrifices from those who choose to emphasize the less individualistic elements of personality and thus it may encourage men to become less competitive as well.

As in the humanist feminist tradition, the basis of inequality in the workplace in this approach is understood to lie in the privatization and separation of household and childrearing functions. Such privatization, as many scholars have noted, perpetuates the inequality of women in the household, is characterized by dependence on male support, and is upheld by the value placed on femininity (Sokoloff 1980). But these inequalities in the home are rooted in contributions and values that some women, as well as men, do not choose to give up. For all that they have been manipulated and abused, notions of nurturance, sharing, and the kinds of relational and affectional qualities of which Gilligan (1982) speaks are nevertheless valued by large numbers of people. Maintaining them has in the past required women to ignore inequality in the workplace and men to consciously foster it. A strategy that revalues these different qualities can create conditions that will enhance equality at home by making some of the real costs of family life and childrearing a social responsibility rather than a private one. This in turn will serve to increase the demand for equality.

I am here not suggesting a new strategy so much as I am urging that we not retreat from an insight that has had mixed results in the past. Yet the attempt to deny differences has been equally mixed. A series of utopian communities in the nineteenth and early twentieth centuries attempted to confront and resolve the issues of childrearing and family care by fostering cooperation to share the burden. All were problematic. Charlotte Perkins Gilman proposed in her pathbreaking essay, *Women and Economics,* that these tasks be removed from the household. Several attempts to set up cooperative kitchens and community laundries provided no continuing model. We must at least consider the notion that such proposals have had little popular appeal because they have ignored what many women have felt was most satisfying about their lives, namely, their relationships to family. More successful have been those few attempts to accommodate the workplace to family. Wartime experiments in housing women with families demonstrated the dramatic increase in productivity and family well-being that resulted from offering well-planned housing with easy supervision of children and on-site day care, laundry and banking facilities, as well as prepared hot meals (Hayden 1981, 1984). This success offers a sharp contrast to the extension of female poverty that has resulted from the systematic decrease in the already minimal community and social services offered to poor women today. And it suggests that an earlier generation of feminists who asserted women's difference deserves a new look. For them, difference meant limiting or regulating the sphere of work for women—a strategy that, as we have seen, in the end undermined equality for women. But within the context of the service economy of the 1980s, difference could mean adapting workplace patterns for all workers to suit family lives.

In contrast to earlier notions of social or woman-centered feminism, the new understanding of difference proudly accepts the attributes associated with women's historically assigned roles, declaring itself antithetical to such male values as competition and achievement for their own sakes. It lacks the moralistic assumption that women's culturally or socially ascribed roles are in any sense more valuable while insisting that such qualities belong in the world and not in a separate sphere. Thus, it argues that women bear responsibility for family lives but insists that they do not bear it alone. This perspective opens the possibility of placing what have previously been private issues onto the public stage. In doing so, it takes assumptions of difference that in Eleanor Roosevelt's time were rooted in biology and therefore isolated women as a group and turns them into a sociocultural form that holds the possibility of genuine equality.

These new arguments from difference suggest that a woman's sense of morality and responsibility, and her behavioral codes (including those that derive from her sense of family and her childbearing capacity) are as much a public as a private resource, and they insist as a matter of social policy that the work force recognize and make room for these alternative approaches to human relationships. Far from believing that women can act like men at work, this position asserts women's differences proudly, insisting that the workplace accommodate to women's biology as well as to society's need for those less individualistic qualities of personality and relationship that are her strength. At its most optimistic, this approach is nothing less than a belief that gender equality will be achieved only when the values of the home (which have previously been assumed to keep women out of the workplace or to assign them to inferior places within it) are brought to the workplace where they can transform work itself. It opens the possibility that an ethic of compassion or tolerance, a sense of group responsibility to the world at large (instead of to self), might in fact penetrate the workplace.[5]

It differs sharply from the implications of a neohumanist feminism that argues that women can respond to the workplace like men and that assumes at heart that women can and will play the game the way men play it. In this form of feminism, personal aspiration and individual achievement measure progress toward the goal of equality. The problem is that this theory makes room in the work force primarily for those who wish to place nurturing roles in a secondary category and/or to acquiesce to the ethic of competition. It relegates to second place those who wish to function by their own more clearly female lights. In contrast, those who assert the validity of difference challenge the rules by which the game has been played, leaving room to extend protections won by women to men (as in the ACLU example) and opening up the opportunity to share the costs of childbearing and childrearing. Because this position accepts domestic life as a necessary part of the wage-work process, it encourages innovative thought in regard to housing programs, transportation systems, childcare, and the allocation of community resources. On the other hand, it insists on the need for compromises in the work situation that fully integrate women's orientations to work. At their most extreme, the two positions juxtapose the power of individualism against the force of some notion of collective good.

But lest it appear that one perspective is more radical than another, let me add that both hold the possibility of major social transformation, and it is for this reason that I suggest what looks like a utopian possibility. Given the numbers of women entering the labor force for perfectly valid demographic, ideological, and economic reasons, and given their pressures to share in the American dream of success, some change in either the family or the work force seems inevitable. If women are to function at work in competitive and achievement-oriented ways, they can and should fulfill all their drives for personal achievement. That goal offers a vision of a world without gender domination in the same breath as it implies the necessity for maintaining some form of hierarchy. It directly threatens the family in its patriarchal form and challenges traditional familial values. It begs the question of how the services normally offered in the home are to be provided in most families. In the end, it threatens the breakup of the family altogether.

The second direction, in insisting that women's orientation be publicly espoused, turns the attention of the state, the community, and extended friendship and kin networks to modifying both workplace and the home. As in our comparable worth example, it places the market in second place behind an ethos of responsibility and fairness. Yet in insisting on shared values, this view challenges individualism, competition, and the profit system.

Both directions hold the possibility of conservative responses. The same group of people who argue that women can and should accept the rules as men have defined them implicitly accept the premises of individualism, namely, that people are by nature competitive, that some will not survive the struggle, and that although no one need starve, self-help is the key to eventual equality. Those who believe that difference should be honored, however, could respond positively to the New Right position that social order rests on reinforcing distinctions, not on accommodating them. The logic of that argument is that women really belong at home.

If women's values become a force in creating and influencing work culture, if women can resist efforts to use their understandings to enforce old roles, then exciting possibilities could confront us in terms of cooperation and shared goals in the workplace and in family lives. As the material and other costs of rearing children and running households are shared or socialized, then no woman need fear an Equal Rights Amendment. Once women's values are fully integrated into social relations, women will no longer constitute a "special group."

Notes

Acknowledgments: An earlier version of this chapter was delivered at the Eleanor Roosevelt Centennial Conference, Vassar College, October 15, 1984. My thanks to Louise Tilly and Marilyn Blatt Young for suggestions as to revisions.

1. Long before Gilligan (1982) articulated the differences between men and women in terms of their moral stance, historians spoke of a socialization process that yielded differentiated male and female stances toward the world. See, for example, Welter's classic "The Cult of True Womanhood: 1820–1860" (1966). For a discussion of the uses of these different relationships in the work force, see Kessler-Harris (1975). Gilligan's work sustains these earlier notions but is not necessary to it.

2. Evidence on this point is ambiguous. In her concluding remarks to the most recent survey and evaluation of occupational segregation to date, Blau notes rather pessimistically that "sex segregation in employment remains a pervasive feature of the labor market and a major cause of women's lower earnings" (1984:313). She reaches this conclusion despite the relatively optimistic account of Beller and Rosenfeld in the same volume and in view of research findings by Bielby and Bowen, also in the same volume. Note also the comments of Pamela Stone Cain on this issue. Thanks to Louise Tilly for drawing this volume to my attention. Blau and Ferber suggest (1985) that a modest decline in the rate of occupational segregation in the seventies may be due to the shifting priorities of younger women vis-à-vis paid work and home work. If this is so, then some way of narrowing the separation between home and work becomes ever more crucial as this generation confronts conflicts between home and work in the future.

3. Marcia Greenberger (1980) cites lack of federal enforcement as well as the inadequacy of some of the laws themselves as responsible for slow progress.

4. For unemployment figures see the U.S. Department of Labor, Bureau of Labor Statistics (1983). Despite the generally high ratio of female unemployment to male, during the recession of the early 1980s women's level of unemployment dropped below that of men, indicating their persistence in occupationally segregated areas that were less vulnerable in this downturn. For female earnings and the level of poverty among wage-earning women, see report number 663 (1981), which indicates that the median earnings of female household heads were less than half those of male household heads.

5. Contrast this with the New Right position that, still wedded to the old notion of difference, reasserts the importance of the work/family dichotomy by implying that women will be returned to the home. See Ruddick (1980).

References

Anderson, Mary. 1925. "Should There Be Labor Laws for Women? Yes." *Good Housekeeping*, September, p. 4.

Baer, Judith A. 1978. *The Chains of Protection: The Judicial Response to Women's Labor Legislation*. Westport, Conn.: Greenwood.

Baker, Elizabeth Faulkner. 1964. *Technology and Women's Work*. New York: Columbia University Press.

———. 1969. *Protective Labor Legislation: With Special Reference to Women in the State of New York*. New York: AMS Press.

Becker, Susan D. 1981. *The Origins of the Equal Rights Amendment: American Feminism Between the Wars*. Westport, Conn.: Greenwood.

Blackwelder, Julia Kirk. 1983. *Women of the Depression: Caste and Culture in San Antonio, 1929–1939*. College Station: Texas A & M University Press.

Blau, Francine. 1984. "Concluding Remarks." In B. Reskin (ed.), *Sex Segregation in the Work Place: Trends, Explanations, and Remedies*. Washington, D.C.: National Academies Press.

Blau, Francine, and Marianne A. Ferber. 1985. "Women in the Labor Market: The Last Twenty Years." in Laurie Larwood, Ann H. Stromberg, and Barbara A. Gulek (eds.), *Women and Work: An Annual Review*. Vol. 1. Beverly Hills, Calif.: Sage, pp. 19–49.

Degler, Carl. 1980. *At Odds: Women and the Family in America from the Revolution to the Present*. New York: Oxford University Press.

Epstein, Cynthia F. 1971. *Woman's Place: Options and Limits in Professional Careers*. Berkeley: University of California Press.

Fuller, Margaret. 1971. *Woman in the Nineteenth Century*. New York: W. W. Norton.

Gilligan, Carol. 1982. *In a Different Voice: Psychological Theory and Women's Development*. Cambridge: Harvard University Press.

Gilman, Charlotte Perkins. 1898. *Women and Economics*. Boston: Small and Maynard.

Greenberger, Marcia. 1980. "The Effectiveness of Federal Laws Prohibiting Sex Discrimination in Employment in the United States." In A. S. Ratner (ed.), *Equal Employment Policy for Women: Strategies for Implementation in the United States, Canada, and Western Europe*. Philadelphia: Temple University Press.

Hamilton, Alice. 1953. Personal communication to Miss Magee, May 15. Wayne State Archives in Labor History and Urban Affairs, Detroit, Michigan.

Hayden, Dolores. 1981. *The Grand Domestic Revolution: A History of Feminist Designs for American Homes, Neighborhoods, and Cities*. Cambridge: MIT Press.

———. 1984. *Redesigning the American Dream: The Future of Housing, Work, and Family Life*. New York: Norton.

Hill, Ann Corinne. 1979. "Protection of Women Workers and the Courts: A Legal Case History." *Feminist Studies* 5:no. 2:24–85.

Kanter, Rosabeth Moss. 1977. *Men and Women of the Corporation*. New York: Basic Books.

Kessler-Harris, Alice. 1975. "Stratifying by Sex: Notes on the History of Working Women." In R. Edwards, David Gordon, and Michael Reich (eds.), *Labor Market Segmentation*. Lexington, Mass.: Lexington Books.

———. 1982. *Out to Work: A History of Wage-Earning Women in the United States*. New York: Oxford University Press.

Milkman, Ruth. 1976. "Women's Work and the Economic Crisis: Some Lessons from the Great Depression." *Review of Radical Political Economics* 8:(Spring) 73–97.

Piore, Michael. 1979. "Fragments of a "Sociological" Theory of Wages." In Michael Piore (Ed.), *Unemployment and Inflation: Institutionalist and Structuralist Views*. White Plains, N.Y.: M. E. Sharpe.

Pratt, Norma. 1957. "When Women Work." *American Federationist* 64 (August):7–9, 25.

Reasons for Opposing the Equal Rights Amendment. N.d. Wayne State Archives in Labor History and Urban Affairs, Detroit, Michigan.

Roosevelt, Eleanor. 1933. *It's Up to Women*. New York: Franklin A. Stokes.

———. 1944. Personal communication to Rose Schneiderman. Eleanor Roosevelt Collection, Franklin Delano Roosevelt Library, Hyde Park, New York.

Ruddick, Sarah. 1980. "Maternal Thinking." *Feminist Studies* 6, no. 2:342–67.

Ryan, Mary P. 1983. *Womanhood in America: From Colonial Times to the Present*. New York: Franklin Watts.

Shuler, M. M. 1923. "Industrial Women Confer." *The Woman Citizen*, January 27, p. 12.

Smith-Rosenberg, Carroll. 1971. "Beauty, the Beast, and the Militant Woman: A Case Study in Sex Roles and Social Stress in Jacksonian America." *American Quarterly* 23:562–84.

Sokoloff, Natalie J. 1980. *Between Money and Love: The Dialectics of Women's Home and Market Work*. New York: Praeger.

Thibert, M. S. 1933. "The Economic Depression and the Employment of Women: II." *International Labor Review* 27.

U.S. Department of Labor, Bureau of Labor Statistics. 1983. Report no. 663. Washington, D.C.: Government Printing Office.

Welter, Barbara. 1966. "The Cult of True Womanhood, 1820–1860." *American Quarterly* 17:151–74.

Woloch, Nancy. 1984. *Women and the American Experience*. New York: Knopf.

Young, Iris. In press. "Humanism, Gynocentrism and Feminist Politics." *Hypatia: A Journal of Feminist Philosophy*.